DAY BY DAY IN
NEW YORK
YANKEES
HISTORY

A publication of
Leisure Press.
597 Fifth Avenue; New York, N.Y. 10017
Copyright © 1983 Leisure Press
All rights reserved. Printed in the U.S.A.

Library of Congress Catalog Card Number 82-83934

ISBN 0-88011-102-X

DAY BY DAY IN
NEW YORK
YANKEES
HISTORY

by Mark Gallagher

LEISURE PRESS

NEW YORK

Dedication

This book is dedicated to the legions of loyal fans of the New York Yankees.

Photo Credits

I am grateful for the assistance offered by Howard Eskenazi of Photoworld, Eugene Ferrara of the *New York Daily News*, Laura Tosi of the Bronx County Historical Society, Tom Freeman of Wide World Photos and Harry Collins of Brown Brothers.

I extend special thanks for their excellent advice to Brian Elias and Bob Green, both of Photo Communications in Rockville, Md., and to Mike Cornelius of Kansas City, Kansas, who kindly volunteered the use of several photographs within these pages.

Some of the other photos which are uncredited come from the author's personal collection. Otherwise, the photo credits are as follows:

Bronx County Historical Society
Brown Brothers; Sterling, Pa.
George Brace Photos; Chicago, Ill.
New York Daily News
New York Yankees
Photoworld; New York, N.Y.
Requena, Louis; New York, N.Y.
Wide World Photos; Washington, D.C.

Contents

Acknowledgements

An author, if he is to get the job done, requires a wealth of active and passive resources.

The active ones take part in the process, and no one took a stronger role than Neil and Louise Gallagher whom I have come to regard as "associates" as well as parents. They furnished inestimable hours of research, editing support and typing.

We took a team approach, really, and we had a four-member team. The fourth member was Walter LeConte, Jr., a fellow member of the Society for American Baseball Research who lives in Baker, La. Walter has researched virtually every game the Yankees ever played and was gracious enough to lend his time and expertise to the enterprise, both in large portions. I don't know of anyone who has a better understanding of Yankee history than Walter does. A thousand thank you's to Walter.

Another SABR member, Fred Stein, a friend, writer and expert on the old New York Giants, must be thanked for putting me in touch with Walter. I am also indebted to David Szen and his assistant, Bill Nicky, of the Yankees' front office; Clifford Kachline, the renowned baseball historian; Bill Guilfoile, director of public relations at the Baseball Hall of Fame; Shirley Povich, the widely acclaimed Washington sportswriter; Bob Hoie, another fellow SABR member; Mort Shanerman, another expert on the Yankees down through the years; Jack Lang, secretary-treasurer of the Baseball Writers Association of America; Helen Strong of the Baseball Commissioner's Office; Jack Galvin of Rockville, Md., for his assistance in obtaining research materials; and Mrs. Bea Neeb for her gracious hospitality in Florida.

I would also like to thank all the people at Leisure Press, especially Dr. James Peterson who suggested that I write this book.

Now for the passive resources—the books, records, newspaper files and indices, old magazines, clippings, scrapbooks, yearbooks, media guides, game programs, personal recollections, old baseball cards, and, of course, the reference works and body of baseball literature.

A number of books have helped me to understand eras and personages that preceded my own "Yankee cognizance," which had its beginning in the late 1950s. Marshall Smelser's *The Life That Ruth Built* and Robert Creamer's *Babe: The Legend Comes to Life* were important for their coverage of the Babe Ruth era. George DeGregorio's *Joe DiMaggio: An Informal Biography* helped me through the DiMaggio years. Peter Golenbock's *Dynasty* covered the years, 1949-64. Among many other books, I also drew from *The New York Yankees; An Informal History* by Frank Graham, *The Great All-Time Baseball Record Book* by Joseph L. Reichler, *This Date in New York Yankees History* by Nathan Salant and *The Yankees: The Four Fabulous Eras* by Dave Anderson, Murray Chass, Robert Creamer and Harold Rosenthal. And, as always, the various baseball encyclopedia were helpful statistical references.

Preface

For a time while working on my first book, *The Yankee Encyclopedia*, I found myself date-riddled. I respected dates but I didn't necessarily like them. Gradually, however, my attitude altered. Dates began to take on a precious quality.

What I did next was to take these dates, these gems, and strew them along a trail. Follow the trail, gem by gem, and you have the history of the New York Yankees.

Typically, "date" books cluster the gems. All events taking place on July 17th, for example, are bunched together, regardless of the years in which they reside. It is a format that forbids storytelling. It is impossible to follow a career or pennant drive without chronological order. The approach taken here was aimed at achieving the best of both worlds—at putting the gems with the individual settings they deserve and arranging these along a storyline trail. The object was to not only capture the sparkle of the day but to gain narratives on campaigns and careers and the whole of the Yankees' 80 years of baseball.

Not every gem is necessarily included. Your favorite Yankee's four-for-four day in 1940 may have been excluded. Not that I high-handedly rejected anything, but because of the requirements of editorial balance and space limitations. Nor is every included gem guaranteed to be free of a minor rough spot. Conflicting information was not always easy to reconcile. An occasional date may be off by a day or two.

I attempted to present the news of each date as exactly that—news. From time to time I inserted what I call "elaborations," asides that amplify on a situation or personality, the rough equivalent of a news analysis. But I have an advantage analysts can only wish they had. I can see the future. I can say that a pitcher traded away by the Yankees will go on to compile a 164-97 record in the majors; I have the 20-20 vision of hindsight. (Incidentally, when a pitcher's record is shown in parentheses, it is his record for the *entire* year. In other words, his record might actually be 6-3 on June 1, 1953, but it will appear as 18-1—his 1953 record.)

Enough said. I hope you enjoy reading this book as much as I enjoyed writing it.

MARK GALLAGHER

Rockville, Maryland
March, 1983

1903-1919
BIRTH AND ADOLESCENCE

1903-1919

The first 17 seasons of New York's AL franchise will be years of frustration. The club will not be without stars—Willie Keeler, Jack Chesbro and Hal Chase, for example—yet will repeatedly fail, although the Highlanders will go to the wire in 1904 and again in 1906. Some terrible teams follow and the club will wallow until Jake Ruppert and Til Houston become its owners in 1915. A few years later, Miller Huggins will become manager, and, with a few more player acquisitions, the pieces to a winning aggregation begin to come together. The final piece will be added in the winter of 1919-20. That piece is Babe Ruth, and with the Babe there dawns a new day for the Yankees and indeed for baseball.

1903

Jan 9— New Yorkers Frank Farrell and Big Bill Devery lay out $18,000 for an American League franchise languishing in abandonment in Baltimore. They plan to bring it to New York.

— Farrell and Devery are enjoying rewarding careers, which for both happen to begin as bartenders. Farrell owns a gambling house and a racing stable, and Devery, a former New York City police chief, is doing well in real estate. They are not without presence, means and influence, but in this transaction the two friends are the foot soldiers of AL President Ban Johnson. Looking ahead to a third year of major league status for his league, Johnson is waging a winning war against the National League. Johnson has reason to dislike the kingpins of the NL's New York Giants, John T. Brush and John J. McGraw. He would like nothing better than to give them competition. More importantly, he knows he has to have a team in New York if his league is to be a major league in the complete sense. He places his faith in a colorful pair of turn-of-the-century entrepreneurs.

Jan 10— To put an end to player raiding and other destabilizing practices afflicting big-time baseball, representatives of the American and National Leagues enter into a peace treaty under which the New York market is opened to the junior circuit.

— The agreement is reached at a meeting in Cincinnati. It is not accepted by Giant owner John T. Brush, however. Brush is determined to keep a rival team out of New York. But AL President Ban Johnson, insisting as a condition of lasting peace that his league have a club in New York, is equally determined. A bitter personal struggle between Brush and Johnson intensifies.

Jan 20— NL brass again meets in Cincinnati and overrules the Brush rejection of the treaty. Brush yields to the will of the other owners.

— But Brush will belittle the new kids in town. And Andrew Freedman, a man with ties to the Tammany Hall political machine, intends to make it difficult for the AL to find a playing field. Freedman is a former owner of the Giants and is still connected with the club. He is also a close friend of Brush.

Mar 12— Members of the AL officially vote New York into their league.

— The vote is a formality since the only "vote" that counts belongs to Ban Johnson, and he is already at work building a strong team for New York. The team, grandly tagged The Greater New York Club of the American League, will be called the Highlanders and will also be known as the Americans and Hilltoppers. The press, notably Jim Price of the *New York Press* and Mark Roth of the *New York Globe,* will prefer "Yankees," which in 1913 is adopted as the official nickname.* Owners Frank Farrell and Bill Devery install Joseph W. Gordon as the club's first president.

Mar 22— The club announces plans to build a ballpark at 168th Street and Broadway, in the Washington Heights neighborhood of upper Manhattan.

— The ballpark will not be much. It will be "blasted out of a rockpile" on land leased for 10 years from the New York Institution for the Blind. But it *will* be built, and with the announcement, tickets go on sale. Ban Johnson is pleased. John T. Brush, Andrew Freedman and John J. McGraw have been outflanked.

Mar 26— The Yankees open their exhibition season at Piedmont Park in Atlanta and beat the home club, 9-0.

— Ernie Courtney, who will be traded after hitting .266 in 25 regular season games, is the first New York player to bat. He walks and scores the first Yankee run posted in competition. New York sweeps five games from Atlanta before moving on to New Orleans, there to take three of five games from the Pelicans.

Apr   22—New York starts its inaugural season in Washington and loses, 3-1.

— Taking the field for New York before 11,950 fans are Jack Chesbro, the losing pitcher, Jack O'Connor (C), John Ganzel (1B), Jimmy Williams (2B), Wid Conroy (3B), Herman Long (SS), George "Lefty" Davis (LF), Dave Fultz (CF), and Wee Willie Keeler (RF), who scores the club's lone run. Ban Johnson has stocked New York with quality players, some of whom were recruited in raids against the NL before the two leagues entered their peace pact. Highly regarded Clark Griffith, recently of the White Sox, is New York's manager. Charley Comiskey hates to lose Griffith, but the White Sox owner is told by Johnson, "We need the best that we have in New York, and that is Griff." Manager Griffith also pitches.

**While "Highlanders" is acknowledged as the team's official nickname in its formative years, this book uses "Yankees' throughout for simplicity's sake.

The Yankees' first manager, Clark Griffith, doubled as a pitcher and won 31 games. The Old Fox pitched the first shutout in Yankee history on June 16, 1903.

Apr   23   New York defeats the Senators, 7-2, for its first win. Handsome Harry Howell is
            the winning pitcher.

Apr   30   Upwards of 16,000 turn out to see New York's new team beat Washington,
            6-2, behind Jack Chesbro.

            — It is a beautiful day and happy pre-game ceremonies include a parade to
            the flagpole led by Ban Johnson, AL president, and Joe Gordon, club presi-
            dent, who is instrumental in Hilltop Park's development. The players, each
            carrying a small American flag, are part of the procession. and the band plays
            "The Star Spangled Banner," "Yankee Doodle Dandy," and "Columbia, the
            Gem of the Ocean," as the crowd sings along. Owners Frank Farrell and Bill
            Devery are pleased by the turnout at old Hill Top.* Hilltop Park, also known as
            American League Park, Highlander Park and Hilltopper Park (there is a ten-
            dency to call the Highlanders the Hilltoppers and the ballpark, accordingly,
            Hilltopper Park) is built on a leveled hill that is Manhattan's highest point.
            There is a deep ravine in right field. Wee Willie Keeler on the first play of
            today's game stops himself just short of this dangerous precipice, and a
            relieved Farrell and Devery soon have the ravine filled in.

            — The Yankees can't afford to have anything happen to Keeler. He is the
            drawing card, the club's first superstar. Willie, who jumped from Brooklyn of
            the NL, gives the Yankees seven solid seasons, hitting over .300 in the first
            four of those seasons (making 15 consecutive Keeler seasons of .300 or
            better!). The greatest place hitter in baseball history thrills the fans by "hit-
            ting 'em where they ain't." On this date he has two doubles and two walks. He
            scores three runs and is out trying to score a fourth in a bang-bang play at
            the plate.

May 7—   Boston and New York meet for the first time and launch an 80-year rivalry.
            The Pilgrims, as the Red Sox were then known, are 6-2 winners.

May 8—   New York defeats the Pilgrims, 6-1, behind Jack Chesbro's six-hitter.

May 11—   The first home run in Yankee history is hit on the road by first baseman John
            Ganzell off Detroit's George Mullin. Wid Conroy also homers as New York
            breezes to an 8-2 win.

Jun 10—   The Yankees in their first major trade acquire Kid Elberfeld (SS) and John
            Deering (P) from Detroit for Herman Long (SS), Ernie Courtney (INF) and
            Patsy Greene (3B).

            — Elberfeld is the key of the trade. He will play great shortshop for New York,
            but curiously, while having hit .341 for Detroit, he bats only .287 over the
            remainder of the season in New York. (The Yankees' early years are riddled
            with disappointments.)

Jun 16—   Manager Clark Griffith pitches the first shutout in Yankee history and needs it
            to beat Chicago 1-0.

---

*Crowd estimates of over 20,000 customers are padded. The stands will not be completed until the
Yankees return from a long road trip on June 1, by which date Hilltop Park will have about
15,000 seats and standing room for several thousand more.

1904

Apr 22— Jack Chesbro allows a leadoff single by Washington's Kip Selbach, then refuses to give up another hit in leading New York to a 2-0 win.

Jun 16— First baseman John Ganzel hits the first grand slam homer in Yankee history. Ganzel, who also owns the club's first homer, will have a total of six fourbaggers this season, establishing the Yankee home run record that will stand until Wally Pipp's 12 homers in 1916. (Ganzel's record was tied in 1912 by Guy Zinn.)

Jul 4— Pitching ace Jack Chesbro wins his 14th consecutive game, establishing an AL record that Walter Johnson will better in 1912 with 16 straight wins. But Happy Jack's streak will remain the Yankee club record. (It will be tied in 1941 by Whitey Ford.)

Jack Chesbro won 129 games for the Yankees, 41 of them in 1904 to establish a 20th Century record for season wins.

Aug 10—   Jack Chesbro, after completing his first 30 starts, is finally knocked out (by
the White Sox). He sets several AL records in 1904: most wins (41), most
games started (51) and most complete games (48).

Oct 7—   On a Friday afternoon at Hilltop Park, New York defeats Boston, 3-2, and
takes a ½-game lead over the Red Sox in the pennant race. The win gives
Jack Chesbro his 41st victory of the season.

Oct 8—   Boston takes two from New York and moves into first place by 1½ games.

— Frank Farrell leases Hilltop Park to Columbia University for a Saturday football game and the doubleheader is switched to Boston. Manager Clark
Griffith instructs Jack Chesbro to remain behind and rest for another doubleheader with Boston on Monday. But as the team prepares to leave Grand
Central Station, Griffith sees Chesbro and invites him along. "He looked so
hurt, I couldn't leave him behind," Griffith says. When the Yankees arrive in
Boston, Chesbro insists on pitching the opener. He gets knocked out (for only
the third time all year), and Boston coasts to a 13-2 victory, then nips New
York in the nightcap, 1-0.

Oct 10—   Following a day of rest on Sunday, Boston and New York meet in a Hilltop
Park doubleheader that the locals must sweep for the pennant. New York is
done in by a wild pitch.

— Some 28,000 fans squeeze into the tiny ballpark to see whether Jack
Chesbro (who else?) can beat Bill Dinneen, who had a fine 23-14 season, in
the first game and set up a second game climax. Boston ties the game in the
seventh inning on a throwing error by second baseman Jimmy Williams. In
the ninth, Boston's Lou Criger reaches first on an infield hit, takes second on
a sacrifice and gets to third on a groundout, the second out. Chesbro unleashes one of his famous spitballs (then a legal pitch) for a wild pitch, the
ball sailing over catcher Red Kleinow's head, allowing Criger to score. New
York fails to score in the bottom of the ninth. Boston is handed a 3-2 win and
the AL pennant. The heartbroken Yankees win the nightcap, 1-0, to end
the season 1½ games from the summit. And poor Happy Jack is to·be remembered as much for his wild spitter as for having had one of the greatest
seasons in the history of pitching.

1905

Aug 30—   Jack Chesbro allows an 18-year-old his first big league hit, a double, and
loses, 5-3. The 18-year-old is Ty Cobb, and the Cobbs seem to be going to
the Detroits.

— The New York franchise has frustrating personnel problems in the early
years. Around the league, ready to blossom into stardom, along with Cobb,
are such future Hall of Famers as 22-year-old Chief Bender of Philadelphia,
24-year-old Ed Walsh of Chicago and 25-year-old Addie Joss of Cleveland.
And in two years Washington will have Walter Johnson. Except for a few
"flashes," New York will play aging warriors in its first decade. However, there
is one player of Hall of Fame caliber who this year begins his career with New
York. Hal Chase, 22, is a magician at first base. But Prince Hal suffers from
what can be called "a lack of dedication." Lou Gehrig will be the first player to
start his career with the Yankees and make the Hall of Fame.

1906

Aug 22— At Hilltop Park, Chicago wins, 11-6, extending to 18 a winning streak that will end at 19. Chicago's Hitless Wonders do some good hitting, taking a four-game series by scores of 10-0, 4-1, 6-1 and 11-6, as Big Ed Walsh captures two wins. The White Sox had earlier swept a three-game series from New York in Chicago.

Aug 25— Double Zip. Slow Joe Doyle, in his major league debut, wins, 2-0, and Walter Clarkson captures the nightcap, 7-0, as New York keeps Cleveland scoreless in a doubleheader.

Aug 30— First of Doubleheader String. Slow Joe Doyle wins his second shutout in a row, 5-0, becoming the first AL pitcher ever to win his initial two games in the bigs by shutouts. Only three others will follow Doyle in this feat. Hal Chase in the nightcap of this doubleheader with Washington becomes the first player in Yankee history to make four extra-base hits in one game, lashing out three triples and one double in New York's 9-8 win in 10 innings. The Yankees in quick order will tie four more doubleheader sweeps to this date's twin killing.

Aug 31— The Yankees again sweep a doubleheader from Washington at Hilltop Park, winning 7-5 and 20-5. The nightcap is called after six innings.

Sep 1— For the third consecutive day at Hilltop Park, the Yankees win two games from the Senators, 5-4 and 5-3. Washington leaves town with six losses in three days. The victors will enjoy a day of rest on September 2.

Hilltop Park, a 15,000-seater in Washington Heights, was the home of the Yankees from 1903 through 1912. Some 20,000 fans descended on the tiny park for a September 3, 1906 doubleheader with Philadelphia.

Sep 3— New York takes a fourth doubleheader in five days and moves into first place.

— The double win over Philadelphia is memorable for its incidents. Kid Elberfeld is so unsportsmanlike in the first game that even the 20,000 home fans turn against him. Angered by a decision against the Yankees, Elberfeld chases an umpire around the field with the clear intent of inflicting physical harm. The police rescue the poor umpire and remove the Tabasco Kid from the playing field. Trailing 3-0 in the nightcap, the Yankees rally to tie in the ninth. They are helped by a basepath play involving Wee Willie Keeler and alleged interference, according to the vociferous arguments of the A's. Connie Mack pulls his team off the field and refuses to return. The umpires award a victory by forfeit to New York.

Sep 4— New York wins its fifth doubleheader in six days, a big league record, and is enmeshed in what it will not experience again until 1920—a pennant race.

— Walter Clarkson and Al Orth beat Boston, 7-0 and 1-0. It is the Yankees' second double shutout in 10 days and the third in two months. New York has now swept doubleheaders from Washington August 30 and 31 and September 1, Philadelphia September 3 and Boston on this date. The 10 wins by doubleheader are the centerpiece of a 15-game winning streak. New York and the White Sox, the so-called Hitless Wonders, will battle through September for the pennant, but a 19-game Chicago winning streak will prove too much, eliminating the gritty New Yorkers in the final week.

Sep 26— In Detroit, the Yankees lose, 2-0, after losses of 7-4 and 6-5, closing out their chances of winning the pennant. This comes after New York has put the heat on the White Sox by winning a series in Chicago. But now the Yankees are mortally wounded and will finish three games out; they will not get close again until Babe Ruth comes to town in pinstripes.

1907

Jun 28— New York catcher Branch Rickey allows 13 stolen bases (an AL record) as Washington tramples New York, 16-5, at Hilltop Park. Baserunners get good jumps on Yankee pitchers Earl Moore and Lew Brockett.

Aug 28— In his big league debut, Tacks Neuer of Hazleton, Pa., blanks Boston, 1-0. He will win three more games in a one-month career. Two of these will be by shutouts, too. He finishes 4-2 and disappears from the majors.

1908

Jun 24— New York changes managers for the first time, replacing Clark Griffith, their leader since Day One, with infielder Kid Elberfeld.

— In Philadelphia and near the end of a disastrous road trip, the Yankees are 24-32 and in sixth place. They struggle to a 6-6 tie. An angered owner is Frank Farrell. He goes into a tirade and Griffith resigns. New York loses a fine baseball man who will one day enter the Baseball Hall of Fame. Under Elberfeld, restricted by a leg injury to playing only 19 games, the club will be even worse, winning 27 and losing 71. One other consequence of Griffith's departure: reportedly star first baseman Hal Chase is peeved over not being asked to succeed Griffith.

Jun 30—   Cy Young pitches his third career no-hitter at Hilltop Park at the age of 41
           years and 3 months (the oldest man ever to throw a no-hitter). Young, who
           issues only one free pass, helps his cause with three hits as the Red Sox
           coast to an easy 8-0 win, roughing up pitchers Rube Manning, Doc Newton
           and Joe Lake along the way.

Jul 31—   The Yankees lose, 16-3, at Cleveland and with a July record of 6-24 for a .200
           winning percentage, conclude the worst month in the history of the franchise.

Sep 3—   Californian Hal Chase jumps the Yankees and signs with Stockton of the out-
           law California State League. "I am not satisfied to play under a management
           that sees fit to give out a story detrimental to my character and honesty," he
           says. "Such a story appeared in a New York Sunday paper August 23. I feel
           that I could not do myself justice under such conditions, and therefore I have
           decided to quit. I never had managerial ideas." Frank Farrell denies Chase's
           allegations, calling them a smokescreen for his jumping the team.

Sep 7—   Washington's Walter Johnson beats the Yankees, 4-0, in the top of a Monday
           doubleheader for his third shutout of New York in four days. He blanked the
           Yankees on six hits the previous Friday, held them scoreless on four hits Sat-
           urday, and, after a day of rest imposed by the ban on Sunday baseball,
           returns on this date to starve them on two hits.

Oct 1—   Happy Jack Chesbro in his final game as a Yankee starting pitcher beats
           none other than Washington's Walter Johnson. Chesbro's five-hitter edges
           the Senators, 2-1.

Oct 6—   In Boston the Yankees lose, 11-3, their 100th loss of the season.

           — New York will lose three more games to finish at 51-103, 39½ games
           behind first-place Detroit and a distant 17 games behind seventh-place
           Washington. The 103 defeats will remain the most in the club's history. Chi-
           cago's Big Ed Walsh singlehandedly accounts for nine of the losses. George
           Stallings will soon be summoned and asked to take over as manager.

1909

May 3—   Hal Chase reports to the Yankees after a bout with smallpox and receives a
           silver loving cup from his teammates. Before the season's start he paid a
           $200 fine for playng in the outlaw California State League and is now reinstat-
           ed in organized baseball by a decision of the National Commission, base-
           ball's ruling body.

           — Chase signs his New York contract for $4,000, making him one of this era's
           highest paid players. All the previous September's bitterness between
           Chase and owner Frank Farrell is erased. Chase's declaration of the pre-
           vious fall that he would never again play in the East is not only forgotten but
           the controversial first baseman is welcomed back with open arms. He is, after
           all, one of the top drawing cards in baseball and the game's fanciest fielder.
           He will hit .284 over his nine seasons with the Yankees, with a high of .323 in
           1906 and a 27-game hitting streak in 1907.

Aug 27—   Jack Chesbro makes his final appearance for New York. In a relief role,
           Happy Jack is hit hard as Detroit romps over New York, 17-6.

           — Before the month's end, Chesbro, the first great pitcher in the team's history, is released to the Red Sox where he finishes the season with a combined 0-4 record and closes out his career. The spitballer can look back with pride on a major league record of 199-127, including a 129-88 mark in New York. Jack Chesbro has set the standard by which future Yankee stars will be measured.

Dec 16— New York sells the contract of Kid Elberfeld to Washington.

— What is considered a large sum—$5,000—is involved. Gone is one of the premier players for the New Yorkers. The Tabasco Kid hit .268 over seven years with the club. He played a steady shortstop and provided fiery leadership. He even managed the club when asked to in 1908. Elberfeld will give Washington two solid seasons, his final years as a big league regular. New York, meanwhile, can't find a shortstop to play more than 100 games until Roger Peckinpaugh will come along to solidify the infield in 1914.

1910

Aug 30— First Yankee No-Hitter. Tom Hughes pitches the first no-hitter in Yankee history, actually hurling 9⅓ hitless innings, but in the end loses to Cleveland, 5-0, in 11 innings. The Indians' first safety with one out in the 10th does not result in a score and the game enters the 11th inning. Here Hughes runs out of gas and Cleveland scores five runs on seven hits to deal him a heartbreaking loss. Justice will be served in 1916 when Hughes will *win* a no-hitter for the Boston Braves, following Cy Young as the second pitcher to author no-hitters in both major leagues.

Sep 23— The resignation of New York Manager George Stallings is forced amid controversy over Hal Chase.

— Stallings is recalled to New York from a road trip to explain reports in the *New York Times* that he plans to quit if Hal Chase remains a Yankee. Owner Frank Farrell and AL President Ban Johnson are on Chase's side. Stallings believes Chase is throwing games and he is not the only one. Many close to the game wonder about the greatest fielding first baseman in the story of baseball, questioning his commission of errors at critical moments. But Farrell and Johnson do not see eye to eye with Stallings and the manager is gone. It is a strange time for Stallings' ouster. In this, his second season, he has the Yankees in second place, only two years after the New Yorkers were cellar-dwellers. But he is high-strung, with a short temper, and he has long been upset over the interference and second-guessing of owners Farrell and Devery. His resignation is inevitable with or without the Chase episode.

Sep 24— Hal Chase is the new Yankee manager. The team wins 9 of its remaining 11 games but ends the campaign a distant 14½ games behind first-place Philadelphia.

— Chase's appointment is more than interim; Prince Hal later signs a $6,000 contract to be a player-manager for 1911. Owners Farrell and Devery fly in the face of Chase's unsavory reputation and neither the league nor National Commission posts any warnings. Baseball is unconcerned about the integrity of baseball.

Oct 21— New York's Giants beat New York's Yankees, 6-3, at the Polo Grounds to win the New York City Series, four games to two with one tie (a game called in extra innings because of darkness).

— It is a runners-up series growing from the fact that both the Yankees (88-63) and Giants (91-63) finished second in their leagues, and in New York it closely rivaled the World Series for attention. The games alternated between Hilltop Park and the Polo Grounds. The Yankees win two games and tie one at Hilltop, while the Giants win all four at the Polo Grounds. The undisputed hero of the Series: 27-game winner Christy Mathewson, winning pitcher in all four Giant victories!

1911

Apr 14— A fire that can be seen throughout Manhattan, the Bronx and Queens severely damages the Polo Grounds after only the second Giants' game of the season. Coming to the Giants' aid, Frank Farrell offers them the use of Hilltop Park and the Giants readily accept, bringing to an end the animosity between the two clubs. The Giants beat Brooklyn, 6-3, at Hilltop Park the next day. The Polo Grounds will reopen on June 28. The grateful Giants will invite the Yankees to move in with them for the 1913 season, after the latter's lease on the Hilltop site has run out.

Jul 12— Yankee third baseman Roy Hartzell has 8 RBIs in one game, setting an AL record that will stand until Jimmie Foxx gets 9 RBIs in a 1933 game.

— Hartzell is the first American Leaguer to have a home run and double in the same inning, and his grand slam homer is the first by a Yankee in nearly five years. In his 11-year big league career, Hartzell has more than 38 RBIs only twice, but this uear he has 91 RBIs—the Yankee club record until 1916 when Wally Pipp will drive in 93 runs.

Jul 24— Russ Ford, All-Star. In a benefit game played with Cleveland for the widow of Cleveland's Addie Joss, a group of the AL's best (they win, 5-3) includes Yankees Hal Chase and Russ Ford.

— Ford, who joins with Walter Johnson and Smokey Joe Wood to form the All-Stars' pitching corps, is a riches to rags story. As a Yankee rookie right-hander in 1910, he set AL rookie pitching records for wins (26) and shutouts (8). He pitched 300 innings, fanned 209 hitters, won 12 straight games and had a 1.65 ERA. Ford never recaptures these numbers, although he will go 20-6 in 1914 after jumping to Buffalo of the Federal League. But the Federal League will fold following the 1915 season, and the career of the Canadian-born Ford, owner of the lowest Yankee career ERA (2.54), will fold with it.

Sep 20— The Yankees commit 12 errors in a doubleheader, seven in the first game and five in the second, but still manage to gain a split with Cleveland.

— New York makes 328 errors this year, one of five seasons (1907, 1908, 1909, 1911 and 1912) in which the team committed more that 300 errors. There are no other years in Yankee history of 300 errors.

Sep 28— In an 18-12 win over St. Louis, New York sets the AL record for stolen bases in a nine-inning game with 15. Birdie Cree and Hal Chase each steal four bases in the contest. New York steals six bases in the second inning alone in a game that has 20 walks and 11 errors by both clubs.

— The Yankees steal 270 bases this year, only 18 shy of the club record established the previous year. That the Yankees are a running team in their early years is exemplified by the fact that Chase, a first baseman, no less, will set the Yankee record with 248 career stolen bases. Chase and Cree with their four steals on this date set a Yankee single-game record that will be tied several times over the ensuing years.

Nov 21— Hal Chase is asked to step down as manager—his disorganized team having finished sixth—to make way for Harry Wolverton. As a player, Chase hit .315 for the season, and in spite of his reputation as a defensive wizard, leads AL first basemen in errors with 36. Chase agrees to return in 1912 as a player. Wolverton, a colorful character and a successful pilot in the minors, arrives in New York wearing a sombrero and smoking a long cigar, his trademarks. He will take the Yankees to the top, Wolverton proclaims.

1912

Apr 20— The Yankees are the Red Sox' opponents in the first official-AL game at Boston's brand new Fenway Park. The Red Sox win the first of their 105 victories this year, 7-6. They will win the AL pennant by 14 games.

Apr 21— The Yankees lose, 11-2, in a benefit game with the Giants for the survivors of the sunken liner Titanic.

Warming up in 1911 with Harry Ables (left), pitcher Hippo Vaughn had a 8-11 record for the year and was traded the following year. He went on to enjoy four 20-game seasons.

May 15— Tiger star Ty Cobb enters the Hilltop Park stands to fight with a fan. After warning Yankee Manager Harry Wolverton that trouble would result if a heckler, Claude Lueker (Lucas, in some accounts) failed to quiet down. Cobb exchanges words with Lueker and then jumps into the stands and attacks his antagonist. Lueker is seriously cut and bruised. Fans come to Lueker's assistance and Detroit players join in the fray, precipitating a near riot. The brawl results in a suspension for Cobb and, more lastingly, in tighter security at league ballparks.

Jun 26— The Yankees let pitcher Hippo Vaughn get away, selling his contract to Washington on waivers. Vaughn, up from Macon of the South Atlantic League in 1908, started slowly because of an injury and built a 22-30 record, pitching mostly for poor Yankee teams. His 12-11/1.83 ERA season of 1910 was especially promising. Vaughn will finish his career with a record of 176-137. He will have four seasons with the Chicago Cubs when he wins more than 20 games.

Jul 12— The only Yankee pitcher ever to steal home, Jack Warhop, does it against the Browns on this date. It is the second time as a Yankee that Warhop steals home. He did it against the White Sox two years earlier.

Jul 25— Outfielder Bert Daniels in a game on this date singles, doubles, triples and homers to become the first Yankee to hit for the cycle.

Aug 15— Guy Zinn steals home twice and swipes a total of four bases. The Yankee outfielder steals second, third and home in the first inning, then in the sixth provides the winning margin for New York's 5-4 win over Detroit by stealing home. The Yankees in 1912 set a big league record with 18 steals of home.

Oct 1— New York loses to Philadelphia, 4-3, for its 100th loss, and with two more losses, will finish a dreadful season with a 50-102 record. The .329 winning percentage will remain the lowest in Yankee history. One-year Manager Harry Wolverton's optimism at the start of the campaign appears to have been unjustified.

Oct 5— The Yankees play their final game at Hilltop Park, getting a three-run homer out of Hal Chase and beating Washington, 8-6. The 10-season residence on the Old Hill Top is over; the Yanks will play their games at the Polo Grounds.

1913

Jan 8— Owners Frank Farrell and Bill Devery announce the signing of the legendary Frank Chance as Yankee manager. The winner of four NL pennants (while managing the Cubs), Chance is lured from a planned California retirement by a lucrative three-year contract. Chance is supposed to be of the stature of the Giants' John J. McGraw and is expected to bring a dying Yankee club back to health.

Mar 4— The Yankees open spring training camp in Bermuda. They are the first big league team to train outside the United States. The Bermuda camp is the brainchild of Yankee business manager Arthur Irwin, and for new manager Frank Chance it affords an opportunity to impose discipline in a distraction-free atmosphere. New York plays exhibition games on the island with the Jersey City Skeeters of the International League.

First stringer Ed Sweeney, far right, and Yankee catcher prospects in 1913. Sweeney was a Yankee from 1908 through 1915 and hit a combined .265.

Apr 10— In the season's opener at Washington, President Woodrow Wilson throws out the first ball and Walter Johnson throws smoke, winning, 2-1, over George McConnell and the YANKEES who, for the first time, begin the season officially known as the Yankees.

Apr 17— New York's home opener is a doubly special event. They have a new ballpark in the Polo Grounds and a new manager in Frank Chance. The new skipper is honored in "Chance Day" festivities, but the visiting Washington Senators mar the merriment with a 9-3 win.

May 20— The Yankees get Roger Peckinpaugh from Cleveland for Jack Lelivelt (OF) and Bill Stumpf (SS) in what probably is the best trade of the Farrell-Devery regime. Peckinpaugh will be the glue of the Yankee infield for nine seasons while hitting a respectable .257. Peckinpaugh is the player around whom the Yankees will build a winning team.

May 31— The Yankees trade their best player, Hal Chase (1B), to the White Sox for Rollie Zeider (INF) and Babe Borton (1B). In the words of Mark Roth, reporter for the *New York Globe,* "The Yankees traded Chase to Chicago for a bunion and an onion." (Zeider had bunions and Borton was not highly regarded.) The trade, so obviously one-sided in Chicago's favor in spite of Chase's current .212 batting average, is the product of fast-moving events. A few days earlier, Manager Frank Chance told two sportswriters that Chase is "throwing games on me." Chase was deliberately letting good throws elude him at first base, Chance said. Heywood Broun in the *New York Tribune* reports only that Chance feels Chase in not "playing up to his ability" and is hurting the

Yankees with loose play in the field. The next day Frank Farrell lets Broun know he thinks a cheap shot has been taken at his first baseman. Broun answers, "I only said something that Chance told Fred Lieb and me, and he told us a lot more than I wrote in the paper." Now, on this date, Chance learns from Yankee catcher Ed Sweeney that Prince Hal has been entertaining the team with mocking imitations of the manager behind Chance's back. The Peerless Leader, as Chance is known, is livid. He confronts Chase, telling him, "Get out. You'll never wear that uniform again," and on the night of this date Chase is unloaded in a deal Chicago couldn't refuse.

Jun 6— The Yanks are beaten by Cleveland, 2-1, at the Polo Grounds for the 13th consecutive defeat. It will remain the longest losing streak in Yankee history.

Jun 7— The Yankees edge Chicago, 3-2, breaking their 13-game losing streak as the White Sox' Hal Chase, a Yankee of a week ago, undergoes a chorus of cheers and boos from the Polo Grounds crowd and goes two for four at the plate.

Sep 11— Marty McHale shuts out St. Louis, 4-0, in his first major league game. McHale is one of the most colorful players in Yankee history. He sings in vaudeville for 12 years and is known as The Baseball Caruso. His poor Yankee record (12-27 in 51 games over three seasons) is largely the result of his having pitched for poor Yankee clubs.

1914

Apr 2— The Yankees help Brooklyn open a brand new Ebbets Field with an exhibition game several days before the start of the regular season.

Apr 17— Third baseman Fritz Maisel steals four bases, tying a Yankee single-game record. Maisel will lead the Al in steals with 74 and will set the Yankee club record.

Aug 3— Yankee catcher Les Nunamaker nails three would-be base stealers at second base in the second inning of a game with Detroit. It will remain the only time in the 20th century that a big league catcher throws out three thieves in one inning.

Sep 15— With New York mired at 61-76, Frank Chance resigns as Yankee manager.

— Chance walks away from the club but not before trying to slug owner Bill Devery, a gutsy action since at the time Big Bill is surrounded by hulking New York cops loyal to their former chief. Later in the evening, Chance departs for California without speaking to the Yankee owners again. Chance is used to baseball excellence and is frustrated by his New York experience. Saddled with inferior talent, The Peerless Leader at first requests, then demands, better players from Devery and co-owner Frank Farrell who in turn believe that Chance erred in trading away for far too little his one quality player, Hal Chase. The stormy relationship among Chance, Farrell and Devery deteriorates step by step into a triangle of bickering.

Sep 16— Roger Peckinpaugh is only 23 but is named the Yankees' shortstop-manager for the rest of the season. He will remain the youngest big league manager in baseball history. The Yankees go 9-8 under Peckinpaugh, team captain from 1914-21, and finish tied for sixth place. Peckinpaugh will return to shortstop-only status in 1915.

1915

Jan 11—   Fed up with the Yankees and, for that matter, with each other, Frank Farrell
          and Bill Devery sell the franchise to Colonel Jacob Ruppert, a multimillionaire
          brewer, sportsman, socialite and dandy from New York, and wealthy Captain
          Tillinghast L'Hommedieu Huston, a fun-loving, unsophisticated soldier-
          engineer from Ohio.*

          — On a tip from John J. McGraw, Ruppert and Huston approach Devery and
          Farrell about buying the Yankees. Negotiations are brief. Farrell, who is in
          some financial distress, and Devery on this date unload the inartistic
          franchise for $460,000. Ruppert assumes the office of president, Huston that
          of vice president. Wild Bill Donovan will become their first manager on the
          advice of the fraternity of baseball writers. The task of making the club a
          success will not be easy. Ruppert says he now owns "an orphan ball club,
          without a home of its own, without players of outstanding ability, without
          prestige." The Yankees will first taste glory under two men who are as
          different as night and day. Ruppert is born to wealth, Huston is a self-made
          man. Ruppert guards his privacy, Huston is open and gregarious. Ruppert is
          an impeccable dresser, Huston is sloppy and rumpled. Yet, their combined
          wealth and mutual love of baseball make their partnership, however short-
          lived, a successful if bumpy working relationship.

Apr 22—   The Yankees take the field wearing pinstriped uniforms for the first time. The
          pinstripes are the idea of owner Jake Ruppert, a snappy dresser himself,
          who in 1923 will buy two sets of uniforms and make the Yankees the first team
          to wear clean uniforms every day.

May 6—   Boston's Babe Ruth hits a tremendous blast off Jack Warhop that lands in the
          second deck of the Polo Grounds' right field grandstand, his first home run in
          the majors. Ruth loses a tough game as a pitcher, however—the Yankees
          winning, 5-3, in 13 innings. Ruth's homer comes on his 18th trip to the plate
          in the big leagues; over his career he will hit one home run in every 11.76 at
          bats.

Jun 2—   Babe Ruth again takes Yankee pitcher Jack Warhop deep at the Polo
          Grounds. In the second inning, Ruth hits a mighty two-run homer even fur-
          ther into the right field second deck than his blast of a month earlier. Ruth
          permits only five hits and Boston wins, 7-1.

Jun 4—   Detroit beats New York, 3-0, as Ty Cobb steals home for the fifth time against
          the Yankees. It is the second time Cobb steals home while Ray Caldwell is on
          the mound. The victimized Caldwell is so upset with the umpire's call that he
          throws his glove high into the air and is ejected.

Jun 11—   Yankee Ray Caldwell pinch-hits a home run and becomes the first American
          Leaguer to hit consecutive pinch-hit homers, a feat that will not be duplicated
          in the league until 1943 (Joe Cronin). Caldwell will remain the only AL pitch-
          er to pinch-hit consecutive homers.

Jun 12—   Pitcher Ray Caldwell, while beating St. Louis, blasts his third home run in
          three days.

---

*Ruppert's title is honorary. Huston will reach the rank of colonel in World War I and together
Ruppert and Huston will be known as "the colonels." Huston's friends will continue to call him "Cap."

— The 27-year-old Caldwell has a fantastic all-round season. He is 19-16/2.89 ERA as the circuit's second winningest southpaw. He scores 27 runs, a total that will remain the second most by a ML pitcher, and leads the AL in pinch-hit at bats (33). Caldwell leads AL pitchers in fielding (.988) and is one of the finest baserunners in the AL.

Jul 7— The Philadelphia Athletics sell the Yankees the contract of pitcher Bob Shawkey.

— This transaction, reportedly involving $85,000, indicated owners Jake Ruppert and Til Huston are serious about building a winner. The colonels picked a fine nucleus around which to build a great pitching staff. Shawkey is a combined 10-13 with the A's and Yanks in 1915 but the 24-year-old righthander from Pennsylvania will go on to compile a Yankee record of 168-131, pitching through 1927. He will be the Yankees' first four-time 20-game winner.

1916

Jan 16— Pitcher King Cole dies at the age of 29 in Bay City, Mich. Cole had records of 11-9 and 2-3 with the Yankees in 1914 and 1915. He was a 20-game winner with the Cubs in 1910.

Feb 15— The Yankees buy the contract of Frank Baker, the best third baseman in baseball, from Connie Mack's Athletics for a reported $35,000.

— Baker, who sat out the entire 1915 season on his Maryland farm, brings class to the Yankees, but his best years are behind him in Philadelphia. His lifetime batting average of .307 is lowered by his six-season .288 average in New York. But Home Run Baker hits 48 of his 93 lifetime fourbaggers while with the Yankees.

Apr 12— For the third time in three season starters, Walter Johnson defeats the Yankees on Opening Day. He beats Ray Caldwell, 3-2, in 11 innings at the Polo Grounds.

Jun 21— Boston's George Foster throws a no-hitter against the Yankees at Fenway Park. The Red Sox win, 2-0, as Bob Shawkey takes a tough loss. Foster allows three free passes, strikes out three and there are no Boston errors. (It is the second no-hitter dealt the Yankees in their 13½-year history.)

1917

Apr 24— New York's George Mogridge pitches a no-hitter against Boston. It is the first ever *won* by a Yankee pitcher. (See August 30, 1910.) Mogridge's no-hitter will remain the only hitless game thrown by a Yankee southpaw. Amazingly, George records his no-hitter at Fenway Park, a famous graveyard for left-handers with its short left field wall. Six Red Sox reach base, three by walks and three on Yankee errors, and one scores as the Yankees triumph, 2-1.

May 19— The Yankees take the AL lead but hold it for only one brief day.

— In the first two years of the Ruppert-Huston ownership, slow but steady progress is made. But after reaching the top rung of the ladder on this date, the Yankees gradually slide down the AL standings, finishing in sixth place.

This is a disappointment. Since finishing eighth in 1912, the Yankees in each of the following years improve in the final standinga by one place, finishing fourth in 1916. At season's end, Jake Ruppert summons Manager Wild Bill Donovan to the brewery. "I like you, Donovan," he says, "but we have to make some changes around here." And Donovan answers, "I know it, Colonel." After this, his third season, the popular Donovan departs.

Jun 23— In a deal with Louisville of the Southern League, the Yankees purchase the contract of Aaron Ward.
— The versatile Ward is an important addition. Playing both second and third bases, he will be a big asset over 10 seasons, his best in 1921 when he will hit .306 and help New York to its first pennant.

Jul 10— In one of the great pitching efforts in Yankee history, Ray Caldwell does not allow a hit over 9⅔ relief innings and gets the win as the Yankees outlast St. Louis, 7-5, in 17 innings

Aug 17— Yankee first baseman Wally Pipp hits the Yankees' sole grand slam home run of the season.
— Pipp is on his way to his second consecutive AL home run title. He is the first Yankee to lead the league in homers. In his 11 seasons with New York (1915-25), Pipp hits a combined .282 and has five 90-plus RBI years. In the championship years of the early 1920's, Pipp teams with Babe Ruth and Bob Meusel to form a powerful trio of run producers. Pipp and Hugh High came to the Yankees from Detroit in 1915 for the waiver price of $7,500. (Tiger owner Frank Navin is the only AL owner to make good on his word to the colonels to help restock the depleted Yankees.) Pipp's excellence at his Yankee position of first base suffers from the sandwiching of his career between that of the greatest fielding first baseman of all time, Hal Chase, and

Frank "Home Run" Baker is at the far right in the front row, Bob Shawkey is fourth from the left in the third row, and Roger Pechinpaugh is second from the right in the third row. The leader of these Yankees, Manager Wild Bill Donovan, is in the middle of the second row. This team photo was made in either 1916 or 1917.

the greatest hitting first baseman in history, Lou Gehrig. Indeed, he probably is best remembered as the man Gehrig replaced. But Wally Pipp was an outstanding ballplayer.

Oct 26— Miller Huggins signs a two-year contract to manage the Yankees.

— The hiring is done solely by Jake Ruppert although AL President Ban Johnson, an admirer of The Mighty Mite, acts as advisor. Cap Huston wants Uncle Wilbert Robinson for the job, but Huston is in France with the war effort and his influence is diminished by distance. Huggins isn't anxious to join the Yankees but is persuaded by J.G. Taylor Spink, publisher of *The Sporting News,* to see Ruppert. The two meet at the brewery and like each other's sales pitch. To his astonishment, Huggins accepts the position of Yankee manager. The signing of Hug is, of course, a tremendous step in the right direction for the Yankees. But Huston refuses to see it that way and never forgives Ruppert for not hiring his friend, Uncle Wilbert. The co-ownership is irreparably damaged; Huston will leave the club within a matter of a few years. In the meantime, Huggins must suffer Huston's constant criticism. Huggins, who learned the game on the sandlots of Cincinnati, turned pro in 1899 and played 13 seasons (1904-16) in the majors. Hug was a headsy second baseman and was a law school graduate. Over the previous five seasons he was happily engaged as manager of the Cardinals.

1918

Apr 15 In the Yankees' opener at Washington, New York wins, 6-3, as Allan Russell defeats Walter Johnson. It is the only occasion in four Opening Day meetings that the Yankees beat the Big Train.

May 6— Three years to the day he hit his first major league home run at the Polo Grounds, Boston's Babe Ruth for the first time plays a position other than pitcher, again making history at the Polo Grounds. Ruth fields well at first base, bats sixth and hits a home run. Yankee President Jacob Ruppert, watching this display, offers to buy Ruth's contract. But Harry Frazee, the Red Sox owner, laughingly turns Ruppert away.

May 23— General Enoch Crowder, provost marshal of the armed forces, issues a "work or fight" order and sets July 1 as the deadline for men in nonessential work (like baseball) to take war-related jobs or be drafted. Later, Secretary of War Newton D. Baker relaxes this deadline. The major leagues decide to end the season on Labor Day, with the World Series following.

May 24— The Yankees play the longest game, by innings, in the Polo Grounds' long history.

— Cleveland beats New York, 3-2, in 19 innings. Stan Coveleski of the Tribe goes the entire route, allowing 12 hits and 6 walks, in a real test of endurance. Another Indian hero is Smokey Joe Wood, the one-time great Boston pitcher now playing the outfield. He hits two home runs, including a game winner in the 19th. George Mogridge is the loser. New York third baseman Frank Baker makes 11 assists, tying an AL record for third sackers in an extra-inning game.

Aug 26— The National Commission awards the contract of Jack Quinn, the fine spitball pitcher, to the Yankees. Quinn's contract has been a matter of dispute between the Yankees and White Sox, sowing seeds of discord in the AL.

— It is Ban Johnson who casts the deciding vote in favor of the Yankees, and Charley Comiskey of the White Sox never forgives the AL president. There is only a week left in the 1918 season so Quinn joins New York in 1919. In his career, he has two Yankee stints (1909-12 and 1919-21) and has a combined 81-64 record. Quinn will pitch in the majors until he is 49. He will win a total of 247 games.

Sep 2— The season ends. New York plays 123 games (60-63) and finishes fourth in Miller Huggins' first season. The Yankees lost 14 roster players to military service during the season, including stars Wally Pipp, Bob Shawkey, and Ray Fisher, the latter missing the entire season. All in all, it was not a fair test of Huggins.

1919

Mar 15— New York sells the contract of pitcher Ray Fisher to the Cincinnati Reds.

— Fisher, a teacher during the off-season, goes 73-77 in eight Yankee seasons, after starring on his Middlebury College baseball team in Vermont. He misses the entire 1918 baseball season while serving in the military but will bounce back in 1919 to go 14-5 and help the Reds win the NL pennant. Then follow 38 seasons as University of Michigan coach. Several months before his death at 95 in late 1982, Ray Fisher will be a special guest at Yankee Old Timers' Day ceremonies. It will be his first visit to Yankee Stadium.

May 1— The season is opened late because the owners, who lost money in 1918, are overly cautious and design a shortened, 140-game schedule in an attempt to save money.

— The owners miscalculate. After the war, the game is more popular than ever. At home, the Yankees break their attendance record by more than 100,000. The club under Miller Huggins is greatly improved, finishing third after occupying first place from June through late July. The Yankee record is 80-59. And for the first time the Yankee line-up is described as Murderers' Row.

May 11— The Polo Grounds is treated to a great pitching duel. Jack Quinn of the Yankees and Walter Johnson of the Senators battle for 12 innings before darkness intervenes. Quinn allows 10 hits in the scoreless tie. Johnson is even better, getting nicked for only two hits and retiring 28 Yankees in a row between Peckinpaugh's first-inning single and Baker's 10th-inning walk. (Batting leadoff for the Yankees, football great George Halas goes 0 for 5.) The next day the teams play to a 4-4 tie in a game called after 15 innings.

May 30— After defeating Walter Johnson the day before to begin a personal 10-game winning streak, Bob Shawkey shocks the Washington fans by beating Johnson for the second straight day.

Jun 2— Shortstop Roger Peckinpaugh is walked five times, tying Eagle Eye Hemphill for the most walks in one game. Hemphill drew five on August 3, 1911, to establish the Yankee club record.

Jun 8— Bob Shawkey one-hits the White Sox and pitches to only 30 batsmen as New York wins, 4-0, at the Polo Grounds.

Jul 9— Shawkey's 10-game winning streak is snapped as New York loses in Cleveland, 2-0. But Roger Peckinpaugh hits safely in his 29th consecutive game.

Peckinpaugh's 29-game hitting record (later tied by Earle Combs) will remain the Yankee record until Joe DiMaggio hits in 56 straight games in 1941.

Jul 30— New York obtains the contract of pitcher Carl Mays from the Red Sox for $40,000 and pitchers Allan Russell and Bob McGraw. It is a deal that nearly tears the AL apart. (See Sidebar—The Carl Mays Dispute of 1919). While the league slugs it out over the transaction, Mays finishes the season 9-3 with New York (with a 1.65 ERA) after going 5-11 for Boston.

Sep 10— Former Yankee Ray Caldwell pitches a no-hitter against the Yankees at the Polo Grounds as Cleveland beats Carl Mays and New York, 3-0. Two Yankees reach base, one on a walk, the other on an error. Incredibly, Caldwell's no-hitter comes less than three weeks after being hit by lightning while on the mound! The Yankees' trade of Caldwell the previous December hurts them today, but the trade will have more lasting consequences in 1920 when Caldwell's 20-10 record helps Cleveland win the pennant, finishing three games ahead of New York.

Sep 27— Bob Shawkey in a winning cause (9-2) strikes out 15 Athletics in a nine-inning game, a club record that will stand until Ron Guidry strikes out 18 batters in a 1978 game. Shawkey has a 20-11 record this year; 10 of his wins are consecutive victories.

Dec 26— Babe Ruth's contract passes from the Red Sox to the Yankees and baseball will never again be the same. The contract of sale is signed today but not announced for several days.

— For some time, Colonels Ruppert and Huston have sought Ruth. Now, with Boston owner Harry Frazee, who is first and foremost a theatrical producer, needing cash to get out of debt and produce some promising shows, the situation ripens. Frazee receives somewhere between $100,000 and $125,000, plus a personal loan from Ruppert of $300,000 to $350,000. (Reports vary as to the exact financial terms. As collateral against the loan, Ruppert takes out a mortgage on Fenway Park.) All theColonels want, and get, in return is Ruth. It is a huge sum of money for the Yankees to lay out but even Red Sox fans know the Yankees have obtained the most exciting ballplayer and biggest drawing card on the baseball scene. Now the Yankees are ready to become the *Yankees.*

THE CARL MAYS DISPUTE OF 1919

Jul 13— Red Sox pitcher Carl Mays, disgusted with his team's lack of hitting support, jumps the club. He deserves suspension but Red Sox owner Harry Frazee wants to make some money and shops Mays around.

Jul 30— The Mays contract is sold to the Yankees ($40,000 and two second-line pitchers). AL President Ban Johnson doesn't like the precedent that is being set and orders Mays' return to Boston. It is the beginning of Johnson's downfall; Yankee owners Jake Ruppert and Til Huston have no intention of returning Mays.

Aug 3—   The Yankees petition Justice Robert F. Wagner of New York for a temporary court injunction restraining Johnson from interfering with the Mays deal. Detroit owner Frank Navin says his Tigers might not play the Yankees until Mays is returned.

Aug 6—   Justice Wagner issues a temporary injunction and calls for additional briefs. Meanwhile, the Yankee owners instruct Manager Miller Huggins to pitch Mays.

Aug 9—   Carl Mays pitches his first game as a Yankee as a court clash threatens to divide the league. In fact, the AL is already in chaos, with the Colonels of New York, Harry Frazee of Boston and Charley Comiskey of Chicago squaring off against five other owners and Ban Johnson.

Oct 25— The season long over, Justice Wagner grants a permanent injunction in the Mays case. Wagner rules that AL clubs have the right to regulate their business without interference from Johnson. Johnson's power is greatly diminished.

Oct 29— The National Commission meets and refuses to recognize New York's third-place finish in the AL. The result is the withholding of the Yankee players' share of the World Series money. (The three top teams in the AL share in the World Series pool. Navin of the fourth-place Tigers argues that New York games won by Mays not be allowed because Mays was under a Johnson-imposed suspension.)

Nov 5—   Ruppert and Huston pay the Yankees their World Series money out of their own pockets.

THE 1920's
THE BLOSSOMING
OF A FRANCHISE

RUTH RULES BASEBALL
THE FEUDING AND FIGHTING
RUPPERT-BARROW-HUGGINS LEAD CLUB
THE RAPE OF THE RED SOX
YANKEE STADIUM OPENS
SIX PENNANTS WON
HOYT AND PENNOCK STAR ON MOUND
MEUSEL-COMBS-RUTH CHASE FLIES
GEHRIG BECOMES A STAR
THE GREATEST TEAM EVER
BACK-TO-BACK WORLD TITLES
HUGGINS PASSES AWAY

YANKEE-GIANT GATE COMPARISON

The Yankees and Giants for 10 years presented their offerings from the same stand, the Polo Grounds. Almost without exception, the Giants outdrew the Yankees until the arrival of the Sultan of Swat. Then the Yankees had the larger gates. Even though the Giants also enjoyed a decided upswing in attendance in the early 1920's.

	Yankees		Giants
1913	357,551		630,000
1914	359,477		364,313
1915	256,035		391,850
1916	469,211		552,056
1917	330,294		500,264
1918	282,047	—World War 1—	256,618
1919	619,164		708,857
1920	1,289,422	—Arrival of Ruth—	929,609
1921	1,026,134		945,809

1920

The Yankees will finish third with a 95-59 record, three games behind pennant-winning Cleveland, one game behind Chicago. Babe Ruth will belt 54 homers, drive in 137 runs and bat .376. Incredibly, his home run total will nearly double his previous year's total of 29, the major league record. He as an individual player will hit more home runs than any opposing *team*. Carl Mays will win 26 games and Bob Shawkey 20 games.

Jan 5—   The Babe Ruth deal is announced. The press is called to Jacob Ruppert's brewery office after Miller Huggins, in California where Ruth is vacationing, wires that Ruth has agreed to terms. New York fans are ecstatic. In Boston they threaten to tear down Fenway Park. But Red Sox owner Harry Frazee insists Boston will benefit from the Ruth sale. Yankee outfielder Ping Bodie has his own interpretation: "I suppose this means I'll be sent to China."

— Announcement of the complicated deal was delayed to give Huggins and the Yankees time to reach a contractual understanding with the Babe. Ruth was unhappy with the two years remaining on his $10,000 per year contract with Frazee. And, if the truth be told, he was not thrilled with having to leave Boston. Nor was he captivated by Hug's authoritative attitude and views as to Ruth's behavior. But Ruth's feelings were soothed with money; technically, he would remain under his old contract but he would get more than $20,000 in bonuses, making the combined pot for the 1920-21 seasons upwards of $40,000.

Feb 10— The AL owners reach the following settlement at a showdown meeting: (1) Johnson is stripped of most of his powers, ending rule by one man. (2) Carl Mays is reinstated and new York's third-place standing of 1919 is upheld. (3) A two-man board of review (Ruppert and Clark Griffith) will review penalties and fines in excess of $100 or suspensions of more than 10 days. (A Federal judge in Chicago will decide cases if the board members cannot agree.) This reduces Johnson, who will retire seven years later, more or less to figurehead status. It is a big win for the New York ownership.

Apr 1— Ruth hits his first home run in spring training (Babe's only homer in 20 exhibition games). Babe's wallop clears the fence at the 429-foot mark in center field. Ruth eventually hits over .300 for a spring training made memorable not by Ruth but by a highly successful barnstorming tour the Yankees make in the South.

Apr 22— The Yankees open the regular season in Philadelphia and lose, 6-5. Ruth manages two singles. He plays center field (the Yankees are short of outfielders) and makes an error that costs New York the game.

— With two on and two outs in the eighth, Ruth dropped Joe Dugan's fly ball and the winning runs scored. (The next day, Dugan had a brown derby, a symbol of ineptness, delivered to Ruth at home plate. Babe wore it, laughed and waved to the crowd.) Ruth played both right and left fields this year, always playing in other than the "sun field." He was in right field at home and more often than not in left field on the road.

May 1— Ruth finally hits his first regular season homer as a Yankee, his 50th career fourbagger, as New York beats Boston, 6-0. It's a tremendous blast over the right field roof at the Polo Grounds. Ruth had done this trick before, and he and Shoeless Joe Jackson were the only ones to do it.

— Ruth was mired in a slump in the early season and then left the line-up with an injury. In the same period, Boston was 10-2 and by the final day of April had defeated New York four times in the young season. The Yankees were in the second division and Harry Frazee was looking smart. The Babe's home run (along with his double) helped New York win the second game of a five-game series with Boston. The Yankees would take two more in the set and the two teams would begin moving in opposite directions in the AL standings.

May 7— Yankee business manager Harry Sparrow dies. Sparrow, in poor health since a near-fatal illness three years earlier, left the ballpark, went home and there died of heart failure.

— The Orange, N.J., native played baseball and football with the famous Orange Field Club. A friend of John J. McGraw, he made spring training trips with the Giants and in the winter of 1913-14 he served as business manager for a Giants-White Sox world tour. On McGraw's recommendation, Sparrow joined the Ruppert-Huston Yankees in 1915 and did a great job.

May 31— The Yankees set another attendance record at the Polo Grounds when 38,688 pay to see the second game of a morning-afternoon twinbill in which Ruth homers off Washington's Walter Johnson. New York wins both ends, 7-6 and 10-7.

— It was a great month for Ruth homers and Yankee attendance. Ruth hit 12 home runs on the month, 11 of them either leaving the ballpark or stopping in the upper deck. The Polo Grounds' maintenance crew painted a vertical white foul line in right field so that Ruth's shots could be more easily called fair or foul. And fans were flocking to see the Babe's show. He would hit 12 more homers in June.

Jun 1—   The Yankee pitching staff is injury-riddled, with Bob Shawkey the latest casualty. On Ruth's insistence, Miller Huggins lets the Babe start on the mound. Ruth faces 17 batters and allows three hits and two runs. He takes over in right field in the fifth inning as Hank Thormahlen comes in to finish the game. The Yankees beat Washington, 14-7, and Ruth, who at one point retired nine Senators in a row, is credited with the win. The Babe singles, doubles and scores two runs in the victory, New York's ninth in a 10-game win streak. The Yankees (24-15) are now in second place, 2½ games behind Cleveland.

Jun 4—   For the second successive day, a Yankee player hits a grand slam homer. Del Pratt does it in the first inning off 23-game loser Rollie Naylor as the Yankees down Philadelphia, 12-5. Ping Bodie had the previous day's bases-loaded roundtripper.

Jun 6—   Rookie outfielder-third baseman Bob Meusel finishes a seven-game hitting streak (.500, 16 for 32).

— The 23-year-old Californian is a tremendous addition to the Yankees, hitting .328 and driving home 83 runs on the season.

Jul 6—   The Yankees bomb Washington, 17-0, scoring 14 runs in one inning, a club record and an AL record until Boston's 17 in one inning in 1953.

Jul 9—   Some 1,000 members of the Knights of Columbus march to the Polo Grounds for a K of C-sponsored Babe Ruth Day. They present Ruth with a diamond-studded watch fob. Babe returns the favor: he unloads his 25th homer and tips his cap to the Knights' seating section.

Jul 13—   For the third time in 1920, the Polo Grounds' all-time attendance record is broken when 38,823 pile in to see the Yankees split a doubleheader with the Browns. The first time was on May 16 when 38,600 showed up to break the old mark of 38,281, set in 1911.

Jul 18—   New York outfielder Ping Bodie hits a grand slam homer in an 8-4 Yankee win over Chicago. Bodie's blast makes him the first Yankee to hit a pair of grand slams in one season.

— Bodie is a witty Italian from California. He is Ruth's roommate but he has been quoted recently as saying, "I don't room with Babe Ruth. I room with his suitcase."

Jul 28—   In St. Louis, a Bob Shawkey winning streak ends at 11 games; he loses, 1-0, even though he pitches one of his best games of the year. Sailor Bob is outdueled by 20-game winner Urban Shocker.

Jul 30—   The Yankees collect 21 hits and wreck the St. Louis Browns, 19-3. Ruth scores four runs and his three hits include his 36th homer which the New York Times describes as a "titanic wallop." The ninth-inning shot clears Sportsmans Park's right field pavilion and lands on the opposite side of Grand Avenue.

— As evidenced by the score, the Yankees had several heavy hitters besides Ruth, including Wally Pipp, Ping Bodie, Roger Peckinpaugh and a great addition to the team, Bob Meusel, who hit .328 and drove in 83 runs on the season. But Ruth was clearly the big gun in the unprecedented power barrage. The Babe would enter August with 37 home runs after a 13-homer July, a July in which he survived unscathed a serious auto accident on a winding road in Pennsylvania.

Aug 16— At the Polo Grounds, Yankee submarine-style righthander Carl Mays beans Ray Chapman, the Indians' excellent shortstop. A sickening sound fills the stands. Yet Chapman somehow manages to get to his feet with assistance and walks toward the center field clubhouse. Then he collapses on the outfield grass and falls into a coma. He is rushed to St. Lawrence Hospital and operated on that night.

Aug 17— Early in the morning, Ray Chapman dies at St. Lawrence Hospital. Major league baseball's first fatality dictates the postponement of today's game.

— Ray Chapman to this day remains the only fatality from a major league baseball game. Carl Mays was exonerated of any criminal charges but around the AL there was an angry outcry against Mays. Several players actually wanted him exiled from baseball. AL President Ban Johnson stated that he did not believe Mays would ever play again. But Mays, a cold and unpopular competitor, gained valuable support from his manager. Although no fan of Mays, Miller Huggins believed that Chapman got his spikes caught and was unable to move away from Mays' pitch. Cleveland's Ray Caldwell saw his teammate actually ducking his head right into the pitch, and Yankee catcher Muddy Ruel stated that Chapman made no effort to avoid getting hit. Mays protested his innocence. The pitch was a curveball, he argued, not the kind of pitch you would throw to bean a batter. The pitch was actually over the plate, some felt. Chapman, known for crowding the plate and crouching, for whatever reason failed to elude the fatal pitch. Mays returned to the mound August 23 and shut out Detroit.

Aug 19— The important three-game series between the Yankees and Indians, completely overshadowed by the Chapman tragedy, concludes with a 3-2 Cleveland victory. The first-place Indians leave the Polo Grounds leading the Yankees by 1½ games after winning two of three. Cleveland's record is 72-41. Chicago, a half-game behind, stands at 72-42, and the Yankees are 73-45.

Sep 18— For the third straight day, the Yankees lose in Chicago, seriously damaging the club's pennant hopes. Today, New York loses, 15-9, following 8-3 and 6-4 defeats. The night before, Til Huston pounded his fist in a Chicago hotel and roared, "This race is not over! Remember what Commodore Perry said at Lake Erie. 'Don't give up the ship until your trunks hit the water!'" But New York is eliminated. The sweep was a mild surprise to some who felt that the Indians and Yankees were the only teams trying. And, indeed, it will be announced September 28 that eight White Sox players were indicted in a 1919 World Series fix, the so-called Black Sox Scandal.

Sep 29— On the final day of the season, Ruth hits his 54th home run off Dave Keefe in Philadelphia as the Yankees sweep a doubleheader.

— In the first season of the "lively ball," the Babe broke his previous season's record by all of 25 homers. The Yankees aside, he personally hit more round-trippers than any AL team! But the pennant belonged to Cleveland, thanks in part to New York's three-game Windy City failure. However, the Yankees wound up with a .617 winning percentage, highest in the AL before or since for a team finishing third. They played to six new attendance records on the road and had a home mark of 1,289,422, which remained the AL record until 1946. The Giants disliked being outdrawn in their own ballpark and the Yankees were flirting with eviction. But the colonels were prepared, having taken out an option on 20 acres in the Bronx.

Oct 29— Ed Barrow becomes the Yankees' business manager (a job later known as general manager), and it is announced that Miller Huggins will return as New York's manager in 1921.

— The middle-aged Barrow left the sinking Red Sox to join the rising Yankees, a club he successfully operated for the next 25 years. A lifelong baseball man, Barrow held a variety of jobs in the game before joining the Yankees. He was both a tightfisted executive and a baseball genius. He moved quickly to assure Miller Huggins of his support and to establish a businesslike atmosphere in the Yankee front office.

Nov 12— Judge Kenesaw Mountain Landis is named Commissioner of Baseball, effective January 1921. The main reason for Landis' appointment is the blow to organized baseball inflicted by the Black Sox Scandal. But the feuding in the AL over the Carl Mays' case is a contributing factor. The Yankees, Red Sox and White Sox had threatened to bolt the AL and join the NL.

Dec 15— Barrow makes his first big trade and it is a whopper. From Boston the Yankees obtain Waite Hoyt (P), Wally Schang (C), Harry Harper (P) and Mike McNally (INF). They give Del Pratt (2B), Muddy Ruel (C), Hank Thormahlen (P), Sammy Vick (OF) and cash.

— The key acquisition for the Yankees was the Brooklyn-born Hoyt, who, in his 10-year career with New York had a 157-98 record, eventually winning 237 games and making the Baseball Hall of Fame. He was 6-6 for Boston in 1920. Schang was the first in the long line of great Yankee catchers and batted .297 in five seasons in New York. Harper and McNally contributed more modestly. Although Pratt hit over .300 in his final four big league seasons, giving up Ruel hurt the Yankees most. Ruel, who hit .275 lifetime, would remain in the bigs (mostly with Washington) through 1934 as one of the game's greatest catchers. Barrow and Huggins always admitted that trading Ruel was a mistake.

1921

The Yankees with a 98-55 record will win the first pennant in their history. They will finish 4½ games ahead of second-place Cleveland. Babe Ruth will set another home run record with 59 and Carl Mays will lead AL pitchers with a 27-9 record. But the Yanks will lose to the Giants in a long World Series. "The strain was too much for us," Huggins will say.

Apr 13— On Opening Day at the Polo Grounds, Babe Ruth goes five for five with two doubles and three singles in the Yanks' 11-1 win over Philadelphia. It is Ruth's first five-hit game as a Yankee.

May 7— Yankee outfielder Bob Meusel hits a single, double, triple and homer in one game. He is only the second Yankee to hit for the cycle, Bert Daniels having done it nine years earlier. Ruth hits a monstrous homer to center field off

Walter Johnson in the eighth inning, the longest homer hit in the Nation's Capital up to this time.

May 25— Ruth blasts his 13th home run. The distance is estimated at over 500 feet, the longest homer hit in St. Louis up to that time.

May 29— Ruth hits his 14th home run, a towering drive that clears the right field roof of the Polo Grounds. He hits it off Dave Keefe of Philadelphia as the Yankees win, 9-4.

Jun 8— Ruth is arrested for speeding on Riverside Drive in Manhattan.

— The Sultan of Swat was slapped with a $100 fine and ordered held, not to be released until 4 p.m. And the Yankees had a game scheduled for 3:15 p.m. Ruth's uniform was delivered, he suited up in jail and at 4 p.m. stepped out to an awaiting crowd. A motorcycle escort led him uptown to the Polo Grounds and he ran through the center field gate to a great ovation. New York was losing, 3-2, but rallied to win, 4-3, and although Ruth did nothing at the plate, he once more stole the headlines!

Jun 13— Ruth blasts a homer for the fourth straight day. He actually hits a pair of fourbaggers, both off Detroit's Howard Ehmke, in leading the Yankees to an 11-8 triumph.

— The Babe began the game pitching and finished in center field. He worked five innings on the mound, striking out Ty Cobb and earning the victory. The Yanks were without a rested pitcher and Ruth volunteered to fill the gap. So Huggins went with him. Ruth allowed four runs but the Tigers were out-produced, thanks largely to Ruth whose second homer landed in the Polo Grounds' right-center field bleachers about 460 feet from home plate.

Jun 14— Hitting two more homers, both off the Tigers' Hooks Dauss, Ruth completes an incredible stretch in which he hits at least one homer in each of five games for a total of seven home runs, an AL record. One streak gives way to another—the Yanks have begun a nine-game win skein. And Ruth will have another personal streak. On August 28 he will begin an AL record-setting streak of at least one extra-base hit in nine consecutive games.

Jul 4— At the Polo Grounds, Ruth hits a "pop-up" that reaches its peak at twice the level of the roof of the Polo Grounds. Second baseman Jimmy Dykes of the Athletics staggers around the infield in a feeble attempt to get under the falling sphere. At last, the ball strikes the tip of Dykes' glove and falls safely to the ground. Dykes is given an error in a scoring decision that has the Babe angry for days.

Aug 11— New York moves into first place, one percentage point ahead of Cleveland (.618 to .617). The Yankees win, 7-3, in Philadelphia, as Ruth delivers a home run and a bunt single. In the next several days, the Yankees and Indians take turns at the top of the AL.

Aug 15— The Yankees are in first place and have a day off. Jake Ruppert takes this opportunity to announce that Miller Huggins will be his manager again in 1922.

— Ruppert was forced to constantly give Hug his support in the face of Cap Huston's open disdain for the Mighty Mite's managerial abilities. Huggins' genius was not yet universally recognized.

Aug 25— Cleveland blasts New York, 15-1, as the teams brawl and the pennant race heats up. Steve O'Neill, the third Indian plunked by pitcher Harry Harper, picks up the ball and whips it back at Harper in anger. Both teams meet in the center of the field for fisticuffs but no one is injured. In baseball action, the normally reliable Bob Meusel makes four errors in the outfield.

Sep 3— The Yankees beat Washington for the sixth consecutive time in five days. They took two games in Washington, then returned to New York for a four-game sweep. New York scores a total of 59 runs and all its wins are about as easy as today's 9-3 triumph. The Yankees' good luck with the Senators, who will finish in the first division, is a key to their winning the pennant.

Sep 5— In the second game of a doubleheader at Boston, center fielder Bob Meusel makes four assists and ties an AL record for outfielders. Overall, New York outfielders make five assists, another still-standing AL record. The Yankees win, 8-0, then lose, 8-2.

— Meusel had one of the greatest throwing arms in baseball history—some experts insist he was the greatest throwing outfielder in the game's long story. He led AL outfielders in assists in 1921 and 1922 before baserunners knew better than to unnecessarily challenge Long Bob's arm.

Sep 9— Ruth ties his single-season home run record, hitting his 54th off Rollie Naylor as the Yankees win, 14-5. Philadelphians say it is the longest ball ever hit at Shibe Park to that time.

Sep 10— New York defeats the Athletics, 19-3, as Carl Mays scatters 13 hits. Leading the Yanks' 21-hit attack is catcher Wally Schang who accounts for five of the hits.

— The understandable fuss over Ruth relegated baseball's best battery in 1921, Carl Mays and Schang, to unsung hero status. Mays pitched 337 innings, a workload never again carried by a Yankee pitcher, and tied the Browns' Urban Shocker for the AL lead with 27 wins. Hitting .343, Mays stroked 49 hits, the third most by a pitcher in AL history. Schang, the strongest man in baseball according to Ed Barrow, was an excellent defensive catcher and in 1921 hit .316.

Sep 15— For the third consecutive season, Ruth breaks a home run standard he himself set. Ruth unloads No. 55 against the Browns as the Yanks sweep a doubleheader at the Polo Grounds, 10-6 and 13-5. New York leads the pennant race. Cleveland will lead tomorrow, New York the day after tomorrow, and Cleveland the day after that. The Yankees will regain first place on September 20.

Sep 23— Cleveland, trailing the Yankees by two percentage points, enters the Polo Grounds for a four-game showdown series to determine the pennant winner. Young but poised, Yankee righthander Waite Hoyt rises to the occasion in the opener, winning 4-2 as the Babe rips three doubles and scores three runs. But Cleveland will rebound to beat the Yankees tomorrow.

Sep 25— Before a standing-room-only Sunday crowd of more than 40,000, the largest crowd to see the Yanks at the Polo Grounds, New York mauls Cleveland, 21-7, and extends its lead to 1½ games.

— While Ruth's bat was relatively silent, Carl Mays, Bob Meusel, Wally Pipp and Roger Peckinpaugh each collected three hits. The contributions of

Pipp and Peckinpaugh this year were invaluable. Pipp hit .296 and knocked in 97 runs. Peckinpaugh hit .288 and was the key to a cohesive infield.

Sep 26— Almost worn to a frazzle by the worrying of his bosses, Jake Ruppert and Til Huston, Miller Huggins arrives at the Polo Grounds uncertain as to whom he will pitch in the series finale, a game that will prove to be one of the greatest in Yankee history. Hug's pitching staff is tired and he is tempted to bring back Hoyt on two days' rest. Instead, he shocks his pitchers by asking them for a candidate. Jack Quinn gets the pitchers' nod. But Quinn allows three first-inning runs and the overworked Hoyt is brought in. Then the Yanks score four runs in their half of the first inning and a see-saw battle is on. The Babe belts his 57th and 58th homers, doubles and walks. Hoyt, displaying a lion's courage, lasts until the eighth inning when, exhausted, he leaves with New York leading, 8-7. Mays is the reliever. In the ninth, Cleveland puts runners on second and third with two outs. The nervous Ruppert seeks solace in the Yankee bullpen and promises his pitchers the brewery if the Yankees win. The crowd is on its feet as Mays runs the count full to Steve O'Neill. Then O'Neill swings, misses and the Yankees win, 8-7, their greatest victory to date. Cleveland leaves town 2½ games out of first place with the race virtually over. New York has beaten Cleveland in 14 of 22 games this season.

Oct 1— The Yankees sweep a doubleheader from the Athletics at the Polo Grounds, clinching their first AL pennant with a 5-3 victory in the opener. In the nightcap, Huggins accedes to the wishes of the crowd and Ruth and permits the Bambino to take the mound in the eighth inning, after Hoyt had staked the Yankees to a 6-0 lead. Pitcher Ruth allows Philadelphia to tie the game, then pitches three shutout innings. The Yanks score in the 11th to win, 7-6. Babe has a tainted victory, his second of the year. But poor Hoyt is deprived of his 20th victory—he will finish 19-13.

— The Yankees' all-time record was evened at 1,412 wins and 1,412 losses with the pennant-clinching win of the first game. By winning the nightcap, the Yankees climbed over the .500 mark, never to drop below .500 again in the franchise's history. New York City was in a swirl over the upcoming World Series between the Yankees and Giants, the first Subway Series. The Yankees were favored to win the Series because of Ruth, Murderers' Row and pitchers Mays, Hoyt and Bob Shawkey. But the Giants were hungry —they had finished second three years in a row.

Oct 2— On the final day of the regular season, Ruth blasts No. 59, a three-run homer that helped the Yankees edge the Red Sox, 7-6.

— Not only did the Babe finish the year with a new home run record and league leadership in slugging (.846), walks (144), RBIs (171) and runs scored (177), but he established other never-to-be-broken marks with 457 total bases and 119 extra-base hits. His run total was the most ever scored by a 20th-century player. He had an incredible season, possibly the greatest year a hitter ever had. His batting average, while third in the league behind Harry Heilmann and Ty Cobb, was a towering .378.

Oct 5— The best-of-nine-game World Series opens with Carl Mays hurling a five-hitter and the Yankees beating the Giants, 3-0, at the Polo Grounds. In the first inning, centerfielder Elmer Miller scores the first Yankee run in World Series history, with Ruth driving him home with a single. That is all Mays needs, but the Yankees add insurance runs in the fifth on Mike McNally's steal of home and in the sixth on Bob Meusel's run-scoring triple. (Meusel himself is declared out for failing to touch first base.) Frankie Frisch gets four hits for the Giants.

Oct 6—   Waite Hoyt puts on one of the greatest pitching shows in World Series annals, stopping the Giants cold on two hits. The Yankees win another 3-0 decision. The Giants' Johnny Rawlings leads off the third with his team's first hit but after that McGraw's team is hitless until Frisch's one-out single in the ninth. (In the first two games, Frisch makes five of his club's seven hits.) Meanwhile, the Yankees themselves manage only three hits off Giant ace Art Nehf, but break through in the fourth on Hoyt's bases-loaded groundout. In the fifth, Ruth walks for the third time and thrills the crowd by stealing second and third. The steal of third is costly; Ruth badly scrapes an elbow that will become infected. The Yankees add two insurance runs in the eighth, capped by Bob Meusel's steal of home.

Oct 7—   Bob Shawkey runs the Giant scoreless streak to 20 innings, and when the Yankees score four times in the top of the third, it looks like lights out for the Giants. But the Giants knock Shawkey out in the third with successive bases-loaded walks, scoring four runs and tying the game, then put the contest out of reach, 13-5, with an eight-run seventh.

Oct 10—   In Game 5, Hoyt and Nehf repeat their earlier pitching duel, the Brooklyn Schoolboy spreading out 10 hits as the Yankees win, 3-1, taking a 3-2 lead in the Series. With the score 1-1, Ruth leads off the fourth with a bunt single and scores on a double by Meusel. Ruth plays with the painful elbow infection, a leg injury and a wrenched knee. All three problems are aggravated by today's action. Ruth's grit wins him the cheers of virtually everyone. But Ruth was sidelined in the next two games, both Yankee losses.

Oct 13—   Pitching on two days' rest, Hoyt is brilliant. But the only run of the game is scored by the Giants in the first inning. It is unearned; with two outs, a grounder goes through shortstop Peckinpaugh's legs and a baserunner scores. Hoyt allows just six hits but counterpart Nehf permits only four. In the ninth inning, Ruth pinch-hits and grounds out. Then Ward walks and Frank Baker is robbed by second baseman Rawlings, who throws him out at first, with Ward attempting to take third. First baseman George Kelly guns Ward down, with Frisch making the tag to end Game 8 and the Series. The Giants are World Champions.

           — Ruth's virtual absence after Game 5 did not help; the Yankees scored one run in the last 25 innings without the Bambino. Miller Huggins talked of a strain on his pitching staff but the strain was certainly not too much for Hoyt. The Brooklyn Schoolboy refused to allow a single earned run in 27 innings of pitching!

Oct 21—   In Scranton, Pa., Yankee co-owner Cap Huston talks Babe Ruth into ending an ill-fated barnstorming tour with more than half the exhibition schedule left to play.* Babe quits his tour, not because he is afraid of a threatening Commissioner Landis, but because Huston convinces Babe that the repercussions could hurt the Yankees.

           — Ruth and a few Yankee teammates had gone barnstorming in direct violation of a major league rule prohibiting touring by World Series partici-

---

*It may have been Ruth's only postseason barnstorming flop, both financially and artistically.

pants. And Commissioner Landis had given plenty of warning of the consequences of any such barnstorming by Ruth and his pals. This was a major crisis in baseball and a threat to Landis' authority.

Dec 5— Commissioner Landis announces his decision. Babe Ruth, Bob Meusel and pitcher Bill Piercy (5-4 for N.Y. in 1921) receive six-week suspensions, beginning at the start of the 1922 season, and forfeiture of their World Series shares of $3,362.26 plus forfeiture of their first six weeks' salary of 1922. A fourth Yankee player who participated in the barnstorming tour, Tom Sheehan (1-0 in 1921), was not punished because he had not been eligible for the World Series. Landis declared the group (he was really aiming at the Babe) in "mutinous defiance." The Yankee owners were not unhappy; they had expected stiffer penalties.

Dec 20— The Yankees announce another blockbuster deal with the Red Sox. In exchange for Roger Peckinpaugh (SS), Jack Quinn (P) and Rip Collins (P) and cash, the Yankees receive Everett Scott (SS), Sad Sam Jones (P) and Joe Bush (P). All three Yankee acquisitions will make big contributions in 1922; Scott playing every game and hitting .269, Jones going 13-13 and Bush having a tremendous 26-7 record.

1922

The Yankees, at 94-60, will win their second consecutive pennant, nosing out the St. Louis Browns by one game. Babe Ruth will lose his home run title even though he hits 35. Bullet Joe Bush will be 26-7 and Bob Shawkey 20-12, making the Yankees baseball's only club with a pair of 20-game winners. But the Yankees will again lose to the Giants in the World Series, and will lose badly.

Apr 12— The season opens in Washington without the suspended Babe Ruth and Bob Meusel. President Harding throws out the first ball. The Yankees lose, 6-5.

Apr 17— The Yankees purchase the contract of Whitey Witt (OF) from the Athletics in an attempt to fill the void created by the suspensions of Babe Ruth and Bob Meusel.

— After the 1921 World Series defeat, Ed Barrow and Miller Huggins decided replacements were needed in a couple of positions, one of them in center field. Witt was an outstanding centerfielder. He led AL outfielders in fielding in 1923 with a .979 percentage. He was a tremendous leadoff man, possessing blinding speed, an eagle batting eye and a stinging bat, and he averaged exactly .300 at the plate over four New York seasons.

May 5— White Construction Company of New York begins construction of Yankee Stadium and will complete the job in 284 working days at slightly more than $2.3 million.

— "Yankee Stadium was a mistake," Ruppert once said, "not mine, but the Giants'!" Giants owner Charles A. Stoneham asked the Yankees to leave the Polo Grounds, ostensibly to allow both teams to accept more Sunday dates but probably out of jealousy over Yankee gate successes. Now the Yankee owners were building a magnificent structure with Til Huston, an engineer, overseeing the operation.

May 20— Their suspensions lifted, Ruth and Meusel return to the line-up of the first-place Yankees. It is like a second opening day at the Polo Grounds and the Bambino assumes his new role as Yankee captain. But Ruth and Meusel are hitless, and Sad Sam Jones loses a heartbreaker to St. Louis. Going into the ninth inning, Jones apparently has a 2-1 lead protected as he steps on first base for the final out. But he drops the ball and the runner is safe. Part of the overflow crowd of some 40,000 goes onto the field. Play stops for several minutes until the field is cleared. Then Jones cannot get the third out. The Browns, given a second life, score seven runs for a stunning 8-2 victory.

May 22— Ruth hits home run No. 1 of the season but shows no joy as he trots around the bases. The Polo Grounds' crowd has been either booing him or mock cheering him when, for example, he catches an easy fly ball. Ruth responds with sarcastic tips of his cap. The Babe has a tough year with the fans who resent his $52,000 contract.

May 27— Ruth enters the Polo Grounds' stands to fight a heckler. The ruckus starts when the Babe tries to stretch a single and is called out. He throws dirt at the umpire and is ejected from the game, the first ejection of his Yankee career. As Ruth reaches the dugout, the heckler enrages him. Ruth charges into the stands after the fast-fleeing fan. A brigade of special police, ushers and players intercepts Ruth, and he walks to the center field clubhouse in a crescendo of boos. AL President Ban Johnson suspends Ruth for one game, fines him $200 and strips him of his six-game Yankee captaincy.

Jun 12— New York loses, 7-1, as Ruth goes down on strikes three straight times at the hands of Hub Pruett. The St. Louis pitcher has legendary success pitching to the Sultan, fanning him 13 times in their first 21 confrontations.

Jun 19— Umpire Dinneen dislikes Ruth's choice of obscenities and ejects him from the game. The Babe had come in from his left field position to argue a call at second base which gave Cleveland's Les Nunamaker a double and ignited a two-run rally in the eighth to give Cleveland a 3-2 win. It also gave the Yanks their eighth loss in a row. Later in the evening, Ban Johnson suspends Ruth for three days for using "vulgar and vicious language." The league president is a little vicious himself, adding that "maybe with Ruth out, (the Yankees) will turn around and win a few..." Unable to let things be, Ruth the next day verbally assaults Dinneen and gets two days tacked onto his suspension. This, his fourth suspension of the year, costs Ruth about $1,500 in lost salary.

Jul 3— For the second time in his big league career, Long Bob Meusel bats for the cycle (a single, double, triple and homer in one game).

Jul 23— The Yankees shore up a weak link by obtaining third baseman Joe Dugan from the Red Sox. The exact deal has Dugan and Elmer Smith (OF) going to New York for Elmer Miller (OF), Chick Fewster (OF), John Mitchell (SS), Lefty O'Doul (P), who will be transferred to Boston after the season,* and cash. Dugan takes over at third from Home Run Baker, who will retire in February, and hits .286 in 60 games.

---

*A more important transfer later in his career moves O'Doul from the mound to the outfield, and he hits .349 lifetime.

— What a furor this trade created! The first-place Browns and their fans cried foul. How could the Yankees arrange a deal in the middle of the pennant race and acquire a player of Dugan's caliber and give what they regarded as so little in return? The St. Louis Chamber of Commerce adopted a resolution denouncing the Yankees for an alleged lack of sportsmanship and Ban Johnson bellowed that this kind of deal was injurious to baseball even though it was within the rules. Soon the rules would be changed, thanks to Judge Landis who instituted a trading deadline of June 15 (except for waiver deals).

Jul 26— In St. Louis, Bob Meusel and Wally Schang fight on the Yankee bench, to be followed by a Babe Ruth-Wally Pipp bout, after Ruth criticizes Pipp for what he saw as a poor fielding effort. Pipp the Pickler pops Ruth and the Bambino roars, "We'll settle this after the game." But then Ruth hits two home runs, Pipp hits one and Schang triples in two runs, helping the Yankees to a come-from-behind 11-6 win. Everyone makes peace in the victorious locker room.

— This may have been the wildest Yankee team in history, a hard-drinking, quick-tempered lot Miller Huggins found all but impossible to discipline. On this particular road trip there were Yankees in a fistfight practically every day. Finally, Huggins used his pocketbook weapon. "I'm running a ball club, not a fight club," he said. "Hereafter, if there is any fighting, you'll pay for it in fines and suspensions." But the club lifestyle was engrained. Back in spring training camp in New Orleans, there had been a headline which said that the Yankees were "Training on Scotch." Jake Ruppert was moved to hire a detective named Kelly who ingratiated himself with the Yankee players and traveled around the circuit with them, partying and turning in incriminating reports. Among other penalties, the bad actors had to undergo a stern lecture from Commissioner Landis on the evils of drinking and playing the horses.

Aug 20— Ruth scores five runs in one game, becoming the first Yankee to do so. The Yankees win the game with Chicago in the bottom of the ninth, 7-5.

Aug 30— At the Polo Grounds, Ruth homers in his first at bat but is called out on strikes in his next plate appearance. The Bambino uses foul language and Umpire Connolly tosses him out of the game.

— Two days later, AL President Ban Johnson handed Ruth a three-day suspension for abusing an umpire. The Babe endured five suspensions in this one season.

Sep 5— The final regular season home run hit by Ruth at the Polo Grounds is given up by Boston's Herb Pennock who on May 1, 1920, also served the Babe his first Polo Grounds homer as a Yankee.

Sep 10— The Yankees sweep a doubleheader from Philadelphia, 10-3 and 2-1, before the largest crowd to date in Polo Grounds' history. General Manager Ed Barrow estimates 40,000 were admitted to the ballpark and another 25,000 turned away. Mob scenes occur and one fan is actually crushed to death. All the excitement is over the Yankees' final game at the Polo Grounds. The club will have to chase the pennant on the road for the remainder of this season, and next season it will be quartered across the Harlem River in the Bronx.

— Bullet Joe Bush and Waite Hoyt, the winning pitchers against Philadelphia, were members of a pitching staff that had one unusual feature: all 154 games were started by *righthanders*—George Murray (4-2), Carl Mays (12-14), Sad Sam Jones (13-13), Hoyt (19-12), Bob Shawkey (20-12) and Bush (26-7), who fought off a finger injury and did well at the plate, too, hitting .326. Lefty O'Doul, while on the staff, was used only in relief. He had no decisions in six appearances.

Sep 11— Ruth blasts two home runs and adds a pair of doubles to register four extra-base hits in one contest. The Yankees win, 9-4, at Philadelphia.

Sep 16— Leading the Browns by a half game, the Yankees arrive in St. Louis for the most important series of the year. The city is crazy with excitement. The Browns have never won a pennant and anti-Yankee feeling (inspired by the Dugan deal) runs high. The Yankees notice that a small brown barrel is placed on every street corner, the significance of which is explained to Yankee players by a cab driver. "A committee of fans is taking up a citywide collection to buy presents for the Browns," says the cabbie, "when they knock you off and clinch the pennant." The opener is a pitching duel between Bob Shawkey and Urban Shocker, a pair of 20-game winners. Sportsmans Park is packed beyond capacity, and fans keep chanting, "Yellow, yellow, yellow!" at Ruth. Shawkey and the Yankees win, 2-1. In the ninth inning, while Whitey Witt and Bob Meusel chase a fly ball hit by Eddie Foster, a bottle is thrown from the crowd and strikes Witt on the forehead between the eyes with such force that it breaks. Witt is knocked out cold and is bleeding. Fans start to come onto the field but police hold them back. One yells, "We'll get you, too, Meusel!" Yankee coach Charley O'Leary smears Witt's blood all over Whitey's face and the crowd is some-what arrested by the sight. Bootnose Hofmann and a few other teammates carry Witt off the field. He has a deep two-inch cut but fortunately a surgeon finds nothing worse. League President Ban Johnson offers a reward for the arrest of the bottle thrower. One fan maintained that Witt stepped on the bottle, kicked it in the air and actually hit himself in the forehead! St. Louis will rebound and win tomorrow's game, 5-1.

Sep 18— The Yankees pull it out, 3-2, in their most critical win of the season. The Browns lead, 2-1, in the ninth inning, when Pruett enters the game, loads the bases and is removed. Witt, still bandaged, singles in two runs, the tying and winning runs of the game. Poetic justice is served in Witt's case, but yesterday's hero, Pruett, takes the loss. As the Yankees head for the train station to leave town, happy with their 1½-game lead, they see all the street-corner barrels kicked over, resting in the gutters. All the collected money will be given to charity, they are told. And the Yankees celebrate all the way to Detroit. They had beaten what was probably the greatest team in Browns' history. George Sisler, who led the league in triples, hits, runs scored and stolen bases, was also the leading hitter at .420!

Sep 30— The Yankees defeat Boston, 3-1, clinching the pennant in dramatic style behind the outstanding pitching of Bush and Hoyt. They now turn their attention to the hard-hitting Giants.

Oct 4— The best-of-seven-game World Series opens with the Giants rallying for a 3-2 win. Breaking up a scoreless game in the sixth inning, Ruth singles home Dugan. Aaron Ward's sacrifice fly in the seventh increases the Yanks' lead to 2-0. But in the eighth, the Giants reach Bush, as Irish Meusel's bases-loaded single ties the game and Frankie Frisch scores the third run on a sacrifice fly.

Oct 5— In one of the most controversial games in World Series history, Game 2 ends, 3-3, after 10 innings, when it is called because of darkness. Bob Shawkey allows three first-inning runs, then puts goose eggs on the Giant side of the scoreboard for nine straight innings. The Yanks, meanwhile, chip away, scoring on Pipp's single in the first, Ward's homer in the fourth and Meusel's double in the eighth. Umpires Hildebrand and Klem call the game with at least 30 minutes of daylight left. Angry fans, who mistakenly figure the game is called by Commissioner Landis, harass Landis all the way down the street from the ballpark. Later, Landis orders the game receipts turned over to charity and the public furor eases somewhat.

Oct 8— In Game 5, the Giants beat the Yankees, 5-3, to sweep the Series (with one tie). The clubs' respective aces, 26-game-winner Bush and 19-game-winner Art Nehf, go all the way. Bush's fifth-inning single ties the score, 2-2, and the Yanks go ahead in the seventh on Everett Scott's sacrifice fly. Bush takes the one-run lead into the eighth, and, after getting into a jam, is ordered by Huggins to issue an intentional walk. Bush answers Hug in loud curses heard by all, then gives up a two-run single to George Kelly in a three-run rally.

— In the aftermath, Huggins and Bush will never be cordial toward each other again. Huston screams for Huggins' resignation, and Ruth is branded the goat because of his .118 batting average (2 for 17). McGraw's reputation as a genius was enhanced since he called every Giant pitch, and the Giants felt that they had reclaimed New York. The Yankees set sail for the Bronx, slightly disorganized.

Dec 12— Jake Ruppert announces he will buy Til Huston's Yankee stock and will become the sole owner of the club.

— The long simmering disagreement between Ruppert and Huston over Huggins' merits was brought to a head. "Miller Huggins has managed the Yankees for the last time," Huston had announced after the World Series debacle. But Ruppert disagreed. In November, Barrow threatened to quit unless one-boss rule was instituted. A short time later Ruppert told Barrow of his desire to become sole owner. Would Barrow stay if Jake were the sole owner? Yes, said Barrow.

1923

The Yankees will take their third straight pennant, their 98-54 record putting them 16 games in front of second-place Detroit. Babe Ruth will win two-thirds of the Triple Crown with 41 home runs and 131 RBIs. He will hit .393, his career high, but 10 percentage points short of Harry Heilmann's .403. Ruth will win the League Award as the MVP. Sad Sam Jones will lead the pitching staff with a 21-8 record. This will be the year—the Yankees' first World Championship!

Jan 30— New York obtains Herb Pennock (P) from the Red Sox for George Murray (P), Norm McMillan (INF), Camp Skinner (OF) and cash.

— Pennock blossomed in a Yankee uniform, compiling a 19-6 record in 1923. He went on to build a 162-90 record over 11 Yankee seasons. Pennock had been an enigma in his previous big league career, never winning more than 16 games in his 10 seasons and going 10-17 in 1922 for last-place Boston, while at the same time being regarded as one of the game's most talented pitchers. Many in baseball thought the Yankees had acquired an over-the-hill Knight of Kennett Square, notwithstanding the fact that Herb was only 29. But the Yankees badly needed lefthanded pitching. "We could win the whole thing," Huggins told Ruppert, "if we could only pick up a strong lefthanded pitcher."

Apr 18— Yankee Stadium opens. Located at 161st Street and River Avenue in the Bronx, the Stadium stands on what once was a lumber yard, and before that, beautiful farmland. The biggest baseball crowd in history to date is at the game. Reportedly, 74,217 fans attend and nearly 25,000 are turned away at the gate.* The festivities begin at 1 p.m. with a musical program by the Seventh Regiment Band. At 3 p.m. the band is led in the National Anthem by John Phillip Sousa. Governor Al Smith and Commissioner Landis pose for pictures at home plate, the Yankees receive a floral horseshoe from a local fan club and Ruth gets a huge bat in a carrying case. Smith throws out the first ball, caught by Yankee catcher Wally Schang, and the game begins at 3:31 p.m. The game is a match-up between New York's Bob Shawkey and Boston's Howard Ehmke. Chick Fewster, leading off for Boston, is the game's first batter, and Yankee leadoff man, Whitey Witt, is the first Yankee to hit in the new sports palace. The game is scoreless until the bottom of the fourth inning when New York plates four runs, highlighted by Ruth's three-run, line-drive homer into the right field bleachers— the first home run hit in the new ballpark and one Babe wanted so badly he had told reporters before the game, "I'd give a year of my life if I can hit a home run in this first game in this new park." Yankee Stadium has its first eruption of cheers as the Babe touches the plate, bows to the crowd. Emke had tried to sneak by a slow curve ball with the count at two and two, and Ruth's 199 career home run is the consequence of the tactic. Shawkey has little trouble with the Boston bats, allowing three hits in going the distance and winning, 4-1. All in all, one of the most memorable days in New York City history.

— Yankee Stadium was financially possible for two reasons. One, of course, was Babe Ruth's drawing power. In Fred Lieb's game story for the *Evening Telegram,* he used the nickname, "The House That Ruth Built," and it stuck. The second was the legalization of Sunday baseball a few years earlier.

May 2— Yankee shortstop and captain Everett Scott plays in his 1,000th consecutive game, a streak he began with Boston in 1916. In Washington, Scott is presented with a gold medal at home plate by Secretary of the Navy Denby amid predictions that here is a record that will never be broken. In the game that follows, the Senators' Walter Johnson records his 100th shutout in beating New York, 3-0.

May 22— Two dramatic things occurred in the Yankee community, one in the front office and one on the playing field. Til Huston sells out to Jake Ruppert and Babe Ruth predicts and hits a home run to win in the 15th inning in Chicago. The Yankees win, 3-1, for Herb Pennock who goes the route, allowing only four hits. In danger of missing the train from Chicago, road secretary Mark Roth is distressed. "Take it easy," the Babe tells him. "I'll get us out of here." And so the Babe does.

---

*Ed Barrow's attendance figure was padded by at least 10,000, as he admitted shortly thereafter. There were more than 60,000 at the game, however, breaking the previous record in baseball by some 20,000. The official Yankee records state the crowd at 62,281.

— Huston did, in fact, elect to sell his Yankee stock to Ruppert and received $1.5 million for the decision. In Chicago, the Yankees were read a wire from Ruppert, stating, "I now am the sole owner of the Yankees. Miller Huggins is my manager." From this moment on, Huggins could be more authoritative. There would be no more of Huston constantly looking over his shoulder, and Hug would be a better manager for it. Huston made a tidy profit, more than six times his original $230,000 investment, but he left reluctantly, a casualty of the bitter Huggins dispute. He saw the writing on the wall—Ruppert, Barrow and Huggins were solidly against him. With Huston gone, Ruth lost the best friend he ever had in Yankee management. The sportswriters lost a colorful figure to write about.

May 31— Tomorrow the Yankee players will take an eight-game lead; today the Yankee brass reorganizes. Col. Jacob Ruppert remains as president. His brother, George, not previously associated with the club, is elected vice president, and Barrow, who buys a small piece of the club, assumes the office of secretary in addition to his duties as general manager.

— Ruppert as the virtual sole owner of the club does the unthinkable as one of his first acts—he buys the team two additional sets of uniforms so that the players can take the field in clean uniforms every day. It was a serious violation of tradition, but, Jake explained, "I want my boys to look neat."

Jul 3— Bullet Joe Bush has an amazing performance, beating Washington, 2-1, in 15 innings. Bush allows only eight hits and his home run forces extra innings. Ruth's leadoff roundtripper in the 15th wins it.

— Bush slipped a bit in 1923, both on the mound and at bat, going from 26-7 to 19-15 and from .326 to .274. But Bullet Joe was still the club's workhorse in spite of his differences with Hug.

Jul 4— The Yankees sweep a doubleheader from Washington, 12-6 and 12-2, before a large Independence Day crowd at the Stadium. In the opener, Yankee shortstop Everett Scott hits the first grand slam homer in the Stadium's history. It is actually nothing more than a hard-hit ground ball. The ball *bounces* over leftfielder Goose Goslin's glove and into the stands for Scott's "slam." (There are no ground-rule doubles.) Scott later adds another homer in the first game, in this one game producing one-tenth of his 13-year-career total of 20 home runs. He will end this year with six.

Jul 17— Huggins, who has been ignoring Carl Mays all season, finally gives in and lets Mays start a game in Cleveland. The Indians win, 13-0. Huggins lets Mays go the route—lets him undergo a 20-hit shelling.

— Hug disliked Mays intensely, deeply resenting the pitcher's insubordinations when things on the club were less stable and the manager's authority less certain. The two had a loud street argument during spring training. But the humiliation of Mays upset a few Yankees. Everett Scott and Wally Pipp removed themselves from the game. The competitive Mays will bounce back a week later and beat the A's, for the 23rd straight time, 9-2.

Jul 18— Yankee rightfielder Elmer Smith (Babe Ruth is in left) turns in a rare unassisted double play in Detroit as the Yankees win, 4-1. Detroit's Del Pratt sends a liner to right field as Harry Heilmann sprints to second base on the hit-and-run play. Smith makes the grab, and, with Heilmann around second, Elmer casually jogs in and tags first base. It is the only unassisted double play ever recorded by a Yankee outfielder.

Yankee Stadium under construction in 1922. The grandstand ends abruptly—it does not make the turn; instead, the huge bleachers (foreground) will bend around to meet the triple-decked covered seats. Note the framework for the famous Gothic facade.

Picked off first base by Giant catcher Frank Synder in Game 2 of the 1923 World Series, Babe Ruth is about to be tagged out by first baseman George Kelly. The Babe's two homers in this game helped the Yankees end an eight-game losing streak to the Giants in World Series play.

Babe Ruth doffs his cap in the 1923 World Series at the Polo Grounds. The Babe, who had three Series home runs, is admired by Eddie Bennett, Yankee mascot and batboy.

— The unassisted double play was something of a Smith specialty. He made four of them as a major league outfielder for various teams. Smith, as a Cleveland Indian, also hit the first grand slam homer in World Series history. As the Yanks' fourth outfielder in 1923, Smith hit .306 in 70 games. The three outfielders in front of him were .300 hitters, too. Ruth hit .393, Whitey Witt .314 and Bob Meusel .313.

Aug 5— At Yankee Stadium, the Bambino hits home run Nos. 26 and 27 against St. Louis' Ray Kolp. But twice in extra innings, as Babe stands smiling in the righthanded box, Elam Vangilder intentionally walks him to load the bases. After the second free pass in the 13th inning, Bob Meusel singles home Waite Hoyt and the Yankees win, 9-8.

— Ruth was frustrated by his 170 walks (a major league record) this year. He wanted to hit and wasn't that what the fans paid to see him do? Still, he had an incredible season. His 205 hits and his walks allowed him to set a major league base-reaching record of .375; with .356 in 1949, baseball's runner-up is Ted Williams. His batting average of .393 (it would remain the Yankee record) was 78 points better than his previous season. Babe gave .400 a good shot—he was hitting .401 after the season's 111th game. However, he ended up 10 points behind Detroit's Harry Heilmann.

Sep 4— Sad Sam Jones hurls a no-hitter against the Athletics and the Yankees defeat Bob Hasty, 2-0. Jones allows only one walk and the Yanks make one error behind him. A's shortstop Chick Galloway is the last man to bat in the bottom of the ninth. He yells at Jones, "I'm gonna break it up if I can," and proceeds to bunt down the third base line. But Jones fields the ball and throws him out for the third no-hitter in Yankee history.

— Jones once said this win was the biggest thrill of his long career, an unbroken string of 22 seasons, an AL record. He compiled a 229-217 record pitching for six AL teams. (The Tigers and A's were the only AL teams for which Sad Sam never pitched.)

Sep 11— Whitey Witt leads off against Boston's Howard Ehmke with a hard grounder off Red Sox third baseman Howard Shanks' chest. Witt gets a hit. Then Ehmke retires 27 Yankees in order to win, 3-0. There is a great furor to have Witt's hit changed to an error. Fred Lieb, the official scorer, regrets that his decision denies Ehmke from becoming the first man to throw back-to-back no-hitters. (Ehmke had no-hit the A's four days earlier.) But Lieb sticks to his guns. Ehmke will go to the opposite extreme before the month's end, allowing 21 hits and 17 runs in six innings' work against New York on September 28.

Sep 20— In St. Louis, the Yankees clinch the pennant in their 141st game with a 4-3 verdict over the Browns, extending their AL lead to 18 games. Following the game, the Yankees have a celebration worthy of the occasion on the train out of town. Eight days later the Giants clinch the NL pennant, setting up a third consecutive Subway Series.

Sep 27— At Fenway Park, 20-year-old Yankee Lou Gehrig belts his first home run in the major leagues. It comes at the expense of pitcher Bill Piercy, once a Yankee, who is 8-17 this year. The blast by Gehrig helps New York to an 8-3 victory.

— Yankee scout Paul Krichell signed Gehrig in June off the campus of Columbia University for a $1,500 bonus and a $3,000 salary. Krichell had been following Gehrig since he saw him play in New Brunswick, N.J., in a

Columbia-Rutgers game, after which he told a bemused Barrow, "I think I saw another Ruth today." Shortly after signing with the Yankees, Gehrig put on an amazing power display at Yankee Stadium. Wally Pipp was established at first base, so the Yanks sent Lou to Hartford where he hit .304, then finished the season in New York making 11 hits in 26 trips (.423). Gehrig almost played in the World Series. Pipp suffered a cracked rib and Commissioner Landis was willing to waive the eligibility rule to allow Gehrig as a replacement but John McGraw would have none of it and Pipp was forced to play in great pain.

Oct 10— The World Series opens at Yankee Stadium and the Giants win, 5-4, running their consecutive-game winning streak to eight games over the Yankees (not including last year's tie game). The score is tied at 4-4 when Giant outfielder Casey Stengel steps to the plate with two outs in the ninth inning. Yankee hurler Joe Bush delivers a change-up and Stengel drills it to deepest Death Valley in left-center field. His shoe coming off, Stengel circles the bases, shouting, "Go legs, go!" He barely beats the relay home for an inside-the-park homer, the game-winning hit.

Oct 11— At the Polo Grounds in Game 2, home runs support Pennock's nine-hit pitching and the Yankees have a critical victory, 4-2, snapping an eight-game losing streak in World Series competition. Solo Yankee homers are hit by Ward in the second, Ruth in the fourth, a blast that sails over the right field roof, and Ruth in the fifth. In the ninth, the Babe hits a 475-foot shot to center field, but Stengel makes a fine catch. With an assortment of dazzling fielding plays at third base, Dugan helps Pennock, who shows heart by hanging in after being hit with a pitch.

— This was not only a big win for the Yankees, but a victory for Ruth over McGraw in their not-so-friendly rivalry. Before the game, McGraw had stated his complete willingness to pitch to Ruth, who, in McGraw's opinion, was not as great a hitter as he was made out to be.

Oct 12— Game 3 at Yankee Stadium is a tremendous pitching duel between Sad Sam Jones and Art Nehf. The game's only run is scored in the seventh inning when the Giants' Stengel pulls a homer into the right field bleachers. As he rounds the bases, Stengel wags his fingers from his nose at the Yankee bench. Ruppert insists that Stengel be punished for "insulting my players, our fans and me," and Stengel pays $50 for the gesture. But Commissioner Landis observes, "Casey Stengel just can't keep from being Casey Stengel." Nehf has now won four World Series games in a row from the Yankees. But the Yankees will win the next three games.

Oct 15— A high water mark date in Yankee history—the Yankees win their first World Championship. In Game 6 at the Polo Grounds, the Yankees prevail, 6-4. Pennock pitches seven innings to get the win and Jones saves it. In the first inning, Ruth hits a long homer into the right field upper deck. But the Giants rally with single runs in the first, fourth, fifth and sixth to take a 4-1 lead. Then the Yankees have a decisive five-run eighth: Ward pops out, Schang singles for the first hit off Nehf since the second frame, Scott singles to right, pinch-hitter Fred Hofmann walks on four pitches to load the bases, pinch-hitter Bush walks on four pitches (forcing in a run and bringing in reliever Rosy Ryan), Dugan also walks on four pitches (bringing in another run), Ruth strikes out for the second out on an ankle high slow curveball, Meusel singles through the box (for two RBIs and a third run scores on a wild throw), and Pipp grounds out. The clutch hit is Meusel's.

— The Yankees had many heroes in this Series. Pennock won a pair of games and saved another, Ward led all hitters at .417, Meusel led everyone with eight RBIs, and Ruth hit .368 and led all hitters in homers (3), runs (8) and walks (8). Ruppert was never happier, giving credit to everyone, but reserving the most credit for his manager, "Little Hug."

Dec 11— Cincinnati obtains pitcher Carl Mays from the Yankees in a waiver deal. All seven other AL clubs failed to claim Mays and his contract passes to the Reds for the inter-league waiver price of $7,500. Huggins writes to Reds' president Garry Herrmann, saying, "I may be sending you the best pitcher I have, but I warn you that Carl is a troublemaker and always will be a hard man to sign."

— Mays and Huggins were happy to part company. Some point to Mays' 20-9 record for the Reds in 1924 as evidence of Huggins' failure with the moody star, but while the Yankees could have used Mays in 1924 when they finished second, it must also be noted that Mays was 3-5 in 1925. Mays was 208-126 in his career and 80-39 for the Yankees.

1924

The Yankees (89-63) will finish in second place, two games behind the Washington Senators. Babe Ruth will lead the AL in six major offensive statistics, including home runs with 46. The pitching ace will be Herb Pennock at 21-9.

Jan 7— New York purchases the contract of outfielder Earle Combs from Louisville. Combs, the most talented and talked about player in the minors, in 1923 had 241 hits and batted .380 for Louisville. He is a disciple of his manager at Louisville, Joe McCarthy.

— Combs was to become a great centerfielder for the Yankees, the beginning of the Combs, then DiMaggio, then Mantle legacy of greatness in New York's center field. However, Combs' 1924 season was ruined by a broken ankle. He made 14 hits in only 35 trips (.400, In Ruth's view, Combs' injury cost New York the pennant.

May 14— Babe Ruth Day is held at Yankee Stadium and the Babe receives his League Award for 1923.* Also, the World Championship flag is raised for the first time in Yankee Stadium. St. Louis wins, 11-1, the Bambino managing to get a mere single.

Jun 13— One of the biggest brawls in Yankee history takes place in Detroit. The Yankees take a 10-6 lead into the ninth inning when Ruth tells Bob Meusel he saw Tiger Manager Ty Cobb instruct pitcher Bert Cole to hit Meusel, and, sure enough, Long Bob is plunked. Meusel charges the mound and both dugouts empty. In the middle of the melee, unfriendly rivals Ruth and Cobb square off but do little except cuss each other out. Umpire Evans ejects Meusel and Ruth but that is not good enough for the hostile Detroit crowd of some 18,000. About 1,000 of them storm the field and others pelt the visitors with various objects. The Yankees manage to reach the safety of

---

*The League Award was the AL's official MVP honor for the years 1922-28. This was Babe's only League Award because of a rule against repeat winners.

their clubhouse, but with further play out of the question, Evans awards a victory by forfeit to New York. This is the third of five wins by forfeiture in Yankee history. Meusel and Ruth receive $100 fines, but more harshly, Meusel and the Detroit pitcher, Cole, get 10-day suspensions. Cobb is slapped on the wrist.

Jul 1— Waite Hoyt gives up 11 hits but blanks Philadelphia, 7-0. Hoyt, who ties a Yankee record set by Jack Chesbro in 1908 for most hits allowed in a shutout game, is as consistent as ever and will go 18-13 this year, pitching 247 innings.

Jul 2— In the second game of a twinbill at Philadelphia, Yankee centerfielder Whitey Witt walks five times as the Yankees win, 10-1. He follows Charlie Hemphill (1908) and Roger Peckinpaugh (1919) as the third Yankee in history to get five free passes in one game. Incredibly, Witt fails to score a run in the game.

— Witt was a fine leadoff man, hitting .297 in 1924, but he was beginning to slow up, most noticeably in center field.

Jul 4— In Washington, the Yankees sweep a doubleheader, 4-2 and 2-0. But on this day that traditionally marks the start of the summer's pennant race, Washington is in first, Detroit is in second and New York is a close third. The surprisin Senators, distant fourth-place finishers the year before, are being driven by 27-year-old player-manager Bucky Harris, called the Boy Wonder.

Aug 14— New York purchases the contracts of outfielder Ben Paschal and pitcher Ray Francis from Atlanta of the Southern League.

— Paschal was an interesting study. The Alabaman was a tremendous hitter, batting .309 over six Yankee seasons, but as a reserve outfielder playing behind the Ruth-Combs-Meusel outfield that many still regard as the greatest outfield in history, he saw little action. Paschal played in only four Yankee games in 1924.

Aug 18— Ruth has his average up to .397 after a torrid stretch (and a 14-homer July). He walks three times in this date's 2-0 win over Chicago.

— Babe won his only batting title this year, finishing with a mark of .378, 19 percentage points ahead of runner-up Charlie Jamieson. Babe's 46 homers easily outdistanced Joe Hauser's 27. And Babe was runner-up in RBIs (121) to Goose Goslin (129), whose productive year prevented Ruth from winning the Triple Crown.

Aug 31— The Senators win in 10 innings, 4-2, and complete a four-game series by taking three victories from the Yankees at Yankee Stadium. This is a cruel blow to New York's hopes of winning four straight pennants. Now the Yankees (71-55) are 1½ games behind Washington (74-55) although the teams are even in the loss column.

Sep 18— Bullet Joe Bush hits a pinch-hit home run in the top of the 10th for the game-winning hit. He is only the second Yankee pitcher to hit a pinch-hit homer and the first since Ray Caldwell's back-to-back pinch-hit homers in 1915. The Bush homer beats St. Louis, 2-1.

— Bush hit .339 (42 for 124) this year, one of the best hitting seasons ever enjoyed by a Yankee pitcher. For his three Yankee seasons, he hit a combined .313 (104 for 332). Many a non-pitcher would like to own those stats.

Sep 20— The Yankees suffer a heartbreaking loss and fall one game behind Washington
with eight games left to play. In Detroit, Shawkey uncorks a wild pitch
with two outs in the bottom of the ninth, allowing Heinie Manush to cross
the plate with the winning run for the Tigers' 6-5 victory. The Yankees
record is 85-61; Washington's is 86-60.

Sep 29— New York is helpless as the Washington Senators clinch their first pennant with
a victory in Boston. Meanwhile, the Yankees are rained out in Philadelphia,
and they are the following day, too. They end their season at 89-63 (with
one tie), two games behind Washington and only one game behind in the
loss column. The Senators finished at 92-62. Had the Yankees made up and
won the last two rained-out games in Philadelphia, they still would have
finished one game out. But it was a gallant effort by the Yankees who won
18 of 22 games through September.

Dec 17— The Yankees obtain Urban Shocker (P) from the St. Louis Browns for Bullet
Joe Bush (P), Joe Giard (P) and Milt Gaston (P).

— In New York, Bush was 62-38. Lifetime, he was 196-181. He was a quality
pitcher but he and Huggins didn't get along and the manager was anxious
to trade him. Shocker was a valuable addition to the Yankees. New York's
trading away Shocker in 1918 was a mistake as evidenced by Urban's
winning of 20 or more games for the Browns for four straight years (1920-24).
His absence cost the Yanks the 1920 pennant. When the trade was
announced, Huggins was asked why the righthanded Shocker was dealt
away in the first place. "Because I was foolish," said Hug.

1925

A disastrous year, 1925. The Yankees will plummet to seventh place, 28½ games
behind the pennant-winning Washington Senators. Their record: 69-85. Babe Ruth will
be ill and play in only 98 games. Bob Meusel will lead the AL with 33 home runs
and 138 RBIs. Herb Pennock's 16-17 record will be tops on the pitching staff.

Apr 5—   The Yankees are barnstorming North after breaking their first spring training
camp in St. Petersburg, Fla., and Miller Huggins states that the Yanks will
win the pennant with what he calls "the strongest team I ever had." The
experts agree. The Yanks are strong pre-season favorites.

Apr 7—   Ruth collapses in Asheville, N.C., with the "bellyache heard around the world."
A severe intestinal attack (the grippe, some reports say; acute indigestion,
others say) brings the Bambino down. He collapses on a railroad station
platform and is taken to the Battery Park Hotel where an Asheville physician
examines him. Ruth rests comfortably, after a day of severe stomach pain.
He then embarks on a tough train trip to New York with Yankee scout Paul
Krichell accompanying the fallen hero. The reports of Ruth's death are
incessant.

Apr 9—   While cleaning up at the Newark stop, Ruth falls and knocks himself out
when his head hits a washbasin. When he reaches New York, the scene at
Penn Station is wild; the Babe is delirious and has several convulsions.
He is ambulanced to St. Vincent's Hospital. He is semi-conscious, running a
high fever and having convulsive attacks. At the hospital, Babe regains
consciousness and his mood brightens. He is placed under observation and
given a bland diet. But in the next several days the Babe's condition does

not improve. Indeed, he is still hospitalized on Opening Day, with a rising fever. He is said to have an intestinal abscess but surgeons will find an ulcer (reportedly the result of careless eating and drinking). Ruth and his new, long scar will leave St. Vincent's on May 26.

Apr 14— It is Opening Day at Yankee Stadium but much of the joy is gone because of Ruth's illness. Babe's substitute, Ben Paschal, hits a home run and the Yankees defeat Washington, 5-1, before some 50,000 fans.

— But before the end of the season's first week, New York found itself in fourth place. Worse, the club was never again that high in the standings over the remainder of the campaign.

Apr 23— Herb Pennock takes a 1-0 lead into the ninth inning in Washington and two Senators reach base. Walter Johnson comes to bat as a pinch-hitter, doubles in the tying and winning runs and Pennock loses a heartbreaker, 2-1.

May 5— Yankee captain, shortstop Everett Scott, plays in his 1,307th consecutive game, an incredible streak of durability begun on June 20, 1916, when he was with the Red Sox.

— This, the longest playing streak in big league history to this date, would be surpassed only once—by Lou Gehrig, now a teammate of Scott's.

May 6— Yankee Manager Miller Huggins benches Everett Scott, thereby snapping the Deacon's consecutive-game playing streak. Huggins feels his 32-year-old shortstop is playing poorly, and, indeed, Scott has slowed down considerably, possibly because of the grind of playing every day.

— Pee Wee Wanninger replaced Scott at shortstop (hitting .236 on the year) and became a part of baseball lore because of his unique association with this streak—and with the one Lou Gehrig will begin within a month. And Scott, hitting only .217, later was claimed on waivers by Washington.

May 20— The Yankees suffer a galling loss in Cleveland, 10-9, when the Indians score six runs in the bottom of the ninth inning. Tris Speaker scores the winning run in a sprint from first base on a mere single.

Jun 1— Ruth is back in the line-up with the Yankees resting in seventh place at 15-25. His return is much too soon. Washington beats the Yankees at Yankee Stadium, 5-3. In the eighth inning, Lou Gehrig unsuccessfully pinch-hits for Pee Wee Wanninger, the start of his streak of 2,130 games played without interruption (and Pee Wee's second connection with a streak). Ruth misses a homer that barely goes foul, gets thrown out at the plate and makes a fine defensive play. He is exhausted when he leaves the game after six innings.

Jun 2— Yankee first baseman Wally Pipp reports to work with a headache, attributed to his having been recently hit on the head with a pitched ball, and asks Miller Huggins for a day off. "You're my first baseman today," Hug tells Lou Gehrig in the clubhouse a few minutes later.

— And the Iron Horse remained the Yankee first baseman for 14 years. He also started a streak of 885 consecutive games at first base, a big league record. "I took the most expensive aspirin in history," Pipp was to lament. Pipp is often remembered only in connection with Gehrig's streak, but he was a fine player in his own right. His 1925 season was disappointing, though (.230 in 62 games), and he was of little use to the Yanks once Gehrig stepped in. So Pipp was dealt to Cincinnati after the season ended and had three fine campaigns with the Reds, retiring four RBIs shy of 1,000.

Jun 17— The Yankees absorb the largest losing margin in their history, losing by 18 runs. Detroit beats them, 19-1, at Yankee Stadium. It was and still is the most runs ever scored by an opponent at Yankee Stadium.

Jun 24— Gehrig steals home for his first stolen base as a major leaguer. It is part of a double steal with Wally Schang stealing second base.

     — Gehrig, believe it or not, stole home 14 times (some sources say 15), establishing a Yankee record that still stands.

Jul 4— Two of the greatest lefthanders in AL history, New York's Herb Pennock and Philadelphia's Lefty Grove, battle in a tremendous pitching duel that Pennock and the Yanks finally win, 1-0, after 15 innings. The Knight of Kennett Square allows only four hits and does not give up a walk. He retires the first 18 and final 21 batters in order.

Jul 23— Gehrig has seven RBIs, three hits and scores two runs, as he leads the Yankees to a 11-7 triumph over Washington at Yankee Stadium. In the fifth inning, Columbia Lou jolts a two-run homer. Two innings later, he belts a bases-loaded homer, the first of his 23 grand slammers, a major league record. It comes off Firpo Marberry, the game's best relief pitcher, who will win eight games and save 15, a league-leading number.

Earle Combs, left, Babe Ruth and Bob Meusel, the Yankee outfield from 1925 through 1929, may have been baseball's greatest all-around outfield. Meusel had a great arm, Combs covered all of center field and more, and Ruth could throw and field with the best of them. Lifetime, Ruth hit .349, Combs .325 and Meusel .309.

— Gehrig enjoyed a fine rookie season, hitting .295 with 20 homers and 68 RBIs. But the rookie season of Combs, all things considered, was superior. Of Huggins' established players, only Meusel, who had a great year, came through for him. Hug had to revamp virtually his entire line-up.

Aug 9— In a game the Yankees lose, 4-3, in extra innings, Huggins sends up Bobby Veach to pinch-hit for Babe Ruth. Veach flies out. This is the only time the Babe is pinch-hit for in his 15-season Yankee career.

— Huggins said he had Veach bat because the Bambino had a wrenched back. In reality, Hug was impatient with Ruth's slumbering bat. On top of this, the Babe was acting grumpy, carrying on more than ever at night and his first marriage was falling apart. All in all, Ruth, who had rejoined the line-up too soon after his spring illness, was in no shape to play baseball.

Aug 29— Showdown time. The differences between Ruth and Huggins come to a head in St. Louis when Hug suspends Babe indefinitely and fines him $5,000. Babe's worsening conduct has been especially flagrant on this western road trip. So, when the tardy Babe steps grandly into the locker room, Hug tells him not to bother suiting up and informs him of the suspension and fine. The enraged Bambino screams obscenities at Hug, and at one point tells the Mighty Mite, "If you weighed 50 more pounds, I'd punch you." To which Hug replies, "If I weighed 50 more pounds, I'd have punched you!" Ruth wants a conference with Jake Ruppert, stalks out and begins his odyssey to New York, stopping first in Chicago to unsuccessfully solicit help from Commissioner Landis.

Sep 1— A more subdued Ruth arrives in New York and goes to the Ruppert brewery. The Babe never has a chance. Unknown to him, Huggins first got the support of Ruppert and Barrow before his disciplining action. After their meeting, Ruppert and Ruth face the gathered press. Babe is grim as Jake announces, "The fine and suspension stand. I told Ruth, as I tell you now in front of him, that he went too far. I told him Miller Huggins is in absolute command of the ball club, and that I stand behind Huggins to the very limit." Babe says how well he has been treated by Ruppert and goes to the Stadium to apologize to Huggins. But Hug will neither accept Ruth's apology nor reinstate him. Babe watches a Yankee win from the colonel's box. "No," he says in cutting off an interview, "I don't want to do any more talking. It only gets me in bad. I did too much of it with those reporters in St. Louis and Chicago." On September 6, Ruth will meet one of Hug's conditions for reinstatement. He apologizes to the manager before the entire team. Huggins, who was actually fond of Ruth, thus establishes his authority over the great star.

Sep 7— Huggins reinstates Ruth on Labor Day and the Babe gets one hit as the Yankees lose, 5-1, to Boston. Amid gossip that he is washed up at 30, Ruth is anxious to prove himself. He will hit 10 homers over the season's final few weeks, including No. 300.

Sep 22— Ben Paschal hits a pair of inside-the-park homers in one game at Yankee Stadium, becoming the first player in AL history to do so. It helps the Yanks beat Chicago, 11-6, but New York loses the second game, 4-2.

— Paschal had a great year, playing whenever Ruth did not. He hit .360 with 12 home runs and 56 RBIs in 247 trips to the plate.

1926

The Yankees will finish at 91-63, three games in front of second-place Cleveland to win the pennant in a remarkable comeback season. Babe Ruth will lead the league in all the power categories, including home runs (47). Herb Pennock's 23-11 record will lead Yankee pitchers. But the Yankees will lose the World Championship in Game 7 of the World Series—a much remembered Game 7.

Apr 11— In the final spring exhibition, played at Yankee Stadium, the Yankees defeat Brooklyn, 14-7. The Yankees finish the pre-season with 16 consecutive wins, including 12 in a row in a running series with the Dodgers. Babe Ruth slaps three doubles to pace the attack.

— The experts in the pre-season looked upon the Yankees as weak, inexperienced, probably second-division material. But as the exhibition winning streak unfolded, Ruth insisted that if the Yankees could do the improbable—sweep a 12-game set with Brooklyn as the two clubs were heading North—then New York would take the pennant in the regular season. With the sweep actually accomplished, the Bambino roared, "Don't forget what I've been saying all along. We'll win the pennant now, sure!"

Apr 13— Only 12,000 fans show up at Fenway Park on a bitterly cold Opening Day to see a barnburner that the Yankees win, 12-11. Ruth demonstrates that his reformation is no joke, hitting two doubles and a single and scoring three runs.

Apr 20— The Yankees in an 18-5 thrashing of Washington pound out 22 hits, five of them off Ruth's bat. The Babe's hits include a two-run homer off Walter Johnson. He scores five runs and drives in eight runs. It is only the second time a Yankee has scored five runs in a single game (it was Ruth who did it previously, in 1922) and it is only the second time a Yankee has eight RBIs in one game (first accomplished by Roy Hartzell in 1911).

— The Yankees enjoyed a fast start and an April that included an eight-game winning streak. They were in first place at the month's end.

May 18— Rookie second baseman Tony Lazzeri belts a grand slam homer off Chicago's Sloppy Thurston (6-8), as the Yankees rally for five runs in the eighth inning to win, 5-3, at Yankee Stadium. It is New York's seventh win in a row.

— Lazzeri deserves much of the credit for the Yanks' great early-season success. The previous season, Lazzeri had 60 homers and 222 RBIs playing the 200-game Pacific Coast League schedule. Yankee scout Paul Krichell made sure the Yanks purchased Lazzeri's contract. This year in New York, Tony will hit .275 with 18 homers and 114 RBIs. A new dimension has been added to the mystique of Murderers' Row—that of a power-hitting second baseman.

May 26— The Yankees defeat Boston, 9-8, completing a four-game sweep at Fenway Park. The win is the Yanks' 16th victory in succession (No. 17 will be denied by Philadelphia as the A's sweep a doubleheader) and breaks the previous club record of 15 wins in a row, set back in 1906. This new club record will stand until the 1947 Yankees win 19 consecutive games.

June 8— Ruth hits a home run that is the longest of his career in a regular season game. A Ruth shot at Detroit's Navin Field is reported to have traveled

602 feet in the air. The ball rolls to a stop on Plum Street, 800-850 feet from home plate. The ball, retrieved by a youngster, is good for $20 from the Bambino himself.

Sep 15— New York is 5½ games up on the Indians but the Tribe is red-hot as the Yankees invade Cleveland for a six-game series. The excitement in Cleveland is at a fever pitch in anticipation of one last run at the Yankees by Tris Speaker's boys. But the Yankees win the opener of a doubleheader, 6-4, with Bob Meusel hitting three sacrifice flies for an AL record. The second game is postponed. But Cleveland will take tomorrow's doubleheader and win two more games after that—Indian pitching giving up three runs over the four games—and Cleveland fans sense that the Yankees are folding.

Sep 19— With the pennant on the line, some 31,000 fans, a record crowd to date for Cleveland's League Park (also known as Dunn Field), anticipate seeing the Tribe creep even closer to the Yankees. All the pressure in the world is on New York but three Yankees—Ruether, Gehrig and Ruth—carry the club to an 8-3 victory. Dutch Ruether, acquired August 27 from Washington, on only two days' rest pushes himself into the ninth inning, before Huggins must relieve the weary veteran. Gehrig has five RBIs and four extra-base hits,

In Game 4 of the 1926 World Series, Babe Ruth walloped three home runs, including one of the longest homers ever seen at Sportsmans Park.

including a homer and three doubles. Ruth homers, singles and scores three runs. Reserve infielder Mike Gazella also has a fine game, especially in the field. The Yankees (88-58) salvage two wins and leave town leading Cleveland (85-62) by 3½ games. Cleveland still has a chance, the Yanks winning only three of their remaining eight games. But the Indians also win only three.

Sep 20— Having just escaped with their lives in Cleveland, the Yankees have the pressure put right back on them. They lose a doubleheader in Chicago, 7-3 and 4-3.

Sep 21— Waite Hoyt saves the day, halting an embarrassing Yankee skid with a two-hitter. Hoyt walks only one batter and shuts out Chicago, 14-0. The Yankee hitters break out of a slump against Chicago's ace righthander, Ted Lyons (18-16). Ruth homers and triples and Lazzeri homers. The victory is made all the more valuable by the Yankees' 2-1 loss to Chicago the following day.

Sep 24— The Yankees arrive in St. Louis the day the Cardinals clinch the NL flag and must endure nightlong partying outside their quarters at the Buckingham Hotel as hundreds of St. Louis fans celebrate the Cardinals' first pennant. The Yankees are expected to be the Cardinals' World Series opponents and the locals want the pinstripers to know where their hearts belong.

Sep 25— New York clinches the pennant with a doubleheader sweep of the Browns. Herb Pennock wins the first game, 10-2, and Waite Hoyt the nightcap, 10-4. Ruth blasts three home runs, including a grand slam, off three different pitchers. His third fourbagger is his 47th, and final, homer of the season.

— Again Ruth just missed the Triple Crown. He was way out in front in two categories, home runs and RBIs (145). The runners-up in home runs and RBIs finished 28 HRs and 31 RBIs behind him. But he finished just six percentage points behind batting champion Heinie Manush, who hit .378.

Sep 26— The Browns sweep a doubleheader from the Yankees in the amazingly swift time of two hours and seven minutes.

— No doubt anxious to hit the road, the Yankees lost the nightcap, 6-2, in a game that took only 55 minutes, the fastest nine-inning game the Yanks have every played.

Oct 1— The day before the opening of the World Series, Ruth travels to Essex Falls, N.J., to visit a sick boy named Johnny Sylvester. A doctor had said that a visit from the boy's hero, the Babe, would be better than any medicine. So the boy's father gets in touch with Ruth, and one of the great legends surrounding the Babe, who promises Johnny that he will hit a home run for him, begins to take form.

Oct 2— The World Series opens at Yankee Stadium and Pennock pitches a brilliant three-hitter to win, 2-1. Pennock gives up two of the three hits and the lone run in the first inning. St. Louis is hitless after that until Sunny Jim Bottomley singles with one out in the ninth. Gehrig breaks up a 1-1 tie in the sixth with a single to score Ruth, and Earle Combs makes a fine eighth-inning catch with a Cardinal on second.

Oct 6— Ruth belts three home runs to lead the Yankees to a 10-5 win and even the Series at two games apiece. The Babe reaches base safely five times and scores four runs, both Series records. His first homer in the first inning is a solo job that clears the right field roof at Sportsmans Park. His homer in the third clears the right-center field roof. The Babe walks in the fifth and in the sixth, on a full count, he belts a two-run homer deep into the center field bleachers. For the first time, someone has hit three homers in a World Series game and even the St. Louis fans cheer. He is walked again in his final trip to the plate in the eighth. Hoyt goes the distance but is in constant trouble, giving up 14 Cardinal safeties. All the while Shocker, Shawkey and Pennock warm up in the bullpen, but Hoyt guts it out to the end. Listening to the game on the radio back in New Jersey—and eating up Ruth's three home runs—is Johnny Sylvester, who is declared on the way to recovery from a case of blood poisoning.

Oct 7— New York wins Game 5, 3-2. The contest goes 10 innings and Pennock picks up his second complete-game victory. Trailing, 2-1, the Yankees tie it in the ninth on Gehrig's opposite-field bloop double, Lazzeri's bunt single and Paschal's pinch-hit single to center. In the 10th, the Yankees take the lead on Lazzeri's deep bases-loaded sacrifice fly. Pennock then retires the Cardinals.

Oct 9— Back in Yankee Stadium for Game 6, Grover Cleveland Alexander pitches an eight-hitter while the Cardinals collect 13 hits, eight of them off Shawkey, the Yanks' starter and loser. Cardinal third baseman Les Bell paces the attack with three hits, including a two-run homer, and four RBIs as the Cardinals win, 10-2.

Oct 10— Game 7 of the Series is to become one of the legendary games in baseball history, but uncertain weather dictates that only 38,093 fans will see it. It is a raw, rainy morning and rumors have it that Commissioner Landis will postpone the game. But in the early afternoon Landis orders the game played. Ruth stakes Hoyt and the Yankees to a 1-0 lead in the third inning with a solo homer off Jesse Haines. Then the Cardinals rally for three runs in the fourth when the defense breaks down behind Hoyt. With one out, St. Louis loads the bases on a clean single, an error by Mark Koenig on a potential double-play grounder, and a bloop single. A run scores when Meusel drops an easy fly to left and two more runs come in when Thevenow follows with a single. The Yankees in the sixth cut the deficit to one run when catcher Hank Severeid doubles home Joe Dugan. Then, in the seventh, with the Cards leading 3-2, New York loads the sacks with two outs. Haines is forced from the game by a blister and Manager Hornsby beckons for Grover Cleveland Alexander, who supposedly is sleeping off a hangover in the Cardinal bullpen. Hornsby meets Alexander in the outfield, examines his eyes, sees they are clear and hands him the ball. Lazzeri takes a ball, a strike, then blasts a drive to deep left field that misses being a home run by a few feet. Alexander has Lazzeri set up. He fans Tony on a curveball, low and away. Protecting his lead, Alexander retires the Yankees in order in the eighth and gets the first two batters in the ninth on ground balls. Ruth is then semi-intentionally walked, his fourth walk of the game and 11th of the Series (and thus he reaches first safely for the fifth time in one game, tying his own record). Ruth attempts a delayed steal of second, but Bob O'Farrell's throw to Rogers Hornsby nails him for the final out of the game and the Series. Babe is branded the goat but he contends his steal attempt is defensible for its surprise element. Alexander enjoys his greatest moment and Lazzeri's strikeout takes on unfortunate dimensions that interfere with fair perceptions and fair memories of Tony as a ballplayer.

1927

The 1927 Yankees—perhaps baseball's greatest team—will win the pennant by 19 games over the second-place Philadelphia Athletics. The Yankee record: 110 wins, 44 losses. Babe Ruth will set a single-season home run record with 60. Lou Gehrig, winner of the League Award as MVP, will lead the AL in RBIs with 175 and Waite Hoyt, at 22-7, will be the league's winningest pitcher. The 1927 Yankees will need only four World Series games to lay claim to the World Championship.

Mar 2— Babe Ruth reaches New York from California and heads for Jacob Ruppert's brewery office at 91st Street and Third Avenue to talk contract. The Babe had returned unsigned a contract that proposed to pay him the same $52,000 he had been making. Ruth and Ruppert meet for an hour and emerge to announce that Ruth has agreed to a three-year contract at $70,000 per year. "The Babe is a sensible fellow," beams Ruppert. The formal signing takes place two days later.

Apr 12— On Opening Day at Yankee Stadium, an unofficial crowd of over 70,000 watches Waite Hoyt defeat the Athletics and Lefty Grove, 8-3. The win puts the Yankees in first place where they remain for 174 days—the entire season.

Apr 15— At Yankee Stadium, Ruth hits home run No. 1 of the season, off Philadelphia's Howard Ehmke. Babe hits only one homer in his first 10 games. The Yankees win, 6-3.

May 1— The Yankees win, 7-3, at Yankee Stadium as Ruth hits homer Nos. 5 and 6 off a pair of Athletic pitchers—Jack Quinn and Rube Walberg. It is Babe's second home run in a little over a week off the southpaw Walberg, who was victimized by a Ruth homer 17 times in his career to gain the distinction as the pitcher allowing the most Ruth homers.

May 6— As they travel through the western section of the AL loop, the Yankees stop in Fort Wayne, Ind., for an exhibition game against a semi-pro team, the Lincoln Lifes. The Yankees are the "home team," so Ruth's two-run homer in the 10th inning gives the Yanks a sudden-death 5-3 victory. Just before delivering the blow, the Babe steps to the plate and telegraphs his intent by signaling to the crowd of some 35,000 to begin filing out the park. In other words, he calls his shot, something he is supposed to have done on several occasions before his famous "called shot" homer in the 1932 World Series. (There was at least one time in Fenway Park when Ruth shut up a loudmouth heckler by calling and hitting a home run.)

May 7— The first home run hit at an enlarged and remodeled Comiskey Park in Chicago belongs to Lou Gehrig, and it is a grand slammer hit off Ted Lyons. It lands in the new right field pavilion and it is Lou's second career grand slam. Among those in attendance to see the Yankees win, 8-0, is the Vice President of the United States, Charles G. Dawes.

May 16— Yankee outfielder Bob Meusel steals second base, third base and home in one game as the Yankees beat the Tigers in Detroit, 6-2.

— It was the second time in history that a Yankee accomplished single-game thefts at the three corners. It hasn't been done since Meusel's feat. Meusel was a key member of the 1927 Yankees, hitting .337, driving in 103 runs, and leading the team in stolen bases with 24. And he had no equal as a throwing outfielder. Meusel played left field instead of right field, where his arm could have been used to better advantage, because Ruth refused to play the "sun field" at Yankee Stadium.

May 22— In Cleveland, the Bambino hits homer No. 10, the ball going a tremendous distance into the air—a high pop-up is what it is—clearing the fence by inches. The Babe wears an Indian bonnet for an inning of this game. New York wins, 7-2, and completes a 13-game western road trip with 10 victories; the Yankees are 23-10 and lead the AL by 4½ games.

May 28— The Sultan of Swat unloads homer No. 12 off Washington. The Yankees win, 8-2, at Yankee Stadium.

May 31— The Yankees sweep a twinbill, 10-3 and 18-5, at Shibe Park and for the fourth day in a row, Ruth homers. He knocks out two, in fact, Nos. 15 and 16. The first comes off Jack Quinn and the second off Howard Ehmke. The Bambino finishes May with 12 home runs for the month. He has hit homers in seven of the eight AL ballparks—every one except Comiskey Park, the league's toughest all-round park to crack with the long ball.

Jun 8— Yankee second baseman Tony Lazzeri*is the hero of a comeback win over Chicago at the Stadium. Lazzeri belts three home runs, the first two coming off Red Faber and the third, a two-run shot in the ninth to cap a five-run Yankee rally that ties the score at 11-11, off Sarge Connally. In the bottom of the 11th, Morehart singles home Durst, who tripled, and New York wins, 12-11. Lazzeri is the first Yankee to hit three homers in a regular season game.

Jun 11— Ruth hits Nos. 19 and 20 at the Stadium off Cleveland's southpaw, Garland Buckeye. On his next trip, Indian catcher Luke Sewell asks the home plate umpire to inspect Ruth's bat. It is ruled legal and the Babe strikes out with it. The Yankees win, 6-4.

Jun 13— Yankee catcher Pat Collins and reserve outfielder Ben Paschal steal the show from Ruth as the Yanks overwhelm Cleveland at the Stadium, 14-6. Collins hits a grand slam homer and Paschal has four extra-base hits—a pair of homers, a triple and a double. Paschal scores five runs, becoming the first Yankee other than Ruth to do so.

Jun 23— Gehrig drives a trio of homers in one game against Boston at Fenway Park, as the Yankees win, 11-4.

— Lou was keeping pace with Ruth in home runs and was on his way to his first great season. He hit .373 this year, leading the AL with 52 doubles and setting a new league RBI record with 175. Gehrig broke Ruth's 1921 record of 171 and will go on to break his own record in 1931 with 184 RBIs.

Jul 4— New York sweeps a doubleheader from Washington at Yankee Stadium by scores of 12-1 and 18-1, before an unofficial crowd of around 74,000 fans, reportedly the largest baseball crowd to date. Gehrig hits two homers on the day, one a grand slam, and passes Ruth in the home run derby. Ruth himself goes five for seven at bat over both games. Washington had been

---

*Lazzeri, in his second year with the Yankees, owned the hearts of the fans, especially members of the Italian community who so frequently implored him to "poosh 'em up," meaning hit a free baseball into the seats, that he became known as Poosh 'Em Up Tony.

hot but New York now leads the AL by 11½ games and the pennant race is over before it can begin.

Jul 9—   Ruth wallops Nos. 28 and 29 in Detroit. Both are at the expense of right-hander Ken Hollaway. Babe has a field day, adding two doubles for four extra-base hits as the Yankees breeze to a 19-7 win.

Jul 24—   After a 12-day homer drought, Ruth belts No. 31 against Tommy Thomas, an excellent 27-year-old righthander (19-16). It is Ruth's first home run of the year at Comiskey Park; the Big Fellow has now conquered every ballpark in the AL for at least one roundtripper. New York wins, 3-2.

Aug 16—   In Chicago, the Yankees win, 8-1, as Ruth hits No. 37, his third homer in a little more than two months off White Sox righthander Tommy Thomas. This is the first homer hit clear out of remodeled-enlarged Comiskey Park. It clears the right field roof and travels over 475 feet. Babe is now only one home run behind Gehrig, who will hit only nine more homers.

Aug 24—   Lazzeri hits a grand slam homer, the fourth "slam" by a Yankee in 1927, establishing a Yankee club record. It leads New York to a 9-5 triumph in Detroit.

Aug 29—   The Yankees beat the Browns, 8-3, and conclude this season's 11-game schedule in St. Louis. Without exception, all 11 games at Sportsmans Park went to New York!

Sep 2—   The Babe hits No. 44 in Philadelphia, his 400th career home run and his fourth of the year off Walberg. It is the first of 17 homers hit by Ruth in September, a big league record for home runs in one month. The Yankees win, 12-2.

Sep 3—   Lefty Grove administers the first whitewash of the Yankees all year, taming Murderers' Row on three singles, two of these by Ruth. Grove needs the whitewash, his A's able to score only one run.

Sep 6—   Ruth blasts three home runs in a doubleheader at Fenway Park. Babe hits Nos. 45 and 46 off Tony Welzer (his second and third homers off Welzer within a week) in the opener and No. 47 off Jack Russell in the nightcap. After winning the opener, 14-2, the Yankees lose the nightcap, 5-2.

Sep 7—   Babe continues his Fenway Park onslaught with two more homers, giving him five in two days and in three games. He hits No. 48 off Danny MacFayden and No. 49 off Slim Harriss as the Yanks win in a typical Fenway slugfest, 12-10.

           — Ruth has now hit his eighth and final homer of the year at Fenway Park, his top road ballpark for home runs in 1927.

Sep 11—   In the 22nd and final meeting of the year between the Yankees and Browns, St. Louis wins for the first time. But Ruth sends No. 50 out at Yankee Stadium.

           — This homer was the fourth of the year Ruth hit off Milt Gaston. The Browns' pitcher thus tied the A's Rube Walberg in allowing the most 1927 homers by Ruth. At this point the Babe began talking about possibly breaking his home run record. He had only 17 games remaining but he did it. All 10 of the homers he was yet to hit were hit at Yankee Stadium.

Sep 13—   New York sweeps a doubleheader from Cleveland at the Stadium by identical 5-3 scores to clinch the AL pennant in the club's 139th game of the year. Ruth hits Nos. 51 and 52, the first off Indian ace Willis Hudlin and the second off Joe Shaute. Hoyt wins his 20th game of the season, although the Tribe gathers 10 hits.

— Hall of Famer Hoyt enjoyed his greatest season this year and was the Yanks' only 20-game winner (22-7). He led the AL in winning percentage (.759) and ERA (2.63) and shared the league lead in wins. Teammate Wilcy Moore (19-7), who was both a reliever and spot starter and who led the AL with 13 saves, had an ERA of 2.28 but failed to meet the technical requirements to gain the ERA championship.

Sep 18— The Yankees sweep a twinbill from Chicago, winning, 2-1 and 5-1, at the Stadium. Gehrig belts his third grand slam of the year and Ruth hits No. 54 in the nightcap against Chicago's great righthander, Ted Lyons, who this year ties Hoyt for most AL victories with a mark of 22-14.

Sep 22— The Yankees beat the Tigers, 8-7, at the Stadium. Ruth hits No. 56 off Ken Hollaway, a pitcher he has taken deep twice this year. (Ruth carries his bat with him and as he rounds third base, a boy grabs the bat; the Babe happily drags both across the plate.) But the hero of the game is Yankee centerfielder Earle Combs. The Kentucky Colonel hits three consecutive triples.

— Combs' contributions to this great club should not be overlooked. He covered all of a big center field and led AL outfielders with 411 putouts. As leadoff man in the Murderers' Row line-up, Combs hit .356 to ignite the attack and set still-standing Yankee records with 231 hits, 166 singles and 23 triples. And Combs was third in the AL behind Ruth and Gehrig in runs scored (137) and behind Gehrig and Ruth in total bases (331).

Sep 24— The Yankees win their 106th game of the season, breaking the AL record for most wins established by the Boston Red Sox with 105 wins in 1912. New York blanks Detroit, 6-0, at the Stadium.

Sep 29— Ruth hits a pair of home runs, including a grand slam homer for the second straight game to set a record, as New York defeats Washington, 15-4. It was the Yanks' seventh grand slam of the year. In the first inning, Babe blasts a solo homer for No. 58, his second of the year off Hod Lisenbee, the Senators' ace at 18-9. In his next trip, Ruth unloads a triple to right-center field. In the fifth, the Babe hits No. 59, a grand slammer off Paul Hopkins, a righthander who this season won his only big league game. Ruth almost gets his 60th homer in his final at bat. He lofts a long fly to right field that travels to the fence and is inches shy of clearing it when Goose Goslin makes the grab.

Sep 30— Ruth hits his 60th home run off Washington's Tom Zachary. The two-run blast provides the winning margin in the Yankees' 4-2 victory in New York's 154th contest, the next-to-last game of the season.* The dramatic moment comes in the eighth inning with the score tied, 2-2, one out and Mark Koenig standing on third base after tripling. The Babe, who earlier had singled twice and walked, steps to the plate a determined man. On a one ball-one strike

---

*An early season Yankee game ended in a tie. This interjected an extra game in the normal 154-game season.

pitch, Babe golfs a fast, knee-high, inside pitch and sends it high toward the Stadium's right field bleachers, the ball hooking toward the foul line and finally landing some 10 feet fair and half way to the top of the bleachers for a home run. It is the third homer Zachary has given Ruth this year and he screams, "Foul ball!" and argues with an umpire as the smiling Babe jogs around the bases enjoying the cheers of 10,000 fans.

— One fan, Joe Forner of Manhattan's First Avenue, is especially happy; he caught Ruth's historic homer. The bleacher brigade demonstrates some more when the Babe assumes his position in the ninth, and Ruth responds with several snappy military salutes. In that ninth inning, Walter Johnson pinch-hits for Zachary and skies out to Ruth, thereby bringing to a close Johnson's phenomenal career. Ruth's 60th homer was his record-setting 17th homer of September. It was also his 28th at Yankee Stadium, a record number bested by Lou Gehrig in 1934. It meant that the Babe personally broke the single-season home run record for the fourth time. Ruth had at least one homer off the winningest pitcher on each AL team. He hit four off 17-game winner Rube Walberg of the A's and four off 13-game winner Milt Gaston of the Browns. On the road, Babe hit eight homers in Boston, five in Philadelphia, four in Cleveland, four in Detroit, four in St. Louis, four in Washington and three in Chicago.

Oct 1— In the final game of the regular season, Ruth goes hitless in three trips. But the Yankees beat Washington, 4-3, and win their 110th game.

— The 110 wins established an AL record that Cleveland topped in 1954 with 111 wins. But no comparison should be made between the two teams.

The Mighty Mite, Miller Huggins, is in the middle of some of his great personnel, circa 1927. From left are Bob Shawkey, Bob Meusel, Babe Ruth and Waite Hoyt.

Cleveland was swept by the Giants in four World Series games. The 1927 Yankees, hailed as the greatest ever, was more than just a one-man team, with all respect due Ruth. Gehrig hit 47 home runs, combining with Babe for 107 fourbaggers, the big league record for teammates until 1961. Ruth outhomered all the other AL *teams* and Larrupin' Lou hit more homers than four of the other seven clubs. The outfield featured a trio of .300-plus hitters. Ruth and Combs both had .356 averages and Meusel's was .337. Second baseman Lazzeri hit .309 and had 18 home runs (third most in the AL behind Ruth and Gehrig) and shortstop Koenig hit a respectable .285. When he was healthy, Joe Dugan was the best third baseman in the league but he played in only 112 games because of injuries and hit .269. The pitching staff was deep. Following Hoyt and Moore were Herb Pennock, 19-8; Urban Shocker, 18-6; Dutch Ruether, 13-6; and George Pipgras, 10-3.

Oct 4—   The day before the World Series opens between the Yankees and Pirates, New York deflates—perhaps intimidates is the word—the opposition with an astounding display of power in batting practice.

— In spacious Forbes Field, Ruth hit four straight balls over the distant fence and suggested to the awestruck Pirates in attendance that if they'd fetch the balls he'd be happy to affix his signature to them. As Waite Hoyt and the Athletics' Eddie Rommel, the latter brought along by the Yanks because of his ability to groove pitches, laid the ball down the middle, Gehrig, Combs, Koenig, Meusel, Lazzeri, Dugan, Collins and Grabowski stepped up and belted balls all around the yard and over the fences. Pirate rookie Lloyd Waner turned to his brother Paul and whispered, "Jesus, they're big, aren't they?" Legend says the Yankees won the Series right here. Whether intimidated or not, the Pirates, with a 94-60 record, were a stronger club than the Cardinal team of the year before that whipped the Yankees. Paul Waner won the NL batting crown at .380, Lloyd Waner hit .355 and Pie Traynor .342. Three other starters hit over .300 but outfield star Kiki Cuyler, feuding with Manager Donie Bush, did not play in the Series. Still, it was a team of pretty fair country hitters, who as a club hit .305, just two points below the Yankees' average.

Oct 5—   The World Series opens in Pittsburgh and the Yankees win, 5-4. The Yanks score in the first frame on Ruth's single and a Gehrig triple that was a short fly Paul Waner let get by him while attempting a shoestring catch. After Pittsburgh ties it, the Yanks tally three times in the third. With the bases loaded, Meusel walks to force in a run, Ruth scores on a forceout and Gehrig, trapped off third, scores when catcher Earl Smith drops a throw. The three-run Yankee rally is accomplished on one hit. Gehrig adds another run with a sacrifice fly in the fifth. Meanwhile, the Pirates nick away at Waite Hoyt, and with trouble brewing in the eighth, Miller Huggins brings in Wilcy Moore who allows a run-producing hit and then puts out the fire. Hoyt gets the win and the Pirates' defense an assist for allowing three unearned runs. Moore, who will have a 36-21 record with 35 saves over two tours with the Yankees, gets the save.

Oct 6—   Urban Shocker is scheduled to start but Huggins switches to his rookie wonder, George Pipgras, and is rewarded when the Danish Viking pitches a complete-game seven-hitter and New York wins, 6-2. Pipgras belies his reputation as a breaking ball pitcher. Throwing only three curveballs, his fastball surprises and bewilders the Pirates. The Yankees, meanwhile, put together three-run rallies in the third and eighth innings.

Oct 7—   With the Series shifted to Yankee Stadium, the Yankees win Game 3, 8-1, taking a 3-0 Series lead. Herb Pennock is sensational, retiring the first 22 Pirates in order and finishing with a three-hitter. His arm stiffens while sitting through a six-run Yankee seventh that is highlighted by Ruth's three-run homer, and Pennock loses his no-hitter in the eighth when Traynor cleanly singles with one out. The Pirates were murder on southpaws and in the victorious locker room, Meusel asks, "Who said a lefthander couldn't beat the Pirates?" A reporter answers, "Plenty of guys. But they meant the lefthanders in the National League. They haven't any like Pennock in that league."

Oct 8—   New York completes what seemed like an inevitable four-game sweep, winning, 4-3, for the club's second World Championship. Ruth singles home a run in the first inning and hits a tremendous two-run homer in the fifth. But the Pirates rally against Wilcy Moore to tie. Moore hangs in the entire game, scattering 10 hits. With Pirate reliever Johnny Miljus on the mound and the game tied in the ninth, Combs walks, Koenig beats out a bunt and Ruth is walked intentionally after a wild pitch. Miljus courageously strikes out Gehrig and Meusel, but with one strike on Lazzeri, he uncorks his second wild pitch and Combs scores the winning run. The surprise hitting star of the Series is Koenig, who hits .500. The Bambino hits .400 with seven RBIs and the only two home runs hit in the Series.

1928

The Yankees will finish at 101-53, good enough to edge second-place Philadelphia by 2½ games, for their third consecutive pennant. Babe Ruth with 54 circuit clouts will retain his home run title, and he will tie Lou Gehrig for the RBI title at 142. George Pipgras, at 24-13, will be the league's winningest pitcher, but Waite Hoyt, 23-7, will have a better winning percentage (.767). The Yankees will again prevail in the World Series for their second consecutive World Championship.

Apr 11—   The Yankees open the campaign in Philadelphia and knock Lefty Grove out in the third inning to win, 8-3. Herb Pennock twirls a seven-hitter and Ruth scores three runs. New York will win the first four games and build a 36-8 spring record.

           — The Yankees were coming off a fish-bowl spring. The publicity lights tracked their many holdouts, most notably Hoyt. (The players naturally wanted salaries commensurate with their newly earned reputation as baseball's greatest team.) And the visible Yankees were made all the more visible after spring training broke by a memorable barnstorming tour through Texas and Oklahoma.

Apr 20—   Yankee Stadium opens its season with triple-deck stands extended on a bending line across the left field line, creating the wrap-around effect that is prominent in the Stadium's present shape. Until the extension, ground-level bleachers ran all the way to the left field foul pole where they met triple-decked stands. Philadelphia spoils the home opener with a 2-1 win.

May 4—   Yankee third baseman Joe Dugan belts a bases-loaded homer at the Stadium, the only grand slam hit by a Yankee all year, and the Yankees beat Chicago, 10-4.

— Dugan was one of many injured Yankees in 1928. He was sidelined for 60 games with knee problems. Second baseman Tony Lazzeri and shortstop Mark Koenig also missed many games this season because of injuries. The only infielder to be healthy all year was first baseman Lou Gehrig. The outfield was afflicted, too. Bob Meusel missed time with a bad ankle and Ruth and Combs suffered various injuries.

Jun 12— In Chicago, New York wins, 15-7. Gehrig is a one-man demolition crew. Lou has four extra-base hits in four trips for a total of 14 bases—a pair of home runs and two triples. He scores five runs and drives in six runs. He has a two-run homer in the first, a run-scoring triple in the third, a three-run homer in the sixth and a triple in the eighth. The other home run twin, Ruth, also belts a homer and scores four runs.

Jul 4— The Yankees split a holiday doubleheader in Washington. New York leads the AL by 12 games, the biggest lead on Independence Day by the eventual pennant-winner in AL history. (A few days earlier, the Yanks led the A's by 13½ games.) The Yankees have a phenomenal record: 53-17.

Jul 26— In the first game of a doubleheader in Detroit, the Yankees score 11 runs in the top of the 12th inning to beat the Tigers, 12-1, but lose the second game, 13-10. In the first game's rally, Gene Robertson has two hits and drives in three runs, Meusel and Lazzeri triple, and Ruth and Grabowski double.

— Meusel had a single, double and home run before his triple. It was the third time in his career that he hit for the cycle, setting a record that still stands. It is only the fourth cycle in Yankee history and is indication of Meusel's amazing hitting versatility.

Jul 29— In Cleveland, the Yankees take a 24-6 whipping, as the Indians score the most runs in history against the Yankees. The Tribe pounds out 27 hits.

— In the first two weeks of the road trip, New York will win only 6 of 16 games. Meanwhile, Philadelphia has turned red-hot. The A's in July go 25-8 to climb right back into pennant contention.

Aug 1— The Yankees win, 12-1, as pitcher Hank Johnson has a memorable day in St. Louis. Johnson's neat, complete-game pitching is accompanied by a five-for-five day at the plate. He hits .241 (19 for 79) this season. Ruth hits his 42nd homer of the year in the first inning off Browns' ace General Crowder (21-5). The ball lands on Sportsmans Park's right field pavilion roof and bounces onto Grand Avenue. Babe is 27 games ahead of his 1927 homer pace.

Aug 23— New York purchases the contract of pitcher Tom Zachary on waivers from the Washington Senators, a move made necessary by an arm injury to Herb Pennock.

— The Pennock injury occurred in a recent three-hitter he pitched against Boston. Pennock was 17-6 and heading for another great season, but he had to be shelved and his absence almost cost the Yankees the pennant. More important, from a longer perspective, the Knight of Kennett Square would never regain his outstanding form. Zachary would go 3-3 for New York over the final weeks of 1928.

Aug 31— The Athletics are within reach of the Yankees, who have played a shade over .500 since the Fourth of July. New York is 84-42 and Philadelphia is 83-45, only two games behind. The Yankees are battered with injuries to their regulars and to the pitching staff.

— Ruth's quest of a new home run record has been stymied. He was well ahead of his 1927 pace as August began. But the Babe hit only six homers on the month.

Sep 1— In the midst of a presidential campaign, Republican candidate Herbert Hoover takes in a Yankee-Senators game in Washington. Arrangements are made for a Hoover-Ruth photograph. Suddenly the always cooperative Bambino bows out. "Nothing doing," he said. "I'm for Al Smith." (Hoover defeated challenger Smith, the Democratic governor of New York, in the 1928 presidential election.)

Sep 7— New York loses a doubleheader to Washington while Philadelphia wins a pair from Boston. The 13½-game lead the Yankees enjoyed at the beginning of July has evaporated—New York and Philadelphia are tied for first place.

Sep 8— Philadelphia wins another doubleheader from Boston while the Yankees take only a single game from Washington. The A's have first place to themselves by a half game.

— New York was abuzz over the Yankee-Athletic doubleheader to be played at the Stadium the next day. So great was the demand for tickets that a riot nearly broke out at the Yankee offices on 42nd Street. Scalpers were asking $25 for $2 seats. Extra subway trains were to be run to the Stadium and extra police were made available to fortify the peace. The streaking A's were coming to town with Lefty Grove, Al Simmons, Mickey Cochrane, 20-year-old Jimmie Foxx and 41-year-old Ty Cobb.

Sep 9— As a huge crowd, reported unofficially at 85,264, watches from inside the Stadium, and another 5,000 or more watch from nearby rooftops, the Yankees sweep a doubleheader from Philadelphia, 3-0 and 7-3, to regain the AL lead. George Pipgras shuts out the A's in the first game, one of the most important wins in this or any year, and Waite Hoyt wins the second game. Ordinarily, the team celebration would be raucous, but as the Yankees storm into the clubhouse, road secretary Mark Roth informs them that Urban Shocker is dead.

— Shocker, afflicted with a swollen heart and who was unable to sleep lying down, died in Denver at the age of 38. The Yankees were sickened by the news. They had had little knowledge of the seriousness of Shocker's condition. They had lost a popular teammate and a great (some would argue Hall-of-Fame great) pitcher. Urban Shocker was 62-37 in two stints with New York and 188-117 overall, for a winning percentage of .616. The Ohio spitballer, whose best years were with the Browns, was aware of the terminal nature of his condition in 1927 when he posted an 18-6 record.

Sep 11— After an open date, New York complete a three-game sweep of the Athletics, winning, 5-3, and the A's leave town 2½ games back (the position they will be in when the season ends). The game is tied, 3-3, in the bottom of the eighth when Ruth unloads a two-run, game-winning homer. Pitcher Hank Johnson beats Lefty Grove, the ace of the A's.

— The biggest factor in the Yankees finishing ahead of the A's may well have been the 22-year-old Johnson's success against them. He beat the A's five times and each time Grove absorbed the loss! For the season, Johnson was 14-9. Grove at 24-9 tied Pipgras for the most wins in the AL. The Yankees were 16-6 for the year against the A's.

Sep 28— In Detroit, Pipgras defeats the Tigers, 11-6, and the Yankees clinch the pennant with only two games remaining. Ruth contributes his 53rd home run, then rents several rooms of a Detroit hotel and throws the team a riotous victory party.

Sep 29— Miller Huggins uses only two regulars against the Tigers, who rap 28 hits in a 19-10 victory over the injury-riddled Yankees. Meanwhile, the Cardinals win to clinch the NL pennant, the final margin being only two games over the Giants, and a repeat of the memorable 1926 Series is in the works. The Cardinals are slight favorites, mostly because of the Yankees' many injuries.

Oct 4— The World Series opens at Yankee Stadium. Behind Waite Hoyt's neat three-hitter, the Yankees down St. Louis, 4-1, before 61,425. The Cardinals do not get a hit until George Harper singles to center with one out in the fifth inning. The other two hits are by Sunny Jim Bottomley, who homers in the seventh and singles in the ninth.

Oct 5— St. Louis starts 41-year-old Grover Cleveland Alexander and the Yankees drive him from the hill in the third inning, going on to win, 9-3. Gehrig starts the rout in the first inning with a monstrous three-run homer, a rising line-drive that strikes the distant scoreboard—one of the most awesome blasts ever seen at the Stadium. George Pipgras is brilliant after allowing three runs in the second inning, pitching a four-hit complete game. Two singles by Frankie Frisch are the only hits Pipgras allows after the second inning.

Oct 7— The Series moves to Sportsmans Park and the Yankees disappoint the home folks by winning Game 3, 7-3. Miller Huggins hands the ball to veteran lefthander Tom Zachary, who rewards Hug's faith in him by going the distance. After St. Louis scores twice in the first, Gehrig gets one run back with a homer that lands on the top of the right field pavilion. In the fourth, Lou hits an inside-the-park two-run homer to put the Yanks ahead, 3-2. But the Cardinals rally to tie in the fifth. The Yankees tally three runs in the sixth—the go-ahead run scoring when Ruth, forgetting his sprained ankle and charley horse, heads for home from second on a force play. He scores when he separates catcher Jimmie Wilson from the ball. Having been shown the way by Ruth, the Yankees execute a perfect double steal, Meusel scoring and Lazzeri going to second. Lazzeri then scores when Gene Robertson, Joe Dugan's replacement for much of the Series, singles.

Oct 9— Sweeping to their second consecutive World Championship, the battered Yankees win, 7-3, taking back-to-back Series in the minimum of eight games. Perhaps more impressively, Hoyt gets his second complete game, meaning that the Yanks have used only three pitchers—Hoyt, Pipgras and Zachary—in winning four Series games! Ruth steals the headlines, however, by hitting three homers and making a great catch to end the Series. Babe's second homer in the seventh inning comes after Bill Sherdel had slipped a called third strike by Babe. But the strikeout is disallowed because it was quick-pitched. The decision causes a rhubarb, then Babe knocks one over the right field pavilion.

— The day's business over, the Yankees held a wild party on the train, lasting all the way to New York. For the Series, Ruth hit .625, still the highest percentage in Series history, and Gehrig .545. Between them, they scored 14 runs, made 16 hits, had 4 doubles, belted 7 homers, knocked in 13 runs and drew 7 walks. But the trio of Yankee pitchers were the unsung heroes. Hoyt's performance rivaled his incredible accomplishment in the 1921 Series. And three pitchers who were so valuable in the campaign— Pennock, Moore and Shocker—did not pitch at all.

Dec 29—   In one of several personnel moves, the Yankees ask for waivers on third baseman Joe Dugan, who is claimed by the Boston Braves. Joe will hit .304 as a part-timer with the Braves in 1929.

— Jumping Joe was increasingly hobbled by a problem knee, and it was with regret that Yankee fans lost this fun-loving pal of Ruth's. Dugan was a .286 hitter and fielder supreme in his seven Yankee seasons. His baseball career ended with the 1931 season, the year the Yanks, with the insertion of Joe Sewell at third, finally filled the hole caused by Dugan's absence. Dugan hit .280 over 14 major league seasons.

1929

The Yankees will finish at 88-66, in second place—18 games behind the Philadelphia Athletics. Babe Ruth will retain his home run championship with 46 and Tony Lazzeri will hit .354 to lead the club. George Pipgras at 18-12 will be the only Yankee pitcher to come close to being a 20-game winner.

Apr 17—   Opening Day at Yankee Stadium is postponed because of rain but Babe Ruth's second marriage takes place as planned. The Babe and the former Claire Merritt Hodgson, a young widow, are married at St. Gregory's Roman Catholic Church on West 90th Street in Manhattan.

Apr 18—   The Yankees defeat Boston, 7-3, for an Opening Day win at the Stadium where they take the field wearing uniform numbers on their backs. The Yankees have the distinction of being the first big league team to wear uniform numbers on a regular basis, home and away. In his first at bat in the first inning, Ruth hits a home run off Boston's Red Ruffing, then tips his cap and blows a kiss to his new wife. Gehrig later adds a homer off Milt Gaston, as a wedding present to the Ruths, Babe says later. The Yanks will win 13 of their first 17 games.

— The players' numbers correspond to their place in the batting order; thus, Combs is No. 1, Koenig No. 2, Ruth No. 3, Gehrig No. 4, Meusel No. 5, and so on. Leo Durocher wears No. 7, a number that will later be made famous by Mickey Mantle.

May 4—   In Detroit, Gehrig blasts three home runs in one game, the first time an American Leaguer has done this since Lou himself did it in 1927. One of Lou's homers, in an 11-9 slugfest won by the Yankees, comes in the middle of back-to-back-to-back homers by Ruth, Gehrig and Bob Meusel. It is the first time in the AL that three homers are hit in a row since a succession of Ruth-Gehrig-Meusel homers in 1925.

— The Athletics who started slow are now red-hot and in the second week of May take first place. The Yanks hung on for awhile, thanks largely to Ruth, but there never was a pennant race.

May 7—   In a relief role, the Yanks' Tom Zachary wins in St. Louis, the Yankees pulling it out in the ninth inning, 6-5.

— Zachary went on to log a 12-0 record, the most wins in big league history without a loss. He won 9 of 11 starts and in 15 relief games he won three and saved two. Seven of his starts were complete games. No AL pitcher has ever won more than nine games without at least one defeat. But as Tom would one day say: "All they remember about me as a pitcher is that Babe Ruth hit his 60th home run off me."

May 13— New York's rookie catcher Bill Dickey makes three assists in the sixth inning, but the Indians win in Cleveland, 4-3, in the first big league game in which both teams wore numbers on their uniforms.

— Dickey remains only one of four AL catchers to make three assists in one game. The famed catcher's contract was bought from the Little Rock, Ark., minor league club in 1928 on the advice of Yankee scout Johnny Nee and the Yanks never regretted the deal. Bill was the second (behind Wally Schang) of a long line of great catchers for New York. After playing 10 games in 1928, Dickey in 1929 established himself as the first regular Yankee catcher since Schang. Dickey hit .324 and was the good news for the Yankees in 1929.

May 19— Tragedy mars this day at Yankee Stadium. A cloudburst sends the crowd looking for shelter and a stampede jams a narrow exit in right field. Panic and hysteria result in two deaths and 62 injured persons. The hospitalized among the casualties, some of Ruth's best fans (people who sat in the right field bleachers known as Ruthville), were visited by the Babe who gave gifts to all the injured.

Jun 3— Ed Wells, a pitcher with a combined 24-28 record (pitching for Detroit) makes his return to the majors memorable after a two-year absence. Now wearing Yankee pinstripes, Wells draws Chicago ace Ted Lyons (14-20) as his opponent at Yankee Stadium. Wells pitches a two-hitter, outduels Lyons (who allows six hits) and wins, 1-0, in a game that takes only one hour and twenty minutes. Both pitchers go the route. Yankee third baseman Gene Robertson, soon to be ticketed to the Boston Braves, knocks in the game's only run and has three doubles. Wells will go on to have a fine 13-9 record making him the Yankees' second biggest winner.

Jun 7— Suffering from a deep chest cold that has prevented him from playing for several days, Ruth enters St. Vincent's Hospital and it is discovered that he has a heart murmur. He is told to take some rest.

— The Ruths left for Maryland's Chesapeake Bay on June 9 for a week of rest, and on June 18 the Babe returned to the Stadium for batting practice. In all, the Babe would miss 17 days and when he returned he trailed Gehrig in homers, 19-10. But from the date of his return through August he would hit 30 home runs.

Jul 13— The Yankees sweep a doubleheader, 4-2 and 6-5, in Chicago. As a team, the Yankees are hitting .303 and have 73 home runs to lead the AL, but New York is 7½ games behind Philadelphia and moving in the wrong direction. Complacency has set in, the critics, including Miller Huggins, maintain.

— The reasons for the Yanks' decline are many. Two pitchers experienced a decided drop-off in victories from 1928, Hoyt going from 23 to 10 and Pennock from 17 to 9. This great righty-lefty combination, which had a combined record of 264-148 from 1923-30, was no longer the heart of the pitching staff. And a back injury limited Hank Johnson to only 12 games, resulting in 11 fewer wins. The left side of the infield was weak and Huggins was unable to find the right third base-shortstop combination from among infielders Gene Robertson, Leo Durocher, Mark Koenig and Lyn Lary. And following two straight great years, Gehrig lost 74 points from his average, dropping to .300 even, but he did have 35 homers and 126 RBIs.

Aug 1—   In the home run derby Gehrig still leads Ruth, 26 to 24, but the Babe's bat is hot—in less than six weeks since his return from illness, the Babe has hit 14 homers to Lou's seven. In today's losing cause, Ruth hits a homer off Chicago's Ted Lyons.

Aug 7—   After hitting a grand slam homer in the second game of the previous day's doubleheader, Ruth hits a grand slammer in the first game of today's twinbill off Howard Ehmke in Philadelphia. It is the second time in his career that he has homered with the bases filled in successive games. And it is his third grand slam of the year. The Yankees win the first game but drop the nightcap.

Aug 11—   In Cleveland, off Willis Hudlin, Ruth hits his 500th career home run, his 30th of the season. The ball clears the right field retaining wall at League Park. But the blast cannot keep the Yankees from losing, 6-5.

Aug 24—   The Yankees reach the low point of their season. For the third consecutive game in St. Louis, a Browns' pitcher shuts them out. This time it is General Crowder who blanks New York, following whitewashes the previous two days by Sam Gray and George Blaeholder.

Sep 5—   The Yankees go up the river to Sing Sing and, with little regard for their personal safety, win 17-3. Ruth plays first base, hits three homers and has a great time exchanging jokes with the prisoners.

Sep 20—   Yankee Manager Miller Huggins, never physically robust and the victim of several health problems over the years, is depressed, restless and unable to sleep worrying about the Yankees. He has an ugly red sore under one eye and he is exhausted. He is hospitalized at St. Vincent's where his temperature will soon rise to 105 degrees.

Sep 25—   Miller Huggins, 50, dies of erysipelas, a form of blood poisoning. The Yankees are playing in Boston. The game is halted for a moment of silence and the flag is lowered to half mast. Many of the Yankees, including Babe, break down in tears in the clubhouse. Tom Meany reports this to his New York paper and a news-hardened copyreader tells Meany to stop overwriting. Insists Meany, "I can't help it. They were crying."

  — Thus ended the reign of the first great Yankee manager. Hug's friend and coach, Art Fletcher, who took over the club when he was hospitalized, finished out the year as manager. But no one had his heart in playing baseball. Lazzeri was so affected that he returned home to San Francisco after Hug's funeral. All AL games were cancelled on September 26. Services were held in New York City on the 27th and Huggins was laid to rest in Cincinnati on the 29th.

Oct 16—   The Yankees sell the contract of outfielder Bob Meusel to the Cincinnati Reds.

  — Meusel will hit .289 in 113 games for the Reds in 1930, his last major league season. Long Bob was nearing the end of a great career as one of the best all-round players in the story of baseball. But he had a 1929 average of only .261, 48 points below his lifetime average of .309. His decline as a player had a direct bearing on the Yanks' decline. In his prime, he hit for average and power, ran the bases with daring and skill, and had perhaps the best throwing arm an outfielder ever had. But Bob Meusel, somehow, has never been inducted into the Baseball Hall of Fame.

Oct 23— Bob Shawkey is named the new Yankee manager. It bears ill tidings for the future, perhaps, that Shawkey is the fourth choice of Jacob Ruppert and Ed Barrow. In order, the Yankees are turned down by Donie Bush, Eddie Collins and Art Fletcher, the latter telling Ruppert, "If it's just the same to you, Colonel, I would rather remain as coach."

The Bambino ends his holdout, agrees to a two-year contract worth a total of $160,000, and he and owner Jacob Ruppert shake on it March 8, 1930, in St. Petersburg, Fla.

THE 1930's
A DYNASTY ESTABLISHED

1930

The Yankees will finish in third place at 86-68, 16 games in back of pennant-winning Philadelphia. Babe Ruth will win his fifth straight home run championship with 49, and Lou Gehrig will win the RBI title with 174. The club's leading pitchers, with 15 wins apiece, will be George Pipgras and Red Ruffing.

Jan 8—   His contract having run out, Babe Ruth meets with Jacob Ruppert and Ed Barrow at the colonel's brewery office to talk dollars and cents. No progress is made, however, and thus begins Ruth's most famous salary fight.

— The ensuing negotiations produced headlines but no settlement, and Ruth went to spring training unsigned, threatening to jump the club. He worked out with the team at St. Petersburg while conducting negotiations with Ruppert. In time the Babe reduced his demands to $85,000 per year for three years. Jake raised his offer to $80,000 per year for two years.

Mar 8—   On an impulse, more or less, Ruth ends his much ballyhooed holdout in St. Petersburg. In essence, he agrees to Ruppert's terms. Of course, no one is calling Babe the loser—he has signed a two-year contract calling for a nice $10,000 raise. The formal signing will take place in two days. When asked if he thought it right that he should make more money than President Hoover, the Babe answers, "Why not? I had a better year than he did."

Apr 25—   The Yankees, after losing five straight, get their first win for Manager Bob Shawkey by beating Boston, 3-2, in 10 innings at Yankee Stadium. They also lost a lot to rain—five early season games were postponed because of rain.

May 5—   Lefty Gomez makes his first big league start and pitches a complete game to defeat Chicago and 41-year-old future Hall of Famer Red Faber, 4-1. Gomez allows only five hits, no walks and fans six. He had less success in middle relief against Washington April 29, his debut, when he was tagged with the loss.

— The Yankees were reported to have paid the San Francisco Seals between $35,000 and $50,000 the previous year for Lefty's contract. He was a promising prospect but he needed polish, and after winning just two of seven decisions, he was sent to St. Paul. As the colorful Lefty would later explain, he got to visit St. Paul after two consecutive runners stole home on him: "Before I could take that third long windup, I wound up in St. Paul." But he returned and attained stardom, combining with a righthander to form the heart of the Yanks' great pitching staff of the 1930's. The righthander, Boston's Red Ruffing, was about to become a Yankee.

May 6—   In one of the best deals in Yankee history, New York obtains pitcher Red Ruffing from the Boston Red Sox for outfielder Cedric Durst and $50,000.

— Durst in 1930 ended his major league career. He hit .245 in 102 games for Boston. Ruffing was just beginning a 15-season Yankee career over which he won 231 games. Yet, at the time of the deal, Ruffing was a study in futility, or at least, bad luck; his career mark was at 39-96, including a 1-14 record against New York. Red led the AL in defeats in both 1928 and 1929, with 25 and 22 losses, respectively. But all that changed in New York.

May 18—   The Yankees beat Boston, 11-0, at Braves Field (for some reason the game is not played at Fenway) and finally climb to .500, a mark that has eluded them throughout a season beginning with five losses in a row. Ruth hits the longest homer ever seen in Braves Field up to this time, a shot over the right field bleachers off Ed Morris.

May 21— As the Yankees lose two games, 15-7 and 4-1, in Philadelphia, Babe Ruth for the first time hits three homers in a regular season game, the first game of a doubleheader. The Babe's first two homers, which give New York a short-lived 5-0 lead, come off George Earnshaw (22-13). The third is off Lefty Grove (28-5) and all three give Ruth six RBIs. The homer off Grove lands on a roof several houses away from Shibe Park. Hitting against former teammate Jack Quinn in the ninth, the Babe has a chance to become the first AL player to hit four homers in one game. He delights the crowd by stepping into the righthanded batter's box! He strikes out, but a classic Ruth barrage of long balls has been launched nonetheless—the Babe in one week will hit nine homers.

May 22— At Shibe Park, the Yankees sweep Philadelphia by scores of 10-1 and 20-13. Gehrig blasts three home runs in one game, a day after Ruth accomplished the same feat. Lou has eight RBIs in the game (the nightcap of the doubleheader). In two days the Yankees will sweep another doubleheader in New York from the A's, winning 10-6 and 11-1. And these A's will win 102 games this season.

May 30— New York deals Waite Hoyt (P) and Mark Koenig (SS) to Detroit for Owen Carroll (P), Harry Rice (OF) and George Wuestling (SS). Of these three players received, only Rice makes much of a mark. He hits .298 in 100 games, knocking in 74 runs, and in a June 12 game with Detroit makes 11 putouts.

— Hoyt quarreled with Manager Bob Shawkey a few weeks earlier after serving a homer to Philadelphia's Al Simmons. Hoyt threw a fastball. No good, says Shawkey—stick to curveballs against Simmons. Hoyt resented these instructions and said as much to Shawkey, who snapped, "You'll pitch the way I tell you to, or you won't pitch for me at all." It was a mistake to trade Hoyt; Waite won 70 games in the majors after leaving the Yankees. And the Yanks were short on pitching in 1930. As for Koenig, he had slowed down but he was still a respectable shortstop. He played in the majors through 1936, finishing with a fine .279 lifetime batting average. Koenig was a .285 hitter and solid fielder in his six seasons with the Yankees.

Jun 17— In Cleveland, the Yankees score eight runs in the second inning and win, 17-2. Gehrig has four hits, including a homer and a double and scores three runs. He even steals a base. Lou's four RBIs give him 10 consecutive games in which he knocks in at least one run (for a total of 27 RBIs).

— Gehrig was on his way to his third RBI championship. He would fall just one RBI shy of his AL record of 175, set in 1927. Gehrig this year made a strong bid for Triple Crown honors. His 174 RBIs were 18 more than runner-up Jimmie Foxx collected. His .379 average was only two points lower than Al Simmons'. And only the Babe outdid Lou (49 to 41) in homers. It was the fourth year in a row that Columbia Lou finished second to the Bambino in home runs.

Jun 28— The Yankees trail Philadelphia by two games but the clubs are even in the loss column. Ruth blasts his 28th and 29th homers of the season as the

Yankees rout Cleveland twice, 13-1 and 14-2, New York making 33 hits for the day and scoring 7 runs in the first inning of each game.

— The Yankees had two amazing hitters in Gehrig and Ruth. Gehrig's batting average was .399 as of this date and led the AL. Ruth was fifth at .380. The Babe had an amazing June, hitting 15 homers to take an insurmountable home run lead. Besides Ruth and Gehrig, the Yankees had four regulars who hit better than .300 on the year (Gehrig hit .379 and Ruth, .359). Combs finished at .344, Bill Dickey at .339, Ben Chapman at .316 and Tony Lazzeri at .303. But hitting was busting out all over with the introduction of an even livelier ball than the one introduced in 1920. Fred Lieb called it "the lively ball at its liveliest." New York led the league at .309 and the entire AL hit a combined .288.

Jul 2—
At Yankee Stadium, Chicago's Carl Reynolds hits three home runs in succession against the Yankees. In trying to catch the second Reynolds' homer, Ruth tears off a fingernail and the crowd watches, amused, as Babe *limps* to the dugout.

— If the Babe was loose, the race was tight. Philadelphia led at 48-26, followed by Washington at 44-25 and New York at 43-26. New York was still even with Philadelphia in the loss column. But the A's would slowly pull away.

Jul 31—
In Boston, Gehrig has eight RBIs in one game, two days after having six RBIs. Lou's barrage is highlighted by a bases-loaded home run, his second grand slam of the year. He adds two doubles. The Yankee win a barnburner, 14-13. ("Did Boston miss the extra point?" asked baseball researcher Walter LeConte.)

— This capped an amazing five-week period when five different Yankees (Tony Lazzeri, Jimmy Reese, Bill Dickey, Harry Rice and Gehrig) hit grand slams.

Sep 18—
In a game he pitches in St. Louis, Ruffing hits two home runs, becoming the sixth AL pitcher ever to hit a pair of homers in one game. He is the first Yankee pitcher to do so. Combs has a gift inside-the-park homer when an outfielder falls down. The Yankees win, 7-6, in 10 innings and Herb Pennock gets the win in relief.

— In his career in the majors, Ruffing hit 36 home runs, the third most ever hit by a pitcher, following West Ferrell's 38 and Bob Lemon's 37. Ruffing hit .364 in 1930.

Sep 28—
Gehrig's streak ends at first base (885 straight games at the position) but Ruth gets the headlines in the Yanks' 9-3 win in Fenway Park. Not having pitched in nine years, Babe takes the mound, pitches a complete game and scatters 11 hits to pick up the win. Babe even strikes out three while walking only two, showing remarkable control after such a long layoff. At bat, the Bambino has a pair of singles, drives in a run and scores a run. And with that, the season ends.

Oct 14—
Joe McCarthy is the new manager of the Yankees, a position he will hold for 16 seasons. At the formal signing, a nervous McCarthy blurts into the news microphone, "Colonel Huston, I..." Everyone laughs good-naturedly at McCarthy's error, including Colonel *Ruppert*. It is one of the few Marse Joe will make in his Yankee employment. Unfortunately, the switch from Shawkey to McCarthy is handled shabbily. Ruppert had assured Shawkey

that his contract would be renewed in the off-season, just as Huggins' contract had been handled. But when Shawkey arrives at Ed Barrow's office on business, he is shocked to see McCarthy, and, realizing the implications, leaves immediately. Shawkey had no way of knowing that Ruppert, Barrow and McCarthy, in the wake of McCarthy's September 23 dismissal as manager of the Cubs, had held a meeting in which the manager's job was offered to McCarthy and McCarthy, who earlier received a "feeler" from Yankee scout Paul Krichell, accepted. "It was a dirty deal," Shawkey will say years later.

— Besides Shawkey, the man most hurt by McCarthy's appointment was Ruth, who wanted badly to manage the Yankees. In his four years under Marse Joe, Ruth was critical of his manager's ability and the two men shared a distant and uneasy relationship. But McCarthy eventually won to his side the remainder of the team. He was a tough disciplinarian but a fair one; he demanded respect but also gave it.

1931

The Yankees will finish in second place (94-59), 13½ games behind Philadelphia. Babe Ruth and Lou Gehrig will tie for the AL home run championship at 46, but it will be Lou's season, clearly. He will set the still-standing AL record for RBIs with 184. Lefty Gomez will lead the pitching staff, posting a sterling 21-9 record at the age of 22. The exceptional catcher, Bill Dickey, will not have a passed ball all year.

Mar 13— Spring training camp opens for the Yankees in St. Petersburg, Fla. Miller Huggins Field is dedicated and a game between the Ruths and Gehrigs is played.

— The Yankees trained in St. Petersburg from 1925 through 1961 except for two breaks. They did not go South in World War II because of travel restrictions, and in 1951 they trained in Phoenix. The Yanks moved into their present winter home in Fort Lauderdale, Fla., in 1962.

Apr 6— In an exhibition game in Nashville, the Yankees crunch the home team, 23-3, as they collect 26 hits. Myril Hoag hits two homers, Gehrig scores four runs, and in general the club looks ready for the season opener a little more than one week away. This in spite of the fact that four days earlier a woman named Jackie Mitchell, pitching for the Chattanooga Lookouts, struck out Ruth, Gehrig and Lazzeri in succession. Chattanooga promoter Joe Engel arranged for the humiliation and the Yankees went along with the fun.

Apr 22— The Yankees win, 7-5, but the triumph in Boston is a painful one for Ruth, notwithstanding his three hits and two runs scored. While running from second to third, Ruth twists his foot, then, in scoring on a short fly ball, has a violent collision with Charlie Berry, the tough Red Sox catcher. Babe seems okay but the next inning as he chases a fly ball, the Bambino falls to the ground in agony. He is carried off the field with a paralyzed nerve center in his thigh, the direct result of his collision with Berry. It is a temporary condition but it sidelines the Babe for 10 days.

— Yankee outfielders took a beating while patrolling the outfield over the next few days. Ruth's replacement, Myril Hoag, hurt his ankle, and Dusty Cooke broke his collarbone.

Apr 26— Gehrig has a home run wiped out and will lose the undisputed home run title as a result. Gehrig's drive, with Lyn Lary aboard, lands in the center field bleachers in Washington. But Lary, who believes the ball was caught (the ball he saw the centerfielder catching was on the rebound from the bleachers), crosses third base and heads into the dugout without touching home plate. Gehrig does not notice Lary's mistake and compounds it by completing his circling of the bases, only to be called out (while credited with a triple) for passing a runner. Also, in this same game, Senator Ossie Bluege has one of history's shortest inside-the-park homers, when his short fly to right field eludes Dusty Cooke, who hurts himself attempting the catch. Before Gehrig can retrieve the ball, Bluege has crossed the plate.

Jun 30— As June ends, Ruth is hitting close to .400 to lead the AL, but it is obvious the Yankees are not strong enough to make a run at the Athletics. New York is in third place, after losing, 8-7, in 11 innings at Detroit, the Yanks' third loss in a row.

— The Yanks finished the season with the AL's third best pitching staff. The team ERA was almost three-quarters of a run higher than Philadelphia's. But offensively the Yanks were awesome, leading the AL in most important categories. The Yanks boasted six .300 hitters in Ruth, Gehrig, Dickey, Combs, Chapman and Sewell; six regulars who scored at least 100 runs were Gehrig, Ruth, Combs, Chapman, Sewell and Lary; and four players with at least 100 RBIs were Gehrig, Ruth, Chapman and Lary. Chapman stole 61 bases, the most in the majors between Ty Cobb's 96 in 1915 and Maury Wills' 104 in 1962. The team scored 1,067 runs, still the big league record.

Jul 2— In Detroit, Ruth establishes a still-standing Yankee record by driving in at least one run in 11 consecutive games. Over the 11-game span, the Babe has 18 RBIs. The Yankees win, 13-1.

Jul 26— The Yankees and White Sox split a doubleheader at Yankee Stadium. In a 22-5 win, the Yankees score all 22 runs over the first four innings: 3, 6, 9 and 4. Pat Caraway (10-24) is tagged with 13 runs, helping to explain his 1931 ERA of 6.22. But Chicago wins the other half of the twinbill, 5-4.

Aug 2— Wilcy Moore, now pitching for the Red Sox (the Yankees having sold his contract) shuts out the Yankees, 1-0. Incredibly, the Yankees will not be shut out for the next 308 games.

Aug 21— Ruth belts his 600th major league home run off George Blaeholder at Sportsmans Park in St. Louis. The Babe pays a youngster $20 to retrieve the ball from Grand Avenue. Later in the game, which the Yanks win, 11-7, the Babe is ejected for arguing with Umpire Van Graflan.

Sep 1— Gehrig blasts a grand slam homer, his third "slam" in four days, setting an AL record for most grand slams in a week that will be tied by Jim Northrup in 1968 and Larry Parrish in 1982. Lou also sets an AL record by hitting a home run in the sixth consecutive game (six homers in all), as Columbia Lou homers in both ends of a doubleheader. Furthermore, for the 10th consecutive game the Iron Horse drives in at least one run for 27 RBIs in all. The Yankees sweep the twinbill, 11-3 and 5-1, against Boston at Yankee Stadium.

— Gehrig enjoyed perhaps the greatest run-producing season of all time. Not only did he set the AL mark with 184 RBIs—topped only in the major leagues by Hack Wilson's 190 RBIs in the NL the year before—but he produced 301 runs (computed by adding the RBI and runs scored totals, 184 and 163, and subtracting homers, 46). No other player, including Wilson, has ever produced more than 288 runs. And Gehrig and Ruth combined to hit 92 home runs, their second highest total after 1927.

Sep 7— The Yankees win two games, 15-3 and 9-4, in Philadelphia. In the opener, Yankee centerfielder Earle Combs walks twice in the first inning when the Yankees score eight runs on only two hits. They receive eight walks, the first eight-walk half-inning in AL history.

    — Combs had a typically impressive season in 1931, hitting .318 and scoring 120 runs. The Kentucky Colonel also hit in 29 straight games, tying the Yankee record that stood until Joe DiMaggio's 56-game streak in 1941.

Sep 17— At Yankee Stadium, the Yankees defeat St. Louis twice, 17-0 and 6-1. Ruffing pitches a shutout, and in the nightcap, Gehrig makes his 200th hit of the campaign. It is Lou's fourth 200-hit season and he will lead the league with 211 hits.

Sep 27— The Yankees beat the champion Athletics, 13-1. The losing pitcher is Lefty Grove, who made his final start of a 31-4 season. Three of Grove's wins were at New York's expense, but today the Yanks drive Grove from the mound in only three innings, bombing him for five runs and eight hits.

Nov 12— Two weeks after Jacob Ruppert and Ed Barrow decide that there will be no farm system in the Yankee organization, Ruppert purchases entire control of the Newark franchise in the International League from Paul Block, a newspaper publisher and the sole owner of the Newark Bears.

    — Branch Rickey's Cardinals had run a successful farm system for almost 10 years, but Ruppert and Barrow for a time believed they could continue to buy talent on the open market. However, more and more minor leaguers were being tied up by big league teams. With the Newark club, bought more or less on impulse, now in hand, Ruppert instructed Barrow to establish a first-class farm system. The search began to find a man to run what would prove to be not only a first-class system but baseball's most successful.

1932

The Yankees will finish at 107-47, good enough to lay easy claim to their seventh AL pennant. Second-place Philadelphia will wind up 13 games behind them. Lou Gehrig will lead the way, hitting .349 with 34 home runs and 151 RBIs. Babe Ruth will hit .341 with 41 homers and 137 RBIs. Lefty Gomez, at 24-7, will pace the pitching staff. And the Yankees will sweep the Cubs in the World Series.

Feb 12— Colonel Ruppert names George Weiss, 38, to head the Yankee farm system. Weiss was vice president and general manager of the International League's Baltimore Orioles.

    — Weiss had success with a semi-pro team he operated in his hometown, New Haven, Conn., and used this success to launch an impressive career as a minor-league executive. At New Haven, he once draw the ire of Ed Barrow when he refused to pay the Yankees for an exhibition game played sans Babe Ruth, the very reason the exhibition was scheduled in the first place. Barrow, who wanted a proven baseball executive to run the Newark

Bears and help build and run a farm system, remembered Weiss. At the minor league meetings in West Baden, Ind., Barrow and Ruppert tagged Weiss as their man, and George began a Yankee association that lasted for 29 baseball seasons.

Mar 16— In St. Petersburg, Ruth and Ruppert end one of their well-publicized contract hassles. Babe is supposed to have signed a blank contract leaving it up to Jake to fill in the amount and Ruppert writes in $75,000 for one year and a percentage of profits from Yankee exhibition games. After the formal signing, the Babe, his wife Claire and Ruppert toss coins into a wishing well. "I wish for another pennant," Ruth says, "so that I can play in 10 World Series." Says Claire, "I wish for many more Yankee contracts." Says the colonel, "I wish I had the money in that well."

Apr 12— In the season opener in Philadelphia, Yankee second baseman Jack Saltzgaver walks four times in his debut, a record for a big league first game. Ruth hits a home run and the Yankees begin a record streak in the AL of hitting at least one homer in the first eight games of the season (20 homers in all). In fact, New York blasts five fourbaggers in winning this game, 12-6. New York, it appears, is determined to end Philadelphia's three-year domination of the American League.

— Ironically, although New York did deny Philadelphia another pennant this year, the Yankees lost the league home run championship for the first time since 1922, and lost it to the Athletics. In fact, with 172 homers, the A's broke the Yanks' AL record of 158, set in 1927. The Yankees, themselves, hit 160 homers to set a short-lived club record. Their run production was down from the previous season's record 1,067 to 1,002.

Babe Ruth has his wife, Claire, by his side, and Yankee owner Jacob Ruppert, second from the right, is accompanied by Col. Fred Wattenberg, a friend and a witness to the signing of a one-year contract paying Ruth $75,000. The four cap the March 16, 1932 signing by feeding a St. Petersburg, Fla., wishing well.

May 30— A monument to the memory of Miller Huggins is dedicated in the outfield at Yankee Stadium. It is the first of three monuments in deep center field and reads in part, "As a tribute to a splendid character who made priceless contributions to baseball and on this field brought glory to the New York club of the American League." The Yankees sweep a doubleheader from Boston, winning, 7-5 and 13-3. They will not relinquish the top spot in the AL which they have held since mid-May.

Jun 3— Gehrig hits four home runs in one game and the Yankees win a slugging marathon in Philadelphia, 20-13. New York has 23 hits and 50 total bases, as the two clubs set an AL record with 77 combined total bases. In the first inning, Gehrig wallops a two-run homer off George Earnshaw to left-center field. He homers off Earnshaw again in the fourth over the right field wall. In the fifth, Lou blasts still another off Earnshaw, this over the left-center field wall. Gehrig's fourth consecutive homer in the seventh comes off Roy Mahaffey and clears the right field fence. Gehrig grounds out in the eighth and in the ninth Lou hits his longest drive of the day, but Al Simmons makes the catch in deep center, near the flagpole and a few steps from the furthest corner of Shibe Park. In all, New York hits seven homers—Gehrig's four and one each by Combs, Ruth and Lazzeri, who hits for the cycle and has five hits on the day. Lazzeri's homer comes with the bases loaded in the ninth.

— Gehrig was the first AL player to hit four homers in one game, and only Rocky Colavito (in 1959) has since managed the feat in a nine-inning game. But Lou displayed a terrible sense of timing: his accomplishment came on the day John J. McGraw retires after 31 years of managing the Giants. The headlines in New York belonged to McGraw. Gehrig, who for so many years played first in the shadow of Ruth and then in that of DiMaggio, found himself in the shadow of still another.

Jun 14— New York defeats Cleveland, 7-6. With the bases loaded, Ben Chapman steals home as the other two runners move up a base to give the Yankees a triple steal.

— Chapman may have been the most exciting player in the league. The year before, Joe McCarthy repositioned the Tennesseean from the infield to the outfield and Ben found a home. His great speed helped him defensively and offensively. He led the AL with 38 stolen bases and hit .299 with 10 homers and 107 RBIs. Chapman's only flaw was his quick temper. He even quarreled with the Bambino on occasion.

Jul 3— In Boston, Earle Combs and Lyn Lary each stroke a pair of doubles in a nine-run sixth and the Yankees win, 13-2. Also in the big inning, Ben Chapman delivers a bases-loaded triple.

— Combs had another fine year at .321 but Lary lost his shortstop job to rookie Frank Crosetti and became a utility infielder. Crosetti pulled the infield together and was a key reason for the Yanks' success in 1932. Crosetti's contract was purchased from the San Francisco Seals.

Jul 4— The Senators sweep a doubleheader from the Yankees, 5-3 and 12-6, in Washington but lose the services of slugging outfielder Carl Reynolds for six weeks after Yankee catcher Bill Dickey breaks Reynolds' jaw in two places with a hard righthanded punch. Scoring on a squeeze play, Reynolds, a solid 200-pounder, steamrolls Dickey at the plate. Dickey, one of the mildest-mannered players in the game, recently has been hammered by baserunners. In a rare fit of anger, Bill picks himself off the ground and punches Reynolds. The one-punch knockout brings Dickey a fine of $1,000 and a suspension of 30 days.

— The Senators, who were 93-61 this season, were badly hurt by the loss of Reynolds, who was hitting better than .360 at the time of the incident. Dickey finished the year hitting .310 and managed to attain the highest totals so far in his career in homers (15) and RBIs (84), in spite of the month's suspension. But Joe McCarthy told Dickey to stop blocking the plate at all costs—he was too valuable to lose in a bang-bang play.

Jul 9—   The Yankees sweep a doubleheader from Detroit, 7-6 and 14-9, at the Stadium, winning the opener behind home runs by Ruth, Gehrig and Joe Sewell and the nightcap behind three consecutive roundtrippers by Ben Chapman. One of Chapman's home runs is a grand slam and two are inside-the-park homers, making Chapman the second player in AL history to hit two inside-the-parkers in one game.

Jul 24—   The Yankees beat Philadelphia, 9-3, at home as Lefty Gomez is twice a strikeout victim in the same inning. Lefty can throw the ball much better than he can hit it. He will have a lifetime batting average of .147. But on the mound, El Goofo rules supreme—he wins 11 consecutive games in 1932, 24 in all. And after Lefty came Red Ruffing with 18, Johnny Allen with 17, George Pipgrass with 16 and Herb Pennock with 9. It was the only staff in the AL to allow fewer than four runs per game.

Aug 4—   Dickey returns from his 30-day suspension with a bang, hitting a grand slam homer and three singles to lead the Yankees to a 15-3 win in Chicago.

Aug 13—   Ruffing does it all to beat Washington, 1-0, in one of the great individual performances of all time. Red strikes out 10 Senators and allows only three hits. He battles Washington's Tommy Thomas for 10 innings before winning his own game with a home run.

Sep 5—   At Yankee Stadium, Combs walks twice in the Yanks' six-run first inning and the Yankees defeat the Athletics, 8-6, as Gomez wins his 23rd game of the year. New York also wins the nightcap, 6-3. A crowd of 70,772 sees the sweep. The Yankees increase their lead to 12½ games and it is apparent now that second-place Philadelphia will be dethroned after three seasons of supremacy.

Sep 7—   Ruth has appendicitis symptoms and returns to New York from Detroit to see the Yankee doctor. For several days, the Babe has a shooting pain in his right side and is sure he has appendicitis.

— In New York, the Babe was kept in bed. He had a low fever but there is no emergency and no operation. So the Babe rested in ice packs for five days as New Yorkers speculated: Would their .341 power hitter be ready for the World Series?

Sep 13—   The still-Ruthless Yankees, in their 143rd game, clinch the AL pennant with a 9-3 win over Cleveland. The victory makes Joe McCarthy the first manager in history to win pennants in each major league.

Sep 21—   In Philadelphia, four days after his first workout since his appendix attack, Ruth plays and goes one for four at the plate. Jimmie Foxx of the A's hits his 54th home run of the year but it appears Ruth's record of 60 is safe at this late date. The A's win, 8-5.

— Two days later Babe played a full nine innings. He was in the line-up for the season's final five games, but made only three hits in 16 at bats. For the first time since 1925 the Babe lost his home run title. Jimmie Foxx' final total of 58 would, however, fall short of the Babe's record.

Sep 24— Phenom Charlie Devens makes his big league debut pitching for the Yankees in Boston. Devens goes the route, walks seven, strikes out four and defeats the Red Sox, 8-2. Ruth and Gehrig each hit home runs.

— Devens was one of the most highly touted young pitchers ever to join the Yankees. The Milton, Mass., native signed with the Yanks out of Harvard University. (Thus, his start in Boston.) Paul Krichell and others were convinced Devens would be great. But Devens' three-year (1932-34) mark in the majors was only 5-3 in 16 games.

Sep 28— The World Series opens at Yankee Stadium and the home team destroys Chicago, 12-6. The Yanks take a 3-2 lead in the fourth inning on Ruth's run-scoring single and Gehrig's two-run homer, then ice the game with a five-run sixth. It is a rude way to greet the NL's best pitching staff.

— Already this had become one of the most bitterly fought Series in history. There was the natural rivalry between the nation's two largest cities, McCarthy's revenge factor—Joe is still bitter about his Cubs' firing—and, most importantly, there is the matter of the Cubs' tightfistedness toward the former popular shortstop on the Yankees, Mark Koenig. The Cubs voted only a partial Series share to Koenig, who had come to the team late in the year and hit .353. Ruth led the Yankees in riding the Cubs about Koenig's small share, and in return the Cubs made the portly, aging Ruth the object of some tough bench jockeying.

Sep 30— In Chicago, the crowds are openly hostile to the Yankees, the winners of the first two games. Ruth, who has predicted a Yankee sweep, and his wife are spat upon by a woman at their hotel. The Chicago fans are fueled with anti-Yankeeism. The Bambino is planning his revenge.

Oct 1— Ruth hits his "called shot" homer at Wrigley Field as the Yankees beat the Cubs, 7-5, in Game 3. Ruth and Gehrig combine to hit four homers, but it is Babe's homer in the fifth inning that is forever etched in history.

— It has never been conclusively determined whether the legend of the "called shot" has its roots in fact or fiction or in something in between. The Babe stepped to the plate in the fifth with the score tied, 4-4, thanks in part to a misplay on his part. Amid the deafening boos of Cub fans and the loud taunts from the Cub dugout, he took a called strike from Charlie Root, raised one finger and declared, "It only takes one to hit it." Babe gestured toward the distant bleachers and exchanged views with the folks in the Cub dugout. The Babe took a second strike and the tension mounted. Then he unloaded a tremendous home run that landed near the top of the old Wrigley bleachers in center field, exactly where he had pointed, legend has it. The Babe laughed, thumbed his nose and shouted at the Cubs as he rounded the bases. The Yankees went wild with delight. Gehrig followed with a homer, but it took veteran Herb Pennock, 38, to quell a Cub uprising in the ninth and preserve Babe's hero laurels. New York governor and presidential candidate, Franklin D. Roosevelt, was witness to the memorable moment. In the clubhouse afterwards, Babe shouted, "Did Mr. Ruth chase those guys back into the dugout? Mr. Ruth sure did!"

Oct 2— New York whips Chicago, 13-6, to sweep the Series in four games and extend the club's winning streak to 12 games in Series play. It is also the fourth consecutive game in which Chicago leads, only to have the Yanks come back to snatch victory. Wilcy Moore receives the win in relief and Pennock gets his second straight save. Lazzeri hits a pair of two-run homers and Combs adds a solo homer. Combs scores four runs to tie a record.

— Gehrig was really the Series hero. He led all hitters in batting (.529), hits (9), runs (9), homers (3), RBIs (8) and slugging (1.118). In his final Series, Ruth hit .333, scored six runs and knocked in six runs. His "called shot" was his 15th and final home run in Series play. Dickey hit .438. And everyone was happy for Pennock, who saved the final two wins.

1933

The Yankees, at 91-59, will finish in second place, seven games behind the Washington Senators. Gehrig will hit .334, but Babe Ruth will drop to .301. Lefty Gomez will fall off his great numbers of the previous season but will still lead the pitching staff with a 16-10 record.

Mar 22— In St. Petersburg, Fla., Ruth gives in and signs for $52,000 to end a bitter contract war. Actually, he gets more than Ed Barrow would have given him. Barrow wanted Colonel Ruppert to stand firm at $50,000, but after Ruppert meets with Ruth they emerge with Babe grinning and happy to announce their grand-a-week agreement.

— Ruppert played hardball in negotiations with Babe. Four days earlier, the colonel had given Ruth until the 29th to either sign or receive a lower offer. Babe dropped his demands to $60,000, then $55,000, then "compromised" at $52,000. It was some compromise—Ruppert went up $2,000 and Ruth went down $23,000. But with the country in economic shambles, no one was crying for the Babe. After all, he was still baseball's highest-paid player. The Yankees successfully argued Depression economics.

Apr 25— In a wild game at Griffith Stadium, the Yankees crush Washington, 16-0, with Earle Combs going five for five and pitcher Russ Van Atta turning in an incredible major league debut. Besides pitching a shutout, Van Atta strokes four hits. He is the second AL player to make four hits in his first game and he will remain the only pitcher to achieve the feat. A second story associated with this game starts when Senator second sacker Buddy Myer is spiked as Ben Chapman breaks up a double play. Myer kicks the stunned Chapman. Both dugouts empty and fans join in the fray, taking punches at Yankees. Gomez uses a bat to ward off attacks, as police unsuccessfully attempt to restore order. Meanwhile, Chapman's buddy and roommate, Dixie Walker, takes up the cause and gets the best of Myer. Finally, police clear the field. Five fans are arrested and the umpires eject Myer, Chapman and Walker. Chapman is cursed as he makes his way to the locker room by Senator pitcher Earl Whitehill and he lands a punch on Whitehill. Now, Chapman and Walker are fighting for their lives against a swarm of angry Senators before the police can rescue them. AL President Will Harridge will suspend Chapman, Myer and Whitehill for five days each, as well as fine them $100 apiece. Senator President Clark Griffith will say that Chapman should have been dealt with more severely.

— Van Atta never lived up to the promise of his maiden game, although he finished at 12-4 in 1933 (the Yanks' third biggest winner) and hit .283.

In 1935, Van Atta left the Yankees with a combined mark of 15-9 in 59 games with the club. Lifetime, Van Atta was 33-41 and hit .228.

Apr 29— At Yankee Stadium, Washington beats the Yankees, 6-3, with the help of one of the daffiest double plays imaginable. In the bottom of the ninth, Lou Gehrig leads off with a single and reaches second base on Dixie Walker's single. Tony Lazzeri has the crowd screaming as he sends a drive into the gap in right-center field. It is an obvious extra-base hit, but Gehrig plays it too safe and when he finally shifts gears and begins motoring, Walker is right on Lou's heels. Meanwhile, rightfielder Goose Goslin makes a strong relay to Joe Cronin, who makes a perfect peg to catcher Luke Sewell. Now comes the bang-bang double play, as Sewell tags out Gehrig, whirls around after the collision, and tags out Walker, too. The astonishing double play kills New York's rally and the contest ends when the next hitter makes the final out.

May 4— The Yankees beat Detroit, 5-2, as Gomez loses a potential no-hitter in the ninth inning when Charlie Gehringer leads off the inning with a home run. Another hit and run follow but the undaunted Lefty finishes the game for the victory.

Three great sluggers of the early 1930's—the Yankees' Lou Gehrig, left, and Babe Ruth, and the Philadelphia Athletics' Jimmie Foxx, who in 1932 hammered 58 home runs.

May 12— The Yankees sell the contracts of pitcher George Pipgras and infielder Billy Werber to the Red Sox for $100,000. The deal seems inverted, somehow, considering that the Yankees were built with Boston's help, but Tom Yawkey now owns the Red Sox and is the freest spender in baseball.

— Pipgras was 2-2 in New York and 9-8 in Boston in 1933. He suffered a broken arm while throwing a fastball, an injury that required the removal of seven chips from his elbow. It brought a premature end to the 33-year-old's career. Pipgras finished with a record of 102-73—93-64 of it in New York— and embarked on a successful umpiring career.

May 27— In a remarkable comeback, the Yankees overcome an 11-3 White Sox lead by scoring 12 runs in a 40-minute eighth inning and win, 15-11. In this inning, the Yankees thump three Chicago pitchers, including starter Ted Lyons. In rapid fire, Chapman singles, Lazzeri walks, Dickey walks, Crosetti singles in one run, pinch-hitter Ruffing singles home one run, Combs walks to force in a run, Sewell singles in one run, Ruth singles in two runs, Gehrig doubles in one run, Chapman is walked intentionally, Lazzeri singles in the tying run and Dickey belts a grand slam homer.

Jun 3— In a slugging marathon, New York outscores Philadelphia, 17-11. The Athletics score 11 runs in the second inning but the Yankees roar back with 10 tallies in the fifth off three A's pitchers. The Yankees trail 11-4 going into the big inning that includes a three-run Chapman homer and two hits each by Lazzeri, Jorgens and Crosetti. In the eighth, Ruth ices the contest with a three-run fourbagger. Yankee reliever Jumbo Brown finishes a game he entered early and in the process strikes out 12 A's. This helps reserve catcher Art Jorgens make 15 putouts, and, coupled with his previous day's 14 putouts, gives Jorgens 29 putouts in consecutive games, an AL record for a catcher.

Jun 4— Yankee hurler Johnny Allen pitches a one-hitter against Philadelphia and wins, 6-0. In the first frame, Ed Coleman, a .281 hitter this season, singles. Thereafter, Allen handles the Mackmen without allowing a hit.

— The fiery Allen, who grew up in a North Carolina orphanage, managed to control his temper often enough to have his second straight fine season in 1933. Johnny was the second biggest winner on the Yankee staff with a log of 15-7.

Jun 10— In Philadelphia, the Yanks' reserve catcher, Art Jorgens has a rare moment in the sun as a slugger when he blasts a grand slam homer and a two-run homer—his only two homers of the year—for six RBIs. It is the third grand slam of the year hit in the AL and all three are hit by Yankees (Lazzeri, Dickey and Jorgens). Jorgens' slam comes off Sugar Cain (13-12) in the second of two games, which the Yankees lose, 9-5, after falling, 8-7.

— The Norwegian-born Jorgens was a Yankee from 1929-39 and played on five World Series winners. Over his entire career he was back-up catcher to Bill Dickey, a job he willingly accepted. Lifetime, Jorgens made 176 hits in 738 at bats for a batting mark of .238.

Jun 23— The day begins with the Yankees and Senators owning identical 37-23 records. But after the Yanks split a doubleheader in St. Louis, winning, 10-6, and losing, 5-4, they find themselves a half game behind the league-leading Senators, who win their single game. It will be a two-team race for the duration of the season.

Jul 4— Washington leads the second-place Yankees by 1½ games after sweeping a doubleheader, 6-5 (in 10 innings) and 3-2, at Yankee Stadium before a frustrated crowd unofficially reported at 77,365. Ruth hits his 18th home run in the nightcap but it is of little consolation to the Yankees. The All-Star Break halts play with the Yankees at 45-28.

— The Yankees failed to make a serious run at the Senators, and, sadly, Ruth was part of the problem. Though his season's numbers might have contended for the Triple Crown in a later era, this was the era of high batting statistics and high earned run averages. He was runner-up in homers with 34 to Jimmie Foxx's 48, but five regular AL outfielders outhit the Babe, and eight hitters, including the Yanks' Gehrig and Lazzeri, drove in more runs than Ruth did. And the Babe was now slow in the outfield.

Jul 6— The first All-Star Game is played at Comiskey Park, and the American League defeats the National League, 4-2. Who else but Ruth is the hero! In the third, the Bambino hits the first home run in the history of the Summer Classic, a two-run shot off the Cardinals' Wild Bill Hallahan. In the eighth, Ruth makes a fantastic catch, robbing Chick Hafey of what would have been a game-tying homer. Ruth also singles. Lefty Gomez, the winning pitcher, surprisingly drives in the first run in All-Star history with a single in the second inning. Yankees Gehrig and Chapman also play in the game.

Aug 3— New York's streak of 308 consecutive games without being shut out comes to an end when Lefty Grove blanks the Yankees, and the Athletics win, 7-0. New York had avoided being whitewashed since August 2, 1931, when Wilcy Moore, now pitching in his last big league season with the Yanks, blanked them. Against Grove, the Yankees manage only five hits.

— Scoring at least one run in 308 straight games would remain a major league record.

Aug 7— A big four-game set opens at Yankee Stadium and the Yankees sweep a doubleheader, 6-5 and 5-4, from Washington. Their two one-run victories breed hope of a sweep, but the Senators rebound the next two days to win, 5-1 and 4-1. Eight games played over two weeks between the league's top two teams prove inconclusive with each team winning four times.

Aug 14— Dramatically, in the bottom of the ninth inning, Red Ruffing's grand slam homer off Boston's Bob Weiland gives the Yankees a 6-2 victory. It is the first grand slam in history hit by a Yankee pitcher. However, the Yankees have slipped several games behind Washington and are not given much chance of catching the Senators. One of the big disappointments is Ruffing, who is 9-14 this year, his only losing campaign in 15 seasons with the Yankees.

Aug 17— Gehrig plays in his 1,308th consecutive big league game, thereby breaking Everett Scott's record of 1,307, which Scott had established from 1916-25. Gehrig began his streak in 1925.

— Gehrig fell off from the previous year in all three Triple Crown categories. But Lou did lead the AL with 138 runs scored. And just before the season ended, on September 29, he married Eleanor Twitchell.

Sep 23— In a demonstration of what is right with the Yankees—hitting—and what is wrong—fielding and pitching—the Yankees beat Boston, 16-12. When the season ends, the Yankees will lead the AL in scoring with 927 runs, plating 52 more runs than Philadelphia and 77 more than first-place Washington.

Oct 1—   Ruth pitches at Yankee Stadium on the final day of the season. With the Yankees' hold on second place assured, his advertised pitching appearance is used to hike attendance. Babe responds with another amazing performance, pitching a complete game and scattering 12 hits in beating Boston, 6-5. Babe also hits his 34th home run in the fifth inning. After the game, Babe is so tired it takes him an hour to dress, but several thousand fans are still waiting outside to cheer him as he departs the Stadium. Babe waves to his admirers with his right hand because his left arm is so sore.

   — Ruth, of course, had been a great pitcher in Boston early in his career. He brought a career record of 89-46 to New York, and, in five pitching appearances with the Yankees, won five games. Thus, his lifetime pitching record stood at 94-46.

1934

The Yankees, at 94-60, will finish second, seven games behind the Detroit Tigers. Lou Gehrig will have a sensational year, winning the Triple Crown. Lefty Gomez will lead AL pitchers in seven major categories, including wins. He will go 26-5.

Jan 5—   The Yankees release pitcher Herb Pennock and third baseman Joe Sewell, two stars who are pointed to the Baseball Hall of Fame.

   — Pennock, the Pennsylvanian with the stylish delivery and the scientific turn of mind, was nearing 40. He left with only good things to say about the Yankees and compiled a 2-0 record in 30 games for Boston in 1934. Sewell, the Alabaman who was the toughest big leaguer in history to strike out, ended his major league career. Sewell hit .282 over his three years with the Yanks after a sensational career at Cleveland. Pennock was inducted into the Hall in 1948, Sewell in 1977.

Jan 15—   Ruth signs his last Yankee contract, a one-year pact at $35,000 for a cut of $17,000. He is still the highest-paid ballplayer in the game but his days as a player are numbered. He has gone from making $75,000 to $35,000 in two seasons. Actually, the Yankees asked Ruth to sign at $25,000. But the Babe salvages $35,000 after a meeting with Jake Ruppert.

Apr 24—   Some 40,000 fans turn out for Opening Day at Yankee Stadium. One of those fans is Gertrude Musier of Flushing, N.Y., a 19-year-old polio victim who has recovered her eyesight after 15 sightless years. She is the guest of the Ruths. The Yankees edge Philadelphia, 1-0.

May 10—   In one game, Gehrig drives in seven runs and makes four extra-base hits, including two home runs and two doubles. One of Lou's homers is a grand slammer, the first of four bases-loaded homers he hits this year. And Gehrig removes himself from the line-up after five innings because of illness! The Yankees beat Chicago, 13-3, at Yankee Stadium.

May 22—   The Iron Horse knocks in at least one run in the 10th consecutive game, the third time in his career that Gehrig has done this. Over the 10-game span, Gehrig nets a total of 22 RBIs. But Cleveland beats New York, 5-1.

Jun 6—   The Yankees split a doubleheader with Boston, winning the opener, 15-3, on the strength of 25 hits, and losing the nightcap, 7-4. In the first game onslaught, Yankee outfielder Myril Hoag makes six singles in six trips. Through 1982, more than 30 players in the AL have made six hits in a game, but Hoag will remain the only Yankee to do so. Hoag scores three times. He adds one single in the second game.

Jun 14— New York defeats St. Louis, 7-0, at Sportsmans Park. Johnny Broaca, a 24-year-old righthanded rookie, pitches a one-hitter. He gives up only a third-inning single to Sammy West, the Browns' outfielder who will hit .326 this year.

— Broaca, a star at Yale who was recruited by scout Paul Krichell, in his first year gave every indication of becoming a great. He was the Yanks' third starter and fourth biggest winner at 12-9. He will go 40-27 for New York over four years.

Jun 20— Red Ruffing pitches the second Yankee one-hitter in a week and New York beats Cleveland, 3-0. Red allows only a fifth-inning single by Hal Trosky, the Indians' first baseman who will hit .330 this year.

— A 30-year-old veteran in his 11th big league season, Rufus the Red enjoyed a great comeback season in 1934, going 19-11. In fact, a case could be made that Ruffing finally found himself as a winning pitcher this year. It was the first of nine outstanding seasons in a row for Ruffing.

Jun 29— Gehrig's playing streak is jeopardized—he is beaned in an exhibition game in Norfolk, Va. The Yankees are playing the Norfolk Tars, one of their farm teams. Columbia Lou hits a first-inning homer but in the second inning he is struck on the head by a wayward pitch from Norfolk's Ray White. He is knocked out cold and is taken to the hospital with little chance of being in the Yankee line-up the next day in Washington. However, Lou finds an overnight steamer to take him the relatively short distance from Norfolk to Washington.

Jun 30— Not only does Gehrig play in Washington, but he strokes three triples in his first three at bats! Unfortunately, the game and Gehrig's stats are washed away after 4½ innings by rain. It is an unofficial game, the Senators not having batted in the fifth inning. But the heroic efforts of Gehrig, who five days earlier hit for the cycle against Chicago, win him even more fans.

Jul 5— Another big day for Gehrig. He hits his fourth and final grand slam homer of the season, establishing a Yankee club record, to be tied by Tommy Henrich in 1948. In the Yanks' 8-3 victory against Washington at the Stadium, Larrapin' Lou goes four for four, including two homers and two singles, and drives home seven runs.

Jul 10— At the Polo Grounds, the AL wins the All-Star Game, 9-7. The game is best remembered for Carl Hubbell's consecutive strikeouts of Babe Ruth, Lou Gehrig, Jimmie Foxx, Al Simmons and Joe Cronin. Bill Dickey breaks the string with a single, then Lefty Gomez fans and later jokes that Dickey cost him a piece of history. Gomez starts the game but is hit hard, as is Ruffing, who pitches the middle innings. The AL's third pitcher, Mel Harder, gets the win. Ruth, who brings his embarrassing .285 average into the game (he was hit on the wrist in June and afterwards went 0 for 21), and Gehrig fail to get a hit, but they each score a run, as does Dickey. Ruffing knocks in two runs and Chapman has a triple.

Jul 13 In Detroit, Ruth hits his 700th big league home run off Tommy Bridges, as the Yankees beat the Tigers, 4-2, and briefly go into first place.* Babe's

---

*At the time, only Gehrig and Rogers Hornsby had hit as many as 300 homers.

third-inning blast is truly a Ruthian clout, the ball clearing the right field wall (before it was double decked) and rolling several hundred feet down a street. The drive is estimated at 480 feet in the air. Babe pays $20 to Lennie Bielski for the ball, plus two autographed balls and a box seat for the rest of the game. Bielski sees the game's winning runs score on Dickey's eighth-inning two-run double. Gehrig is forced to leave early with a severe case of lumbago and his playing streak is again in jeopardy. Tomorrow he will single in the first inning and leave the game.

Jul 17—   At Cleveland's League Park, the Indians beat the Yankees, 13-5. Tribe pitcher Oral Hildebrand walks Babe Ruth twice, the Babe's 1,999th and 2,000th free passes of his major league career.

— The Babe was the first to reach 2,000 walks and only Ted Williams (2,019) would follow him to this mark. With a lifetime total of 2,056, Ruth ranks first on the all-time list.

Jul 18—   New York scores five runs in the top of the ninth, but Cleveland rallies to score three times in the bottom half, winning, 15-14. Worse for the Yankees, Ruth is struck by a line-drive single off Gehrig's bat. Babe is carried off the field, his right shin badly hurt, and in the clubhouse while waiting for the ambulance the Bambino states, "I'm going to get out of this game before I'm carried out." When Babe returns to the line-up a week later, New York trails Detroit by one game in the standings.

Jul 24—   St. Louis defeats New York, 4-2. But the real story is the terrible injury suffered by Earle Combs when he crashes into the center field wall at Sportsmans Park. It is one of the most frightening incidents in baseball history. Chasing a fly ball, the Kentucky Colonel smashes head-first at full speed into the concrete wall in left-center field. He falls to the ground with a fractured skull. Combs is in a very real life-threatening condition as he is rushed to the hospital where he remains in a coma for hours. There Dr. Robert F. Hyland successfully brings Combs through the danger. Several other injuries, including a severe muscle tear in his right shoulder, are also administered to by the doctor. But, obviously, Combs is out for the year.

— The main concern was that Combs pull through his near-fatal accident. But for the Yankees, his loss was a critical blow to the pennant drive. Earle had been hitting .319 and New York could find no adequate substitute for him. Combs made a comeback in 1935, but this injury was career-ending for all intents and purposes.

Jul 28—   New York's Jimmie DeShong, a 24-year-old righthander who goes 6-7 this year, pitches a one-hitter against Philadelphia. He allows only a home run to Jimmie Foxx, who will hit 44 homers in 1934.

— New York pitchers this year hurled four one-hitters to lead the AL in most categories. (For a change, it was the Yanks' offense that let them down.) The Yankee staff was led by Lefty Gomez, who earned the Triple Crown of pitching by leading the league in wins (26), ERA (2.33) and strikeouts (158).

Aug 14—   The Tigers move into Yankee Stadium for a showdown series with the Yankees and an estimated crowd of 80,000 is on hand with some 25,000 turned away. Detroit sweeps a key doubleheader and proceeds to win its first pennant since 1909. The Tigers win, 9-5 and 7-3, extending their current winning streak to 14 games (where it will end). Detroit (73-37), led by Hank Greenberg and Charlie Gehringer, is now 6½ games in front of New York (66-43).

Sep 3—   Lefty Gomez wins his 10th consecutive decision and runs his record to 24-3, as he defeats Philadelphia, 11-7, at Yankee Stadium in the first of two games. The streak began in Chicago back on July 21 when Lefty won, 6-2; it will be snapped in four days when Gomez is the loser in relief in a 6-5 game in Chicago.

Sep 24— Ruth plays his last game at Yankee Stadium. The Yanks lose, 5-0, to Boston, as Detroit backs into the pennant. A crowd of less than 4,000 is on hand to witness the end of an era. Babe walks in the first inning and is pulled for pinch-runner Myril Hoag after limping to first base.

Sep 29— In Washington, the Yankees split a doubleheader, losing, 8-5, and then winning, 9-6, as Babe Ruth hits his final home run as a Yankee in the opener. It is Babe's 659th homer as a Yankee (his 708th as a major leaguer), which remains the club record. (Mickey Mantle is second at 536.) Ruth's home run is hit off Sid Cohen (1-1) who, like Ruth, is Baltimore-born and who has a lifetime record of 3-7.

— Over 10 seasons as teammates, Ruth and Gehrig combined to average 77 homers and 274 RBIs per year. But, unfortunately, the home run twins, once such great friends, no longer were speaking to each other. In October, Connie Mack took a group of all-stars on tour of Japan and Ruth, Gehrig and Gomez made the trip. The iciness Babe and Lou showed toward each other made Mack and the others uncomfortable.

Sep 30— At Griffith Stadium in Washington, Ruth plays his last game as a Yankee and the Senators win, 5-3. Before the game, the Babe is presented a scroll from the appreciative Washington fans, as wife Claire, daughter Dorothy and Senators' President Clark Griffith look on. Also on hand is the St. Mary's Industrial School Band from Babe's childhood home in Baltimore. Babe thanks everyone, including President Roosevelt, for the testimonial of love given him. Ruth is hitless in three trips, walks and scores a run. In Babe's final at bat, he takes two called balls and Senator Manager Joe Cronin steps to the mound and instructs his pitcher to throw strikes so that the mighty Sultan of Swat would have one last chance to blast a ball over the fence wearing a New York uniform. Babe gets his chance but hits a fly ball that centerfielder Jake Powell catches. Babe rounds first base and heads straight to the clubhouse and has a hard time fighting back the tears. Also, Lou Gehrig caps his Triple Crown year by going three for four, scoring two runs and hitting his 49th home run.

— The three hits were critical to Lou's winning the batting title. He finished at .363, only seven points ahead of Charlie Gehringer. Lou's homer was unneeded—he had clinched the home run title, hitting 49 (including a record 30 at Yankee Stadium) to runner-up Jimmie Foxx's 44. Lou's final RBI gave him 165 and a safe margin over runner-up Hal Trosky with 142. Gehrig was the first Yankee to win the Triple Crown and only Mickey Mantle would follow (in 1956). Yet Gehrig did not win the MVP Award. When all the Baseball Writers' ballots were counted, that honor went to Detroit's player-manager, Mickey Cochrane, who hit .320 with two homers and 76 RBIs.

Nov 21— The Yankees send cash (between $25,000 and $50,000) plus players Doc Farrell (INF), Floyd Newkirk (P), Jim Densmore (P), Les Powers (1B) and Ted Norbert (OF) to the San Francisco Seals of the Pacific Coast League in exchange for just one player, Joe DiMaggio (OF). Other big league teams had been willing to offer substantially more for the man who had hit in 61 consecutive games in 1933, but Joe's serious knee injury scared off all the scouts except the Yanks' Bill Essick and Joe Devine. The Yankees give DiMaggio an exhaustive physical examination. Joe is pronounced fit and Jacob Ruppert okays the deal.

— As part of the agreement, DiMaggio remained with the Seals in 1935 and in San Francisco had an MVP season, hitting .398 with 34 home runs and 154 RBIs. His fielding was just as spectacular. Thanks to Essick, Devine, Ruppert and Weiss, DiMaggio would take his rightful place among the Yankee greats, beginning in the spring of 1936.

1935

The Yankees, at 89-60, will finish in second place, three games behind the Detroit Tigers. Lou Gehrig will lead the attack at .329. Red Ruffing, at 16-11, will be the pitching staff's leading winner.

Feb 19— Lou Gehrig signs his 1935 contract for a reported $30,000, meaning Lou is rewarded with a $7,000 raise for his Triple Crown season. But it did not come easy; Lou had to negotiate to get it. Gehrig began negotiations asking for $35,000.

Feb 26— A few days after Ruth returns to New York from a four-month world trip, the Yankees hold a press conference at Jacob Ruppert's brewery to announce that Ruth has been given his unconditional release in order to allow the Babe to sign with the Boston Braves as rightfielder, assistant manager and vice president. Babe is sad that the Yankees are willing to part with him on the one hand, but excited about future possibilities in Boston, which he hopes will include managing. Ruppert tells everyone that in return for the greatest drawing card in baseball history he will receive not one cent. This deal has been in the works since the Babe returned to New York six days ago. Yet, no one quite comprehends exactly what Ruth's duties as vice president will entail. When questioned, Emil E. Fuchs, president of the Braves, says simply, "Advisory capacity. He'll be consulted on trades and so forth." Trying to inject a little humor into a sad day for New York Ruppert quips, "A vice president signs checks. Everybody knows that." The contract of Sammy Byrd, known as Babe Ruth's Legs because he was often a late-inning replacement for the Babe, was sold to Cincinnati in December.

— Ruth's second stint in Boston was disastrous. He never got to manage the Braves, or any other team for that matter. What he really wanted to do was to manage the Yankees, and before leaving New York he made one last bid for the job. But Ruppert and Ed Barrow were happy with Joe McCarthy. Besides, the Babe had turned down their best offer by refusing to manage at Newark. Ruth was no longer useful to them as a player; he was, if anything, a liability because of his anti-McCarthy attitude. To Ruppert, especially, the Boston deal was the most graceful way out of a can't-win public relations situation. What they were dealing with here was a player who skyrocketed the Yankees to the bigtime, a player who lifetime hit 714 home runs, averaged .349, knocked in 1,970 runs and scored 1,959 runs, a player who was not just a person, which is enough in an athlete, but a per- sonage; they were dealing with the greatest, most dimensioned career in the story of baseball.

Apr 16— On Opening Day at Yankee Stadium, Boston beats the Yankees, 1-0. Gehrig plays for the first time as captain of the Yankees, an honorary position he holds until his death. The captaincy had been vacant since the departure of Everett Scott in 1925.

May 16— Joe McCarthy, who was seriously ill with bronchial pneumonia, returns to the Yankees and the club celebrates with a 10-0 win over Cleveland at Yankee Stadium. Bill Dickey goes four for five. Vito Tamulis, who will win 10 of 15 decisions, pitches a seven-hit shutout. Tamulis' three shutouts this year will lead the club. Art Fletcher led the club in McCarthy's absence. The Yanks were 4-6 under Fletcher.

May 18— New York beats Cleveland, 3-0, as Gomez pitches a two-hitter. Both safeties are singles by Indian outfielder Earl Averill, a .288 hitter this season.

Jun 1— At the Stadium, the Yankees in downing Boston, 7-2, stroke six solo homers. This sets a major league record for the most bases-empty homers by one team in one game. Bill Dickey hits two of the homers and Frank Crosetti, Ben Chapman, George Selkirk and Red Rolfe each hit one.

June 24— In Cleveland, George Selkirk walks twice in the fifth inning as the Yankees win, 4-1. It is the first of four occasions in his Yankee career that Selkirk walks twice in the same inning.

Jul 8— The All-Star Game is played in Cleveland and the AL wins, 4-1, the third victory in three games for the junior circuit. Starting for the AL for the third straight time, Gomez allows only one run and three hits in six innings and notches his second win in the Summer Classic. Thanks to Goofy's skill, the NL changes the rules so that a pitcher cannot work more than three innings. Lou Gehrig and Ben Chapman also play in the game.

Jul 28— With his batting average at .282 in 89 games, 36-year-old outfielder Earle Combs retires.

— The Kentucky Colonel was suffering from another injury in an injury-riddled career. He saw the end of the tunnel, although he had made a courageous comeback after the critical head injury of the previous year. Combs retired with a lifetime mark of .325. He remained with the Yankees through the 1944 season as one of Joe McCarthy's coaches.

Jul 30— Yankee pitching ace Red Ruffing begins a streak of 241 consecutive starts. He will not be used as a relief pitcher again and he will pitch through the 1947 season when he wraps up his career with the White Sox. In Philadelphia, Ruffing loses, 6-5, to the A's.

— As great a pitcher as Ruffing was, his hitting was sometimes more spectacular. For the fourth season as a Yankee, Ruffing topped .300, hitting .339. Red had an advantage in winning close games because Joe McCarthy seldom pinch-hit for him. Indeed, Ruffing was .444 this year as a pinch-hitter, getting 8 hits in 18 trips. Whenever Red pitched, the Yankee batting order was awesome, top to bottom.

Aug 5— In the fourth inning against Boston, Myril Hoag pinch-hits for Lou Gehrig, who leaves the game with lumbago. Jack Saltzgaver finishes the game at first base. The Yankees win, 10-2. Hoag is the last man to ever pinch-hit for Gehrig.

Aug 10— Yankee rightfielder George Selkirk, who will finish second on the club behind Gehrig with 94 RBIs this year, drives in eight runs in the first game of a doubleheader. Selkirk gets four of his RBIs with a bases-loaded home run. The Yankees beat Philadelphia twice, 18-7 and 7-2, at Yankee Stadium.

— If ever a man had a difficult act to follow, it was Selkirk, who replaced Ruth in right field and even inherited Babe's No. 3 uniform. George at first heard boos from the Bambino's loyal fans but he responded by hitting .312, the second of four consecutive .300 seasons, and the fans were quickly won to his side. Selkirk conducted himself as a true professional in the face of enormous pressure. McCarthy helped by telling him to forget about Ruth and help the club in his own way.

Aug 26— Zeke Bonura, the White Sox' slow first baseman, steals home in the 15th inning against the Yankees and Chicago wins, 9-8. Not only is this a damaging loss to the Yanks' pennant cause, but it is embarrassing that Bonura, one of the game's top sluggers but perhaps its slowest runner, should score the winning run on a steal of home.

— The Ruthless Yankees were in first place in May but faded as July ended and Detroit grabbed the top spot. Both Gehrig and Gomez fell off from their Triple Crown seasons of the year before, as was only natural, but Yankee management felt they were tired from their off-season travel in Japan. Gomez fell all the way to 12-15 but the New York staff still led the AL in pitching.

Aug 27— In Chicago, the Yankees lose, 4-3, in the second game of a twinbill, as Gehrig walks five times on his way to 132 walks. He leads the AL in bases on balls for the first time in his career. Lou does not score once in this game. The Yankees win the opener, 13-10.

— Without Ruth, Gehrig stood alone as the only genuine power hitter in the Yankee line-up. Opposing teams wisely tried to not let Lou beat them. And without Ruth, the Yankees were perceived as dull. Home attendance was 657,508, the second lowest in Yankee Stadium history. The Yankees not only needed another power hitter to help Gehrig, they needed a drawing card to replace Ruth, and the kid in San Francisco seemed to fit the bill.

Dec 11— New York acquires Monte Pearson (P) and Steve Sundra (P) from Cleveland for Johnny Allen (P) in one of those trades that will help both clubs.

— Pearson was a big factor in the Yankees' pennant-winning 1936 season. The 26-year-old righthander from Oakland posted a 19-7 record as the Yanks' second starter, following a record of 36-31 in four Indian seasons. Sundra would help, too, a few years down the road. Allen in his four seasons in New York was 50-19, for a great winning percentage of .725. He hated to lose and did little of it, but his fierce competitiveness was viewed as hot-headedness by McCarthy. Yet, in the next three seasons in Cleveland, Allen managed to stay cool enough to string records of 20-10, 15-1 and 14-8. In 13 big league seasons, he was 142-75.

1936

The Yankees will win their eighth pennant. They will compile a 102-51 record to win by 19½ games over second-place Detroit, a margin that will prove an enduring AL record. Lou Gehrig will hit 49 home runs to lead the league and will win the MVP Award. Rookie Joe DiMaggio will hit .323. Red Ruffing will pace the pitchers with a record of 20-12. And the Yankees will win their fifth World Championship, defeating the Giants from across the Harlem River in the World Series.

Jan 17—   The Yankees obtain Bump Hadley (P) and Roy Johnson (OF) from Washington for Jimmy DeShong (P) and Jesse Hill (OF). They are making changes to their 1935 starting rotation of Ruffing, Gomez, Broaca, Allen and Tamulis— Monte Pearson and Hadley will be substituted for Allen and Tamulis.

— Hadley, a veteran of 10 big league seasons, was 10-15 for the Senators in 1935. But as the Yanks' fifth starter in 1936, Hadley went 14-4. DeShong did well for himself in Washington with an 18-10 record in 1936. However, this was his only big year.

Jan 29—   Babe Ruth is among the initial five ballplayers elected to the newly established Baseball Hall of Fame, it is announced today. The Baseball Writers are allowed to vote for 10 post-1900 players who in the opinion of each participating writer deserves baseball's highest honor. It takes 75 percent of the total poll to enter the Hall, or 170 of the 226 votes cast. Five greats gain election—Ty Cobb (222), Ruth (215), Honus Wagner (215), Christy Mathewson (205) and Walter Johnson (189). The Baseball Hall of Fame building will open in four years.

Apr 7—   The Yankees' team physician, Dr. Harry G. Jacobi, announces that the foot burns Joe DiMaggio suffered in an unusual accident will keep him out of Opening Day action and have him sidelined for several weeks. Recently, young DiMaggio injured his foot in an exhibition game and underwent diathermy heat treatment. But a machine used in the therapy malfunctioned and Joe's foot was burned. The Yankees have to barnstorm North without him.

— In spring training, DiMaggio received a big press buildup and the New York fans were eagerly awaiting their first glimpse of this talented, shy youngster. Joe traveled to St. Petersburg from San Francisco by car in the company of Tony Lazzeri and Frank Crosetti. All three are silent types and the long trip was made in virtual silence. It culminated in a burst of excitement for young Joe, who later was to say that arriving at St. Pete and meeting the Yankee players was his biggest thrill in baseball. Then Joe thrilled his new teammates by displaying his exceptional all-round baseball skills.

Apr 14—   New York opens the season in Washington where President Roosevelt throws out the first ball and Bobo Newsom pitches a four-hitter to defeat Lefty Gomez, 1-0, in a tense pitching matchup. The game is scoreless until the bottom of the ninth when Cecil Travis singles and Carl Reynolds doubles off the left field wall to win it for the Senators. The Yanks start a line-up of Rolfe (3B), Johnson (LF), Selkirk (RF), Gehrig (1B), Dickey (C), Chapman (CF), Lazzeri (2B), Crosetti (SS) and Gomez.

— Sitting quietly on the bench, the injured DiMaggio watched his first game as a major leaguer without any way of knowing he was setting the wrong kind of precedent for openers. DiMaggio would be out of the line-up for his first three Opening Days and for several more later in his career.

Apr 26—   New York beats the Red Sox, 12-9, at Fenway Park after Boston scores six runs in the bottom of the first inning, only to have the Yankees, who collect 18 hits today, rally for seven runs in the top of the second. Bump Hadley, who lost his first decision, wins in relief to begin a personal 11-game winning streak running through August 12.

— The ability of this team to overcome deficits was amazing. New York hit 182 home runs to set an AL record that stood for 20 years. Six Yankee regulars hit over .300: Dickey, .362; Gehrig, .354; DiMaggio, .323; Rolfe,

.319; Selkirk, .308; and Powell, .306. And these thumpers, one of the original "Bronx Bomber" editions, set a still-standing AL record in having five players drive in more than 100 runs: Gehrig, 152; DiMaggio, 125; Lazzeri, 109; Dickey, 107; and Selkirk, 107. These Yankees set big league records with 995 RBIs and 2,703 total bases.

May 3—   At Yankee Stadium, the Yankees demolish St. Louis, 14-5, as Joe DiMaggio gets three hits in his major league debut. After missing the first 16 games with a foot injury, DiMaggio has recently taken strenuous workouts without pain. So McCarthy bats DiMaggio third in the order, between Rolfe and Gehrig, and sends Joe out to play left field, with Chapman playing center. Wearing No. 9, DiMaggio in his first time up singles crisply to left field against pitcher Jack Knott. Joe later singles, flies out, grounds out, triples to left center and pops up. He scores three runs and drives home one. Leading the New York parade of 17 hits are Gehrig and Chapman, each making four hits. Lou scores five runs and knocks in two.

May 8—   In Detroit, the Yankees win, 6-5. In the top of the eighth, Dickey belts a three-run homer to put the Yankees ahead. But in the bottom of the ninth, Hadley walks Pete Fox and Mickey Cochrane singles him to third. Then Charlie Gehringer flies to DiMaggio. Fox tags up and attempts to score but DiMaggio fires a perfect peg to Dickey, nailing Fox and preserving New York's one-run victory. DiMaggio will lead all AL outfielders this year with 22 assists.

May 10—   DiMaggio hits his first big league homer. It comes at Yankee Stadium against George Turbeville (2-5) of the Athletics and travels at least 400 feet. Joltin' Joe drives in three runs. He also makes a tremendous catch in left field as the Yankees win, 7-2.

           — In one week, DiMaggio established himself as one of the league's best all-round players. In the field, Joe showed a great arm, brilliant judgment and good speed, and on offense, he displayed amazing power, an ability to make contact and hit for high average, and smart baserunning. His 132 runs and 15 triples remain AL rookie records. And his 206 hits, 44 doubles and 125 RBIs rank high on all-time rookie lists. No Yankee rookie before or since DiMaggio has done better than his 29 freshman homers.

May 14—   DiMaggio has a four-hit game just 11 days after his debut. He strokes three doubles and a single as the Yankees win, 6-1, in St. Louis.

May 23—   After an off-day, Lazzeri homers in the first game of a doubleheader in Philadelphia, then blasts two homers and knocks in four runs in the nightcap. Lazzeri has hit four homers in three games. New York wins, 12-6 and 15-1. Resentful fans litter the field with debris and hit at least one Yankee with a tomato.

May 24—   The Yankees beat Philadelphia, 25-2, in the third most lopsided win in AL history (23-run difference). They score the most runs in a single game in the franchise's history. Batting eighth in the order, Lazzeri leads the way by driving in 11 runs, an AL record that still stands. Poosh 'Em Up Tony becomes the first player in major league history to belt a pair of grand slam homers in one game. He adds a solo homer and just misses a fourth fourbagger by inches, having to settle for a two-run triple instead. As it is, he has seven homers in four games. Five homers and 15 RBIs in two games! Chapman, Crosetti and DiMaggio also have big days: Chapman reaching

The Giants' Carl Hubbell, left, had a 26-6 record in 1936 and led the NL with a 2.31 ERA, while Lou Gehrig hit .354 and won the AL home run crown with 49. The two superstars met in the World Series. Gehrig hit two homers in the Series and Hubbell claimed one victory.

base safely seven times in seven trips with five walks and two doubles; Crosetti hitting two homers; and DiMaggio belting a homer, double and single.

May 31— In front of a Yankee Stadium crowd of 41,781, DiMaggio has another heroic day. The Jolter ties the game dramatically with a two-run single in the bottom of the ninth. In the 12th, his triple knocks in Red Rolfe to give the Yanks a 5-4 victory over Boston.

Jun 7— At Yankee Stadium, two brave pitchers go a marathon distance. Red Ruffing pitches 16 innings, allowing 10 hits, and is rewarded for his perseverance with a 5-4 victory over Cleveland. George Selkirk's 16th-inning two-out home run off starter Oral Hildebrand is the decisive blow. But Red is the hero. He has three hits, including a single, double and a home run, and knocks in two runs. Ruffing will hit five homers for the season.

Jun 8— DiMaggio knocks in five runs with a home run, triple and single. He also makes two catches to take away hits and New York beats St. Louis, 12-3, at Yankee Stadium.

Jun 10— New York defeats Cleveland, 18-0, in the second most lopsided shutout in Yankee history, breaking a club record (17-0) set in 1909. The Yanks will win a 21-0 shutout in 1939.

Jun 11— Red Rolfe makes four extra-base hits in one game, three doubles and one triple, and the Yankees beat Detroit, 10-9, in 10 innings at Yankee Stadium.

— Rolfe, a classy gentleman from New Hampshire, scored 116 runs and hit .319 in 1936, his second of seven straight seasons of at least 100 runs scored. He was the underrated star of the Yankees. He was quiet and efficient—McCarthy's kind of player. Signed by Paul Krichell, Rolfe joined the Yankees in 1934 and was shifted by McCarthy from shortstop to third base. He adapted quickly, leading the AL in fielding in both 1935 and 1936. He hit a combined .289 in 10 big league seasons, all with New York and won the overwhelming respect of his Yankee teammates.

Jun 14— The Yankees trade Ben Chapman to Washington for outfielder Jake Powell. McCarthy will now switch DiMaggio from left to center field. He wanted to get Joe comfortable in the majors before putting the pressure of center field on him.

— McCarthy was criticized for this seemingly poor trade, although it was made, of course, with Ed Barrow's blessing. In seven Yankee seasons, Chapman hit a combined .305, stole 184 bases and scored more than 100 runs in four seasons. He was exciting and excellent defensively. He finished 1936 with a .315 average and followed with marks of .297, .340, .290 and .286 before his career went downhill. But Chapman was quarrelsome and hot-tempered, traits McCarthy disliked in his players. Powell was less talented and, although he was tough, was usually (but not always) quiet. Powell fit into the supporting role Marse Joe had for him and finished 1936 hitting .306 for New York in 87 games.

Jun 17— New York sweeps a doubleheader at Cleveland, 15-4 and 12-2, getting 19 hits in each game for a total of 38 on the day. Ruffing wins the opener, makes four hits—two of them homers—and has 10 total bases to establish a still-standing record for an AL pitcher. Pearson wins the nightcap, makes four hits and has four RBIs. It is quite a day for New York pitchers, who crack eight hits!

Jun 24— In Chicago, DiMaggio becomes the third player in AL history to hit two home runs in one inning. In the Yanks' 10-run fifth inning, Joltin' Joe hits a two-run homer off Ray Phelps, Jake Powell hits a grand slam homer and DiMaggio belts a three-run homer off Red Evans. DiMaggio has two doubles in the game for four extra-base hits on the day. The Yankees win, 18-11.

Jul 7— At Braves Field in Boston, the NL wins the All-Star Game, 4-3. Yankee Manager Joe McCarthy pilots the AL team that includes five Yankees— DiMaggio, Gehrig, Dickey, Selkirk and Crosetti. In the seventh inning, Gehrig hits a home run off the Cubs' Curt Davis (13-13).

Aug 15— Gehrig belts a grand slam homer in the eighth inning off 18-year-old Randy Gumpert (1-2) and the Yankees beat the Athletics, 16-2, in Philadelphia.

— Larrupin' Lou had another tremendously productive year in 1936, leading the AL in homers, walks, slugging average and runs scored. He knocked in 152 runs and scored 167. For the first time in history, the Yankees had two players with 200 hits. DiMaggio had 206 and Gehrig 205. The next year, DiMaggio will have 215 hits and Gehrig 200, the only other season a pair of Yankees make 200 hits each.

Aug 28— At Yankee Stadium, New York beats Detroit twice, 14-5 and 19-4. In the nightcap, Yankee pitcher Johnny Murphy makes five singles in five at bats, drives in five runs and scores three runs. Lifetime, Murphy hits only .154 and he is a reliever most of the time, so the odds are very much against Murphy ever making five hits in one game. Murphy has two hits and Selkirk walks twice in the Yanks' 11-run second inning.

— Murphy, a native of New York City, attended Fordham University and joined the Yankees to stay in 1934. Against his better judgment—and the value put on relief specialists at this point in baseball history—Fordham Johnny eventually accepted the role of reliever, then elevated that role to new heights. He was still in the transition stage in 1936, going 5-2 with five saves in relief and 4-1 in five starts.

Sep 9— On the earliest date to clinch a pennant in AL history, a record the Yankees will break in 1941, New York sews up its eighth pennant. It is only the 137th game of the season. The Yankees, having gone into first place in early May, were never threatened. The curtain falls on the race when the Yankees sweep a doubleheader from Cleveland by scores of 11-3 and 12-9. Gehrig, who hit the most recent grand slam in the league not quite a month ago, has another grand slam today.

— The NL race was much more exciting, but the Giants emerged victorious by five games over the Cubs, setting up the first Subway Series since 1923. The Babe and Mugsy McGraw were gone but the Yanks had DiMaggio and Gehrig, and the Giants had their league's home run champ in Mel Ott, who hit 33, and King Carl Hubbell, the NL's leader in wins (26-6) and ERA (2.31) and winner of his last 16 decisions of the campaign.

Sep 30— The World Series opens at the Polo Grounds on a rainy, miserable day. Selkirk starts the scoring when he powers a home run into the right field upper deck, becoming the first Yankee to homer in his first World Series at bat. But then King Carl settles down, blanks the Yanks the rest of the way, pitches a seven-hitter and controls the Bronx Bombers with his screwball, winning, 6-1. A 12-game World Series winning streak by the Yankees is snapped.

Oct 2— In Game 2 at the Polo Grounds, the Yankees romp, 18-4, as Lefty Gomez pitches a six-hitter, while five Giant pitchers are scored upon. Every man in the Bronx Bombers' line-up, including Gomez, makes at least one hit and one run, as the team has 17 hits and nine walks. Crosetti and DiMaggio have three hits apiece. The Crow scores four runs, tying a record. Lazzeri hits the second grand slam homer in World Series history off Dick Coffman in the third, and in the seventh, with the sacks filled again, Tony flies to deep center field. Dickey hits a three-run homer in the ninth. DiMaggio ends the game when he races to deepest center field, near the Eddie Grant memorial, and makes a spectacular catch to rob Hank Leiber of a 475-foot hit. DiMaggio respectfully waits on the clubhouse steps, and when a limousine carrying President Roosevelt drives through the outfield exit, the President gives Joe a big wave.

Oct 3— At Yankee Stadium, the Yankees nip the Giants, 2-1, in a pitching duel between Bump Hadley and Fred Fitzsimmons. The game remains tied on solo homers by Gehrig and Jimmy Ripple until the Yankees score in the eighth inning on a scratch hit by Crosetti off Fitzsimmons' glove. After the game, a reporter tells Joe McCarthy, "I was rooting for you, as you know. But I felt sorry for Fitz." Responds the Yankee manager, "To tell you the truth, I did, too." The teams will split the next two games.

Oct 6— The Yankees win their fifth World Championship, beating the Giants, 13-5, at the Polo Grounds. It is a Gomez-Murphy game, as the former gets the win and the latter the save. The Yankees' early scoring is highlighted by Jake Powell's two-run homer and a run-scoring single by the light-hitting Gomez, and they ice the game with a seven-run ninth inning in which DiMaggio makes a pair of hits. Rolfe, DiMaggio, Powell who led all hitters at .455, and Lazzeri all have three hits in the 17-hit Yankee attack. In the seventh inning, DiMaggio makes his only World Series error. He will follow with 45 errorless games in World Series competition.

1937

The Yankees will finish at 102-52 and will win the pennant by 13 games over second-place Detroit. Joe DiMaggio's 46 homers will win him the AL home run championship, and Lou Gehrig will lead the club in hitting with .351. The Yankees will have the league's only 20-game winners in Lefty Gomez (21-11) and Red Ruffing (20-7). And they will have the World Championship, again beating the Giants in the World Series.

Mar 22— The great Newark Bears of 1937, very possibly the greatest minor league club in baseball history, open their home exhibition season at Fireman's Field in Sebring, Fla., with a 5-3 win over the parent Yankees. In the first inning, Gehrig drives a three-run homer off Atley Donald, then New York is held scoreless. Before the game, Colonel Ruppert, who owns both clubs, says, "I don't care who wins. I can't lose."

— The Bears would have done well in the AL. With players like Charlie Keller, Joe Gordon, George McQuinn, Buddy Rosar and Babe Dahlgren and pitchers like Atley Donald, Spud Chandler, Marius Russo and Steve Sundra, Newark won the International League pennant in 1937 by 25 games.

Mar 26— At New York's winter home in St. Petersburg, Fla., George Selkirk's two-run triple helps the Yankees beat Newark, 4-2, avenging a loss to the Bears four days earlier.

Apr 14— Commissioner Landis rules in Tommy Henrich's favor and against Cleveland General Manager Cy Slapnicka. Landis decides that the Indians are guilty of deliberately preventing Henrich from advancing to the major leagues and declares Henrich a free agent. At least eight big league clubs are interested in signing the talented young outfielder who over three years in the Cleveland organization hit .326, .337 and .346.

Apr 19— The Yankees sign Tommy Henrich for a bonus of $25,000. On this day, Henrich plays in New York's exhibition game at West Point, N.Y., against the Army team, whom the Yankees defeat, 19-4. Henrich scores one run and plays right field. He opens the season in Newark but Joe McCarthy asks Ed Barrow to "bring up the kid in Newark" when Joe becomes dissatisfied with Roy Johnson one week into the season.

Apr 20— Yankee Stadium opens with a new triple-decked grandstand in right field. Thus it takes some 14 years for the Stadium to arrive at the configuration we know today. The new grandstand replaces bleachers and curves around the right field foul pole, ending past the straightaway right field point. The left field grandstand was similarly extended in 1928. Joe DiMaggio has his tonsils and adenoids removed at New York's Lenox Hill Hospital. He misses his second straight Opening Day and will miss the season's first six games. Washington wins, 3-2.

Apr 26— The Yankees beat Philadelphia, 7-1, and make (unofficially) the first triple play in Yankee Stadium history. In the eighth inning with runners on first and second, the A's Chubby Dean grounds to Lazzeri at second base. Tony throws to shortstop Crosetti covering second. Frank fires to first and Gehrig relays to Rolfe at third to nail the lead runner.

May 1— DiMaggio returns as a Yankee regular and makes three hits off Boston's Rube Walberg. New York wins, 3-2, and DiMag has a hand in all three Yankee runs.

May 10— Monte Pearson pitches a one-hitter in Chicago and wins, 7-0. He allows only a first-inning hit by Larry Rosenthal, who will hit .289 in only 58 games this year, and walks two. DiMaggio belts two homers and Selkirk hits one. Bill Dickey is hit on the arm by a Ted Lyons pitch and is forced to leave the game. His injury sidelines him for several games and bothers him the rest of the season.

May 25— An accident at Yankee Stadium nearly claims the life of Mickey Cochrane, Detroit's manager-catcher. In the fourth inning, Cochrane, who previously homered, steps up to bat. Bump Hadley's fastball gets away from him and strikes Black Mike on the side of the head with such force that the ball bounces back to Hadley. Everyone watches in horror as Cochrane rolls in the dirt.

— Yankee Stadium was known for its poor hitter's background; Cochrane lost the ball from the moment it was pitched. It was feared for several days that Cochrane might die, but Mickey pulled through. His great playing career was prematurely concluded, however.

Jun 5— Red Ruffing, the Yankees' righthanded pitching ace, comes through with a pinch-hit home run, helping New York to defeat Detroit, 6-5.

— Ruffing was a holdout this spring and it was easy to sympathize with a man taking up one roster position and holding down two jobs, pitcher and pinch-hitter. As a pinch-hitter he would go 6 for 21 in 1937.

Jun 13— In the second game of a doubleheader at Sportsmans Park, DiMaggio belts three consecutive homers off Browns' pitching, which was pretty badly mauled in the first game, the Yankees winning, 16-9, with a seven-run uprising in the ninth. The nightcap is called because of darkness with the score knotted at 8-8.

Jun 16— Lefty Gomez strikes out the first five Indians—Lyn Lary, Roy Weatherly, Earl Averill, Hal Trosky and Moose Solters—in defeating Cleveland, 4-1, at Yankee Stadium. He fans nine altogether in the game.

Jun 30— New York clips Philadelphia, 5-1, on a one-hitter by Gomez. Goofy allows Bob Johnson, who hits .306 with 25 home runs this year and who earlier in the month spoiled another no-hitter, a home run in the fifth.

— For the second time in four seasons, Gomez won the mythical Triple Crown of pitchers, leading the AL in wins with 21, ERA with 2.33 and strikeouts with 194.

Jul 5— At Yankee Stadium, the Yankees sweep Boston, 15-0 and 8-4. In the nightcap, DiMaggio breaks up a 4-4 tie with his first career grand slam homer, the first of three grand slammers that will be hit by Joe this year. It is DiMaggio's 20th homer of the season and Rube Walberg is the victim.

— DiMaggio had a fantastic July. His 15 homers were the most ever hit in that month and they helped him to the first of his two home run titles. His 46 homers for the season remain the Yankee record for a righthanded hitter. They constitute a remarkable total given the fact that DiMaggio played half of his games at Yankee Stadium, an unfriendly ballpark for righthanded power hitters. Joe's 167 RBI total in 1937 was his career high. As a mark of his consistency, he enjoyed hitting streaks of 20 and 22 games.

Jul 7— The AL wins the All-Star Game, 8-3. The nucleus of Manager McCarthy's squad is made up of Yankees—DiMaggio, Dickey, Rolfe and Gehrig—who each play the entire contest. DiMaggio singles and scores a run. Dickey has a single and double, scores a run and drives one home. Rolfe singles, triples, scores two runs and drives in two runs. Gehrig knocks in four runs, scores a run and makes two hits, including a mighty homer off Dizzy Dean, the ball clearing the right field wall of Washington's Griffith Stadium. Starter Gomez yields only one hit over the first three innings and is the winning pitcher. The Yankees simply steal the show.

— Gomez made the All-Star Game an instrument of his own display, much the way he used the World Series as his own personal showcase. Beginning with the first All-Star Game in 1933, Gomez started five of the first six inter-league clashes, winning three decisions before taking a loss in 1938. Lefty's World Series record: 6-0.

Jul 9— DiMaggio hits for the cycle at Yankee Stadium, getting a single, double, triple and two home runs in the Yanks' 16-2 victory over Washington.

Jul 18— In Cleveland, DiMaggio's two-out, ninth-inning, grand slam homer beats the Indians, 5-1. A crowd of 58,884 turns out to see the Indians' 18-year-old phenomenon, Bob Feller, tame the bats of the Bronx Bombers. Instead, they witness a big day for Joltin' Joe, who also triples and doubles and accounts for all five Yankee runs.

Aug 1— New York mauls St. Louis, 14-5, as DiMaggio hits his third homer in two days, giving him 31 for the year and putting him one game ahead of Babe Ruth's record pace of 1927. Gehrig hits for the cycle for the second time in his career and is on his way to his eighth 200-hit season. (Only Pete Rose and Ty Cobb have had more 200-hit seasons.)

Aug 3— Lou Gehrig Appreciation Day is held at Yankee Stadium, drawing 66,767 fans to honor Lou, who is playing in his 1,900th consecutive game. Lou is presented with a pocket watch by George M. Cohan of show business fame, as a special honor for winning the previous year's MVP Award. In the first game of the doubleheader, Gehrig and DiMaggio both hit three-run homers and Lazzeri adds a solo fourbagger, as the Yankees beat Chicago, 7-2. In the nightcap, the Bronx Bombers trail, 3-1—their only run coming in the second inning on Lazzeri's homer—until the eighth when Dickey belts a grand slam homer, setting off a wild joyous demonstration by Gehrig Day fans. In the sweep, the Yankees hit five homers (all of more than 400 feet) that account for all the New York scoring.

Aug 4— Dickey hits a third-inning grand slam homer off Vern Kennedy (14-13), his second grand slam in as many games, tying a big league record. Babe Ruth and Dickey are the only Yankees to hit grand slams in consecutive games. The Yankees edge Chicago, 10-9, at Yankee Stadium.

— Dickey in 1936 set the still-standing big league record for catchers with a .362 batting average. In this campaign he batted in 133 runs, the still-standing AL record for a catcher. Between 1936-39, when the Yanks were World Champs four years running, Dickey hit over .300 with more than 20 homers and 100 RBIs each season. And he was the game's best defensive catcher. While sometimes measured against another great catcher, Mickey Cochrane, Dickey would seem to have no peer.

Aug 18— At Yankee Stadium against the Senators, DiMaggio makes four hits. Joe's final hit, coming in the ninth inning, is his 35th home run of the season and wins the game for New York, 7-6.

Sep 8— In a thrilling doubleheader at Yankee Stadium, the Yankees beat Boston twice. In the opener, Myril Hoag singles home the winning run in the bottom of the ninth, the Yankees taking a 3-2 decision. With two outs in the ninth inning of the second game, the Yankees are losing, 6-1. But they score eight runs! Clutch RBI hits are delivered by Don Heffner, a two-run triple; Dickey, a run-scoring double; DiMaggio, a run-scoring single to tie the game after a run had scored on an error; and Gehrig, a three-run homer to win the game for New York, 9-6.

Sep 23— New York clinches the AL pennant in the club's 142nd game of the season. At home, the Yankees are beaten by St. Louis, 9-5, but Boston beats second-place Detroit to give New York the championship. The Giants, coming through a tough fight with the Cubs, will again be the World Series opposition.

Oct 6— The World Series opens at Yankee Stadium with the Yankees winning, 8-1. The game has the makings of a classic pitching confrontation, with Gomez pitted against Carl Hubbell, but the Yanks, down 1-0 in the sixth, blow it open with a seven-run outburst. Key bases-loaded singles are delivered by

DiMaggio and Selkirk but Giant mistakes help, too. Gomez leads off the big inning with a walk. Then the Giants make two errors, the first giving Gomez safe status at second base after catcher Gus Mancuso has him picked off. Topping everything, the Giants bring in a relief pitcher other than the one whose name was given the home plate umpire, and after letting the "wrong" pitcher face one batter, they change pitchers again. Four walks are served up in the inning, including two to Gomez, to go with five singles and the two errors. The Yankees win the next two games, 8-1 and 5-1, behind Ruffing, Pearson and Murphy.

Oct 9—   Behind Hubbell at the Polo Grounds, the Giants win Game 4, 7-3, to stay alive. The Giants bomb Bump Hadley for six runs in the second inning as King Carl chucks a six-hitter. One of the Yankee hits is Gehrig's final World Series home run.

Oct 10—   The Yankees settle the Series in five games, winning, 4-2, at the Polo Grounds. Gomez scatters 10 hits to win his second complete game of the Series, yet still finds time for airplane watching while on the mound. The Bronx Bombers score first on Hoag and DiMaggio homers, the latter a tremendous blast that hits a flag pole atop the roof in left field. It is Joe's first World Series home run. Mel Ott delivers the Giants' only fourbagger of the Series in the third, a two-run shot that ties the score. But in the fifth, Lazzeri triples to center, Gomez singles Lazzeri home, and Gehrig doubles home Gomez, completing the scoring off twice-beaten Cliff Melton (20-9), a rookie given to making disparaging remarks about the Yankees. The North Carolinian, who goes by the nickname Mountain Music, is ripe for plucking by the Yankee bench jockeys.

Lefty Gomez is a happy man moments after pitching a six-hitter to defeat the Giants at Yankee Stadium in Game 1 of the 1937 World Series. Friend Joe DiMaggio is there to offer congratulations.

Oct 15— Just five days after he finishes a World Series in which his .400 average makes him the leading hitter, Tony Lazzeri is released. Tony is let go so that he can seize on an opportunity with the Cubs. The Yankees were in a dilemma; Lazzeri was aging, slowing down around second base and hitting (in the just-concluded season) only .244, while in Newark a tremendous homer-hitting prospect named Joe Gordon was playing second base like no one had ever played it before. The dilemma ends when Phil Wrigley of the Cubs calls Ed Barrow and asks to have Lazzeri, who represents that "Yankee spirit" to Wrigley. Lazzeri has no objections so the Yankees give him his unconditional release and he signs with the Cubs at a good salary and nice bonus. In 1938, with Lazzeri as their utility infielder, the Cubs will win the NL pennant.

— Lazzeri was the greatest second baseman in Yankee history. It is hard to believe that Poosh 'Em Up Tony is not a member of the Baseball Hall of Fame. In 12 seasons in New York, Lazzeri hit .293, cracked 169 home runs and drove in 1,154 runs while anchoring second base. Tony Lazzeri—the second baseman with seven 100-RBI seasons!

1938

The Yankees will finish at 99-53, 9½ games ahead of second-place Boston, to win their third consecutive pennant. Joe DiMaggio will hit .324 and collect 32 home runs. Red Ruffing will be the league's only 20-game winner at 21-7. The Yankees will sweep Chicago in the World Series.

Jan 21— Joe DiMaggio, Jacob Ruppert and Ed Barrow fail to agree on DiMaggio's 1938 contract after meeting for all of a half-hour. Ruppert tells the press Joe has rejected his offer of $25,000 and that the two parties are far apart. A bitter holdout has begun.

— DiMaggio had a good case for wanting a sizable raise after two spectacular seasons. Besides, DiMaggio is now the game's greatest drawing card. He lost 1937 MVP honors to Charlie Gehringer by a mere four votes. But a good slice of the public sides with the Yankee management. When spring training begins, DiMaggio, who made $8,000 in his first year with the Yankees and $15,000 in his second, will remain in San Francisco.

Mar 12— Four days after refusing Yankee management's offer of $39,000, Lou Gehrig signs his 1938 contract for $39,000. It is a raise of $3,000 over the previous season.

Mar 29— The Yankess learn as they prepare to break camp that Cap Huston has died on his plantation on Butler Island, near Brunswick, Ga., at the age of 71. Some of the Yankee players had never even heard of him, this only 15 years after Huston sold his interest in the Yankees to Ruppert. Gehrig is the only current Yankee player to have ever seen Huston.

Apr 18— At Boston, the Yankees lose the season's opener, 8-4. DiMaggio still has not reported—he misses his third straight Opening Day—and Myril Hoag plays center field. From California, Joe says of the loss, "It's too bad, but we'll do it again this year."

Apr 20— DiMaggio ends his holdout, agreeing to play in 1938 for $25,000. From San Francisco, DiMaggio informs Ruppert of his decision and Barrow announces the end of the holdout. Ruppert adds, "His pay will be $25,000, no more, no less, and it won't start until McCarthy says it should." DiMaggio immediately boards a train for New York.

— DiMaggio may have lost the battle but he is now the third highest paid player in baseball and the highest paid third-year player in baseball history. Perhaps DiMaggio was persuaded to sign by his friend, Joe Gould, the boxing manager, who phoned DiMaggio, saying, "You have a chance to break a lot of records and then get the money you want. But you can't break any records in San Francisco." DiMaggio will earn his money, hitting .324 with 32 home runs and 140 RBIs.

Apr 30— DiMaggio is in the line-up for the first time this year, his 12-game absence costing him nearly $2,000 in lost pay. The Yankees, who were 6-6 in his absence, defeat Washington, 8-4, at Griffith Stadium, the Jolter contributing a single and colliding with Joe Gordon in the field in his very first game with the new second baseman. Both players lay unconscious in the outfield for a few minutes after cracking heads in shallow center field. Hospitalized overnight, they were released the next morning, having suffered nothing more serious than bruises, although Gordon doesn't play.

May 2— McCarthy places DiMaggio in the fourth slot of the batting order and drops Gehrig, hitless in 11 trips, to sixth. Gehrig has a single, DiMaggio homers and the Yankees beat Washington, 3-2. Joe will hit safely in his first nine games.

May 30— A crowd of 81,841, the largest official crowd in Yankee Stadium history, sees the Yankees sweep a Memorial Day doubleheader from Boston, 10-0 and 5-4, while several thousand other fans are turned away at the gate. Many watch from the elevated train platform and buildings beyond the bleachers. They are witness to a wild fight between Jake Powell and Joe Cronin. After being brushed back and then hit by a pitch, Powell charges the mound after Archie McKain only to be intercepted by Cronin, Boston's shortstop-manager. The two slug each other repeatedly before they are separated and ejected from the game. Tough as bargain stew meat, they want more of each other and resume their Pier Nine brawl under the stands with many members of the Yankees and Red Sox in attendance. Both Powell and Cronin will receive fines and 10-day suspensions. McKain is uninvolved, although inwardly, as the instigator, he must have been amused.

Jul 1— Bill Dickey drives in seven runs in an 8-0 win over Washington. In the fourth inning, Dickey belts a three-run homer off starter Harry Kelley (9-8) and in the very next inning tags Kelley for a grand slammer.

Jul 12— At Yankee Stadium, the Yankees sweep two games from St. Louis, 7-3 and 10-5. New York passes Cleveland and goes into first place for good. The Indians will finish third, 13 games behind the Yankees.

Jul 31— The Yankees edge the White Sox, 7-3, in 15 innings. Spud Chandler, a 30-year-old righthander who this year finally gets his chance with New York and goes 14-5, pitches the entire game and allows only eight hits. The Yanks' Jake Powell makes racist remarks on the air in Chicago after the game and will receive a 10-day suspension. The big leagues might be for whites only, but the hierarchy does not condone mean-spirited talk about blacks.

— Born in Silver Spring, Md., on the Washington, D.C., boundary, Powell was not exactly from the Deep South. Nonetheless, he was a man of intense prejudices. He once broke the wrist of Hank Greenberg in a collision at first base, leaving a lingering question of whether Greenberg was hit with relish because he was Jewish. In the off-seasons, Powell was a sheriff, in the mold, no doubt, of the redneck lawman. As a player, Powell was in in the mold of a Ty Cobb. He was highly competitive and aggressive. He hit .272 in five Yankee seasons (1936-40) before sustaining a beaning that resulted in a severe concussion and the end of his Yankee days.

Aug 7— The Yankees beat Cleveland, 7-0, but Red Ruffing loses a no-hitter in the ninth inning. With one out, Roy Weatherly, a .262 hitter as a part-timer this year, doubles to ruin Red's bid. It is the closest Ruffing will ever get to a no-hitter.

Aug 12— For the second time in his career, George Selkirk has eight RBIs in one game. Selkirk in the nightcap of a doubleheader with the A's hits a run-scoring single, a three-run homer, and a bases-loaded homer, as the Bronx Bombers win at the Stadium, 16-3. New York loses to Philadelphia in the opener, 5-4. Twinkletoes Selkirk has a solo homer in that game.

Aug 20— Gehrig has six RBIs in New York's 11-3 triumph over Philadelphia. The Iron Horse, still plugging away every day, blasts a grand slam homer off Buck Ross. It is Lou's 23rd and final grand slam, establishing a big league record that still stands.

Aug 27— Monte Pearson pitches Yankee Stadium's first no-hitter. He strikes out seven Indians and faces the minimum of 27 batters; he walks two Indians but they are wiped out on double plays. Pearson usually complains of an ailment on his day to pitch and today he is louder than usual in his complaining. The Yankees win, 13-0, after taking the opener of today's doubleheader, 8-7, behind DiMag's three straight triples.

— Pearson, who was on his way to a 16-7 season that included a 10-game winning streak, today hurled the sixth and final no-hitter of the decade in the AL.

Aug 31— Detroit beats the Yankees, 12-6, at Yankee Stadium, as the Yankees conclude a brutal August schedule, playing 36 games in 31 days. But New York wins 28 of them, the most victories ever by a team in one month in the AL.

Sep 4— Joe Gordon has four extra-base hits in one game—a pair of homers and a pair of doubles—as the Yankees defeat Washington, 7-4, at the Stadium.

— Just two years removed from the University of Oregon, Gordon already was a big league star. He had excelled in Oakland and Newark and he excelled in New York, hitting 25 home runs and driving in 97 runs as a rookie. The only other AL second baseman to hit more than eight homers was Detroit's Charlie Gehringer, who had 20. Gordon was the flashiest, most acrobatic second sacker in the league.

Sep 18— Although they lose a doubleheader in St. Louis, the Yankees clinch the pennant—their 10th. They are the first team in history to win 10 pennants. They clinch because their nearest competitor, Boston, is rained out of a doubleheader with Chicago, a doubleheader that will not be rescheduled. This means that even if the Yankees lose all of their remaining games and Boston wins all of its remaining games, Boston will still fall one-half game short. So this Yankee edition, which Joe McCarthy always considered his best, clinches in its 140th game.

— The team led the AL in most batting and pitching stats. Five players hit more than 20 homers each. DiMaggio had 32 homers, Gehrig 29, Dickey 27, Gordon (who batted eighth) 25 and Henrich 22. Of the other three starters, Rolfe hit .311, Crosetti led the AL with 27 stolen bases and Selkirk had 62 RBIs in only 335 at bats. The pitchers were led by Ruffing, 21-7; Gomez, 18-12; Pearson, 16-7; Chandler, 14-5; and reliever Murphy, who led the AL with 11 saves. The Yankees in the World Series would face the Cubs, a team woefully short on power; not one of them had as many as 70 RBIs or 14 homers!

Sep 27— At Yankee Stadium, Gehrig blasts his 29th homer of the season, the 493rd of his career and the final fourbagger he will ever hit in a regular season game. It comes off Washington's Dutch Leonard, the winner of 191 games, exactly 15 years to the day Lou hit his first homer in the majors.

— The 35-year-old Gehrig had slowed down a little but most experts felt he had a few big years left. After all, he still hit .295, drove in 114 runs and scored 115 runs. For the 13th consecutive season, Gehrig both drove in and scored 100 runs, the combination a major league record. In August, Gehrig was presented with a new automobile for being voted the Most Popular First Baseman in a nationwide poll. The season ended with Lou's consecutive game streak total standing at 2,122 games.

Oct 5— The World Series opens in Chicago and Red Ruffing pitches a nine-hitter, walks no one and beats the Cubs' 22-game winner, Bill Lee, 3-1. Bill Dickey paces the attack with four singles in four at bats.

Oct 6— Gomez beats the Cubs, 6-3, with relief help over the final two innings from Murphy, to run his World Series record to six wins without a loss. Dizzy Dean, pitching without his once awesome hummer, puts on a particularly brave performance. New York scores two runs in the second when Gordon's easy grounder gets through the Cubs' left side as their shortstop and third baseman collide. Still, Dean takes a 3-2 lead into the eighth. Then Crosetti hits a two-run homer into Wrigley Field's left field bleachers. In the ninth, DiMaggio ices it with another two-run homer. The Yanks will win the third game also behind Pearson at the Stadium.

Oct 9— New York is the first team to win three World Series in a row, as Ruffing polishes off the Cubs, scattering eight hits in pitching his second complete game of the Series. The Yankees win, 8-3. Their three-run second inning signals to 58,847 Stadium spectators that they are watching the finale in a four-game sweep. In that two-out rally, Ruffing strokes a run-scoring single and Crosetti knocks in two runs with a triple into the left field corner. Henrich homers in the sixth and the suspense ends with a four-run Yankee uprising in the eighth, capped by a two-run, two-base hit by Crosetti.

1939

The Yankees will finish at 106-45 and win an unprecedented fourth straight AL pennant by 17 games over second-place Boston. Joe DiMaggio will win the batting championship with a mark of .381 and will be the American League's MVP. Red Ruffing will be the club's top pitcher at 21-7. And the Yankees will again prevail in the World Series.

Jan 13— Col. Jacob Ruppert, the owner of the Yankees for 24 years, dies at the age of 71. Ruppert had been suffering from phlebitis. Except for relatives and brewery associates, Babe Ruth is the last to visit Jake and the two Yankee greats have an emotional final meeting. Control of the club passes to the Ruppert estate. Six days later, Ed Barrow will succeed Ruppert as Yankee president.

— Ruppert was buried from St. Patrick's Cathedral. The large funeral was packed with mourners and a line of police held back thousands of onlookers. Flags were lowered to half-staff at City Hall and other buildings. Ruppert was a businessman, politician, socialite and sportsman. Still, he lived a protected private life. His determined privacy and a measure of aristocratic aloofness made him seem distant to many fans. With his death, however, emerged a widespread feeling that Ruppert had been good for baseball. The wonder is that the doors at Cooperstown remain closed to Ruppert, the man known as the Master Builder in Baseball, whose clubs won 10 pennants during his lifetime and would win many more after his death.

Apr 13— Lou Gehrig has his last hurrah as a slugger. Moving North to open the season, the Yankees play an exhibition game in Norfolk, Va. Everyone is talking about Gehrig's poor spring training—coming on the heels of his mediocre 1938 season—and about how Lou lacks power and coordination. But on this date against Brooklyn he belts two homers and two singles. His legion of supporters breathes a premature sigh of relief.

Apr 20— On Opening Day at Yankee Stadium, Red Ruffing pitches a seven-hitter and beats Boston, 2-0. Boston's 20-year-old rookie outfielder, Ted Williams, strikes out in his first two appearances against Rufus the Red, then thumps a double off the 407-foot sign in right-center for his first big league hit. Joe DiMaggio, who goes one for two, finally makes an opener after missing the first three of his career.

— Ted Williams may well have been the best all-round hitter the Yankees have ever had to face. He hit exceptionally well for both average (.344 lifetime) and power (521 career home runs). And, of course, Williams' emergence inaugurated 12 years of arguments over who was better—Williams or DiMaggio.

Apr 29— DiMaggio injures his right leg in the field, but luckily the injury is not so severe as it might have been. Tracking a line-drive hit by Bobby Estalella, DiMaggio's spikes stick in a muddy outfield in Washington and he crumbles in terrible pain. It is feared at first that Joe has suffered a leg fracture, but St. Elizabeth's Hospital reports his injury as torn muscles. Still, he will be sidelined in pain for about five weeks.

Apr 30— Gehrig plays in his 2,130th consecutive game. As it turns out, it is his last. Johnny Murphy compliments Gehrig on a routine play at first base and Lou is suddenly aware of the low level to which his game has fallen. His .143 batting average is even more glaringly deficient. The club leaves New York for Detroit. Lou is on the train but he has already decided to remove himself from the next game's line-up. He has played with lumbago, fractured fingers, spike wounds, charley horses, sore muscles and back pains. He has even played the day after being seriously beaned, but he will not play when he cannot give a Gehrig-type performance.

May 2— Gehrig performs his duty as captain, taking the Yankee batting order to home plate before the game at Detroit's Briggs Stadium. The announcement that

Gehrig will not be in the line-up is met with a deadly silence. Then there is a tremendous ovation as Lou walks into the dugout. There, the Iron Horse stands for a long time at the water fountain, tears streaming down his face.

— Gehrig asked Manager Joe McCarthy to remove him from the line-up. "I haven't been a bit of good to the team since the season started," he explained. McCarthy, who deep inside believed there had to be something terribly wrong with his first baseman, was worried that Gehrig might hurt himself. He acceded to Gehrig's wishes but assured Lou that first base was his whenever he wanted to reclaim it. McCarthy later commented: "He's been a great ball player. Fellows like him come along once in a hundred years. I told him that. More than that, he's been a vital part of the Yankee club since he started with it. He's always been a perfect gentleman, a credit to baseball." Gehrig's replacement in the game that ended his streak of 2,130 consecutive games was Babe Dahlgren. Dahlgren hit a home run and double as the Yankees pummeled the Tigers, 22-2. Babe wanted to play but not at the price of replacing his boyhood hero. As the Yankees mounted a big lead, Dahlgren went to Gehrig in the seventh inning and thoughtfully suggested, "Lou, you had better get in there now and keep that streak going." But the Iron Horse slapped Babe on the back appreciatively and protested that he wasn't needed. The Yankees on the field, who besides Dahlgren included rookie Charlie Keller, getting a chance to play in the absence of the still-hospitalized DiMaggio, were "doing fine," Gehrig assured Dahlgren.

May 10— The Yankees beat the Browns, 7-1, and begin a streak of 13 consecutive victories in St. Louis, an AL record for consecutive wins against one club at their home ballpark. New York will win all 11 games this year at Sportsmans Park and the first two games in 1940. The Yankees move into first place during this series.

— The Yankees' superiority over the Browns was hardly surprising. The Yanks of 1939 played at a winning percentage of .702 (106-45), joining the 1927 Yankees as the second AL team to play over .700, while St. Louis finished last with a record of 43-111. This converts to a winning percentage of .279. The Browns finished 64½ games behind New York. The Yankees were the "haves" and the Browns the "have nots" of baseball.

Jun 6— The day after rejoining the club, DiMaggio makes his first game appearance in over five weeks and has a home run, a double and a single. Joe's happy return leads the Yanks to a 7-2 win over Chicago.

Jun 12— Baseball takes a break from its one pennant race—there is no race in the AL with the Yankees leading by nine games—as all the big names of the game gather in Cooperstown, N.Y., for the official opening of the Baseball Hall of Fame. Enshrined in the Hall following four years of elections are Yankees Willie Keeler, who died in 1923, and Babe Ruth, who is on hand. The Babe tells those assembled, "They started something here. And the kids are keeping the ball rolling. I hope some of you kids wil be in the Hall of Fame. I'm very glad that in my day I was able to earn my place. And I hope the youngsters of today have the same opportunity to experience such a feeling." Afterward, a game is played with each big league club sending two players. Representing the Yankees are Canadian-born George Selkirk and Norwegian-born Art Jorgens. Quipped Lefty Gomez: "Leave it to the Yankees to be represented by a couple of foreigners."

Jun 20— A Mayo Clinic report is issued on the condition of Lou Gehrig and the country is shocked to learn that Lou has a deadly disease. Dr. Harold C. Harbein's report reads: "This is to certify that Mr. Lou Gehrig has been under examination at the Mayo Clinic from June 13 to June 19, 1939, inclusive. After a careful and complete examination, it was found that he is suffering from amyotrophic lateral sclerosis. This type of illness involves the motor pathways and cells of the central nervous system and, in lay terms, is known as a form of chronic poliomyelitis—infantile paralysis. The nature of this trouble makes it such that Mr. Gehrig will be unable to continue his active participation as a baseball player inasmuch as it is advisable that he conserve his muscular energy. He could, however, continue in some executive capacity."

Jun 26— For the first time in their history, the Yankees play a regular season game under the lights—at Philadelphia's Shibe Park, where the Athletics defeat New York, 3-2.

Jun 28— In Philadelphia, the Yankees sweep a doubleheader, winning 23-2 and 10-0. For the day, the Bronx Bombers make 43 hits, score 33 runs and hit 13 home runs—eight in the first contest—in setting standing AL marks for homers in one game and consecutive games. The Yanks make 53 total bases in the opener, a standing Yankee record. In the day's awesome display of long-ball hitting, DiMaggio, Dahlgren and Gordon each hit three home runs, and Dickey, Selkirk, Henrich and Crosetti hit one homer apiece. In the nightcap, Lefty Gomez pitches a shutout; not that he needs to, what with his mates belting five homers and 16 hits.

Jul 4— Lou Gehrig Appreciation Day is held at Yankee Stadium and 61,808, including Lou's wife and parents, are on hand for one of baseball's most legendary afternoons. Thirteen members of the 1927 Yankees,* Lou's first World Championship team, march to the flagpole and raise the 1927 World Championship flag. Among the 1927 Yankees present is George Pipgras, now an AL umpire. Pipgras will officiate at today's game. Also present are Everett Scott, whose playing record Gehrig broke, and Wally Pipp, whose job Gehrig took. Sid Mercer is toastmaster. Ed Barrow supports Lou as the former players are introduced and Lou is presented with a large silver trophy from his present-day teammates. Babe Ruth chucks the fact that he and Gehrig have not been on friendly terms for years and impulsively hugs Lou. The Iron Horse receives gifts and hears cheers, as the crowd alternatively laughs and cries in the finest tribute ever given a ballplayer. Speeches are made by Mayor LaGuardia, former Mayor Walker, Postmaster General Farley and Manager McCarthy. Gehrig, choked with emotion, is not expected to speak, but he takes the microphone and delivers a few words from the heart to a crowd well aware of his terminal condition. "I may have been given a bad break," Lou says, "but I have an awful lot to live for. All in all, I can say on this day that I consider myself the luckiest man on the face of the earth."

Jul 9— A home run by Joe Cronin helps Boston beat New York, 5-3, and sweep a doubleheader. It is the Red Sox' fifth consecutive win against the Yankees

*Actually, with so many former players on hand, this was the first Old Timers' Day although it was not so named.

in a five-game series at Yankee Stadium. Boston wins by scores of 4-3, 3-1 and 3-2 (DH), and 4-3 and 5-3 (DH). The series sweep, allowing Boston to extend a winning streak to 12 games, momentarily puts the Red Sox back in the pennant picture. But the Yankees, after losing six straight, turn back the challenge by starting an eight-game winning streak of their own.

Jul 11— For the first time, an All-Star Game is played at Yankee Stadium and it is won by the AL, 3-1. AL Manager Joe McCarthy starts six of his own players— Rolfe, DiMaggio, Dickey, Selkirk, Gordon and Ruffing, who opens and hurls three solid innings. The hometown fans—the game is played in New York because of the World's Fair—are ecstatic when DiMaggio blasts a fifth-inning home run off the Cubs' Bill Lee, a 19-game winner this year. One NL fan murmurs before the game, "They ought to make Joe McCarthy play an All-Star American League team. We can beat them, but we can't beat the Yankees."

Jul 25— Yankee pitcher Atley Donald wins his 12th consecutive game since May 9, setting a standing rookie pitching record in the AL, as the Browns fall, 5-1, at Yankee Stadium. Donald also ties a Yankee record with 12 wins at the start of a season, a record later broken by Ron Guidry, the Yankee pitcher recruited through the draft by Yankee scout Atley Donald!

— At 13-3 in 1939, Donald was the Yanks' second biggest winner behind Ruffing. Donald, also known as "Swampy," could not impress Yankee scout Johnny Nee as a pitcher for Louisiana Tech, nor could he get a reaction from Ed Barrow after writing a letter to the Yankee boss. But in an uninvited spring training tryout, Donald impressed Joe McCarthy enough to be signed. Having climbed the farm ladder, Swampy was a combined 35-9 over the 1937-38 seasons in Newark. Then in New York from 1938-45, he posted a 65-33 record and was a valuable swing pitcher. He played his entire big league career in a Yankee uniform.

Jul 26— Dickey hits three consecutive home runs, leading the Yankees to a 14-1 victory over St. Louis at Yankee Stadium. The Yankees tie a major league record by scoring in every inning. They score 2-1-1-4-1-3-1-1 runs and do not need to bat in the ninth. Ruffing allows the Browns three hits, while New York collects 20.

Aug 2— Joe DiMaggio makes what many consider the greatest catch in Yankee Stadium history. It comes in Detroit's 7-2 victory before a crowd of 12,341. Hank Greenberg sends a tremendous blast into the vast open center field pasture, some 460 feet from home plate. Joe gets a great jump on the ball, taking off the instant Hank connects. He races with his back to the plate and with an instinct as to where the ball will descend from the sky. Just two feet shy of the 461-foot sign, right next to the famed monuments, Joe clutches the ball without looking back! Greenberg is robbed of a sure inside-the-park homer.

Aug 12— Dahlgren has a great day in Philadelphia as the Yankees romp, 18-4. Babe goes four for six, drives in eight runs and scores four runs. In the seventh inning, he unloads a grand slam homer off A's pitcher Lynn Nelson.

Aug 13— After losing the first game of the doubleheader, 12-9, the Yankees rebound to rout the Athletics, 21-0, in a game called after eight innings. It is the most lopsided shutout in AL history. Dahlgren and DiMaggio each hit a pair of home runs and Ruffing, besides his shutout, contributes four hits himself.

— Known as a great slugging team, the Yankees as a pitching team were not unaccomplished. Ruffing's shutout of the A's helped New York pace the AL in shutouts for the third consecutive year, and, more impressively, the Yanks' team ERA of 3.31 gave New York the team ERA title for the sixth straight year! And it was Ruffing who led the staff, winning at least 20 games for four consecutive seasons. Over those four years—all World Championship years for the Yankees—Ruffing's combined record was 82-33. Ruffing also hit .307 to go with 21 wins in 1939, and only two AL pitchers since then have hit .300 with 20 wins in the same season.

Aug 25— In St. Louis, the Yankees win twice, 11-0 and 8-2, and for the 17th and 18th consecutive games, Red Rolfe scores at least one run, setting an AL record that still stands. Rolfe scores two runs in each contest. Over the remarkable streak, Rolfe, as the second-place hitter in the batting order, scores a total of 30 runs. He is on his way to his greatest season. He will hit .329 and lead the AL in hits (213), doubles (46) and runs scored (139).

Aug 28— In Detroit, the Yankees romp, 18-2, and DiMaggio knocks in eight runs. He blasts a grand slam homer and a three-run fourbagger, giving him 22 home runs for the year, and singles home a run. He has a batting streak of 14 straight games and his average is close to .400.

Sep 1— In Cleveland, Bob Feller is thwarted in his attempt to win his 20th game for the first time, as New York bombs him, 11-8.* DiMaggio drives in six runs on two triples and a single, extends his hitting streak to 17 games and finishes the western road trip with 27 hits in 53 at bats. The Yankees have won 10 of 12 games.

— DiMaggio was by no means the only hard-hitting Yankee outfielder. The Yanks started an all-.300-hitting outfield with DiMaggio at .381, Charlie Keller at .334 and George Selkirk at .306. The fourth outfielder, Tommy Henrich, hit .277 in 99 games.

Sep 3— In the first game of a doubleheader in Boston, the Red Sox beat the Yankees, 12-11, then New York wins the nightcap by forfeit. In the second game,. the Yankees break up a tie game to go ahead, 7-5, with the 6:30 Sunday curfew only a few minutes away. Both teams realize the situation and act accordingly; the Yanks doing everything possible to make outs, including ill-fated attempts at stealing home, and the Sox trying to prolong the inning so that the curfew will salvage a tie for them. Finally, Boston Manager Joe Cronin charges the field and maintains that the Yanks are doing something illegal. But Umpire Hubbard says New York is playing within the rules and the angry crowd pelts the Fenway Park field with garbage. Every time the field is cleared, the Bostonians throw out more junk. One wonders if the Fenway faithful came to the park armed with garbage, but, in any event, the game cannot be resumed and the Yankees are awarded the forfeit victory.

Sep 8— DiMaggio raises his batting average to .408, and, at this late date, is given an excellent chance of being the majors' first .400 hitter in nine years. But over the season's final weeks, the Yankee Clipper is plagued by a bad cold and "slumps" to his final .381 mark. He will finish with 30 homers and 126 RBIs.

---

*Feller finished the year with a record of 24-9.

They burst upon the American League scene in 1936 and immediately captured the public's imagination. By 1939 they were recognized as the best hitter and pitcher in baseball. That year Joltin' Joe DiMaggio won the AL batting championship with a .381 average and Rapid Robert Feller led the AL in wins with 24.

Sep 15— Yankee second baseman Joe Gordon makes 11 assists in one game, tying an AL record broken later. The Yankees beat Detroit, 10-3, at Yankee Stadium.

— The Yankees had one of the best double play combinations in AL history. Gordon took part in 116 DPs and shortstop Frank Crosetti in 118. Gordon led second sackers in putouts, assists and double plays, while Crosetti led shortstops in fielding average, putouts and double plays. They were the best in the majors, but some experts thought the Yanks had an even better double-play combination in the minors in the persons of Jerry Priddy and Phil Rizzuto.

Sep 16— Rookie Marius Russo, who wins 8 of 11 decisions this year, wins the pennant clincher by defeating Detroit, 8-5, the Yankees clinching in their 139th game of the year. Cincinnati will later clinch in the NL.

Sep 30— On the final day of the season, Yankee pitcher Steve Sundra loses his only game of the year, as Boston beats him, 4-2, after New York had won the opener, 5-4. Sundra finishes with a near-perfect record of 11-1. He is 8-1 in 11 starts and 3-0 in 13 relief games.

— In December 1935, the native of Pennsylvania came to the Yankees in the Allen-for-Pearson deal as a "throw in." But Jake Ruppert once revealed the inside story. Said Jake, "We told Cleveland 'Allen for Pearson' wasn't an even exchange and we mentioned a few players we knew the Indians wouldn't give up. Then we mentioned Sundra, the man we wanted all the time." Sundra starred at Newark, then went 21-11 in four seasons with the Yankees.

Oct 4— The World Series opens at Yankee Stadium and Ruffing outpitches Paul Derringer (25-7). The Yankees win, 2-1. Cincinnati's McCormick opens the scoring with a run-scoring single in the fourth inning, but the Yankees tie the game in the fifth on Gordon's single and Dahlgren's double. Ruffing retires the Reds in order in the sixth, seventh, eighth and ninth. In the bottom of the ninth, Keller rifles a one-out triple to the right-center field wall and DiMaggio is walked intentionally. Cincinnati Manager McKechnie elects not to walk the bases loaded and clutch-hitter Dickey delivers a single to end the game. Ruffing pitches a four-hitter; Derringer loses a tough six-hitter.

Oct 5— New York defeats Cincinnati, 4-0, behind the brilliant two-hit pitching of Pearson, who strikes out eight batters. Pearson is not reached for a hit and walks only one until Ernie Lombardi's one-out eighth-inning single. Bucky Walters (27-11) goes the route but for the second straight day one of the Reds' aces is outpitched. The Reds now have no chance; they lose Game 3 with Keller becoming the first rookie to hit two homers in a World Series game.

Oct 8— In Cincinnati, the Yankees win, 7-4, completing their four-game Series sweep, and giving them a record four consecutive World Championships (broken in 1953) and 28 victories in the Yanks' last 31 World Series games! Cincinnati uses both Derringer and Walters in their last ditch effort. In the ninth, the Reds blow a 4-2 lead with poor fielding and allow the Yankees to tie the game. In the 10th, Crosetti walks, Rolfe sacrifices and Keller reaches on shortstop Billy Myers' second error of the game. Then DiMaggio singles home Crosetti, and when the ball is kicked around in right field, Keller scores, flattening catcher Ernie Lombardi in the process. Lombardi falls to the ground, dazed, and DiMaggio alertly scores the third run of the play. Murphy escapes trouble in the ninth and the Series ends when Crosetti catches Wally Berger's line drive.

— During the Series, a Reds' fan was heard to exclaim, "Break up the Yankees, hell! I'll be satisfied if they'll just break up Keller." Indeed, the 23-year-old rookie paced all hitters with a .438 average. His amazing Series capped a meteoric rise to baseball's highest echelon. The strong farm boy from Frederick, Md., was a star at the University of Maryland, where as a sophomore he hit .506. He was signed at dawn one morning by Yankee scouts Paul Krichell and Gene McCann, who roused Keller from his bed in Kinston, N.C., where he was playing semi-pro ball during summer vacation. His first two years of pro ball were spent at Newark where Keller hit .353 in 1937 and .365 in 1938. With the Yankees in 1939, he hit .334, nine points shy of the all-time high for an AL rookie. He was a star at the ripe old age of 23.

Dec 8— Lou Gehrig is elected to the Baseball Hall of Fame by special election. The Baseball Writers, realizing the seriousness of Gehrig's illness and that he may not survive the required five-year waiting period upon retirement, elect Lou by acclamation at their annual meeting in Cincinnati and Lou is allowed to smell the roses. No real need to wait anyway to select a man who, over 17 big league seasons, hit .340 with 493 home runs, drove in 1,991 runs and scored 1,888 runs. Lou had made his final appearance in uniform in the final game of this year's World Series—he had remained with the club as captain through the season—and was preparing to start a job on the New York City Parole Commission, an appointment made by Mayor LaGuardia.

THE 1940's
DISRUPTION AND
REASSERTION

1940

The Yankees will finish at 88-66, two games behind pennant-winning Detroit and one game back of the Cleveland Indians, who will finish second. Joe DiMaggio will win his second straight batting crown at .352 and Red Ruffing will lead the pitching staff with a record of 15-12.

Apr 14— Joe DiMaggio, who in March signed a $30,000 contract ($2,500 better than his previous pact), will miss his fourth season opener in five big league seasons. Joltin' Joe strains a tendon in his right knee while running out a double in a game with Brooklyn the day before the season's start. Di-Maggio misses the first 15 games.

May 8— Cleveland hands the Yankees their fifth straight defeat, 10-4, and New York is in undisputed possession of last place. The Yankees' record is 6-11. They will remain associated with the cellar through May 25, emerging a couple times only to fall down the stairs again in one of the most dismal season starts in Yankee history.

May 11— The last-place Yankees suffer their eighth consecutive loss, all at home, no less, bowing 9-8. It is the second day in a row that the Yankees lose an extra-inning game to the Red Sox. New York has won only six of its first 14 games and the rest of the league is eating it up. The Yanks will snap the losing streak by beating Boston tomorrow.

May 26— New York "floats" out of the cellar. The Yankees are idle but the seventh and eighth-place teams lose and the Yankees end the day in sixth place. It will be 19 years before they get to play in the cellar again.

Jul 4— The Yankees win a doubleheader in Boston, 12-4 and 7-3. But on this tradi-tional date of the start of the pennant race, they find themselves in fourth place, six games behind the front-running Indians. Cleveland is 44-28; Detroit, 41-27; Boston, 38-30; and New York, 36-32. The Yanks' hitting is weak and so is their pitching. Lefty Gomez has been ailing with a bad back and a sore arm and will finish with only six decisions (3-3).

Jul 13— The Yankees sweep a doubleheader from St. Louis, 10-4 and 12-6, with DiMaggio getting nine RBIs on the day. The Yankee Clipper's two homers and two singles drive in seven runs in the opener. His two-run homer in the nightcap is followed by a Charlie Keller grand slam homer.

Jul 19— The day after hitting a grand slammer, backup catcher Buddy Rosar shocks everyone by hitting a single, double, triple and home run. It is only the ninth cycle in Yankee history. The Yankees rout Cleveland, 15-6, and sweep the key three-game series. Rosar will hit .298 in 73 games this year. Dickey will hit .247 in 106 games.

Jul 26— New York routs Chicago, 10-2, behind a great individual performance by Spud Chandler. The Georgia native goes all the way on the mound and at the plate has three hits, two of them homers and one of the homers a grand slam. He drives in six runs and scores two runs. His "slam" is the Yankees fourth in 13 days.

Jul 28— At Comiskey Park, Keller belts three home runs, DiMaggio adds two four-baggers and the Yankees pull out a one-run victory, 10-9. After this dramatic win, New York breaks even on the day as Chicago takes the nightcap, 8-4.

Jul 30— DiMaggio hits safely in his 23rd consecutive game. It is the longest streak in the majors this year. It will end with his next game, six games short of the Yankee club record.

Aug 8— The Yankees complete a disastrous trip to Fenway Park, losing, 6-5. The Red Sox win four in a five-game set.

— New York's record was 50-51 and the Yankees were in the middle of the AL standings. Cleveland and Detroit were fighting for league leadership. Most experts had the Yankees written out.

Aug 12— Ernie Bonham, the Yanks' star righthanded pitcher on their Kansas City farm club, is finally summoned to the big club. Bonham will go 9-3, complete 10 of 12 starts and post an ERA of 1.90, lowest in the AL. (But Bonham does not pitch enough innings to qualify for the official ERA title.)

— Most contemporary experts believe the Yankee braintrust made an uncharacteristic mistake in not bringing Bonham up earlier, and that this error cost them the pennant. In the spring, Bonham should have made the club, but Joe McCarthy, George Weiss and Ed Barrow felt he needed another year on the farm. Even as the Yankee pitching sagged all spring and through the summer months, the club failed to make a move. If Bonham had been recalled earlier . . . eight consecutive pennants?

Aug 13— DiMaggio drives in eight runs in one game, the first time the AL has seen so many personal RBIs in one game since DiMaggio knocked in eight a year ago.

Aug 22— With a nine-run second inning spearheaded by DiMaggio's grand slam homer and helped by George Selkirk's two walks (the fourth time George received two walks in one inning), the Yankees overwhelm Cleveland, 15-2.

Aug 24— Against Cleveland's Bob Feller, DiMaggio leads off the ninth inning with a triple and scores on a sacrifice fly to give New York a 3-2 win. Unfortunately, he pulls a leg muscle and will be sidelined for several days, just when the Yankees are making a run that Joe happens to be leading.

Aug 29— DiMaggio pinch-hits with the Yankees losing to the Browns, 4-1, with two on and two outs in the ninth. He hits a three-run homer off St. Louis ace Eldon Auker to tie a game the Yankees win in the 13th inning.

— DiMaggio had a great stretch drive and almost led the Yankees to a miracle pennant. He finished with 31 home runs and 133 RBIs. He would claim a batting title won in a race that was almost as exciting as the pennant fight. For the first part of the year, Rip Radcliff of the Browns led with Luke Appling of the Wite Sox challenging. The big boys, DiMaggio and Ted Williams, got hot late in the summer and climbed up the leader board. The final averages: DiMaggio, .352; Appling, .348; Williams, .344; and Radcliff, .342.

Sep 2— After winning the opener of a twinbill, the Yankees complete an incredible string of 21 wins in 24 games (since August 9) and are in a virtual tie for second place with Detroit, both teams trailing Cleveland by 3½ games. The schedule has the Yanks playing all 24 games at home except for a doubleheader in Philadelphia.

Sep 8—   Joe Gordon hits a single, double, triple and home run to hit for the cycle, the mark of the versatile as well as proficient hitter.

— Flash Gordon and King Kong Keller were among the few regulars to join with DiMaggio in having productive years in 1940. Gordon hit 30 home runs, most ever by a Yankee second baseman, and drove in 103 runs. Keller hit 21 fourbaggers and knocked in 93 runs.

Sep 11—   The Yankees play a crucial doubleheader in Cleveland. After winning the opener with Bonham defeating Feller, 3-1, New York goes into first place by half a game. (The Yankees are 25-6 in their last 31 games.) The stay at the top is brief; Cleveland wins the nightcap, 5-3, pushing the Yankees back into second place, and it is hard to imagine a more discouraging loss. The game is played on a rain-soaked field and is interrupted for 30 minutes because of the rain. Up 2-0, the Yankees hand the Indians five runs in the third inning, Dahlgren and Ruffing committing errors. New York is held scoreless in the top of the sixth and the umpires call the game because of darkness. Little do they know it, but the darkness has set in for good for the Yankees who will drop their next two games in Detroit.

Sep 16—   The Browns score seven runs in the bottom of the first and dominate 16-4 for their third straight home win over the Yankees. St. Louis' Johnny Lucadello becomes the first switch-hitter in AL history to hit homers from both sides of the plate, the only two fourbaggers Lucadello hits in 17 games this season.

— The next day, New York would win, 9-0, but the lowly Browns, who would finish sixth, had dealt the Yankees a crippling blow. After their third St. Louis loss, the Yankees were in third place, 4½ games off the lead. Cleveland led 82-60, followed by: Detroit, 81-60; New York, 77-64; and Chicago, 78-65. The Tigers would grab the lead by a half game on September 17.

Sep 26—   New York sweeps Philadelphia in a twinbill, extending a win streak to eight games. The idle frontrunners, Detroit and Cleveland, have three games left with each other, and the Yanks still have hope. Detroit (89-62) leads Cleveland (87-64) by two games and New York (86-64) by 2½ games.

Sep 27—   With four games left, the Yankees pitch Marius Russo, who will finish at 14-8, and face Philadelphia's Johnny Babich, who will finish at 14-13. Babich, who felt he was not given a fair chance when he was with the Yankee organization, is bitter. He has already beaten the Yankees four times this year and he gets a pre-game pep-talk from Manager Connie Mack, who has vowed that the Yankees will not win five pennants in a row. Babich is hit hard but hangs in. His fielders catch everything and he gets hitting support from Sam Chapman. He wins, 6-2, eliminating New York from contention. It takes 90 wins to capture the flag and the Yankees' total will be 88. It is only the second time in McCarthy's reign that the Yankees fall short of 90 victories.

1941

The Yankees will finish at 101-53, rebounding to win the pennant by 17 games over second-place Boston, and Joe DiMaggio will hit safely in 56 straight games. DiMaggio will also lead the league in RBIs with 125 and will be the AL's MVP. Lefty Gomez and Red Ruffing with 15 wins apiece, will lead a balanced mound corps. New York will defeat Brooklyn in the World Series.

Smallish Brooklyn-born Phil Rizzuto joined the Yankees in 1941 and for 13 years played shortstop with exceptional skill. Casey Stengel rated Rizzuto a better fielder than Honus Wagner. "If I were a retired gentleman," Stengel said, "I would follow the Yankees around just to see Rizzuto work those miracles every day."

Feb 25—   The Yankees sell the contract of first baseman Babe Dahlgren to the Boston
Braves. Dahlgren, who has played first base in every Yankee game since
replacing Lou Gehrig, has good pop in his bat and is considered one of the
majors' best defensive first basemen. But to Joe McCarthy the six-foot
Dahlgren has arms that are "too short" and "makes easy plays look hard."
In 1941, playing for two NL teams, Dahlgren will hit .267 with 23 home
runs and 89 RBIs. Not a bad year.

— Dahlgren, of course, would always be remembered as the man who followed Gehrig at first base. He did not fill Gehrig's shoes—who could?—but
played quality ball for New York. In 1939, Dahlgren hit 15 homers and knocked
in 89 runs. The next year he raised his average from .235 to .264.

Apr 14—   On Opening Day in Washington, Marius Russo three-hits the Senators and
wins, 3-0. Joe DiMaggio manages to play in this opener and goes two for four.

— With Dahlgren gone, Joe McCarthy drastically revamped his infield. The
outstanding double-play combination of Jerry Priddy (2B) and Phil Rizzuto (SS)
was up from the minors and McCarthy had wanted to start Priddy and Rizzuto
and shift Joe Gordon to first base. But an ankle injury and an anemic batting
average would relegate Priddy to a utility infielder role. Another rookie up from
Kansas City, Johnny Sturm, took over at first base, played 124 games and
hit .239. Gordon, who felt strange at first base, returned to second where
he felt more at home. Gordon played 131 games at second and 30 games at
first. Red Rolfe anchored the infield at third base. When McCarthy finally got his
personnel aligned, he had a fine infield, one that turned at least one double
play over 18 consecutive games for a club record.

Apr 23—   New York's rookie shortstop, Phil Rizzuto, hits his first home run in the majors.
In the 11th inning at Yankee Stadium, with George Selkirk aboard, Rizzuto
homers off Boston's Charlie Wagner (12-8) to give the Yankees a 4-2 victory.

— Upon graduation from Richmond Hill High School in Brooklyn, the 5'6"
Rizzuto had tryouts with both the Dodgers and Giants. He was told he was too
small for pro ball. Scout Paul Krichell and Joe McCarthy of the Yankees believed
differently and Rizzuto in 1936 was planted in the farm system. He worked
his way up and in 1940, playing for Kansas City, was the minor leagues'
Player of the Year. The Scooter was on his way to a .307 season with the
Yankees.

May 2—   Joe DiMaggio reaches base safely and a streak of getting on base in
84 consecutive games is begun. But the Yankees lose, 8-1, in Chicago.

May 15—   It is Jimmy Dykes Day at Yankee Stadium in honor of the White Sox
manager who recently announced his retirement as a player. The White Sox
celebrate by beating the Yankees, 13-1, the Yank's eighth loss in 10 games.
New York rests in fourth place, 5½ games behind Cleveland, and the newspapers are describing this club as the weakest hitting Yankee team in years.
The Bronx Bombers need a lift. In the first inning, DiMaggio singles off
southpaw Edgar Smith (13-17). It is the only hit of the game for Joe, whose
average is .306, but it begins a phenomenal hitting streak.

May 24—   The Yankees trail, 6-5, with runners on second and third in the seventh inning
at the Stadium and DiMaggio due to bat. Joe has gone hitless and Boston
Manager Joe Cronin orders 22-year-old southpaw, Earl Johnson (4-5), to
pitch to the Yankee Clipper. Bad strategy. DiMaggio lines Johnson's first pitch
for a two-run single, giving the Yankees a victory and extending Joe's hitting
streak to 10 games.

May 27— In Washington, DiMaggio goes four for five against three different Senator pitchers, knocks in three runs and scores three runs. He also hits a home run in extending his hitting streak to 12 games. New York wins, 10-8.

May 28— Hitting in his 13th straight game, DiMaggio triples and scores a run in a night game at Griffith Stadium, the first game played under the lights in his streak. His triple is off Sid Hudson (13-14), who also gives George Selkirk the first pinch-hit grand slammer in Yankee history. New York wins, 6-5.

— This was the fourth career grand slam for Selkirk, one of the most underrated run-producers in Yankee history. Playing his entire, injury-hampered career with New York, Selkirk batted over .300 five times and had 100-plus RBI years in 1936 and 1939. Twinkletoes was a reserve outfielder in 1941-42, his playing career soon to give way to service with the Navy. Lifetime, Selkirk hit .290.

Jun 2— DiMaggio raps a pair of hits off the great Bob Feller (25-13), running his streak to 19 games, in a 7-5 loss in Cleveland. Afterwards, the Yankees travel to Detroit where, upon arrival, Joe McCarthy is informed by the hotel manager of Lou Gehrig's death. McCarthy and Bill Dickey (one of Lou's best friends) lead a delegation to New York for the funeral.

— Gehrig, who remained the Yankee captain throughout his illness, died at his home in the Riverdale section of the Bronx. He had been bedridden with amyotrophic lateral sclerosis for some time. The funeral was held two days later from the Christ Episcopal Church in Riverdale. His No. 4 uniform, the first retired by the Yankees but kept ready for him by clubhouse man Fred Logan, waited in a locker that is now sealed. Gehrig died 17 days before his 38th birthday, 16 years to the day he replaced Wally Pipp as the Yankee first baseman.

Jun 7— In St. Louis, DiMaggio makes three hits off three different pitchers, scores two runs and drives in one run, as he hits safely in his 22nd game in a row. Charlie Keller contributes a grand slam homer. The Yankees win, 11-7.

— The Yankee outfield of Keller-DiMaggio-Henrich may have been the club's— all of baseball's?—greatest, and 1941 was a banner year for the trio. Each of the outfielders hit at least 30 home runs—the first time in big league history for three teammates to perform the feat. They combined for 94 of New York's league-leading 151 fourbaggers. All three Yankee outfielders scored more than 100 runs and all three were excellent defensively.

Jun 8— New York sweeps a doubleheader in St. Louis by scores of 9-3 and 8-3 and extends its winning streak to eight games as DiMaggio extends his hitting streak to 24 games with a fabulous afternoon. In eight at bats, Joe makes four hits, including three homers and a double, knocks in seven runs and scores four runs. Dickey executes a rare catcher's unassisted double play—the first in Yankee history—in the first game. With the Browns' Johnny Berardino running from first base on the pitch, Bob Swift pops a foul down the first base line. Dickey makes the catch and touches first base for the second putout.

Jun 17— DiMaggio hits in his 30th straight game and establishes a new Yankee record. Joe's only hit is a bad-hop single that bounds off Chicago shortstop Luke Appling's shoulder—one of the few breaks DiMaggio gets in the streak. The hit, off Johnny Rigney (13-13), betters the 29-game club record jointly held by Roger Peckinpaugh and Earle Combs. But Chicago wins, 8-7.

Jun 24— At Yankee Stadium, the Browns' Bob Muncrief (13-9) retires DiMaggio the first three times Joe bats. But in the eighth inning, in Joe's final plate appearance, DiMaggio singles to extend his streak to 36 games. Muncrief's manager asks why he didn't walk Joe in his last appearance, and the rookie pitcher answers, That wouldn't have been fair—to him or to me. Hell, he's the greatest player I ever saw." The Yankees win easily, 9-1.

Jun 26—   Marius Russo hurls a one-hitter against St. Louis, the Browns' only hit a homer by George McQuinn, as the Yankees win, 4-1, and the DiMaggio streak stays alive. DiMaggio is hitless and due to bat fourth in the eighth inning. Red Rolfe walks with one out and McCarthy grants Henrich permission to sacrifice, thereby preventing any chance of his hitting into a double play and depriving Joe of a chance to keep his streak alive. Henrich executes a bunt and DiMaggio cracks a run-scoring double on the first pitch thrown by Eldon Auker (14-15). Joe's streak now stands at 38 games and the Yankees stand in first place. New York (39-25) leads Cleveland (41-27) by six percentage points.

Jun 28—   Philadelphia's Johnny Babich says he will halt DiMaggio's streak at Shibe Park. The Yankee Clipper soon learns that Babich plans to pitch around him. Joe walks in his first trip to the plate and nearly walks in his second at bat. He takes three balls, then strikes an outside pitch through the legs of Babich for a base hit. Joe later doubles. His streak is now at 40 games, tying him with Ty Cobb, until this date the sole holder of the second longest streak in AL history. And the Yankees are victorious again, 7-4.

Jun 29—   In a doubleheader played in 98-degree heat at Washington (the Yankees sweep by scores of 9-4 and 7-5), DiMaggio hits in his 41st and 42nd consecutive games, tying and breaking the 41-game AL record of George Sisler. In the opener, the Jolter bangs a sixth-inning double off the Senators' ace pitcher, Dutch Leonard (18-13), that rolls to the 423-foot sign. Joe experiences frustration early in the second game, lining out twice and flying out deep. In the seventh inning, DiMaggio is brushed back by Red Anderson (4-6). Then Joe strokes a line-drive single to left field to break Sisler's record. Most of the some 31,000 fans cheer wildly.

—   A streak of consecutive games in which the Yankees hit one or more home runs was snapped on this date at 25. This is a major league record.

Jul 1—   Before a packed house at Yankee Stadium DiMaggio hits in his 43rd and 44th consecutive games and reaches another milestone. He ties Wee Willie Keeler—holder of the *all-time* record. (Keeler in 1897 hit in 44 consecutive games for the NL's Baltimore Orioles under somewhat easier rules for the hitter.) The Yankees beat Boston, 7-2 and 9-2, the second game shortened by rain.

Jul 2—   In stifling 95-degree heat at Yankee Stadium, DiMaggio hits in his 45th consecutive game, breaking Keeler's record and setting a new big league record. Not that it is easy. Joe is robbed of hits in his first two at bats. But in his third trip the Yankee Clipper belts a three-run homer off Boston ace Dick Newsome (19-10). Joe receives a tremendous ovation from 52,832 fans as he rounds the bases and is told by Lefty Gomez, "You not only broke Keeler's record. You even used his formula—you hit'em where they ain't!" Gomez adds a bases-loaded two-run single in the six-run rally and New York wins, 8-4.

Jul 6—   The Yankees dedicate a monument to Lou Gehrig in center field two years and two days after Lou spoke to the Stadium crowd on his "day." It is a "tribute from the Yankee players to their beloved captain and teammate." In today's action, a doubleheader with Philadelphia, DiMaggio not only hits safely in games 47 and 48 but has a field day, going six for nine and knocking in four runs before a Stadium crowd of 60,918. Play stops for the All-Star Break following this 8-4 and 3-1 sweep by the Yankees. The Yankees have won nine consecutive games and lead Cleveland by 3½ games.

Jul 13— The Yankees extend a winning streak to 14 games and DiMaggio hits safely in both ends of a doubleheader before 50,387 in Chicago, his hitting streak reaching 52, then 53 games. In the opener, Joltin' Joe raps three singles, two of them off Ted Lyons (12-10), and scores two runs. He gets a single in the nightcap off Thornton Lee (22-11). The Yankees win twice, 8-1 and 1-0 in 11 innings.

Jul 16— At Cleveland's League Park DiMaggio hits in his 56th straight game, erasing the suspense early by hitting the first pitch thrown him by Al Milnar (12-19) in the first inning. He adds another single and a double and scores three runs, and the Yankees win, 10-3. Since breaking Keeler's record, Joe collects 24 hits in 44 official at bats; he hits for an average of .545 over the 11 games since the Keeler topper.

Jul 17— Before 67,468 at Municipal Stadium in Cleveland (the Indians used the larger Municipal Stadium for their big dates), DiMaggio's hitting streak is brought to a close. It ends at 56 games. DiMaggio is stopped only because of the defensive brilliance of Indian third sacker Ken Keltner, who robs Joe of two doubles. Al Smith (12-13) starts on the mound for Cleveland. Keltner fires to first in the first inning to nail Joe after backhanding his wicked two-bouncer over third base. DiMaggio walks in the fourth and in the seventh takes another Smith pitch for a hot smash to third. But Keltner again handles and nips Joe at first. In the eighth, DiMaggio faces reliever Jim Bagby (9-15) and drills a hard grounder up the middle that takes a bad hop, but shortstop Lou Boudreau fields it cleanly and begins a double play. Displaying no anger although his streak is all but ended, DiMaggio rounds first base and jogs to his position in center field. The Indians rally for two runs in the bottom of the ninth and the Yanks lead by a 4-3 score. One more Indian run—a tie score—and Joe might have another chance in extra innings. But Johnny Murphy puts out the fire and Lefty Gomez has his eighth victory, his sixth win in a row. The Cleveland management is ecstatic about stopping Joe's streak—except for the next day when the ballpark is less than half full.

— DiMaggio's hitting streak was stopped just five games short of Joe's personal best, his 61-game streak in the Pacific Coast League in 1933. Over the 56 games, Joe hit .408 (91 for 223) and had 16 doubles, four triples and 15 home runs. Coincidentally, Joe made 56 singles, scored 56 runs and had 55 RBIs. Not coincidentally, Joe's streak led a Yankee resurgence in the standings. New York rested comfortably in first place, seven games ahead of the second-place Indians. The win on this date was the Yanks' 17th in 18 games and 31st in 36 games. And from June 7 through the first game on July 27, the Yankees would go 40-6! No doubt about it, Joe's streak ignited the club.

Jul 18— Against Bob Feller, DiMaggio hits safely and starts a new, 16-game hitting streak. The Yankees will win 14 of the 16 games. When this mini-streak ends, DiMaggio will have hit safely in 72 of 73 games!

Jul 20— DiMaggio makes four extra-base hits in one game—three doubles and a home run. The Yankees win, 12-6, in 17 innings in Detroit.

Jul 31— The Yankees complete a blistering July, compiling a 25-4 record for an .862 winning percentage, the highest percentage for one month in AL history. The current AL standings reflect the shambles New York is making of the race. At 67-30, New York leads second-place Cleveland (55-42) by 12 games and third-place Boston (50-46) by 16½ games.

Aug 1— Lefty Gomez walks 11 batters and still manages to pitch a shutout. He sets a still-standing big league record for most walks in a shutout victory. Lefty also allows only five hits in beating the Browns, 9-0, at the Stadium.

— Following his poor 3-3 record of 1940, Gomez rebounded with a fine 15-5 mark in 1941, good enough to put Lefty back on top of the Yankee pitching staff. It was his final big season.

Aug 29— The Yankee players throw a party in DiMaggio's honor at Washington's Shoreham Hotel. They present Joe with a sterling silver cigar humidor on which their names are engraved below the following inscription: "Presented to Joe DiMaggio by his fellow players on the New York Yankees to express their admiration for his consecutive-game hitting record, 1941."

— There was little argument over who was the chief factor in the Yankee pennant runaway. It was DiMaggio. And when the ballots for the Most Valuable Player were counted, DiMaggio would edge Ted Williams, 291 points to 254. Besides winning the RBI title, Joe would hit 30 homers and bat .357. Williams would finish at .406 (the last time a big leaguer hit over .400) and would win the home run title with 37. But the Baseball Writers felt DiMaggio's hitting streak was the season's outstanding accomplishment.

Sep 4— The Yankees defeat the Red Sox, 6-3, at Fenway Park and win the pennant on what will remain the earliest clinching date in big league history. They gain their 12th pennant in their 136th game behind the five-hit pitching of Atley Donald.

— The Yankees ran away with the pennant—their record on this date was 91-45 for a winning percentage of .669—with only three .300 hitters (DiMaggio, Rizzuto and Ruffing) and two 15-game winners (Ruffing and Gomez).

Sep 11— Charlie Keller chips a bone in his ankle sliding into second base and his foot goes into a cast for three weeks. But Keller will be in the line-up for the opening of the World Series.

— At the time of his injury, Keller had 122 RBIs to DiMaggio's 112 and Williams' 111. He trailed Williams in homers by only one, 34 to 33. But Keller had no more RBIs or homers while sidelined and finished as the AL's runner-up to DiMaggio in RBIs and runner-up to Williams in homers.

Oct 1— The first-ever World Series between Brooklyn and New York opens at Yankee Stadium and Red Ruffing wins his fifth straight complete game in World Series play, 3-2. For the Yankees, Joe Gordon hits a solo home run in the second, Bill Dickey has a run-scoring double in the fourth and Gordon has a run-scoring single in the sixth. But the Dodgers will even the Series the next day, snapping the Yankees' 10-game winning streak in World Series play.

Oct 5— The Yankees win Game 4, 7-4, and take a three-games-to-one lead in one of wildest games in World Series history. Brooklyn takes a 4-3 lead into the top of the ninth. Hugh Casey retires two batters and gets Tommy Henrich to swing at strike three. The Ebbets Field faithful let out a collective cheer; they figure the Series is knotted. But the elusive pitch, probably a spitball, gets by catcher

Mickey Owen. Henrich alertly sprints to first base to keep the Yankees alive. What follows is the only sustained Yankee barrage of the Series—DiMaggio singles to left, Keller doubles (his fourth hit) off the right field wall for two runs, Dickey walks and Gordon doubles in two more runs. No one in the ballpark can believe the rapid turn of events. The winning pitcher in relief, Johnny Murphy, retires the disheartened Dodgers in order in the bottom of the ninth.

Oct 6—   The Yankees wrap up the Series with a 3-1 victory in Game 5 at Ebbets Field. It is New York's 32nd win in their last 36 games in World Series competition, and their eighth consecutive World Championship in as many World Series appearances. Joe McCarthy's sixth World Series triumph breaks a tie with Connie Mack. The game lacks suspense with Ernie Bonham pitching a four-hitter. Henrich contributes a home run in the fifth inning, following which there is almost a fight. Wyatt twice knocks down DiMaggio, before Joe flies deep to Pete Reiser in center field. As Joe trots toward the dugout, he exchanges words with Wyatt. They start to go for each other and both dugouts empty, but a fight is averted by the umpires. When the Dodgers go down one-two-three in the bottom of the ninth, the Yankees begin their celebration and the Dodgers look forward to next year. Gordon leads all hitters, batting .500, and the deep Yankee pitching staff has an ERA of 1.80.

The day after Mickey Owens' famous missed catch of a strikeout pitch in the 1941 World Series, Ernie "Tiny" Bonham, center, pitched a four-hitter against Brooklyn to wrap up the Series for New York. Mobbing Bonham, from left, are Red Rolfe, Phil Rizzuto, Johnny Strum and Joe Gordon.

1942

The Yankees will finish at 103-51 and repeat as pennant winners, nine games in front of second-place Boston. The club will be led by Joe Gordon, who will hit .322 and win the MVP, and Joe DiMaggio, who will drive in 114 runs. Ernie Bonham will finish at 21-5 to lead the pitching staff. A great season except for its climax; the Cardinals will take the World Series in five games.

Jan 15— In reply to Commissioner Landis' plea for guidance on baseball's role in a time of total war, President Roosevelt, some five weeks after the Japanese attack on Pearl Harbor, says, "I honestly feel it would be best for the country to keep baseball going... These players are a definite recreational asset to their fellow citizens—and that, in my judgment, is thoroughly worthwhile." But before spring training begins, the Yankees will have lost reserve catcher Ken Silvestri and first baseman Johnny Sturm to the Armed Forces.

Mar 12— Three days after holdouts Red Ruffing, Bill Dickey, Joe Gordon, and Charlie Keller come to terms, Ed Barrow signs Joe DiMaggio following a one-hour meeting. Thus ends a bitter holdout, similar to the one in 1938. It began when Barrow suggested that DiMaggio take a pay cut, this coming after his great 1941 season. But the Yankee Clipper signs for $43,750, a raise over his $37,500 contract of the previous year.

Apr 14— On Opening Day in Washington, Red Ruffing, who will go 14-7 this year, three-hits the Senators and wins, 7-0. Ruffing contributes two singles and two RBIs toward his cause. For the second straight year, Joe DiMaggio plays in the opener and has a single, a run scored and an RBI.

Apr 15— DiMaggio leads New York to a 9-3 win over Washington with a homer, double and single and five RBIs. In the fifth inning, DiMaggio wallops his first four-bagger of the year, a clout off Bobo Newsom that flies 450 feet into Griffith Stadium's center field bleachers, bounces a few times and stops more than 500 feet from home plate.

Apr 22— At Yankee Stadium, DiMaggio hits his 200th career homer and two triples, all of them long blasts. The home run travels over 400 feet, one triple goes over 430 feet in the air to center field, and the second triple is to Death Valley in left-center field.

— DiMaggio would finish at .305 with 21 homers, but he would not lead the league in any offensive categories. For him it was an off-year. In June, he would suffer a batting slump and hear, at home and on the road, what he had not heard since the days immediately following his 1938 holdout—boos. But for the first time in his Yankee career, DiMaggio played in all 154 games.

May 5— At Yankee Stadium, the Yankees trail Chicago, 4-0, then win, 5-4. DiMaggio leads the rebellion. He has two homers and his 10th-inning triple wins it for New York in a great individual effort.

Jun 14— Gordon hits safely in his 29th game, tying the second longest streak in Yankee history. Begun May 13, Flash's streak is snapped in the second game of today's double win over St. Louis (6-1, 5-4) at Yankee Stadium. Joe is having his greatest season, hitting .322 with 18 home runs and 103 RBIs. Two of his homers are grand slams. He will win the MVP Award.

Jul 6—   The All-Star Game, played at the Polo Grounds, is won by the AL, 3-1, under
           Joe McCarthy. Starter Spud Chandler yields only two hits over four scoreless
           innings (the three-inning rule is waived this year) and earns the win. DiMaggio
           goes two for four, Henrich doubles and scores a run in four trips, and Gordon
           is hitless in four at bats. Game proceeds go to war charities.

Jul 12—   New York drops the first game of a doubleheader at Yankee Stadium but
           rebounds to win the second, but not without a struggle. With one out and Dickey
           on base in the bottom of the 13th, Hassett belts a two-run homer to give the
           Yankees and pitcher Marv Breuer a 3-1 win over 21-year-old Hal Newhouser.
           Afterwards, Joe McCarthy tells Hassett that his homer was all-important and
           that the pennant will now be won by the Yankees. The contenders are still
           relatively close, the Yankees (53-28) leading Boston (48-32) by 4½ games
           and Cleveland (49-36) by 6 games.

Jul 18—   Bill Dickey is hurt and the Yankees turn to Dickey's backup, Buddy Rosar. But
           without permission, Rosar returns to hometown Buffalo to take a police can-
           didate's exam. He rejoins the Yankees three days later and is fined $250.
           Rosar says he wants to be able to provide for his family in case the war-caused
           uncertainties of the time torpedo baseball.

           — Rosar was discovered by Mrs. Joe McCarthy who spotted his play in an
           amateur game. She told Joe about Buddy who in turn passed the information
           on to Yankee scout Gene McCann. Buddy was signed and, as an expert
           receiver and high-average hitter, he moved up the Yankee farm ladder. From
           1939-42, as Dickey's backup, he hit .273. But his future with New York was
           closed out with the AWOL episode. He would be traded in December and go
           on to have many more fine seasons in the AL.

Aug 12—   Keller hits his second grand slam homer of the year. The clout helps the
           Bombers defeat Boston, 8-4, at home. Charlie is having another big season.
           He will hit for a .292 average and knock out 26 homers.

Aug 14—   The Yankees turn seven double plays, a still-standing AL record, against
           Philadelphia.

           — The best double-play act in the AL in 1942 was the Gordon-Rizzuto com-
           bination. Gordon and Rizzuto were league leaders in turning double plays at
           their respective positions and their combined total of 235 remains the third
           highest by a double-play combination in Yankee history.

Aug 23-   Between the games of a doubleheader at Yankee Stadium, Babe Ruth faces
           Walter Johnson in a benefit for a War Bonds Campaign. He hits Johnson's
           first and 21st pitches into the right field stands to the delight of some 69,000
           spectators. With the second shot, which is a tad foul, the tiring Babe goes into
           his classic home run trot one last time in the House that Ruth Built.

Aug 30—   Tommy Henrich plays in his last Yankee game before joining the Coast Guard.
           When Henrich comes to bat for the last time, the Stadium public address
           announcer informs the large Sunday crowd of Henrich's impending departure.
           The spectators rise as one and give Henrich, who has three hits on the day,
           one of the greatest ovations in Stadium history. Roy Cullenbine, whose con-
           tract was purchased from Washington, is Henrich's replacement and will hit
           .364 in 21 games for New York.

Sep 2—   Hank Borowy, who will be 15-4 this year, would have had a no-hitter against
           St. Louis except for Harlond Clift, who gets the only hit off him. Clift, who will be

a .274 hitter this year, has a habit of personally messing up no-hitters. He has spoiled three in the last four years.

Sep 14— New York clinches its 13th pennant with Ernie Bonham notching his 20th win of the season, 8-3, in the Yanks' 145th game. Bonham gets most of his support from the Yankee Clipper, who belts a home run and lashes three singles. It would be several days before the Cardinals clinched the NL with a record of 106-48 (better than the Yanks' 103-51).

Sep 30— The World Series opens in St. Louis and Red Ruffing wins his fifth Series opener, beating the Cardinals, 7-4. Ruffing has a no-hitter until Terry Moore singles with two out in the eighth. The Yankees grab a 7-0 lead on the strength of four errors by the Cardinals, three hits by DiMaggio, two runs scored by Rolfe and two RBIs by Hassett. But the Cardinals throw a scare into the AL champs by scoring four runs in the bottom of the ninth. The Redbirds drive Ruffing from the mound and load the bases. Then Spud Chandler retires Stan Musial on a grounder to Hassett for the game's final out. Their confidence restored, the Cards will win the next three games.

Oct 5— Winning, 4-2, the Cardinals capture the Series in five games. Johnny Beazley (21-6) wins his second complete game in the Series while Ruffing loses after six straight wins in World Series competition. Going into the ninth, the score is deadlocked at 2-2, but Whitey Kurowski's two-run homer puts St. Louis ahead in the ninth. In the bottom of the ninth, Gordon singles and Dickey reaches on an error. But Gordon is picked off second by catcher Walker Cooper and the rally goes flat. The next two hitters are retired and the game and Series are over. Phil Rizzuto, who homers in this game, leads all hitters at .381.

— In the minds of most people, the Cardinals were huge upset winners of the 1942 Series. And the team that was supposed to win drew criticism. Asked Joe McCarthy, in reference to the critics: "Have they forgotten that this ball club had won eight World Series in a row? What do you have to do—win all the time? Well, I got my name in the papers this time, anyway."

Nov 6— Frank Crosetti and Joe Gordon are punished for their part in an argument in Game 3 of the World Series. For pushing Umpire Summers, Crosetti is suspended for the first 30 days of the 1943 season and is fined $250. For a lesser role in the incident, Gordon is fined $250 but escapes suspension.

— The Yankees were put into a bind at shortstop. Phil Rizzuto entered the Navy with the end of the World Series and would miss three baseball seasons. Now, with the 31-year-old Crosetti sacked for the first 30 days of 1943, the job falls to 24-year-old infielder Snuffy Stirnweiss, who would hit .219 in 83 games in 1943. In addition, third baseman Red Rolfe, after a .219 season in 1942, retires to coach college baseball.

Dec 29— Red Ruffing is inducted into the U.S. Army Air Corps, and, at the age of 38, his baseball future is very much in doubt. Ruffing, missing four toes on his left foot (he lost them in a coal mine accident as a teenager) is accepted for non-combat duty.

1943

The Yankees will finish at 98-56 and win their third consecutive pennant, 13½ games in front of second-place Washington. Charlie Keller will hit 31 home runs, Nick Etten will drive in 107 runs and Bill Dickey will hit .351. Not only will Spud Chandler be the league's leading pitcher at 20-4, but he will lead all players in the MVP competition. The Yankees will win their 10th World Championship.

Jan 22— The Yankees obtain Nick Etten (1B) from the Philadelphia Phillies for Tom Padden (C), Al Gerheauser (P) and a sum reported at $10,000. A new Philadelphia owner, William Cox, will attempt to get Etten back in the spring by having Commissioner Landis void the deal. But Landis upholds the transaction.

— Etten was a fine first baseman who in 1941 hit .311 for the Phillies. With Hassett in the Armed Forces, Etten was the Yanks' regular first sacker through the 1946 season. He would be remembered somewhat unfairly as the classic wartime ballplayer. In three consecutive seasons, Etten drove in 107, 91 and 111 runs, leading the league with the latter figure in 1946. And in 1944 Etten won the league home run title with 22.

Jan 25— The Yankees sell the contract of pitcher Lefty Gomez to the Boston Braves. Gomez, released by the Braves in the spring, will sign with Washington, pitch one game, lose and retire.

— Gomez had a sensational 13 years with the Yankees, posting a record of 189-101. The Yankees lost (within a month) both sides of the greatest righty-lefty combination in club history. Between 1930-42, Red Ruffing and Gomez combined for a record of 408-221. Only two righty-lefty tandems of the early 20th century—Christy Mathewson and Hooks Wiltse, who combined for 438 wins, and Chief Bender and Eddie Plank, who combined for 419 wins—produced more victories than Ruffing and Gomez in major league baseball.

Feb 16— Joe DiMaggio's North Beach, Calif., draft board calls the Jolter to the Armed Forces. The induction of a star like DiMaggio dramatically paints the picture of the lean days in store for baseball as the war effort soaks up the game's stars.

— When asked about a remark by the nation's coordinator of manpower, Paul V. McNutt, asserting in effect that baseball was not essential, Barrow barked, "Who ever said it was?" The big leagues were asked to train close to home and Joe McCarthy and Paul Krichell selected Asbury Park, N.J., as the site for the Yanks' spring camp. The weather could not have been worse.

Apr 22— The first of the three "war seasons" opens at Yankee Stadium, one day late because of rain. The Yankees beat Washington, 5-4, and quickly assume first place. Joe McCarthy had predicted that the Senators, a seventh-place team in 1942, would be the team to beat. Although there will be no real pennant race, McCarthy will be proved right.

May 31— At Yankee Stadium, Joe Gordon hits a bases-loaded homer, the Yanks' only grand slam in 1943 (after hitting five in 1942), in the second game of a doubleheader with Chicago which the Yanks win, 10-4, after dropping the opener, 10-5.

— Gordon was off the marks of his 1942 MVP season, this slippage coming after signing late and being even later in reporting to spring training. Flash's average (he hit only .095 in the 1942 World Series) fell from .322 to .249; his RBIs dropped from 103 to 69. But he would still hit 17 home runs, second most on the club, and play second base with his customary acrobatic skill.

Jun 26— Boston's ace righthander, Tex Hughson, who will go 12-15 this year for the seventh-place Red Sox, personally beats the Yankees for the eigth time in a row.

Joe Gordon is honored early in the 1943 season for winning the AL's MVP Award for 1942. Taking part in the ceremony is New York political leader and former U.S. Postmaster General, James A. Farley. Joe McCarthy can be seen between Farley and Gordon.

Jul 13—   The AL wins the first All-Star Game played at night, 5-3, with little help from Yankees. Manager Joe McCarthy of the AL has six members from his Yankees on the roster, but uses not a single one. He is aparently stung by accusations that in the past he has favored his own players. McCarthy wins in Philadelphia's Shibe Park without Yankees. Spud Chandler, Ernie Bonham, Bill Dickey, Joe Gordon, Charlie Keller and Johnny Lindell have only to relax and watch the proceedings.

Jul 25—   In the second game of a Sunday doubleheader at Yankee Stadium, an announcement is made that the Italian dictator, Mussolini, has resigned. Cheers and dancing in the aisles follow; Mussolini is the first of the Axis leaders to bite the dust in World War II.

Jul 28—   In a benefit for the Red Cross, Babe Ruth plays in his final baseball game, and fittingly, it is played at Yankee Stadium. Ruth manages a bunch of old timers who call themselves the Yanklands. The Yanklands play a Ted Williams-managed team called the University of North Carolina Pre-Flight Cloudbusters. The 'Busters are ex-big leaguers training for naval flight commissions. Ruth's team loses, 11-5, and as a pinch-hitter, the Babe walks off Johnny Sain. Babe also hits a foul ball off Sain, the last time he ever hit a pitched ball. About $30,000 is raised for the Red Cross.

Aug 11—   A home run by Charlie Keller ruins a bid for a no-hitter by former Yankee teammate Steve Sundra of the Browns.

             — Without DiMaggio and Henrich, the Yankees were left with one-third of their great outfield—Keller. Charlie would hit 31 percent of the Yanks' league-leading total of 100 home runs. Detroit's Rudy York and Keller would battle to the end for the home run crown. York won it, 34 to 31.

At Yankee Stadium, the Yankees beat Detroit, 2-1, in 14 innings and clinch the AL pennant in their 144th game of the season. The Yankees are victorious because they take the one-run games. They will win 38 games by margins of a single run. St. Louis in the NL has an easier time, winning by 18 games.

Oct 5— The World Series opens at Yankee Stadium and Spud Chandler hurls a seven-hitter to defeat St. Louis, 4-2. The Cardinals score a run in the second but from right field Tuck Stainback nails Danny Litwhiler at the plate, preventing any additional scoring. In the bottom of the fourth, Frank Crosetti reaches on pitcher Max Lanier's error, steals second, moves to third on Billy Johnson's bunt single and scores as Charlie Keller hits into a double play. Joe Gordon follows with a 450-foot homer, giving the Yankees a 2-1 lead. St. Louis rallies to tie but New York scores twice in the sixth; Crosetti singles, Johnson singles, and on Lanier's wild pitch, Crosetti scores from second and Johnson goes from first to third. Johnson scores on Bill Dickey's bloop single.

Yankee Frank Crosetti steals second base in the fourth inning of the opening game of the 1943 World Series. He will later score as the Yankees defeat St. Louis, 4-2.

Oct 6— St. Louis wins Game 2 at Yankee Stadium, 4-3, behind Mort Cooper's courageous six-hitter, this coming several hours after learning of his father's death. His brother, Walker, is the catcher.

Oct 7— Hank Borowy allows only two runs in eight innings, Johnny Murphy retires the side in the ninth and the Yankees win Game 3, 6-2, at Yankee Stadium. The Yankees trail, 2-1, in the eighth inning when they have the most important rally of the Series. Johnny Lindell singles and continues to second on an error. Snuffy Stirnweiss bunts and the first baseman's throw to third is in time to cut down Lindell, but Whitey Kurowski drops the ball after Lindell crashes into him. Stirnweiss moves to second on a fly ball and Crosetti is intentionally walked. Billy Johnson follows with a bases-loaded triple. The Yankees score five runs before they are finished. The Series shifts to St. Louis where the Yankees will win Game 4 behind Marius Russo.

Oct 8— Ed Barrow, the 75-year-old president of the Yankees, is admitted to New Rochelle Hospital with a heart ailment, fatigue and arthritis. He will be allowed to listen to the final two games of the Series. His condition is serious but this is not made known. He will remain hospitalized until November 24 and will not return to his office until the spring.

Oct 11— Chandler pitches a seven-hit shutout, winning, 2-0, and the Yankees win their 10th World Championship in a pitching duel between Chandler and Cooper, who strikes out the first five Yankee batters. Cooper slips only once. With two out in the sixth, he gives up a single to Keller and a two-run homer to Dickey. Chandler manages a shutout only through grit, stranding 11 Cards on the bases. The Series ends with Chandler stranding two runners and getting Debs Garms to ground out to Gordon.

Joe McCarthy gleefully pats Spud Chandler on the head following Chandler's shutout victory over the Cardinals in the finale of the 1943 World Series. McCarthy is especially euphoric because the Yankees avenged their conquest at the hands of the Cardinals in the 1942 World Series.

— Marty Marion led all hitters at .357. Billy Johnson, the AL's top rookie during the regular season with 94 RBIs, was the only Yankee to hit .300 and he hit exactly that. But the Yanks' pitching staff, led by Chandler with two wins, allowed only seven earned runs for an ERA of 1.46, and pitching proved the difference. The conquest of the Cards was Joe McCarthy's seventh and final World Series triumph and in many ways it was his sweetest. His first World Series win in 1932 over Chicago avenged his firing by the Cubs; similarly, this one avenged the loss to the Cardinals in the 1942 Series. And McCarthy proved he was not a "pushbutton" manager, winning in a year when DiMaggio, Henrich, Rizzuto, Selkirk, Hassett and Ruffing were in the service.

1944

The Yankees will finish at 83-71, in third place and six games behind the pennant-winning St. Louis Browns. Snuffy Stirnweiss will lead the AL in hits with 205, and Nick Etten will capture the home run crown with 22. Hank Borowy, at 17-12, will lead the Yankee twirlers.

Apr 18— The Yankees, who held their spring training camp in Atlantic City, open the season in Boston with Hank Borowy blanking the Red Sox, 3-0, before a sparse crowd of 8,520. Johnny Lindell hits a solo homer. Joe McCarthy starts the following line-up (in batting order): Snuffy Stirnweiss (2B), Bud Metheny (RF), Nick Etten (1B), Lindell (CF), Don Savage (3B), Ed Levy (LF), Oscar Grimes (SS), Mike Garbark (C) and Borowy (P).

— As a result of the war, the Yanks fielded a team made up of the available. Not *one* of this team's members had started for the Yankees on Opening Day in 1941. Of the starters from that year's opener, eight were in the military and the ninth, Red Rolfe, was coaching college ball. The club's roster quality was definitely reduced.

Apr 22— At Yankee Stadium, Spud Chandler makes a start against Washington, his only appearance in 1944. The Yankees win, 6-3, but Chandler, who is relieved by Atley Donald in the seventh inning, gets no decision. Donald, a 13-game winner this year, gets credit for the win. Chandler is now Army-bound and will not return to the club until late in the 1945 season.

Apr 25— New York centerfielder Johnny Lindell belts a grand slam homer at Yankee Stadium as the Yankees lose to Philadelphia, 8-4.

— Lindell joined the Yankee organization in 1936, and spent several years as a highly promising righthanded pitcher. He pitched in 25 games in 1942 and was 2-1 with one save. But with Joe DiMaggio in the military service, Lindell made the club in 1943 as a reserve outfielder. He proved to be the best centerfielder the Yankees had. He played the position regularly and hit .245. In the 1944 campaign, just two years after working as a pitcher, Lindell would hit .300 with 18 homers and 103 RBIs while patroling the fabled center field real estate that belonged to DiMaggio.

Jun 26— More than 50,000 fans trek to the Polo Grounds to witness the first, and only, three-sided baseball game, an idea of New York sportwriters to raise funds for the War Bonds campaign. The "tripleheader" among the Yankees, Giants and Dodgers is actually a nine-inning game with each team playing two innings, at bat and in the field, then sitting out a full inning. Thus, each team plays a full six innings. The final score: Dodgers 5, Yankees 1, and Giants 0. Several field events are also held (the Yanks' Snuffy Stirnweiss winning the sprint competition) and more than $6,500,000 is raised in the bonds campaign.

Jul 11— The NL wins the All-Star Game, 7-1, the proceeds from which go to buy sports equipment for the members of the Armed Forces. Joe McCarthy is the losing manager. The Yanks' Hank Borowy starts the game, blanks the NL on three hits over three innings and knocks in the AL's only run. Yankee catcher Rollie Hemsley, who will hit .268 this year in 81 games before going into the military, starts the game and is hitless in two at bats. The game is played in Pittsburgh and the Yanks' Joe Page, winner of four of his first five decisions and a resident of the Pittsburgh area, is on the AL roster. Page has many supporters and figures to have a fun All-Star night, but a tragic turn is taken when Joe's father suffers a stroke and dies. Page doesn't get to perform in the game.

Aug 4— Frank Crosetti starts his first game of the season. Crosetti had been voluntarily retired and was working at a defense job in Stockton, Calif. But the Crow reconsidered, joined the team in July and today makes his first start. Crosetti will hit .239 in 55 games playing his familiar shortstop position and replacing Mike Milosevich, who hit .247 in 94 games.

— Joe McCarthy began the season with only Nick Etten back from his 1943 infield. Joe Gordon and Billy Johnson were in the service. Gordon's replacement at second base, Snuffy Stirnweiss, would lead the AL in four offensive statistics, including stolen bases with 55. Johnson's replacement at third base, Oscar Grimes, would hit .279.

Aug 13— At Yankee Stadium, in his team's 10-1 win in the first of two games, the Yankees' Russ Derry hits a grand slam homer. Chicago wins the nightcap, 11-3. Derry, one of a legion of spare outfielders, hits .254 in 38 games.

Aug 17— The Yankees beat Cleveland, 10-3. Yankee centerfielder Johnny Lindell ties an AL record by rapping four consecutive doubles in one game. He remains the only Yankee to ever accomplish the feat. Lindell drives in two runs and scores twice.

Sep 4— The Yankees sweep Philadelphia, 10-0 and 14-0, their first double-shutout sweep since 1917. Monk Dubiel wins the opener and Mel Queen, who will win six of nine decisions this year, blanks the A's in the nightcap.

Oct 1— The Browns defeat the Yankees while Detroit loses, allowing the Browns to finish the season in first place, one game ahead of the Tigers. It is the only pennant in the Browns' history. Pitcher Sig Jakucki beats the Yankees in St. Louis, 5-2, in what turns out to be his last big league victory. The Browns sweep the four-game series. But back in New York, Ed Barrow praises his team and McCarthy. Barrow feels McCarthy never managed better. Joe had been ill for much of the early season. Art Fletcher managed in the games that he missed.

1945

The Yankees will finish at 81-71, in fourth place but only 6½ games behind pennant-winning Detroit. Snuffy Stirnweiss will win the batting championship with a .309 average and Nick Etten will have a league-leading 111 RBIs. Bill Bevens, 13-9, will have the most wins on the Yankee pitching staff.

Jan 26— For only the second time in history, the ownership of the Yankees completely changes. The Ruppert heirs sell the club to Larry MacPhail, Dan Topping and Del Webb for $2.8 million. The transfer includes the Yanks' minor league clubs in Newark, Kansas City and other smaller cities that form the farm chain run by George Weiss. MacPhail, who put the deal together and who reportedly ventured far less cash than either Topping or Webb, says he plans to remain in the background and let Ed Barrow run the club. The war continues but the new owners are already looking to a prosperous and progressive post-war era.

— The new owners were a varied and visible trio. MacPhail was a dynamic and bombastic veteran baseball executive who had done wonders for Cincinnati and Brooklyn, and who, among other things, brought night baseball to the majors. He went to war as a major and returned as a colonel. Topping was a playboy heir to millions but was a sound businessman in his own right. Webb, a construction engineer and contracting tycoon in Arizona, had played baseball professionally as a young man but did not fulfill his dream of making the majors. He was a great fan of the game.

Feb 21— Larry MacPhail replaces Ed Barrow as president and general manager of the Yankees. Three months shy of his 77th birthday, Barrow becomes chairman of the board, a position that entails little.

— Barrow disliked the MacPhail style and gradually withdrew from the club. MacPhail would move the Yankees' business offices from 42nd Street to fashionable Fifth Avenue. Legend has it that Barrow, who hated phoniness and pretentiousness in all forms, walked into the lavish new quarters, grunted, and walked out, not returning for some time.

Apr 17— On Opening Day against Boston at Yankee Stadium, following a second spring at Atlantic City, Yankee outfielder Russ Derry unloads a grand slam homer in an 8-4 New York win.

— As the Yanks' fourth outfielder in 1945, Derry would hit only .225 but have 13 home runs and 45 RBIs in only 253 at bats. Nick Etten would be the only Yankee to outhomer Derry, and he would hit 18 homers. Derry would hit another grand slam homer (his third as a Yankee) in just 12 days. His 17 homers over 1944-45 were hit in only 367 at-bats.

Jun 21— The Yankees enjoy their most productive inning since 1920 (when they scored 14 runs in one inning), scoring 13 times in the fifth inning at Boston. The Yankees use five singles, four doubles, four walks and one Red Sox error in the rally and win, 14-4, for Monk Dubiel, who will finish the year at 10-9 and who scores three runs in the game.

— One of the catalysts of the uprising, Snuffy Stirnweiss, had a great 1945. He would finish the year leading the league in seven major offensive categories, including batting average—.309, the lowest since Elmer Flick hit .306 to lead the league in 1905—yet he would lose the MVP Award to Detroit's Hal Newhouser, who led AL pitchers in eight major categories and went 25-9.

Jul 16— After two and a half years of military service, 41-year-old Red Ruffing returns to the Yankees and finds a lot of new faces. Of all the players from his last Yankee team in 1942, the only ones remaining are Frank Crosetti, Tuck Stainback, Hank Borowy, Ernie Bonham, Atley Donald and Jim Turner.

— The Yankees lost Johnny Lindell, who hit .283 in 41 games, to the service during the season. But others were beginning to return from the Armed Forces. Besides Ruffing, Charlie Keller returned from the Merchant Marine and would hit .301 in 44 games. Catcher Aaron Robinson returned and hit .281 in 50 games. And Spud Chandler, taken by the Army after pitching just one game in 1944, returned to go 2-1 in four starts.

Jul 26— Red Ruffing makes his first appearance since the 1942 World Series and pitches six shutout innings against Philadelphia. Almost unbelievably, Ruffing will finish the year winning 7 of 10 decisions and with an ERA of 2.89. All of this from a 41-year-old who was 30 pounds overweight when he was released from the service (he lost half of it in early workouts) and who suffers from assorted aches and pains.

Jul 27— The Yankees sell the contract of pitcher Hank Borowy to the Chicago Cubs for a reported $97,500 after Borowy clears waivers in the AL. Borowy is the Yanks' best pitcher with a 10-5 record. MacPhail is asked why the Yankees would sell their top pitcher when they have a chance to win the pennant. "A hundred thousand dollars," answers MacPhail. He is asked if the Yankees need the money that badly. "No," says Larry. "But this was a good chance to sell a pitcher who never has been a winner in the last month or so of a season." But Borowy makes MacPhail look bad. He leads the Cubs to the NL pennant, winning 11 of 13 decisions and a pair of games in the World Series. In another controversial aspect of the deal, some wonder how a pitcher of Borowy's ability can clear waivers. But MacPhail vigorously denies any complicity or "gentlemen's agreements" among the AL owners. Unconvinced, contending NL clubs are outraged, and more strict waiver rules are made as the result of this deal.

— Borowy, a native of Bloomfield, N.J., who attended Fordham University, began his Yankee career in 1942 and posted successive won-lost marks of 15-4, 14-9, 17-12 and 10-5. He was a combined 21-7 for the Yanks and Cubs in 1945, after which he never enjoyed the same kind of success. His departure from the Yankees undoubtedly was without the blessing of Joe McCarthy, who was ill at the time with a stomach ailment and was resting at his farm near Tonawanda, N.Y. MacPhail was busy denying rumors of Marse Joe's resignation.

Aug 19— In the first game of a twinbill at Chicago, the Yankees win, 4-2, and snap a nine-game losing streak, their longest since 1913. But the Yanks lose the nightcap, 2-0.

— The losing skein proved a key factor in the Yankees' failure to finish first. After all, it took only 88 wins to win the pennant and New York fell seven short. Another big factor was the Yanks' 3.45 ERA, fifth highest in the AL and 53 points behind the Senators' staff. The Bronx Bombers led the AL in several offensive categories, including homers (93) and runs scored (676).

Aug 30— Yankee righthander Bill Bevens pitches a one-hitter against Boston and wins, 7-1, at Yankee Stadium. The Red Sox are hitless until Bob Johnson doubles home Catfish Metkovich in the seventh inning. Johnson, a .280 hitter this year, also destroyed a no-hit bid by Lefty Gomez eight years earlier. Frank Crosetti supports Bevens with a grand slam homer off Boo Ferriss in the fourth inning.

Sep 1— In Washington, Yankee outfielder Hersh Martin, who hits .267 this year in 117 games, becomes the sixth Yankee to be walked five times in one game. But New York loses, 3-0.

Sep 2— In the second game of a doubleheader at Washington, Bill Zuber loses by shutout for the third straight time, the Senators winning, 3-0.

— The Yankees lost 14 games by shutout this year and Zuber lost seven of them, a Yankee club record and only three less than Walter Johnson's AL record of 10 in 1909. Zuber would have an ERA of 3.19 and finish 5-11. Probably no Yankee pitcher has ever pitched so well and fared so badly.

Sep 4— Paul Schreiber, the Yanks' batting practice pitcher since 1937, makes a relief appearance for the team.* In relief of Al Gettel in the sixth inning, Schreiber goes 3⅓ innings, allowing zero hits, two walks and striking out Paul Richards. What makes this outing so remarkable is that Schreiber, one month shy of his 43rd birthday, has not pitched in a professional game since he was with Allentown of the Eastern League in 1931 or in a major league game since he was with Brooklyn in 1923! Schreiber will pitch in two games without a decision. Gettel is charged with the loss in Detroit's 10-0 win at Yankee Stadium.

Sep 13— At Yankee Stadium, Chicago beats the Yankees, 7-0, in 10 innings. Zuber carries a one-hitter into the 10th inning, the only hit coming from Johnny Dickshot (.302) in the seventh, before he and reliever Jim Turner are shelled. The defeat drops New York to fourth place, eight games behind first-place Detroit.

Sep 14— Joe DiMaggio is released from the Army. He had been suffering from a duodenal ulcer, and, while hospitalized, had received a call from Larry MacPhail, who assured Joe he was wanted back with the Yankees in 1946 at his pre-war salary.

Nov 20— At the Yankee offices, DiMaggio formally signs his Yankee contract for the 1946 season. He notes that dealing with MacPhail is much easier than dealing with Barrow. The Japanese have surrendered, the war is over—and wartime baseball is no more.

1946

The Yankees will finish at 87-67, 17 games behind pennant-winning Boston and in third place. Charlie Keller will hit 30 home runs with 101 RBIs and Joe DiMaggio will hit 25 homers with 95 RBIs. Spud Chandler, 20-8, will lead the pitching staff.

Feb 19— Joe DiMaggio hits a home run in an exhibition game, the first of 14 homers he will hit in spring training season after not playing big league ball since the 1942 World Series or any kind of baseball since June of 1944 when he was with a service team. DiMaggio's blast is hit in Balboa, Panama. Larry MacPhail has the Yankees in the Canal Zone for preliminary training and will move them to St. Petersburg in March.

Apr 19— The Yankees beat Washington, 7-6, before 54,826 fans, then the largest official home opener crowd at Yankee Stadium.

— The Stadium was given a sprucing up by MacPhail. Among the changes: lights have been installed, new box seats have replaced grandstand seats,

---

*The Yankees were the first team to carry a regular batting practice pitcher.

lounges have been built, the Yankees have a new clubhouse, and the Yankees move from the third-base dugout to their new dugout on the first-base side.

Apr 30— Bob Feller pitches the first no-hitter against the Yankees since 1919 and Cleveland wins, 1-0. The only Indian run off Bill Bevens comes in the top of the ninth when Frank Hayes, who hits only five homers all year, parks one in the Yankee Stadium seats. Feller walks five and strikes out 11. His teammates make two errors but shortstop Lou Boudreau makes a great play when Snuffy Stirnweiss sends a low chopper behind the mound. Boudreau deftly fields the ball and nails the fleet-footed Stirnweiss.

May 2— MacPhail promotes a Yankee Stadium fashion show and gives away 500 pairs of nylons, and Nick Etten's grand slam homer helps the Yankees trounce Cleveland, 8-2.

— MacPhail introduced a slew of promotions to the Yankees. Ed Barrow believed that the game itslf should be the only promotion to draw fans, and, in fact, opposed night baseball on the grounds that baseball under the lights was a gimmick. But MacPhail opened a whole new approach to the merchandising of baseball.

May 9— DiMaggio has one of the few poor fielding days of his career. At Yankee Stadium, the Browns are leading, 3-1, in the eighth inning when Frank Mancuso hits a fly ball to center field. DiMaggio drifts under it, then drops the ball for a two-base error. After a double, Glenn McQuillen singles to center and Joe bobbles the ball for his second error of the inning. It is one of the few times DiMaggio hears the Stadium boo-birds. Joe will make up for the miscues tomorrow with a grand slam.

With World War II over, Charlie Keller, left, and Joe DiMaggio return to the Yankee line-up. Once again they prove to be the heart of the Yankee batting order.

May 11— Yankee pitcher Ernie Bonham, who wins only 5 of 13 decisions this year, snaps Boston's 15-game winning streak by shutting out the Red Sox, 2-0. But by now first-place Boston is well on the way to winning the pennant.

May 13— The Yankees become the first major league team to fly regularly. It is the first scheduled swing around the league by air. At LaGuardia Field, the Yankees board the "Yankee Mainliner," a chartered four-engine United Air Lines plane that gets them to Lambert Field in St. Louis 4½ hours later. Five players are allowed to make the trip by train. One is Red Ruffing, who excused himself from the flight to Panama a few months earlier. "I got my belly full of flying in the Army," Red had explained.

May 21— On the Yanks' flight from Cleveland to Detroit, Joe McCarthy, who has been in poor health and is upset about today's 7-2 defeat in Cleveland, plants himself in the seat next to Joe Page and loudly berates his young southpaw. McCarthy has been fighting a losing battle trying to get Page to curb his night-life, but this scene is most unlike McCarthy, who usually spoke to players behind closed doors. But Joe is irritable, upset about the Yanks' fortunes. He is having gall bladder troubles and is drinking a bit too much, and his Irish temper gets the better of him. As embarrassed passengers turn the other way, McCarthy says all the things he has kept pent up inside him, perhaps unleashing some of the frustration he has built up in his sour relationship with Larry MacPhail, too. McCarthy is in no shape to manage the club and he remains in his Detroit hotel for a day or so before returning to his Tonawanda, N.Y., farm. Coach Johnny Neun will run the club.

May 22— In Detroit, the Yankees win, 5-3, thanks to a triple play for which Tommy Henrich comes in from the outfield to put a tag on Dick Wakefield for the third out. But Henrich gets spiked in the process and needs several stitches.

May 24— Joe McCarthy resigns after 16 years as Yankee manager. He is replaced by Bill Dickey, the Yankee catcher who hits .261 in 54 games this year. MacPhail receives the following wire from McCarthy: "It is with extreme regret that I must request that you accept my resignation as manager of the Yankee Baseball Club, effective immediately. My doctor advises me that my health would seriously be jeopardized if I continued." At a hastily called press conference on an off-day in Boston, MacPhail announces the change of managers. MacPhail says George Weiss was sent to Tonawanda to try to change Joe's mind. But, says Larry, Joe, and especially Mrs. McCarthy, were firm in the retirement decision. So after eight McCarthy pennants and seven World Championships, the guard changes and the 39-year-old Dickey has a tough act to follow.

— There is no question that McCarthy both needed and deserved a rest. But it appeared that McCarthy was also happy to be disassociated from MacPhail. Larry rubbed a lot of people the wrong way, and McCarthy was one of them. World War II had prevented Marse Joe from establishing an untouchable winning record and the coming of MacPhail meant the end of the quiet, supportive relations he enjoyed with Ed Barrow. It had been a great McCarthy era but it had run out. Joe was not finished with baseball—he would return in 1948 as the Red Sox' manager.

May 26— The Yankees win their first game under Manager Bill Dickey, beating the Red Sox in the second game of a doubleheader, 4-1, in seven innings. DiMaggio contributes his 10th home run of the year. Boston had won the opener, 1-0, also beating the Yanks the previous day.

— Dickey was an especially popular choice as McCarthy's successor among the fans and press. He took over with the club in second place, only five games behind Boston, but he was stuck with a talented team rusty from wartime layoff. The hitters were especially weak.

May 28— The first night game in Yankee Stadium history is played and 49,917 brave a raw, windy, misty Tuesday night to attend the historic contest, won by Washington, 2-1. The first ball is thrown out by General Electric President Charles E, Wilson. This is also Dickey's home debut as Yankee manager.

— Night baseball was highly regulated in New York City in 1946. All three of the city's big league teams agreed that each would play only seven games under the lights. Special permission was needed to turn on the lights for a late day game, and, in fact, many day games were called early.

Jun 9— At Yankee Stadium, the Yankees and Indians play before 66,545 fans, as the Yankees surpass the one million mark in home attendance on what is the earliest date (up to today) in big league history.

— The bigger post-war market, the Stadium lights and MacPhail's creativity helped the Yankees have a season of as yet unparalleled success at the gate. For the first time since 1930, the Yanks drew over one million customers. The Yanks, in fact, would draw over two million! The figure of 2,265,512 would break the existing home mark set in 1920 at the Polo Grounds by nearly one million customers. And this club record would be broken two years later.

Jun 13— Clark Griffith, Frank Chance and Jack Chesbro are inducted into the Baseball Hall of Fame. First New York Manager Griffith and fifth New York Manager Chance are cited for general achievements or accomplishments realized elsewhere. The citation of pitcher Chesbro is Yankee-specific. He is honored for his great lifetime record, most of which was compiled with New York and for his 41-win season as a Highlander in 1904.

Jun 29— The Yankees lose, 2-0, to Philadelphia and fall eight games behind Boston. Worse, they lose the services of Red Ruffing, who suffers a broken kneecap when hit by a hot liner off the bat of Hank Majeski. The injury virtually ends Ruffing's great career in New York. Ruffing, 42, sustains his first loss today after winning his first five games and posting a 1.77 ERA.

Jul 2— Spud Chandler defeats Boston, 2-1, before a Stadium crowd of 69,107 fans. The Red Sox are hitless with one out in the ninth inning when Bobby Doerr singles—the only Red Sox hit in the game.

Jul 7— DiMaggio tears cartilage in his left knee and sprains his left ankle in a slide into second base at Shibe Park. The injury will sideline Joe until August and the Yankees by then will be out of the pennant race., At the All-Star Break, the front-running Red Sox lead the Yankees by 7½ games.

— It was a discouraging year for DiMaggio. He wanted badly to have a great comeback season and worked hard over the winter to get in shape. But he started the season slowly and developed a bone spur from a bruise suffered in May. The Stadium fans, who had expected the Yankees to regain their pre-war place at baseball's top rung, were occasionally rough on Joe, who was finally getting it in gear when he got hurt. He ended the year with 25 homers and 95 RBIs but for the first time hit under .300 at .290. There was talk, in Boston especially, that Joe's brother, Dom, his replacement in the All-Star line-up and a .316 hitter on the season, was the best player in the DiMaggio family.

Jul 9—   The AL wins the All-Star Game, 12-0, at Fenway Park and three Yankees do well. Keller starts the rout by crunching a two-run first-inning homer. Gordon has a double and two RBIs and Stirnweiss singles and scores a run. Dickey is unsuccessful as a pinch-hitter.

Aug 8—   Looking for more punch at first base, Dickey benches Nick Etten—a .232 hitter this year—and has the versatile and reliable Tommy Henrich play first in a doubleheader against Washington. Henrich played only 10 games at first before this season but today dazzles the fans by making several sensational plays at the position. In the nightcap, he homers and doubles to knock in five runs.

           — Henrich hit 19 homers and knocked in 83 runs in 1946. He would often play first base and do an outstanding job there over the remainder of his career.

Sep 8—   Bill Dickey, the great Yankee catcher who broke in with the club in 1928, plays in his final major league game. He pinch-hits for pitcher Al Gettel in the eighth inning and comes through with a single on this day when the Yankees lose twice to the Senators in extra innings.

           — Dickey hit .261 in 54 games in this, his final playing season. Concerned primarily with managing the club, Dickey turned over most of the catching chores to Aaron Robinson, who finished at .297 with 16 homers in 100 games.

Sep 12—   Dickey resigns as Yankee manager and coach Johnny Neun will finish the campaign as the club's skipper. Whether MacPhail planned to keep Dickey is open to conjecture, but Bill must have felt his number was up with the recent hiring of Bucky Harris in an executive capacity.

           — Dickey, who was 57-48 as a manager, would rejoin the club as coach after MacPhail departed. Neun was the third manager of the 1946 season, a circumstance that would not be duplicated in Yankee history until 1982. The Yankees finished 1946 winning eight of 14 remaining games under Neun. MacPhail regarded Neun as strictly an interim manager and would be searching for a more experienced pilot to steer the ship in 1947. MacPhail insisted that Harris would not be that manager.

Sep 20—   Red Ruffing is released by the Yankees. Ruffing won 231 games for the Yankees, a record that Whitey Ford will surpass in 1965. Red was having a great season until he was injured in late June. The White Sox will sign Ruffing in December and Red will go 3-5 for Chicago in 1947. The emotional toll is heavy in New York. Since May, the Yankees have lost McCarthy, Dickey and Ruffing, three of their greatest.

Sep 22—   The Yankees call up a quartet of hot prospects—Vic Raschi, Yogi Berra, Bobby Brown and Frank Colman—from their Newark farm team and three of them make their major league debuts in a doubleheader sweep, 4-3 and 7-4, over Philadelphia at Yankee Stadium. Catcher Berra belts a two-run homer. Brown plays shortstop and gets one hit. In the nightcap, Brown has another hit and rightfielder Colman goes two for two, one of his hits a home run.

Sep 23—   Vic Raschi wins his first big league game, beating the Athletics, 9-6, in a complete game. Raschi, a hardthrowing righthander from Springfield, Mass., allows nine hits but strikes out eight. Berra, who will have 8 hits in 22 at bats (.364) in the final days of the season, makes a single and hits his second home run in as many days. But the Yanks' home finale is played before only 2,475 fans.

LIES, CONDUCT DETRIMENTAL TO THE GAME, AND OTHER EXCESSES

1946

Oct 3—   Leo Durocher ends speculation that he will join old boss Larry MacPhail
in Yankeeland. He will stay in Brooklyn "until the day I die." He was offered
the job of Yankee field boss, the Brooklyn manager will insist, but turned it
down. The Lip tried for the job, MacPhail will counter, but the Yankees turned
him down.

1947

Mar 3—   The "Durocher Says" column in the *Brooklyn Eagle* begins: "this is a
declaration of war. I want to beat the Yankees..." Durocher, with presumed
reference to Rickey and the Dodgers, says that MacPhail "tried to drive a
wedge between myself and all these things I hold dear." Leo is steamed
over Chuck Dressen's leaving the Dodgers to become a Yankee coach
without "the courtesy of a phone call." Dressen broke his Brooklyn contract
by making the move, Durocher contends. "What does this mean to Bucky
Harris?" Leo asks a little wedge-driving of his own.

Mar 4—   In Caracas, Venezuela, the Yankees beat Brooklyn, 17-6, while MacPhail and
Durocher feud about everything and anything. But the principle contention
of each is that the other is a liar.

Mar 9—   The Yanks and Dodgers get together again in Havana, Cuba, and Durocher
charges that MacPhail is seated with gamblers. Dick Young, then a reporter
for the *New York Daily News,* finds that the men fingered by Leo as
gamblers are separated from MacPhail by a narrow stairway, that they are
not in Larry's box.

Mar 13—   Baseball Commissioner Happy Chandler is fed up with Durocher. "Maybe it
is time Durocher decided whether he is a baseball manager or a columnist,"
Chandler observes.

Mar 15— MacPhail files charges with the Commissioner against Durocher, Rickey and Harold Parrott, the Dodger road secretary who is ghosting Leo's column in the *Eagle*. Dressen charges Durocher and Rickey with falsely accusing him of acting in bad faith.

Mar 24— In a four-hour closed-door meeting in Sarasota, Fla., Chandler listens to Durocher and MacPhail, among other witnesses. Rickey is absent. Nothing is made public from the meeting.

Mary 28— In St. Petersburg, Fla., Chandler has another meeting, this one lasting four hours and 22 minutes. MacPhail and Rickey are there, and, whatever is said, it makes Happy very unhappy.

Apr 9— Commissioner Chandler flat out suspends Durocher for the 1947 season. Yankee Coach Chuck Dressen in suspended for 30 days for failure to keep a verbal agreement with the Dodgers, and Harold Parrot is fined $500 and ordered to discontinue his column. The Dodgers and Yankees are each fined $2,000 for engaging in a public controversy detrimental to baseball. A rule of silence is imposed on everyone involve.

Apr 10— MacPhail publicly states his regret over the penalty given Durocher and strongly objects to Chandler's "gag order." He says he "will continue to release any and all factual information pertinent and proper with the operation of this club."

Apr 22— MacPhail says in an interview he feels Durocher was dealt with too severely by Chandler.

May 1— Chandler and MacPhail meet in Cincinnati and have nothing to say afterward. Apparently MacPhail was summoned to explain why he violated the silence edit. MacPhail had said in his interview that "so far as any evidence developed at the Sarasota and St. Petersburg hearings is concerned there was nothing to justify even a five-minute suspension of Durocher."

May 2— Chandler makes it clear that no one outside of the inner circle of the major leagues will ever know how he punished MacPhail for "insubordination."

May 4— Chanderl and MacPhail have another long meeting. Again, neither will talk about the meeting afterwards.

May 15— Yankee Coach Chuck Dressen's 30-day suspension ends and Bucky Harris welcomes him back to the club. Dressen had been working out with the team prior to games early in the season but Chandler put a halt to his being in uniform before the suspension period was ended.

Sept 11— In Cincinnati, MacPhail has another locked door "no comment" conference with Chandler. The Colonel had again broken the silence order. He had insinuated in Washington that Durocher was suspended because Rickey wanted it that way, and he took the trouble to roast Chandler, too. Rumors are afloat now that MacPhail plans to retire if the Yankees win the World Series. Nothing would make Happy Chandler happier, from all appearance.

Oct 19—   The Yankees obtain Allie Reynolds (P) from Cleveland for Joe Gordon (2B) and Eddie Bockman (INF) in a swapping of malcontents. Gordon, who hits only .210, is told by MacPhail that he will be traded. His career will revive in Cleveland where he teams with Lou Boudreau to form one of the game's greatest double-play combinations, drives in 124 runs and leads the Indians to the 1948 pennant. Gordon will end his career after the 1950 season with 253 home runs, the AL record for second basemen. Reynolds joins the Yankees, beginning with an impressive 19-8 mark in 1947. In short, this is one of the few trades that ends up benefitting both clubs, although Reynolds' remaining career will run longer than Gordon's.

           — The Yankees were offered a choice of several Indian pitchers in the deal. MacPhail was ready to take Red Embree, who was 8-12 in 1946, and Bucky Harris seemed to concur. But at the World Series, DiMaggio was asked by Harris and Dan Topping for his opinion. DiMaggio favored Reynolds and the Yankees went with Joe's advice.

Oct 21—   The Yankees trade Ernie Bonham to Pittsburgh for Art Cuccurullo, a pitcher for a pitcher. Bonham will have a record of 11-8 in 1947 with the Pirates but on September 15, 1949, will die of complications following surgery. In seven years with the Yankees, Tiny Bonham was 79-50.

Nov 5—   Bucky Harris is named Yankee manager, following rumors that Leo Durocher, Billy Herman, Frankie Frisch or Charlie Dressen would get the job. Dressen does leave Brooklyn and joins the Yankees as a coach. Standing in the crowded press room of the club's Fifth Avenue offices, MacPhail states, "Harris is the manager on a two-year contract, and Dressen is his first assistant." Since joining the Yanks' front office on September 9 in an executive capacity, Harris kept saying he wanted no part of managing. But he accepts the position with the understanding that he may return to the front office in the near future. He came to New York from the International League's Buffalo club where he was GM. He has 20 years of managing in the big leagues in his resume. Johnny Neun had already resigned the Yankee post to accept Cincinnati's managing job.

Nov 21—   Ed Barrow, under whom the Yankees won 14 pennants, resigns his position as chairman of the board. Under his three-year contract, Barrow exercises his option to cancel the pact after two years. Reportedly, he is another of the old guard who is unhappy with MacPhail. But Barrow *is* 78 years old. Barrow will say in the official announcement in January, "We are parting on very friendly terms. When a man gets to be as old as I am, well, I'm afraid he's getting pretty old."

Dec 10—   New York signs free agent first baseman George McQuinn after his release from the Athletics. McQuinn hit only .225 in 1946 and Connie Mack, saying the 37-year-old had hung on one season too long, let him go. But McQuinn felt he could still play and told Bucky Harris so.

           — McQuinn surprised everyone by making the Yankees in spring training and winning a regular job, after the club unsuccessfully tried to acquire Mickey Vernon. (Hank Greenberg also almost became a Yankee.) So McQuinn finally got to play with the Yankees, who in the 1930s had Lou Gehrig and let McQuinn go. He would lead the AL in batting next season as late as June 1. He would finish hitting .304 with 13 home runs and 80 RBIs. And he would play the bag better than anyone on the Yankees since Hal Chase.

1947

The Yankees will finish at 97-57, winning an unexpected pennant by 12 games over Detroit. Joe DiMaggio will hit .315 and be MVP, and Allie Reynolds will lead Yank pitchers at 19-8. Joe Page will win 14 and lead the AL in saves with 17. New York will win the World Championship.

Jan 2—   Frank Crosetti is named a Yankee player-coach under Bucky Harris. The fast-thinking, slick-fielding shortstop will bat once this year and 14 times in 1948, ending up with an average of .245 and with 1,006 runs scored in 17 seasons with the Yankees.

Jan 7—   Joe DiMaggio has a bone spur removed from his left heel in an operation at Beth David Hospital in New York City. The operating surgeon says he should be ready for spring training. But by February's end, DiMaggio will be a patient in Baltimore's Johns Hopkins Hospital.

Feb 14—   Bucky Harris heads a group of 30 Yankees leaving New York's LaGuardia Field on a six-hour flight to Puerto Rico. (A second group of Yankees will work out in St. Petersburg, Fla.) This group will play six games in Puerto Rico and another six in Venezuela. Brooklyn will be the opposition for several games in both countries.

Mar 11—   The Yankees travel to their winter headquarters in St. Petersburg. The players coming off the 4,000-mile tour are in a bad frame of mind (they were un-willing tourists) and discover that their teammates in St. Pete are equally dis-traught. The former feel they were turned into a sideshow by MacPhail and latter are sure they won't get a fair chance to impress Harris, whose mind right now is very much on his centerfielder. Joe DiMaggio undergoes a skin-graft operation on his heel today and doctors are not offering assurances that he will be ready for the season's start. He has yet to play in spring training.

Mar 12—   The Yankees and World Champion Cardinals dedicate 6,000-seat Al Lang Field, the new ballpark named for the man who induced big league teams to train in St. Petersburg. The Cardinals win, 10-5.

Apr 3—   In St. Petersburg, DiMaggio takes his first workout in a special shoe designed for his tender heel. The Yankees will break camp tomorrow but the Yankee Clipper will remain in St. Petersburg for exercises and drills. The Yankees have little hope for a pennant without Joe.

Apr 14—   New York releases veteran relief star, Johnny Murphy, who will sign with the Red Sox. Murphy in Boston will save three games, have no decisions and then retire for good. He had come out of retirement for a 4-2 season with seven saves for the Yanks in 1946.

             — While it was Wilcy Moore who had the first great relief season in Yankee history, Murphy was the club's first consistently effective reliever, and his success did a lot to change baseball's views about relief specialists. In 12 Yankee seasons, Murphy led the AL four times in saves and six times in games won in relief. Murphy—known to the fans as "Grandma" because of his rocking chair delivery—posted a fine Yankee career record of 93-53, with 104 saves, second only to Goose Gossage among righthanders.

Apr 15— The Yankees open the season at Yankee Stadium and lose to Philadelphia, 6-1. Spud Chandler takes the loss and Bucky Harris loses his debut as Yankee manager. Harris starts Robinson (C), McQuinn (1B), Stirnweiss (2B), Johnson(3B), Rizzuto (SS), Keller (LF), Lindell (CF) and Berra (RF). DiMaggio is in uniform but is unable to take part in a season opener for the sixth time in his nine big league seasons. He will make his first appearance of the year as a pinch-hitter in four days.

Apr 20— DiMaggio defies the gloom-sayers by making an early-season start. He not only starts, but belts a three-run homer in the first of two at Philadelphia. The Yankees win, 6-2, and take the second game, too, 3-2, which DiMaggio sits out.

Apr 23— In his second game as a Yankee and first at Yankee Stadium, Allie Reynolds pitches a two-hitter and collects his second shutout, beating Boston, 3-0. Rudy York gets both hits against Reynolds, who will be hit hard in his next start in St. Louis. Allie's first shutout was over Washington April 18.

Apr 24— In his major league debut, Frank Joseph "Spec" Shea gives up only three singles but loses, 1-0. Boston's Tex Hughson is a little better allowing only two hits. Shea will follow with seven straight wins.

Apr 27— It is Babe Ruth Day in every ballpark in organized baseball. The Babe appears at Yankee Stadium showing the effects of the cancer that will claim him 16 months later. About 60,000 turn out to honor the ailing legend, including NL President Ford Frick, Commissioneer Happy Chandler, Mel Allen and Francis Cardinal Spellman. Babe makes a short and eloquent speech in which he tells the crowd that "the only real game in the world, I think, is baseball." In the game itself, Sid Hudson outduels Spud Chandler and Washington wins, 1-0.

May 12— Mired in the second division, the 9-10 Yankees begin a homestand that starts well. They defeat St. Louis, 9-1, with Reynolds pitching a three-hitter. Keller, DiMaggio and Lindell hit consecutive home runs in the sixth and Keller has two homers on the day.

May 18— Cleveland wins, 5-3, on "I am an American Day" at the Stadium, and in his first game against the Yankees since being traded, Joe Gordon singles, walks, singles, walks and homers.

— Gordon later talked about the troubles he had with the Yankees in 1946. He had no problems with Manager Bill Dickey, he said. (There were stories that Dickey pulled rank on Gordon in the military and that Gordon never forgave his onetime good buddy.) Not so, said Gordon. His problems were strictly with MacPhail, who had called Gordon onto the carpet more than once and who had no sympathy for Joe's physical setbacks. Gordon said he was glad to be in Cleveland, away from MacPhail, who, already having more than his share of bad press, was stung by the Gordon comments.

May 22— With the Yankees still struggling and hints of dissension surfacing, MacPhail fines several players in amounts ranging from $25 to $100. He cites various infractions, including failure to pose for promotional pictures and failure to attend banquets. Six players are fined, including—most startling of all—the conscientious Joe DiMaggio. It is Joe's first fine as a Yankee. He failed to cooperate with Army Signal Corps photographers, he and others feeling the time might be better spent in the batting cage inasmuch as MacPhail was unhappy with the club's hitting. Joe gets the heaviest fine ($100). When

MacPhail later tries to return it, DiMaggio gives the $100 to the Damon Runyon Cancer Fund.

May 23— Opening a key four-game series at Yankee Stadium, the Yankees defeat Boston, 9-0, Reynolds notching his second two-hitter of the season against the Red Sox. Keller hits a home run and the Yankees move into a tie for fourth place. Tomorrow, Chandler will blank the Bosox on two hits.

May 25— Banging out 17 hits, the Yankees destroy Boston, 17-2. DiMaggio gets four hits and Stirnweiss scores five runs. Bill Bevens has a no-hitter for six innings and a shutout until the ninth inning when Ted Williams hits a two-run homer that keeps New York pitchers from matching an AL record of four consecutive shutouts.

May 26— The Yankees complete their four-game sweep of Boston, winning, 9-3, before what remains the largest crowd ever to see a single night game at the Stadium—74,747. But the big story is Joe Page's success. And it is the turning point of his career. With the Yankees trailing, 3-1, Page relieves in in tne third with two runners on base. Ted Williams reaches on an error and the bases are full of Red Sox and no one is out. Page runs the count to three and nothing to both Rudy York and Bobby Doerr, then strikes them out. Page extinguishes the fire and gets the win when the Yankees rally. DiMaggio hits a three-run homer. Harris later admits that Page was "one pitch from Newark," adding, "If Page had walked York, he was through as a Yankee." Next to DiMaggio, Page will be the Yanks' most important player the rest of the way.

— The finally untracked Yankees' sweep of Boston was their first over the Red Sox since September of 1943. New York scored 40 runs in four games, forcing Manager Joe Cronin to use all 10 of his Red Sox pitchers. DiMaggio had nine hits and drove in eight runs, hustled in the field and on the bases and showed no bitterness about his recent fine. New York would jump from sixth to second place during the homestand.

Jun 5— In Detroit, the Yankees win, 7-0, and move to within one game of the the first-place Tigers. Chandler scatters three hits and Henrich belts a pair of homers. Keller is forced out of the game with what is believed to be recurring back strain. It is thought that the league leader in home runs and RBIs needs only a few days of rest.

— Keller's injury was much worse than thought. He would make a couple of pinch-hit appearances but was in great pain. Keller finally had an operation for a ruptured intervertebral disc and the seriousness of his injury was only then put into the proper light. For Charlie Keller, with 13 homers and 36 RBIs, the 1947 season was ended.

Jun 15— At Yankee Stadium, the Yankees sweep a twinbill from St. Louis and 55,691 fans see a catcher's unassisted double play, only the second one in Yankee history. The Browns' Jeff Heath breaks for the plate as batter Johnny Berardino attempts a suicide squeeze. The bunt dribbles in front of the plate and Berra pounces on it with catlike quickness and tags Berardino and Heath in rapid succession. It is a breathtaking display of both mental and physical agility. Yogi will have another unassisted DP on August 17, 1962 to establish an AL record.

Jun 16—   The Yankees beat Chicago, 4-3, in stirring game witnessed by 52,633 at the Stadium. The Yankees score twice in the eighth to tie the game. Rizzuto singles and Stirnweiss apparently forces the Scooter at second for the third out. But Umpire Rommel rules that Cass Michaels' foot is off the base and three White Sox are ejected in the ensuing rhubarb. Then Henrich's triple knots it. In the ninth, the Yanks load the bases and Rizzuto lays down a perfect suicide-squeeze bunt, scoring DiMaggio.

Jun 20—   At Yankee Stadium the Yankees beat Detroit, 5-3, and for the third time in three meetings Spec Shea defeats the Tigers' great Hal Newhouser. Shea fans nine and allows only four hits, two of them homers by Eddie Mayo, the only runs scored by Detroit off Shea in 27 innings. New York goes into first place and will stay there for the season's duration. Two days later Shea will be honored with a "day" at the Stadium. The Naugatuck Nugget is bursting on the Yankee scene like no other rookie pitcher since Hank Borowy in 1942.

           — The fun-loving Irishman captured the imagination of the fans and press with just the right combination of skill and cockiness. The folks back home in Naugatuck were wild about Shea. Reports of high truancy and absenteeism on days when he pitched were rampant. If not for a sore arm, Shea might have shattered many a rookie pitching mark. Yet he still managed to go 14-5.

Jul 6—   The Yankees sweep their fifth home doubleheader in five tries, beating Philadelphia, 8-2 and 9-2. In the opener Page gets eight of the final 11 outs by strikeouts. At the All-Star Break, New York is 47-26 and working on an eight-game winning streak.

Jul 8—   The AL wins the All-Star Game, 2-1, at Wrigley Field. Spec Shea is the winning pitcher with three solid innings of work. He is the first rookie pitcher to win an All-Star Game but it may have been in this appearance that Shea develops arm miseries. Shea's arm stiffens and he will be shelved for much of the mid-season. Page pitches well. DiMaggio, McQuinn and Tommy Henrich also play.

Jul 13—   Behind pitchers who have just joined the team, the Yankees win two games in Chicago, 10-3 and 6-4, for 14 in a row. They lead second-place Detroit by 10½ games. Bobo Newsom spins a five-hitter, Rizzuto hits a grand slam homer and Johnson has five singles. Vic Raschi wins the nightcap with relief help from Page and Reynolds.

           — Newsom and Raschi, with completely different personalities and backgrounds, were crucial to the pennant drive with Chandler and Shea injured. The much-traveled Newsom was obtained on waivers from Washington. The Yankees had a hard time finding a size 50 uniform to fit the brash South Carolinian, who first broke in with Raleigh in 1928 and whose contract had now changed hands 22 times. Bobo would win his first four Yankee decisions and finish 7-5. Raschi was a quiet but determined New Englander. He had grown a little tired of wallowing in the minors, but under Jim Turner's tutelage in Portland, he pitched impressively and was 8-2. He was called up when phenom Don Johnson disappointed. Raschi would go 7-2 in New York, at last establishing himself, at 28, as a major leaguer.

Jul 15—   New York wins its 15th and 16th games in a row, tying a club record set in 1926, before 62,355 fans in Cleveland. It is New York's third sweep in four days! In the opener, Lindell hits a three-run triple, as the Yankees win, 9-4. The nightcap is a duel between Bob Feller and Bill Bevens, who wins his first game, 2-1, in nearly two months. The tie is broken in the ninth when DiMaggio singles and Johnson triples him home.

— Johnson and Lindell were the unsung stars of the team. Johnson had platooned at third with Bobby Brown but began playing regularly after Brown broke a finger in May. Johnson took advantage of the opportunity by driving in 95 runs in 494 at-bats. Lindell had been rumored as part of various trades all spring but the Yankees could not move him for one reason or another. When Keller went down injured, Lindell got his chance to play regularly. He hit .275 with a ton of clutch hits, then batted .500 to lead all hitters in the World Series.

Jul 17— In Cleveland, the Yankees win their 18th and 19th consecutive games, tying the AL record set in 1906 by the White Sox. Newsom wins the opener, 3-1, for his 200th major league victory. McQuinn's two-run homer is the key hit. Raschi wins the nightcap, 7-2. Billy Johnson has three RBIs.

19-GAME WINNING STREAK OF 1947

Win No. and Date	Opponent	Home or Away	Score and NY Hits	Pitcher (C) = Compl. Games	Winning Attendance
1. Jun 29	Washington	A	3-1 (6)	Don Johnson	27,883
2. June 30	Boston	A	3-1 (6)	(C) Spec Shea	34,705
3. Jul 2	Washington	H	8-1 (11)	(C) Allie Reynolds	53,520
4. Jul 4	Washington	H	7-3 (10)	(C) Spud Chandler	56,717
5. d-header	Washington	H	4-2 (9)	Joe Page	—
6. Jul 5	Philadelphia	H	5-1 (10)	(C) Spec Shea	30,173
7. Jul 6	Philadelphia	H	8-2 (14)	Randy Gumpert	51,957
8. d-header	Philadelphia	H	9-2 (13)	(C) Allie Reynolds	—
9. Jul 10	St. Louis	A	4-3 (9)	Joe Pgae	9,874
10. Jul 11	St. Louis	A	3-1 (3)	(C) Allie Reynolds	2,171
11. Jul 12	St. Louis	A	12.2 (17)	Butch Wensloff	4,949
12. d-header	St. Louis	A	8-5 (11)	Karl Drews	—
13. Jul 13	Chicago	A	10-3 (16)	(C) Bobo Newsom	43,102
14. d-header	Chicago	A	6-4 (10)	(C) Vic Raschi	—
15. Jul 15	Cleveland	A	9-4 (10)	(C) Allie Reynolds	62,355
16. d-header	Cleveland	A	2-1 (9)	(C) Bill Bevens	—
17. Jul 16	Cleveland	A	8-2 (14)	Butch Wensloff	46,988
18. Jul 17	Cleveland	A	3-1 (5)	(C) Bobo Newsom	22,296
19. d-header	Cleveland	A	7-2 (10)	(C) Vic Raschi	—

The 19-games winning streak of the 1947 Yankees tied an AL record set by Chicago in 1906, although the White Sox' streak was stained by a tie. Over the streak, New York outscored the opposition 119 to 41, averaging 6.3 runs per game to the opponents' 2.2. When the streak began, the Yankees led second-place Boston by 3½ games. When it reached 19 games, Detroit was in second place by 11½ games and Boston was 12½ games off the pace. The Yankees won most of their games on the road and swept six doubleheaders. They used 11 pitchers.

Jul 18—   The Yanks' 19-game winning streak is snapped in Detroit by 18-game
            winner Fred Hutchinson, who throws a two-hitter, walks no one, strikes out
            nine, pitches to only 28 men and wins, 8-0. The tired Yanks are ready for
            plucking on this day. But New York still leads the AL by 10½ games.

Aug 16—   The Yankees defeat Boston, 1-0, at home. Earl Johnson blanks New York
            for eight innings, but in the bottom of the ninth Allie Clark leads off with
            his fourth hit and McQuinn singles him to third. Johnson then walks and
            Lindell singles to win the game for Newsom. The game is saved in the
            sixth when Clark, a .375 hitter in 24 Yankee games after his recall from
            Newark earlier this month, races to deep right-center field to catch Bobby
            Doerr's shot with Ted Williams on base. The Yankees continue to win with an
            outfield that is sometimes Berra (LF), Lindell (CF) and Clark (RF), an
            indication of the club's depth.

Aug 26—   In St. Louis, the Yankees lose, 4-3, but it is a big night for hometown
            lad Yogi Berra. In fact, it is officially "Yogi Berra Night" at Sportsmans Park.
            Yogi and his parents receive many gifts from his neighbors on The Hill
            and Berra is most gracious although he has been hospitalized recently with
            a throat infection. He is also a little nervous. He has a couple of lines
            rehearsed but this slips out: "I want to thank everyone for making this
            night necessary."

Sep 15—   The Yankees clinch their 15th pennant. The Yankees happen to be rained
            out, but they learn that Boston has lost and that they are officially league
            champions. New York's record is 90-53 after 143 games. MacPhail con-
            gratulates Harris and tells the press, "This is a big moment for me, but all I
            can say is it couldn't have happened to a nicer guy, meaning Bucky Harris."
            In turn, Harris praises his players, especially Page. Indeed, it has been one
            of the great team efforts in Yankee history, and an unlikely one, at that,
            considering the spring turmoil.

Sep 28—   On the final day of the regular season, MacPhail has a tremendous
            collection of old timers play two innings for the benefit of the Babe Ruth
            Foundation Inc. before the Yanks take on the Athletics. Many Yankee stars,
            as well as some of the game's all-time greats, play in the benefit. Del Webb
            has Ty Cobb picked up in a private plane in Las Vegas and flown to New York
            for the event. The Bambino is most appreciative.

Oct 2—   In the World Series, the Yanks win the first two at home, but the Dodgers
            today come to life, winning, 9-8, at Ebbets Field. The Yankees, who trail 6-0
            after two innings, keep coming back. DiMaggio has a two-run homer, and
            Berra hits a solo homer in the seventh inning to bring the Yankees within
            one run. Pinch-hitting for Sherm Lollar, Berra's blast is the first pinch-hit
            homer in World Series history. But Hugh Casey holds the Yankees scoreless
            over the final 2⅔ innings. In a courageous relief effort, sore-armed Spud
            Chandler makes his final appearance in a big league game and allows two
            runs in two innings.

Oct 3—   Game 4 goes down as one of history's most famous. Brooklyn does not
            make a hit off Bill Bevens, who is wild, until two outs in the bottom of the
            ninth, yet the Dodgers win the game, 3-2. The Yankees lead, 2-0, when
            the Dodgers score in the fifth on two walks, a sacrifice and a fielder's choice.
            In the ninth, the Yankees load the bases with one out, but Casey enters
            and needs only one pitch to get Henrich to bound into a double play, ending
            the threat. Bevens takes the mound, protecting both a one-run lead and a

no-hitter. Leading off, Bruce Edwards flies to deep center. Carl Furillo walks. Spider Jorgensen fouls out to McQuinn for the second out. Al Gionfriddo runs for Furillo and Pete Reiser is called on to pinch-hit in spite of a bad ankle. When Gionfriddo steals second, Bucky Harris defies the rule against putting the winning run on base and, with the count at three and one, orders Bevens to issue his 10th walk of the game. Eddie Miksis runs for Reiser, and Cookie Lavagetto, pinch-hitting for Eddie Stanky, doubles off the right field wall to score Gionfriddo and Miksis and win the game, 3-2.

Oct 4—
The Yankees rebound to win a nailbiter, 2-1, and take a three-to-two lead in games. Shea pitches a four-hitter and singles home the Yanks' first run. DiMaggio homers in the fifth to put New York ahead, 2-0, and makes two fine catches in center field. In the bottom of the ninth, with two outs and the tying run on second, Shea strikes out yesterday's hero, Lavagetto, to end the game. The team is so moved by Shea's clutch performance, his second win of the Series, that they carry him off the field.

Oct 5—
The Dodgers win a Game 6 made memorable by a great Gionfriddo catch. Brooklyn takes a quick 4-0 lead but the Yanks tie with a four-run third inning. After New York takes the lead on Berra's run-scoring single, the Bums jump all over Page in a four-run sixth inning to go ahead, 8-5. In the bottom half, DiMaggio steps up with two on and two out. Joe smokes a tremendous drive heading on a line for the left field bullpen, but Gionfriddo, running with all he has to give, turns around at the last second, leaps and makes an incredible catch at the 415-foot mark. He later says, "It certainly would have gone into the bullpen alley for a home run if I hadn't got it. The ball hit my glove and a second later I hit the gate." Disappointed after he thought he had tied the game, DiMaggio stops at second base and kicks the dirt in a rare display of anger. The Yankees score one run in the ninth, but it is not enough and the Series turns on Game 7. Larry MacPhail is angered by the loss and barks at trainer Eddie Froelich, Lindell and Harris.

Oct 6—
Thanks to great relief pitching by Joe Page, the Yankees beat Brooklyn, 5-2, in Game 7 at Yankee Stadium and are World Champions once again. Page faces 15 batters and records 15 outs. Brooklyn goes out to a 2-0 lead in the second inning but Rizzuto cuts down one runner at the plate, then in turn singles home a run in the bottom of the inning. In the fourth inning Bobby Brown delivers a run-scoring double, his third hit in three pinch-hit at-bats in the Series, and Henrich's single knocks in the go-ahead tally. The Yankees later add a pair of insurance runs and Page makes the lead hold.

— With the Series victory Larry MacPhail announced his retirement in a tearful statement and congratulated individual Yankees. There followed a wild and stormy celebration at the Biltmore Hotel. The $10,000 Victory Dinner was given by Yankee owners MacPhail, Topping and Webb for the Yankee players and friends of the owners. But it turned into a boxing arena for MacPhail, who arrived at the party telling reporters to "stay away or get punched." He was in a foul mood and berated his partners, George Weiss, an unnamed Yankee player, and he punched John McDonald, his former road secretary at Brooklyn, for defending Branch Rickey's name during an argument. Although he had announced his retirement, he fired Weiss, leaving Mrs. Weiss in tears and stirring scout Paul Krichell to say he'd like a "poke" at MacPhail. Finally, Topping told MacPhail, "I have taken enough—come with me and we will settle this thing once and for all," and pushed Larry into a kitchen. Some time later, MacPhail returned, somewhat cooled down. Mrs. MacPhail was deeply concerned; her husband was a "mighty sick, nervous man," she said.

Oct 7—   In a big front office shakeup, Larry MacPhail sells his one-third share of the
           Yankees to Topping and Webb for $2 million. MacPhail's contract was to
           have run through 1950, at $50,000 per year as club president, so he is in
           part compensated for that loss. Topping will become president and Weiss,
           "fired" the night before by MacPhail, is named general manager. At the press
           conference held in a suite at the Waldorf-Astoria, Topping explains that
           MacPhail in September agreed to leave and that Chandler has been notified
           of the happenings at the Biltmore the previous night. MacPhail's formal re-
           signation, drawn at a hurried meeting, read: "I have this day resigned as pres-
           ident, treasurer, director and general manager of the Yankees."

Oct 14—   In Atlanta, Spud Chandler has an operation on his pitching arm. Cartilage
           scraps and bone chips are removed from his elbow. The 39-year-old had
           pitched his final season in which he was 9-5. He won the ERA title with
           2.46 and lived up to his reputation as a bulldog competitor, completing 16
           of his 17 starts. Chandler, one of the finest pitchers in Yankee history, will
           be released on April 12. His winning percentage of .717 remains the best
           in the majors among retired pitchers with at least 100 wins.

Nov 17—   DiMaggio has two small bone particles removed from his throwing elbow.
           The arm problem was kept silent during the season because it hampered
           his throwing ability. Joe played the entire 1947 season with a "dead arm,"
           in effect, decoying baserunners all year. And he endured great pain every
           time he threw. The operation is performed at Baltimore's Johns Hopkins
           Hospital.

Nov 27—   DiMaggio is named his league's MVP for the third time by the Baseball
           Writers, based on his .315 average, 20 homers, 97 RBIs and the leadership
           qualities that led New York to the pennant. DiMaggio beats Ted Williams by
           one vote, 202 to 201. Joe Page is fourth and George McQuinn sixth. One writer
           did not list Williams, who won the Triple Crown, among his top 10 choices—
           a 10th place vote would have given Ted the necessary two points to pass
           DiMaggio.

1948

The Yankees, at 94-60, will finish third and two games behind the Indians and Red
Sox who tie. The final margin will be 2½ games when Cleveland defeats Boston in a
one-game playoff. Joe DiMaggio will lead the AL wth 39 home runs and 155 RBIs.
Tommy Henrich will knock in 100 runs and Vic Raschi will lead the pitching staff at 19-8.

Feb 24—   New York obtains Eddie Lopat (P) from the White Sox for Aaron Robinson (C).
           Bill Wight (P) and Fred Bradley (P). Robinson, the Yanks' transition catcher
           between Bill Dickey and Yogi Berra, hit .284 over four Yankee seasons.
           He will play in the majors through 1951 and hit .260 lifetime.

           —Lopat was the key to the trade, coming off a fine year in Chicago in 1947
           when he was 16-13 with a 2.81 ERA. The kid off the streets of New York City
           was a craftsman, dazzling hitters with a variety of off-speed "junk." He would
           go 17-11 in 1948, and, together with Vic Raschi and Allie Reynolds, form
           a "big three" that would dominate the AL for several years.

Feb 27—   It is announced that former Yankee pitcher Herb Pennock has been elected
           to the Baseball Hall of Fame by the Baseball Writers. The election comes a
           month after Pennock's death. Of the 121 total ballots cast, Pennock, who was
           general manager of the Phillies at the time of his death, gets 94 votes and

Pie Traynor, 93, to gain membership in the Hall. Pennock won 241 games over 22 major league seasons. He was 162-90 for the Yankees between 1923-33, and he was 5-0 with three saves as a Yankee in World Series play.

Mar 15— In an exhibition game against the Phillies in Clearwater, Fla., Yogi Berra badly sprains an ankle. He will return to action 12 days later but will collapse when his weakened ankle gives way. He will be hurt again on April 12 when he hurts his hand in a game with the Birmingham Barons.

Apr 21— Joe DiMaggio sparkles but the Yankees lose to the Senators, 6-3. In the top of the first inning, DiMaggio hits one of the longest home runs in Griffith Stadium's history, a wallop of over 450 feet off Mickey Haefner. Joe also makes a great throw to cut down Mickey Vernon by five feet at third base, putting to rest lingering worries about his healthy-again throwing arm.

Apr 23— The home opener at Yankee Stadium celebrates the 25th anniversary of the Stadium's opening. The Seventh Regiment Band plays the National Anthem, just as it had done 25 years earlier, and the hero of that first game sits behind the Yankee dugout. Babe Ruth is now a very sick man. The new World Championship flag is raised and DiMaggio receives his MVP Award, both rewards for jobs well done in 1947. Joe McCarthy is now managing the Red Sox who win, 4-0.

May 20— DiMaggio has a single, double, triple and *two* home runs. It is the second cycle for Joe; they come 11 years apart and both come with an extra home run. New York smothers Chicago, 13-2.

May 23— DiMaggio belts three consecutive home runs in the same game for the second time in his career. Two of them are off Bob Feller. Joe also singles and drives in all six Yankee runs, as New York beats Cleveland by one run in the first game of a doubleheader. But the Tribe wins the second game, 5-1. A crowd of 78,431 sees the games in the baseball-mad city on Lake Erie.

Jun 11— At Yankee Stadium, Berra is thrown out of a game for arguing balls and strikes with Umpire Hubbard whose ejection of the beloved Yogi nearly starts a riot. Tommy Byrne is working on the mound and Berra feels Hubbard is squeezing the strike zone on Byrne, who has enough problems with control as it is. Berra communicates his thoughts to Hubbard and the fans, sensing the problem at home plate, begin booing Hubbard unmercifully. Finally, Hubbard ejects Berra, bringing Manager Bucky Harris and Coach Dressen into the fray and moving the usually mild-mannered Stadium fans to bombard the playing field with fruit, beer cans, newspapers and anything else they can find to throw. Harris leads Berra away while Hubbard seethes. A heavy imbiber jumps the wall in right field and zig-zags down the foul line toward Hubbard, stopping short to deliver an empty beer can pitcher-style. The can bounces harmlessly at the umpire's feet. Luckily for the trespasser, a security cop reaches him before Hubbard, a 265-pound one-time pro footballer, can get to him.

Jun 13— Babe Ruth makes his final appearance at Yankee Stadium on Old Timers' Day before a crowd of 49,641. Ruth's illness makes it difficult to take part but he is pleased to see so many old friends. The Yankees are celebrating the 25th year of the Stadium and their first World Championship team of 1923. The Silver Anniversary's highlight is a two-inning game involving the players of 1923. Babe wears his old No. 3 uniform, which is finally retired, and, along

with his Stadium locker, will be sent to the Baseball Hall of Fame.* Bat in
hand, Babe walks to the plate and hears the crowd's cheers for the last time.
He manages a smile through all the pain.

On June 13, 1948, the Yankees celebrated the 25th anniversary of their first World
Championship team, members of which played a two-inning game and gathered for
this group photo. Front row, from left, are Sad Sam Jomes, Wally Schang, Carl Mays,
Whitey Witt, Bootnose Hofmann and Mike McNally. Back row, from left, are Hinkey
Haines, Waite Hoyt, George Pipgras, Bullet Joe Bush, Oscar Roettger, Babe Ruth (who
died two months later), Bob Meusel, Joe Dugan, Wally Pipp and Elmer Smith.

---

*Many players wore No. 3 after Ruth last wore it in 1934. Cliff Mapes is the last one.

Jun 20— DiMaggio blasts three home runs in the Yanks' doubleheader sweep of the Browns in St. Louis. Joltin' Joe's ninth-inning fourbagger gives the Yanks a 4-2 victory in the first game. His solo homer in the eighth and a two-run shot in the ninth win the nightcap for the Yanks, 6-3. The Yankee Clipper will hit seven homers in six days.

Jun 23— Tommy Henrich belts a grand slam homer, first of four bases-loaded homers he will hit this year. Tommy's 11th-inning blast breaks a 1-1 tie and gives the Yankees a 5-1 win before 65,000-plus fans in Cleveland. Henrich will hit his fourth grand slam in Washington on August 17, tying Lou Gehrig's 1934 Yankee club record.

Jul 13— For the 11th time in 15 games, the AL wins the All-Star Game, taking a 5-2 verdict at Sportsmans Park in St. Louis. Vic Raschi is unscored upon over the middle three innings and gets credit for the victory. George McQuinn plays the whole game at first base, makes two hits in four trips, scores a run and steals a base. Henrich plays left field but is hitless in three trips. DiMaggio, who missed his only game of the season just prior to the Break, is still bothered by a sore heel and bad knees and does not start the game. Joe does come through for Manager Bucky Harris with a sacrifice fly as a pinch-hitter.

Jul 17— Old Reliable receives a car, piano, rifle, luggage and other gifts on Tommy Henrich Day at Yankee Stadium. Ed Lopat pitches an 11-hit shutout and wins, 4-0, over St. Louis. Lopat throws just 88 pitches and the game is played in well under two hours. On his Day, Henrich makes a double and a single.

Jul 25— DiMaggio has three singles in the opener and two homers and a double in the nightcap, a game delayed several times when kids trot out to center field to ask for Joe's autograph, as New York takes two from Chicago, 5-3 and 7-3.

Aug 14— Bucky Harris makes a line-up change that will send the Yankees streaking. Berra, who is having troubles behind the plate, is switched to right field, replacing Henrich, who moves to first base in place of McQuinn, who has finally run out of gas at age 39. After his great comeback season of 1947, McQuinn will slump to a .248 finish this year.

— The Yankees won on this date, dropped a doubleheader the next day, then won 15 of 18 games through September 1. Berra, who had been languishing at the .271 mark, no longer had to concentrate on catching and went on a hitting tear, making 34 hits in 85 at-bats for a .400 average over the first 21 games he played in right field. Berra would finish the year at .305 and drive in 98 runs in only 125 games.

Aug 16— Babe Ruth dies of throat cancer at the age of 53 in New York City. The nature of the Babe's illness had been kept secret but the worst is signaled shortly before his death by his hospitalization at Memorial Hospital Center for Cancer and Allied Diseases. The baseball community and the general public, accordingly, are somewhat prepared for the bad news. Indeed, the compassionate are relieved that Babe is finally freed from the pain he so stoically endured. The whole country reacts to Babe Ruth's death much as it would to the loss of a President. Tomorrow the body will be brought to Yankee Stadium's main entrance where more than 100,000 people (some estimates are as high as 200,000) will file past the coffin to pay their last respects. More than 6,500 people will pack St. Patrick's Cathedral on the 19th for funeral Mass celebrated by Francis Cardinal Spellman. The procession passes thousands of solemn onlookers on Fifth Avenue and takes the Babe to his final resting place in the Gate of Heaven Cemetery in Mount Pleasant, N.Y.

Aug 29— With Boston, Cleveland and New York all bunched near the top of the AL, Bucky Harris experiments and lets Joe Page start his only game of the season. But Detroit gets 10 hits and five runs off the Gay Reliever in 5⅔ innings.

— Page had an off-year after his great 1947 season. He saved 16 games but his ERA ballooned from 2.48 in 1947 to 4.26 in 1948. Joe would finish with a 7-8 record and league-leading stats in games pitched (55) and relief losses (8).

Sep 6— The Yankees win their ninth consecutive game, beating Philadelphia, 6-4, then drop the second game, 6-2, at Yankee Stadium. Rightfielder Hank Bauer makes his major league debut in the opener and singles in three trips to the plate. In the nightcap, Bauer plays left field and singles. But Bauer can't keep up the pace, finishing at .180 (9 for 50) in 19 games. In 23 days, Bauer will hit his first homer, also against the A's.

Sep 10— The Yankees beat Boston, 11-6, at Fenway Park, ending a nine-game winning streak of the Red Sox. In the 10th inning of a 6-6 tie, DiMaggio faces Earl Caldwell with two out and the bases loaded. Joe blasts a 420-foot grand slam homer, the Yanks' seventh "slam" this year. At day's end, first-place Boston (84-49) leads New York (82-52) by 2½ games and Cleveland (81-53) by 3½ games.

Sep 14— Charlie Keller, who had hit a pinch-hit homer two days earlier, belts his second home run in as many pinch-hit appearances. Keller is only the third player in AL history to accomplish this feat.

— Keller, who was attempting a comeback after his serious back problems of 1947, broke a bone in his hand in 1948, ending his days as a first stringer. Keller would hit .267 with six homers in 247 at bats. But the Yankees had three outfielders—four, including Berra—who hit over .300. DiMaggio hit .320, Johnny Lindell, .317, and Henrich, .308. Henrich would lead the league in runs scored (138) and triples (14) and would finish second in doubles (42). Old Reliable hit 25 homers and knocked in an even 100 runs in his best over-all season at the plate.

Sep 16— The Yankee Clipper swats his 300th home run as a major leaguer. DiMaggio joins seven previous entries into the exclusive 300-homer club, including Ruth, Gehrig, Ott, Foxx, Hornsby, Klein and Greenberg.

Sep 24— At day's end, there is a three-way tie for the league lead among the Red Sox, Indians and Yankees; all have 91-56 records. The AL announces that if the season ends this way, the Red Sox and Indians will have a playoff to determine who plays the Yankees for the championship. Each team has seven games remaining. The tie is created when the Yankees defeat Boston, 9-6, to begin a three-game series at Yankee Stadium. But the next day, the Bosox will rebound to win, 7-2, and the Yankees will fall one game off the pace.

Sep 26— A crowd of 69,755 comes to Yankee Stadium to see the Yankees and Red Sox complete their three-game series. This remains the Stadium attendance record for a single day game. The Yankees win, 6-2, knocking Boston into a second-place tie with them. Cleveland leads both by one game.

Oct 2—   The Yankees journey to Boston needing a sweep of a two-game series to force a playoff. On the next-to-last day of the season, the Yankees lose, 5-1, and are mathematically eliminated from the pennant struggle. Eighteen-game winner Jack Kramer beats eight-game winner Tommy Byrne. Ted Williams hits a home run. Boston and Cleveland continue the fight. This is one of the few close races involving the Yankees that New York does not win.

Oct 3—   On the final day of the season, Boston again beats New York, 10-5, while Cleveland loses to Detroit, and the Red Sox and Indians finish the season in a first-place tie. (The Yankees in 1948 win 2 of 11 games at Fenway.) Joe DiMaggio is magnificent, playing his heart out against brother Dom's team even though the Yankees are already eliminated. Joe strokes four hits, including two doubles, and drives in three runs. When he is removed from the game for a pinch-runner, the Fenway faithful give him a loud ovation. Joe will enter Johns Hopkins Hospital in Baltimore on November 11. He will have bone spurs removed from his right heel and will remain on crutches for six weeks following his discharge.

           — For better than the final month of the season, DiMaggio played with a painfully tender heel, a charley horse in his left thigh and other nagging injuries. But he still had his best post-war season. He had set personal goals of 35 homers and 150 RBIs and exceeded them with 39 and 155 to lead the AL in both categories. No one came close to him in either category. He finished second to Cleveland's Lou Boudreau in the MVP voting.

Oct 6—   Bucky Harris is released as manager of the Yankees. This comes as a shock to the fans and players, with whom Harris is popular, but not to the press, which has been reporting rumors of Harris' impending demise for weeks. The players had been relaxed all year under Harris. Too relaxed, believes George Weiss, who is upset about the poor records of Joe Page (7-8) and Spec Shea (9-10) after their great 1947 seasons. Both of these pitchers are known to burn the candle at both ends and Weiss feels that discipline was lacking.

           — Weiss and Harris, who simply did not like each other, had several disputes. The friction began when Larry MacPhail brought Harris to the Yankees as his top aide late in the 1946 season. After spending 14 years in the organization, Weiss believed he was being snubbed. Following MacPhail's departure, Weiss still viewed Harris as a "MacPhail man." Harris was known as the "four-hour manager" and Weiss was annoyed when he could not reach Harris away from the ballpark. Then there was the Bob Porterfield controversy—Harris wanted the young pitcher in New York and Weiss felt he belonged in Newark. Weiss had detectives follow certain players, and this upset Harris. And Harris in the pre-season predicted a Yankee pennant, a pennant not won in a year Weiss felt it should have been won.

Oct 12—   Casey Stengel is hired as Yankee manager. The announcement is made at the "21" club with Joe DiMaggio in attendance. Casey says, "I want first of all to thank Mr. Bob Topping for this opportunity." Everyone has a good laugh. Bob Topping, of course, is Dan Topping's brother and is not affiliated with the club. This is right in keeping with Stengel's reputation as baseball's premier clown. The 58-year-old Casey, who derived his name from the initials of Kansas City, his hometown, had a poor managing record with the Braves and before that with the Dodgers. Some experts feel he has been brought in for laughs while Weiss rebuilds the team. Casey is no youngster at age 58, either.

— Weiss and Stengel had been friendly since their days together in the mid-1920's in the Eastern League. In 1945, Weiss had Stengel manage the Yanks' Kansas City farm club and had come to admire Stengel's work with youngsters. Weiss knew Stengel would do well with the many prospects the Yankees had coming up, and that Casey would work well with him. Also instrumental in the decision to hire Stengel was Del Webb, who once thought of Casey as a favorite player. Webb was impressed with Stengel's recent record at Oakland in the Pacific Coast League.

1949

The Yankees will win a rousing pennant race with a 97-57 record, beating out Boston in the final two games of the season and winning by a one-game margin. Joe DiMaggio will be injured much of the year but will hit .346. Yogi Berra will drive in 91 runs and Tommy Henrich, 85. Vic Raschi will win 21 games and Joe Page will lead the league with 27 saves. The Yankees will triumph over Brooklyn in the World Series.

Feb 7— In signing his Yankee contract, Joe DiMaggio becomes the first $100,000-per-year player in baseball history. Joe is appropriately rewarded for his many years of exciting baseball, for his loyalty to the Yankees and for his productive and gritty 1948 performance. The Yankees had offered $90,000 plus an attendance bonus. This was attractive to Joe, but his friend, the restauranteur Toots Shor, persuaded him to negotiate for a flat $100,000. Dan Topping and Del Webb agree to the historic amount.

Mar 1— The Yankees report to spring training in St. Petersburg, Fla. Yogi Berra, whose hitting has been excellent since reaching the majors but who lacks polished catching skills, has a new tutor. He is Bill Dickey, returning to the Yankees as one of Casey Stengel's coaches. The polishing of Berra is the spring's biggest project. It is a productive and quotable undertaking. "Bill Dickey is learning me all of his experiences," says Yogi, who is on his way to becoming the best defensive catcher in the league.

Mar 2— DiMaggio wakes up the day after his first workout with a terrible pain in his right heel. There is immediate concern for the 34-year-old centerfielder, who over the past two years has had three operations, two for bone spurs in each heel and a third for bone chips in his elbow. He is sent back to Baltimore's Johns Hopkins Hospital and to Dr. George Bennett (who performed the three operations). No need to operate again, Bennett says, and Joe returns to camp. But the pain continues.

Apr 11— His spring batting average at .216, DiMaggio comes out of a game in Texas telling Casey Stengel that the pain in his hot heel is unbearable. It is apparent that DiMaggio will miss his eighth season opener in 11 seasons. He leaves for Johns Hopkins tomorrow. There doctors will say Joe's condition is caused by "immature calcium deposits in tissues adjacent to the heel bone." The Yankee Clipper will return to New York, and become a virtual recluse for almost two months, his baseball future in serious question.

Apr 19— Tommy Henrich hits a home run with two out in the bottom of the ninth inning and the Yankees defeat Washington, 3-2, on this Opening Day in which the Babe Ruth monument in centerfield, next to the monuments to Miller Huggins and Lou Gehrig, is dedicated. Among the 40,075 present are Gov. Thomas E. Dewey and Mayor William O'Dwyer. The Babe's widow, Mrs Claire

Ruth, unveils the memorial. Cliff Mapes plays centerfield today while DiMaggio, wearing an overcoat, sits in the dugout.

— New York began well and built an early-season record of 18-7. This success could be attributed largely to Henrich, who was the club's big gun with DiMaggio sidelined. Henrich would produce the game-winnig hit in almost half of the Yanks' first 40 victories.

May 8— Gene Woodling scores five runs, Henrich goes four for four and Tommy Byrne pitches a two hitter, as the Yankees win in Detroit, 12-0, before 52,891 fans.

— Outfielder Woodling, a new member of the cast, had four minor league batting titles to his credit, most conspicuously the 1948 Pacific Coast League crown as a .385-hitter for the San Francisco Seals. Woodling's play with the PCL impressed Casey Stengel, who urged George Weiss to purchase Gene's contract. In 112 games for New York in 1949, Woodling would hit .270.

Jun 27— Joe DiMaggio, who has been working out since his heel pain vanished about a week ago, plays in his first game since April 11. It is the Mayor's Trophy Game with the Giants but it will do. Joltin' Joe hits one into the Stadium's left field stands in the home run hitting contest. He goes hitless in four trips in the game but plays all nine innings, pleasing 37,637 fans. After missing the season's first 65 games, Joe is ready for a real game.

Jun 28— The Yankees, who lead third-place Boston by 5½ games with DiMaggio as yet to play a game, take the morning train to Boston. DiMaggio joins them later in the afternoon and tells Casey Stengel he feels ready to play. A crowd of over 36,000 flocks to Fenway Park in anticipation of DiMaggio's first game of the season. Boston has won 10 of 11 games and recently climbed from sixth to third, and New York has been playing .500 ball for some three weeks. The crowd is eager. The Yankees win, 5-4. Against Mickey McDermott in the second inning Joe lines a single to left field. Johnny Lindell walks and Hank Bauer wallops a three-run homer, giving the Yankees a 3-0 lead. In the third, Phil Rizzuto singles and DiMaggio takes McDermott deep, putting a two-run homer into the screen above the Green Monster. Rizzuto cannot contain his glee, shouting, "Holy Cow! Holy Cow!" as he circles the bases. The rest of the Yankees give Joe a spirited reception. But from a 5-0 deficit, the Red Sox close to 5-4 and have the tying run on base in the bottom of the ninth inning. Joe Page gets Ted Williams to fly deep to DiMaggio and disaster is averted. It is a spectacular return for the Yankee Clipper and an important win for the Yankees.

Jun 29— DiMaggio is the hero again. He hits two more home runs and the Yankees win, 9-7, on a day the 34-game hitting streak of Joe's brother, Dom, is broken. Boston leads, 7-1, but Joe cracks a three-run fifth-inning homer to make it, 7-4. In the seventh, Gene Woodling ties the score with a bases-loaded double. Against Earl Johnson with two outs in the eighth, DiMaggio blasts a towering shot that clears the left field wall, screen and all, and disappears into Boston. Stengel pops out of the dugout and takes a deep bow to the grandest player in the game as he circles the bases. Even the Fenway faithful are now cheering Joe. Page pitches three scoreless innings and gets the win.

Jun 30— DiMaggio's three-run homer leads the Yankees to a 6-3 victory and a three-game sweep of Boston. A plane towing a large banner reading THE GREAT DIMAGGIO circles Fenway prior to the game. There are two DiMaggio's present and one of them is only very good. So the banner is assumed to refer to Joe. After Snuffy Stirnweiss and Tommy Henrich single in the seventh, Joltin' Joe blasts a full-count Mel Parnell pitch with such force that it ricochets off a left field light tower all the way back to second base. The three-run shot puts the Yankees ahead, 6-2.

— Mere words fail in describing Joe's Boston show. Suffice it to say that in 11 at bats, and without having faced competitive major league pitching for more than two and a half months, DiMaggio had five hits—four of them homers— and drove in nine runs. No longer was he merely a sports hero; he was a national hero. And the Yankees closed out June leading the Indians by 5½ games and the Red Sox by 8½ games.

Jul 4—   A crowd of 63,876 turns out at Yankee Stadium to see the Yankees sweep a doubleheader from Boston. The Yankees win the opener, 3-2, in a thriller, thanks to a great play by Mapes and Berra. Vic Raschi starts the ninth by striking out Dom DiMaggio. Johnny Pesky singles, Ted Williams singles and Vern Stephens walks. Play is halted for five minutes while a dust storm blinds everyone on the field. Then, Al Zarilla hits a soft liner to right and Pesky can't decide if he should tag up at third. The ball drops in for a hit and rightfielder Cliff Mapes handles it cleanly and fires a perfect strike to the plate, where Berra touches the plate before Pesky. The home plate umpire is as confused as everyone in the ballpark, but Yogi quickly and forcefully argues that the play is a force-out—that he was not required to tag Pesky, and the ump calls Pesky out. Raschi gets Bobby Doerr to fly out to Mapes and the game is over. Mapes, who has a great arm, has saved the game with a tremendous throw. And Berra has demonstrated quick thinking. The nightcap is delayed by rain and wind (the center field screen blows down) but the Bronx Bombers win, 6-4, in 7½ innings.

— With the loss of both ends of the Independence Day twinbill, Boston's losing streak went to eight games. The first-place Yankees (48-25) led the fifth-place Red Sox (35-36) by 12 games. The A's, of all teams, were in second place as of this date, 4½ games back at 44-30.

Jul 12—   At Brooklyn's Ebbets Field, the AL wins the All-Star Game, 11-7, and Vic Raschi is the winning pitcher. The Springfield Rifle pitches the final three innings, allowing only one single and no runs. DiMaggio, who is named to the squad by AL Manager Lou Boudreau, adds to the legendary feats of this comeback year by hitting a double and single and knocking in three runs. Berra, who had finished second in the balloting behind Birdie Tebbetts, catches the last six innings as proof of his new-found receiving skills.

Jul 15—   Berra hits his first home run in his hometown of St. Louis as a Yankee, and it takes him two and a half years to do it. against Ned Garver, the Browns' ace, Berra knocks two fourbaggers over the right field pavilion roof at Sportsmans Park and the Yankees win, 6-0.

Aug 5—   At Yankee Stadium, the Yankees defeat St. Louis twice, 10-2 and 10-5. Berra hits a grand slam homer in the opener and gets thumbed by Umpire Summers in the nightcap. "I don't mind a little beefing now and then," said Summers. "But this was more than I could take. He kept it up...batter after batter. I finally told him that one umpire in the game was enough and that I was the one who was staying."

Aug 7— The Bronx Bombers make 22 hits and maul the Browns, 20-2, in the first game of a doubleheader that degenerates into a bean-ball battle. DiMaggio knocks in four runs, Rizzuto goes four for seven and scores four runs, and Berra hits a three-run homer. The next time up Yogi is hit on the left thumb by pitcher Dick Starr and gives way to his backup, Gus Niarhos. Mapes just gets out of the way of a head hunter and throws his bat at Starr. Later, reliever Karl Drews plunks Henrich on the right elbow and hits Niarhos and Jerry Coleman. Yankee pitcher Tommy Byrne, attempting to protect his hitters, retaliates by brushing back Starr in the fifth and Drews in the eighth. Stengel is irate after the doubleheader (the second game ends in a 2-2 tie), particularly with Starr and Drews, both former Yankees. At Lenox Hill Hospital, Henrich is discovered to have a bad bruise and will be sidelined briefly. Yogi has still another injury, a broken thumb (the Yanks' 50th injury of the season) and will miss several weeks.

— With Berra sidelined, perennial backup catcher Charlie Silvera played regularly and had his best major league season, hitting .315 (41 for 130) in 58 games. On the Sunday before the season's close, Silvera himself was injured. Silvera would be Yogi's backup from 1948-56, hitting a combined .291 in 201 games. He would play on seven pennant winners yet would bat only twice in World Series competition.

Aug 13— The Yankees win a cliffhanger, 9-7, in Philadelphia. Page pitches 1⅔ innings and is the winner, but he is scored on for the first time in 11 appearances. The next day Page pitches in both ends of a doubleheader and is not touched for a run.

Aug 22— The Yankees purchase the contract of slugger Johnny Mize for $40,000. Giant Manager Leo Durocher is unloading his maulers so that he can build a team around players with speed and finesse—in the mold of a young Durocher. Casey Stengel is anxious to add such a dangerous power-hitter to his arsenal and the deal will prove to be a bargain.

— The 36-year-old Mize began a five-season Yankee career by winning two games with clutch hits. But then he fell on his right shoulder and could be used only sparingly the rest of the year. The Big Cat finished the year with six hits, including a homer, in 23 at bats (.261).

Sep 5— The Yankees win two games, 13-4 and 5-2, against Philadelphia. In the opener, DiMaggio knocks in five runs and smashes a third-inning bases-loaded homer off Lou Brissie (16-11), and Billy Johnson goes five for six— three singles, a double and a home run.

Sep 7— Only 1½ games back, Boston comes to Yankee Stadium riding a five-game winning streak. Yankee starter Allie Reynolds has a 3-2 lead in the eighth when Bobby Doerr triples with one out. Page enters and gets Al Zarilla to pop out, then fans Billy Goodman. In the ninth, Page strikes out Birdie Tebbetts, Matt Batts and Dom DiMaggio to end the game. Page strikes out the final four batters on only 15 pitches. Reynolds and Page have been a great combination this year. Page, after a disappointing 1948, will lead the AL in saves (27) and in games pitched (60). It is a big win for the Yankees even though Boston will come back after tomorrow's postponement to beat the Yanks, 7-1. It marks the return of Berra, exactly one month after he fractured his thumb. Yogi will be in and out of the line-up and will use a sponge inside his mitt to ease the pain while catching. He can swing the bat with only one arm.

Sep 18— The Yankees lead the Red Sox by 2½ games, but DiMaggio is again forced to the sidelines. After taking batting practice, Joe is ordered to bed with a 102-degree temperature. He is suffering from a viral infection and pneumonia and will be bedridden for more than a week. Joe will lose 18 pounds in 10 days. Mapes plays center field in a big game against Cleveland, which draws 64,549 to the Stadium. The Yanks go over two million in home attendance for the fourth year in a row. Hank Bauer and Page, who hurls three scoreless innings, are the heroes in a 7-3 victory. Rightfielder Bauer, himself a recent injury victim, has a single, double, triple and three RBIs. In the final game of the set tomorrow, the Indians will waste their last chance— they will finish eight games out. Henrich will return from the injury he suffered August 28 when he ran into the outfield wall in Chicago. Wearing a bulky corset, he will knock in two runs.

Sep 25— The Red Sox, who won yesterday, beat the Yankees again today, 4-1, and move into a first-place tie with New York. Both teams have identical records of 93-55. It caps an amazing Red Sox comeback since being counted out of the race on the Fourth of July. Six games remain.

Sep 26— In a make-up game at Yankee Stadium, the Red Sox win, 7-6, to surge into the AL lead by one game. It is New York's first time out of the top spot all season. Things look dim for the Yankees, who are still playing without DiMaggio. Page allows four runs in 3⅓ innings and loses his third game in three appearances. Stengel, Mapes and Ralph Houk are all thrown out of the game. With darkness approaching and Johnny Pesky on third base, Bobby Doerr squeezes home Pesky, although first baseman Henrich's throw to catcher Houk seems to beat Pesky. But Pesky is called safe and the Yankees protest at the top of their lungs. For their protesting, Houk and Mapes will be fined $200 each and Stengel $150. The Yankees have three games left with the A's and two against the Red Sox.

Oct 1— The Red Sox invade Yankee Stadium for the final two games of the season. They lead the Yankees by one game. Boston needs just one victory to clinch the pennant, while New York must win both games to take the AL Champ-ionship. It is Joe DiMaggio Day and 69,551 fans turn out to honor the Yankee centerfielder. Mel Allen is the master of ceremonies and Ethel Merman sings some of her show tunes. Joe receives gifts, as does his mother and son. On Joe's insistence, all cash gifts to him are donated to his favorite charities. Also honoring Joe is Joe MacCarthy, DiMaggio's former manager, who is now piloting the Red Sox. The Yankee Clipper speaks a few heartfelt words, summing up by saying, "I want to thank my fans; my friends; my manager, Casey Stengel; my teammates, the gamest, fightingest bunch of guys that ever lived. And I want to thank the Good Lord for making me a Yankee." Then Joe, coming off a bout with pneumonia and looking drawn and weak, returns to the line-up despite the chilly weather and gets two hits. The pitching matchup is Allie Reynolds against Mel Parnell. The Bosox score a run in the first inning and in the third Reynolds walks the bases loaded with no outs. A resulting bloop single puts the Yankees in a 2-0 hole. Page comes in and promptly walks in two more runs and puts the Yankees in a 4-0 hole. But thereafter, Page is sensational, fanning the last two batters in the third and holding the Bosox to one hit over the final 6⅔ innings. No Red Sox player will even reach second base over the final six frames. Meanwhile, the Yankee hitters come to life. In the fourth, DiMaggio doubles, Berra singles Joe home, Johnny Lindell singles Yogi to third base and Yogi scores on a sacrifice fly. In the fifth Phil Rizzuto singles, Henrich singles, Berra singles home Rizzuto (Joe Dobson relieves Parnell), DiMaggio has an infield hit to load the bases and Billy Johnson bounds into a double play as Henrich plates the tying run. In the eighth, Lindell gets hold of one of Dobson's offerings and lines a game-winning solo homer into the lower left field seats. It is only Johnny's sixth homer of the season, and his first since July, but it gives the Yankees a stirring 5-4 triumph. Now New York and Boston are tied for first place with identical 96-57 records. After the game, Page, who is gasping after his longest relief stint of the campaign, tells reporters, "When I came into the game so early, I knew it would be pretty tough going. But when I got a little tired in the late innings, I just took another look at that guy in center field and told myself that if DiMag can keep playing as weak and as sick as he still is, then I ought to be able to pitch forever!"

Oct 2— Yankee Stadium is packed on a hot autumn afternoon for the game to determine the AL champion. Stengel sends out Vic Raschi, who is going for his 21st win. McCarthy counters with Ellis Kinder, who already has 23 wins against only five defeats. In the first, Rizzuto triples and scores on Henrich's ground-out. After that, both Raschi and Kinder assume command and neither side can break through as the seat-squirmer progresses inning after inning. But in the eighth, after Kinder has been lifted for a pinch-hitter, the Yankees rough up relievers Mel Parnell and Tex Hughson. Henrich launches a solo homer into the right field stands; then the Yanks load the bases. Jerry Coleman clears them with a two-out bloop double that rightfielder Al Zarilla just misses catching. The Yanks have a 5-0 lead. Through eight innings, the Red Sox have managed only two hits off Raschi, but the Bostonians courageously fight back in the ninth for three runs. When Bobby Doerr's triple sails over Joe DiMaggio's head, the weary centerfielder calls time and removes himself from the game. He has given all he can and the huge crowd gives Joe a tremendous ovation as he drags his weary body from the field. With three runs home, a runner on base, two outs and the tying run at the plate, Berra goes out to calm Raschi. "Gimme the goddam ball and get the hell out of here," growls the fiercely competitive Raschi. He induces Birdie Tebbetts to hit a high pop that first baseman Henrich catches in foul territory and the Yankees win the game, 5-3, and the pennant. Coach Bill Dickey is so excited that he leaps into the air, bangs his head against the dugout ceiling and knocks himself out cold. In the clubhouse, Stengel emotionally thanks his players for this "greatest thrill" and adds, "and to think that they pay me for managing so great a bunch of boys."

— Stengel brought a wounded team to the top. These Yankees sustained upwards of 70 assorted injuries. Stengel's big guns— DiMaggio, Henrich and Berra— were in the line-up together for only 12 of the first 148 games. But Casey manipulated the club brillantly, replacing the wounded and platooning at third base and in the outfield . Rizzuto was the only player to get into more than 130 games and bat more than 450 times. The Scooter played 153 games, had 614 at bats and batted .275. From his hospital bed, Henrich had said, "We have nothing to worry about as long as Rizzuto remains healthy." And Tommy was right. DiMaggio's leadership inspired everyone. In the 60 games in which Page pitched, the Yankees won 42, lost 17 and tied one. And Casey trotted out four first-rate starters: Raschi (21-10), Reynolds (17-6), Byrne (15-7) and Lopat (15-10).

Oct 5— The World Series opens at Yankee Stadium and the Yankees defeat the Brooklyn Dodgers, 1-0. This is a tremendous pitching duel between Reynolds, who allows only two hits and strikes out nine, and Don Newcombe, who allows only five hits and strikes out 11 Yankees. But the fifth Yankee hit is a leadoff homer by Henrich on a two ball-no strike count in the bottom of the ninth, ending the game. The Dodgers will turn the tables tomorrow, winning 1-0.

Joe DiMaggio, with Mel Allen at his side, waves to his legion of fans during Joe DiMaggio Day at Yankee Stadium. Joe received many gifts, including his team's defeat of Boston to set up a final-game showdown for the 1949 AL championship.

— The Series naturally began with a scent of anticlimax in the air. Both the Yankees and Dodgers won the pennant on the final day of the season, the Dodgers also winning by one game and with the same 97-57 record.

Oct 7—   The Series shifts to Ebbets Field and the Yankees prevail, 4-3. The game enters the ninth inning tied, 1-1, thanks to the opposing shortstops— Rizzuto has a run-scoring sacrifice fly in the third and Pee Wee Reese homers in the fourth. In the ninth, with the bases loaded, Johnny Mize knocks in two runs with a pinch-hit single off the right field fence. Coleman singles in a fourth run. Page, who wins the game in relief, allows a pair of solo homers in the ninth, but holds on for the win. The Yanks win tomorrow, too.

Oct 9—   The Yankees outslug Brooklyn, 10-6, and win the World Series in five games. New York races to a 10-1 lead, and, when winner Raschi falters in the seventh inning, the peerless Page enters and holds Brooklyn scoreless over the final 2⅓ innings. Coleman drives in three runs, Bobby Brown and Gene Woodling each have three hits, and DiMaggio hits a home run. The leading hitter of the Series is Brown (.500), but the Babe Ruth Award, presented to the Series MVP, goes to Page. And Page ends the Series in style. With the lights turned on for the first time in World Series history, giving the proceedings an eerie glow, Page strikes out Duke Snider, Jackie Robinson and Gil Hodges in the ninth inning.

THE 1950's
A SWEET, SWEET TIME

EIGHT PENNANTS
FIVE CONSECUTIVE WORLD TITLES
CASEY IS THE BRAINS
DiMAGGIO LEAVES IN STYLE
THE KID FROM OKLAHOMA
TAPE MEASURE HOME RUNS
REYNOLDS-RASCHI-LOPAT WIN BIG ONES
FORD BECOMES THE ACE
CASEY AND YOGI KEEP THEM LAUGHING
THE SCOOTER STARS AND DEPARTS
MARTIN'S AGGRESSIVE BASEBALL
A PERFECT GAME
REVENGE OVER BROOKLYN
REVENGE OVER MILWAUKEE

1950

Finishing at 98-56, the Yankees will win their 17th pennant by three games over second-place Detroit and by four over Boston. Phil Rizzuto will hit .324, make 200 hits and win the MVP Award. Joe DiMaggio will hit 32 homers and have 122 RBIs. Vic Raschi will lead the pitching staff at 21-8. The Yankees will bowl over the Whiz Kids of Philadelphia in the World Series.

Jan 12—   The Chicago Cubs purchase the Newark Bears, the Yanks' top farm club since 1932, with plans to move the franchise to Springfield, Mass. The Bears, who in 1949 finished last in the International League, were drawing poorly. Yankee General Manager George Weiss tells the press, "Attendance did not warrant our continuance of a Newark club..."

Mar 11—   The talk at spring training camp centers on an aggressive infielder from Berkeley, Calif., Alfred Martin, who insists that everyone call him "Billy." Martin, obtained over the winter along with Jackie Jensen, came from the Oakland Oaks where he once played for Casey Stengel. Casey starts Martin at shortstop in an exhibition game against the Cardinals at Al Lang Field in St. Petersburg, Fla. Martin contributes two singles and two walks, a "highly impressive showing," writes John Drebinger of *The New York Times*.

Apr 15—   The Yankees take an exhibition game from the Dodgers, 6-4, before a crowd of 12,632 at a Yankee Stadium spruced up with a new scoreboard, press box and visiting clubhouse. Rookie Martin, already popular with Yankee fans, plays great defensive ball, knocks in a run with a double and bothers Dodger pitcher Preacher Roe with his base running and vocal taunts. In the fifth inning, Joe DiMaggio robs Roy Campanella of a possible inside-the-parker with one of the greatest catches in Stadium history. Later Joe homers to break up a 0-0 tie.

Apr 18—   The Yankees overcome a 9-0 deficit and win at Fenway Park on Opening Day, 15-10. Billy Martin, who replaced Jerry Coleman, gets a run-scoring hit in his first official major league at bat in the eighth. Later in the same inning, Billy singles in two more runs. So Martin in his first major league game, in his first two at-bats, makes two hits in one inning. Boston uses five pitchers in the eighth inning as New York scores nine times. DiMaggio today has a single, double and triple and two great defensive plays. When the game is over, Casey Stengel dances as though he had won the pennant. New York is in first place and will stay in or around first over the season.

Apr 21 — Bad weather holds the crowd to 27,877 but the spirits of those who attend the Yanks' home opener are boosted by a 14-7 victory over Washington. The day begins when the Yankees ride in a morning jeep parade to the Bronx County Courthouse for a welcome from borough officials and ends with a dinner at the Concourse Plaza Hotel. DiMaggio's seventh-inning homer breaks a 7-7 tie. Yogi Berra scores four runs and his four hits include a home run. Byrne and Henrich also hit homers.

May 4—   Bob Cain five-hits the Yankees in his first major league start and the White Sox beat the Yankees, 15-0, before only 8,764 at Yankee Stadium. Chicago ties the record for the most runs scored against the Yankees in a shutout. Phil Rizzuto makes three hits and raises his average to .419!

May 14— The Yankees demote Billy Martin to the Kansas City Blues, their top farm club. Martin does not like it, and, on Stengel's advice, sees George Weiss. Martin and Weiss get into a shouting match; from this point on, Weiss has it in for Billy.

— Martin was recalled on June 15 when infielder Snuffy Stirnweiss was traded, opening up a roster spot. Stirnweiss, outfielder Jim Delsing and pitchers Don Johnson and Duane Pillette and $50,000 went to the Browns for three pitchers, Tom Ferrick, Joe Ostrowski and Sid Schact, and third baseman Leo Thomas. Stirnweiss, one of the most popular Yankees of all time, hit .274 over eight Yankee seasons. Martin would be used sparingly in 1950. He would finish at .250 (9 for 36) in 34 games.

May 15— The Yankees sell the contract of outfielder Johnny Lindell to the Cardinals on waivers. In only seven games with the Yankees this year, Lindell hits .190 (4 for 21). He will be deeply hurt by the deal and bat only .186 (21 for 113) for St. Louis. He had a poor 1949 season and he is one of the Old Guard Casey is weeding out.

— In 10 Yankee seasons, Lindell hit .275, belted 63 home runs, drove in 369 runs, came through with scores of clutch hits and provided comic relief as one of the club's top practical jokers. He was a tremendous team player who always gave everything he had.

May 16— New York takes over first place in the AL—Detroit and Boston are within a half game. The Yankees, now 15-8, win big in St. Louis. An eight-run eighth inning powers the New Yorkers, whose Allie Reynolds pitches a five-hit shutout, to an 11-0 triumph. The offensive punch comes from Billy Johnson (a grand slam homer and a total of five RBIs) and Phil Rizzuto (four hits).

Jun 20— DiMaggio gets the 1,999th and 2,000th hits of his careeer in an 8-2 win in Cleveland. Joe's first hit, off Bob Lemon, knocks in two runs in the third inning. His second is a run-scoring single in the seventh off Marino Pieretti. No. 2,000 is stroked in his 6,050th trip to the plate. The only other active players with 2,000 hits are Luke Appling and Wally Moses. The Italian-born Pieretti personally presents the Jolter with the prized ball.

Jun 23— The second great winning Yankee manager, Joe McCarthy, retires today as skipper of the Red Sox, and from baseball. The Yankees he once proudly managed, meanwhile, combine with Detroit to hit 11 homers (a big league record) at Briggs Stadium. Detroit wins, 10-9, when Hoot Evers hits a two-run inside-the-park homer (his second homer of the game) in the bottom of the ninth, *after* Henrich had given the Yanks a 9-8 lead with his two-run pinch homer, *after* the Tigers had overcome a 6-0 Yankee lead to go ahead, 8-6, on fourth-inning homers hit by Evers, Dizzy Trout, Jerry Priddy and Vic Wertz. Pitcher Trout hits his homer with the bases loaded. Yankee homers, besides Henrich's, are hit by Bauer (2), Berra, Coleman and DiMaggio.

— Detroit's win was the start of something not good. The Tigers would dominate the series, winning three out of four, and take a firm grip on first place. With a record of 40-19, they led the Yankees by three full games.

Jul 1— Whitey Ford, just called up from the Kansas City farm club where he won six of nine decisions, makes his major league debut in relief of Tommy Byrne against Boston. Byrne gets the loss, but young Whitey doesn't help, giving up seven hits, six walks and five earned runs in 4⅔ innings. Boston wins in a cakewalk, 13-4.

— This was Ford's only poor outing of the season. He would prove to be the difference in the pennant race, going 9-1. The pennant could not have been won without Ford's great pitching.

Jul 3—   Casey Stengel, worried about production from first base with Henrich and Mize hurting and rookie Joe Collins slumping, makes a mistake and starts DiMaggio at this position in a game with Washington. The Senators win, 7-2. DiMaggio had not played the bag since he was a kid. Although he handles 13 putouts flawlessly, he is hitless in four trips; he sweats bullets and feels out of position, which, of course, he is. This is the only time in DiMaggio's career that he plays a position other than outfield. Late in the game, Bauer injures his right ankle and DiMaggio returns to his home in the outfield (where he will be for tomorrow's holiday doubleheader).

Jul 11—   Seven Yankees see action in an All-Star Game the NL wins, 4-3, in 14 innings. Raschi is the starting pitcher and allows two runs in three innings. Reynolds also goes three innings and allows only one hit and no runs. DiMaggio, Berra, Coleman and Henrich all go hitless, but Rizzuto makes two hits. Stengel loses his first game as a manager in the Summer Classic.

— For a time, the double-play combination in the AL infield was Rizzuto and Coleman, who this year put on an amazing display of infield acrobatics. Rizzuto had his greatest year at the plate in 1950 and would also lead AL shortstops in fielding average and putouts. Coleman also had his greatest year as a hitter, batting .287 with 69 RBIs, and like the Scooter, Jerry was a marvelous fielder. He would help turn 137 double plays. Added to Rizzuto's 123, these two wizards totaled 260 double plays, sixth highest in baseball history. It may have been the greatest all-round season at the shortstop-second base positions in Yankee history.

Jul 17—   Whitey Ford wins his first major league game. He beats the White Sox, 4-3, with relief help from Tom Ferrick in the eighth inning. The Stadium audience sees the start of an era, and they have a new, local-boy hero to cheer.

Aug 6—   Second baseman Billy Martin lets loose with his first major league homer. Billy has three RBIs and scores two runs and Rizzuto has two doubles, a triple and a single as New York beats the Indians in Cleveland, 9-0. Tommy Byrne, who has a no-hitter for six innings, settles for a three-run shutout.

Aug 18—   After a week's rest, DiMaggio returns to the line-up and hits a dramatic ninth-inning upper-deck home run to break a 2-2 tie in Philadelphia. Even the 6,054 partisan Athletic fans cheer Joe, whose teammates mob him around the plate.

— DiMaggio would hit over .400 through the next 11 games, 10 of them Yankee wins, as New York made its run at first-place Detroit. Joe was in there, leading the way, having one of his best-ever periods of hitting. From this date through the season's close, Joe would hit .376 to raise his final average to .301. The Jolter would capture the slugging title with a .585 mark.

Sep 2—   Three days after going into first place, the Yankees win their sixth game in a row and their 15th victory in 17 games. DiMaggio hits a home run and has five RBIs in the 9-2 conquest of Washington at the Stadium. The standings of the principal competitors: New York, on the way to winning 16 to 18, 82-46; Detroit, 78-47; and Boston, only 3½ games out, 79-50. Several days later the Tigers reassume the top spot.

Sep 10— DiMaggio becomes the first player to hit three home runs at Washington's Griffith Stadium. Joe's double gives him a fifth career game of four extra-base hits. He scores four runs in the 8-1 Yankee win and has four RBIs, passing the coveted 100-RBI mark for the ninth time in 12 seasons. All three of Joe's homers travel over 400 feet. They have to: Griffith Stadium rivals Yankee Stadium as the league's toughest park for righthanded hitters—405 feet down the left field line and 420 feet to dead center.

Sep 14— New York arrives in Detroit for a crucial three-game series. The Yankees win the opener, 7-5, and regain first place by a half game, as Raschi wins his 20th game. DiMaggio, Mapes and Mize hit homers.

Sep 15— The Tigers win, 9-7, and take first place. Heroic in defeat, Mize hits three of the longest homers in Briggs Stadium history, accounting for six of New York's runs. It is the sixth game in Big Jawn's major league career in which he has hit a trio of roundtrippers, a major league record that still stands, and he joins Babe Ruth (whose widow is John's cousin) as the second player to hit three homers in one game in both big leagues.

— Mize spent much of the early season nursing an injured throwing arm and was with the Kansas City farm club for a spell. Later he took over at first base, ending Stengel's No. 1 headache. He would hit 25 home runs in only 274 at bats, a pace that would have given the 37-year-old some 50 homers over a full season!

Sep 16— In the season's most important game, played before a packed house, Whitey Ford goes the route and wins his seventh consecutive game without a loss, DiMaggio hits his 30th homer and the Yankees defeat Detroit, 8-1. The score is tied at 1-1 until the Bronx Bombers strike for seven runs in the ninth inning. New York leaves the Motor City with an 89-51 record; Red Rolfe's surprising Tigers are 88-51.

Sep 17— The Yankees score five runs in the ninth inning to beat St. Louis, 6-1. Recently acquired Johnny Hopp's pinch-hit grand slam homer, the second such fourbagger in Yankee history, is the hit of the rally.

Sep 20— In Chicago, Ford wins his eighth consecutive game without a loss, 8-1, on a three-hitter. It is Whitey's 11th start and New York had won them all. New York and Detroit continue to run even in the loss column. The Yanks lead the Bengals by a half game and the Bosox by two games. Ford will beat Washington on September 25 for his ninth win without a loss but will lose in relief two days later in Philadelphia.

Sep 23— The Red Sox are hot and trail the Yankees and Tigers by only two games, with the prospect of pulling up to New York if they can sweep both games of the set that brings them to the Stadium. A crowd of 63,998 is on hand to see the Boston hopes deflated, 8-0. Lopat wins his 18th game of the year. DiMaggio's two-run first-inning homer is enough to get things rolling.

Sep 24— Before 66,924 fans on Johnny Mize Day at the Stadium, the Yankees beat Boston again, 9-5, as Rizzuto has a single, double and homer. Berra contributes three singles and a triple and Raschi wins his 21st game. Meanwhile, Cleveland defeats Detroit for the third consecutive time.

Sep 28—   New York clinches a tie for the pennant by beating Philadelphia, 8-6, in
          10 innings. The Yankees with a record of 97-55 have two games left. The
          Tigers, at 94-57, are 2½ back with three games left. Rizzuto is big in
          today's win with four hits, including a game-winning single.

Sep 29—   The Yankees sit out a rainout in Boston, but clinch the AL pennant; Cleveland
          beats the Tigers, who fall three games behind with only two games to play.
          Stengel's Yankees have won their second straight miracle pennant. DiMaggio's
          bat has led them. Joe had nine homers and 30 RBIs in September.

Oct 4—   The World Series with the Phillies opens in Philadelphia. Raschi's two-hitter
          wins for the Yankees, 1-0. The Phils start Jim Konstanty, whose 74 game
          appearances this year are all in relief, and the strategy works well, except
          for the fourth inning when Bobby Brown doubles, moves to third on Bauer's
          long fly and scores on Coleman's sacrifice fly. The Phillies, known as the Whiz
          Kids, are making their first World Series appearance since 1915.

Oct 5—   In the 10th inning, the Yankee Clipper nails a Robin Roberts pitch and drives
          it into the upper left field stands of Shibe Park, and the Yankees win, 2-1.
          Reynolds and Roberts duel for the full 10 innings. But Reynolds is a little
          better, scattering seven hits, and popping up Richie Ashburn and striking out
          Dick Sisler with the tying run on second base in the bottom of the 10th.
          The Yankees will win still another one-run contest in Game 3 at the Stadium.

Oct 7—   Rookie Whitey Ford pitches the Yankees to their 13th World Championship.
          Ford, who will enter the military for two seasons after the Series, tames the
          Phils on five hits and one walk through eight innings and gets first-inning
          support on run-scoring hits from Berra and DiMaggio. Berra's homer and
          Brown's triple are the key hits in a three-run sixth inning. With two runners
          on in the top of the ninth and two out, it appears Ford has a shutout but
          he has to settle for a 5-2 win. Woodling, playing the Stadium's infamous
          "sun field" in left, loses sight of a fly ball in the autumn haze for a two-run
          error. After another hit, Stengel is forced to bring in Reynolds, who strikes
          out pinch-hitter Stan Lopata to end the Series. Woodling and Hamner are the
          leading hitters of the Series at .429, but Jerry Coleman, who figures in so
          much key scoring, is the winner of the Babe Ruth Award as the Series' star.
          The Yankee pitching staff's ERA is a staggering 0.73—the Phillies score only
          five runs in four games and only three of the runs are earned. It is only the
          seventh Series sweep in history (six of them belonging to the Yankees).

Dec 18—   Old Reliable, Tommy Henrich, retires. He will be one of Casey Stengel's
          coaches in 1951. Henrich had been sidelined much of 1950 with a bad knee.
          He hit .272 in only 151 at-bats. His injury kept him off the World Series
          roster, Johnny Hopp replacing him.

          — Henrich, one of the Yankees all-time greats, was a steady hitter with
          good power, who saved his best hits for the most critical situations. He
          was a tremendous fielding rightfielder who could also ably handle first base,
          a heads-up player who was always two thoughts ahead of the opposition.
          In 11 big league seasons, all with the Yankees, the Ohio native hit .282 with
          183 homers. He scored over 100 runs four times and totaled 901 runs.

1951

The Yankees will finish at 98-56 to win their third consecutive pennant by a five-game margin over second-place Cleveland. MVP-winner Yogi Berra will lead the offense with 27 home runs and 88 RBIs. Both Ed Lopat and Vic Raschi will be 21-game winners. The New York Yankees will defeat the New York Giants in a six-game World Series.

Mar 1— Spring training opens in Phoenix, Ariz., the Yankees having traded camp sites with the Giants, who are in St. Petersburg, Fla. Del Webb and Giant owner Horace Stoneham made the switch and Webb gets the chance to show off his club to his West Coast friends. Three rookies—Tom Morgan, Gil McDougald and Mickey Mantle—are waiting as the veterans report. The latter is already the talk of camp, as he rockets balls tremendous distances from either side of the plate and runs faster than anyone can remember anyone ever running. But Mantle does not look good playing shortstop, so Stengel begins his conversion to outfielder.

— Mantle, McDougald and Morgan got a chance to impress Casey at the Yanks' Instructional School camp, which opened in Phoenix in early February. Some 40 minor leaguers and bonus babies were invited to attend, and besides the three who stuck with the big club, the likes of Andy Carey, Bill Skowron, Bob Cerv and Tom Sturdivant, who didn't for the moment stick, also were impressive. Another New York phenom, Jackie Jensen, will impress in an upcoming game in which he hits two homers a triple and a double. Packing all-time great Joe DiMaggio and exciting youngsters, the Yankees enjoy a great West Coast tour. They draw an overflow 22,000 to Los Angeles' Wrigley Field and 26,000 to a morning-afternoon set with the Oaks and San Francisco Seals in San Francisco. Mantle in particular is causing a stir.

Apr 14— Having failed his Army physical for the second time in Miami, Okla., Mantle boards a plane for New York and the Yankees' final exhibitions of the pre-season. How could a 19-year-old stronger than Ruth and faster than Cobb be classified 4-F? Osteomyelitis, a condition Mickey developed as a high school football player when he was kicked in the leg, automatically pre-empts military sevice. But Mickey will be subjected to criticism.

Apr 15— Mantle plays in New York for the first time and has a homer and three singles. Prior to the game, which is with the Dodgers at Ebbets Field, Stengel takes Mantle out to right field to show him how to play the wall. Young Mickey finds it hard to believe that Casey once played the position. "For crissakes," sputters Casey, "you think I was born old?"

— Mantle may not have been familiar with Stengel's playing career, but he was definitely ready for the Yankees. He finished the pre-season with 41 hits in 102 at bats for a .402 average, and he had nine homers and 31 RBIs. His performance exceeded his tremendous press buildup.

Apr 17— Vic Raschi shuts out Boston on Opening Day at Yankee Stadium, 5-0. Stengel starts three rookies—Mantle (RF), McDougald (3B) and Jackie Jensen (LF). (Another rookie, Tom Morgan, will go into the starting rotation on the strength of 25 consecutive scoreless innings pitched in spring training.) Mantle bats four times and has one hit, a line-drive single that drives in a run. He accepts his first fly, hit by Ted Williams, and is so nervous he leaps off the ground to catch it.

May 1—   Mantle hits his first major league homer, a 450-foot blast at Chicago's Comiskey Park off Randy Gumpert, a former Yankee.

May 3—   Gil McDougald becomes the fourth player in AL history to have six RBIs in one inning. The sensational rookie hits a two-run triple and a grand slam homer as New York scores 11 times (an AL record) in the ninth to beat the Browns in St. Louis, 17-3.

— McDougald would be named Rookie of the Year, the first Yankee so honored by the Baseball Writers since the award's 1947 inauguration. McDougald would finish with an average of .306 and hit 14 home runs. The San Franciscan would switch from third base (82 games) to second base (55 games) in mid-season and handle both positions like a veteran. Rogers Hornsby, Gil's manager in 1950, was proud of him.

May 30— Mantle strikes out five straight times in a doubleheader against Boston. The strikeouts are becoming a disturbing pattern. Mickey is upset, and he tells Stengel, "Put somebody in there who can hit. I can't." Casey reminds the prodigy that neither DiMaggio nor Berra had a hit today, either. Mickey will have 52 strikeouts in 246 at-bats and on July 13 the Yanks will send him down to Kansas City where his slump will continue. He comes out of the slump when his father, Mutt, offers him a lifetime of coal mining in Oklahoma.

Jun 15— At the trading deadline, the Yankees obtain Bob Kuzava (P) and Bob Ross (P) from the Washington Senators for Bob Porterfield (P), Tom Ferrick (P) and Fred Sanford (P), and in a separate deal for Tommy Byrne (P) and $25,000, Stubby Overmire (P) from the Browns.

— The best pitcher of the lot was Byrne. "Sure, he's wild, but he won 15 games for us last year and the year before," complained Stengel, who didn't approve of the Byrne deal. "Who's gonna do that for us now?" (The Yanks would reacquire Byrne, but not until 1954.)

Jul 12— Allie Reynolds pitches a no-hitter against Cleveland. It is the fifth Yankee no-hitter and the first since Monte Pearson's in 1938. The loser of the 1-0 night game in Cleveland is Bob Feller, who no-hit the Tigers just 11 days ago. Reynolds walks three and the Yanks commit one error. The Big Chief sends the final 17 Indians back to their wigwam in order. Reynolds, who missed spring training because of bone chips in his elbow, now has 10 wins, half of them shutout victories.

— Sometime before this game, Stengel was asked why he didn't allow his relievers to ride to the mound in golf carts. Casey said Yankees travel only in Cadillacs. Indian General Manager Hank Greenberg had a Caddy waiting in the New York bullpen on the night of the no-hitter. It would be gone the next night.

Jul 20— Boston, Chicago, New York and Cleveland are within a couple of games of one another at the top of the AL when Stengel shakes up his infield. Casey benches Jerry Coleman, who will hit .249 this year, switches McDougald to second base and plays Bobby Brown at third base.

— Although Brown would finish at only .268, his streak-hitting spurred New York to 17 wins in 20 games. He provided the needed spark, hitting safely in 18 of 20 games, once given the role as the Yanks' regular third baseman.

Jul 30— The Yankees celebrate Stengel's 61st birthday with a 5-4 win over Detroit at the Stadium. The Tigers take a late 4-2 lead when DiMaggio makes an uncharacteristic mental mistake that allows a runner to tag up and score from second base. Joe catches a fly and, wrongly believing it is the inning's third out, trots toward the dugout. The Yankee Clipper atones in the ninth, singling in the deciding run.

Aug 2— Fresh out of the military, Billy Martin plays his first game of the season in the second of two games with the Tigers. A shortstop, Billy makes several great fielding plays and starts a pair of double plays. He has three hits, one of them a triple. Billy leads the Yanks, who lost the opener 9-8, to a 10-6 win.

Aug 23— New York loses the first game of a key three-game series in Cleveland and drops three games behind the first-place Indians. Bob Lemon pitches a three-hitter and defeats Vic Raschi, 2-1.

Aug 24— Up from Kansas City, Mantle joins the Yankees and assumes his position in right field. The Yankees beat Cleveland, 2-0, as Stubby Overmire (1-1) and Joe Ostrowski (6-4) combine to shut out the Tribe. Gene Woodling hits a two-run homer off Early Wynn.

— Woodling and Hank Bauer were part of Stengel's outfield platoon system. Each played more than he sat. Woodling in 1951 played in 120 games and Bauer got into 118 games. Gene would finish at .281 with 71 RBIs and Bauer at .296 with 54 RBIs. Both were excellent defensively, each making only two errors all year. They were complete, solid-as-rock ballplayers. Woodling, 28, batted lefty and played left field; Bauer, also 28, hit righty and played right field. The mirror images were big reasons the Yankees were in the pennant race.

Aug 25— The Yankees beat Cleveland, 7-3, and are now only one game behind the Indians (Cleveland is 78-45; New York is 77-46). Mantle leads the way with a two-run homer off Mike Garcia. He will wind up his rookie year hitting .267 with 13 homers and 65 RBIs.

Aug 28— In St. Louis, Berra is upset with a call and he and Umpire Hurley push each other. But before any real damage can be done, Stengel hauls Berra to the dugout. Fearing a long suspension, Casey has Yogi apologize to Hurley after the game. The umpire's report to AL President Harridge takes the apology into account and Berra is merely fined $100.

Sep 3— The Yankees win, 3-1, then lose, 3-2, in a Labor Day doubleheader in Philadelphia. Johnny Sain, obtained August 29 from the Boston Braves for pitcher Lew Burdette and $50,000, makes his first New York start in the opener and pitches a five-hitter. Johnny, who starts a Yankee rally with a double, is a four-time 20-game winner. Burdette, 0-0 with the the Yanks this year, will win 203 major league games.

Sep 16— Cleveland charges into Yankee Stadium for the season's most important series, albeit a two-gamer. The Yankees trail by one game. Feller (22-8) is matched with Reynolds, and upwards of 68,000 attend. Reynolds is the better today, limiting the Indians to five hits, and wins, 5-1. In the fifth inning, Mantle doubles and Berra is intentionally walked. The Yankee Clipper comes up and blasts a triple to Death Valley, putting the game out of reach. The Yankees are in first place by .003.

Sep 17—   Rizzuto and DiMaggio work a beautiful suicide squeeze play, Lopat wins his
          20th game, 2-1, and the Yankees move a full game (plus a few percentage
          points) ahead of Cleveland with 12 games remaining. In the bottom of the
          ninth of a 1-1 tie, Rizzuto steps to the plate with one out and DiMaggio
          dancing off third. The Scooter signals Joe that he will squeeze. As the pitch
          is cocked, DiMaggio breaks for the plate, and Bob Lemon, sensing that the
          squeeze might be on, fires the toughest pitch to bunt, a fastball high and
          inside. But Rizzuto works the play to perfection and DiMaggio scores the
          winning run. Lemon throws the ball and his glove into the stands in disgust.
          There will be no catching the Yankees.

Sep 28—   The Yankees need only two victories to clinch the pennant with five games
          remaining. And they take a doubleheader in one of the most dramatic days
          in Yankee Stadium history. In the opener, Reynolds pitches his second no-
          hitter of 1951, beating Boston, 8-0.* He becomes only the second major
          leaguer to pitch two no-hitters in one season. With two out in the ninth
          inning, and with 39,038 fans pulling for Allie, the great Ted Williams pops
          up in foul territory. But Berra drops the ball. On Reynolds' next pitch, a
          fastball, Williams again pops up. This time Yogi catches it, three feet from
          the steps of the Yankee dugout, ending the game. Del Webb tells Berra,
          "When I die, I hope they give me a second chance the way they did you."
          Woodling homers in Reynolds' support, just as he had in Allie's first no-hitter.
          In the nightcap, Raschi wins, 11-3, and the Yankees clinch their 18th
          pennant. The Yankees score seven runs in the second inning. Later,
          DiMaggio hits a three-run home run off Chuck Stobbs, Joe's 361st and final
          regular season homer in the majors. The Giants will complete the Miracle
          of Coogan's Bluff, coming from 13½ games back to tie Brooklyn and then
          beating the Dodgers on a Bobby Thomson home run. They will battle
          the Yankees in the World Series.

Oct 5—   Losers of Game 1 in the World Series, the Yankees rebound to win, 3-1,
          behind Lopat's five-hitter and Joe Collins' key second-inning solo homer.
          Mantle, who had led off the bottom of the first with a bunt single and who
          scored the first run, is seriously injured in the fifth inning when his spikes
          catch in a drain cover of a sprinkler head in right-center field. He is carried
          off the field on a stretcher with a badly injured right knee, an injury that will
          haunt Mickey for the rest of his career. Mickey will have to undergo an
          operation. The Giants will win tomorrow at the Polo Grounds.

Oct 8—   Stengel in a closed-door meeting before Game 4 appeals to Yankee Pride.
          Casey is lucky that the game the day before was rained out; he can now
          bring back Reynolds. Reynolds scatters eight hits and wins, 6-2, to even
          the Series. The Yankees score two early runs, then, in the fifth, DiMaggio
          wallops a two-run homer to give the Yanks a 4-1 lead. It is Joe's eighth
          and final home run in World Series play.

Oct 9—   The Yankees romp, 13-1, and take a three-games-to-two lead. Lopat pitches
          a five-hitter, wins his second game of the Series and runs his ERA to 0.50.
          But after talking with reporters and drinking a few beers, Lopat can't lift
          his left arm (it is a cold and windy day) and the injury will remain with
          Steady Eddie for the remainder of his career. The Yanks' 12-hit attack is

---

*This was the last regular-season no-hitter by a Yankee pitcher (through 1982).

led by Gil McDougald, who belts a grand slam homer; Rizzuto, who hits a two-run homer, knocks in three runs and scores three runs; and DiMaggio, who has a double and two singles and drives in three runs.

Oct 10— Raschi leads the Yankees to a 4-3 win at the Stadium and the World Championship in six games. Bauer's bases-loaded triple in the sixth inning drives in three key runs, giving the Yankees a 4-1 lead. Sain enters the game in the seventh and gets out of Raschi's jam, then in the eighth escapes a bases-loaded pickle of his own doing. In the top of the ninth, Sain again loads the bases, and Stengel brings in Bob Kuzava with no outs. Irvin hits a sacrifice fly to left, as all runners move up and the score is 4-2. Thomson also hits a sacrifice fly and the margin is 4-3 with two out. Pinch-hitter Sal Yvars buzzes a liner to right field, and, with the tying run streaking for the plate, Bauer makes a fantastic catch, the ball just inches above the ground, to end the Series. Irvin at .458 is the Series' leading hitter but Rizzuto (.320) wins the Babe Ruth Award.

— This was DiMaggio's final game of baseball. In the eighth inning, Joe doubled to right field off Larry Jansen in his last at bat. He was out at third on a fielder's choice and as he trotted off the field, the 61,711 fans rose and gave the Clipper a tremendous ovation. In the locker room afterwards, Joe took off his uniform and said, "I've played my last game." One by one, Joe's teammates got him to autograph various items for them.

Nov 8— Yogi Berra learns he has won the MVP Award. Allie Reynolds is third in the voting. Yogi is named on 23 of 24 ballots, Ned Garver of the St. Louis Browns on 20, and Reynolds on 12.

Dec 11— At the Yankee offices on Fifth Avenue, Joe DiMaggio announces his retirement. A reporter asks him why he has made his decision, and Joe replies, "I no longer have it."

— Obviously, it was an emotional day. But Joe left with his dignity intact. Topping and Webb had wanted him to continue drawing his $100,000 salary and to play whenever the aches and pains were not too severe. DiMaggio appreciated the offer but felt this kind of arrangement would not be fair to himself or his fans. He had been doing a lot of traveling and everywhere he was hounded by those who wanted to know if he was really going to retire. But he remembered the working press back in New York. "I said I'd announce it in New York," Joe would say, "and it wouldn't be fair to the sportswriters there if I said anything now. That's where I work, so I'm making the announcement there."

Joe DiMaggio announced his retirement from baseball on December 11, 1951. With DiMaggio, center, are from left, General Manager George Weiss, Manager Casey Stengel, and owners Del Webb and Dan Topping.

1952

Finishing at 95-59, the Yankees will win their fourth successive pennant by a mere two games over second-place Cleveland. Yogi Berra will knock in 98 runs and Mickey Mantle will hit .311. Allie Reynolds will lead the pitching staff at 20-8. And for the fourth straight time the Yankees are World Champions.

Apr 6—   The Yankees open the regular season by beating the A's, 8-1, in Philadelphia behind Vic Raschi. The Yank outfield has Bauer in left, Jensen in center and Mantle in right. Mantle gets three hits, including a two-run double. Through the end of April, Jensen, Cerv and Woodling will share center field, with Mantle staying in right. The Yankees open with Yogi Berra, Joe Collins and Billy Martin sidelined with injuries. Raschi is now 21-2 against the A's.

May 3—   The Yankees obtain Irv Noren (OF) and Tommy Upton (INF) from the Washington Senators for Jackie Jensen (OF), Spec Shea (P), Archie Wilson (OF) and Jerry Snyder (INF). Stengel continues to worry about center field, and with Mantle still hobbling, the presence of Noren, a solid centerfielder, eases the tension.

        — Noren was a fine ballplayer, although he would hit only .235 in 93 games for New York this year. But his price was high. Jensen would blossom into one of the league's best players. He would win three RBI titles with the Red Sox and 1958 MVP honors. Shea, 29-21 in 100 games for the Yankees, would never recapture the magic of 1947, but his trade was also a mistake. Shea would rebound with 11-7 and 12-7 seasons in 1952-53 for the second-division Senators.

May 6—   Mickey's father, Mutt Mantle, who was most responsible for Mickey's becoming a major leaguer, dies in a Denver hospital. Mr. Mantle had been critically ill for several months with Hodgkin's Disease.

May 13— In Cleveland, Mantle is shocked when Stengel sends him into the game in the fifth inning as Bobby Brown's replacement at third base. It is a puzzling move. Mantle makes two errors in four chances. He also makes two hits but the Yankees lose, 10-6.

         — In mid-May the Yankees trailed Boston and Cleveland by four games and Stengel was forced to make a number of changes. During the month, Jerry Coleman was called into the Marines (Coleman made 17 hits in 42 at bats for a .405 average) and McDougald went to third. Collins and Mize were both hurt, so Stengel was forced to bring Noren to first base and to put Cerv in center. Mantle sat on the bench for several games following the third base experiment. Martin, hurt March 12 while demonstrating the art of sliding for a macaroni commercial, returned to his second base position.

May 20— A big day in Mantle's career. Stengel starts Mickey in center field and bats him third. Mantle has his first four-hit game of the season, getting two singles batting lefty off Chicago's Ken Holcombe and two singles batting righty off Chuck Stobbs. His average leaps to .315. Johnny Sain pitches a six-hitter and the Yankees win, 3-1.

         — More significantly, from this day on, Mantle is the Yanks' regular center-fielder. He was to be groomed for center field but he reported to camp limping badly from his World Series injury. He made his spring debut in centerfield in Atlanta on April 5 but after a week had to surrender the position to Bob Cerv and Jackie Jensen. He was not ready for the strain involved in playing center.

May 24— Martin fights Jimmy Piersall under the grandstands during a game at Fenway Park. It starts when Piersall, teasing Martin about his nose, calls him Pinocchio. Billy gets in two good licks before Coach Bill Dickey and others break it up. Stengel is happy and hopes Martin's fighting spirit spreads throughout the team. "Ill have to ask him to confine the fighting to his opponents," Casey jokes. "He knocked Dickey's cap off and damned near spiked him trying to get at Piersall again. I don't want to lose any of my coaches."

May 27— The Yankees defeat Washington, 7-2. Reynolds hurls a splendid two-hitter and Berra belts two home runs in his support.

         — The Yankees would finish May with a mediocre 18-17 record. But Reynolds was great, opening the season with 15 complete games in a row. Berra was about to catch on fire. In 12 June games, Yogi would blast 10 home runs. He would finish with 30 homers, establishing the AL record for catchers. He came within two homers of being the only catcher in AL history to lead the league in homers; outfielder Larry Doby of Cleveland would hit 32.

Jun 5—   Joe Collins singles home Mantle in the 13th inning and the Yankees beat the White Sox, 4-3. Mickey makes four hits off Billy Pierce and raises his average to .333.

         — In his fifth year with the Yankees, Collins, a native of Scranton, Pa., finally established himself as the regular first baseman after shaking off an early-season injury. He would have a fine year, batting .280 in 122 games with 18 homers.

The 1951 season ended one comparison of two active players and launched another. The great rivalry between Ted Williams and Joe DiMaggio, left, drew to a close after 12 years of arguments among fans over who was better. Williams played beyond 1951. But baseball enthusiasts were finding a new comparison in two formidable rookies, Mickey Mantle and Willie Mays, right.

Jun 14—   New York goes into first place. Berra, Mantle and Woodling, who is batting
           .330, propel the Yankees to 10 wins in 11 games in early June. Today the
           Yankees beat Cleveland, 11-0. Raschi pitches a four-hitter and Berra has a
           homer and five RBIs.

Jul 12—   Martin and the Browns' Clint Courtney clash at Yankee Stadium. In the
           second inning, Courtney slides hard into Martin at second, and in the sixth
           he barrels into Berra at the plate, although he is out by 10 feet. He is still
           not through. In the eighth, on a delayed steal, Courtney comes into second
           long after Berra's peg has arrived, his spikes flashing. Martin deftly but
           forcefully slaps the tag on Courtney's face for the final out. Courtney charges
           Martin but Billy is ready and lands two punches flush on the catcher's
           face. The fans roar their approval as both dugouts empty and several
           scattered fights take place. Two umpires are knocked over. When peace is
           restored, Courtney is ejected but Martin is allowed to continue playing.

Jul 29—   The Yankees crawl into Chicago, having lost six of seven games. They now
           lead the second-place Indians by only three games. Chicago's Billy Pierce
           has a seemingly safe 7-0 lead. But the Yankees break through with three
           seventh-inning runs. With one out in the top of the ninth, Woodling singles,
           Berra walks, pinch-hitter Mize singles home Woodling. After a groundout
           and an error make the score 7-5, with two out, southpaw Chuck Stobbs
           enters and walks Collins to fill the bases. Noren fouls off seven pitches
           with a full count before walking to force in the Yank's sixth run. Then, Mantle
           wallops Stobbs' first pitch into the lower left-center field stands and the
           Yankees have a dramatic 10-7 victory. It is Mickey's second grand slam
           homer in four days and his 16th homer of the season.

           — Many fans believed the 20-year-old Mantle was the most exciting player
           in the AL. He was not quite the most valuable; that honor belonged to Berra.
           But Mickey would finish the season with fine stats, hitting .311 with 23 homers
           and 87 RBIs. He and Berra led this team but it was certainly a team
           effort. The only individual batting title won by a Yankee was the strikeout
           crown; Mantle would share that with Larry Doby, both acquiring 111. Yet
           Mantle would finish third in MVP voting.

Aug 4—   Vic Raschi gets his 11th straight win. He pitches a tough six-hitter at
           Washington and the Yanks win, 1-0. His streak, which includes a one-hitter
           (on July 13 against Detroit) will be broken in Boston on August 9, the Red
           Sox winning in 10 innings, 3-1.

Aug 25—   At Yankee Stadium,. Detroit's Virgil Trucks pitches a controversial no-hitter
           and wins, 1-0, with Bill Miller taking the hard-luck loss. Trucks strikes out
           eight, walks one and has two errors made behind him. But there are those
           who believe one of the errors was a hit. Rizzuto beats out a grounder to
           deep shortstop and is given a hit. But Johnny Pesky, the Tiger shortstop,
           later in the game tells the official scorer that he couldn't get the ball out
           of his glove. The scorer then gives Pesky an error, taking away the Yanks'
           one hit. A tainted no-hitter? Not according to Trucks, who years later
           maintained the scoring should have been incidental because Rizzuto was
           "thrown out by a step" at first base. Said Trucks, "We argued about it,
           but the umpire called him safe. He should have been called out, and there
           wouldn't have been any controversy."

Sep 2—   The Yankees sweep two games from Boston, winning by double shutouts,
           at Yankee Stadium and prepare to embark on their final western road trip

with a 3½-game lead over the Indians. Tom Gorman, a rookie righthander from New York City, wins the opener, 2-0. Ewell "The Whip" Blackwell, recently obtained from Cincinnati for $35,000 and four players, in the second game displays the form that made him a 22-game winner in 1947. Blackwell wins, 4-0. Another pitcher recently obtained, Ray Scarborough, whose contract was bought from the Red Sox for the waiver price, will win five or six decisions down the stretch.

— Stengel was desperately patching together a pitching staff. Gorman would go 6-2 and Blackwell would win one and save one in five games. A shoulder injury held Lopat to only 19 starts, but he was 10-5. Various journeymen and youngsters had their chances but it was Sain (11-6), Raschi (16-6) and especially Reynolds (20-8), who would lead the league in ERA, strikeouts and shutouts, who held the staff together. By comparison, Cleveland had 23-game-winner Early Wynn, 22-game-winner Mike Garcia and 22-game-winner Bob Lemon. The Yankee staff would win the club ERA title, however.

Sep 5—   The Yankees lose in Philadelphia, 3-2, and after boarding a train for Washington, the players order large steaks and settle down to a merry game of Twenty Questions. What's this? Casey has a question? "I gotta question to ask you fellers," he barks. "WHO WON TONIGHT?" The press dutifully noted the lecture that followed.

Sep 7—   In the sixth inning at Washington, Johnny Mize delivers a pinch-hit grand slam homer over the high right field wall off Walt Masterson and the Yankees win, 5-1. Mize has now homered in every big league ballpark. The Yankees appear to be on a roll following Stengel's eruption.

Sep 14—   In Cleveland, a crowd of 73,609 turns out for the final meeting of the year with the Yankees. Having won nine in a row, Cleveland is hot and now trails the Yanks by only 1½ games. Mike Garcia, 4-0 against the Yanks this year, gives up four runs in the third inning, the key hit a bases-loaded single by Berra. The Yankees go on to win, 7-1. Bauer and Mantle each knock in two runs, Mickey hitting a double off Garcia and homering off Lou Brissie. Lopat, who has pitched three complete games in a row after a summer of inactivity, pitches with heart into the later innings before giving way to Reynolds, who saves his second straight game. The Yankees (86-57) now lead Cleveland by 2½ games.

Sep 20—   At Yankee Stadium, the day after Bobby Shantz blanked the Yankees, Lopat beats the Athletics, 2-0. The Junkman pitches a four-hitter, winning his fifth straight game and his 10th victory of the year.

Sep 26—   The Yankees clinch their 19th pennant in Philadelphia, winning 5-2, in 11 innings. Irv Noren hits an eighth-inning homer to tie game, 2-2, and Billy Martin breaks it up with a two-out, two-run single in the 11th. Lopat pitches into the ninth and Sain takes over and gets credit for the victory. Brooklyn will provide the resistance in the World Series.

— It was a pennant worth celebrating. Cleveland and New York each lost only once since their meeting September 14. Stengel won with what some experts thought was his worst Yankee team. But Berra wondered aloud when this team would get some respect. "They said we couldn't win in 1949," said Yogi. "They said we weren't good enough in 1950. They gave us a chance in 1951. In 1952 all the experts said Cleveland was going to win. We won again. And we will keep winning..."

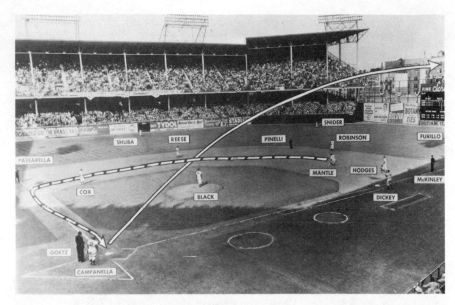

The arrow shows the flight of Mickey Mantle's clutch home run in the sixth inning of Game 4 of the 1952 World Series at Ebbets Field. The fourbagger broke up a tie game, giving the Yankees a lead they would not relinquish.

Oct 4—   In Game 4 at the Stadium, Reynolds pitches a four-hitter and whiffs 10 Bums in winning his rematch against Black, 2-0, before 71,787. Mize unlocks a scoreless game with a leadoff homer in the fourth. Mantle triples and scores when Reese throws the relay into the stands in the eighth, and the Series is now even.

Oct 5—   Brooklyn wins, 6-5, and takes a three-games-to-two-lead. Down, 4-0, the Yankees score five runs in the bottom of the fifth, capped by Mize's three-run roundtripper. Then Sain relieves Ewell Blackwell, who leaves for a pinch-hitter in the uprising, and pitches six strong innings. But the Dodgers nick him for one run in the seventh and the game moves into extra innings. In the 11th, two Dodger singles and Snider's double put the Flatbushers ahead. Carl Furillo makes a leaping catch to rob Mize of a game-tying fourbagger in the 11th. Carl Erskine pitches a courageous game, retiring the final 19 Yankee hitters and allowing only five hits over 11 innings.

Oct 6—   Back in Brooklyn, the Yankees win do-or-die Game 6, 3-2. Vic Raschi and Billy Loes settle into a pitchers' duel. The ice isn't broken until Snider hits a sixth-inning solo homer. Brooklyn fans can smell a Series triumph at last. But in the seventh, Berra sends one over the right field screen, Woodling singles and is balked to second, and scores on Raschi's single off Loes' leg. ("I lost it in the sun," Loes later explains.) Leading off the eighth, Mantle homers into the left-center field stands for the first of his 18 World Series homers and none more important. In the Dodger half, Snider homers, and when George Shuba doubles with two out, Reynolds comes in and strikes out Roy Campanella. Superchief retires the side in the ninth inning, too, and the Series is back to even.

Oct 7—   The Yankees gut out a 4-2 victory in a Game 7 played in Brooklyn and tie
           the record of the 1936-39 Yankees with their fourth consecutive World
           Championship. Stengel uses Lopat, Reynolds (winner), Raschi and Kuzava
           (save). The score tied 2-2, Mantle steps up to face Black, who starts on only
           two days' rest, with one out and none on in the sixth inning. The Mick
           drives one to his liking over the right field scoreboard and the Yanks
           have the lead for keeps. Mantle adds a run-scoring single in the following
           inning. Brooklyn loads the bases in the bottom of the seventh and Stengel
           waves in Kuzava. The southpaw gets lefthanded-hitting Snider to pop up
           for the second out and the crowd gasps when Casey lets Kuzava face the
           righthanded Robinson. With the runners breaking on a 3-2 pitch, Jackie
           pops up to the right of the mound. No Yankee makes a move, until Martin
           races in and saves the game with a lunging, shoestring catch. Kuzava stops the
           Dodgers cold over the final two innings to preserve one of the Yankees'
           greatest triumphs. Mize, whose .400 leads all hitters, wins the Babe Ruth
           Award.

1953

The Yankees will finish at 99-52 and win a record-breaking fifth consecutive pennant,
outclassing second-place Cleveland by 8½ games. Yogi Berra will knock in 108 runs
and Mickey Mantle will drive in 92. Whitey Ford will lead the pitching staff with
18-6, but Ed Lopat will win the ERA title with 2.42. Again it's Brooklyn in the World
Series, and again, the Yankees will be World Champions.

Apr 10—   In an exhibition game in Pittsburgh, Mickey Mantle smashes a home
           run over the 100-foot-high two-tiered grandstand at Forbes Field, a feat
           previously achieved only by Babe Ruth and Ted Beard. Mantle finishes an
           awesome pre-season with a .412 average.

Apr 17—   The season is barely begun when Mantle shocks the baseball world by
           belting a Ruthian homer in Washington. It is Mantle's most famous right-
           handed home run (some still consider it the longest home run in major
           league history), although Babe Ruth is supposed to have hit a 602-footer
           in Detroit. Batting against southpaw Chuck Stobbs, Mantle rips into a
           medium-high fastball and sends it toward the tall left-center field bleachers.
           He drops his bat in disgust, figuring he missed the sweet spot, but none
           of the Senators moves a muscle. The ball leaves the field at the 391-foot
           mark, keeps climbing and glances off the top of a beer sign on the football
           scoreboard to the rear of the bleacher wall. It clears the ballpark, sails
           over 5th Street and lands in a backyard at 434 Oakdale Street. There is
           silence in the Yankee dugout as the players look at each other in utter
           disbelief. The sparse crowd of 4,206, however, cheers wildly. Red Patterson,
           the Yanks' publicity director, bolts from his seat to find the ball, which he
           does, and to make measurements and calculations. It was a 565-footer,
           he concludes. The age of the tape measure home run is ushered in.

           — Built in 1924, the 32 rows of seats in Griffith Stadium's left-center had
           never been cleared, although Ruth and Jimmie Foxx came close and Joe
           DiMaggio bounced one out off the seats. It was 66 feet to the back of
           the bleacher wall where the beer sign stood 60 feet above ground. Patterson
           found 10-year-old Donald Dunnaway holding the ball. The boy showed him
           where he picked it up. Patterson used a tape measure to establish the
           distance from the bleacher wall to the backyard spot where the ball was

found—108 feet. Adding the 391 feet from home to the outfield wall to the 66 feet of bleacher space, and the sum to the 108 feet from the ballpark to the backyard, Patterson came up with the 565-foot distance.

Apr 28— Mantle hits a righthanded three-run home run off Bob Cain that travels 500 feet, clearing the scoreboard in St. Louis' Sportsmans Park, where catcher Clint Courtney and the Yankees continue their brawling. With the score tied, 6-6, in the top of the 10th inning, Gil McDougald knocks over his minor league roommate at the plate, separating Courtney from the ball and scoring the go-ahead run. In the bottom half, Courtney steps to the plate and tells Yogi Berra that "someone is going to pay." He singles to right field, and with no chance of making two bases, continues to second. He slides spikes first into Phil Rizzuto, ripping open the Scooter's right leg. Several Yankee players take pokes at Old Scrap Iron. Brawls erupt around the field and Umpire Stevens dislocates his collarbone attempting to restore peace. There is a long delay as the angry Sportsmans Park crowd showers the field with debris. A bottle narrowly misses Gene Woodling, and the Yankees have reason to fear for their lives with only three cops in the ballpark. Six fines will be handed down, Courtney receiving the heaviest, $250. Also fined are the Browns' Billy Hunter and the Yankees' Billy Martin, McDougald, Joe Collins and Allie Reynolds.

Jun 3— After hitting two home runs yesterday, one of them a game-winner, Joe Collins today strokes four hits to pace a 19-hit attack in Chicago. The Yanks win, 18-2, for Whitey Ford, who has three RBIs himself.

Jun 14— New York extends a winning streak to 18 games by winning two, 6-2 and 3-0, before 74,708 in Cleveland. Berra homers in the first game and triples in the winning run in the nightcap. The Yankees now lead Cleveland by 10½ games. The remarkable thing about the winning streak is that 15 of the 18 games are played on the road.

Jun 16— St. Louis beats the Yankees, 3-1, snapping the Yanks' winning streak one game shy of the AL record of 19, set by the 1906 White Sox and tied by the 1947 Yankees. Satchel Paige is the winning pitcher, besting Whitey Ford, who won his first seven decisions of the season after spending two seasons in the military. Johnny Mize makes his 2,000th hit in this game, connecting off starting pitcher Duane Pillette to drive in the Yanks' lone run.

Jun 18— The Yankees sweep a doubleheader from the Browns, winning by double shutouts, 5-0 and 3-0, behind Ed Lopat and Jim McDonald.

— Lopat would finish at 16-4 and McDonald at 9-7. The Yankee pitching staff would lead the AL in several categories, including ERA (3.20) and shutouts (16).

Jul 2— New York snaps a surprising nine-game losing streak with a 5-3 victory at Boston. In the 10th inning, Mize delivers a pinch-hit, run-scoring double and Martin's single scores Mize. Mize is a tremendous pinch-hitter in his final season, leading the league with 19 pinch-hits in 61 trips and making five consecutive pinch-hits at one point.

— During the Yankee winning streak, Stengel was brutal with his players, criticizing every move.* But during the losing streak, which reduced the

*Later in the season he would be tough on Mantle, who was photographed blowing bubbles in center field. He publicly spanked Mickey, and Mickey promised not to be so unprofessional again.

Yankee lead over Cleveland and Chicago to six games, he turned into a teddy bear, not saying a word to further rock the boat (though he did bar reporters from the clubhouse after the eighth loss). Once the losing streak ended, Casey let his players have it but good in a team meeting.

Jul 6— Mantle hits a pinch-hit grand slam homer that clears the left-center field roof of Philadelphia's Shibe Park, another amazing shot. The ball goes "beyond the sight, grasp, or measurement of anyone in the park," according to one account,. Mickey is spreading his long shots around the league.

Jul 7— The team bus has an accident on the way to the train station after a game in Philadelphia. The bus crashes under a low-clearance abutment and the top of the bus is destroyed. Yankee personnel are thrown everywhere and the driver is unconscious. Red Patterson quickly evacuates the bus and no one is thought to be seriously injured. But the next day Allie Reynolds awakens with terrible back pains from an injury that will continue to hound him. Allie will one day win an out-of-court settlement from the bus company.

Aug 4— The Yankees blitz Detroit, 15-0. Besides pitching a shutout, Vic Raschi gets three hits and knocks in seven runs, setting an AL record for RBIs in one game by a pitcher. Raschi will make only nine hits and bat .143 for the season.

Aug 7— Second-place Chicago, five games out of first and the only team within shouting distance of New York, invades Yankee Stadium for a key four-game series. Chicago Manager Paul Richards has said he knows how to beat the Yankees. Stengel, as usual, has an answer: "If he's so smart, why can't he beat the Philadelphia A's?" The Yankees win the opener, 6-1. Lopat pitches seven strong innings and Reynolds nails it down. Mantle, Berra and Martin homer.

Aug 8— Over 68,000 fans turn out for a Ladies' Day doubleheader and they see perhaps the greatest day of pitching in Yankee history. In the opener, Ford pitches a five-hitter and beats Chicago, 1-0, for his 13th win of the campaign. (Ford will finish 5-0 vs. the Chisox this year.) Chicago's Sandy Consuegra is equally excellent through eight innings, but the Yanks pick up a run in the bottom of the ninth. In the nightcap, Bob Kuzava, who will finish 6-5 and make only six starts in 33 games this year, carries a no-hitter into the ninth inning. But with one out, Bob Boyd, a .297 hitter this year, gets a clean double. Kuzava finishes with a one-hitter and wins, 3-0. In the opener, Mantle's right knee buckles as he plants his right foot to make a throw, tearing ligaments. He must wear a knee brace for the remainder of the season. His average .360 on May 20, will fall to its final .295 mark.

Aug 9— Chicago salvages the final game of the series as Billy Pierce pitches a three-hitter. But the White Sox leave town trailing the Yankees by seven games. The pennant race appears to be over. Chicago will finish third, behind Cleveland.

Aug 12— The Yankees score 22 runs and make 28 hits—one homer, two triples, three doubles and 22 singles—against Washington. Hank Bauer personally scores five runs in the game.

— Bauer was one of several consistent hitters who helped the Yankees lead the AL in hitting at .273, although Cleveland outhomered New York, 160 to 139. Among the starters, Woodling hit at .306, followed by Bauer .304, Berra .296, Mantle .295, McDougald .285, Rizzuto .271, Collins .269 and Martin .257. (Martin knocked in 75 runs.) Nothing spectacular, but very consistent. And all the regulars except the Scooter would hit homers in double figures.

Sep 12— In New York's 13-4 win over Detroit at the Stadium, Mickey Mantle, batting righthanded, hits a line-drive homer off Detroit's Billy Hoeft into the upper left field grandstands that some witnesses feel might have left the Stadium if it had been hit toward the bullpen area. The ball was hit that hard. It was still rising when it hit at a point 80 feet above the ground and 425 feet from home plate.

Sep 14— The Yankees clinch a record fifth pennant in a row, erasing a 5-0 deficit and beating Cleveland, 8-5. Martin drives in four runs and Berra hits a two-run homer. The team coolly accepts the inevitable and is entertained at the Stadium Club with a victory dinner. Brooklyn will represent the NL in the World Series. Many Dodger followers insist that this is the greatest team in Brooklyn history; it is the winner of 105 games.

Sep 28— Ed Barrow, who ran the Yankees for nearly 25 years (1920-45) as general manager, and the last six years as president, is named to the Baseball Hall of Fame by the new Committee on Veterans. Barrow's plaque recalls his 50-plus years in baseball, his conversion of Babe Ruth from pitcher to outfielder, his discovery of Honus Wagner and the fact that he "built New York Yankees into outstanding organization in baseball." Barrow will die in less than three months in Port Chester, N.Y., at the age of 85.

Sep 30— The World Series opens at Yankee Stadium. The Yankees defeat Brooklyn, 9-5, Johnny Sain winning in a strong relief effort. Martin's bases-loaded triple in the first inning gets New York rolling, knocking out Carl Erskine. Berra's fifth-inning homer gives the Yanks a 5-1 lead but the Dodgers battle back to tie. Then, with two out in the seventh, Collins hits a clutch homer, breaking the deadlock. The Yanks add three insurance runs in the eighth, two on Sain's double.

Oct 1— The Yankees win Game 2, 4-2, behind Lopat's crafty nine-hitter. New York trails, 2-1, when Martin leads off the seventh with a homer. In the eighth, Bauer singles and Mantle follows with a two-run homer, pulled to left field off southpaw Preacher Roe. Lopat escapes trouble in the ninth, getting Duke Snider to ground out to end the game.

Oct 4— Brooklyn wins twice at home, then critical Game 5 goes in the Yankee column, 11-7, as the teams combine for 25 hits, 47 total bases and trot out seven pitchers. Woodling leads off the contest with an opposite-field home run on the first pitch, a rarity for Gene. In the third inning, Mantle cracks a grand slam homer off Russ Meyer, giving the Yankees a 6-1 lead. It goes into the left-center field upper deck, a good wallop for a lefthanded batter, and a sign of Mickey's grit; he is playing with painful legs. Martin belts a two-run homer in the seventh and McDougald adds a solo homer in the ninth.

Oct 5— Back at the Stadium, the Yankees win, 4-3, taking the Series in six games. Erskine and Ford match up. The Yankees pick up two runs in the first inning on Berra's run-scoring double and Jim Gilliam's error (Martin getting an RBI). Rizzuto scores the third run in the third inning on Woodling's sacrifice fly. But Brooklyn scores once in the sixth and ties it in the ninth on Carl Furillo's two-run homer off Reynolds, who cannot save Ford's win. In the bottom of the ninth, reliever Clem Labine walks Bauer, Berra lines out, Mantle beats out an infield chopper and Martin singles home Bauer with the Series' winning run.

— Martin hit .500 and led all hitters. The Babe Ruth Award was his. Almost singlehandedly, Martin stole the show. For Stengel, who joined the Yanks with a buffoon's image, the Series victory capped an incredible story—five World Championships in five seasons as Yankee skipper. Billy and Casey shared a special relationship and this was their finest hour together. It was also a great moment for 12 players—Bauer, Berra, Coleman, Collins, Houk, Lopat, Mize, Raschi, Reynolds, Rizzuto, Silvera and Woodling—all members of all five consecutive World Championship clubs. No one before or since could make that claim.

Nov 3—   A piece of torn cartilage is removed from Mantle's right knee in Springfield, Mo. The Mick is hospitalized for three days, then returns to his home in Commerce, Okla. Doctors say his knee should be healed in three months.

Dec 16—   The Yankees make a six-for-five trade with the Philadelphia A's. Most of the players involved are "no names," although the Yankees do pick up Eddie Robinson, who will lead the AL in 1954 in both pinch-hits (15) and pinch-hit at bats (49). Among the departees from the Yankees organization is minor leaguer Vic Power, a talented first baseman many felt would become the first black ballplayer on the Yankees.

    — The Yankees—and George Weiss, in particular—have been faulted for being slow to open their roster to blacks. There was no official policy against blacks, but Weiss' statement that the Yankees were looking for a black "good enough to make the Yankees" seemed either a contradiction of factual circumstances, a deft "code" message or a cover-up. The majors had numerous outstanding blacks; it seemed harder to avoid a good black than to recruit one. In the early 1950's, the Yankees signed such blacks as Artie Wilson, Ruben Gomez, Vic Power, Frank Barnes and Elston Howard, and Weiss would point to them as evidence that the Yankees were equal opportunity employers. Power was generally expected to break the color-line on the Yankees. After all, he hit .349 with the Yanks' Kansas City club to lead his league in hitting. And now the most promising black was dealt away. The Yankees' explanation: Power was a showboat, or hot dog in today's terms. He proved to be a fine player, hitting .284 over 12 big league seasons and playing the bag like few others could.

Dec 17—   The Yankees get the approval of the AL to sell Yankee Stadium and Blues Stadium in Kansas City to Arnold Johnson, wealthy Chicago industrialist-businessman, for approximately $6.5 million. Johnson leases back the Stadium to the Yankees in a multi-year deal. Johnson also buys the Blues and now has territorial rights to Kansas City. He will buy the Athletics and move them to Kansas City in 1955.

1954

The Yankees will have a great record (103-51) but finish in second place, eight games behind Cleveland. Yogi Berra will hit .307 and knock in 125 runs as the league's MVP. Mickey Mantle will hit .300 and drive in 102 runs. Rookie Bob Grim will lead the pitching staff at 20-6.

Feb 2—   Mantle is admitted to a Springfield, Mo., hospital for the removal of a fluid-filled cyst from the back of his right knee which was operated on in November. He will be discharged in three days. Doctors say the cyst was caused by too much post-surgery activity. The Mick will not be able to run until late in spring training, much to Casey Stengel's displeasure.

Feb 23— The Yankees sell the contract of pitcher Vic Raschi to the St. Louis Cardinals for $85,000. Raschi will finish his career with records of 8-9 and 4-7 for a lifetime mark of 132-66. George Weiss faces 12 holdouts this spring and Raschi, who ruined his knees helping the Yankees win six World Championships, becomes part of a larger picture.

— Raschi and Weiss fought annually over his contract. After winning only 13 games the previous season, Raschi's 1954 contract called for a 25-percent cut. Vic returned it unsigned. When he arrived in St. Petersburg, Fla., to continue negotiations, he learned of his sale. Weiss did not bother to inform him. "Mr. Weiss, you have a very short memory," Raschi told him. But Weiss achieved the desired results—the holdouts fell into line and signed. However, bitterness lingered. The Yankee players were furious and so was Stengel, who had no voice in the Raschi deal. The Springfield Rifle was one of the greatest righthanders in Yankee history, winning 120 of 170 decisions. His winning percentage of .706 was the second highest for an inactive pitcher in club history. Off the field, he was quiet and conservative. On the field, he was ornery and scowling, a tremendous competitor who could play with pain. He had heart. Raschi *never* missed a starting assignment as a Yankee pitcher!

Apr 13— In Washington, the Yankees open their season with a 5-3 loss, when Mickey Vernon hits a two-run 10th-inning homer. Mickey Mantle is in the Opening Day line-up and in center field but goes zero for five at the plate. He will get off to a brutal start. Over the first two weeks of the season, Mantle will hit .167, 6 for 26 against lefthanders and 0 for 10 against righthanders. His knee is troubling him and there are some who are predicting a premature end to his career, à la Pete Reiser.

— But the Mick would soon get himself on track and have a great year. He would lead the AL in runs scored with 129, 10 more than runner-up Minnie Minoso. By June, Mantle's knee would be fully recovered and his play would be much improved in all aspects of the game. Mickey's 20 assists would lead all outfielders. But New York's other two centerfielders, Willie Mays of the Giants and Duke Snider of the Dodgers, stole some of Mickey's luster. Mays won the NL batting title at .345 and belted 41 homers. Snider hit .341 with 40 homers and 130 RBIs.

Jun 12— After a slow season's start, the red-hot Indians go into first place. They will remain there for the rest of the season. The Yankees help by beating close contender Chicago, 2-0, on a Ford two-hitter.

— Cleveland would win 111 games, breaking the AL record of 110 victories, set by the 1927 Yankees. But Cleveland's image of invincibility would be shattered in the World Series when the Giants sweep in four games. The 103 wins the Yankees earn would be the most in Stengel's 12-season reign. The Yanks' .669 winning percentage remains the highest in history for a second-place team in the AL. But they missed the traded Raschi, the retired John Mize and Billy Martin, who was recalled by the Army.

Jul 1— The day after making two hits in his final game, Bobby Brown retires as a ballplayer to begin his hospital internship and eventually become a cardiologist in Fort Worth, Tex. His replacement at third base, Andy Carey, a California bonus baby, who received approximately $60,000 to sign with New York, will hit .302.

— Yankee scout Joe Devine scouted Brown on the West Coast and watched him at Stanford University and at UCLA where he was a Navy premedical student. The Yankees signed Brown to a big bonus in 1946. He proved to be an outstanding hitter but never was any great shakes with a glove. In eight Yankee seasons, Brown hit .279. He missed most of the 1952 season and all of 1953, serving in the military. When he returned in 1954, he hit only .217 in 28 games, but because he had been attending medical school in his off-seasons, Brown was ready for his next profession when he gave up professional baseball.

Jul 13— At Cleveland's Municipal Stadium, the AL gives Casey Stengel his first win as AL manager in the All-Star Game, an 11-9 victory over the NL. Whitey Ford, the AL's starting pitcher, hurls three strong innings and allows only one hit. Berra gets two hits and scores twice. Mantle also makes two hits and scores once, and Bauer is one for two. Irv Noren gets into the game but does not bat.

— Noren would have his best Yankee season this year, finishing with a .319 average. He would hit around the .350 mark until September, then go into a late-season slump that would cost him the batting title to Cleveland's Bobby Avila, a .341 hitter.

Jul 19— Allie Reynolds pitches a three-hitter for his fourth shutout and 10th consecutive win. (Allie's streak will be broken July 30 in Baltimore where he is knocked out after four innings and loses, 10-0.) Mantle has a grand slam homer, his first righthanded home run since May 23, as New York downs Detroit at the Stadium, 8-0.

— This was Reynolds' final season. He would conclude with a New York record of 131-60. But records and statistics aside, Allie was truly great—one of the greatest two-way pitchers of all time, as his 41 saves while serving with the Yankees indicate. He would end his Yankee career with 27 shutouts. Lifetime, the Oklahoma native would win 182 major league games.

Jul 25— New York beats Cleveland at Yankee Stadium, 4-3 in 11 innings, after the Tribe wins the first two of a three-game set. Cleveland leaves town leading the Yanks by one game.

Aug 9— It is a big day in Cooperstown, N.Y., for the Yankee family. Bill Dickey, who received 202 of 252 votes cast by the Baseball Writers, is inducted into the Baseball Hall of Fame. His plaque states that Dickey was a member of seven World Series winners, that he hit .313 lifetime and that he "set a record by catching 100 or more games in 13 successive seasons." In the annual Hall of Fame Game, the Yankees, helped by homers from Mantle and Bob Cerv, rally to win, 10-9, after trailing Cincinnati, 9-1, going into the seventh.

Aug 17— In Philadelphia, New York wins, 11-1. Yankee rookie Bill "Moose" Skowron belts a pinch-hit grand slam homer off Al Sima of the Athletics, capping a six-run, ninth-inning uprising. It is Moose's first career slam. Skowron will finish with a tremendous first-year .340 average in 87 games. And he will hit another grand slammer as a pinch-hitter (on July 14, 1957), making him one of only two Yankees (Berra is the other) to hit two pinch-hit "slams."

Aug 21— Gene Woodling breaks his thumb, ending his season, as New York loses in Boston, 10-9, in 12 innings. Woodling crashed into a wall chasing a ninth-inning triple by Harry Agganis. Today's game will prove to be Woodling's last Yankee game. He will be traded following this season. The Yanks will lose at Fenway again tomorrow and fall 5½ games out of first.

— Woodling hit .250 in 97 Yankee games in 1954. Sometimes called Old Faithful for his clutch hits, Gene batted .285 over his six Yankee seasons. True to his nickname, he hit .318 in World Series play. His lifetime fielding average of .989 is one of a fine all-round ballplayer.

Sep 3—   The Yankees purchase the contract of pitcher Tommy Byrne, 34, from Seattle of the Pacific Coast League. Byrne had won 20 games at Seattle after developing a couple of breaking pitches to compensate for having lost something off his fastball. Stengel is most pleased to have Byrne back after a three-year hiatus. In his first start for the Yankees, Byrne will beat Baltimore (where he was born), 8-2. He will finish with a 3-2 record.

Young Whitey Ford and Bob Grim are deep into the 1954 season and doing well. Ford finished the year with 16 wins and Grim took Rookie of the Year honors with 20 victories.

Sep 6—   At Yankee Stadium, the Yankees use 10 pinch-hitters in a pair of one-run
          games against the Red Sox. New York wins the opener, 6-5, on a pinch-hit
          homer by Joe Collins. But the Bombers squander a 7-0 lead and lose the night-
          cap, 8-7. Five pinch-hitters are used in each game. The only real success
          is with Collins who, hitting for Jim Konstanty, homers. Only three of the
          pinch-hitters are for pitchers. As a matter of fact, it is a pitcher, Byrne, who
          bats for Rizzuto in both games. Rizzuto is struggling at .190 and will finish
          at .195. But how can he start to hit when he is being pinch-hit for? By a pitcher
          yet, albeit a .368 hitter. It is easy to understand why Casey was not Phil's
          favorite manager.

Sep 9—   Baltimore's Joe Coleman, a 13-game winner this year, pitches a one-hitter
          against the Yankees. Enos Slaughter makes the only Yankee hit. It is the
          third time in his career that Slaughter has broken up a no-hitter. A broken
          wrist limits Slaughter's play this year to 69 games and he hits only .248.

Sep 12—   New York comes into Cleveland for a doubleheader (having just lost a tough
          10-inning game in Chicago), trailing the first-place Indians by 6½ games.
          a crowd of 86,563, largest in AL history, packs Municipal Stadium for the final
          Bomber-Tribe meeting of 1954, and the Yankees' last chance to stay in the
          pennant race. Bob Lemon beats the Yankees, 4-1, on a six-hitter in the
          opener, and Early Wynn wins the nightcap, 3-2. The Yankees fall 8½ games
          off the pace, and Yankee followers realize there will be no sixth pennant
          in a row.

Sep 21—   Bob Grim beats Washington, 3-1, at the Stadium, to run his record to 20-6.
          He is the first New York rookie to win 20 games since Russ Ford did it in
          1910. (And he is the last rookie in the AL to win 20.) On hand for the
          Yankees' 101st win is a crowd of 1,912, an all-time low to date but one that will
          be broken later.

Sep 26—   In a meaningless game, Stengel, presumably looking for power, starts a
          crazy infield of Eddie Robinson (1B), Moose Skowron (2B), Mickey Mantle
          (SS) and Yogi Berra (3B). The gimmick does not work, however, and the A's
          win, 8-6.

Nov 18—   The Yankees and Orioles announce Part I of an 18-player deal that is
          completed on December 1. The complete trade sends to the Yankees: Bob
          Turley (P), Don Larsen (P), Billy Hunter (INF), Dick Kryhoski (INF), Jim
          Fridley (OF), Ted Del Guercio (OF), Darrell Johnson (C) and Mike Blyzka (P),
          and to the Orioles: Gene Woodling (OF), Harry Byrd (P), Jim McDonald (P),
          Hal Smith (C), Gus Triandos (C-1B), Willie Miranda (INF), Bill Miller (P), Kal
          Segrist (INF) and Don Leppert (INF). With all that, Baltimore still owes New
          York one player to be named later!

          — The keys to the deal, from the Yankees' standpoint, were the two right-
          handed pitchers, Turley and Larsen. With Raschi gone, Reynolds retiring and
          Lopat in his final years, George Weiss was rebuilding his pitching staff.
          Turley was believed to be the hardest thrower in the AL and in 1954
          led the league in both strikeouts (185) and walks (181). Bullet Bob would
          win 17 games for the Yankees in 1955. Weiss felt Larsen had even more
          natural talent than Turley, regardless of his 3-21 record with the seventh-
          place Orioles. Larsen would win nine of 11 decisions in 1955.

1955

The Yankees will finish at 96-58 and win the pennant, finishing three games ahead of second-place Cleveland. Repeat MVP winner Yogi Berra will knock in 108 runs and Mickey Mantle will win the home run championship with 37. Whitey Ford will tie for the league lead in wins at 18-7. In the World Series, Brooklyn will finally get its revenge.

Jan 29— John William Cox purchases Yankee Stadium and its grounds from Arnold Johnson for $6.5 million. The Knights of Columbus will buy the Stadium grounds from Cox for $2.5 million. In 1962, Cox will bequeath the Stadium to Rice University.

Mar 26— During a Yankee-Dodger exhibition game at Al Lang Field in St. Petersburg, Casey Stengel is accused of kicking and cursing Branan Sanders, a *St. Petersburg Independent* photographer, who was blocking his view. He is arrested and hauled off to the station house. He later agrees to apologize and the charges are dropped. Casey, in having the apology prepared, says, "Put in there that I couldn'a kicked him because he's a veteran. I have great respect for veterans, having been one myself from the Navy in World War I, and you can look it up."

Apr 13— Only 11,251 are at Yankee Stadium for Opening Day (following a rainout) but those who show up see Whitey Ford and the Yankees level Washington, 19-1. Ford, who pitches a two-hitter and knocks in four runs, will win six of his first seven games, three by shutout.

Apr 22— Jerry Coleman breaks his left collarbone as New York beats Boston, 3-0, at the Stadium.

— Coleman was having a tough time. He returned from the military in 1954 to hit only .217 in 107 games. After the injury sustained on this date, in a collision at the plate in an unsuccessful double steal attempt, he would play in only 43 games in 1955 as a utility infielder, hitting .229.

Apr 26— Bob Turley pitches a one-hitter, beating the White Sox in Chicago, 5-0. Turley strikes out 10 and walks nine. Moose Skowron hits a home run and raises his average to .438.

— Bullet Bob would get off to a great start with New York, mowing down hitters with his blazing fastball. He would win eight of his first nine decisions. While he showed a pattern of walking almost as many batters as he struck out, he also seemed to be able to work out of jams. He would strike out 210 in 1955, most on the club since Jack Chesbro's 239 in 1904, while also leading the league in walks, giving up 177 in 247 innings.

May 6— New York wins in Boston, 6-0, on a Bob Turley two-hitter. Turley fans 13 Bosox while walking five.

May 13— In a 5-2 victory over Detroit at Yankee Stadium, Mickey Mantle goes four for four, and three of his hits are home runs. He knocks in all five Yankee runs. Mantle also switch-hits homers in the same game, becoming the second AL player ever to do so (Johnny Lucadello of the Browns was the first in 1940). In the first inning, batting lefthanded against Steve Gromek (13-10), Mantle hits a 400-foot homer into the right-center field bleachers with Andy Carey aboard. In the third inning, the Mick singles home Hank Bauer.

In the fifth, still against Gromek, Mickey whales a two-ball-pitch into the right-center field bleachers for a solo home run measured at 430 feet. Against 19-year-old Bob Miller (2-1) in the eighth, Mantle bats righthanded and on the first pitch deposits his third home run of the game into the right-center field bleachers.

— This would be Mantle's only three-homer game and the first of 10 career games in which he switch-hit home runs. Mickey enjoyed an injury-free spring for a change and came out of the chute smoking. In one stretch in May he got on base 15 consecutive times, nine times by walks. Bob Turley, one of the great readers of pitchers in the history of the game, would detect tell-tale signs in a pitcher's delivery and relay the kind of pitch that would be coming to the awaiting Mantle. That Mickey would have his biggest home run years with Turley on the club was more than just a coincidence.

May 15— Irv Noren, a .253 hitter in 132 games this year, belts a grand slam inside-the-park homer as New York wins in Kansas City, 8-4, to split a double-header. Suitcase Simpson missed a shoestring catch in center field and Noren went all the way.

Jun 5— At Chicago's Comiskey Park, Mantle's righthanded homer off Billy Pierce may have traveled 550 feet. The ball cleared the left field upper deck.

Jun 6— The Yankees win, 7-6, in Detroit as Eddie Robinson knocks in four runs. The Yanks crack five homers, including two by Robinson and one each by Mantle, Gil McDougald and Billy Hunter. Mantle's drive clears the screen in dead center field at the 440-foot mark. The Yankees are hot and by mid-June will lead the AL by 5½ games.

Jun 21— Mantle blasts the first homer ever hit into the bleachers at dead center field at Yankee Stadium. The ball lands in the ninth row and is measured at 486 feet. Hitting righthanded, Mantle supplies all the power—he hits a change-up! Witness Bobby Shantz of the A's: "For sheer force and velocity, I never saw anything like it. It actually sounded like an explosion." Other witnesses cite the explosion effect. Bill Dickey says it went even further than Lou Gehrig's homer in the 1928 World Series. Mickey's blast is the first one ever to clear the hitters' backdrop, which is 30 feet high and to the right of the 461-foot mark.

Jul 12— The NL wins the All-Star Game, 6-5, in 12 innings. Mantle, who goes two for six, belts a three-run first-inning home run off the Phillies' Robin Roberts (23-14) that travels some 430 feet over the center field fence in Milwaukee's County Stadium. Berra starts and Ford pitches—these are the only three Yankees to compete, although Turley is also on the All-Stars.

Jul 22— Chicago goes into first place. The Yankees had led the league by five games at the All-Star Break, but once play resumed, New York went into a slump extending over 25 games, the Yankees losing 16 of them. The Yanks lose, 3-1, at Kansas City today. They have Chicago two percentage points in front and Cleveland only two games behind; they will be back in first in two days.

Jul 23— For the first time in AL history, two pinch-hitters hit home runs in the same half inning. In the ninth inning of a losing effort in Kansas City, Bob Cerv and Elston Howard each hit pinch-hit homers; Cerv off Alex Kellner and Howard off Tom Gorman.

— The Yankees had a tremendous bench. In fact, of their 175 homers, 44 were hit by reserves. Cerv would hit a staggering .341 (29 for 85) as a part-time player. Howard survived the pressure, hoopla—and in some cases the humiliation—of being the first black Yankee ballplayer and hit a resounding .290 as a 26-year-old rookie. Ellie played 75 games in the outfield, nine games behind the plate and was not allowed to live with the other Yankees at the Soreno Hotel in St. Petersburg, Fla., during spring training.

Jul 25—   Joe DiMaggio, who led the voting of the Baseball Writers, receiving 223 of 251 votes cast, and Frank Baker are among a chosen few inducted into the Baseball Hall of Fame. DiMaggio's plaque mentions his having "played in 10 World Series" but neglects to point out that Joe and the Yankees won in nine of those Series, and that Joe had a .325 lifetime average. Nor does it cite the grace with which he played center field. He was, in fact, the most well-rounded player in the game's history. It was Joe who led the Yankees to those 10 pennants. Baker gave the Yankees several fine years, but his plaque naturally focuses on his more spectacular days with the A's when he was part of Connie Mack's $100,000 infield. He was selected by the Committee on Veterans.

Jul 26—   Tommy Byrne pitches a four-hitter at the Stadium to beat Chicago, 1-0. Yogi Berra's sixth-inning homer wins it for New York. Byrne is typically wild, issuing five walks, hitting two batsmen and throwing a wild pitch.

— Byrne would be named Comeback Player of the Year, finishing with a 16-5 record and a league-leading win percentage of .762. He no longer had his great fastball but was more successful than ever. He was cocky. He would talk to hitters, ask a few personal questions to get them smoldering. Then he would serve guile, at carefully varied speeds. His last season would be 1957 which he closed by hitting a game-winning pinch-hit homer. He would finish with a 72-40 Yankee record and an overall major league mark of 85-69.

Jul 30—   The Yankees waive pitcher Ed Lopat, who is 4-8, to the Baltimore Orioles, where he will go 3-4 and end a great major league career. A roster spot is now open for Don Larsen, who won nine of 10 decisions pitching for the Yanks' Denver farm club.

— With the departure of Lopat, the great Yankee pitching trio of Raschi-Reynolds-and-Lopat was no more. Lopat, who won 166 games in the majors, was 113-59 for a winning percentage of .657 as a Yankee, besides winning four of five decisions in World Series competition. He threw junk, but he was also smart, a winner and a leader. One other fact about Lopat—he was 40-12 lifetime against contending Cleveland.

Jul 31—   Yankee third baseman Andy Carey helps turn four double plays in one game, an AL record (which Carey still holds with two other third sackers). Carey will lead AL third basemen this year in double plays (37), assists (301), putouts (154) and total chances per game (3.5).

Sep 1—   The White Sox surge into first place with the Yankees, Cleveland and Boston right behind. Three days later, the Indians will take over the top spot in the standings and are confident of repeating their 1954 pennant year.

Sep 2—   Stengel calls a team meeting and takes his club to task for its recent poor play. This is the first day back from the Army for Billy Martin and he lets his teammates know that he plans on spending some World Series money. Casey, thrilled to death at having his sparkplug back, inserts Martin at second base, shifts McDougald to third and benches the slumping Carey. Then Ford goes to the mound against Washington and allows only a seventh-inning single by Carlos Paula, winning , 4-2. Mantle blasts a three-run homer. New York trails Chicago by a half game and the club is beginning to gel. Martin will hit .300 (21 for 70) in 20 games.

— Mantle's home run was his 36th of the season. He was practically assured of the home run title (runner-up Gus Zernial would finish with 30), yet would hit only one more homer (on September 4) after severely pulling a thigh muscle. He would finish the campaign playing in great pain and would be able to play in only three of the seven World Series games. Another kind of hurt was bothering the crowd-shy 23-year-old—he was being booed unmercifully by fans never satisfied with his extraordinary accomplishments. Mantle did not measure up to the memory of DiMaggio, in the view of many Stadium fans. In fact, supporters of Willie Mays and Duke Snider argued that Mantle was the third best centerfielder in New York. After all, Mays would lead his league with 51 homers and Snider would knock in 136 runs to pace the NL.

Sep 7—   Whitey Ford, already establishing himself as one of baseball's greatest money pitchers, tosses his second consecutive one-hitter, an AL record. Ford downs Kansas City, 2-1, allowing only a seventh-inning double by Jim Finnigan.

Sep 10— Chicago beats New York, 9-8, at the Stadium as Stengel juggles his line-up and has Bauer catching, the only major league game Hank will ever work behind the plate. Hank has one passed ball. He is one of three catchers used in the game, Casey having previously used Berra and Silvera.

Sep 11— The Yankees and Indians split a doubleheader at Yankee Stadium in a two-game series. Tommy Byrne pitches a four-hitter to win the opener, 6-1. Ford's eighth-inning wild pitch allows the Indians to capture the nightcap, 3-2, in 12 innings and remain in first place by 1½ games over New York and 3½ games over Chicago. But the Yankees are about to embark on an eight-game winning streak.

Sep 16— With less than two weeks left in the season, the Yankees score a dramatic 5-4 victory over Boston at the Stadium and go into first place by a half game with 10 games remaining. The Yankees open a three-game series against the always-tough Red Sox, who fight back from a 3-0 deficit to go ahead, 4-3. But in the bottom of the ninth Hank Bauer hits a game-tying homer down the left field line off Ellis Kinder. Kinder gets the second out, but Berra, who had homered earlier off Frank Sullivan, hits the first pitch deep into the rightfield seats. The Bronx Bombers are in first place and will remain there. The only bad news concerns Skowron, who hits .319 in his sophomore year, and Mantle, both of whom are injured.

Sep 18— Phil Rizzuto Day is held at the Stadium and 54,501 attend. It is a big day for the lucky Phil, who yesterday was beaned by Boston's George Susce. Phil's helmet saved him and he is able to play in today's game. The Yanks edge the Red Sox, 3-2, behind Bob Grim, who will be 7-5 this sore-arm year; he has a no-hitter for seven innings and finishes with a three-hitter. New York is now two games in front of Cleveland after sweeping Boston.

Sep 23— The Yankees' eight-game winning streak is snapped, 8-4, in the opener of a Boston doubleheader. But Larsen wins the nightcap, 3-2, to clinch. Martin, who ignites the Yankees to nine wins in their final 10 games, contributes two hits. Says Stengel of Billy the Kid, "That feller can shame others into winning. He never went to college but he's smart. He doesn't have to think two seconds to do the right thing..."It was Eddie Robinson, however, who delivered the key pinch-hit. The Yankees will face Brooklyn in the World Series.

Sep 28— The World Series opens at the Stadium on the earliest date (except in 1918) in history. A moment of silent prayer for President Eisenhower's recovery from a heart attack precedes the game. Then the fireworks in the form of home runs—five of them, three by New York—go off. Ellie Howard becomes the second Yankee ever to homer in his first World Series at bat, going deep with a two-run homer to tie the game in the second. Joe Collins gets two home runs off Don Newcombe, whom Joe hit well in the minors. The first breaks a 3-3 tie and the second, coming with Berra aboard in the sixth, is a tape-measure job into the right-center field bleachers and the Yanks lead 6-3 and ultimately win, 6-5. Whitey Ford gets the win.

Sep 29— Tommy Byrne wins, 4-2, on a five-hitter and becomes the first southpaw to pitch a complete-game victory over the Dodgers in 1955. The Yankees are trailing, 1-0, in the fourth when they score four runs with two outs. Berra singles, Collins walks, Howard singles home Berra, Martin singles home Collins, Robinson is hit by a pitch to load the bases and Byrne singles home two runs. Bauer, who will lead all Series hitters at .429, pulls a muscle trying to steal in the first inning and joins Mantle on the sidelines.

Sep 30— No teams ever won the World Series after losing the first two games but the Dodgers will try. They win a must-win Game 3 at Ebbets Field, 8-3. Turley is knocked out in the second inning and Johnny Podres, of Witherbee, N.Y., celebrates his 23rd birthday by winning in a breeze. The Dodgers rock four Yank pitchers for 11 hits and seven walks (two coming with the bases loaded). Mantle insists on starting but his thigh is so sore that he shifts to right field in the second inning, moments after blasting a 400-foot homer. The Bums gather momentum and will win their next two home games.

Oct 3— Back in the Bronx, Ford keeps the Yankees alive with a 5-1 victory in Game 6. Whitey pitches a masterful four-hitter and strikes out eight batters. The Yanks score all their runs in the first inning; Rizzuto walks and steals second on a strikeout, McDougald walks, Berra singles home Rizzuto, Bauer singles home McDougald and Skowron delivers a three-run homer. Bauer returns to the line-up and has three hits but Mantle is sidelined again.

Oct 4— In the happiest day in Brooklyn baseball history, the Dodgers win Game 7, 2-0, as Podres scatters eight hits. The Dodgers break the ice against Byrne in the fourth inning on Campanella's double and Hodges' single. Hodges adds a sacrifice fly in the sixth inning. In the bottom half, Martin walks and McDougald beats out a bunt. Berra slices a long fly to left field and Sandy Amoros makes an unbelievable catch just inside fair territory. He relays to Pee Wee Reese who throws to Hodges, doubling up McDougald and snuffing out the potential rally. With two out in the seventh, Howard singles, but pinch-hitter Mantle pops out. Then in the eighth, Rizzuto and McDougald single around an out, but Berra flies out and Bauer strikes out. The Yanks go down in order in the ninth. Podres says he thought the Yanks would look for his change up, adding, "That's why I had to go to my harder stuff."

Nov 20— The Yankees leave Japan after a month-long barnstorming tour of the Far East. In baseball-happy Tokyo, two million fans lined the streets to welcome the Yankees. Against the best players of the Pacific region, the Yankees in 24 games won 23 and tied one. Everyone had a good time and Stengel saw Johnny Kucks pick up a slider pitch from coach Jim Turner and learned that Gil McDougald can play a sensational shortstop.

Dec 4— Yogi Berra is named the Most Valuable Player of the AL for the second consecutive year and the third time in five seasons. Yogi receives a total of 218 points to runner-up Al Kaline's 201 in balloting conducted by the Baseball Writers. Yogi has finished no worse than fourth in the MVP voting since 1950, an amazing standard of consistency.

1956

The Yankees at 97-57 will finish in first place, nine games ahead of Cleveland. Mickey Mantle will win the Triple Crown and establish himself as the undisputed best player in the game. Yogi Berra will hit 30 home runs and knock in 105 runs and the pitching staff will be led by Whitey Ford, who goes 19-6 and wins the ERA title at 2.47. The Yankees will defeat Brooklyn in the World Series.

Jan 24— Mickey Mantle signs his 1956 contract for $30,000, a raise of $10,000 over his $20,000 salary for 1955. It is believed Mantle may be the highest-paid 24-year-old in the story of baseball.

Mar 28— Mantle slides into second base and bruises his right leg in an exhibition game in St. Petersburg, Fla. Mickey will miss the next 10 days of the spring training season.

— This was a disappointing development but only a temporary snag. Mantle had reported to camp with a great attitude, opening up to reporters like never before. More importantly, he was laying off bad pitches, striking out only once in his first 36 trips. Shirley Povich of The Washington Post wrote, "In Florida one feeling has been inescapable for the past month. This...is Mickey Mantle's year."

Apr 17— Opening the season in Washington, the Yankees win,10-4, as Mickey Mantle belts a pair of awesome home runs for four RBIs, exactly three years to the day after his 565-footer at Griffith Stadium. Both blasts are hit batting lefty against Camilo Pascual (who will lose seven times in seven decisions to New York this season) and are estimated at 500 feet. Both homers clear the right-center field bleachers, and the second shot is said to be the longest ball ever hit to that section of the ballpark. Few players will hit the ball over Griffith's center field fence but Mantle will do it five times in his career.

Apr 22— Don Larsen, the Yanks' fine hitting pitcher, hits a grand slam home run to help New York to a 13-6 win over Boston at the Stadium. It is only the third bases-loaded homer ever hit by a Yankee pitcher.

May 5— Batting lefthanded, Mantle hits a tremendous home run off Kansas City's Moe Burtschy. The shot hits the upper-deck facade down the right field line with such force that it rebounds more than 100 feet. It is a line drive that leaves witnesses awestruck. Kansas City Manager Lou Boudreau thought it was going out of the park. Mantle's blast wins the game for the Yankees. He had a homer earlier and has three hits on the day. He is batting .433 with a slugging average of .950!

May 6— The Yanks starve Chicago twice at the Stadium, 4-0 and 4-0. The first shutout is Whitey Ford's. Rip Coleman and Jim Konstanty combine for the second.

May 13— Tom Sturdivant gets his big chance in the nightcap of a doubleheader with Baltimore after the Yanks win, 11-2. He does well, allowing only four hits and three runs over 7⅓ innings, but loses, 5-1. Stengel is impressed. Instead of farming Tom out, as was expected, Casey releases Konstanty. Good move: Sturdivant will go 16-8.

May 16— In the fourth inning against Cleveland, Casey Stengel calls in reliever Tom Morgan, who retires all 17 Indians he faces in a Yankee victory. The Yankees go into first place and remain there for the rest of the campaign. Morgan will win six games and save 11.

May 18— For the third time in his career, Mantle switch-hits home runs in the same game. His slugging in Chicago helps the Yankees to an 8-7 come-from-behind win in extra innings. He goes four for four, adding a double and a single to his pair of homers, and scores four times. His first homer is a two-run shot off lefty Billy Pierce that goes 12 rows into the upper deck. Then batting lefty against Dixie Howell, Mickey hits a towering solo homer deep into the right field seats to tie the game. Mantle now has 15 homers and Berra, who also hits one today, has 12. Both are ahead of Ruth's 1927 pace. Pitchers can't work around Yogi, who is hitting in the .350 neighborhood, with the Mick on deck.

May 22— The Kansas City pitching staff seems intent on starting a riot in a game in Kansas City. The A's Jose Santiago is so wild over the early innings the Yankees are convinced that he is throwing at them deliberately. In retaliation, Don Larsen brushes back Harry Simpson in the bottom of the third. The game is halted while the umpires warn both teams against further head hunting. But late in the game, Tom LaSorda brushes back Hank Bauer. The next pitch heads straight for Hank's head but he hits the dirt in time. Martin yells at LaSorda, as Mantle steps to the plate, "Knock him down and we'll chase you out of the park and into the river!" LaSorda walks toward New York's dugout. It takes Stengel and four Yankees to control Martin. The fans scream some cruelties Billy's way and he has to be restrained from entering the stands.

— Later, Martin and LaSorda would become friends. Martin, who suffered from depression, anxieties over family matters and hypertension throughout his Yankee career, had a new source of concern—a promising 20-year-old second baseman named Bobby Richardson. Martin became more determined, intense and aggressive on the field, hustling all the time. He would hit .264 in 121 games, 105 of them at second base. As usual, Gil McDougald's versatility saved the Yankees. McDougald would play 92 games at shortstop, 31 at second and five at third, batting .311. Martin's spark and McDougald's flexibility were leading factors in Yankee successes.

May 24— Eddie Robinson's grand slam home run and Mickey Mantle's five-for-five hitting power New York to an 11-4 win in Detroit. Mantle has a homer and four singles. Robinson's "slam" is the first of two for the Yanks in as many days; Bob Cerv will hit one tomorrow in a 10-2 win over Baltimore.

May 30— In a doubleheader sweep of Washington, 4-3 and 12-5, that puts the Yankees six games in front of the second-place White Sox, Mantle hits one of his most famous homers. Pedro Ramos (12-10) is protecting a one-run lead when Mantle steps in with two runners on base in the opener's fifth inning. Batting lefthanded, Mickey connects squarely and socks a drive to a point above the Yankee Stadium roof. Cutting through a breeze, the ball starts to descend and strikes the facade crowning the right field third deck, only 18 inches from becoming the first homer hit completely out of the Stadium in its storied, 33-year history.

— The blast off the facade made Mantle a national celebrity. He made the cover of several magazines, including *Time* and *Newsweek*. Yet he would later call the home run "a long high fly" compared to an even more impressive shot off the facade in 1963. Mantle at this point had 20 home runs, a record 16 of them hit in May, and a .414 average. A week later, he would be leading the AL in hitting (.407), runs (46), RBIs (52), hits (70) and homers (21).

Jun 18— Batting lefthanded, Mantle slams a high fastball from Paul Foytack and clears the right field roof at Detroit's Tiger Stadium.* He joins Ted Williams as only the second player to hit a fair ball out in Detroit. The ball, hit against an 18 mph wind, clears the 94-foot-high roof at the 380-foot mark and travels over 500 feet. Two days from now Mantle will hit a pair of 500-footers in Detroit and go ahead of Ruth's 1927 homer pace.

Jul 1— The Yankees sweep a doubleheader from Washington, 3-2 and 8-6, at the Stadium. In the nightcap, Mantle switch-hits homers for the fourth time in his career; Mickey hits No. 28 batting righty off Dean Stone and No. 29, a game-winning shot in the bottom of ninth, hitting lefty off Bud Byerly.

— Mickey's home run hitting would slow down in July when his knee bothered him again, forcing him to wear a brace. The pain would not substantially ease until August. He would hit only three more homers before July 30.

Jul 10— At Washington's Griffith Stadium, the NL wins the All-Star Game, 7-3. Stengel is the AL manager. Mantle hits a home run off Warren Spahn, Yogi Berra goes two for two at the plate and has 11 total chances behind the plate to set an All-Star Game record, Whitey Ford pitches one inning and Martin is unsuccessful as a pinch-hitter. Mantle comes into the game as the top vote-getter (206,524).

Jul 12— The Yankees begin the season's second half with an important three-game series with Cleveland. Bauer delivers a pinch-hit grand slam homer off Don Mossi, making a 9-5 winner of Johnny Kucks, who will defeat the Tribe four times this season. Tomorrow Tom Sturdivant will throw a two-hitter at the Tribe and win, 10-0. Like Kucks, Sturdivant will defeat Cleveland four times in 1956. And the next day Mantle will hit his 30th homer (off 20-game-winner Herb Score) and rap a bases-loaded single to beat a declining Bob Feller, 5-4, in 10 innings and sweep the series. The Yankees are into an 11-game winning streak.

*Formerly Briggs Stadium.

Jul 20— In defeating Kansas City, 6-3, Ford fans six consecutive A's to tie an AL
          record since broken. Whitey begins by striking out Joe Ginsberg to end
          the second inning. In the third, he strikes out the side—Joe DeMaestri,
          Clete Boyer and Jack McMahan. Hector Lopez and Al Pilarcik strike out in
          the fourth, before Enos Staughter flies out. Ford finishes with eight strikeouts.

Aug 23— Mantle hits a memorable tape-measure homer batting righthanded in the
          nightcap of a twinbill at the Stadium that Chicago sweeps. Mickey puts a
          Paul LaPalme pitch 20 rows deep in the left field upper deck. The ball misses
          going over the roof by a mere 20 feet.

Aug 25— The Yankees reacquire Enos Slaughter, purchasing his contract from Kansas
          City* for an amount in the $50,000 range. In 24 games, Slaughter will hit
          .289 over the final weeks for the Yankees. To make room for Slaughter on
          the roster, the Yankees cut veteran shortstop Phil Rizzuto, who is hitting
          .231 in 31 games as a reserve shortstop behind McDougald. It is Old Timers'
          Day and Rizzuto is called to Stengel's office for a meeting with the manager
          and George Weiss. The Scooter is asked who he feels should be let go
          now that Slaughter will be added to the roster. Rizzuto, honored to be
          included in the braintrust, names several little-used players, but Weiss
          says he needs each of them. As the charade dawns on Rizzuto, Weiss
          finally tells him he will be the one to go. Those who believe Weiss to be a
          cold fish are sustained in their belief.

          — Rizzuto was a loyal and valuable member of the Yankees, and with his
          release the last link to the great Joe McCarthy era was gone. In 13 seasons,
          the Scooter hit .273, was the best bunter of his day and one of the best
          baserunners. He played shortstop gracefully and expertly. Over his Yankee
          career Joe DiMaggio, Berra and Mantle were the best players in the game,
          but Rizzuto was probably the one player the Yankees could least afford
          to lose. In short, he was one of the greatest shortstops of all time. It is
          regrettable that he is not in the Baseball Hall of Fame. Shortstops and
          catchers are the two most important everyday players, but their jobs are
          defensively oriented and their offensive stats are generally not impressive.
          They don't have to be impressive, but the Hall voters can't accept this.

Aug 31— The Yankees have a so-so 16-15 record in August but it is a good month
          for Mantle who hits 12 home runs, giving him 47 for the season. He is hitting
          .366 and has 118 RBIs to lead the league in all three categories. He gets
          his final August roundtripper in Washington off Pascual—his fifth base hit
          off Pascual for 1956, and all of them homers. President Eisenhower asked
          Mickey to "hit one for me" before the game, although Ike told him he was
          rooting for Washington. But in September, Mantle will slump and pull a groin
          muscle, ending his chase of Ruth's record.

Sep 3—   Kucks wins his 18th and final game of the regular season, beating Baltimore,
          6-1, in the opener of a doubleheader at the Stadium. The 22-year-old's
          emergence is a vital factor in the Yanks' pennant. Larsen wins the second
          game, 5-0.

Sep 14— Yogi Berra hits a home run in the Yankees' 5-1 win in Detroit and, with
          237 lifetime homers, passes Gabby Hartnett on the all-time list for catchers.
          Yogi will hit his 30th of the season on the final day, tying his own AL

*Kansas City GM Parke Carroll once worked for George Weiss and is receptive to transactions
proposed by the Yankees.

single-season record. (He hit 30 in 1952.) Don Larsen pitches a four-hitter. He will win two more games on the season, beating Boston both times.

Sep 18— In Chicago, the Yankees win, 3-2, in 11 innings to clinch the pennant. In the top of the 11th inning, Mantle hits his 50th home run off southpaw Billy Pierce (20-9). Ford pitches a strong game to get his 19th win in a duel between two of the league's best southpaws. New York had tied the game in the ninth when Martin tripled leading off and scored. Brooklyn will lay claim to the NL pennant on the final day of the season.

Catcher Yogi Berra hit his 237th home run late in the 1956 season. This put him one homer ahead of catcher Gabby Hartnett. Yogi's next homer put him at 30 for the year and tied his own record for homers by a catcher in one season, a record broken by Lance Parrish of Detroit in 1982.

Sep 21— Mantle hits a 500-foot home run, his 51st, at Fenway Park. It is a line drive that reaches the center field back wall "in a second," in the words of Tom Sturdivant. Mickey's lefthanded wallop strikes the rear retaining wall 10 inches from the top. It barely misses clearing the wall and leaving the ballpark.

— The main interest in Boston was in the batting race between Mantle and Ted Williams. Mickey made six hits in nine trips in the series and passed Williams, who was held by Yankee pitching to two hits in 11 trips. Mickey would finish at .353, eight points above Ted.

Sep 26— In his final attempt at his first 20-game season, Ford pitches a great game but loses, 1-0, in Baltimore. With one out and Ford on third base in the ninth inning, pinch-hitter Mantle pops out. Whitey is beaten by 21-year-old Charlie Beamon who in his major league career wins only three games.

— The season would end a few days later with Mantle joining Lou Gehrig as the only Yankee ever to win the Triple Crown, hitting .353, with 52 homers. He would get his 52nd homer September 28 at the Stadium off Washington's Bob Porterfield. His home run total bested runner-up Vic Wertz of Cleveland by 20. His 130 RBIs were two more than the total of Detroit's Al Kaline. Mantle also led the AL in total bases, runs and slugging. The Yankees hit 190 home runs as a team, breaking the league record of 182, held by the 1936 Yankees. Besides Mantle, the top home run hitters were Berra, 30; Bauer, 26; Skowron, 23; and McDougald, 13.

Oct 6— Down two games to none in the World Series, the Yankees win, 5-3, behind Whitey Ford at the Stadium. Martin homers off Roger Craig to tie the game but the Dodgers go ahead, 2-1, in the sixth. However, in the bottom half, Bauer singles, and with two out, Berra singles. Then Slaughter strokes a three-run homer, the most important and timely hit of the Series.

Oct 7— Tom Sturdivant pitches a six-hitter in Game 4 and beats the Dodgers, 6-2, evening the Series at two games apiece. Berra knocks in the game's first run but Brooklyn ties. In the bottom of the fourth, Mantle walks and steals second. The Dodgers walk Slaughter to get to Martin, who destroys the strategy by singling home Mantle. McDougald's sacrifice fly scores Slaughter. Icing the contest later, Mantle hits a towering homer and Bauer smacks a two-run roundtripper.

Oct 8— Don Larsen accomplishes the unthinkable—a perfect game in World Series competition. He beats the Dodgers, 2-0. Larsen takes the mound hoping to redeem himself for a poor effort in Game 2. Mantle gets the first hit off Maglie, a fourth-inning solo home run. The Yankees add an insurance run in the sixth when Bauer singles home Carey. Larsen has several close calls. Swift Jackie Robinson lines a shot off third baseman Carey's glove, but shortstop McDougald grabs the deflection and nips Robinson at first. Mantle makes the most spectacular play, robbing Hodges in deep left-center field with a backhanded catch. Carey makes a nice shoestring catch of a line drive, again hit by Hodges. In the ninth, Furillo fouls off four pitches before flying out to Bauer. Campanella hits a long foul ball, then grounds out to Martin. Pinch-hitter Dale Mitchell takes a called strike three and Larsen goes into the history books. Later, Larsen admits, "I was so weak in the knees out there in the ninth inning I thought I was going to faint..." He adds, "Let me tell you, I'm glad I had Yogi back there. He did all my thinking for me..."

— Larsen had some great games in September—three four-hitters and a three-hitter. He experimented with a no windup delivery and was getting great results. He finished the year 11-5. Larsen was involved in an early-morning car accident in spring training and Weiss was all set to unload Don, but Stengel persuaded the GM to keep him.

Oct 10— After Brooklyn won Game 6, Johnny Kucks, winner of 18 games and key to the Yankee pennant success, pitches a brillant three-hitter, the Yankees win, 9-0, and the World Championship rests again in the Bronx. Berra blasts a pair of two-run homers early off Newcombe. Howard adds a solo homer and Skowron salts away the Series with a seventh-inning grand slam homer. The exciting Series ends when Berra, after dropping a third strike, throws out Jackie Robinson. Berra sets a record with 10 RBIs, leads all hitters at .360 and calls a perfect game.

Nov 14— Mickey Mantle becomes the second man in history to be a unanimous selection for AL MVP honors. He receives all 24 first-place votes. Berra finishes second.

— Mantle also won the Hickok Belt as the year's top professional athlete. He was now looked upon not only as the best centerfielder in baseball but the best in New York City. Mickey this year outdid Willie Mays of the Giants and Duke Snider of the Dodgers in runs, hits, homers, RBIs, walks, batting and slugging. Mays was the Major League Player of the Year in 1954, and Snider in 1955. But the award given by *The Sporting News* this year went to Mantle.

Dec 18— Phil Rizzuto, the one-time greatest shortstop in Yankee history who was so unceremoniously released by George Weiss the previous summer, is hired to broadcast Yankee games. He joins the profession's two greatest broadcasters, Mel Allen and Red Barber. Rizzuto will continue to broadcast games into the 1980's. "Holy Cow!" will be his stamp.

1957

The Yankees will finish at 98-56 and win their third consecutive pennant by eight games over second-place Chicago. League MVP Mickey Mantle will hit .365 and Yogi Berra will hit 24 home runs. Tom Sturdivant will lead the pitchers with a record of 16-6, and Bob Grim will have a league-leading 19 saves. Milwaukee will defeat the Yankees in a seven-game World Series.

Feb 19— The Yankees and Kansas City A's swing a major deal. The Yankees obtain Art Ditmar (P), Bobby Shantz (P), Clete Boyer (INF), Jack McMahon (P), Curt Roberts (INF) and Wayne Belardi (INF). The A's acquire Irv Noren (OF), Tom Morgan (P), Mickey McDermott (P), Rip Coleman (P), Billy Hunter (INF), Milt Graff (INF) and Jack Urban (P). There is just one snag: Commissioner Frick will rule that Boyer, a talented bonus baby, must stay with the A's until the expiration of his bonus term. Boyer will transfer to New York on June 4.

— Noren and Morgan were the top players surrendered by the Yankees. Noren was a good contact hitter and a fine defensive outfielder. Over five seasons with the Yankees, he hit .272. He played with painful knees even after operations on both of them. Morgan finished his Yankee career with a 38-22 record and 26 saves as a starter and reliever. The Californian, whom Mel Allen nicknamed Plowboy, would pitch in the majors until 1963 and finish at 67-47. The key gains for the Yanks were Boyer, the accomplished Bobby Shantz, and Art Ditmar. Ditmar was only 12-22 for the A's in 1956, but George Weiss liked his looks. He would go 8-3 in New York in 1957. Shantz, a little southpaw from Pottstown, Pa., would go 30-18 with 19 saves over four New York seasons.

Apr 16— In the Yanks' home opener, Whitey Ford pitches a six-hitter and defeats Washington, 2-1, before 31,644 at the Stadium. The Yanks score the winning run in the ninth when Berra, who earlier homered, singles, McDougald doubles and Carey singles.

May 4— Ford retires the first five White Sox hitters and then must leave the game with what is diagnosed as tendonitis. Whitey developed the problem on a cold April day when his arm tightened during a long Yankee rally. Ford is able to throw only off-speed pitches. He will make only one start over the next two months, finishing the year with a record of 11-5 and a fine 2.57 ERA.

— With Ford sidelined, Bobby Shantz would play an important role. Shantz, a cute 5'6" Ed Lopat-style pitcher from Pottstown, Pa., won 24 games for the Philadelphia A's—and the MVP Award—in 1952, and then, because of arm and shoulder miseries, failed to have a season of more than five wins after 1952. Now he would be the savior of the Yank staff, finishing 11-5 and winning the ERA title at 2.45.

May 7— In Cleveland, Gil McDougald drives a ball into Herb Score's face. The pitcher is semi-conscious and is bleeding profusely from the nose and mouth. He is taken to Lakeside Hospital where doctors treat three broken bones and save his damaged right eye.

— Score won the strikeout championship in his first two seasons and was a 20-game winner as a 23-year-old in 1956. He would never regain his sensational early form, returning in 1958 with a 2-3 mark and finishing his career in 1962 at 55-46 lifetime. McDougald, too, was adversely affected. In going up the middle, he was doing exactly what good hitters should do, but the sensitive Gil was shaken by the accident and vowed he would quit baseball if Score lost his eye. Gil's aggressive style of baseball, the style that had made him one of the league's best players, seemed to drain out of him. He stopped trying to hit up the middle and his batting average suffered. Even while dropping 22 points (from 1956), he still had a fine .289 year at the plate.

May 15— Ah, the Copacabana! One of the most famous off-field fights in baseball history starts innocently. Mantle, Ford, Berra, Bauer, Kucks and their wives and Martin hold a celebration of two birthdays—Martin's 29th (the following day) and Berra's 32nd (a few days past). The ballplayers settle in to see Sammy Davis, Jr., perform at the Copacabana. A group of drunken bowlers directs racial slurs toward Davis. Bauer suggests that the bowlers desist, words are exchanged and several members of each group step outside. The details of what happens next are fuzzy, but bowler Edward Jones, a delicatessen owner in the Bronx, is out cold on the men's room floor. Jones may have been floored by a bouncer. In any case, the partying Yanks attempt a discreet rear-exit departure but are spotted by a newspaper columnist who investigates and digs up the story.

— Bauer would be accused of slugging Jones, a charge that he vehemently denied. But Jones filed a suit for damages and a grand jury would investigate. Testimony from the Yankees involved was taken, and Bauer was cleared of any criminal charges. When Yankee lawyers suggested filing a countersuit, Bauer said, "Forget it. What would I do if I won? Take the guy's delicatessen?"

May 16— George Weiss awakens to see the *New York Daily News* headline: "Bauer in Brawl in Copa." He calls all party-goers to the Yankee offices. The players are guilty of nothing except creating bad publicity, but Dan Topping (in consultation with Weiss) levied stiff fines ($1,000 for all but Kucks, who is made $500 poorer).

— The large headlines steamed Weiss, who wrongly blamed Martin for the entire episode. Martin, whom Weiss never liked, was made the scapegoat. Now with Richardson playing so well at second and Carey back at third (where Martin had played 13 games while Andy was injured), Weiss was presented with the moment he had been waiting for—the chance to trade Billy while Stengel's resistance was low.

Jun 8— In Detroit, the Yankees lose, 7-4, while the White Sox beat Baltimore. Riding a nine-game winning streak, first-place Chicago now leads the stumbling Yankees by six games. Chicago is 32-13, New York 27-20.

Jun 13— Yesterday Minnie Minoso almost set off a brawl when, upset over a close pitch, he threw his bat toward the mound. Today the Yanks and White Sox do go at it at Comiskey Park. In the bottom of the first inning, Art Ditmar allows a walk and an infield single. Ditmar gets two strikes on Larry Doby, then fires a pitch that knocks Doby down, eludes Ellie Howard and rolls to the backstop. Ditmar rushes in to protect the plate, and, there, exchanges words with Doby. Doby swings at Ditmar and both benches empty. Fights break out everywhere. White Sox pitcher Bob Keegan jumps the bullpen fence yelling, "Whitey Ford is my man!" then falls splat into a water puddle. It takes 30 minutes for police to restore order and, when the brawls are finally ended, Slaughter's uniform shirt is torn apart (by Walt Dropo) and Doby, Dropo and Slaughter are ejected. In the interval before resumption of play, Martin finds out that Doby had threatened Ditmar and he goes after Doby, landing several punches. The Yankees win, 4-3. Four games behind the White Sox after today's win, they are off on a 10-game winning streak.

Jun 15— The Yankees trade Billy Martin (INF), Ralph Terry (P), Woodie Held (INF-OF) and Bob Martyn (OF) to the Kansas City A's for Ryne Duren (P), Harry "Suitcase" Simpson (OF-1B) and Jim Pisoni (OF). Duren is the key for the Yankees. Yankee players had told Stengel and Weiss in the spring to either get Duren or ban him, because they couldn't hit him. The Yankees announce that Simpson will be the regular leftfielder but Suitcase will hit only .250 in 75 games.

— Emotionally this was a tough deal for Stengel to take. Martin himself was moved to tears. He felt Casey did not fight Weiss hard enough to keep him, that Casey could have prevented Weiss from trading him. It would be several years before Martin would talk to Stengel, but eventually they made their peace. The fire had gone out of Martin's play; he would play for six teams after leaving New York, finishing in 1961 with a lifetime .257 average. In seven Yankee seasons, Martin hit .262—.333 in World Series play.

Jun 17— The Yankees beat Kansas City, 4-3, but Martin stars in his first game against his former teammates. Billy sparkles in the field and has a single and home run and scores three runs. Elston Howard drives in the winning runs in the ninth inning.

Jun 30—   The Yankees finish June with a record of 21-9 for the month. They beat Kansas City twice at the Stadium today, 2-1 and 5-1. They are now in first place—where they will stay.

Jul 3—   Berra has an incredible eight-RBI performance against Boston. Yogi belts a three-run homer, a pair of two-run singles and knocks in a run with a groundout.

    — Berra began the season mired in a deep slump but rebounded strongly and would finish with 24 homers and 82 RBIs. He played all summer suffering from painful headaches, aftermath of a broken nose.

Jul 9—   The AL wins the All-Star Game, 6-5, in St. Louis with Stengel the winning skipper. The NL rallies for three runs in the ninth inning but Casey brings in his own Bob Grim, who gets Gil Hodges to line out to left field, ending the game. Skowron has two hits, Mantle and Berra one apiece. McDougald, Mantle and Skowron each score once.

Jul 22—   Former Yankee Manager Joe McCarthy is inducted into the Baseball Hall of Fame, his plaque noting that Joe was an "...outstanding manager who never played in major leagues. The major league teams managed by him during 24 years never finished out of first division..." McCarthy, who retired from baseball during the 1950 season as the Red Sox' manager, was elected by the Committee on Veterans.

Jul 23—   Mantle hits a single, double, triple and homer at the Stadium for his only cycle as a major leaguer and the first by a Yankee since DiMaggio hit for the cycle in 1948. Mickey's homer travels 465 feet to the next-to-last row of the right-center field bleachers, the closest anyone has ever come to clearing Yankee Stadium in this direction. It follows by one month another home run, also hit off Chicago pitching, that would have traveled at least 550 feet had it not been stopped by the facade hanging from the roof of the right field stands. Mickey's triple today was a bases-loaded game winner, the Yanks trouncing Chicago, 10-6. He leads the AL at .367 and has 69 RBIs.

Aug 7—   For the second game in a row, Bauer leads off with a home run against Washington. Stengel loves lead-off homers, and with Bauer batting first there is always the possibility of one—Hank will hit 18 homers this season. Lifetime, he will hit 18 homers to lead off a game, putting him among the all-time leaders.

Aug 10—   Mickey Mantle collects four hits in five trips, as the Yanks win in Baltimore, 6-3, behind Turley. Mantle's homer travels 460 feet to the base of the center field scoreboard. It is the first time a ball has ever cleared a hedge in Memorial Stadium's center field. The Mick is playing sensationally and seems to have a shot at a second straight Triple Crown. But "wheel" problems lie ahead.

Aug 27—   Their 7½-game lead of only a few weeks ago now down to 3½, the Yankees arrive at Chicago for a three-game series with the White Sox. Berra assumes command (with both Mantle and Ford ailing). He knocks in six runs, half of them with a game-winning three-run homer. New York wins, 12-6, behind Grim (his 11th in relief), and will win again tomorrow, 5-4.

Aug 29— Over 40,000 fans jam into Comiskey Park for the series finale, a match-up between Tom Sturdivant and Dick Donovan. Bauer belts an early homer but the White Sox scramble back to tie. Ford relieves in the middle innings and holds the Chisox in check. Leading off the 11th inning, Slaughter homers to put New York ahead, 2-1. Ford retires Chicago in order in the bottom half and the Yankees barely make their getaway train. They leave the Second City with a 6½-game lead—the White Sox wasted their chance.

Sep 13— After being hospitalized for several days with shin splints, Mantle returns to the Yankees, who will win seven of their next eight games. They defeat Chicago, 7-1, today and the taped-up Mantle has a double and a triple. But no longer is he a Triple Crown prospect. His .365 average will finish second to Ted Williams' .388, his 34 homers will finish third and his 94 RBIs will be sixth. Mickey will, however, lead the league in runs scored and walks.

Sep 21— Tom Sturdivant defeats Boston, assuring the Yankees of a tie for the pennant; later today Kansas City beats Chicago, meaning that the Yanks have won their 23rd AL flag. It will be Milwaukee in the World Series.

— Stengel won with one of his most balanced pitching staffs. The double-figure winners numbered six: Sturdivant, 16-6; Turley, 13-6; Grim, 12-8; Shantz, 11-5; Ford, 11-5; and Larsen, 10-4. All except Larsen finished with earned run averages of less than three runs per game. One of them, Grim, may have been the best unpublicized pitcher in the Stengel era. After hurting his arm in 1955, Grim, went to the bullpen and this year would lead the league with 19 saves. Grim, part of a June 15, 1958 trade with Kansas City, would be 45-21 with 28 saves with New York and 16-20 with nine saves in his post-Yankee career.

Oct 5— In Milwaukee's County Stadium, the New Yorkers pulverize the Braves, 12-3, to take a two-games-to-one lead in the World Series. Larsen relieves Turley in the second inning and allows only two runs the rest of the way in his first World Series appearance since his perfect game. Larsen retires the first seven batters he faces to give him an amazing record of 11 ⅓ consecutive perfect innings in World Series play. Mantle has a two-run homer but incurs a significant injury. On a pickoff play, Mantle dives back into second base safely, only to have Red Schoendienst fall on his shoulder. The injury will force Mickey to miss the fifth and sixth games and will plague him the remainder of his career. Tony Kubek, a Milwaukean, has a big day in his hometown. Kubek hits two home runs. He joins Charlie Keller as the second rookie to homer twice in a World Series game. Kubek has three hits in all, scores three runs, and drives home four runs.

— When Mantle sprained ligaments in his left foot in spring training, Tony Kubek was sent to center field to take his place. Kubek looked great. Casey took a liking to him—he knew Tony's dad from the minor leagues—and kept him with the club for the regular season. Kubek played in the outfield and infield. He hit .297 and won Rookie of the Year honors.

Oct 10— Burdette bests the Yankees, 5-0, in Game 7 and the Braves are World Champions. Working on two days' rest (Spahn has the flu), Burdette gets his third win and his second shutout. The onetime Yankee farmhand allows only two runs in 27 innings. It is one of the great efforts in World Series history. Stengel starts Larsen, the loser, but ends up using five pitchers. The Braves put the game on ice with a four-run third-inning after a Yankee error opens the door. Eddie Mathews doubles home two runs and scores on a single by Hank Aaron, who will eventually score. In the bottom of the ninth, the Yankees load the bases but third baseman Mathews robs Skowron of a hit to end a World Series overshadowed everywhere but in Milwaukee by the news in New York—the Giants of upper Manhattan and the Dodgers of Brooklyn would embark for California.

— Yankee pitchers held the Braves to a feeble .209 batting average. Hank Aaron was Milwaukee's only consistent hitter, leading everyone with .393. And Burdette was the Braves' standout pitcher. His club's ERA of 3.48 would have ballooned without his 0.67. In summary, a two-man effort—Burdette and Aaron—beat New York, and for the first time since 1948, the City of New York was without the World Championship.

Nov 22— For the second successive season, Mickey Mantle is named the AL's most Valuable Player in balloting conducted by the Baseball Writers. Mickey collects 233 points, one more than Ted Williams draws. Boston fans scream that Williams has again been robbed by a Yankee, and Williams did lead the AL with a .388 average. But Mantle, intervening injuries aside, might will have won another Triple Crown. And Mantle's team won the pennant.

Dec 9— Jerry Coleman, a Yankee infielder since 1949, is released. Coleman retires as a player and will go to work in the Yankee front office, eventually becoming one of the team's broadcasters. Coleman leaves in style, as the Yanks' leading hitter in the recent Series at .364 (8 for 22). This follows a nine-year career in which Jerry hit .263 and played a beautiful second base.

1958

The Yankees will finish at 92-62 and win their fourth consecutive pennant by 10 games over the second-place Chicago White Sox. Mickey Mantle will lead the league with 42 home runs and Yogi Berra will hit 22 with 90 RBIs. Bob Turley will win the Cy Young Award as the AL's only 20-game winner (21-7), and the Yankees will give Casey what may have been his most satisfying Series triumph.

Mar 20— The Yankees sell the contract of first baseman-outfielder Joe Collins to the Philadelphia Phillies. But the deal is voided when Collins decides to retire rather than report to the Phils.

— Collins played his entire 10-year career with the Yankees, hitting .256, platooning at first base but playing there more often than anyone on the Yanks since Lou Gehrig. He was steady, if unspectacular, a player Casey Stengel called "my meal ticket." Collins was the quintessential team player, welcoming the talented Bill Skowron to the team in 1954 without a trace of malice toward a rival for his position.

Apr 7— The Yankees hit six home runs and beat Philadelphia, 20-1, in an exhibition game at Greenville, N.C. Moose Skowron hits two homers. One of them is his third grand slam homer in seven days.

— Skowron, a Chicagoan and a one-time football and baseball star at Purdue, joined the Yankees in 1954 and hit .340, .319, .308 and .304 over successive seasons. He had tremendous power to center and right field, his opposite field. He was leading the Yankees in spring training in both home runs (11) and RBIs (30). Moose would carry his sensational hitting into the regular season, hitting .373 in early May and drawing comparisons to Lou Gehrig. Then on May 11, in fielding a grounder, he collapsed with a badly torn back muscle. He was hospitalized for several weeks, and Marv Throneberry filled in at first base. Moose did not regain his sensational early-season form when he returned and finished at .273—his first sub-.300 season in the majors—in 126 games.

Apr 18— Whitey Ford defeats Baltimore in the Yankee Stadium opener, 3-1. It is Ford's fourth straight Opening Day win at the Stadium.

Apr 22— Tom Sturdivant's shoulder pains, and he drops out of today's game, which Boston wins 12-7, and out of the Yankee rotation,. His problem developed several days earlier on a cold and rainy day in Boston when he sustained ligament damage. This after Tom, a spring holdout following back-to-back 16-win seasons, missed most of spring training.

May 25— The Yankees, who went into first place on the fourth day of the season, today sweep a doubleheader in Cleveland and at 25-6 lead the AL by nine games. Yankee pitchers are giving up less than two runs per game.

Jun 3— Whitey Ford strikes out six straight White Sox batters and shuts the Sox out, 3-0. It is the second time in Ford's career that he fans six in a row.

Jun 4— Against Chicago's southpaw ace Billy Pierce (17-11), Mantle hits a 478-foot homer into the 19th row of the Stadium's left-center field bleachers. It is only the seventh time that these faraway bleachers have been reached. Yankee Stadium superintendent Jim Thomson does the measuring.

— Mantle was playing with an assortment of injuries, including a strained right shoulder which especially bothered him when he hit lefthanded. In compensating for the shoulder, Mickey would do further damage to his weak right knee. However, Mickey who had only four homers through May, went on a power spree over the summer, hitting 10 homers in June, 14 in July and 9 in August. But in mid-June, his average batting lefthanded was around .230. The Stadium fans, totally unsympathetic with Mickey's physical woes, took to booing him terribly.

Jul 8— The AL wins the All-Star Game, 4-3, at Baltimore's Memorial Stadium. Stengel is the winning manager. Jackie Jensen (Red Sox) flanks Mantle in right field and Bob Cerv (A's) plays left. All three outfielders were once the jewels of the Yankee organization and all three in 1952 had a chance to succeed Joe DiMaggio in center field. Turley, McDougald, Skowron and Berra perform.

Jul 9— In Washington, Stengel and Mantle testify before the Senate Subcommittee on Anti-Trust and Monopoly. The committee is considering a bill to exempt baseball and the three other major professional sports from anti-trust laws. Casey gives a rambling dissertation on his baseball past, complete with stories of such places as Kankakee, Ill. Everyone is enthralled and baffled. Up steps Mickey, who is asked his opinion concerning the applicability of the anti-trust laws to baseball. "My views are just about the same as Casey's," deadpans Mantle.

Jul 12— With a 10-0 defeat of Cleveland, New York is now 52-26 and leads by 12 games. The rest of the pack is being called the Sorry Seven. Zack Monroe and Art Ditmar combine for a three-hitter today, as Andy Carey has a pair of homers and five RBIs.

— Carey in his next game would have a triple, double and two singles in four at-bats. He would hit .286 in 102 games on the season. Another hot hitter around this time was Jerry Lumpe, who won a few games in July. Stengel was getting production from his two third basemen, righthanded Carey and lefthanded Lumpe. Stengel had the touch and the horses, including young, oncoming Norm Sieburn who would hit an even .300 in 134 games.

Jul 16—   The Tigers win, 12-5, at Yankee Stadium with Frank Lary beating the Yankees for the fifth straight time. Detroit's Billy Martin, who contributes a double, plays a brillant defensive game in the infield, taking hits away from Bauer, Carey and Berra. Lary's hold on the Yankees in the face of averages is uncanny. He will gain his Yankee killer tag by beating the Yanks seven times this year. He will go 16-15 on a 77-77 team that will be 10-12 against New York.

Jul 22—   Don Larsen two-hits Detroit while he and his teammates pile up 16 hits to win 15-0. McDougald has four hits and Elston Howard has the game's only homer. Howard is having another year as the best three-way (C-OF-1B) player in the game. He will hit .314.

Jul 24—   Yankee relief ace Ryne Duren, who is leading the AL in saves (17) and ERA (1.38), is beaned by Detroit's Paul Foytack. Duren's glasses and helmet go flying and he falls to the ground a bloody mess. Ryne is carried from the field on a stretcher and taken to Detroit's Memorial Hospital. Luckily, no permanent damage has been done and Duren will be out for a little over a week. He will return in early August to pitch no-hit ball over three innings against Baltimore.

Jul 25—   Whitey Ford hurls his third consecutive shutout! He beats the Indians in Cleveland, 6-0. Ford, whose record is 13-4 (6 wins by shutout) has worked his ERA down to 1.68. The streak, which includes a shutout over Kansas City, began 11 days ago when Whitey blanked Chicago.

Aug 2—   Art Ditmar beats Chicago for his seventh win in nine decisions. The Yankees are now on top by 17 games, the biggest lead as of this date in the history of the majors. New York's pitching is deep and formidable. The club's batting average of .278 is 11 points higher than the next-best hitting team, the Tigers. Joe Gordon, recently named Cleveland's manager, says about this time that "in this league, there are no pennant contenders. There is just the Yankees and no one to challenge them."

— As it turned out, the Yankees were fortunate to have built such a big lead. They would limp home with a 25-28 record over the final 53 games. Skowron, McDougald and Bauer all hit less than .225 in the final two months. Skowron and McDougald were bothered by back problems and Bauer turned 36 in July. The pitching staff finished the season poorly, too. But when the campaign ended, the Yankees would lead the AL in hitting (.268), two points higher than Detroit, and in ERA (3.22), 18 points lower than Baltimore.

Aug 8—   Ford blanks Boston. It is Whitey's seventh shutout (he will lead the AL with seven shutouts in 1958) and he runs his record to 14-5. But it is his last victory of the season.

— Two days later he would hurt his elbow in relief. He could not pitch without pain the rest of the year and did not return to the rotation until mid-September. Whitey would lose two games and finish 14-7. But he would win the ERA championship with a sparkling 2.01.

Aug 12— Plagued by arm trouble, Tom Sturdivant starts and beats the Orioles for his third and final win of the season. But a week later Sturdivant goes on the disabled list and is fined $250 when he is spiked on the heel while "horsing around." He will finish at 3-6.

Sep 6— Washington wins, 8-3, at the Stadium but it is the Yankees who turn a triple play. Clint Courtney lines to McDougald who goes to Kubek at second who pegs to Skowron at first; runners are doubled up off both bases.

Sep 12— Turley wins his 21st game of the season, 5-0. He hurls a four-hitter at Chicago. He wil complete 19 games in only 31 starts and he will lead the league with a .750 winning percentage. He will make three more starts in the regular season but in the eyes of the Cy Young Award voters he has already proved he is 1958's best pitcher.

Sep 14— The Yankees make it official, clinching their 24th pennant by sweeping a doubleheader from the Athletics. Afterwards, the Yankees have a victory party at Kansas City's Muhlenberg Hotel, then board a train for Detroit. Fireballing Ryne Duren is more than a little fired up on alcohol and begins to pester Coach Ralph Houk. Duren pushes at Houk's lit cigar and Houk backhands him, accidentally scratching Duren's head. Duren swings at the coach and several players pull the reliever away. The incident draws head-lines. The Yanks, meanwhile, look ahead to another World Series matchup with Milwaukee.

Sep 15— The Yankees are followed by private detectives hired by George Weiss, who along with Stengel is disturbed over the team's mediocre record since early August. Ford, Mantle and some others have fun leading the detectives on goose chases through Detroit and then losing the private eyes when they become bored. Bobby Richardson and Tony Kubek, both clean livers, are among a group of players followed to a YMCA for a night of ping-pong. Most of the players are upset at being trailed. Says Kubek, "I'm going to ask for a raise next year and tell them to give me what they paid the cops to follow us."

Sep 20— In Baltimore, 35-year-old Hoyt Wilhelm, considered washed up as a relief pitcher, throws a no-hitter against the Yankees and wins, 1-0. Dazzling the Bronx Bombers with his famed knuckler, the recently obtained Wilhelm walks only two and strikes out eight as the Orioles play errorless ball behind him. Losing a heartbreaker is Don Larsen, who knows a thing or two about no-hitters. Larsen's only mistake is allowing a seventh-inning home run to Gus Triandos, who hits 30 this year to tie Berra's AL record for catchers.

— No pitcher has since no-hit the Yankees, who have escaped a number of near misses. The next season, Wilhelm would pitch a one-hitter against the Yankees, allowing only an eighth-inning single by Jerry Lumpe.

Sep 24— Mickey Mantle hits his 42nd home run in Boston and wins his third home run title, finishing ahead of Rocky Colavito, 41; Roy Sievers, 39; Bob Cerv, 38; and Jackie Jensen, 35. Mickey has a great stretch drive, hitting .331 over the final two months. He will finish with 97 RBIs, a league-leading 127 runs, 129 walks and 120 strikeouts.

Sep 28— The Yanks beat Baltimore twice, 7-0 and 6-3, in New York on the final game of the season. Larsen, Duren and Kucks combine for a two-hitter in the opener. Mantle gets three singles in the nightcap and finishes at .304.

Oct 4— The Yanks lose the first two games of the World Series. Today, at the Stadium, Don Larsen and Duren combine to shut out the Braves on six hits as the Yankees win 4-0. Larsen goes seven innings for the victory and Duren finishes for the save. Bauer, with three of the Yankees' four hits drives in all four runs with a two-run single and a two-run 400-foot homer.

— Bauer extended a remarkable World Series record of hitting in 17 consecutive World Series games. The skein would be snapped in Game 4. Bauer hit safely in all seven games in both the 1956 and 1957 Series, and again in the first three games of the 1958 Series. In this, Hank's ninth and last Series as a Yankee, he would hit .323 and lead all batters in at-bats (31), hits (10), homers (4), RBIs (8) and runs (6).

Oct 6— The Yankees send Turley after the Braves whose three-games-to-one lead in the Series has made them boastful. Bob pitches a five-hit, 10-strikeout shutout as the Yankees win, 7-0, and force the Series to return to Milwaukee. After four consecutive World Series losses to Lew Burdette, the Yankees finally get to him. Gil McDougald instills happiness when he drills a third-inniing homer. In the top of the sixth, Bill Bruton makes a lead-off single. Red Schoendienst lines to short left where Ellie Howard makes a great catch and throws to first to double up Burton. The play by Howard, who is making his first start since a Game 2 injury, seems to lift the entire team. The Yankees explode for six runs in the bottom half.

Whitey Ford delivers one of many good Ford pitches in Game 4 of the 1958 World Series. Ford's fine effort proved inadequate, with Milwaukee's Warren Spahn whitewashing the Yankees on two hits. The Braves won, 3-0.

Oct 8— Back at County Stadium, the Yankees win again, 4-3, and force a seventh game. But it takes 10 innings to beat Warren Spahn. Bauer's first-inning homer gives the Yankees a short-lived lead and Berra's sixth-inning sacrifice fly ties it, 2-2. Ditmar and Duren pitch brilliantly in relief. In the 10th, McDougald homers and with two out Howard, Berra and Skowron bunch singles, giving the Yanks a two-run lead. In the bottom half, Aaron delivers a two-out run-scoring single and goes to third on Adcock's single. Stengel brings in Turley, who gets the final out. A key play is Howard's perfect throw from left field to nail Andy Pafko at the plate in the second inning.

Oct 9— Completing their dramatic comeback with a third straight win, the Yankees defeat Burdette once again, 6-2, giving Stengel perhaps his most satisfying Series triumph. It is Casey's seventh World Championship, tying Joe McCarthy for the record. Larsen starts but gives way to Turley, the winner, who allows only one run over the final 6⅔ innings—he has a hand in all of the Yanks' final three wins. The score is 2-2 as the Yankees come up in the eighth. After Burdette sets down the first two batters, Berra doubles, Howard singles home Yogi, Carey singles off Eddie Mathews' glove and Skowron delivers a three-run homer. The Braves have two on and two out in the bottom of the ninth when Turley retires Red Schoendienst on a liner to Mantle.

— Back in New York, normally restrained Yankee fans went wild in a demonstration of civic pride. There were many Yankee heroes; Howard won the Babe Ruth Award and Turley was named MVP by *Sport* magazine. Last year's hero, Burdette, finished with a fat 5.64 ERA. Mathews hit .160 and struck out 11 times.

1959

The Yankees, at 79-75, will finish third, 15 games behind pennant-winning Chicago (and 10 games behind runner-up Cleveland). The season is disappointing for almost all the Yankees, although Mickey Mantle will hit 31 home runs. Whitey Ford will lead the pitching staff at 16-10.

Feb 28— In St Petersburg, Fla., Mickey Mantle ends his one-day holdout and signs for $72,000, a raise of $2,000 over his 1958 salary. George Weiss had offered $60,000 (a cut of $10,000); Mantle requested $85,000.

— Several other regulars were unsigned when the camp opened, and they included Ford. Some of the contract battles became bitter. Casey Stengel, himself,was unsigned until the start of spring training, and there was concern for the 69-year-old Casey's condition.

Apr 12— Bob Turley wins the Yanks' home opener, beating Boston, 3-2, after two days of rain delay. Yankee Stadium has a new, huge, $300,000 scoreboard built beyond the right-center field bleachers. It boasts the first changeable message area in the majors. It is an electronic scoreboard with a simple message area that is eight lines high and eight spaces wide. The scoreboard is the third in the Stadium's history.

Apr 18— The Yankees beat Baltimore, 16-7. Elston Howard has five hits and Andy Carey has four, and Carey and Bill Skowron have four RBIs apiece. This is one of the few positive early-season games. Injuries plague the team. Mantle hurts his shoulder on a throw and chips a bone in his right index

The 1959 season was bitterly disappointing for both Mickey Mantle and the Yankees. Mickey flings his bat in disgust after striking out April 25 in a close game with Baltimore. But even in this "off year" Mickey delivered 31 home runs!

finger. Larsen and Sturdivant have sore arms, McDougald and Carey would have hand injuries and Skowron plays in pain.

— Howard had a fine season, hitting 18 homers with 73 RBIs. He played 50 games at first base, 43 games behind the plate and 28 games in the outfield.

Apr 22— The day after Mantle hits his 250th career homer, Whitey Ford puts on an amazing show in Washington, striking out 15 Senators and winning, 1-0. In 14 innings! Skowron finally gives Whitey a lead with a 14th-inning solo homer and Ford makes it hold up in the bottom of the 14th.

May 3— Charlie Maxwell of Detroit, who is to New York pitchers what the Tigers' Frank "Yankee Killer" Lary is to Yankee batters, clubs four homers on the day, as Detroit takes a doubleheader, 4-2 and 8-2. Maxwell continually hits hard against the Yankees. The Yankees will win only 8 of 22 games against Detroit.

May 7— A crowd of 93,103, the largest ever to see a baseball game, gathers at the Los Angeles Coliseum for a benefit exhibition game for Roy Campanella, the crippled great of the Dodgers' recent past. The Yankees beat the Los Angeles Dodgers, 6-2, but the Yanks suffer still another injury when Skowron tears a hamstring muscle running out an infield hit.

May 10— The Yankees sweep a doubleheader from Washington at home, winning 6-3 and 3-2 in 10 innings. Catcher Yogi Berra plays the final game of his big league record 148 consecutive errorless games in which he accepts 950 chances. His string began on July 28, 1957. He will make an error in his next game (day after tomorrow, on his 34th birthday).

May 20— Detroit's Frank Lary defeats the Yankees, 13-6. The Bronx Bombers, in last place for the first time since May 1940, become the Basement Bombers. Injuries and the Asian flu have taken a severe toll; no one is hurting more than Mantle. Mickey, who is hitting .275 and playing in spite of a bad shoulder, broken finger and the flu, is taking terrible abuse from the Stadium fans. As he circles the bases after his two-run homer off Lary today, Mickey is subjected to sustained and lusty booing.

May 24— Whitey Ford beats the Orioles, 9-0, allowing only two hits (both by Bob Nieman) in the first of two in Baltimore. The Orioles win the nightcap, 2-1. Mantle hits a three-run homer in the first game but also fans three times in a row, the third time taking three strikes as though he weren't interested. Mantle apologizes to both Stengel and his teammates afterwards. New York is out of the cellar briefly with the first-game win, then falls back in. The Yanks will languish in last place until a 3-0 win over Washington on May 31 lifts them out of the cellar.

May 30— New York has two big games in Washington, winning 11-2 and 11-0. Elston Howard hits a pair of two-run homers in the opener and Mantle's perfect four-for-four game includes a two-run homer. In the second game, Kubek has four hits and five RBIs. Ditmar pitches a five-hitter in the first game and Larsen a four-hitter in the second.

Jun 17— The Yankees beat Chicago, 7-3, Mantle unloading a 450-foot home run that lands 10 rows deep in the right field upper deck at the Stadium. The shot on a 3-0 Ray Moore pitch is Mickey's 14th homer and is good for three runs. "It was the best one I've hit in two years," Mickey says after the game.

Jun 18— Mantle's 10th-inning homer off Gerry Staley beats the White Sox, 5-4.

The winner is Bobby Shantz, who pitches three hitless innings in relief. Shantz will have a fine year, winning seven of 10 decisions.

Jun 23— Mickey Mantle hits his fifth home run in a week. His two-run shot off Rip Coleman in Kansas City is his 18th of the year. The Yanks are winning and moving up in the standings.

— Mantle's homer would be his final homer for the month. Indeed, between this date and August 4 he would hit only two more homers. It would be an unpleasant as well as unproductive summer. Mantle and the entire Yankee team would be booed loud and long by the Stadium crowd through the hot days of 1959.

Jun 26— The Yankees beat Chicago, 8-4, with Duren pitching the final three innings and striking out eight of the nine men he faces. In the seventh, Duren fans the side—Earl Torgeson, Suitcase Simpson and Sherm Lollar. In the eighth, he strikes out Billy Goodman and Johnny Callison. In the ninth, he again fans the side—Luis Aparicio, Nellie Fox (who whiffed only 13 times in 624 at bats in 1959) and Torgeson once again. New York is only 1½ games out of first place, which is occupied by Cleveland.

— Duren who would go 12-15 with 43 saves in a four-year Yankee stint, was as intimidating in his era as Goose Gossage is today. His fastball was a blazer. But he didn't always have control of it, nor did he have good eyesight. In fact , Ryne wore extremely thick glasses. And for good measure he usually threw his first warm-up pitch to the backstop. As Casey said of Duren, "He takes a drink or 10, comes in with them Coke bottles, throws one on the screen, and scares the shit out of 'em." Ryne probably had his best season in 1959. He posted 14 saves and had an astonishing 1.87 ERA. But injuries would catch up with him too; with only 10 days left in the season he broke his right wrist in a dugout spill.

Jun 28— In a Comiskey Park doubleheader the day after they defeat Bob Turley (8-11), the White Sox sweep two games, beating both Ford and Larsen in 100-degree heat. Reserve catcher Earl Battey wins both games with home runs. They are Battey's only homers of the season! The Yankees are now in fifth place, four games behind the Indians, who aren't running as scared as they were a couple of days ago. And the Yanks are about to be forewarned of a disastrous July: Mantle will badly injure his right ankle the day after tomorrow, and a few days after that will reinjure his right shoulder. These problems will arise as Mantle is getting it going, having hit at a .326 clip from May 25 through June 29. The Yankees will go 12-16 (with one tie) in

Jul 4—   In an Independence Day doubleheader with Washington, Tony Kubek has seven singles and a double in 10 at-bats. Tony, who will hit .279 this year, falls one hit shy of the AL record of nine hits in a doubleheader.

Jul 13— Boston completes its sweep of a five-game series with New York at Fenway Park, 13-3. The biggest blow is a grand slam homer by Gene Stephens, who will hit three homers all year. Stephens enters the game as a pinch-runner for Ted Williams.

— This series spelled disaster for the Yankees. They left Boston in fourth place, 7½ games out of first. The Yanks' pitching was horrible and the Red Sox feasted, scoring 40 runs. The Bosox romp over the Yankees came almost exactly 20 years after Boston swept a five-game series at the Stadium.

Jul 16—   With two out in the 10th at Yankee Stadium, Mantle homers off righthander
           Gary Bell (16-11) to beat Cleveland, 7-5, in the first of two. The Yanks
           also take the nightcap, 4-0, but sustain serious injuries. Leftfielder Tony
           Kubek and shortstop Gil McDougald collide in short left field while going
           after a Rocky Colavito pop fly. Kubek, who is knocked out cold, suffers
           a concussion and will have lingering pains in the neck and shoulder.
           McDougald will have dizzy spells. To make matters worse, Andy Carey, who
           has been bothered by back problems, comes down with mononucleosis this
           week and is lost for the year.

Jul 25—   In Detroit, the Yankees suffer the final blow to any comeback hopes when
           Skowron breaks his arm in two places. Moose, who less than 24 hours
           earlier had had his back examined at the Mayo Clinic, reaches for a bad
           throw at first and Coot Veal runs into him. Moose's season is over; he
           finishes at .298 with 15 homers and 59 RBIs (at the time the second most
           in the AL behind Harmon Killebrew) in 74 games. The injury is the latest
           in a string of injuries to both Skowron and the Yankees. (Marv Throneberry
           will play first and hit .240.) New York wins the game, 9-8, on Berra's ninth-
           inning two-run homer. But the Yankees are now merely playing out the string.

Aug 3—   The year's second All-Star Game is played in the Los Angeles Coliseum, and
           the AL and Stengel win, 5-3. Berra blasts a two-run homer off the Dodgers'
           Don Drysdale. Mantle goes one for three and Kubek pinch-hits, walks and
           scores.

Aug 28-   Art Ditmar, on his way to a fine 13-9 season, pitches a two-hit shutout
           in Washington and the Yankees win, 4-0. Ditmar hits a home run and a
           bases-loaded single, driving in three runs. It is a sensational one-man
           performance. The low-key Ditmar, a valued member of the Yankee pitching
           staff over five seasons, will go 47-32 in New York.

Sep 3—   Ditmar has a no-hitter against Washington through seven innings. The
           Senators finally get to him for four safeties, but Art wins, 9-2, at the Stadium.

Sep 13—   The Yankees put a severe crimp in Cleveland's chances of catching the
           White Sox by handing the Indians a double defeat. Joe Gordon's charges go
           down, 2-1 (in 11 innings) and 1-0 at the Stadium. The Tribe will finish five
           games out. Mantle hits his 29th homer in the opener and a Bauer single
           knocks in the only run in the second game, a six-hitter by Duke Maas. Five of
           Maas' 14 wins this year are at Cleveland's expense. (Frank Lary and Don Mossi
           of Detroit both beat the Yanks five times as did Cal McLish of Cleveland.)

Sep 15—   Mantle switch-hits homers in one game for the seventh time in his big league
           career. Batting righthanded, Mantle hits a two-run homer off Billy Pierce
           (14-15) and later, batting lefthanded, he hits his 31st homer off Bob Shaw
           (18-6). But Chicago wins anyway, 4-3, at the Stadium.

Sep 19—   Yogi Berra Day is held at Yankee Stadium. Yogi receives some 58 gifts,
           including a new station wagon from the Yankee owners, a silver tray signed
           by Yankee teammates, a silver plate from the Baseball Writers and a watch
           from Joe DiMaggio. Yogi receives $9,800, which he gives to Columbia
           University, and a Berra Scholarship Fund (paying $500 a year tuition to a
           meriting scholar-athlete) is established. He also receives a truckload of
           baseball equipment, which he and his wife personally deliver to some
           grateful kids in Italy. The Yankees beat Boston, 3-1. Yogi goes hitless,

but Ford wins his 15th game on a four-hitter and Marv Throneberry goes three for three, including a homer.

— This was Berra's final season as a fulltime catcher. He would remain a regular in 1960 but split his time between catching and outfielding, turning the regular catching chores over to Elston Howard. Yogi had a decent year in 1959, batting .284 with 19 homers and 69 RBIs in 131 games, but the Yankees will need another power hitter to complement Mantle. At 34, Yogi in 1959 would miss playing in the World Series for only the third time since his full season with the Yanks in 1947.

Dec 11— In the last important trade made by George Weiss—with the A's, not surprisingly—the Yankees obtain Roger Maris (OF), Joe DeMaestri (INF) and Kent Hadley (INF) for Hank Bauer (OF), Norm Sieburn (OF), Marv Throneberry (1B-OF) and Don Larsen (P).

— Maris is the best player New York could get to regain its supremacy. He would win MVP Awards in 1960 and 1961. Nevertheless, Maris was a gamble. He was coming off a .273 year in which he hit only 16 homers, and the Yankees gave up a lot to get him. Bauer's loss hurt the most. Over 12 seasons, Bauer proved one of the Yankees' greatest all-round outfielders. He was a fine defensive player, made few mistakes, ran well, hit .277 (his career average), belted 158 homers and was a team leader. Larsen, too, would be missed, but his perfect game would never be forgotten. He had been suffering from a sore arm, yet he finished his Yankee career with an impressive 45-24 record and a winning percentage of .652. Don's career mark would end at 81-91, as he drifted through the majors until 1967. Sieburn, whose career was retarded by Stengel's constant criticism, would blossom as a first baseman for the A's. In three seasons with New York, Sieburn hit .273. In 1962, he would put it all together and hit .308 with 25 homers and 117 RBIs. Throneberry, a .238 hitter over three seasons with the Yankees, would go on to fame and fortune with the expansion Mets and later in beer commercials. No one will ever say, "I still don't know why the Yankees traded Marv Throneberry." Also sent to the A's earlier this year, on May 26, were Tom Sturdivant (P), Johnny Kucks (P) and Jerry Lumpe (INF), for Ralph Terry (P) and Hector Lopez (INF-OF). Lopez would hit .262 over an eight-year Yankee career. Terry, a returnee, would go 76-55 with 8 saves through 1964.

THE 1960's
FALL FROM
THE MOUNTAINTOP

FIVE CONSECUTIVE PENNANTS
STENGEL AND WEISS "RETIRE"
HOUK INSTILLS CONFIDENCE
THE M&M BOYS AND 61 FOR ROGER
THE GREATNESS OF 1961
MANTLE IS GAME'S BEST
BERRA WINS PENNANT AND IS FIRED
CBS BUYS CLUB
THE DYNASTY COLLAPSES
HOUK REPLACES KEANE
THE LAST-PLACE FINISH
GOOD-BYE TO FORD AND MANTLE
SOME IMPRESSIVE KIDS

1960

The Yankees will finish at 97-57 and in a comeback season will win the AL championship by eight games over second-place Baltimore. Roger Maris will win the RBI title with 112 and will hit 39 homers. He will also win the MVP Award. Mickey Mantle's 40 home runs will win him the homer title. Art Ditmar, with a 15-9 record, will be the club's top pitcher. The World Series will be an exciting seven-game struggle from which Pittsburgh will emerge victorious, thanks to a sorely remembered Mazeroski home run.

Mar 11— Mickey Mantle meets behind closed doors with George Weiss in St. Petersburg, Fla., and signs for $65,000, ending a 10-day holdout. His pay is cut $7,000 from his 1959 salary. Says Mickey when the "compromise" is announced: "They gave me a pretty stiff cut."

— It was Mantle's most bitter contract fight. Originally, the Yankees sent Mickey a contract for $55,000—a $17,000 cut. Thinking the proffered contract a mistake, Mantle returned it unsigned. Weiss straightened things out. "It was no misprint," he told Mickey, who fully acknowledged that 1959 was a poor season for him. But Mickey did not feel a large cut was warranted. He wasn't happy with the settlement, and in an effort to prove Weiss wrong, he did too much in the early camp and aggravated old injuries. Casey Stengel wasn't happy with the way Weiss humiliated his star.

Apr 19— The Yankees celebrate Opening Day with a 8-4 win in Boston. The big slugger is Roger Maris, who in his debut as a Yankee hits two homers, makes four hits in all and drives in four runs. Moose Skowron also has a four-hit day.

Apr 22— Whitey Ford shuts out Baltimore, 5-0, to give the Yanks their seventh straight home opener win.

— The Yankees came off an unpromising 11-21 spring training record, the worst of the AL. Most experts predicted that Chicago would repeat as AL champions. Stengel began the season with only two set starters, Ford and Bob Turley. Unfortunately, Ford would have arm problems so severe at times that he was unable to throw a curve. He would finish at 12-9. Turley would go 9-3 in his last winning year.

Apr 30— In Baltimore, New York wins, 16-0, as Jim Coates pitches an eight-hit shutout. Maris gets three hits, including two doubles and a homer, and drives home four runs.

— The Yankees' powerful attack, led by Mantle, Maris, Skowron and Berra, kept them afloat until Stengel could plug holes in the club's pitching. Maris, exactly what the Yanks needed, fitted in well, although he had expressed dissatisfaction on having to leave Kansas City. Maris played splendidly in right field, hustled non-stop and by the end of May was leading the AL in homers. By July, Maris would be ahead of Babe Ruth's 1927 home run pace, but an injury would take him from any pursuit of the Babe's record. The Mantle-Maris duo took over where the Mantle-Berra duo left off. And an injury-free Skowron would finish with 91 RBIs.

May 28— Stengel is hospitalized with a virus and a high fever and will miss 13 games, seven of which are won by the Yankees under Coach Ralph Houk, who shakes things up in running the team. He plays Clete Boyer at third base for the first time, inserts Hector Lopez in left field, allows Johnny Blanchard to catch occasionally and places Art Ditmar back into the starting rotation. Basically, Casey will allow the changes to stand when he returns. The Yankees today beat Washington, 5-1, as Mantle hits a solo homer off Jim Kaat.

— Ditmar held the staff together and had a fine year as the club's biggest winner with 15 victories. Expected to work out of the bullpen, Ditmar responded brilliantly when switched to starting assignments. Over one stretch of the summer the fierce competitor won seven games in a row.

May 30— New York winds up a Memorial Day doubleheader with Mantle catching a fly ball for the final out, but Mickey's trot to the dugout is not uneventful. A hundred or so young fans charge the Mick, pulling at his cap, glove and uniform. A punch is thrown and Mantle takes it flush on the jaw, then struggles to the dugout. The x-rays show no fracture but Mickey has to go on a soft diet for four days. In baseball, Washington won the first game, 2-1, while New York took the second, 3-2.

Jun 1— In Baltimore, Mantle's home run ruins a no-hitter by Baltimore's Hal Brown (12-5), as the Yankees are beaten, 4-1, in the middle game of a three game set they drop to the Orioles. The sweep puts New York six games behind the first-place Baby Birds, the majors' youngest team.

Jun 7— After losing the first game of a big four-game set at Yankee Stadium, the Yankees beat Chicago, 5-2, behind Jim Coates' four-hitter and begin a 15-game stretch in which they win 13, lose one and tie one.

Jun 8— The Yankees are off and running—winning consistently for the first time since the summer of 1958—as Casey returns and tells sportswriter Dick Young, "They examined all my organs. Some of them are quite remarkable and others are not so good. A lot of museums are bidding for them." Turley three-hits Chicago, Mantle booms two long homers and the Yankees win, 6-0. Mantle will hit another homer tomorrow in a 5-2 Yankee win, New York taking the series three games to one.

Jun 17— The Yankees begin a four-game set in Chicago that will produce four wins for the New Yorkers. The Yankees sparkle in more ways than one. White Sox owner and Yankee-baiter Bill Veeck had just installed a new $300,000 scoreboard that is programmed to go crazy (rockets, the works) when a Chicago player hits a home run. It is totally unresponsive to similar feats by the opposition. Casey and the boys in the dugout and bullpen decide to do something about this. They equip themselves with sparklers before the first game and when Clete Boyer hits a tater they parade up and down and around with their sputtering sparklers held aloft. They repeat the scene after a Mantle homer. Everyone thinks the sparkler show is funny, everyone but Veeck.

Jun 29— At Yankee Stadium, the Yankees cream Kansas City, 10-0, as Jim Coates pitches a three-hitter and wins his ninth game without a loss and his 13th consecutive game over two seasons. Maris belts a pair of fourbaggers and has four RBIs.

— Coates would lose his next decision, in Boston. In 14 starts prior to that loss, he benefitted from 117 New York runs, an average of 8.4 runs per game. Coates, a lanky righthander with a good fastball, was a tough guy who liked brushing back hitters. He would toil for the Yankees until the spring of 1963 when he would leave by trade. He would have a Yankee record of 37-15 and would be regarded as one of the best long reliever-spot starters the Yanks ever knew.

Jul 13— Only 38,362 turn out for the second All-Star Game in three days and the second ever played at Yankee Stadium. The NL wins this one, too, 6-0. Both teams use the roster of two days earlier when the NL won in Kansas City. Ford starts for the AL, goes three innings, allows three runs and takes the loss. Mantle and Skowron each have one hit. Maris is hitless in four trips and Berra is hitless in two.

Aug 14— The Yankees lose a doubleheader to Washington, 5-4 and 6-3 in 15 innings, and tumble to third place, a half game behind both Baltimore and Chicago. There are two lowlights—the first is the grand slam Senator pitcher Camilo Pascual hits off Bob Turley, and the other is a Mickey Mantle goof. In the sixth inning of the nightcap, Mantle bats with the score tied and two runners on base. He grounds to third, and, believing there are two outs, jogs slowly to first. But there is only one out and the Senators turn an easy double play, even though Maris injures some ribs (and will miss several games) at second base attempting to break up the double play. Mantle is showered with boos and an enraged Stengel replaces Mantle with Bob Cerv.

— This was when Mantle's career, in terms of his relationship with both the fans and Stengel, was at its lowest. But Casey knew better than anyone (except the team doctor) of the painful knee on which Mickey had been playing uncomplainingly.

Aug 15— First-place Baltimore, winners of 13 of its last 14 games, comes to Yankee Stadium. The introduction of Mantle in the first inning evokes a highly negative reaction from the crowd. The boos grow louder after Mantle grounds out. When Mickey next bats, the Orioles are leading, 2-0. Mantle draws some support by belting a two-run homer into the Yankee bullpen. Elated, Mickey tips his cap to the house as he crosses the plate and with the gesture wins over spectators. Jackie Brandt's eighth-inning homer puts the Orioles ahead, 3-2. In the bottom half of the inning, Mantle faces Hoyt Wilhelm with a mate aboard and hits a foul pop that catcher Clint Courtney drops. Given a reprieve, Mantle lines a shot into the right field stands for his second two-run homer. The fans are unrestrained in their cheers. It is a magic moment in Mantle's career. The Yanks win, 4-3, and when Chicago also loses, New York is back in first place. With a 1-0 win over Baltimore tomorrow, first-place New York (64-45) will have a modest edge on Chicago (66-48) and Baltimore (65-49).

— Mantle never had to worry again about being booed at Yankee Stadium. He became one of the most popular athletes in New York City history. (Unfortunately, the wrath of the boo birds was deflected to Maris.) Mantle used this August 15 turning-point date as a springboard for a great final six weeks. Prior to today's game, Mantle trailed Maris in homers, 27 to 35. But Mickey would finish ahead, 40 to 39, and would win his fourth and final home run crown.

Aug 26— The Yankees sweep Cleveland, winning 7-6, in 11 innings, and 7-5 at the Stadium. In the first game triumph, four Yankee pinch-hitters deliver safeties—Gil McDougald, Johnny Blanchard, Roger Maris and Bob Cerv—all singles.

Aug 27— On Moose Skowron Day, the Yankees sweep the Tribe again, 7-4 and 3-0. In the opener, Bill Stafford wins his first major league game. Ralph Terry pitches a two-hit shutout in the nightcap. New York now leads both Chicago and Baltimore by 2½ games.

— Stafford, recently recalled from the Richmond farm club, would go 3-1 in 11 games with a 2.25 ERA over the final 1½ months, and the Yankees would win seven of Stafford's eight starts. The 21-year-old righthander had a great arm and more talent than any Yankee rookie pitcher since Whitey Ford in 1950.

Sep 10— At Tiger Stadium, Mantle homers over the right field roof for the third time. And no Tiger has yet done it! The 560-foot blast goes through a light tower, clears Trumbell Avenue and lands in a parking lot across the street.

Sep 16— The first-place Yankees host a four-game series with the Orioles who trail by .002 in the standings. The Yankees lost three out of three in Baltimore earlier in the month when the Orioles went ahead by two games. The Yankees scored only two runs in that series, but they will score 18 in this set and sweep the series, 4-2, 5-3 and 7-3 and 2-0 (a doubleheader). Maris hits his 39th and final home run of the campaign in the opener.

— The Yankees would finish with 15 straight wins. Their sweep behind solid pitching in the Baltimore series gave them a four-game lead and all but assured the pennant. Then they beat Washington twice at home; Boston three times on the road; Washington three times on the road; and Boston three times at home.

Sep 25— Ralph Terry's 4-3 win over Boston clinches it for the Yanks; they have their 25th pennant. Pittsburgh, after years of futility, is winning in the NL.

Oct 2— On the final day of the season, the Yankees tie a knot on their 15-game win streak with an 8-7 victory over Boston.

— The pitching staff, a major source of concern for Stengel early in the season, was outstanding in the stretch. Ford won his final three starts, Terry allowed only two runs in 22⅔ innings and Stafford gave up just three runs in 19⅓ innings. Relievers got credit for seven of the final 11 wins. The run-scoring was potent all year and the Yanks' total of 193 home runs set a new AL record, breaking the 1956 Yankees' mark of 190. "In my mind he is my most valuable player," Stengel says of Mantle. The Baseball Writers would select Maris by a three-point margin over Mantle for the MVP Award.

Oct 6— After losing the World Series opener, 6-4, New York pounds six Pirate pitchers for 19 hits and breezes to a 16-3 triumph. Among the hitting stars are Tony Kubek and Bobby Richardson, who each make three hits and score three runs. But the big gun is Mantle, who drives in five runs and hits two titanic homers. His second homer, against southpaw Joe Gibbon, sails over the 457-foot sign in dead center field, making Mickey the first righthanded hitter to clear that sign in Forbes Field history. The drive goes at least 475 feet.

Oct 8— The Yankees batter Pittsburgh again, 10-0, as the Series shifts to Yankee Stadium. Bobby Richardson, who had only one homer all season, hits a first-inning grand slam homer and sets a single-game World Series record with six RBIs. The Yankees have a six-run first and a four-run fourth. Mantle has four hits, including a two-run homer into the left field bullpen off Freddie Green. Chipping in two hits apiece are Howard, Skowron and Cerv, as the Yanks post 16 hits off six Pirate hurlers. Whitey Ford has no such difficulty, pitching a beautiful four-hit shutout. But the gritty Bucs will not roll over;

they win the next two games, 3-2 and 5-2.

Oct 12— Back at Forbes Field, the Yankees romp, 12-0, as Ford pitches a seven-hitter and wins his second shutout. The Yanks stroke 17 hits off six Pirate hurlers. Maris, John Blanchard and Berra make three hits apiece, and Berra scores three runs. Richardson rips a pair of triples and knocks in three runs. The Series is tied at three games apiece.

Oct 13— Bill Mazeroski's dramatic ninth-inning homer gives the Pirates Game 7, 10-9, and the World Championship. Pirate Manager Danny Murtaugh starts Vern Law; Stengel counters with Bob Turley (although there are those who scream for Stafford). Turley, who will never regain his Cy Young form of 1958 and who will finish (in 1962) in New York with an 82-52 Yankee record, is knocked out in the second. The Yankees are down, 4-0, when Skowron gets one back with an opposite field homer in the fifth. In the sixth, Richardson singles, Kubek walks and Roy Face strides into the game. After Maris fouls out, Mantle singles home Richardson, and Berra hits a three-run homer. Numb Pirate fans watch the Yankees increase their lead to 7-4 with a two-run, two-out rally in the eighth. Bobby Shantz, who has tamed the Bucs on one hit over five innings, allows a lead-off single in the bottom of the eighth. Then Virdon sends a perfect double-play grounder toward shortstop, but the ball takes a crazy hop on a poor Forbes Field infield and strikes Kubek in the throat. The runners are safe and Tony must be taken to a hospital. Dick Groat singles home a run, with Virdon holding second and no outs. It is a sure bunt situation, but, curiously, Stengel replaces Gold Glove fielder Shantz, a southpaw, with Jim Coates, a righthander, and with the lefthanded Nelson on deck. Shantz, seemingly on his way to hero status, will never again pitch for the Yankees. After the obligatory sacrifice, Coates retires Nelson for out number two. Roberto Clemente chops one to Skowron that goes for a run-scoring single when Coates is slow covering first base. Hal Smith follows with a three-run homer, putting the Bucs in the lead, 9-7, and sending the Steel City slightly wild. In the ninth, Richardson singles, pinch-hitter Dale Long singles, Maris fouls out and Mantle singles home Bobby. (McDougald runs for Long at third base.) Berra rockets a grounder down the first base line that Nelson spears, touches the bag for the second out and turns to throw to second. But a heads-up Mantle, with the force off, dives back into first as McDougald scores from third to tie the game. Skowron grounds out to end the rally. Ralph Terry, who has been warming up several times and who is now tired, faces Mazeroski leading off in the bottom of the ninth. The ball Maz hits sails over the left field wall and concludes the Series, but a two-day Pittsburgh party is just beginning.

— The Yankees were stunned in defeat. Mantle was inconsolable and wept openly. Stengel replied, when asked if the better team had won: "What do you think?" The Yankees set World Series records for most runs (55), hits (91), extra-base hits (27) and batting average (.338). New York had a team ERA of 3.54, compared to Pittsburgh's 7.11. Ellie Howard led all regulars with a .462 average, followed by Mantle's .400. In fact, 14 Yankees hit higher than the Pirates' .256 average, including all eight regulars. Bobby Richardson, who set a new record with 12 RBIs, was named the MVP by *Sport* magazine, the only time a player on the losing team would be so honored.

In 1960, his final season as Yankee manager, Casey Stengel led the team to a great comeback after the debacle of 1959, taking the Yankees to a pennant that was Casey's 10th. Casey wanted badly to beat Pittsburgh in the World Series, but that was not to be.

Oct 18— At a poorly staged press conference in Manhattan's Savoy Hotel, the Yankees announce what had been rumored for weeks—the "retirement" of Casey Stengel. Dumping the popular Stengel is public relations problem enough, but the Yankee owners compound the seeming coldheartedness of their action by saying the move is necessary because of Casey's advanced age. Casey reads a prepared statement, then opens up and speaks bitterly of his ouster. "I guess this means they fired me," the broken-hearted Stengel tells a sympathetic press. "I'll never make the mistake of being 70 again."

— Dan Topping and Del Webb looked unappreciative toward a man who generated excitement and color and 10 pennants in 12 seasons. Beloved by the fans and the press, Casey was hardly the darling of some of his own players. He would get the headlines and the players would get the criticism—from Casey, and with some sting—and they had grown weary of it. But there was no question of Stengel's positive contributions. And he would come back to haunt the Yankees as manager of the expansion New York Mets.

Oct 19— The Yankees make Ralph Houk Stengel's successor. In Houk, they are getting a World War II hero, a one-time catching back-up to Yogi Berra (1947-54) and an organization man who has displayed talent as a coach and minor league manager in the New York farm chain. Houk may later fail in his relations with the press, and he may never win the public's affection. but his players will love him. He builds them up and lets the glory be theirs.

— The biggest mistake Topping and Webb made in the change of managers was their failure to stress that Houk was being promoted because they feared they would lose him. Houk, who had been groomed to replace Stengel for some time, had been wooed by other clubs. It would be months before Webb explained the real motive in the change—that the Yankee owners simply wanted to reward a man whom everyone knew would be a good big league manager, and they wanted to make the move before another team stole him. But many fans felt that the fact of the firing was without reason, and that the way it was done, its lack of justification aside, was without style.

Nov 2— George Weiss is "retired" as general manager of the Yankees and is replaced by his assistant, Roy Hamey. This comes after 29 baseball seasons of service in the Yankee organization. Weiss hands out a one-sentence statement at a press conference in the Savoy Hotel. It says that George is retiring as of December 31, 1960, but will continue in an advisory capacity through 1965. Then Weiss, a man the press and much of the public regard as a cold fish, breaks into tears. Few cry with him.

— Weiss was forced out much the same as Stengel was. He was shattered. Baseball was his whole life. Despite his flaws, his exclusion of blacks and his penny-pinching on salaries, Weiss was still sharp. So sharp, in fact, that this year he was named the Major League Executive of the Year by The Sporting News. His Maris deal alone made him the natural winner of the award. Weiss would take over as chief executive of the New York Mets; he would be the architect of the Mets miracle team of 1969. Weiss said the Yankees had five more good years left, and that would be it. He was right.

Dec 14— The Yankees lose several players in a confusing expansion draft, created to help fill the rosters of the Los Angeles Angels and the new Washington Senators. Bob Cerv and Gil McDougald are the biggest Yankee names lost, both to the Angels. Cerv will later return to New York for the third time.

— In spite of a lucrative offer from the Angels, McDougald hangs up

his spikes after 10 years with the Yankees over which he batted .276, hit
112 home runs and scored 697 runs. He was a scrappy player on the field
and a classy gentleman off the field. Through the decade of the 1950's,
only Mickey Mantle and Yogi Berra were more valuable players in the AL.
Gil would remain the only Yankee in history to be a starter at third base,
second base and shortstop. And he mastered each position; three times he
led the AL in turning double play—and at all three positions. McDougald's
versatility gave Casey Stengel tremendous flexibility in the make-up of his
infield.

1961

The Yankees will finish at 109-53, winning the pennant by eight games over second-place
Detroit. Roger Maris' 61 homers will break Babe Ruth's most famous record, and Mickey
Mantle will be close behind him with 54. The 1961 Yankees will hit a still-standing
major league record of 240 homers. Their record total of six 20-homer men also
includes Bill Skowron, 28; Yogi Berra, 22; Elston Howard, 21; and Johnny Blanchard, 21.
Whitey Ford will lead the AL in wins and percentage at 25-4 and .862, and Luis
Arroyo will have a league-leading 29 saves. Maris will receive the MVP Award and
Ford will win the Cy Young Award, and Ralph Houk will become the third manager
in baseball history to win the World Championship in his freshman year.

Apr 26— In Detroit, the Yankees win, 13-11, in 10 innings. Paul Foytack grooves a high
fastball and Roger Maris deposits it into the right field seats for his first
home run of the season, after going homerless in the season's first 11
games. Mantle switch-hits homers for the eighth time in his career. He hits
a two-run blast off Jim Donohue hitting lefthanded and a two-run shot
righthanded off Hank Aguirre. They are Mick's sixth and seventh homers.

— There were no signs to indicate it, but Maris was beginning an assault
on Babe Ruth's single-season home run record that would make him a
celebrity—and a nervous wreck. He would soon be dealing day-to-day with
media attention that had him losing clumps of hair by season's end. He
also faced a legion of hostile fans, although they would become more vocal
in 1962. Sometimes Maris felt his own front office was against him, especially
when the Yankees remained silent on Commissioner Frick's decision in July
that "Babe Ruth's record can only be broken only in 154 games."

May 2— In Minnesota, Mantle belts a grand slam homer off Camilo Pascual in the top
of the 10th inning and New York wins, 6-4. It is Mickey's eighth homer.
Tomorrow Maris will hit his second homer, the only one he hits this year
at Metropolitan Stadium.

May 17— Maris hits No. 4, his first at Yankee Stadium, off Washington's lefty Pete
Burnside. Struggling at .218 in mid-May, he is encouraged to start swinging
for the fences.

May 28— Against Chicago in a doubleheader, Maris wallops No. 9 off Cal McLish
and Cerv belts a tape-measure pinch-hit grand slam homer into the
Stadium's right-center field bleachers off Early Wynn. The Yanks win, 5-3,
after losing, 14-9. Cerv will play in 57 games, hit .271 and hit six homers,
three as a pinch-hitter in his third Yankee stint.

May 30— The Yankees put on an awesome display of power in their 12-3 win over
Boston at Fenway Park. The Bronx Bombers blast seven homers, two apiece

by Maris (Nos. 10 and 11), Mantle (Nos. 12 and 13), Skowron (Nos. 6 and 7) and one by Berra. It is only the fifth time that three batters on one team hit two homers each in the same game. It is also the first occasion this season that Maris and Mantle hit back-to-back homers. This year's Yankees will break the AL team record for homers that they set the previous year. They will hit 240 taters, besting the old record by 47.

Jun 11—   Maris, who is practically hitting a home run a day, unloads two in New York's doubleheader sweep over Los Angeles at Yankee Stadium. No. 19 comes off Eli Grba and No. 20 off Johnny James, who was a teammate of Roger's as late as last month. Mantle swats his 18th, a three-run blast off Grba. The Yanks win, 2-1 and 5-1.

Jun 18—   A big three-game series in Detroit concludes with the Yankees salvaging one victory, 9-0. The Tigers (40-23) remain in first place, a half game ahead of the Indians (40-24) and one game up on the Yankees (38-23). Maris hits No. 24 off Jerry Casale in the eighth inning. He will hit 15 this month, tying a major league record for homers in June.

Jun 21—   In Kansas City, New York wins, 5-3, as Mantle hits his 21st and 22nd homers, the first a three-run clout and the second a two-run shot (Mickey accounts for all five Yankee runs). Both are off veteran righthander Bob Shaw, who says they are the hardest-hit balls ever hit off him. The first hits Municipal Stadium's right-center field scoreboard, going a distance of about 475 feet. The second travels about 525 feet, clears two fences in right field and bounces onto Brooklyn Avenue. The second fence has been cleared only three times, twice by Mantle.

Jun 26—   In Los Angeles, the Yankees win, 8-6, and Yogi Berra gets his 2,000th hit in the majors, all as a Yankee. A huge cake is wheeled out to celebrate Yogi's milestone achievement.

           — Yogi at 36 was still a vital cog in the pinstriped machine. This year he would play 87 games in the outfield and 15 games behind the plate, hitting 22 homers and driving in 61 runs in 395 at bats. He would hit a respectable .271.

Jun 30—   Ford goes the route in beating Washington, 5-1, and becomes the first lefthanded pitcher in AL history to win eight games in one month. Whitey runs his record to 14-2 and the Yankees win their 22nd game in June. Mantle hits his 25th homer, a two-run inside-the-parker off righty Dick Donovan that carries some 450 feet in the air and rolls to the Stadium wall. The centerfielder doesn't even attempt a return throw. Mickey will hit five inside-the-park homers in his career, a Yankee record.

Jul 1—   The Yankees pull out a dramatic 7-6 victory over Washington at the Stadium. Mantle hits his 26th and 27th homers but the Senators lead, 6-5, as the Yankees come to bat in the bottom of the ninth. Tony Kubek singles and Maris faces righthander Dave Sisler. Displaying his sweet home run swing, Roger unloads No. 28 to plate the tying and winning runs. It is his first roundtripper in more than a week.

Jul 2—   The Yankees put on another show of raw power at the Stadium, as they overwhelm Washington, 13-4. Maris hits No. 29 off Pete Burnside in the third inning and No. 30 off Johnny Klippstein in the seventh. Mantle cracks a two-run homer, his 28th, off Klippstein. Skowron whips a one-handed homer into the left-center field bleachers in deepest Death Valley, Howard bats a 400-foot homer into the left field stands and Cerv rips a two-base hit off the left-center field wall at the 457-foot sign.

Jul 4—   A holiday crowd of 74,246—largest at the Stadium since a May 1947 date against Boston—watches the Yankees beat Detroit, 6-2, then bow, 4-3, in 10 innings. Maris adds No. 31 off the Yankee Killer Frank Lary. Detroit (50-28) maintains its one-game lead over New York (48-28).

Jul 13—   In Chicago, the Yankees win, 6-2, as Maris and Mantle hit back-to-back homers for the second time this season, victimizing future Hall of Famer Early Wynn. It is No. 34 for Maris and No. 30 for Mantle. Mickey's wallop, his 350th lifetime, is a 500-foot line drive that reaches the upper deck in the center field corner of the stands above the bleachers and bounces off the scoreboard. (Mickey will hit another long one tomorrow that sportswriter Tommy Holmes writes "could have carried the month's wash of a large family.") Kubek stars defensively. With Luis Aparicio on first base, Nellie Fox hits a grounder into the hole between shortstop and third base. Shortstop Kubek fields the ball and fires out Fox. Kubek anticipates Aparicio's next move and beats little Luis to third. There, Tony accepts the return throw and sticks the tag on Aparicio to complete a double play.

          — The power-packed line-up and slew of pitching stars tended to obscure the spectacular fielding of middle infielders Kubek and Richardson. Their combined total of 245 double plays (136 for Bobby/109 for Tony) is the second highest for a double-play combination in Yankee history. They were solid, if unspectacular, place hitters. Kubek hit .276 and at one point batted safely in 19 consecutive games. Richardson hit .261. Batting at the top of the line-up, they combined for 164 runs and 95 RBIs.

Jul 15—   Maris hits No. 35 off Ray Herbert, his fifth roundtripper of the year at Comiskey. But the Yankees are trailing, 8-7, when Bobby Richardson leads off the ninth inning with a walk and goes to second base on Kubek's sacrifice. Maris doubles to tie the game. In the 10th, Clete Boyer doubles and Kubek singles him home for a 9-8 victory.

Jul 16—   Mantle hits a ball that clears the center field fence in Baltimore and hits the scoreboard on one hop; then, in the ninth, he singles home Tony Kubek from second to give the Yankees a 2-1 victory.

Jul 21—   In Boston, New York wins a wild one, 11-8, and the Yankees and Tigers are virtually tied for first place. Against Bill Monbouquette, Maris snaps a 0-for-19 slump with homer No. 36. Mantle follows with another, the third time this season that the M&M Boys hit back-to-back homers. Going into the ninth inning, however, the Red Sox lead, 8-6. After Maris and Mantle draw walks, Berra singles in Maris, and on the play, Mantle and Berra each advance one base on an error by Jackie Jensen. Skowron is walked intentionally and Houk sends up Johnny Blanchard, an unheralded, bench-warming catcher, to hit for Boyer. Facing Mike Fornieles with two outs, Blanchard lines a grand slam homer deep into the Red Sox bullpen in right field. Luis Arroyo halts the Bosox in the bottom half, the Yanks have an important victory, and Blanchard has begun a streak of four homers in four trips to the plate, making him an instant celebrity.

Jul 22—   Blanchard is the hero of New York's 10-9 win in Boston, as the Yankees keep pace with Detroit. Again, with two out in the ninth inning, and the Red Sox ahead, 9-8, Blanchard bats for Boyer, and again Johnny homers.

He becomes the fifth player in AL history to deliver consecutive pinch-hit home runs. His blast ties the score and the winning run scores when Arroyo doubles off Gene Conley and Richardson singles. Now it is back to the bench for Blanchard, who will not play for the next four days.

Jul 25— At Yankee Stadium, the Yankees sweep a doubleheader from Chicago, 5-1 and 12-0, as Maris blasts four home runs, two in each game, to tie the AL record for the most fourbaggers in one twinbill. Roger hits the quartet of longballs off four different White Sox pitchers—Frank Bauman, Don Larsen, Russ Kemmerer and Warren Hacker. Maris has eight RBIs for the night. When the games are over, Roger has 40 homers and is 24 games ahead of Ruth's home run pace of 1927. Mantle also homers, his 38th.

Jul 26— Houk gives Howard a rest and starts Blanchard at catcher against Chicago. In the bottom of the first, Mantle whales No. 39 and Blanchard immediately follows with another home run. In the fourth, Blanchard wallops still another homer, his fourth in his last four at bats to tie a major league record. In the seventh, Blanchard sends a high fly ball to deep right field that Floyd Robinson catches right in front of the fence. The crowd gives Blanchard a standing ovation anyway.

— The Yankees would finish July with a month's record of 20-9. Maris would have 40 homers and Mantle 39, and Ford would be 19-2. August would be even better—a 22-9 record—and September would be New York's fourth straight 20-win month.

Aug 4— At the Stadium against Minnesota, Maris hits No. 41 off Camilo Pascual in the first inning. It is Roger's first homer since his doubleheader rampage nine games earlier. The score is 5-5, when Blanchard bats with two on and two out in the 10th. He delivers a three-run homer and the Yankees win, 8-5.

Aug 6— The Yankees sweep two games from Minnesota, 7-6 and 3-2, as Mantle belts three home runs. The Mick hits his 41st and 42nd in the opener to pass Joe DiMaggio on the home run list with 362, then unloads his 43rd in the nightcap. The Twins lead the opener, 6-5, when Blanchard swats a 10th-inning fourbagger to tie a game the Yanks win in the 15th.

— Blanchard had a remarkable season; he was the most valuable part-time player in baseball history. He hit 21 homers in only 243 at bats. And of his first 15, five tied games that New York eventually won and two were game-winners. He also hit .305. Houk had to find a place in the line-up for him but that was difficult what with Ellie Howard leading the league much of the year in batting and finishing at .348, Berra still producing, and Hector Lopez and Cerv coming through with so many clutch hits. There was no designated hitter, so Houk had to cleverly manipulate his line-up to get his players their at-bats. Blanchard played in 48 games as catcher, 15 games as outfielder and 26 games as pinch-hitter.

Aug 10— At the Stadium against the Angels, Ford wins his 20th game of the season and his 14th in a row, tying Jack Chesbro's Yankee record. He wins, 3-1. It is Whitey's first 20-win season. He had previously won 19 games once and 18 games twice, but never 20, primarily because Casey Stengel held Ford back for the top teams and did not give the league's best pitcher enough starts to win 20. Five days later, Ford will lose a tough 2-1 decision to Chicago to snap his streak at 14 straight wins.

Aug 16— Maris homers in his sixth straight game, hitting two, in fact, Nos. 47 and 48, off Billy Pierce of the White Sox. It is "Babe Ruth Day" at the Stadium, commemorating the 13th anniversary of the Babe's death. Mrs. Ruth attends the game. Maris has now passed Mantle, with whom he was tied at 45 three days ago, for good, and he is well ahead of Ruth's 1927 home run pace.

Aug 20— In Cleveland, the Yankees sweep a doubleheader, 6-0 and 5-2, behind the pitching of Rollie Sheldon and Ralph Terry. Maris unloads No. 49 off Jim Perry, his third homer of the year off the righthanded Perry. Mantle hits a three-run homer, his 46th.

— Sheldon was a 24-year-old righthander out of the University of Connecticut. He was signed to a nice bonus by the Yankees and went 15-1 in Class-D ball in 1960. Ralph Houk defied the odds and kept Sheldon this year, and Rollie had a fine 11-5 season as the team's fourth starter. Terry, 25, came into his own in 1961 with a splendid 16-3 record for a winning percentage of .842, second only in the AL to Ford's. The work of Bill Stafford (14-9) and Jim Coates (11-5) gave this staff great depth. Luis Arroyo, obtained from Jersey City of the International League on July 22 of last year, and Stengel's bullpen stopper in 1960 with Duren having an off-year, is looming ever more important with Duren having been dealt from the Yanks early in the season.

Aug 22— In Los Angeles, Maris belts No. 50 off the Angels' ace, Ken McBride. Maris thus becomes the first player in history to hit his 50th homer in the month of August. But the Angels win, 4-3.

Sep 1— The clawing Tigers, at the Stadium for the first of a three-game series, trail the first-place Yankees by only 1½ games. Some 65,000 fans watch Don Mossi hold the Yankees scoreless through eight innings while the New York trio of Ford, Daley and Arroyo hold the Tigers in check. In the bottom of the ninth, Howard, Berra and Skowron bunch singles and the Yankees win, 1-0. Arroyo gets the victory, his 10th, and probably most important, win in a row.

Sep 2— About 54,000 fans brave sweltering heat for a Saturday afternoon game, round two with the Tigers. In the sixth, Maris breaks a 6-for-60 slump and a 2-2 tie with a line-drive homer (No. 52) off Frank Lary. Later, Kubek singles in two more runs and Maris hits No. 53 off southpaw reliever Hank Aguirre. The Yankees win, 7-2, Ralph Terry's record going to 12-2 and Luis Arroyo gaining his 26th save.

Sep 3— The Yankees win, 8-5, and Detroit leaves town 4½ games out of first place and totally demoralized. (The Tigers will continue to lose and soon slip out of contention.) Mantle, who plays in severe pain, his arm taped up, is today's star. Batting lefthanded against Jim Bunning in the first inning, he rips his 49th home run into the right field seats. Later, Mantle robs Bunning with a spectacular catch over his shoulder on a shot drilled into left-center field. But Detroit is up by one run as Mantle leads off the bottom of the ninth facing righthander Gerry Staley. The large crowd goes looney when Mickey smashes his 50th homer, a tremendous clout of some 450 feet, tying the game, 5-5. Then two runners get on base and Howard deposits his 15th homer into the left field stands off Ron Kline and the Yankees have a sudden 8-5 win. Howard's average is raised to .359. And the Yanks are now off on a 13-game winning streak.

Sep 9— Against the Tribe's Mudcat Grant, their biggest winner, Maris hits No. 56 in the seventh inning. Maris and Mantle now have 108 combined homers to break the Ruth-Gehrig record of 107 homers hit as teammates in 1927. Mantle-Maris will finish with 115. Arroyo wins his 12th straight game in relief since July 1, setting an AL record.

— Arroyo, the cigar-smoking southpaw reliever had one of the greatest seasons in the history of relief pitching. He consistently came out of the bullpen and stopped the opposition with his screwball. Little Luis went 15-5 with 29 saves and led the AL in games won in relief, saves and games pitched (65), breaking Joe Page's club record of 60 appearances in 1949. Many of his saves benefitted Ford, including Whitey's 25th win, in Boston.

Sep 10— The Yankees conclude a five-game sweep of the Indians with two wins, 7-6 and 9-3, at the Stadium. In the first inning against Jim Perry, Mantle belts his 53rd homer and it is another long one. Mickey's arm and legs are paining him terribly and the next day he will get a penicillin shot for a bad head cold.

— The Yankees would leave on their final road trip with Mantle a physical wreck. He continues playing but will hit only one more homer, a three-run shot in Boston 13 days later. Mickey would develop an infection where he took the penicillin shot, and a temperature of 103 degrees. Then he contracts a virus.

Sep 12— In Chicago, New York wins, 4-3, for their 13th straight win. This is the final win in a streak that has broken a close race wide open. New York (100-45) leads second-place Detroit (88-56) by 11½ games.

Sep 19— The Yankees come into Baltimore for a four-game set with Maris needing three homers to break Ruth's record before Commissioner Frick's allotted timetable runs out. The Yankees and Orioles split a doubleheader, as Steve Barber, Hal Brown and Hoyt Wilhelm blank Maris. There is a strong wind blowing in from right field during both games. The Yankees lose, 1-0, and win, 3-1, under conditions favorable to the pitchers.

— Frick's asterisk rule held that any record set after 154 games would be inserted in the record book with an asterisk. This was unfair to Maris. Frick never made similar rulings for other records set under the longer 162-game schedule. Happily, the asterisk rule is no longer countenanced by the baseball public.

Sep 20— The Yankees play their 155th game, but since one tie is included, this is the final game in Frick's 154-game "record season." The first time up Maris hits a long fly ball to right field. Then, in the third, he takes Milt Pappas deep for No. 59. It is Roger's first and only homer hit in Baltimore all year. Maris hits several long foul balls, then faces Hoyt Wilhelm in the ninth. Wilhelm is told by Manager Paul Richards that if he throws anything but a knuckleball it will cost him $5,000. Maris' last chance to tie Ruth within Frick's schedule is gone when he tops a grounder to Wilhelm. But the Yankees are happy; they beat the Orioles, 4-2, and clinch their second straight pennant. The Yanks will have a date with Cincinnati in October.

Sep 26— After a series in Boston, Maris returns to the Stadium still looking for his 60th homer. In the first inning, Maris singles up the middle off Baltimore's Jack Fisher. In the third inning, Fisher works the count to two-two against Maris. Then he hangs a high curveball and Roger jumps on it. Roger stands at the plate and watches No. 60 strike the upper deck—fair by several feet—

and bounce back onto the field. The sparse crowd of less than 20,000 cheers loudly and Roger bows to the fans. He has a rare enjoyable moment in a long, hot summer. Roger joins Mantle on the sidelines tomorrow.

— Late this month, Mantle would be hospitalized with a hip abscess. But Mickey had a tremendous year. He hit .317 and finished as the top man in the AL in slugging (.687), walks (126) and runs scored (132). He was tabbed by Houk as the team leader and he responded well. Generally, the Yankees' attitude was a good one. Houk had a set team and every one knew his job. Whitey Ford responded well to a regular rotation and finished with a league-leading 39 starts.

Sep 29— The Red Sox come into the Stadium for the season's final three games. On this Friday night, Bill Monbouquette (14-14) keeps Maris hitless. Roger will manage only one single tomorrow.

Oct 1— Maris hits No. 61 in the season's final game off Boston's Tracy Stallard. Actually, Stallard pitches his best game of the year, allowing only five hits and one run. In the fourth, Maris takes two balls, then catches a fastball over the plate and sends No. 61 into the lower right field seats, about 360 feet from home plate. Calling the action, broadcaster Phil Rizzuto screams, "…Hit deep to right, this could do it! Way back there! Holy Cow, he did it! Sixty-one home runs!" The crowd of 23,154 is just as excited. A fan comes out of the stands and shakes Roger's hand as he rounds third and Roger pumps Coach Frank Crosetti's hand, too. The entire team greets Maris and will not let him into the dugout until he takes four bows to the cheering fans. Stallard fans Maris in the sixth and Roger pops up in the eighth. The Yankees win, 1-0. It is the first 1-0 game in his career that Maris has won with a home run. New York wins its 109th game and finishes with a home record of 65-16 for a winning percentage of .802. The club plays 163 official games; Maris plays in 161.

— The historic home run ball was retrieved by 19-year-old Sal Durante, a truck mechanic from Coney Island, who caught the ball about 10 rows deep and 10 feet to the right of the Yankee bullpen, then had to fight to hold onto it. A California restauranteur put up $5,000 for the ball and most of the fans packed in the right field areas were aiming to get rich. Roger's homer gave both the club and his partner, Mantle, now famous record totals of 240 and 115. It gave Roger the RBI title, 142 to 141, over Baltimore's Jim Gentile. The homer also tied Roger with Mantle for the AL lead in runs scored at 132 apiece. The homer was Roger's 30th at the Stadium, tying Lou Gehrig's Stadium record set in 1934.

Oct 7— The Yankees and Reds split the first two World Series games at the Stadium and the series shifts to Cincinnati's Crosley Field where the Yankees pull out a nailbiter, 3-2. The Reds go ahead, 2-1, in the last of the seventh. Bob Purkey breezes into the eighth and retires the first two Yankees. Then pinch-hitter Johnny Blanchard homers to tie the game. Leading off the ninth, Maris homers off Purkey, a hit Cincinnati Manager Fred Hutchinson will call "the most damaging blow of the Series." Arroyo pitches the final two innings without allowing a run and gets the win.

Oct 8— Whitey Ford and Jim O'Toole face each other in Game 4. With the game scoreless in the top of the fourth, Maris walks and Mantle hits what should have been a double, but he can only limp to first, where Lopez pinch-runs for him. Mantle leaves the game to the cheers of the Cincinnati crowd and his own teammates. Ford does not come out to pitch for the bottom half after sustaining an ankle injury. But Whitey, who won Game 1 by a shutout, has broken Babe Ruth's scoreless-inning record with 32 straight shutout innings. Jim Coates allows only one hit over the final four innings and New York has a 7-0 win.

Oct 9— Even with Mantle and Berra sidelined with injuries, the Yankees rout Cincinnati, 13-5, at Crosley Field and capture their 19th World Championship. The Bronx Bombers knock out Joey Jay in a five-run first inning and are never seriously threatened. The runs in the big inning score on Blanchard's two-run homer, Skowron's single, Lopez' triple and Boyer's double. The Yanks score five more runs in the fourth, highlighted by Lopez' three-run homer over the center field fence. Reliever Bud Daley, the biggest winner on the A's staff when acquired from Kansas City on June 14, and who would be 8-9 with New York, pitches the final 6⅔ innings, allowing only a two-run homer over that span, and gets the win. The Yankees make 15 hits and are led by two substitutes—Lopez, with five RBIs, and Blanchard, with three hits and three runs scored.

— Ford won both the Babe Ruth Award and the MVP given by *Sport* magazine. Blanchard was the hitting leader of the Series at .400. New York's pitching staff compiled an ERA of 1.60. And Ralph Houk became the third rookie manager to win the World Series. One of history's greatest teams proved its depth in this Series.

Yankee third baseman Clete Boyer makes one of several dazzling plays against Cincinnati in the 1961 World Series. Nine years later the Orioles' Brooks Robinson would make similarly great plays in a World Series, as would Graig Nettles 17 years later.

Roger Maris unloads his 61st home run of the 1961 season on October 1 at Yankee Stadium. The homer was hit off Boston's Tracy Stallard and it did more than establish a new single-season record for home runs. It brought a buy-back windfall of $5,000 to Sal Durante, the fan who caught what Roger's eyes were following.

1962

The Yankees will overcome several injuries to finish at 96-66 and win their 27th pennant by five games over second-place Minnesota. League MVP Mickey Mantle will hit .321 and belt 30 homers, and Roger Maris will hit 33 homers and knock in 100 runs. Bobby Richardson will hit .302 and lead the AL with 209 hits. Ralph Terry will lead the league in wins, posting a 23-12 record. In an exciting seven-game World Series with San Francisco, the Yankees will prevail.

Feb 28— New York's first spring training camp at Ft. Lauderdale, Fla., opens, the Yankees having switched training sites from Florida's West Coast (St. Petersburg) to southern Florida on the Atlantic side where there is a new Ft. Lauderdale Stadium.

— Spring training is the stage for a spirited battle between youngsters Tom Tresh and Phil Linz for the open shortstop job, with Tony Kubek having been called into military service. In 1961, Tresh hit .315 at Richmond, New York's top farm club, while Linz won the Texas League batting crown at .349 for Amarillo. Both rookies impressed Ralph Houk and made the club, with Tresh winning the starting position.

Apr 10— The Yankees defeat Baltimore, 7-6, on Opening Day at the Stadium. Ralph Terry gets the win in relief of Whitey Ford. Mickey Mantle hits his 375th career homer.

— Terry would follow his fine 1961 season with his best year in the majors. Besides leading the AL in wins, Terry would lead in games started (39) and innings pitched (299). He would be Ralph Houk's workhorse with his slider, the big pitch that Johnny Sain taught him. He would win 25 games in all, including two in the World Series, most by a Yankee righty since George Pipgras won 24 in 1928.

Apr 13— Detroit fans give Roger Maris a bad time and someone comes close to seriously injuring him. Standing in right field, Maris is grazed on the arm by a liquor bottle that comes flying from the upper deck and barely misses Roger's head. Maris calls time out, protests and asks for police protection. After five minutes, he returns to his position, gives the fans the finger and goes back to baseball.

— Maris had just spent the worst spring training of his life. He reported to camp hoping the pressures from the media were behind him now that the Ruth chase was in the past. But the press hounded him more than ever. Writers from around the country took unfair shots and the public was given the impression that Roger was a surly red-neck who was cruel to children and envious of Mantle. (In fact, he and Mickey were close friends.) Maris was an uncomplicated, straightforward, small-towner, who wanted to play baseball, be with his family and be allowed a little privacy. But the fans and press treated Maris brutally and he withdrew. Roger was the best rightfielder in the league—both offensively and defensively. And he would prove it this year.

Apr 22— The Yankees play Cleveland in a doubleheader at Yankee Stadium. Maris receives a terrible booing each time he bats from the Easter Sunday crowd. The fans even take to throwing Easter eggs at him. "Sometimes," said Maris, withdrawing even more, "I wish I never hit those 61 home runs. All I want is to be treated like any other player." But the booing will go on all year.

May 17— Mantle displays his versatility in scoring the winning run in the top of the ninth inning in Boston. He walks, steals second, takes third on a wild throw and scores on a sacrifice.

— Mantle would lead the AL with 122 walks (he will have 121 hits), despite playing in only 123 games, leading the league for the fifth time. Mickey's string of nine consecutive seasons of scoring at least 100 runs would be broken, but he would still score 96. And he would lead the AL with a .605 slugging average, besides winning the Gold Glove and his third MVP Award. The Yankees were only a .500-team when Mantle was sidelined with injuries.

May 18— The Yankees bow to Minnesota and Mantle suffers a serious injury. With two out in the last half of the ninth and the tying run on second base, Mantle hits an infield grounder. He strains to beat it out and keep the Yanks alive, but 10 feet short of first base Mantle falls to the ground with a severely torn muscle on the inside of his right thigh, as well as damage to his left knee.

— The timing of the injury was devastating. Mantle, who would be out until June 16, was hitting close to .400 and with his customary power, running the bases with abandon and playing the best center field of his career. The Yankees would slump wihout Mickey and so would Maris, who was hitting over .300 in mid-May. Pitchers worked around Maris, who fished for bad pitches and went 21 for 110.

May 20— Luis Arroyo, the relief star of 1961, is placed on the disabled list with a sore arm, and for all intents and purposes his career is finished. He will win one of four decisions and will save seven games this year, completing a New York record of 22-10 with 43 saves.

May 22— At Yankee Stadium, Whitey Ford, Jim Coates, Bud Daley and Bob Turley combine on a one-hitter and the Yankees beat the Angels, 2-1, in 12 innings. Coates allows the only Angel hit, a one-out ninth-inning single by Bob Rodgers, a .258-hitter this season. Ford is pitching a no-hitter when he has to leave the game in the seventh inning because of a strained muscle in his pitching arm and back pain. Ford will be lost for a month; the Yankees lose their third key player in less than a week. Maris experiences the frustration of hitting without Mantle behind him; he draws five walks and four of them, an AL record, are given intentionally.

May 23— The Yankees beat Kansas City, 13-7, at the Stadium as Joe Pepitone, a 21-year-old rookie from Brooklyn, belts two home runs in one inning. Pepitone is only the second Yankee to hit two homers in the same inning, joining none other than Joe DiMaggio, who also did it in his rookie year, 1936. Leading off the Yanks' nine-run eighth inning, Pepitone homers off Dan Pfister and later in the frame, Joe belts a three-run shot off John Wyatt. Another rookie, Phil Linz, gets his first major league hit today— a home run.

Jun 9— Yogi Berra plays in his 2,000th game as a Yankee in New York's 7-3 win over Baltimore at Yankee Stadium. Up to now, only Lou Gehrig and Babe Ruth have played in more Yankee games than Berra.* Yogi celebrates by hitting his 343rd pinstriped homer with two men aboard.

— For the first time since 1947, Berra, who was 37, was a part-time player. In 86 games, he would hit 10 homers and drive in 35 runs.

Jun 12— In Detroit, the Yankees win, 2-1, the victory sandwiched between three straight losses to Baltimore and four upcoming defeats in Cleveland. After this worst stretch of the year (seven losses in eight games), the Yankees find themselves in fourth place, four games behind first-place Cleveland.

Jun 16— Mantle makes his first appearance since his May 18 injury. He has even the die-hard Indian fans in Cleveland cheering after he belts a three-run, 450-foot, pinch-hit homer. Mantle is unable to speak, he is so choked up. The Indians win, 10-9.

— During the 30 games that Mantle missed (with Ford sidelined, too), the Yankees were only 15-15. Mantle was the indispensable Yankee. But his legs were finally betraying him and his well-being was always uncertain. Mantle would continue to pinch-hit for awhile before starting in the outfield.

Jun 21— In Baltimore, Ford returns to the mound and pitches a neat three-hitter, winning, 3-0. Whitey will follow with a two-hitter and four-hitter and will win nine of 10 starts.

Jun 23— Berra hits a pinch-hit grand slam off Phil Regan as the Yanks and Tigers split a doubleheader in Detroit. He becomes only the second Yankee to hit two pinch-hit grand slams in his carrer.

*Through 1982, Mantle is first on the all-time Yankee games played list, followed by Gehrig, Berra and Ruth.

Jun 24—   The Yankees and Tigers play a seven-hour marathon. Reserve outfielder Jack Reed hits a two-run homer in the top of the 22nd inning and the Yanks prevail, 9-7. It will be Reeds' only major league homer in 129 at bats. This is the longest game by time in AL history and the longest extra-inning game in Yankee history. New York makes 20 hits and Detroit has 19, but until Reed's homer, all the scoring is done in the first six innings. Jim Bouton, who will soon replace Rollie Sheldon in the starting rotation, pitches the final seven innings and allows no runs and three hits to gain the victory. Bobby Richardson bats 11 times in the game, setting an AL record for an extra-inning game. Thirty-seven-year-old Yogi Berra, catching in his first game of the season, squats behind the plate for the entire 22 innings and at bat goes three for 10.

Jul 6—   In Minnesota, Mantle homers twice against 20-game winner Camilo Pascual in his first two at-bats, giving him four consecutive homers to tie a big league mark and seven homers in 12 at bats, an accomplishment achieved last in 1947 by Ralph Kiner. The Yankees win, 7-5. With Mantle swinging a torrid bat, Maris begins to see better pitches and will soon go on a home run spree himself.

Jul 8—   The visiting Yankees edge Minnesota, 9-8, in the final game before the All-Star Break and finally go into first place. At the Break, New York (46-33) leads Cleveland (47-36), Los Angeles (45-37) and Minnesota (45-41) in a tight race.

Jul 20—   At Yankee Stadium, the Yankees defeat Washington, 3-2, behind Mantle's two-run homer and pair of singles. Batting righthanded against Steve Hamilton, Mantle's homer crashes into the left field upper deck and bounces halfway back to the infield. According to Hamilton, the ball "would have left the country had the stands not gotten in the way." It is one of four space shots Mantle hits in his career into the third tier in left field at the Stadium. The Yankees will beat Washington tomorrow for their ninth straight win.

Aug 7—   Three days after rejoining the Yankees, Tony Kubek, who missed the season's first four months while in military service, makes his first start and in his first at-bat cracks a three-run homer against Minnesota at Yankee Stadium. Every Yankee shakes Tony's hand and so does Umpire Hurley. Tony also makes two spectacular plays in left field against the second-place Twins. Tresh hits a pair of long homers and the Yankees win, 14-1.

   — Several days later, Houk would insert Kubek back into his shortstop position, and with Skowron-Richardson-Kubek-Boyer, the Yankees had the best infield in the league. In 45 games, Kubek would hit at a .314 clip. Tresh was switched to left field where he fitted in immediately and played spectacular defense, although he had not played the outfield since he was a youngster. The Tresh-Mantle-Maris outfield was one of baseball's best. Tresh would hit .286, with 20 homers and 93 RBIs.

Aug 19—   In Kansas City, the Yankees win, 21-7. Ellie Howard drives in eight runs, the last time a Yankee has had as many as eight RBIs in one game. Mantle is right behind Howard. The Mick, who hits a grand slam off righthander Jerry Walker, drives in seven runs.

Sep 1—   Ralph Terry beats Kansas City, 3-1, at home and becomes the first of four AL pitchers to gain his 20th win. Terry makes three hits at the plate. Ellie Howard delivers the game-winning hit, a two-run sixth-inning triple.

Sep 6—   At Yankee Stadium, the Yankees beat Los Angeles, 6-5, gain a split of a four-game series and open a little breathing room in an uncomfortably close race. First-place New York (83-59) leads Minnesota by three games. The Angels are also in contention but waste their best opportunity to make a real fight of the race. Nevertheless, after finishing eighth in their maiden season last year, the Angels have stubbornly remained in the race.

Sep 10—   In Detroit, Mantle returns after missing a week or so of games with a strained rib muscle and wallops his 400th career home run, a solo shot off southpaw Hank Aguirre (16-8) to tie the game. Pinch-hitter Hector Lopez' ninth-inning single wins it, and Ralph Terry captures his 21st win of the year.

   — Stan Musial was the only active player who had more home runs than Mantle, who as of this date was in seventh place on the all-time list. Mantle trailed only Babe Ruth (714), Jimmie Foxx (534), Ted Williams (521), Mel Ott (511), Lou Gehrig (493) and Musial.

Sep 11—   Berra cracks a 10th-inning homer, the 350th of his career, and the Yankees beat the Tigers. Bouton gets the win in relief. Minnesota loses and falls 4½ games behind the first-place Yankees. The Twins will not get any closer and their surprising threat is over.

Sep 25—   At Yankee Stadium, Ford defeats Washington, 8-3, and the Yankees clinch the pennant. It is fitting that Ford gets the clincher. Since recovering from his spring arm injuries, he has pitched some of the best baseball of his career and will finish the year at 17-8 with an ERA of 2.90, third lowest in the AL. The Yankees will have to wait for the Giants to win a playoff in the NL.

   — Besides Mantle, Maris and Ford, there were plenty of other stars on this Yankee team. Richardson, who would finish second in the MVP voting, was the first Yankee since Phil Rizzuto in 1950 to reach the 200-hit plateau. Tresh was Rookie of the Year, Skowron hit 23 homers, Boyer hit a career high .272, Howard knocked in 91 runs, Lopez hit .275 and Blanchard hit 13 homers.

Oct 7—   The first two games of the World Series are split in San Francisco and the Series moves to Yankee Stadium where the Yankees prevail, 3-2, behind Bill Stafford's four-hitter. Stafford and Billy Pierce put goose eggs on the board through six innings. In the seventh, Tresh and Mantle each single and move up an extra base on Felipe Alou's bobble of Mickey's hit. Maris follows with a two-run single, and Roger takes second on Willie McCovey's error. Maris scores on a fly and a grounder. Ed Bailey's two-out, two-run, ninth-inning homer cuts the final margin to one run. Stafford courageously finishes, although he takes a smash on the leg in the eighth that inspires a lump the size of a grapefruit. Stafford, who on the season had the same 14-9 record as the previous year although his 3.67 ERA was virtually a run higher, can barely walk off the mound to accept congratulations and will not appear in the Series again. The Giants will battle back in Game 4 to win, 7-3.

Oct 10—   After a one-day rain-caused postponement, the Yanks win an exciting Game 5 at the Stadium as Ralph Terry goes the route. With the score tied, 2-2, and with one out in the bottom of the eighth and Kubek and Richardson on the bases via singles, Tresh strokes a three-run homer for the key hit of the Series. The Giants nick Terry for a run in the ninth, but afterwards he enjoys his first-ever World Series victory in the clubhouse with his old manager, Casey Stengel, who had lost his last Yankee game when Terry allowed

Mazeroski's homer in 1960. There is something poetically beautiful about their reunion today. "I'm only sorry I couldn't have done it for you," Terry tells Casey.

San Francisco's Matty Alou can't reach Tom Tresh's three-run homer that broke up a tied Game 5 in the 1962 World Series. The home run ball gets an excited reception in Yankee Stadium's right field stands.

Oct 14— Game 6 in San Francisco's Candlestick Park is a washout as Typhoon Frieda makes play impossible for the third successive day. Some of the suspense has been drained out of the Series which has had its fourth postponement and will eventually tie the 1911 Series for the longest in history, 13 days. While helicopters dry the field, the Yankees journey to Modesto, Calif., where they can work out under sunny skies. The San Francisco skies will clear tomorrow and the Giants will win, 5-2, on a soggy Candlestick turf.

Oct 16— The Yankees win Game 7, 1-0, and with it, their 20th World Championship. Ralph Terry pitches a tremendous four-hitter to outduel Jack Sanford and Billy O'Dell, who are also magnificent. The game, at Candlestick, is scoreless in the top of the fifth inning, when singles by Skowron and Boyer and a walk to Terry load the bases with no outs. Kubek's double-play grounder kills the rally but scores Skowron with the game's only run. With one out in the seventh, Willie Mays, who earlier had been robbed by Mantle, lines a drive down the left field line that Tresh catches one-handed. McCovey then triples but is stranded, and Tresh's grab takes on great importance. Matty Alou leads off the bottom of the ninth with a bunt single, but Terry bears down and strikes out Felipe Alou and Chuck Hiller. Now it is up to Mays and Willie lines a shot into the right field corner, where Maris handles the ball perfectly and quickly. Maris relays to Richardson, who fires home, as Alou hugs third. With Cepeda on deck and first base open, Terry elects to pitch to McCovey. On a one-strike pitch, McCovey tears the cover off the ball but Richardson catches the liner for the final out. Bobby does not move a step and makes the grab chest-high. As usual, he is in the right place at the right time. And so finally is Terry, who captures both the last two Yankee wins and is named the winner of the Babe Ruth Award and MVP by *Sport* magazine. He is carried off the field.

Nov 26— The Yankees trade first baseman Bill Skowron to the Los Angeles Dodgers for pitcher Stan Williams. This trade is made primarily to open up first base for young Joe Pepitone. Williams will go 10-13 in 50 games for the Yankees over the 1963-64 seasons.

— The Moose, of course, was extremely popular with Yankee fans and the big guy was as gentle as he was strong. Moose hit .294 with 165 homers over nine Yankee seasons. He battled both Death Valley, which he beat by hitting opposite field homers, and constant injuries. Moose would play until 1967 with four more clubs, finish with a lifetime .282 mark and be a favorite of fans wherever he played.

1963

The Yankees will finish at 104-57 (their fifth highest win total) to claim their fourth consecutive pennant. They will leave second-place Chicago 10½ games behind. Mickey Mantle, one of the more injury-hampered Yankees of 1963, will hit .314 in only 65 games. League MVP Elston Howard will hit 28 home runs and have 85 RBIs. Two 20-game winners—lefthander Whitey Ford, 24-7, and righthander Jim Bouton, 21-7—will lead the pitchers. But the club runs into a buzzsaw in the World Series and loses to the Dodgers in four straight games.

Apr 9—   Joe Pepitone, who is filling the shoes of the departed Bill Skowron (now with the Dodgers) unloads two home runs in an 8-2 win on Opening Day in Kansas City.

— It would be a fantastic first full season for Pepitone. He started well, batting over .300 and leading the team in home runs through the spring, and would finish with 27 homers and a club-leading 89 RBIs. He was great around the bag and showed much more range than Skowron. Already he was being favorably compared with the all-time defensive first basemen. The addition of Pepi made the Yanks' infield one of the finest defensively in baseball history.

Apr 11— In New York's home opener, Baltimore spoils the festivities with a 4-1 victory over Whitey Ford, who loses his first two decisions of the season.

— Then Ford got tough and rolled to his third sensational season in a row, at one point winning 12 games in a row. He would lead the league in four major categories, including wins (24) and winning percentage (.774). He pulled off that difficult double championship two years earlier when he won 25 games. But Whitey had a better season in 1963—his 2.74 ERA was 47 points lower than 1961's.

May 12— Jim Bouton makes his first start of the season in Baltimore and pitches a two-hit shutout. He will remain in the rotation after this outing in which he keeps Baltimore hitless over the first 6⅓ innings. New York wins, 2-0.

— It took career-shattering injuries to Bill Stafford and Bud Daley for Bouton to get his chance. Both Stafford (4-8) and Daley hurt their arms pitching on the same 30-degree night in the early season. Bouton would be 10-2 before the All-Star Break. The players were suspicious of his intellectual leanings but they admired his bulldog determination, which in 1963 got him 21 wins, six by shutout.

May 22— Mickey Mantle hits the most awesome home run of his career. The ball all but clears the right field roof at Yankee Stadium. It had the best chance any ball ever had of leaving the famous ballpark. "It was the hardest ball I ever hit," said Mickey. Leading off the 11th inning, Mantle, upset that his team had blown a 7-0 lead, bats lefthanded against Bill Fischer (9-6). Mickey unleashes a vicious swing and sends a rocket that smashes into the facade over the third deck in right field. It is an instant from the time the ball leaves Mantle's bat to the time it strikes the facade, just a few feet from clearing the roof. The ball is still rising when it reaches the facade! Scientists will estimate that if Mantle's game-winning homer had cleared the facade, it would have traveled from 620 to 700 feet, or from over two to nearly two and and half football fields. Experts believe Mantle's shot was the hardest ball ever hit.

Jun 5— Mantle breaks a bone in his left foot and does cartilage and ligament damage to his left knee when he runs into a chain link fence in Baltimore. Mickey chases Brooks Robinson's drive to right-center field, and as the ball clears the playing area, Mickey's spikes catch in the fence. He lies in agony while many in the crowd at Memorial Stadium cheer and concerned teammates offer quick assistance. Mickey will miss 61 games and endure the most frustrating period of his career.

— Mantle, who became a $100,000 ballplayer in 1963, had been hitting well, feeling strong and was on his way to another great season. He still had a good year. In only 172 at bats, Mickey hit 15 homers. His was one of several injuries to test the resourcefulness of Manager Ralph Houk. Roger Maris was injured and then Phil Linz, who was replacing the injured Tony Kubek, was hurt. For several games, Houk played Clete Boyer at shortstop and Harry Bright at third base.

Jun 11— The day after his recall from Richmond, Al Downing is given a starting assignment, his first of the season. In 95-degree heat in Washington, Downing pitches a two-hit shutout, striking out nine Senators. New York wins, 7-0, but drops the second of a doubleheader, 1-0.

— The 22-year-old southpaw from Trenton, N.J., had a fastball that was so alive he was called "the black Sandy Koufax." He would put together a string of great, low-hit games over the summer and finished at 13-5, an ERA of 2.56, and 171 strikeouts in 174 innings. Along with Ford, Bouton and Ralph Terry (17-15), Downing gave New York, which by mid-June took over first place, the strongest four-man rotation in baseball.

Jul 2— Al Downing in one of the four spectacular shutouts he hurls over the summer allows Chicago only one hit. Cam Carreon, a .274-hitting catcher, in the seventh inning makes the only safety as the Yankees win, 3-0, at the Stadium.

Jul 11— Roger Maris is hospitalized for rectal fissure surgery. Back aches will bother him when he returns in August and he will be played sparingly. Maris is leading the Yankees in batting (.294) and home runs (19). He has 42 RBIs and basically has been carrying the team in Mantle's absence. But Roger's season is now ruined. He will play in only 90 games and hit .269 with 23 homers and 53 RBIs.

Aug 4— Mantle makes a dramatic return in the second game of a Yankee Stadium doubleheader against Baltimore before nearly 40,000. The Yanks bow, 7-2, in the opener and trail, 10-9, in the late innings of the nightcap. Houk sends up Mantle, who has not played since his Baltimore mishap. As soon as Mickey touches a bat in the rack, the crowd begins to roar and the noise becomes deafening. Mickey feels goose-bumps as he is announced. He composes himself and on lefthander George Brunet's second pitch hits a 410-foot homer into the left field seats to tie the game and send the Stadium fans slightly berserk. The Yankees go on to win in the 10th, 11-10, on Kubek's single, Richardson's hit-and-run single and Berra's sacrifice fly.

— This was one of the great moments in Mantle's storied career, and one of the most personally rewarding. "The ovation actually chilled me," said Mickey, who by now is one of the most popular players in baseball history. It came after a long convalescence sprinkled with rumors that Mickey might retire. Indeed, Mantle was so discouraged that he had given retirement some thought. But now he was back and basking in the adulation of the fans. He would not actually start a game until September, but thousands of fans kept turning out and calling for the most famous pinch-hitter in the game.

Aug 6— After losing the first game of a doubleheader in Washington, 8-5, the Yankees win the nightcap behind Stan Williams' one-hitter. Williams, who will go 9-8 this year as a valuable fifth starter, allows only a double to Don Blasingame, a .246-hitter. It is the second of four occasions that the pesky Blasingame will personally ruin a no-hit bid.

— Williams' one-hitter would be followed by four more excellently pitched complete games, in Washington and Los Angeles. In order, Downing pitched a three-hitter; Terry, a six-hitter; Bouton, a five-hit shutout; and Ford, a five-hitter that would have been a shutout but for an unearned run.

Aug 15— The Yankees, who now enjoy an 8½-game lead over Chicago, win in

Boston, 10-2. Once again, the heroes are substitutes and non-stars. Johnny Blanchard hits two homers, including a grand slam, and drives in six runs. Phil Linz makes three hits and has a dazzling game in the field. Hector Lopez adds three hits and Stan Williams pitches a six-hitter.

— Blanchard would have another grand slam (against Boston) a week later, and in a period from late July to late August would hit 10 homers and have 40 RBIs in only 35 at bats! Blanchard would lead the bench with 16 homers and 45 RBIs in 218 at bats. Phil Linz would hit .269 in 186 at-bats and Yogi Berra, a player-coach, .293 with eight homers and 23 RBIs in 147 at bats, and Hector Lopez, heretofore a valuable fourth outfielder, would play regularly and hit 14 homers with 52 RBIs in 433 at bats.

Aug 18— This was the all-she-wrote date of the season. If the White Sox win the doubleheader in Chicago, they are within 6½ games of the first-place New Yorkers. But the Yanks sweep by scores of 8-2 and 8-4, dropping Chicago into a tie with Minnesota, 10½ games back. The Yankees at day's end are 78-43.

Aug 21— Pepitone is the center of a wild brawl at Yankee Stadium. Early in the game, Joe is hit on the wrist by Cleveland's Barry Latman. Stan Williams retaliates by throwing some inside pitches and keeping the Tribe's batters on their toes. In the eighth inning, Gary Bell's first pitch brushes back Pepi, who has reached base 10 times in his last 12 trips. When the next pitch hits him, Joe has to be restrained by Umpire DiMuro, who immediately fines Bell $50 for intentional throwing. Pepitone, on first base, and Bell begin jawing back and forth. Finally, Joe charges the mound. Indian first baseman Fred

Mickey Mantle, pinch-hitting at Yankee Stadium on August 4, 1963, after missing 61 games because of an injury, lines a home run into the left field seats to tie a game the Yankees went on to win from Baltimore. Mantle was "chilled" by a great ovation. Dick Brown is the Oriole catcher.

Whitfield attempts to intercede but is decked by Pepitone. Both teams pour onto the field for a fight that by baseball standards is action-packed. Bodies and punches are flying everywhere; both clubs sustain injuries.

Aug 27— At Yankee Stadium, the Yankees sweep a doubleheader by double shutouts from the Red Sox. Jim Bouton comes within three outs of the first no-hitter in the AL this season. But Russ Nixon, a .268-hitter this year, leads off the ninth with a single. Bouton settles for a two-hitter, winning 5-0 for his 18th victory. Boyer makes a great eighth-inning play to keep the no-hit bid intact on the 25th anniversary of the first no-hitter ever pitched at the Stadium. Ralph Terry hurls a five-hitter and beats the Red Sox, 3-0, in the second game.

— These two great games followed shutouts by Ford and Downing. Downing's game, on the 25th, carried to the eighth inning before Chicago got the first of its two hits. After today there would be a two-run 11⅓-inning effort by Williams, followed by Ford's one-run five-hitter. Thus Yankee pitching allowed only three earned runs in 56⅓ innings.

Sep 1— In Baltimore, the Yankees are behind, 4-1, in the eighth inning. Boyer singles, Mantle (still being used as a pinch-hitter) wallops a long, two-run homer off southpaw Mike McCormick, Richardson singles and Tresh unloads a two-run roundtripper off righthander Dick Hall and the Yankees win, 5-4. Tresh, who homered for the first Yankee run, becomes only the third player in AL history to switch-hit homers in the same game.

Sep 15— In Minnesota, the Yankees win, 2-0, and clinch the pennant. Bouton pitches a six-hit shutout for his 20th victory and Pepitone and Blanchard hit solo home runs. Meanwhile, the Los Angeles Dodgers are closing in on the NL flag.

Sep 21— Against Kansas City's Moe Drabowsky (7-13), Yogi Berra belts his 358th career homer in a game at Yankee Stadium. It turns out to be Yogi's final fourbagger. As a catcher, Yogi hit 313 homers, setting an AL record that still stands.

Sep 24— Tresh, out with a hand injury, returns to the Yankee line-up for a home game against Los Angeles and for the first time since June 1 Houk starts all eight of his "regulars" who were not in the line-up together from June 5 to September 5.

— For the season, the M&M Boys played a total of only 155 games and together had 484 at bats. Which is why Elston Howard's great season was so important. Although Howard won several early-season games with late-inning hits, he was more consistent than spectacular. Behind the plate he was brilliant, a big factor in the team's pitching success. Ellie earned a Gold Glove for his fielding.

Oct 2— The World Series opens in Yankee Stadium with each league's best pitcher taking the mound. Whitey Ford of the Yankees and Sandy Koufax of the Dodgers—two native-born New Yorkers—are in a face-off. Koufax is a little better, going the route to win, 5-2. Koufax strikes out 15 Yankees including the first five batters he faces. Los Angeles scores four runs in the second inning that begins with Frank Howard's mighty double off the left-center field wall, some 457 feet from home plate. Bill Skowron, who had a miserable year (.203, 4 HRs, 19 RBIs), singles home Howard, and after light-hitting Dick Tracewski singles, John Roseboro hits a three-run homer down the right

Whitey Ford and the Dodgers' Sandy Koufax, opposing pitchers in the opener of the 1963 World Series. Koufax won, fanning 15.

field line, a 300-foot fly ball. Los Angeles will win Game 2, 4-1, behind Johnny Podres.

Oct 6— The day after Don Drysdale wins, 1-0, the Dodgers again win in Los Angeles to sweep the Series in four games. Ford outpitches Koufax, allowing only two hits in seven innings, but Koufax wins, 2-1. Frank Howard breaks a scoreless tie with a mammoth solo homer in the bottom of the fifth. In the seventh, Mantle, who will have a knee operation after the Series, gets the run back with his 15th World Series homer to tie Babe Ruth's record. In the bottom of the seventh, lead-off man Gilliam grounds to Boyer, but Pepitone loses Clete's throw in the white-shirted crowd and Gilliam goes all the way to third as the ball rolls to the box seats. Gilliam scores on Willie Davis' sacrifice fly. The Yankees have one last chance in the ninth when they put runners on first and second with two out. But Lopez grounds out to Maury Wills and the Series is over. The Dodgers outhit the Yankees, .214 to .171.

Oct 22— In a press conference in the Crystal Suite of the Sheraton-Plaza Hotel in New York City, it is announced that Yogi Berra has been named the Yankee manager and that Ralph Houk will become general manager, replacing Roy Hamey, who is retiring. "I was surprised they offered me the job," Yogi states, "but this is not a joke." He also tells the press, "I've been with the Yankees 17 years, watching games and learning. You can see a lot by observing."

— So after three pennants in three years as manager, Houk moved upstairs where his considerable field talents were wasted. Berra's new job meant his tremendous playing career was over. And the Mets, who have Casey Stengel managing them, will be given a run for the money in the publicity department. Actually, it was a rare bold stroke by Dan Topping, and Berra would do a better job than some people were willing to credit him with doing.

1964

The Yankees will win their fifth consecutive pennant under rookie Manager Yogi Berra. In a tough season-long fight, New York will finish at 99-63, beating out Chicago by one game and Baltimore by two. Mickey Mantle will have his last great season, hitting .303 with 35 home runs and 111 RBIs. Elston Howard will hit .313 and Joe Pepitone will have 28 homers and 100 RBIs. Jim Bouton, 18-13, and Whitey Ford, 17-6, will lead the pitchers. The Yankees will bow to St. Louis in an exciting seven-game World Series.

Apr 26— Mickey Mantle pulls a hamstring muscle in his right leg and will be out for four days. It is the first of a series of Mantle leg injuries this year, and it comes after still another knee operation in the off-season.

— Roger Maris and Tom Tresh also pulled leg muscles around this time and Manager Berra was starting Hector Lopez, Pedro Gonzalez and Johnny Blanchard in the outfield.

May 26— Mantle strains a muscle in his left thigh and will miss several games. With recent injuries to Al Downing and Jim Bouton, the club's young pitching jewels, and a Tony Kubek neck injury that limits his playing time, the club has fallen well off the pace in the AL race. New York is running fourth.

Jun 12— The 1964 Yankees could thank their lucky stars for two June sweeps of Chicago. At the Stadium today, New York takes a doubleheader from the White Sox, 6-1 and 3-0. The Yankees will win tomorrow, 6-3, and on the next day claim two more from the Chicagoans, 8-3 and 4-3, for a five-game sweep.

June 22— New York completes the sweep of a four-game set in Chicago with a 6-5 win. This follows Yankee wins of 1-0 (11 innings), 2-0 and 2-1 (17 innings) and gives New York nine wins over Chicago in 11 days.

— Ellie Howard knocked in three of the five Yankee runs in the first three games. Whitey Ford, after pitching the 1-0 shutout for his 10th straight win since losing his first decision, now has 43 scoreless innings against the White Sox. This exercise in prolonged denial began August 16, 1963. The sweep temporarily puts the Yanks in first place, with Baltimore, Chicago and Minnesota snapping at their heels.

Jun 25— In a game against the second-place Orioles, Berra shifts Clete Boyer from third base to shortstop (regular shortstop Tony Kubek is sidelined with a pulled groin muscle) and inserts Phil Linz, who is hitting just under .300, at third. He lifts starter Rollie Sheldon for a pinch-hitter with the Yanks leading 7-2. Pete Mikkelson doesn't pitch badly but a succession of ground-ball singles passes through the revamped infield. A couple of grounders that Boyer might have handled elude Linz. A seven-run Baltimore rally gives the Orioles the win and underlings blame Berra for the Yankee loss.

Jul 15— Ford starves the Orioles on three hits and leads the Yankees to a 2-0 win and the top spot in the AL standings. But the Yankees will lose to Baltimore tomorrow, 6-1, and the O's reclaim first place.

Jul 27— Miller Huggins is posthumously inducted into the Baseball Hall of Fame in Cooperstown, N.Y. Hall of Famer Joe McCarthy is on hand and says of Huggins, "This is the man who cut the Yankee pennant pattern." Huggins was elected by the Committee on Veterans.

Aug 4— The Yankees invade Kansas City with a record that is 25 games over the .500 mark. But New York loses, 5-1, beginning a tailspin of 18 losses in 30 games, the poverty period running until September 3 and the low point coming August 20.

Aug 11— Pitcher Mel Stottlemyre is called up to the Yankees from their Richmond farm club, where his record is 13-3 with an ERA of 1.42.

— Stottlemyre would prove to be the Yanks' savior. He would defeat New York's pennant competitors, Chicago and Baltimore, in his first two starts. Stottlemyre would go 9-3, pitch two shutouts and have an ERA of 2.06. Mel joined Bouton, Ford, sidelined for the big games with Chicago and Baltimore by a hip ailment, and Downing (13-8) to form a formidable four-man rotation. His promotion, however, meant less work for swingmen Ralph Terry (7-11), who made 14 starts this year; Rollie Sheldon (5-2), who had 12 starts; and Stan Williams (1-5), who had 10 starts.

Aug 12— Mantle and Stottlemyre give the Yankees a much-needed shot in the arm as the Yanks beat Chicago, 7-3, at the Stadium and finish the day three games behind first-place Baltimore and 1½ games to the rear of Chicago. Stottlemyre makes his big league debut and goes the distance, scatttering seven hits. Mantle, who three days ago pulled a groin muscle, hits home runs from both sides of the plate for his 10th and final time, establishing a big league record. One of his homers is the longest "measured" homer ever hit at Yankee Stadium. Batting lefthanded against Ray Herbert (6-7), Mickey hits a high drive that backs centerfielder Gene Stephens to the 461-foot sign in dead center. Stephens runs out of room and watches in amazement as the ball clears the 22-foot-high black background screen. It is the second and final homer hit to this area in the Stadium (Mantle hit the other). The ball lands 15 rows up in the center field bleachers, a measured distance of 502 feet from home plate. In the clubhouse afterwards, Mickey says, "I didn't hit it all that good. I got it up into the wind. I thought it was going to be caught. In fact, I almost banged my bat down in disgust ..." Mantle's other homer, hit righthanded, is an opposite-field smash.

Aug 14— Dan Topping and Del Webb sell 80 percent of the Yankees to the Columbia Broadcasting System for an estimated $11.2 million. CBS will purchase the other 20 percent later, the total sale price reaching close to $14.4 million.

— Most baseball people were bothered by the idea that a large corporation would soon be running the Yankees. Houston President Ray Hofheinz called it "the blackest day for baseball since the Black Sox Scandal." But the AL owners will approve the sale by an eight-to-two vote, and the official transfer of the club will take place in November. Topping will remain as club president.

Aug 20— The Yankees have lost 10 of 15 recent games against their two top rivals, Baltimore and Chicago. With a loss today they have dropped four straight to Chicago and are 4½ games out of first place. On the team bus, predictably caught in traffic on the way to O'Hare Airport, Phil Linz begins to play "Mary Had a Little Lamb" on his harmonica. The usually controlled Berra becomes angry and orders him to stop. Linz makes music and then tosses the harmonica to Berra who slaps it away. It is a disagreeable little scene that is quickly laid to rest (although Linz is fined $200—a small price to pay for the $20,000 contract he will get from the Horner Harmonica Company).

— The press used this incident to discuss the so-called dissension on the Yankees. Indeed, there were several players who were critical of Berra as a manager and they made their views known to GM Houk. The relief brigade was the unhappiest, but out of that rubble, Berra would get a league-leading 45 saves. His best reliever, Pete Mikkelson (7-4, 12 saves), is given a chance and performs well. Whether or not Berra's fit of temper had anything to do with it, the Yankees would begin playing with verve after the incident.

Aug 22— The Yankees, who lost the first two games in Boston to extend their losing streak to six and fall six games behind Baltimore (Chicago is in second place), have Mantle in the line-up although he is still limping badly from an August 14 knee injury in Baltimore. New York drops the first game of today's doubleheader, 5-3, but Mel Stottlemyre halts the Sox and the Yankee slide with an 8-0 win in the second game. The Mick, literally forcing himself to play, nails a two-run homer.

Sep 4— In Kansas City, the Yankees outlast the A's, scoring four runs in the 10th inning to win, 9-7. Mantle hits a two-run homer and Elston Howard adds a solo shot. Playing on one wheel, Mickey plays left field while Tresh patrols center. (Mickey works right field at home—he must play the field with the least area to defend.)

Sep 5—   The Yankees, still in third place, purchase the contract of pitcher Pedro
            Ramos from Cleveland. After the season, the Indians will receive pitchers
            Ralph Terry and Bud Daley, thereby completing the deal. Terry was a
            78-game winner for New York. This is Topping's trade. Houk doesn't
            think the Yanks are close enough for Ramos to make a difference, but
            Ramos is obtained anyway. Ramos saves eight games and wins another in
            13 September relief games. He literally saves the pennant.

Sep 7—   For the second consecutive game, Tony Kubek leads off a game by hitting
            a homer, becoming only the fourth American Leaguer to accomplish the
            feat. The third-place Yankees beat Minnesota, 5-4, in 11 innings.

            — A serious back problem greatly reduced Kubek's performance. He wasn't
            able to play up to his talents and he finished the year at .229 in 106
            games. Two weeks before the end of the season, the frustrated Kubek
            punched the dugout door and severely sprained his wrist. He was through
            for the year, including the World Series. Kubek was not quite 28 but his
            back problems were putting his career in serious jeopardy.

Sep 16—   At Yankee Stadium, the Yankees beat Los Angeles, 9-4, in the start of an
            11-game win streak. Maris breaks a tie with a two-run homer, his 22nd of
            the year and his 1,000th hit in the majors. Maris will finish with 26 homers
            and a .281 average, his highest average since 1960.

Sep 17—   The Yanks climb into first place (for good this time), and, typically, it is
            Mantle who leads them. They beat the Angels, 6-2, behind Stottlemyre.
            Mickey fights off a 2-for-28 slump and singles, doubles and homers. He
            receives a standing ovation after his 2,000th hit and ringing applause
            for his 450th home run. After a 42-day absence from the top spot, New
            York is 86-59 for a winning percentage of .593, two points better than
            Baltimore and Chicago, who are both 88-61 for .591.

Sep 18—   Ford pitches a seven-hitter and blanks Kansas City for his eighth shutout
            of 1964, tying a club record for season shutouts held by another Ford, Russ,
            who did it in 1910. The Fords' club record will fall in 1978 when Ron Guidry
            will pitch nine shutouts.

Sep 20—   Bouton pitches a two-hitter and defeats Kansas City, 4-0, for his 17th
            victory. New York (89-59, .601) leads Baltimore (90-62, .592) by one game
            and Chicago (89-63, .586) by two games. The Yankees have 14 games
            remaining. The Orioles and White Sox each have 10 games left.

            — Bouton, off to a slow start after missing two weeks of spring training in
            a bitter contract hassle with GM Houk, did not have the same velocity early
            in the year that he had in his great 1963 season. But he regained his
            strength and won 13 games over the season's second half.

Sep 23—   The Yankees play their second doubleheader in Cleveland in two days.
            Ellie Howard, who catches 146 games, drives in 84 runs and is generally as
            valuable as he was last year when he won MVP honors, catches four games—
            all won by New York—in a 30-hour period. At bat, Ellie has three singles,
            two doubles and a game-winning 11-inning homer. He has four RBIs and
            scores four runs. Behind the plate, the 35-year-old Howard catches 10
            pitchers and plays all 38 innings. The winning pitchers in Cleveland:
            Stottlemyre by a 5-3 score; Ford, 8-1; Mikkelson, 4-3 in 11 innings; and
            Sheldon by a score of 6-4. Mikkelson and Sheldon are today's winners.

Sep 25— Maris is the hero in the Yanks 10th successive victory. With the Yankees trailing, 5-2, Maris hits a two-run homer. In the ninth, with the score tied, 5-5, he hits another roundtripper for the game-winner in Washington.

Sep 26— The Yankees win their 11th straight game, defeating Washington, 7-0. Stottlemyre pitches a two-hitter and goes five for five at the plate.

Oct 2— Ford beats Cleveland, 5-2, at Yankee Stadium to clinch a tie for the pennant. Ford is struggling. He has a circulatory blockage problem in his left pitching shoulder. It will ruin his World Series—he pitches only briefly in Game 1— and necessitate a post-season operation.

Oct 3— The Yankees defeat Cleveland, 8-3, on the next-to-last day of the season to clinch the pennant. Mikkelson is the winner in relief and Ramos retires the side in the ninth. New York scores five runs in the bottom of the eighth to break a 3-3 tie.

— This is a great triumph for Berra, who never panicked or wavered in his belief that the Yankees would make a comeback. Many members of the press, and, perhaps the front office, believed the Yankees were out of it late in August, but Berra never gave up. Several players made outstanding contributions to New York's 22-6 September record. Pepitone had 12 homers and 30 RBIs in September, Mantle hit over .400 in the final few weeks and Howard close to .400, and Maris played great all-round ball down the stretch. The pitching was splendid. Defensively, the Yankees played 91 errorless games, the most in club history. The club had a fielding average of .983, one point better than the previous year's average, to set a new club fielding record. The Cardinals also won the NL flag by one game.

Oct 10— The Yanks and Cards trade wins in the World Series' first two games and the Series moves to New York. The Yankees pull out a dramatic 2-1 victory as Jim Bouton hurls a six-hitter. Curt Simmons is tough, too, but Clete Boyer drives in a second-inning run with a single. In the fifth, Tim McCarver singles, takes second on rightfielder Mantle's error and scores on Simmons' single. Both Stottlemyre and Simmons escape bases-loaded jams in the sixth and Simmons is lifted for a pinch-hitter in the ninth. Leading off the bottom of the ninth, Mantle, still feeling guilty and bristling over his error, faces knuckleballing Barney Schultz. After telling Howard, "If he throws the first ball over, I'm going to hit it out," Mickey does just that; his game-winning homer lands in the third deck of the right field stands, as Yankee fans bring the house down. It is Mantle's 16th World Series homer, putting him one ahead of Babe Ruth for first place on the all-time list. But St. Louis will knot the Series again tomorrow.

Oct 12— Bob Gibson goes the full 10 innings, strikes out 13 Yankees and wins, 5-2. Down, 2-0, the Yanks tie the game, 2-2, in the bottom of the ninth, but a great play by Gibson prevents New York from winning outright. Mantle reaches on Dick Groat's error, Howard fans and Pepitone sends a smash up the middle that Gibson deflects, pounces on and fires to first to nip Pepitone on a close and questionable call. Tresh follows with a two-out, two-run homer off Gibson to force extra innings. But McCarver's three-run homer in the 10th settles matters.

Oct 14— Back in St. Louis, the Yankees win Game 6, 8-3, to force a seventh game. Bouton gets his second win and ties the game with a two-out, fifth-inning, run-scoring single. In the sixth, Maris and Mantle blast long back-to-back homers. In the eighth, Howard singles home a run and Pepitone wallops a grand slam homer completely out of the ballpark, sealing the win.

Oct 15—   Returning after only two days rest, Gibson pitches a complete game, strikes out nine and defeats Stottlemyre, 7-5, and the Cardinals win the Series in seven games. The Cardinals break up a scoreless tie with three fourth-inning runs. They are helped by some poor New York fielding. Downing takes the mound in the fifth and surrenders three more runs, including Lou Brock's homer. In the sixth, Mantle's three-run homer, his last in World Series competition, cuts New York's deficit to 6-3. Ken Boyer homers off Hamilton in the seventh, making it 7-3. In the ninth, Tresh fans, Clete Boyer homers, Blanchard fans, Linz homers and Richardson pops out to end the Series.

— Gibson was the Series star, winning two games and striking out 31 batters in 27 innings. McCarver led all regulars with a .478 batting average. Richardson, who hit .406, made 13 hits to set a Series record. Ford played in his last Fall Classic and finished with a 10-8 record, the most wins in history, but lost his final four decisions. Mantle, playing on one leg, led all batters in six categories, including runs scored and RBIs. Mickey finished with World Series records in homers (18), RBIs (40), runs scored (42), total bases (123) and walks (43). The Yankees would not see another World Series until 1976.

Oct 16—   Berra is released as Yankee manager. At the same time, Johnny Keane resigns as Cardinal manager, secure in the knowledge that he will become the next Yankee manager. Both teams hold press conferences on the subject of the departing managers on this same day. Four days later it is announced that Keane is New York's new manager.

— Berra was given one of the shabbiest deals of all time. GM Houk had decided to fire him as far back as mid-summer. Meanwhile, Yogi was bringing an aging, injured team to a first-place finish although he received no support from his boss, Houk. Yogi made some rookie managerial mistakes—but what rookie manager hasn't? Basically, Yogi did a first-rate job that wasn't appreciated until after he was gone. Yogi would soon join the Mets as a coach and the Queens club would have two of the Yanks' most popular personalities, Berra and Casey Stengel. The Yankees further compounded their public relations problems by firing popular broadcaster Mel Allen over the off-season.

1965

The Yankees will tumble to sixth place, finishing 77-85, 25 games behind pennant-winning Minnesota. Tom Tresh will lead the club with 26 homers and 74 RBIs. Mel Stottlemyre (20-9) and Whitey Ford (16-13) will be the only starting pitchers to enjoy winning seasons, and Pedro Ramos will save 19 games. The 1965 Yankees, ravaged by age and injury, will be the first of a series of no-cigar editions out of the Bronx.

Feb 18—   Elston Howard, five days shy of his 36th birthday, signs a 1965 contract for around $70,000, making Ellie the highest-paid catcher in baseball history to this date. Howard over the past four years may well have been the league's second most valuable player, behind Mickey Mantle.

— Age and injuries would finally catch up with Howard this year. He would be played by Manager Johnny Keane in spite of a nasty arm injury. He would appear in 110 games and bat 391 times. His average would fall from 1964's

.313 to .233; his RBIs from 84 to 45; and his home runs from 15 to nine.

Apr 9—   The Houston Astrodome opens with an exhibition game with the Yankees, and the Astros win, 2-1, in 12 innings. President Johnson attends and Texas Gov. John Connally pitches the first ball. Mickey Mantle belts the first home run in Astrodome history.

Apr 25—   At Yankee Stadium, the Yankees beat the Angels, 3-2. Rightfielder Roger Maris saves the game by robbing Bobby Knoop of a home run. Mantle hits a solo homer off a 20-year-old flame thrower by the name of Rudy May (4-9).

          — Maris took countless homers out of the Stadium's right field stands through the years. But his days as a star player are over even though he is not quite 31. Maris would suffer a severe hamstring injury and a fractured bone in his right hand. Roger would play in only 46 games this year, hitting .239 with eight homers and 27 RBIs.

May 28—   The White Sox defeat the Yankees, 2-0, in Chicago. The struggling Yankees find themselves in eighth place and eight games behind the first-place White Sox. They will remain in eighth place for some six weeks. It is plain that this is more than an early-season slump, painfully plain to Yankee fans. The June 21, 1965 cover of *Sports Illustrated* will show a weary Mickey Mantle wiping his brow, accompanied by type that asserts: NEW YORK YANKEES: END OF AN ERA.

Jun 4—   Chicago beats the Yankees in 15 innings, 2-0. By now, no one is shocked when the Yankees are shut out. The team will hit a dismal .235, 18 points off its collective average for the previous season.

Jun 5—   In his first at bat since surgery for bone chips a month earlier, Elston Howard strokes a game-winning pinch-hit single in the 10th inning and Chicago goes down, 4-3.

Jun 6—   The Yankees sweep a doubleheader from the White Sox, 12-0 and 6-1, at Yankee Stadium. Tom Tresh, this year's most successful Yankee, hits three straight homers in the nightcap. He has switch-hit homers in the same game for the third and final time of his career.

Jun 8—   Baseball's first amateur free-agent draft is held at the Hotel Commodore in New York City. In the first round, the Yankees draft Bill Burbach, a 17-year-old pitcher from Dickeyville, Wis., who will go 6-11 in 37 games when he gets his chance with the Yankees in 1969-71. The Yankees also pick Stan Bahnsen, who will have a more successful big league experience.

          — In a manner of speaking, the draft was an attempt to "Break up the Yankees!" Traditionally employing the finest brigade of scouts, besides possessing the magic name to lure youngsters—and the money to pay them—the Yankees had an unfair advantage, the lords of the game decided. Only the Yankees, Mets and Dodgers were opposed to this draft.

Jun 18—   At Yankee Stadium, the Yankees defeat Minnesota, 10-2, as Mickey Mantle belts a grand slam homer against Mel Nelson, a southpaw, in the first inning. It is Mickey's eighth career homer with the bases loaded.

          — It was in June that Mickey sustained his second leg injury of the year. He strained to score on a passed ball and tore a hamstring muscle in Kansas City. His shoulder would bother him all season, preventing him from making his usual strong throws. And since he would no longer charge the ball or make sudden stops because of his bad wheels, baserunners took liberties. His knees often buckled after a big swing. Many wondered how he could play at all. Mickey would miss 40 games in 1965 and hit .255 with 19 homers. He would hit only two homers after August 18.

Jun 22— Ray Barker of the Yankees hits a pinch-hit home run for the second time in two pinch-hit appearances (he homered two days earlier) and ties an AL record held by six others, including Yankees Ray Caldwell, Charlie Keller and Johnny Blanchard, as of this date. Barker, obtained from Cleveland in May, enjoyed his day in the sun. He would finish the year hitting .254 with seven homers in 98 New York games.

Jul 20— Yankee pitcher Mel Stottlemyre, one Yankee besides Tom Tresh and Pedro Ramos who is having a good year, hits an inside-the-park grand slam homer at Yankee Stadium. He hits it off Boston's Bill Monbouquette in the fifth inning. New York wins, 6-3.

Aug 20— In Baltimore, 25-year-old Jack Cullen of the Yankees outduels 209-game winner Milt Pappas and defeats the Orioles, 1-0, on three hits.

— Cullen went 3-4 and had an impressive 3.05 ERA in a partial season with New York, after a 14-5 mark at Toledo, the Yanks' top farm club, in 1965. Red-headed John Patrick was born in Newark and lived in Nutley, N.J., and came from Irish stock. With all of that going for him, he would win only one major league game after this season.

Aug 29— The Yankees edge Kansas City, 4-3, with rookie Roger Repoz scoring the winning run on a passed ball.

— Repoz was a highly regarded outfielder from Bellingham, Wash. He had hit 14 homers for the Yanks' Toledo club in the season's first half. He joined the Yankees in mid-season and hit 12 homers in only 218 at bats. But he might have been oversold. Traded in 1966, Repoz would hit 82 homers and average .224 over nine big league seasons.

Sep 14— At Washington's D.C. Stadium (later to be named after Robert F. Kennedy), 19-year-old Bobby Murcer belts his first major league home run with Bobby Richardson aboard, and the Yankees win, 3-1.

— Murcer joined the Yankees late in the season, played 11 games at shortstop and hit .243 (9 for 37). There was no doubt that Murcer was the crown jewel of a depleted Yankee farm system, although his similarities to Mantle were perhaps overly emphasized. Bobby was coming off a great year at Greensboro where he was named Player of the Year in the Carolina League after hitting .322 with 16 homers and 90 RBIs. He was being groomed as Kubek's eventual successor at shortstop.

Sep 18— Mickey Mantle Day is held at the Stadium and some 50,000 fans turn out to honor the Mick and see him play in his 2,000th game as a Yankee, injuries or no injuries. Among those on hand is the Yankee Clipper himself, Joe DiMaggio, who joins Mickey in waving to the crowd. The two remind the fans of bygone days that were better than the present, symbolized by today's 4-3 loss to Detroit in 10 innings. More than $32,000 is raised in Mantle's name and contributed for research in the fight against Hodgkins Disease, the ailment that took the life of Mickey's father.

Sep 21— Another promising rookie, Horace Clarke, hits his first big league home run—

a grand slam, to boot. This shot helps the Yankees defeat Cleveland, 9-4, at Yankee Stadium.

— Clarke, a 25-year-old infielder from the Virgin Islands, played mostly at third base in 51 games with the Yankees, hitting .259, after his recall in mid-season. Clarke started in the Yankee farm network in 1958 and hit .301 in his last two Class-AAA seasons.

Oct 2— Mel Stottlemyre caps a sensational season by beating the Red Sox, 6-1, in Boston. It is Mel's 20th victory. He will lead the AL in innings pitched (291) and complete games (18), and will win 11 more games than he loses on a team that finishes eight games under .500 (and out of the first division for the first time since 1925).

Oct 3— Ford beats the Red Sox, 11-5, at Fenway on the final day of the season for his 232nd victory. It is not one of Whitey's greatest games, but it allows him to break a tie with Red Ruffing and become the winningest pitcher in Yankee history. He still is.

A 19-year-old joined the Yankees in 1965 and got to play with his T-shirt heroes, Mickey Mantle, left, and Roger Maris—the M&M Boys. Bobby Murcer hit his first ML home run this year.

Nov 29— The Yankees trade infielder Phil Linz to the Philadelphia Phillies for Ruben
Amaro (SS), a good-field, no-hit type who will be plagued with a knee injury
in three seasons with New York and hit .214 in 191 games. The Yankees
had hoped that Amaro would play regularly at shortstop. Linz was a free
spirit and a valuable utility man—a Supersub. In four years with the Yankees,
he hit .246.

— The search for a shortstop was necessitated by the retirement of Tony
Kubek after the 1965 season and the inexperience of Bobby Murcer.
Back and neck ailments took their toll on Kubek who was told he risked
paralysis with further play. His batting average had fallen from .314 in
1962 to .257 to .229 to .218 in 1965. Some had forgotten just how good an
all-round player the quiet and conversative Milwaukean once was. Tony's
.266 lifetime average fails to do justice to his hitting ability. And he was a
smooth shortstop with good range.

1966

The Yankees will finish in 10th place—at the bottom. With a 70-89 record, it will be a
dismal season. Except for some home run power, with Joe Pepitone hitting 31 homers,
Tom Tresh 27 and Mickey Mantle 23, and the good mound work of Fritz Peterson
and Mel Stottlemyre, each of whom won 12 games, there will be little for Yankee fans
to feel good about.

Mar 1— Mickey Mantle reports to spring training in Ft. Lauderdale, and at a press
conference talks about January's shoulder operation at the Mayo Clinic.
Mickey reinjured his chronically painful right shoulder the previous fall
while playing touch football with his brothers and son.

— Most experts gave Mickey little chance of being ready for Opening Day.
Two days later he would take a dozen swings in batting practice and wince
with every lefthanded cut. A week later he would hit two balls over the
left field fence in batting practice.

Apr 12— Mantle proves the experts wrong and is ready for Opening Day. He is
greeted by thunderous applause from a Stadium crowd of 40,006 every
time he appears at the plate, handles his one chance cleanly in the field
and strokes a couple of hits. But Detroit beats Whitey Ford, 2-1.

— Mantle would go on to have a fine comeback season, but injuries confined
his play to 108 games. Mickey would hit .288 and have a first-rate slugging
average of .538, tying him with Harmon Killebrew for the second highest
in the league behind MVP-winner Frank Robinson.

May 7— Johnny Keane is fired as manager and GM Ralph Houk steps down to take
over for him. Houk makes the move at the request of Dan Topping, who is
still club president. In their first game under Houk since the 1963 World
Series, the Yankees win, 3-1, in California. They thus snap a four-game
losing streak and climb to 5-16.

— Johnny Keane, an outstanding manager in St. Louis, was mismatched
with the Yankees. He suffered from a heart ailment and would die just
eight months after his Yankee discharge. The players and fans were happy
to have Houk back managing—where he should have been all along—
although some players resented certain Houk actions taken as general

manager. For the next three weeks, the Yankees would go 13-4, as witnesses shook their heads in disbelief.

May 9—   Pepitone's ninth-inning home run against Minnesota wins, 3-2, for the Yankees and Manager Houk. The ball hits the foul pole. Just six days earlier a potential game-winning Pepitone homer barely went foul in the ninth inning, making a loser of Keane. A few inches make the difference between a losing manager and a manager in triumphant return.

Jun 28—   In Boston, Mantle hits two lefthanded homers off Jose Santiago, Boston's top winner with 12 victories this year. They account for three Yankee runs as New York bows, 5-3. Mickey today begins a streak of 11 homers over 11 days, recalling better times.

Jun 29—   Mantle hits two more lefthanded homers at Fenway, both off former team-mate Rollie Sheldon. Mickey's three-run blast and solo homer lead the Yankees to a 6-5 win. Richardson, Mantle and Pepitone hit consecutive homers in the third inning.

Jul 2—   In Washington, Mantle hits a pair of righthanded homers off Mike McCormick. Both are solo shots and the Senators survive to win, 10-4. Mickey is on one of his greatest longball streaks; it is his third two-homer game in five days.

Jul 8—   Mantle has his fourth two-homer game in 11 days. At the Stadium, he homers off two righthanded Washington pitchers, Dick Bosman and Jim Hannan. Mantle's streak of homers will be broken when he tears a hamstring muscle trying to score from second on a wild pitch.

Jul 16—   The Yankees win, 9-4, in extra innings in Kansas City. Horace Clarke hits a grand slam homer. He has hit two homers in the majors and both are with the bases loaded. Used mostly as a shortstop this year, Clarke will hit .266 in 96 games.

Jul 25—   Casey Stengel is inducted into the Baseball Hall of Fame in one of the Cooperstown shrine's greatest days. Casey gives thanks to all those he has been associated with in his wonderful career and adds, "I want to thank my parents for letting me play baseball, and I'm thankful I had baseball knuckles and couldn't become a dentist." Casey, elected by the Committee on Veterans, goes into the Hall with Ted Williams.

Jul 29—   Mantle breaks a tie with Lou Gehrig and goes into undisputed possession of sixth place in the all-time home run derby. He hits his 494th homer off Chicago's Bruce Howard. Elston Howard walks with the bases loaded and the Yankees win, 2-1. Al Downing, who earlier in the season won six consecutive games and who will finish with a record of 10-11, 200 innings pitched and 30 starts, gets the win today.

Aug 6—   Clarke's eighth-inning homer off reliever Luis Tiant brings the Yankees a 5-4 victory. Unlikely relief pitcher Whitey Ford keeps the Indians scoreless over the final 2⅔ innings and gains the victory. This will be the last decision of the campaign for Ford who is now 2-5.

          — Ford, who spent most of June on the disabled list, was suffering from an old ailment, a circulatory blockage in his left shoulder. Ford made only 22 appearances, had nine starts and no complete games on the year. Yet he posted a fine 2.47 ERA.

Aug 19—   In a wild doubleheader with the A's at the Stadium, the Yankees win the opener, 7-5, handing sensational rookie Jim Nash (12-1), recalled from the minors in July, his only defeat in 1966. The A's win the nightcap, 1-0, amid controversy. A Bert Campaneris eighth-inning shot to the right field wall, with a runner on first, is ruled a ground-rule double when it is touched by a fan. The umpires feel the baserunner would have scored, so they wave him home. The only run of the contest stands in spite of Ralph Houk's protests. Houk is ejected and so is a teenager who an inning later runs onto the field and throws a punch at Plate Umpire Salerno, missing.

Aug 25—   Several days after Whitey Ford is put on the disabled list for the remainder of the season, clouding his baseball future (he is only two months shy of his 38th birthday), surgery to correct a blocked artery in Ford's left shoulder is termed "eminently successful." The outlook brightens for Ford, whose circulatory problem was so bad that Whitey suffered from cramps in his pitching hand. He had been used solely in relief for his last seven weeks of activity.

Aug 26—   The Yankees stage a dramatic comeback and defeat Detroit, 6-5, on a ninth-inning pinch-hit homer by Mickey Mantle with one on. It is Mickey's first game appearance in 11 days, having pulled a hamstring muscle for the third time this season. Pepitone hits his 29th homer and Steve Whitaker his first major league homer to give the Yankees a 3-3 tie in the sixth. But the Yanks trail, 5-3, as they come up for their last licks. Howard doubles and is singled home by Boyer. Mantle then drives southpaw Hank Aguirre's second pitch into the Stadium's right field stands to end it. It is Mickey's 23rd and final homer of the season. On the down side, Jake Gibbs sustains a broken thumb that will sideline him for the rest of the year.

           — Gibbs was a bonus baby the Yankees signed for a reported $105,000 in 1961 out of the University of Mississippi, where he was a sensational football player. He was converted from third baseman to catcher and was brought along slowly in the minors. He suffered no fewer than four broken bones while learning the techniques of the position. This year, Gibbs worked in 54 Yankee games behind the plate and hit .258 with three homers. Ellie Howard, behind the plate for an even 100 games (and at first base for 13 games), hit .256 with only six homers.

Aug 27—   New York defeats Detroit, 11-1, with Jim Bouton winning his second game of the year on a seven-hitter. It is Bouton's first victory at Yankee Stadium since September 30, 1964, and follows 12 consecutive home losses. But Bouton cannot shake arm troubles and will finish the year at 3-8. Steve Whitaker has three hits, including two doubles and an inside-the-park homer, for the second straight game and is eight for 19 since his recall from Toledo.

Aug 28—   Whitaker concludes a fabulous first week in the majors with his third home run in three days—a grand slam homer—as the Yankees defeat Detroit, 8-1.

           — Whitaker, a 23-year-old from Tacoma, Wash., who was just out of the military, was given a big buildup after his great start. He would finish the season hitting .246 with seven homers in 31 games. As a starter the next year, he would hit .243 with 11 homers. For his three-year Yankee career, Whitaker would hit .231 with 18 homers in 181 games.

Sep 7—   The Yankees drop the fourth game of a four-game series, losing, 3-2, to the first-place Orioles. This final defeat, after losses of 5-4, 7-4 and 4-1, sends the Yankees into last place for the first time in the month of September since 1913. The Yankees and Red Sox will wage a month-long battle to escape the cellar.

Sep 11— Yankee rookie John Miller belts a home run in his first major league at bat and New York beats Boston, 4-2, in 10 innings. Miller will make two hits in 23 at-bats in his brief Yankee trial. He will resurface with the Dodgers in 1969 and as a Dodger will hit his second and final homer in the bigs.

Sep 17— Bobby Richardson Day is held at Yankee Stadium. At the tender age of 31, Bobby has announced his retirement with season's end. His Day benefits several charities with which he has been associated, including the YMCA, the Christian Service Brigade and Youth Development, Inc., and Minnesota benefits with a 4-2 win. Bobby separates from the Yankees with his customary class. He will hit .251 in his final season.

— Richardson was one of the greatest second basemen in Yankee history. He had incomparable range and finesse around second base, winning the Gold Glove Award over five straight years (1961-65). Over 12 seasons, all with the Yankees, the native of Sumter, S.C., was on seven All-Star teams and hit .266. He had two .300 seasons. He received a five-year contract in 1966—one year as a player and four years as a Yankee scout covering the Carolinas. This would allow Bobby to pursue a life in Christian service. A year before his contract was to run out, the Yankees would release Bobby so that he could coach baseball at the University of South Carolina.

Sep 20— As the Yanks's most dismal season nears completion, the CBS-owned Yankees undergo a front-office shake-up. Mike Burke is named club president, replacing the departed Dan Topping, who has sold the remainder of his Yankee stock to CBS. At his first press conference, Burke says, "I'm in the baseball business from today on. CBS has no intention of selling the Yankees, and Ralph Houk will be retained as manager, with a general manager to be named after the World Series." A network vice president, Burke is a former college football player.

— In October, Lee MacPhail, one-time Yankee minor league director under George Weiss, became New York's new general manager. The triumvirate of Burke-MacPhail-Houk would in 1967 put into motion their so-called "five-year plan" to restore the Yankees to baseball's upper echelon, which would include some heavy housecleaning. The trio would have some notable successes—the development of Murcer and Munson, and the trades for Lyle and Nettles, for example—and some failures. Some terrible trades were made, too. But the team of Burke-MacPhail-Houk never really had a chance. CBS had bought an aged team that seemed to have more than its share of career-shortening injuries. The once-bountiful Yankee farm system had dried up and CBS was reluctant to give Burke-MacPhail-Houk the financial capability to reverse things. The status quo would prevail until George Steinbrenner would come in to shake things up and put the Yankee ship back on a winning course.

Sep 22— On a rainy Thursday afternoon in the Bronx, only 413 fans show up at Yankee Stadium. It is the smallest paid crowd in the Stadium's history. The handful of witnesses see Chicago defeat the Yankees, 4-1. A ramification of the sparse crowd: broadcaster Red Barber will not be rehired after a dispute over his insistence on showing on TV the abundance of empty seats at Yankee Stadium. The Yanks' home attendance declines for the fifth consecutive year to only 1,124,648, lowest since World War II.

Nov 29— The Yankees trade infielder Clete Boyer to the Atlanta Braves for outfielder Bill Robinson. The newest Yankee has been to bat only 11 times in the majors but is expected to become a superstar. He has tremendous power and a rifle-like arm. Unfortunately, Robinson will have trouble getting acclimated to major league pitching and will hit only .196 in 116 games in 1967.

— The Yankees made a mistake giving up Boyer, who in 1967 would enjoy his best season at the plate, hitting 26 homers with 96 RBIs for the Braves. He would go on to have four more fine Atlanta seasons and finish his career with a reputation as one of baseball's greatest-ever defensive third basemen. Boyer hit .241 over eight Yankee seasons.

Sep 30— In Chicago, the Yankees lose in 10 innings and clinch last place with only two games remaining. Stottlemyre loses his 20th game, the most losses by a Yankee pitcher since Sad Sam Jones' 21 defeats in 1925. Stottlemyre leads the league in defeats and has gone from a 20-game winner to a 20-game loser in one season.

— The Yankees finished the season only a half game behind the ninth-place Red Sox, who played three more games than the Yankees and actually lost one more game than New York. However, silly as it might sound, this was the best last-place team in AL history, with a winning percentage of .440 (70-89). The Mets consistently lost more than 90 games without instilling outrage, but this Yankee club was held in disgrace. For the record, they were not *that* bad, and certainly not as bad as the last last-place Yankee team, the 1912 Yankees who went 50-102. And the team was only seven games under .500 under Houk.

Nov 29— The Yankees trade infielder Clete Boyer to the Atlanta Braves for outfielder Bill Robinson. The newest Yankee has been to bat only 11 times in the majors but is expected to become a superstar. He has tremendous power and a rifle-like arm. Unfortunately, Robinson will have trouble getting acclimated to major league pitching and will hit only .196 in 116 games in 1967.

— The Yankees made a mistake giving up Boyer, who in 1967 would enjoy his best season at the plate, hitting 26 homers with 96 RBIs for the Braves. He would go on to have four more fine Atlanta seasons and finish his career with a reputation as one of baseball's greatest-ever defensive third basemen. Boyer hit .241 over eight Yankee seasons.

Dec 8— The Yankees trade outfielder Roger Maris to the St. Louis Cardinals for third baseman Charlie Smith. Maris, who had hit only 13 homers in 119 games, has been damaged physically by injuries and mentally by years of unfair treatment from the fans. Roger during the 1966 season told Ralph Houk of his plans to retire, but Houk persuaded him to wait until spring, and Lee MacPhail assured him the club would allow him to retire. Now comes the shocking news of his trade for Smith, who in his entire 10-year career will hit only nine home runs more than Maris hit in 1961 alone. Smith over two New York seasons will bat .224 in 181 games.

— A happier Maris helped the Cardinals win two NL pennants and then retired with 275 home runs (203 with the Yankees) and 851 RBIs. Maris was perhaps New York's greatest defensive rightfielder. Hack Wilson hit 244 homers and had 1,062 RBIs but was nowhere nearly as good defensively as Maris. Yet Wilson made the Hall of Fame, basically because of his record of 190 RBIs in 1930. With similar career stats and far superior defensive play, and for his 61 homers in 1961, Maris would seem a logical inductee for the Hall.

Dec 17— Mantle announces he will be happy to go along with the club's plans to play him at first base in an effort to save his aching legs. Says Mickey, "I've never played first base before, but . . . I'll do anything to help." Typically unselfish, Mantle is willing to change positions at this stage of his career—a willingness not many players of his caliber would have.

— The Yankees in 1965 started the great all-round infield of Pepitone-Richardson-Kubek-Boyer. Next season, the starting quartet would be Mantle-Clarke-Amaro-Smith. The slide is obvious defensively, and, except for Mantle, even more drastic offensively.

1967

The Yankees will go 72-90 and finish ninth, 9½ games in front of the last-place Athletics and 20 games behind the first-place Red Sox. Mickey Mantle will hit 22 home runs and Joe Pepitone will lead the club in RBIs with 64. Horace Clarke will be the highest-hitting regular at .272. Mel Stottlemyre (15-15) and Al Downing (14-10) will allow less than three runs per game but will seldom enjoy a comfortable working margin, pitching for a club that hits .225 as a team.

Jan 30— Yank President Mike Burke announces a Yankee Stadium modernization and refurbishing program to be completed before the opening of the 1967 season. The $1.5 million program is the most complete facelift since the Stadium was built in 1923.

Feb 16— Red Ruffing, who won 231 Yankee games over 15 seasons and collected 273 major league victories in all, is elected to the Baseball Hall of Fame. The Baseball Writers belatedly recognize one of the greatest pitchers of all time. Ruffing, who has been retired since 1947, gets 266 votes of 306 cast, and is the only candidate to gain the necessary number of votes in this year's election. As Ruffing's Hall plaque will note, he won 20 or more games in four consecutive seasons and seven of nine World Series decisions.

Mar 1— The Yanks' full team begins spring training in Ft. Lauderdale and Mickey Mantle, who on January 31st signed his fifth consecutive $100,000 contract, begins workouts at first base. Mantle will become a more than adequate first baseman after much hard work, surprising many experts who didn't think he could make the transition.

Mar 6— Bobby Murcer is inducted into the Army and will lose two seasons from his promising big league career. Murcer will come off the military list in December of 1968.

Apr 10— President Johnson throws out the first ball and the Yankees whip the Senators, 8-0, on Opening Day in Washington. Mel Stottlemyre, who today starts a streak of 272 consecutive starting assignments, pitches a two-hitter. Stottlemyre's sinkerball induces 18 groundouts. Mantle, who makes his regular season debut at first base, pulls a hamstring muscle and will be out of the line-up for several days. Bill Robinson homers in his Yankee debut. Elston Howard also homers, but will not hit another home run until June 9th.

Apr 14— The Yankees are all but no-hit in their home opener, which Boston wins, 3-0. Elston Howard singles with two outs in the ninth for the first and only hit off lefthander Billy Rohr, who is making his major league debut. Rohr will

The big story from the Yankees' 1967 spring training camp was Mickey Mantle's switch from the outfield to first base, a move that was made to ease the strain on Mantle's ailing legs. Mick looked a bit uncertain on the camp's March 1 opening day but surprised many by making a smooth transition.

win a total of two games this year and wind up with a lifetime record of 3-3.

Apr 16— In an 18-inning game at the Stadium, the Yankees defeat Boston, 7-6. In the 18th, Jake Gibbs walks, steals second base and scores on Joe Pepitone's single. The winner is Al Downing, who pitches the final five innings. The game takes just 10 minutes short of six hours to play, the longest AL game in four years. On July 26, the Yankees will lose an 18-inning game, 3-2, to Minnesota at the Stadium.

Apr 19— Ford wins, 3-0, pitching the Yankees into first place. Whitey scatters seven singles in Chicago, winning his 235th major league game over hard-throwing Tommy John. It is also Ford's 45th, and final, shutout. Through 1982, Ford remains the Yanks' all-time leader in shutouts.

Apr 25— Ford hurls an eight-hitter at the Stadium and beats Tommy John (who will one day mirror Ford's pitching style) for the second time in less than a week, 11-2. Whitey's 236th win (as it turns out) is his last major league victory.

Apr 29— At Yankee Stadium, Fred Talbot two-hits the Angels and wins, 5-2, as the Yankees go into a first-place tie with Boston. Mantle, who has yet to make an error at first base, leads the way with three RBIs and a two-run homer. The Mick's first extra-base hit of 1967 goes well over the 407-foot sign in right-center field.

Apr 30— Mantle's three-run homer in the 10th inning beats California, 4-1, in the opener of a Cap Day doubleheader before 47,980 at the Stadium. The Yanks lose the nightcap, 4-2, and get knocked out of first place, but Mantle has a pinch-hit double to pass Joe DiMaggio in hits with 2,215. Lou Gehrig and Babe Ruth, through 1982, are the only players with more Yankee hits than Mantle.

May 14— Mantle hits his 500th home run in a 6-5 win over Baltimore at Yankee Stadium. Batting lefthanded, Mantle's seventh-inning game-winning homer off Stu Miller is hit on a 3-2 pitch. Mickey receives three standing ovations from the crowd of 18,872, who acknowledge only the sixth player to reach 500 homers. Today's home run begins a streak of eight Mantle homers over 13 games and makes a winner of Dooley Womack.

May 24— Downing allows only two hits—to Luis Aparicio and Andy Etchebarren—and wins in Baltimore, 2-0. Al strikes out 13 men. (On July 7th, Downing will pitch another shutout in Baltimore and fan 12.) Mantle's two-run opposite-field homer in the third inning off southpaw Steve Barber produces the game's only runs.

May 28— Amid persistent rumors that the Yankees will relocate in New Jersey, Mike Burke asserts that the club "is definitely not planning to move out of Yankee Stadium."

— Perhaps Burke's greatest contribution to the Yankees was his insistence that they remain housed in the House that Ruth Built. The football New York Giants agreed to move to New Jersey, and the Garden State was making a strong bid to lure the Yankees, too. But Burke was able to convince the right people in New York City that it was essential that the Stadium be renovated and that the Yankees keep their ties with the Bronx.

May 30— Whitey Ford announces his retirement. Whitey had an operation in 1966 for a circulatory blockage in his left shoulder and recently a painful bone spur in his left elbow has worsened. Eight days earlier, Dr. Sidney Gaynor had examined Ford's ailing elbow and said, "The situation is not too encouraging." This comes after a one-inning outing by Whitey. He retires with a season's record of 2-4 but with a fantastic 1.64 ERA.

— The greatest pitcher in Yankee history remained with the club in various capacities in the years to follow. As a pitcher he spent 16 seasons with the Yankees and retired with a winning percentage of .690, highest of all 200-game winners in the 20th century. Whitey Ford Day, by proclamation of Mayor Lindsay, would soon be celebrated in New York City.

Jun 5— At Yankee Stadium, the Yankees overcome Mike Epstein's first big league homer, a 200-foot inside-the-parker, and down Washington, 4-2, behind Thad Tillotson's six-hitter. Tillotson has won his first three decisions but will finish 3-9. He is given the unenviable task of replacing Ford in the starting rotation. Mantle leads off the bottom of the eighth with a slicing homer to right field off southpaw Darold Knowles to break up a 2-2 tie.

Jun 21— In a beanball battle at the Stadium, Thad Tillotson hits Joe Foy in the head with a pitch. When Jim Lonborg hits Tillotson in the shoulder with a retaliatory pitch, Tillotson, Foy and Lonborg get into a brawl. So many fights break out on the field that it takes 12 special security cops to restore order. Pepitone suffers a sprained wrist in the melee and leaves. The game resumes and Tillotson puts Lonborg on his seat with a brushback pitch. The next inning Lonborg beans Dick Howser, who slumps to the ground and has to be replaced. This is getting dangerous, and the umpires meet with Boston Manager Dick Williams and New York Coaches Frank Crosetti and Loren Babe. (Ralph Houk had been ejected earlier; amid a deadly beanball war, Houk, the only one banished, was thrown out for arguing a call!) Boston is an 8-1 winner.

— Also on this date, the Yankees signed Ron Blomberg, an 18-year-old slugger from Atlanta who was the No. 1 pick in the recent draft of amateur players. Blomberg signed for a reported $60,000 bonus and was assigned to Johnson City, where he would hit .297 in 66 games.

Jun 24— Mantle leads off the bottom of the ninth inning with a home run off Fred Gladding to beat Detroit, 4-3. Mickey bats lefthanded to hit his 14th homer. He has made the game-winning hit in eight games. Seven of the hits were homers.

Jun 25— New York beats Detroit, 3-2, to complete a three-game sweep of the Tigers, who will finish just one game behind pennant-winning Boston. With runners on first and second bases in the fifth, Detroit's Jerry Lumpe lines to second baseman Horace Clarke who goes to shortstop Ruben Amaro at second for the second out. Amaro then fires to Mantle at first to complete a crucial triple play.

Jul 4— Batting lefthanded, Mantle hits two homers off Mudcat Grant in the first game of a doubleheader swept by Minnesota. The first ties Mel Ott at 511 and the second puts him above Ott on the all-time list. Mantle now trails only Babe Ruth, Willie Mays, Jimmie Foxx and Ted Williams.

Jul 14— The Yankees sweep a doubleheader from Cleveland, winning 2-1 and 2-0, with Fritz Peterson and Al Downing both pitching five-hitters. It is the first sweep of a doubleheader by the 1967 Yankees.

Aug 3— The Yankees trade catcher Elston Howard to Boston for the $20,000 waiver price and two players to be named later (they will be pitchers Ron Klimkowski and Peter Magrini). Ellie hit .196 with the Yanks this year, and while hitting only .147 for the Bosox, will lend stability to the pitching staff in Boston's successful pennant run.

— Howard was one of the all-time Yankee greats, although he did not have a regular job for his first five seasons. When he finally became the regular catcher, he proved to be one of the game's best receivers, winning two Gold Gloves, setting a single-season Yankee fielding record for a catcher and handling pitchers with just the right touch. Over 13 years, Ellie hit .279 for the Yankees.

Aug 11— Al Downing strikes out 12 Indians and becomes only the sixth AL pitcher to strike out the side on only nine pitches. He wins, 5-3, in a doubleheader split with Cleveland.

— Downing had a great fastball and when he was on, he was as awesome as any of the game's great power pitchers. Downing would lead the Yanks in strikeouts for the fourth straight season.

Aug 13— Cleveland's Sam McDowell takes a 4-0 lead into the sixth inning and loses 15-11. New York has 18 hits in the run-prolific comeback by a club that scores only 522 runs, least in the AL. Reserve catcher Bob Tillman has six RBIs. In his 22-game Yankee career, Tillman will have a total of nine RBIs.

Aug 29— A crowd of 40,314 for a twi-night doubleheader sees the longest game by innings in Yankee Stadium history after Boston wins the first game, 2-1. The nightcap goes 20 innings and takes well over five hours to complete, with the Yanks winning, 4-3. John Kennedy, Fred Talbot and Horace Clarke bunch singles in the 20th to win it for Talbot, who will be 6-8 this year.

Sep 3— Mantle poles his 22nd home run of the year, hitting lefthanded off Washington's Dick Bosman. It is only his third homer since July 25th and he will not hit another in 1967.

Sep 25— Downing pitches a four-hitter to pin a 2-0 loss on Detroit at the Stadium, as 22-game-winner Earl Wilson take the loss. It is a tough loss for the Tigers, who fall back 1½ games from first place in one of the wildest pennant races in AL history.

Nov 30— The Yankees purchase the contract of infielder Gene Michael from the Los Angeles Dodgers. The rescuing of Michael, who hit only .202 in 98 games for the Dodgers after a long minor league apprenticeship, will prove profitable for the Yankees.

1968

The Yankees will finish in the first division. With a record of 83-79, they will place fifth, 20 games behind the pennant-winning Detroit Tigers. The Bronx Bombers will hit a weak .214, with Roy White the club's leading hitter at .267. In his last major league season, Mickey Mantle will hit 18 home runs and will lead the club in that category. A fine pitching staff will be headed by Mel Stottlemyre, who will finish with a 21-12 record.

Apr 10—   Mel Stottlemyer defeats California, 1 0, in what proves to be a harbinger of
            low-scoring games. The 1968 Yankees will score 3.3 runs per game, while
            Yankee pitchers will allow 2.8 earned runs per game. Only 15,744 fans show
            up for today's home opener.

            — Stottlemyer would have one of his greatest seasons. He would finish with
            a career-high 21 wins and tie Luis Tiant for third place in the league, behind
            Denny McLain's 31 wins and Dave McNally's 22. Mel, who was a sinkerball
            pitcher extraordinaire, would pitch to an ERA of 2.45 and complete 19 of 36
            starts. And Stottlemyre would throw six shutouts, exceeded in the AL only
            by Tiant, with nine.

Apr 22—   The Yankees set a club record by using six switch-hitters in a game against
            Oakland. New York's line-up includes switchers Horace Clarke (2B), Mickey
            Mantle (1B), Tom Tresh (LF), Roy White (RF), Gene Michael (SS) and Fritz
            Peterson (P).

May 6—   In the first inning at the Stadium, Mantle hits No. 522 off Cleveland's Sam
            McDowell. The two-run shot isn't enough—Cleveland wins, 3-2—but it
            pushes Mantle past Williams on the all-time homer list. The Mick now holds
            fourth place by himself. Gene "Stick" Michael and Indian first baseman Tony
            Horton have a personal contest. They exchange punches after Horton
            makes a hard tag on Stick. Both are ejected.

May 24—   Stan Bahnsen and Chicago's Tommy John hook up in a duel neither wins.
            Bahnsen allows five hits in 10 innings and John scatters six hits over nine
            innings. In the bottom of the 13th, with both starters departed from the score-
            less game, Bobby Cox doubles and scores when Chicago third baseman
            Sandy Alomar fields a sacrifice bunt and throws the ball away.

            — Bahnsen was to become AL Rookie of the Year, the first Yankee to win
            the award since 1962 (Tom Tresh). At the tender age of 23, the native of
            Council Bluffs, Ia., would go 17-12 with a spectacular 2.05 ERA in 267⅓
            innings. But as a batter, Bahnsen had only four hits in 81 trips for an
            average of .049.

May 30—   A smallish Stadium crowd of 28,197 sees the Yankees and Senators split
            a holiday doubleheader. In the opener, the Yankees win their fifth straight
            game, 13-4, as Mantle goes five for five. Mickey has two circuit clouts,
            one of them landing in the third tier in right field. The Yankees drop the
            nightcap, 6-2.

Jun 3—   The Yankees field their 21st triple play. It begins when Minnesota's Johnny
            Roseboro hits a line drive up the middle, with runners on first and third.
            Pitcher Dooley Womack spears it and gets the second out by going to third
            baseman Bobby Cox, who relays to first baseman Mantle for the third out.

            — A native of Columbia, S.C., Womack signed with the Yankees in September
            of 1958 and spent eight seasons in the minors before making the club in
            1966. In three Yankee seasons, Dooley was a top-notch 15-16 reliever with
            24 saves and an ERA of 2.58. Womack saved 18 games in 1967.

Jul 12—   The Yankees obtain pitcher Lindy McDaniel from the San Francisco Giants
            for pitcher Bill Monbouquette, 11-12 over two seasons with the Yankees.

            — This was an excellent trade for New York. Monbouquette, winner of 114
            games lifetime, would not win another game in the majors. McDaniel would
            rank among the great relief artists in Yankee history. He would finish 1968

with a 4-1 record, 10 saves and a 1.76 ERA. Over a one-week period in late August, he retired 32 consecutive batters over four games. In six seasons with the Yankees, the forkballer would go 38-29 with 58 saves.

Aug 10— Minnesota beats the Yankees, 3-2, at the Stadium, as lefthander Jim Merritt allows only four hits—two of them solo homers by Mantle, his 12th and 13th of the year and 530th and 531st of his career. It is the 36th and final time Mantle will hit a pair of homers in one game.

Aug 22— In Minnesota, Jim Merritt three-hits New York to win, 3-1. Mantle pinch-hits a Merritt pitch into the seats to again ruin a shutout bid by the lefty. The homer is Mickey's 534th and ties him with Jimmie Foxx for third place on the all-time list.

Aug 25— New York takes a doubleheader from Detroit and reaches the .500 level (63-63) for the first time since April 30. In an effort to rest his weary bullpen, Ralph Houk turns to Rocky Colavito, who in 1958 pitched in one game for the Indians. Rocky pitches 2⅔ innings, holds Detroit to only one hit and gets the win as the Yankees, down 5-0, come back to win, 6-5. And he scores the winning run. But there's more! He plays right field in the nightcap and leads the Yankees to a 5-4 win with a homer.

— What a tremendous series the Yanks enjoyed against the soon-to-be AL champs! New York won four one-run games (a fifth game ends in a 19-inning tie). Stottlemyre gained one of the wins, 2-1, against Denny McLean, on a two-run Roy White homer.

Aug 26— Houk, faced with his third doubleheader in four days, again turns to a non-pitcher to do some mound work. In the nightcap of a Yankee Stadium twinbill, he brings in shortstop Gene Michael to mop up after the Yanks fall badly behind the Angels. Michael pitches three innings without allowing an earned run. He gives up five hits, walks none and strikes out three.

Sep 7— In a season of pitiful Yankee hitting, the Bronx Bombers finally get around to bombing. They rout the Senators in a doubleheader before 20,613 at the Stadium, 16-2 and 10-0. Gibbs, Pepitone and White all hit two-run homers in the first game. In the second game, Frank Fernandez hits a three-run homer and Colavito has a two-run blast. Stottlemyre wins his 19th in the opener and Peterson pitches a two-hitter in the nightcap.

— The twin-killing began a 10-game Yankee winning streak that would include seven victories over Washington. Mantle may have been one of the reasons for the mastery over the Senators. He had two hits in this date's doubleheader and at this point in the year was 15 for 32 (plus 10 walks) against Washington pitching.

Sep 13— Stottlemyre gains his 20th victory in the opener and Bahnsen takes the nightcap as the Yankees win twice in Washington, 4-2 and 2-1.

Sep 14— Yankee third baseman Mike Ferraro makes 11 assists at third base, tying an AL record for a nine-inning game. Ferraro and Washington's Ken McMullen continue to share the record.

Sep 16— In Detroit, the Yankees lose, 9-1. Not only does the loss snap the Yankees' 10-game winning streak, but it initiates a string of six defeats in a row for the Yanks.

Sep 19— Detroit's Denny McLain beats the Yankees, 6-2, for his 31st win of the season, but gains headlines for serving up Mantle's 535th home run. Mickey's first homer in almost a month pushes him past Jimmie Foxx into undisputed possession of third place on the all-time home run list.

— After the game, McLain admitted he gave Mantle a nice pitch to hit, thus creating a small controversy. But as Madison Square Garden boxing director Harry Markson said, "When a guy has bought 534 drinks in the same saloon, he's entitled to one on the house."

Sep 20— Mantle tags his 536th, his final career home run. It is hit off Boston's Jim Lonborg. It is Mickey's 373rd lefthanded homer (he hit 163 righthanded). It is his 266th at the Stadium (he hit 270 on the road), seven more than Ruth's total, giving him the Stadium homer record.

Sep 24— Against Cleveland's Mike Paul, Rocky Colavito hits his 374th home run. It will be the Bronx native's final career home run.

— Wrapping up his big league career, Colavito, now 35, hit .220 with five homers and 13 RBIs in 39 games for the Yankees.

Sep 28— Mickey Mantle plays in his final major league game before a large, appreciative crowd at Fenway Park. Mickey bats in the first inning and receives a tremendous ovation. He makes an out and is replaced by Andy Kosco, who ends up hitting the game-winning home run (one of 15 Kosco hits this year).

— Mantle played his final season on courage alone—an 18-season epidemic of injuries left him all but crippled. Still he played in 144 games in 1968 to finish first on the Yanks' all-time games played list at 2,401. But his reflexes had slowed and he hit only .237, his career low. He had more walks (106) than hits (103) in his final season.

Oct 29— Dick Howser, the Yanks' utility infielder who hit .211 in 148 games over two seasons, retires as a player and signs with the Yankees as a coach. Howser replaces Frank Crosetti, who retires after more than 35 years with the club both as a player and as a coach.

Dec 6— Bobby Murcer is discharged from the military. He is still considered one of baseball's most talented young players and will get a chance to prove it when he rejoins the club in February.

1969

For the first time in history, baseball's two major leagues are split into four divisions. The Yankees, placed in the AL East along with Baltimore, Detroit, Boston, Washington and Cleveland, will finish fifth in the six-team division with a record of 80-81. Joe Pepitone and Bobby Murcer will supply the power, with 27 and 26 homers respectively. Roy White will lead the club in hitting with a .290 average, and Mel Stottlemyre (20-14) and Fritz Peterson (17-16) will be the only pitchers to win in double figures.

Mar 1— Mickey Mantle announces his retirement. Mickey, who had met with Manager Ralph Houk before meeting with the press in Ft. Lauderdale, Fla., quits with with opening of spring training. "I just can't play any more," Mickey says.

— With Mantle's not-unexpected retirement, the fallen Yankee Dynasty lost its last connection with the glory days. The Yankees were now just another ball club. These were hard times for Yankee fans, who had come to expect excellence. As for Mickey, he had gained everyone's respect—especially that of the pitchers. Only Babe Ruth and Ted Williams have been walked more often than the Mick.

Apr 7— Mel Stottlemyre wins his third straight season opener, 8-4, and Bobby Murcer makes a triumphant return to baseball by hitting a home run in Washington before President Nixon and some 45,000 others.

— The mantle (pardon the expression) of Yankee leadership was passed from Mickey Mantle to Bobby Murcer on this day. Still a month shy of his 23rd birthday, Murcer became a Yankee regular for the first time and would have an amazing season in many respects. In spite of the pressure of succeeding Mantle as the Yanks' kingpin, Bobby scored 82 runs and drove in 82 runs, besides hitting a respectable .259. He began the season at third base—out of position—then moved to the outfield (mostly right field) where he did a fine job.

Apr 12— Mel Stottlemyre wins 4-0 on a one-hitter that Jim Northrup, who in his career ruins three no-hitters, spoils with a fifth-inning double.

Apr 15— Fritz Peterson beats Washington, 8-2, in New York's home opener. The musical team of Simon and Garfunkel is on hand and long-time Yankee fan Paul Simon throws out the first ball. The symbolism is rich in irony. "Where have you gone, Joe DiMaggio?" is a line from Simon and Garfunkel's hit song, *Mrs. Robinson,* and now the Stadium fans look upon a Yankee squad devoid not only of DiMaggio but, for the first time since 1950, without the great Mickey Mantle.

Mickey Mantle Day—June 8, 1969. Mick addresses the crowd, and for many of those present the day signified not just the retirement of Mantle's No. 7 but the closing of a great chapter in Yankee history.

Apr 17—   Joe Pepitone hits the final grand slam homer by a Yankee player in 1969. (Frank Fernandez hit the only other grand slam a week earlier.) It comes with two outs in the bottom of the 10th and the Yankees beat Washington, 7-3, in the first of a doubleheader. Washington wins the second game, 5-2.

            — Pepitone had a fine comeback year, hitting 27 homers with 70 RBIs, his best season since his 31-homer, 83-RBI year of 1966. Pepitone would also win his third Gold Glove Award for his defensive work at first base. But Joe was gaining more headlines for his carefree lifestyle and stylish long hair. Around the league, fans flocked to boo or cheer the ballplayer who exemplified the Woodstock generation.

Jun 8—   Mickey Mantle Day at the Stadium is celebrated with a doubleheader sweep of Chicago, 3-1 and 11-2. A crowd of 60,096 is present for the retirement of Mantle's No. 7. Joe DiMaggio and Mickey exchange plaques that will be placed on the center field wall at the Stadium. Mickey tells the crowd that "playing 18 years in Yankee Stadium for you folks was the best thing that could ever happen to a ballplayer." Mickey takes a ride around the field in a golf cart and hears the roar of appreciation.

            — Joe DiMaggio himself would be accorded a tremendous baseball honor this season. In celebration of baseball's centennial year, DiMaggio would be voted the game's "Greatest Living Player." Another Yankee, Babe Ruth, would be selected as baseball's "Greatest Player Ever."

Jun 14—   The Yankees trade shortstop Tom Tresh to the Detroit Tigers for outfielder Ron Woods. Tresh, hitting .182, returned to shortstop last year after five seasons in the outfield. He will play 94 games for the Tigers, hit .224 and retire after this season.

            — Tresh never fulfilled the promise of his spectacular rookie season in 1962 when he was prematurely labeled "the next Mickey Mantle." But he was much more than a one-year wonder. He hit 140 homers for the Yankees, three times scored over 90 runs and was a fine all-round player. A succession of disabling injuries caught up with him; over his last five Yankee seasons, his batting average steadily declined from .279 to .233 to .219 to .195 to .182.

Jul 8—   Yankee Ron Woods spoils Oriole Mike Cuellar's no-hitter three times over. All three Yankee hits are made by Woods, who will make just 30 hits in 172 at-bats for a 1969 average of .175.

Jul 23—   Mel Stottlemyre has the honor of being the AL's starting pitcher in the All-Star Game at Robert F. Kennedy Stadium in Washington but gives up three runs and takes the loss. The NL wins, 9-3. Roy White strikes out as a pinch-hitter.

Jul 28—   Yankee pitching great of the 1920's, Waite Hoyt, the winner of 237 games in 21 seasons, who gained election in February from the Committee on Veterans, is inducted into the Baseball Hall of Fame. Waite was also a great broadcaster for many years at Cincinnati. Also inducted is Hoyt's contemporary, Stan Coveleski, who won 214 games. Coveleski was 5-1 for the Yankees in 1928, his final big league season.

Aug 10—   New York defeats Oakland, 5-1, at the Stadium, shocking pitcher Lew Krausse with back-to-back-to-back homers in the sixth inning. They are hit by Bobby Murcer, Thurman Munson and Gene Michael. It is Munson's first big league homer. It is the sixth (and last) time that the Yankees have hit three consecutive homers in one inning.

— Munson was a squatty but athletic 22-year-old catcher from Ohio, who starred at Kent State University and whom Yankee scout Gene Woodling made the Yanks' No. 1 draft pick in June 1968. Thurman received a reported $75,000 bonus to sign with the Yankees. He hit .301 at Binghamton in 1968 and this season was called into the Army and split time between Fort Dix, Syracuse (where he blistered International League pitching at a .363 clip), and New York (where he hit .256 in 26 games).

Dec 4— The Yankees trade first baseman-outfielder Joe Pepitone to the Houston Astros for outfielder-first baseman Curt Blefary. It is a swap of two Brooklyn-born players. Blefary, who began his career in the Yankee organization used to brutalize the Yanks as a power-hitter for Baltimore, but in his coming two Yankee seasons he will hit only .210 with 10 homers in 120 games.

— Pepitone would play for three teams in the next four seasons, bringing a great time wherever he went and having some pretty good seasons along the way. He would hit 26 homers in 1970, then in 1971 enjoy a career-high .307 with the Cubs. Four times in eight Yankee seasons he had more than 20 homers and three times he won Gold Glove Awards. Joe had beautiful natural talent.

THE 1970's
THE RETURN TO GLORY

A ROOKIE-OF-THE-YEAR CATCHER
HOUK'S SURPRISING SECOND-PLACE CLUB
MURCER GOES TO THE TOP OF THE CLASS
STEINBRENNER COMES TO TOWN
THE RENOVATION OF THE STADIUM
VIRDON'S PENNANT CHASES
THE BIG APPLE GETS BONDS AND HUNTER
THE RETURN OF BILLY THE KID
A 12-YEAR DROUGHT ENDS
JACKSON STORMS ONTO THE SCENE
TWO WORLD CHAMPIONSHIPS
A MIRACLE COMEBACK
LOUISIANA LIGHTNING
THE TRAGIC LOSS OF MUNSON

1970

The surprising Yankees will finish at 93-69 and capture second place, although a full 15 games behind pennant-winning Baltimore. The Yankees will have two .300 hitters in Thurman Munson (.302) and Danny Cater (.301) and two 20-homer sluggers in Bobby Murcer (23) and Roy White (22), the latter the club's best all-round hitter at .296 with 94 RBIs. Southpaw Fritz Peterson will be 20-11 and reliever Lindy McDaniel will save 29 games.

Apr 12— Plaques presented to Joe DiMaggio and Mickey Mantle the previous June are dedicated. The plaques are now mounted on the Stadium's center field wall. DiMaggio's cites "his singular excellence" and his "legacy of greatness." Mantle's recognizes Mickey's "true greatness in the Yankee tradition" and his "unequaled courage." The plaques are dedicated between doubleheader games when Mantle and DiMaggio come onto the field riding in golf carts. Police have to restrain chasing admirers. The Yankees and Indians split today's doubleheader.

Apr 22— In Washington the Yankees lose, 2-1, in 18 innings. The Yanks trail, 1-0, when Bobby Murcer raps a ninth-inning homer to necessitate extra innings. After eight more scoreless innings, the Nats pull it out on a walk, single and sacrifice fly. Ron Klimkowski, who will have a 6-7/2.66 ERA season is the loser.

May 7— Roy White switch-hits homers in the same game, joining Mickey Mantle and Tom Tresh as the third Yankee player ever to do so.

— White enjoyed his finest season in 1970. Often batting clean-up, the Los Angeles native in 162 games would have 180 hits, 58 of them for extra bases. He would score 109 runs, walk 95 times and swipe 24 bases, and he would make only two outfield errors.

May 21— The Yankees beat Washington, 2-0, in an unusually wild game for Stottlemyre, who walks 11 men in 8⅓ innings. Southpaw reliever Steve Hamilton, entering in the ninth inning with the bases loaded and only one out, saves the game.

— Hamilton was the third member of an outstanding relief corps that included Lindy McDaniel (29 saves) and Jack Aker (16 saves). Hamilton himself, while recording only three saves in 35 appearances, would dazzle spectators with the Folly Floater, his version of the blooper.

Jun 24— Murcer homers on each of four consecutive official at bats, tying an AL record for consecutive homers in back-to-back games. In a doubleheader with Cleveland, Bobby hits one in the ninth inning of the first game and the other three (which are interrupted by a walk) in the nightcap.

— By mid-June, the Yankees, who on April 26 were in last place, were second only to Baltimore. Their climb to prominence was led by Murcer, Thurman Munson, Roy White and Fritz Peterson. Ralph Houk had stuck with Munson despite a 1-for-30 early-season batting slump, and Thurman would go on to win the Rookie of the Year Award. Besides hitting above .300, Munson would nail 23 out of 38 would-be base stealers.

Jun 25— A young Cleveland righthander, Steve Dunning, faces the Yankees, and Manager Al Dark, fearful that Murcer might set a record for most consecutive home runs against his team, calls Dunning's pitches from the dugout.

Cautious pitching is the result and Murcer walks the first three times he bats. In his fourth trip, Bobby widens the strike zone and pops up on a 3-1 pitch.

Jul 2— For the third time within a month, the Yanks' Horace Clarke, a .251 hitter this season, ruins a no-hitter—and for the third time with a ninth-inning hit! Detroit's Joe Niekro pitches 8⅓ innings before Clarke singles for New York's one hit. The Tigers win, 5-0.

— On June 4, Clarke broke up a no-hitter by Kansas City's Jim Rooker in the ninth and the Yankees went on to win, 2-1, in 12 innings. Then on June 19, he was the wedge in the ninth that destroyed a no-hitter bid by Boston's Sonny Siebert. His was the first of four Yankee hits, but Siebert held on to win, 7-4.

Jul 14— At Cincinnati's Riverfront Stadium, the NL wins the All-Star Game, 5-4, in extra innings. Fritz Peterson pitches to one batter in the ninth, allows a hit and is relieved by Stottlemyre. Mel is perfect for 1⅔ innings.

Jul 20— The Yankees acquire southpaw Mike McCormick, who while with San Francisco in 1967 won the NL's Cy Young Award with a 22-10 record. In a curious statistical oddity, McCormick and John Cumberland, who was traded away for Mike, were both 3-4 before the trade and 2-0 afterwards.

Jul 27— Earle Combs, the Yanks' first great centerfielder, is inducted into the Baseball Hall of Fame. His Cooperstown plaque describes the Kentucky Colonel as the "lead off hitter and center fielder of Yankee champions of 1926-27-28-32" and notes that he "batted .350 in four World Series." He is a selection of the Committee on Veterans.

Aug 8— Before a crowd of 47,914 on Old Timers' Day, the Yankees retire Casey Stengel's No. 37 uniform. In pre-game ceremonies, Whitey Ford and Yogi Berra present their old manager with his uniform and a choked-up Casey speaks to the crowd. In their own way, the club is patching things up with Casey for his unceremonious release almost 10 years ago. Baltimore wins the game, 4-2.

Aug 30— Mickey Mantle leaves NBC as a baseball announcer and returns to the Yankees as a first base coach for the remainder of the season. The Mick on his return receives a standing ovation from the Stadium crowd. The Yankees beat Minnesota, 5-2, as Mickey's old teammate, Roy White, smokes a grand slam homer.

Sep 8— Switch-hit triples—a real rarity—are hit by Roy White in a 7-3 win over Washington.

Sep 9— New York sells the contract of relief pitcher Steve Hamilton to the Chicago White Sox. The veteran lefthander, 4-3 with the Yankees, will have no decisions with the White Sox.

— A 6'7 Kentuckian who once played basketball in the NBA, Hamilton had been a popular member of the Yankee cast since 1963. He was difficult for lefthanded batters to hit. Lifetime, Steve won 40 games, 34 of them for the Yankees (against 20 losses), and had 36 saves.

Sep 23— The Yankees clinch second place with a 6-4 win over Washington. The happy band of Yankees celebrate with a champagne party, doubtless provoking a wince or two among erstwhile Yankees and Yankee followers used to richer successes.

Sep 30—   On the season's final day, Fritz Peterson beats the Red Sox, 4-3, and reaches the coveted 20-win plateau for the only time in his career. He does it by winning his final three decisions and by winning for the first time ever at Fenway Park.

— The victory gave the Yankees a surprisingly high total of 93 wins. Although they never threatened Baltimore, Ralph Houk's charges had reason to be proud of their season.

1971

The Yankees will finish at 82-80 and slip to fourth place, 21 games behind pennant-winning Baltimore. But Bobby Murcer will emerge as one of the game's genuine stars, with an average of .331, 25 home runs and 94 RBIs. Roy White will have another fine year, hitting .292. Mel Stottlemyre, at 16-12, will lead a group of five double-figure winners on New York's pitching staff.

Apr 9—   The Yankees obtain Felipe Alou (OF-1B) from the Oakland A's for Ron Klimkowski (P) and Rob Gardner (P). Alou will hit .289 in 131 games for the Yankees this year. He will play 80 games in the outfield and 42 at first base.

Apr 13—   Stan Bahnsen, who will go 14-12 this season, wins the Yanks' home opener, beating Detroit, 5-2. The Yankees had opened on the road with two wins in five games.

Jun 1—   In the third round of the amateur free agent draft, the Yankees select Ron Guidry on the recommendation of their former pitcher and scout, Atley Donald.

— Guidry was a product of Lafayette, La., where he was a track standout in high school and a baseball star at the University of Southwestern Louisiana. Because of his wide-ranging athletic skills, Ron was given a chance of making the majors as either a pitcher or outfielder. He was assigned to the Yanks' Johnson City farm club in the Appalachian League.

Jun 18—   In the third inning at Baltimore, Andy Etchebarren barrels into Thurman Munson at the plate and Thurman is knocked out cold. He drops the ball for his only error in 615 chances this season; his .998 fielding average will tie Elston Howard's 1964 Yankee record. Jake Gibbs replaces the tough-as-nails Munson. Also in the third, Roy White leaves the game with a pulled hamstring muscle. The Yankees blow a 4-0 lead and lose, 6-4.

— Munson will one day return the favor to Etchebarren by knocking out the Baltimore catcher in a similar play at home plate.

Jun 25—   The Yankees obtain outfielder Ron Swoboda from the Montreal Expos for outfielder Ron Woods. The popular Swoboda was one of the first stars developed by the Mets and will be one of 27 players to wear the uniforms of both the Yankees and Mets.

— Most players who played for both teams were one-time Yankee stars wrapping up their careers with the Mets. Swoboda, one of the first to make the trip from Queens to the Bronx, was hitting .253 for the Expos and would finish the season hitting .261 in 54 Yankee games. In three Yankee seasons, Swoboda would bat .235 (69 for 294), ending his major league career in 1973 when he hit .116 (5 for 43).

Jul 13—   The AL breaks an eight-game losing streak and wins the All-Star Game, 6-4, at Tigers Stadium. Starting centerfielder Bobby Murcer gets a hit in three trips and Thurman Munson spells Bill Freehan behind the plate.

Jul 18—   The Yankees sweep a twinbill from Chicago. In the nightcap, Yankee southpaw Mike Kekich, who will finish with a record of 10-9 as the fifth starter, throws a one-hitter and wins, 6-1. Mike Andrews takes Kekich deep in the fifth inning for one of his 12 homers this season.

Jul 25—   In the second game of a doubleheader in Milwaukee,* Bobby Murcer hits the 12th pinch-hit grand slam in Yankee history. It is the first since Yogi Berra's pinch-hit "slam" in 1962, and it will be the Yankees' only bases-loaded homer of this season. The Yanks take both games, 6-2 (in 11 innings) and 11-9.

    — In this season Murcer established himself as one of the game's elite players. He began a three-season string of 80 homers and 285 RBIs (and an average of .308). Bobby scored 94 runs in 1971 and knocked in 94, third highest RBI total in the division. He battled Tony Oliva to the final week for the batting crown, but lost by six points to Oliva's .337. Bobby also played well in center. However, leftfielder Roy White made no errors in 145 outfield games; his 1.000 fielding average would remain the club record for outfielders.

Aug 9—   George Weiss is inducted into the Baseball Hall of Fame. His Cooperstown plaque credits the Yankee executive of 28 years with developing the "best minor league chain" and points out that he was general manager of the Yankees from 1947-1960 when the team won 10 pennants and 7 World Series. Weiss, who will die on August 13, 1972, was elected by the Committee on Veterans.

Sep 7—   Boston Manager Eddie Kasko uses an entirely different set of 10 players for each game of a doubleheader the Yanks take at the Stadium, 5-3 and 3-0.

Sep 30—   In the final major league game ever played in Washington, the Yankees are awarded a 9-0 forfeit victory when many of the 14,460 spectators storm the playing field in the ninth inning, with the Senators ahead, 7-5. Mike Kekich allows Frank Howard's 26th homer and huge Hondo—the most popular Senator of his generation—believing Ralph Houk and Thurman Munson purposely called for fastballs, thanks Munson as he crosses the plate. With two down in the ninth, fans pour onto the field. They are angry—the franchise is moving to Texas. Some are in tears. A Yankee victory is declared; the forfeit win puts the Yanks above the .500 mark with a record of 82-80. The curtain falls on Washington baseball. Bucky Harris, a two-year Yankee skipper and a long-time manager in Washington, witnesses the death of big league baseball in the nation's capital.

Dec 2—   In one of the worst Yankee deals of recent vintage, pitcher Stan Bahnsen goes to the Chicago White Sox for infielder-outfielder Rich McKinney. In five Yankee seasons, Bahnsen went 55-52 and had an ERA of 3.10.

    — In 1972, Bahnsen would win 21 games and help keep the second-place Chisox in their division race with the A's. Bahnsen would follow with seasons

---

*This year Milwaukee is in the AL West. In 1972 the Brewers will move to the AL East with the transfer of the Washington franchise to Texas.

of 18, 12 and 10 wins, and would retire after 1982 with 146 victories. McKinney, a valuable all-purpose player for Chicago, played out of position at third base for New York in 1972. He would hit .215 with three extra-base hits in 37 games and move on to Oakland in 1973.

1972

The Yankees at 79-76 will finish fourth, but only 6½ games behind division-leading Detroit. The club will be led by Bobby Murcer, who will hit .292 and belt 33 of New York's 103 homers. Reliever Sparky Lyle will save 35 games, and Fritz Peterson (17-15) and Steve Kline (16-9) will lead the starters.

Mar 22— In one of New York's most spectacular steals, the Yankees obtain Sparky Lyle (P) from Boston for Danny Cater (INF) and minor leaguer Mario Guerrero (SS). The Yankees are desperate for bullpen help—the entire Yankee bullpen recorded only 12 saves in 1971.

— Cater, a solid .276 lifetime hitter, batted .290 in two years as a Yankee regular. He would hit only .237 for the Red Sox in 1972 and would never again play as a regular. Guerrero would hit .233 in 66 games as a Bosox rookie in 1973 but would not become a regular shortstop until 1978 (with Oakland). But Lyle blossomed. He would begin a brilliant seven-year Yankee career in 1972 with 35 saves, a 9-5 record and an ERA of 1.91 over 59 games.

Apr 6— The Yanks' Opening Day game against Baltimore is cancelled. For the first time in major league history, the season is late in starting because of a players' strike that will last nine days. The Yankees will have seven games cancelled, including the opening four-game series scheduled at home against Baltimore.

Apr 16— The strike is settled and the season starts where the schedule dictates. Actually, the makeshift opener was postponed yesterday in Baltimore and rain ruins today's doubleheader, too. But the Orioles manage to capture a seven-inning first game, beating Mel Stottlemyre, 3-1. The nightcap is postponed by rain. Yankee pitching coach Jim Turner is wearing a professional baseball uniform for his 50th season, and it is believed he is the first man able to make that claim.

Apr 18— The Yankees for the first time open with a home night game at the Stadium (only home opener the Yankees ever play under the lights) and blank Milwaukee, 2-0, with Steve Kline pitching a three-hitter. Only 11,319 fans attend.

— The Yankees drew fewer than one million fans for the first year since 1945, this in a season in which they would be part of a pennant race for the first time since 1964. True, the Yankees lost four home dates to the strike, and some fans, moreover, were turned off by the strike. But the Mets had loads of enthusiastic supporters; Yankee fans were growing weary of the agonizing slow rebuilding of their club. Yet, New York would go 46-31 at home.

Jun 1— Milwaukee beats New York, 9-8. In the bottom of the 12th inning, Yankee reliever Jim Roland takes the mound and walks four batters on 16 pitches to lose his only decision in his 16-game Yankee career.

Jun 3—   The Yankees beat Chicago, 18-10, with an eight-run 13th inning highlighted by three-run homers by Thurman Munson and Bobby Murcer. Bobby becomes the 11th Yankee to score five runs in one game. He is the first Yankee to score five runs since Hank Bauer in 1953. (No Yankee has scored so many runs since this date.)

— Ralph Houk pointed with pride to Murcer and Munson, who happened to be good friends and the best all-round players in the AL at their positions. Murcer would win the Gold Glove in center field this year and Munson was one year away from beginning a streak of three Gold Gloves in a row. Murcer would pace the AL with 102 runs and his .537 slugging average was only one point behind Carlton Fisk in the AL East. Fisk, the Boston rookie, posed a threat to Munson's newly won position as the league's top catcher. Thurman hit .280 and led the Yanks in game-winning hits in 1972.

Jul 21— The Yankees hang double shutouts on California, Fritz Peterson winning the opener, 6-0, and Mel Stottlemyre the nightcap, 3-0. Half of Stottlemyre's 14 wins this year (against 18 losses) will be by shutout. He is riding a stretch of four consecutive shutouts against the Angels.

Jul 25— The NL wins a 10-inning All-Star Game, 4-3, in Atlanta. Bobby Murcer, the only Yankee to take part, is hitless in three at bats, and AL Manager Earl Weaver strikes out with Yankee fans.

— Sparky Lyle's conspicuous absence from the AL squad infuriated Yankee fans, who faulted Weaver for neglecting the sensational reliever. Lyle was almost single-handedly keeping New York in the pennant race, sometimes saving two games in one day. He would finish with 35 saves, breaking Ron Perranoski's 1970 major league record of 34. To many, the failure to enlist Lyle's support was not only a snub of Sparky but was hurtful to AL chances. (Lyle's save record has since been broken; however, he retains the Yankee club record for saves in one season.)

Aug 7—   Colorful Yankee greats Yogi Berra and Lefty Gomez are inducted into the Baseball Hall of Fame. Berra, who gathered 336 of the 339 Baseball Writers' votes cast, has a little fun with his famous slip-up of 25 years ago, telling those assembled, "I guess the first thing I ought to say is that I thank everybody for making this day necessary." Gomez was selected for induction by the Committee on Veterans. Berra's Hall plaque notes that the three-time MVP winner "played on more pennant-winners (14) and World Champions (10) than any player in history." Gomez' points out that he "won 20 or more games four times in helping Yankees to win seven pennants."

— Bernie Allen in the annual Cooperstown game hit three home runs and Murcer had one as the Yanks beat the Dodgers, 8-3. Allen had nine homers on the season.

Aug 8—   On the day the Yankees sign a 30-year lease (beginning in 1976) to play in city-owned Yankee Stadium, the Tigers, 4½ games in front of the Yanks in a tight AL East race, arrive for a four-game stay. New York wins the opener of the series, 4-2. Tomorrow the teams will split a doubleheader.

Aug 10— The Yankees complete their first crucial series in eight years by beating Detroit, 1-0, behind the pitching of Steve Kline and take three of four games in the set. More than 45,000 pennant-hungry fans attend on a Thursday afternoon. New York (55-49) is only 2½ games behind Detroit (58-47). And the Yankees are the hottest team in the league, having gone 19-11 in July and working on a 19-14 August.

Aug 12—   Johnny Callison belts a grand slam homer in the seventh inning, helping
           the Yankees defeat Milwaukee, 10-6, at the Stadium.

           — Callison, a one-time star for the Phillies, having hit 30-plus homers with
           100-plus RBIs in both 1964 and 1965, was an aging veteran in his first
           Yankee season. He would hit only nine homers with 34 RBIs in 92 games.
           In 1973 he would hit .176 for the Yanks and end a fine 16-year career in
           the majors.

Aug 29—   Bobby Murcer hits for the cycle in an 11-inning game. He is the first Yankee
           to hit for the cycle since Mickey Mantle did it in 1957. The Yankees and Texas
           split a twinbill.

Sep 8—   In Boston, the Yankees lose for the third straight day and the Red Sox' sweep
           is a severe setback to the Yanks' pennant hopes. New York loses the series
           by scores of 2-0, 10-4 and 4-2.

Oct 24—   In the first of a series of excellent trades, the Yankees obtain infielder
           Fred "Chicken" Stanley from the San Diego Padres for minor league pitcher
           George Pena.

           — Stanley would spend most of the 1973-74 seasons with the Syracuse
           farm club, although he also played a little for the Yankees. In 1975-76,
           Chicken split the shortstop job on the Yanks with Jim Mason. In 1976,
           as a member of the Yanks' first pennant winner in 12 years, he would
           set a club fielding record at shortstop with .983. He would follow this
           with four seasons as the club's utility infielder, hitting .222 (224 for 1,008)
           over eight Yankee seasons.

Nov 24—   New York acquires Matty Alou (OF) from the Oakland A's for Rob Gardner
           (P) and Rich McKinney (INF). Gardner, who was 8-5 for the Yankees in 1972,
           will win one more major league game. McKinney will play four more seasons
           as a reserve and has a lifetime average of .225.

           — Matty joined his brother, Felipe, on the Yanks. The NL batting champ
           was coming off a season's average that matched his lifetime average (for
           15 seasons), .307.

Nov 27—   The Yankees obtain Graig Nettles (3B) and Gerry Moses (OF) from Cleveland
           for Johnny Ellis (C-1B), Charlie Spikes (OF), Rusty Torres (OF) and Jerry
           Kenney (INF-OF). Ellis, Spikes and Torres are three of the Yanks' best
           prospects in the post-Dynasty era; Lee MacPhail and Ralph Houk agree
           that "we are trading tomorrow for today." But none of the three youngsters
           achieves the stardom thought to lie ahead for them. Kenney was a military
           veteran who in five years for New York hit .237 and was the regular third
           baseman from 1969-71. He will play in just five games for the Tribe in 1973,
           his last big league season.

           — The acquisition of Nettles, the greatest all-round third baseman in Yankee
           history, would benefit both "today" and "tomorrow," Nettles in 1983 beginning
           his 11th season with the Yankees. Nettles played in the minors for Billy
           Martin, reached the Twins in 1967, became one of the AL's top power hitters
           with the Indians in 1970 and made himself into an excellent defensive
           player at the hot corner. By the time he became a Yankee, Nettles was the
           league's best third baseman and would remain so for many years. In his first
           10 Yankee seasons, he would hit 230 homers with 759 RBIs.

Two all-time Yankee greats and two of the most quoted players in baseball history were inducted into the Baseball Hall of Fame on August 7, 1972. Commissioner Bowie Kuhn presents Hall plaque miniatures to Lefty Gomez, top, and Yogi Berra, left.

1973

The Yankees at 80-82 will finish fourth, 17 games behind first-place Baltimore. Bobby Murcer will hit .304 and Thurman Munson .301. Both Murcer and Graig Nettles will hit 22 home runs. Mel Stottlemyre will lead the starters at 16-16 and Sparky Lyle will pace the relievers with 27 saves. George Steinbrenner will contemplate the restoration of the Yankees' winning tradition.

Jan 3—   Following weeks of negotiation, a group headed by George M. Steinbrenner buys the Yankees from CBS for a reported $10 million. Reportedly, Steinbrenner's original investment is about 30 percent of the sales price. Mike Burke announces that the 12-member ownership group will be headed by himself and Steinbrenner. But Burke will soon step aside. Steinbrenner says he will not be active in the day-to-day operations of the club. But the Steinbrenner years, perhaps the most charged era in club history, are about to unfold. Steinbrenner, a shipbuilder, will exert a decisive presence in the rescue of once-proud Yankees, now fallen to mediocrity and possibly even to stagnation.

— CBS was expanding when it bought the Yankees in 1964. Its adventure into uncharted waters cost the corporation about $4 million. The enterprise was as artistically dismal as it was an investment bust—from 1965, when CBS bought in, the club finished as high as second only once. CBS Chairman William Paley in 1972 offered the club to Burke, the club president, but Burke couldn't find the necessary big-money partners. Not until Gabe Paul introduced Burke to Steinbrenner did the ball start rolling.

Apr 6—   Boston defeats the Yankees, 15-5, to win its opener at Fenway Park with the designated hitter rule used for the first time. Yankee DH Ron Blomberg (the first DH to come to the plate) walks with the bases loaded in the first inning. Ralph Houk starts the following line-up: Horace Clarke (2B), Roy White (LF), Matty Alou (RF), Bobby Murcer (CF), Graig Nettles (3B), Ron Blomberg (DH), Felipe Alou (1B), Thurman Munson (C) and Gene Michael (SS). Mel Stottlemyre is the pitcher. Nettles homers off Luis Tiant in his Yankee debut.

— Blomberg, an outstanding hitter against righthanded pitching, would fit nicely into the DH mold. He would be the Yanks' DH in 55 of the 100 games he played, hitting a robust .329 with 12 homers on the season. Jim Ray Hart, the solid righthanded power hitter the Yanks would obtain from the Giants within two weeks, would DH in 106 games and hit .254 with 13 homers in 114 games. He would burn up the league early in the year. Celerino Sanchez would DH in 11 games and Johnny Callison in 10 games. Also DH'ing, in fewer than five games apiece, would be Nettles, Munson, Matty Alou, Ron Swoboda, Gerry Moses, Bernie Allen and Duke Sims.

Apr 9—   The Yankees, behind Fritz Peterson who will have a disappointing 8-15 season, lose the Yankee Stadium opener, 3-1, to Cleveland. It is Golden Anniversary Day, marking the 50th anniversary of Yankee Stadium. Bob Shawkey, who pitched and won the first game at the Stadium in 1923, throws out the first ball. Lengthy traditions are fine but lengthy hair must go. Steinbrenner asks Houk to ask several long-haired players to get a haircut.

Apr 29—   Mike Burke resigns as Yankee president but retains his small interest in the club, which he maintains into the early 1980's. Burke quotes from the poem, "An Irish Airman Foresees His Death," and leaves the front office without apparent bitterness. Steinbrenner now can run the club through Gabe Paul, one of the limited partners, who will become the Yanks' chief operating officer.

— This is the start of a major changeover in the Yankee organization. Ralph Houk would leave in the autumn and become skipper in Detroit, and GM Lee MacPhail would leave to become AL president and to be succeeded by Gabe Paul. The Burke-MacPhail-Houk triumvirate would be gone less than a year after the new ownership took over.

May 16— The Yankees beat first-place Milwaukee, 11-4. Thurman Munson's three hits include a homer and a double and he picks off a runner at third base. Sparky Lyle, dazzling the Brewers with his slider, has five straight strikeouts.

May 20— The heretofore stumbling Yankees defeat Cleveland twice, 4-2 and 7-3. In the fourth inning of the nightcap, Roy White hits a grand slam homer, the first of two slams by Roy this year, seemingly igniting the Yankees, who will go 24-12 through June 24.

— White played in all 162 Yankee games, and although his average slipped to .246, he hit 18 homers and stole 16 bases. Roy also led the AL with 639 at bats. And in August he would switch-hit homers for the second time in his career. Having broken in with the Yanks in 1965 (along with Murcer and Clarke), Roy was a nine-year veteran. Only Stottlemyre was his senior in Yankee service.

May 31— Oakland's Ken Holtzman, a 21-game winner this season, beats the Yankees, 6-0, handing New York its sixth shutout this month.

Jun 7— The Yankees, suddenly playing like division contenders, make two big acquisitions—both star pitchers—that many believe will make them the team to beat in the AL East. From San Francisco, at a cost of at least $100,000 (some reports say $150,000), they get Sudden Sam McDowell, who is 1-2 in 18 games for the Giants. From Atlanta, they get Pat Dobson, who is 3-7 in 12 games for the Braves. The Dobson price: Wayne Nordhagen (OF), Frank Tepedino (1B-OF) and two minor league pitchers, Alan Closter and Dave Cheadle.

— McDowell and Dobson would be disappointments. McDowell, who won five AL strikeout championships with Cleveland from 1965-70, won his first two Yankee decisions but would finish 5-8. Dobson, who had won 20 games for Baltimore as recently as 1971, would have a 9-8 year with an ERA of 4.18. Dobson would rebound to have an excellent 1974, however.

Jun 20— The Yankees behind Stottlemyre defeat Baltimore, 2-1, and charge into first place where they will remain until August 1. This is the latest date for New York to be in the top spot in a decade.

— New York City and all of Yankeeland were alive with excitement. Fans were finding their way to 161st Street again notwithstanding publicity about muggings at the Stadium, and not to mention irritating parking problems for motoring Stadium-goers. The Yanks' final home attendance of 1,262,077 would be the highest since 1964. It would also begin a remarkable streak for George Steinbrenner; in each of his first eight seasons as principal owner, the Yankees would improve their home attendance numbers!

Jun 22—   It is a bad day for Detroit and Tiger Manager Billy Martin, the day after dropping the first game of their series in New York. First, the Tigers get tied up in New York City traffic, and, fearing they would miss the game's start, Martin leads his starters off the bus and onto the subway. but they get on the wrong train and don't arrive at the Stadium until 10 minutes after the team bus arrives. In the game, Martin and two of his players are ejected. And the Yankees win, 5-4.

Jun 23—   The Yankees beat Detroit, 3-2, for their sixth straight win, their third over the Tigers. Murcer's three-run homer provides all the scoring McDowell needs. The Stadium organist is moved to play "It Seems Like Old Times."

Jun 24—   The first-place Yankees win twice, 3-2 and 2-1, sweeping their five-game set with Detroit. The twin-killing extends New York's winning streak to eight (where it will end) and concludes a five-week Yankee rampage.

           — The defending division champion Tigers would never really recover from their dismal four days in the Big Apple and would finish third, 12 games behind Baltimore.

Jul 4—   The first-place Yankees are looking good with 30 wins in 45 games. But they drop both ends of a holiday doubleheader with Boston, 2-1 and 1-0, before 41,693 vocal fans at the Stadium. Murcer's line-drive homer in the opener holds up until the Bosox win with two runs in the ninth off Stottlemyre and Lyle, who are not to be faulted; the Yankee infield literally throws the game away. The nightcap features exceptional pitching by Doc Medich and Roger Moret. The crowd is at first supportive but grows antagonistic and rowdy. Fans boo, firecrackers explode and fights break out. The news that Baltimore has swept its doubleheader and trails New York by only two games is a further irritant. Ron Blomberg, who had his average up to .408 and who, with Murcer, graced the *Sports Illustrated* cover, sees his average dip below .400 for the first time in several days. No one since Ted Williams in 1941 had hit over .400 so late in the season.

Jul 13—   Murcer hits three home runs off Kansas City's Gene Garber at the Stadium. Bobby has a three-run homer and follows with solo homers to account for all New York's five runs. Stottlemyre wins on a shutout, his 39th, putting him in a second-place tie with Red Ruffing on the all-time Yankee list. Stottlemyre will pitch one more shutout, breaking the tie.

Jul 20—   The Yankees sweep a doubleheader from Chicago. Wilbur Wood, who goes 24-20 this year, starts both games and loses both.

Jul 24—   The NL wins the All-Star Game, 7-1, in Kansas City. Murcer and Munson go hitless in five combined at bats. In pitching a scoreless inning, Lyle strikes out Willie Mays on three pitches. It is Mays' final at bat in All-Star competition.

           — Lyle had a tremendous first half. At one point in June he alone had more saves (19) than any combined bullpen total in the league. The second half would not be as spectacular for Sparky, and he would absorb a $500 club fine for giving the finger to a loud-mouth spectator, the gesture made as Lyle left the field after being cuffed around.

Aug 1—   The Yankees lose, 3-2, in Boston. With the game knotted in the top of the ninth, Gene Michael misses a squeeze bunt effort as Munson barrels home—a dead duck. Munson blasts into Carlton Fisk and the pair come up fighting. The Red Sox win in the bottom half when Mario Guerrero singles off Lyle. It is probably the only time that the Cater-and-Guerrero-for-Lyle deal looks good to Boston fans. Fans of both teams can add a new page to the Munson-Fisk rivalry. The two catchers will scrap again in the future.

— Knocked out of first place, the Yankees began to fold. They lost three of four games at Fenway park and suffered through a miserable 9-18 August. They would be 9½ games out of first by month's end. September would not go much better; an 11-16 September record would put the Yankees 27 games out at season's end.

Aug 4— Lindy McDaniel, the long man out of the Yanks' bullpen, who will be 12-6 with 10 saves in 47 games this year, enters in the first inning after a pulled muscle disables Fritz Peterson. He wins, 3-2, in a gutty performance when Horace Clarke belts a 13th-inning home run.

Aug 29— California's Nolan Ryan should have had—but does not—the first no-hitter against the Yanks since 1958. For the Yanks, it is their eighth straight loss (all on the road) and all but ends their pennant chances. Two Angels call for a Munson pop and neither follows through for the only Yankee hit (in the first inning). Ryan wins, 5-0.

Sep 6— The Yankees trade both of the Alou brothers. Felipe's contract is sold to the Expos and Matty's to the Cardinals. Felipe, who hit .271 over three Yankee seasons, hit .236 in 93 games for the Yanks this year. Matty hit .296 in 123 games.

Sep 8— The Yankees defeat Milwaukee, 15-1, and Fred Stanley belts the last grand slam home run at the "old" Yankee Stadium. Chicken's slam strikes the left field foul pole.

— Stanley hit only six homers in his eight-season Yankee career. Everett Scott, another shortstop, who hit the first grand slam at the Stadium, hit only 13 homers in his four seasons (1922-25) as a Yankee.

Sep 30— The Yankees complete their 50th anniversary season at Yankee Stadium. After the game (a Yankee 8-5 loss to Detroit), the doors are closed and renovations begin so that a "new" Yankee Stadium can open for the 1976 season. It is a nostalgic day and many of the some 32,000 leave with souvenirs and momentos from the last game ever played at the "old" Stadium. Manager Ralph Houk, a member of the Yankee organization since the 1940's, resigns. He and George Steinbrenner did not establish the best of working relationships, it appears.

Oct 1— Shortly before the actual dismantling of the Stadium begins, Mrs. Babe Ruth is presented with home plate and Mrs. Lou Gehrig with first base.

Dec 6— The Yankees purchase the contract of shortstop Jim Mason from the Texas Rangers for a reported $100,000. Mason hit .197 in 1972 and .206 in 1973, but he will have a fine 1974 season, hitting .250 in 152 Yankee games.

Dec 7— In a spectacular Yankee trade, the Yankees obtain Lou Piniella (OF) and Ken Wright (P) from the Kansas City Royals for Lindy McDaniel (P).

— McDaniel enjoyed five fine years in New York. He would go on to pitch in a total of 987 games, second most behind Hoyt Wilhelm in baseball history. After going 6-5 over two seasons with the Royals, he would wind up a 21-year career with 141 wins. Piniella, on the other hand, was in his prime. He had two .300 seasons under his belt and would hit .305 in 140 games in New York in 1974. He would give the Yankees a top-notch hitter with a professional, hard-nosed attitude, and he would begin an instant love affair with Looouuu-chanting Yankee fans.

Dec 18— The Yankees sign Dick Williams as manager. Williams is riding high after winning two World Championships in a row in Oakland and he is considered baseball's top skipper. He recently quit the A's because of problems with Charley Finley, the owner.

Dec 21— AL President Joe Cronin rules that Oakland Manager Dick Williams is still bound to the A's and that the contract he signed with the Yankees is not to be honored. Cronin also rules that Ralph Houk is free to sign with the team of his choice, leaving the Yankees without a manager.

— As it turned out, Charley Finley, the A's owner, would have released Williams only if the Yankees agreed to surrender two minor leaguers—Otto Velez and Scott McGregor. For their part, the Yankees were unwilling to give up their two most prized prospects.

1974

With an 89-73 record, the Yankees will finish in second place, two games behind Baltimore. They will boast a trio of .300 hitters in Ron Blomberg, .311; Lou Piniella, .305; and Elliott Maddox, .303. Bobby Murcer will lead the club in RBIs with 88. A pair of 19-game winners, Pat Dobson and Doc Medich, will lead the pitching staff.

Jan 3— George Steinbrenner signs Bill Virdon as Yankee manager after Ralph Houk steps down and Steinbrenner is thwarted in his attempt to bring in Dick Williams.

— Virdon came up through the Yankee organization in the 1950's and later was an outstanding NL centerfielder. As a manager, he won the NL East title in 1972 for the Pirates but was fired late in the 1973 season. Virdon would keep the Yankees in the race until the final days of the season and would be named Major League Manager of the Year by *The Sporting News*.

Jan 16— The Baseball Writers elect Mickey Mantle and Whitey Ford to the Baseball Hall of Fame. It is the first time that teammates are elected on the same day. Of 365 votes cast, Mantle, one of the few to be elected in his first year of eligibility, receives 322 votes. Ford, in his second year of eligibility, receives 284 votes.

Feb 3— Thurman Munson signs a 1974 contract calling for $75,000, making Munson the highest-paid Yankee catcher to date.

Mar 23— The Yankees purchase the contract of outfielder Elliott Maddox from the Texas Rangers for an amount ranging from $35,000 to $100,000, according to reports.

— Maddox, an East Orange, N.J., native, hit no better than .252 in his four previous major league seasons. But in 1974 he would hit .303 in 137 games. In May, Bill Virdon would make his most controversial decision, shifting Bobby Murcer from center to right and inserting Maddox in center. Maddox responded by drawing favorable comparisons with Paul Blair, the AL's best defensive centerfielder.

Apr 2— In a Yankee-Mets exhibition game in Columbia, S.C., Thurman Munson suffers an injury that will have long-range effects. He is struck in the meat hand by a batter's follow-through. X-rays reveal no fracture but Munson's hand will grow worse and more painful. Twice early in the season he will aggravate the injury and miss week-long periods.

— Munson had a severe inflammation of the medial nerve which made it difficult for him to grip the ball. Then he developed bursitis in his throwing shoulder, an injury that didn't completely heal until 1977. But Munson played in pain, throwing side-arm, and played 137 games behind the plate. He would lead AL catchers with 22 errors but would still win a second straight Gold Glove for fielding excellence.

Apr 6— The Yanks in their home opener at Shea Stadium—their temporary two-season home while Yankee Stadium is being renovated—beat Cleveland, 6-1. A crowd of 20,744 sees Graig Nettles smoke a two-run homer, as Mel Stottlemyre racks up the first of what will be four straight Yankee wins.

Apr 14— Nettles is the 10th AL player to hit four home runs in a doubleheader (split with Cleveland) and the first since Bobby Murcer did it in 1970.

— Nettles, usually a slow season starter, had the baseball world abuzz with his start this year. He would hit 11 home runs in April, setting an AL record for the month. Graig would hit 22 homers on the season with 75 RBIs and 74 runs scored.

Apr 24— Nettles has at least one RBI in his 10th straight game, as New York edges Kansas City, 4-3. His streak will end in the next game, one short of the club record set by Babe Ruth.

Apr 26— Stottlemyre beats Texas for his fourth win but afterwards the team is shocked and angered to learn that Gabe Paul has sent half the pitching staff packing— the Friday Night Massacre, it is to be called. Later—years later—Paul will point with pride to this trade. "It broke up the country club," he will say. "There was great camaraderie on those losing clubs." Paul does plenty of trading this spring; in fact, the Yankees will use 44 players, including 19 pitchers, this year.

— The Yankees traded four pitchers to Cleveland in the first of what would be six Yankee deals over a two-week period. Dealt were Fritz Peterson, Steve Kline, Tom Buskey and Fred Beene. The combined record of the four in New York was 156-148, most of this belonging to Peterson (109-106) and Kline (40-37). The four would go a combined 18-32 with the Tribe in 1974. The Yankees received Chris Chambliss (1B), Dick Tidrow (P) and Cecil Upshaw (P). Upshaw would save six games, Tidrow would go 11-9 and Chambliss would hit .243 in 400 Yankee at bats. The latter two would do a tremendous job for the Yankees over the remainder of the 1970's.

May 18— Dan Topping dies and in less than two months (on July 4) Del Webb will also die. Topping and Webb (Larry MacPhail was a third partner in the first three years of the ownership) owned the Yankees from 1945 to 1964. With George Weiss already deceased, Casey Stengel, released in 1960 because he was too old, will be the only surviving kingpin from the 1949-60 mini-dynasty.

May 27— In the third inning of a Yankee loss to Chicago, New York leftfielder Lou Piniella makes two assists, tying a big league record. It is a record held by many but Sweet Lou is only the second Yankee outfielder to make two assists in one inning. (Ben Chapman is the other.)

— The jokes have been many through the years about Piniella's defensive play. Indeed, for a long time he was thought of strictly as a hitter. But studious Yankee fans know there has seldom been a more dependable outfielder than Piniella, who has the knack of making clutch plays. He may not be pretty but he gets the job done, and then some.

May 31— The Yankees sell the contract of Horace Clarke to the San Diego Padres. After seven years as the regular second sacker, Clarke is eclipsed and the position is tangled. Clarke, who played 20 games, is expendable with the recent acquisition of Fernando Gonzalez, who will play 42 games at second. Gene Michael (45 games) and Fred Stanley (15 games) will also work at second.

— In half of his 10 seasons with the Yankees, Clarke, who hit .257, led the Yanks in hits. He was a sure fielder who for six straight seasons (an AL record) led AL second basemen in assists. His play drew (unfair) criticism from the media.

Jun 11— Stottlemyre makes his 272nd consecutive start to set an AL record. But Mel, whose string of straight starts began April 10, 1967, gets no decision in New York's 5-4 loss to California at Shea Stadium. Bill Sudakis accounts for all the Yanks' runs with a grand slam.

Jun 15— The Yankees purchase Rudy May's contract from California for close to $100,000. The Angels were using May in relief. He was 0-1 with two saves.

— May broke into the majors with the Angels in 1965 as one of the best-looking, hard-throwing prospects ever to come into the league. His lifetime mark on coming to New York was 51-76 (pitching for mostly poor teams).

Jun 23— Rudy May in his Yankee debut defeats Detroit, 4-1, on a four-hitter at Shea Stadium. May would have an amazing start in pinstripes; he would next four-hit Baltimore and then six-hit Texas. Rudy would pitch five four-hitters in 1974.

Jul 8— Yankee shortstop Jim Mason ties a major league record with four doubles in a nine-inning game the Yankees win in Texas, 12-5.

— Also on this date, the Yankees solved their sticky problem at second base by purchasing the contract of Sandy Alomar from California for $50,000. Alomar, who was hitting .222 as the Angels' utility infielder, would hit .269 in 76 games and solidify the Yankee infield. New York would win 50 of 80 games after adding Alomar to the roster.

Jul 9— In Kansas City, the Yankees win, 8-2. Graig Nettles hits his first Yankee grand slam homer off Yankee nemesis Paul Splittorff.

Jul 11— Yankee pennant hopes are dampened as Rudy May goes on the disabled list. May suffers a shoulder injury and will not come off the list until August 1.

— May would finish his Yankee season at 8-4 and with a 2.29 ERA. He was one of the AL's outstanding pitchers. With May disabled, Doc Medich took up the slack. The Aliquippa, Pa., native would be named the AL Player of the Month for July.

Aug 12— Mickey Mantle and Whitey Ford are inducted into the Baseball Hall of Fame. Mantle's Hall plaque in part says that Mickey "won league homer title and slugging crown four times" and that he "batted .300 or over in each of ten years with top of .365 in 1957." Ford "paced A.L. in victories and winning pct. three times and in earned-run average and shutouts twice." Both made eloquent speeches, but following the ceremonies, Casey Stengel, as is his custom, put it best. "Yes sir," said Casey. "They were fairly amazing in several respects, and that's the damned truth!"

Aug 18— New York calls up pitcher Larry Gura from Syracuse after Mel Stottlemyre is put on the disabled list with a serious shoulder injury. Gura will win five games in a row, two by shutouts.

— Stottlemyre, the classy sinkerballer, finished his season with a 6-7 record. He would attempt a comeback in next year's spring training, but he has pitched his last game, finishing with a record of 164-139 and an exceptional ERA of 2.97. A healthy Stottlemyre would have meant at least a division title for the Yanks in 1974. And a healthy starting five of Stottlemyre, Dobson, Medich, May and Gura would have been the hottest, if not the best, in baseball.

Aug 31— The Yankees win, 18-6, as Roy White goes five for seven in Chicago. His seven at-bats tie a big league record for a nine-inning game.

Sep 9— The Yankees beat the slumping Red Sox, 6-3. It is New York's first win at Fenway Park since July 31, 1973.

— The Yankees went into first place on September 5 and would capture 12 wins in 14 games thereafter. Meanwhile, Boston, in first place as September began, would lose 10 of 12 games, 7 by shutout, and Baltimore would win 10 straight games, 5 by shutout.

Sep 10— The Yankees purchase the contract of Rangers' outfielder-designated hitter Alex Johnson, who makes his way to Boston where the Yanks and Bosox are playing an extra-inning game. Johnson, the AL's batting champ in 1970, pops a 12th-inning homer to beat Boston, 2-1, and thrust New York into first place. Second baseman Sandy Alomar had saved the game in the bottom of the 11th with a tremendous stop and throw from shallow right field, preventing the winning run from scoring.

Sep 11— The first-place Yankees, in Baltimore for a twi-night doubleheader, try to improve a one-game lead over the Orioles. The opener goes 17 innings and the Birds win, 3-2, on Boog Powell's single. The nightcap is completed well past midnight; behind Gura, the Yankees prevail, 5-1.

Sep 12— Mike Wallace, a young southpaw who wins all six of his Yankee decisions this year, makes his only start in 23 games and combines with Dick Tidrow to outpitch Jim Palmer. New York wins, 3-0. The league-leading Yankees (78-68) vacate Charm City with a two-game lead over the Orioles (75-69).

Sep 14— In Detroit, the Yankees win, 10-7, as the Nettles brothers, Graig and Jim (of the Tigers), each homer.

Sep 17— The Orioles invade Shea Stadium for a three-game series, trailing the Yankees by 2½ games. New York had just scored 10 runs in each of two wins in Detroit. This is the key series of the year, and Baltimore gets off to a winning (4-0) start.

Sep 18— Behind Mike Cuellar (22-10), the Orioles beat the Yankees, 10-4. The Orioles play fine defense, get clutch pitching and make the cerebral plays, too.

Twice after Bobby Grich walks, designated hitter Tommy Davis executes perfect hit-and-run plays, both of which result in runs.

Sep 19— Using only 88 pitches, Dave McNally blanks the Yankees, 7-0. Baltimore (81-70) charges into first place and leaves the Big Apple a half game ahead of New York (80-70).

— The Orioles had an incredible stretch drive, winning 28 of their last 34 games—15 of their wins were one-run victories. The Yankees would courageously rebound from the Oriole series debacle—after many had counted them out—to sweep a four-game home series from Cleveland.

Sep 24— The Red Sox, who will finish in third place, seven games out, and who carry the stigma of folding in the stretch, come into Shea for a twinbill. The Yankees are back in first place by one game, but the Bostons take two, 4-0 and 4-2, inflicting a mortal wound on the Yanks. Luis Tiant pitches a six-hitter in the opener for his 21st victory. Rudy May suffers the loss. In the nightcap, New York's infield makes two errors and Larry Gura loses his only game in six decisions since his recall. Roger Moret gets the win. Meanwhile, the Orioles rally to beat the Tigers and take the top spot. The Shea crowd of 46,448 grows rowdy and the second game is halted for some time while special police break up several brawls in the stands. Questioned afterwards about the violent fans, a frustrated Bobby Murcer, seeing his best chance at playing on a championship team going down the drain, says, "I don't blame them. Tonight, I wanted to get up there and whale with them."

Oct 1— In Milwaukee, the Yankees lose, 3-2, and are eliminated from the race on the next-to-last day of the season. Baltimore wins its fifth division title in six seasons. It is a cold, wintry night and County Stadium is empty. The Brewers tie the game in the eighth inning on a catchable hit to right field that Murcer probably would have eaten up. But Bobby is not in the line-up. Murcer was hurt playing peacemaker in a hotel lobby fight between teammates Rick Dempsey and Bill Sudakis. Milwaukee wins in the 10th inning. Gracious in defeat, George Steinbrenner throws a party for his team after the game. The next day, New York beats Milwaukee and an exciting season is past.

— Besides the familiar group of heroes—Murcer, Munson, Nettles and Lyle— two others had special reason to feel good about their play down the stretch. Chris Chambliss, who had felt unwanted by his teammates and who struggled at the plate, hit in 18 consecutive games for the longest streak by a Yankee in 14 seasons. Pat Dobson, who had been a disappointment in 1973 and in the first half of this season, finished with 13 wins in his last 17 decisions.

Oct 22— In the biggest one-for-one trade in Yankee history, New York deals outfielder Bobby Murcer to San Francisco for outfielder Bobby Bonds. It is the first-ever even-up trade of two $100,000-salaried players, and it shocks Murcer, an institution at the Stadium, and Yankee fans. This is Gabe Paul's deal; Murcer never becomes accustomed to power-hitting at Shea Stadium, hitting only 10 homers in 1974, and the Yankees are overstocked with lefthanded hitters. So Paul is looking for righthanded power to protect against all the southpaws the Yanks saw in 1974. But he trades away a player with strong psychological ties to Yankee fans, a player with five 20-homer seasons and two .300 seasons. And a player who is only 28 years old. Several fine seasons would follow for Bobby, first with the Giants and then the Cubs, before his return to the Yankees in 1979.

— Bonds was perhaps the most talented all-round player in the game, but he was coming off a down season (.256, 21 HRs, 71 RBIs). Bonds, who had two seasons (1969 and 1973) of 30 homers and 30 stolen bases, was fast, powerful, versatile and strong-armed. He was also a strikeout king, having led the NL in that department three times.

Dec 31— Catfish Hunter signs a five-year contract with the Yankees worth about $3.35 million. The package includes a salary, a deferred salary, a signing bonus, a deferred bonus, life insurance policies for the family, provisions for legal fees, etc. It is a milestone in baseball contracts; the previous high salary was around $250,000, drawn by Dick Allen. Hunter's signing adds special joy to New Year's Eve celebrations for Yankee fans.

— Hunter was probably baseball's best pitcher, having won 21, 21, 21 and 25 games over the last four seasons. Catfish had been declared a free agent after the 1974 World Series when an impartial arbiter, Peter Sietz, ruled that Oakland owner Charley Finley failed to honor certain contractual obligations he had with Hunter. The bidding for Hunter began December 18 with nearly every major league club entering the auction. Clyde Kluttz, the Yanks' minor league director and the scout who originally signed a teenaged Hunter for Finley, was still close to Catfish and proved instrumental in signing the fellow North Carolinian.

1975

The Yankees at 83-77 will finish third, 12 games behind first-place Boston. It is a disappointing season for a team that many experts picked to win. Newcomer Bobby Bonds will hits 32 homers and steal 30 bases, Thurman Munson will hit .318 with 102 RBIs, Graig Nettles will have 91 RBIs and Chris Chambliss will hit .304. Catfish Hunter at 23-14 will share for the league leadership in wins.

Mar 29— Dick Tidrow, the Yanks' third biggest winner in 1974, begins the first of two stints on the disabled list. He will come off on April 19 and go back on the list on August 19 for the rest of the season. All 37 of his outings in relief, he will finish 6-3 with five saves.

— The pitching staff would sorely miss Tidrow during his disabled periods. Especially the bullpen, which recorded a disappointing 20 saves! Sparky Lyle would have his least productive season as a Yankee, going 5-7 with six saves in 49 games.

Apr 8— On Opening Day in front of 56,204 fans in Cleveland, Bobby Bonds makes his Yankee debut and goes hitless in four at bats. But the Indians have a debut of their own and it is decisively more successful: in his first at bat as the new player-manager of the Tribe, Frank Robinson—baseball's first black manager—wallops a crowd-pleasing home run off Doc Medich. The Indians win, 5-3.

Apr 11— The Yankees play their second, and last, home opener at Shea Stadium before 26,212, including New York Gov. Hugh Carey, Mayor Abe Beame, former mayor John Lindsay, Toots Shor, Robert Merrill and anti-war demonstrators. Catfish Hunter, in his Yankee debut, is beaten by Detroit, 5-3. Bobby Bonds, who singles and doubles, fans with the sacks filled in the seventh.

Apr 13— Doc Medich snaps a three-game losing streak by shutting out Detroit, 6-0, for New York's first win of the year. However, the Tigers win the nightcap of today's doubleheader, 5-2.

Apr 29— Yankee first baseman Bob Oliver takes part in six double plays, tying an AL record for first basemen, and five twin-killings are started by Fred Stanley, who ties a major league record for the most double plays started by a shortstop. But Cleveland wins, 3-1.

May 31— In Texas, Catfish Hunter pitches a brilliant one-hitter and wins, 6-0. Cesar Tovar's sixth-inning single is the only Ranger hit. It is the fifth time since 1967 that Tovar personally has spoiled a no-hitter.

— After a slow start, Hunter responded with his fifth 20-win season in a row. He would be the Yanks' first 20-game winner since Fritz Peterson's great 1970 season, and he would tie Jim Palmer of Baltimore for the most wins in the AL with 23. His ERA, thanks in large measure to seven shutouts, would be a sterling 2.58. Catfish would also lead the AL in complete games (30) and innings pitched (328). His complete game total would be the highest in the AL since Bob Feller's 36 in 1946, and his innings pitched total the highest by a Yankee since Carl Mays' 337 in 1921.

Jun 10— It is the liveliest playing of the National Anthem in Yankee history. At Shea Stadium, a U.S. Army unit celebrating a gathering of the Sons of Italy and the Army's 200th anniversary, fires two cannons while the Anthem is played before a game with the Angels. One of the cannons, too close to the center

Rudy May delivers a pitch in his first stint with the Yankees in 1975. The classy southpaw was 14-12 on the year and had a 3.06 ERA.

field fence, blows a huge hole in the fence halfway through 10 volleys. The fence catches fire but the firing continues until all 10 blasts are sounded. Mission completed.

Jun 17— Two of the Yankees' top outfielders, Lou Piniella and Elliott Maddox, go on the disabled list, putting the Yanks' outfield situation in disrepair for the rest of the season. Piniella has an inner ear disorder, undergoes mid-season surgery, returns July 6 and plays occasionally thereafter. Maddox recently suffered a serious knee injury on the wet field at Shea Stadium and is out for the season. He will need two operations and will never regain the form that made him one of the league's better players.

— In 74 games in 1975, Piniella hit a very un-Piniella-like .196; his next lowest average as a Yankee through 1982 would be .277 in 1981. The injury to Maddox may have hurt the club even more. Maddox, who was hitting .307 in 55 games, later sued the City of New York, charging negligence in maintaining the field at city-owned Shea.

Jun 24— The Yankees win in Baltimore, 3-1, and move into first place where they will remain for five days. This is the middle victory of a rare three-game Yankee sweep at Memorial Stadium.

Jun 26— The Yankees charge into Fenway Park for a four-game series that in intensity is reminiscent of the old days. New York is 19-5 so far in June and holds first place by 1½ games over Boston. But the Red Sox win the opener, 6-1, behind Luis Tiant. Carlton Fisk homers in his first game of the year and rookie sensation Fred Lynn has three RBIs.

Jun 27— Boston beats the Yankees, 9-1, and takes a half-game lead in the AL East. Rick Wise blanks the Bronx Bombers until Bobby Bonds hits a towering homer with two outs in the ninth. Both Bonds and Roy White are playing with hobbling leg injuries, compounding the outfield problems for Bill Virdon.

Jun 28— The Yankees down Boston, 8-6, and regain first place. The winning runs score in the eighth inning on No-Neck Williams' run-scoring double and Thurman Munson's sacrifice fly. Munson drives in three runs.

Jun 29— Roger Moret outduels Catfish Hunter and Boston regains first place, winning, 3-2. The Red Sox (40-30) lead the Yankees (41-32) by a half game and will not be threatened again. The series draws 136,187 fans, a new record for a four-game set at Fenway.

Jul 15— The NL wins the All-Star Game, 6-3, in Milwaukee. Bonds, Munson and Nettles go a combined two for nine at the plate and Nettles steals a base. Hunter, who goes two innings plus two batters in the ninth and gets charged with two runs, is the loser.

Jul 27— At Shea Stadium, the Red Sox sweep the Yankees, winning a pair of shutouts. Hunter loses a tough 1-0 opener to Bill Lee and Roger Moret wins the nightcap, 6-0. Bill Virdon's dismissal may be in the winds. The Yanks are sputtering and Billy Martin, fired by Texas, has been out of work for a week.

Aug 2— Billy Martin replaces Bill Virdon as Yankee manager with the club's record at 53-51. Martin's popular appointment is announced to a cheering Old Timers' Day crowd at Shea Stadium. Those old enough remember Billy's tremendous contributions to Casey Stengel's great teams before Billy's exile to Kansas

City in 1957. No one has ever worn the pinstripes with more pride, and the fans appreciate that. The team responds with a 5-3 victory over Cleveland.

— Virdon was victimized by injuries but he never got close to his players or aroused the emotions of the fans. He did not fit the image George Steinbrenner had of a gung-ho leader, and he did not put butts in the seats. Martin's charisma was exactly what the Yankees needed, and his record of turning poor teams into successful franchises was almost unprecedented, even before his grand triumphs in New York and Oakland. Gabe Paul warned Steinbrenner that he and Billy would have conflicts. But the signing was made after negotiations in Colorado, where Martin was fishing. The Yanks would finish 30-26 under Martin, then put it all together in 1976.

Aug 18— Bucky Harris, the Yankees' manager in 1947-48, is inducted into the Baseball Hall of Fame. The Hall plaque for Bucky, elected by the Committee on Veterans, notes that he served "40 years in majors as player, manager and executive, including 29 as pilot..."

Aug 20— Yogi Berra rejoins his old buddy, Billy Martin, on the Yankees as a coach. He was recently fired as manager of the Mets, a club he took to the 1973 NL pennant. Berra was last with the Yankees in 1964, as manager.

Sep 27— The Yankees take a doubleheader from Baltimore, 3-2 in 10 innings and 7-3. Baltimore's double loss gives Boston the division title. Boston will finish 4½ games ahead of the Orioles. Hunter, the first-game winner, bags No. 23.

Sep 29— Casey Stengel dies at the age of 85 in Glendale, Calif. One of Casey's most happy moments in his last months was when he learned of Billy Martin's appointment as Yankee manager, filling his old shoes. Said sportswriter Jim Murray, "Well, God is certainly getting an earful tonight." On November 4 a memorial service will be held for Casey at St. Patrick's Cathedral in New York City, city of his greatest triumphs.

Nov 22— The Yankees obtain outfielder Oscar Gamble from Cleveland for pitcher Pat Dobson, who was 11-14 in 1975 and 39-37 in three Yankee seasons. Gamble is a solid young hitter who hit 15 home runs in 121 games this past season.

— Gamble would excite Yankee fans with his timely hitting in 1976. He would hit 17 homers with 57 RBIs. Dobson would be Cleveland's top winner at 16-12 and would eventually finish with 122 wins in the majors.

Dec 11— In a brilliant day of wheeling and dealing, the Yankees obtain Willie Randolph (2B), Dock Ellis (P) and Ken Brett (P) from the Pirates for Doc Medich (P). Also, the Yankees acquire Mickey Rivers (OF) and Ed Figueroa (P) from the Angels for Bobby Bonds (OF). Randolph, Ellis, Rivers and Figueroa will be key members of the Yanks' 1976 AL pennant-winning team.

— Medich and Bonds were excellent players who were destined to travel from team to team over the next several years. Medich, who put himself through medical school, was 49-40 as a Yankee. He would go 8-11 for the Pirates in 1976. Bonds would enjoy several fine years, yet he always kept his suitcase packed. His one season in New York was an enigma. Although he again reached the 30 homer-30 stolen base plateau, he struck out 137 times and was a more consistent hitter batting first than third. In fairness to Bonds, he played the season with damaged knees. Playing in a new league, foreign city (to Bonds), a tough hitters' park and with a changing cast of outfielders, he still put big numbers on the board.

1976

At 97-62, the Yankees will capture the AL East by 10½ games over second-place Baltimore. It is the first title of any kind for the Yankees since 1964, ending a 12-year drought. League MVP Thurman Munson will drive in 105 runs and Graig Nettles will win the home run championship with 32. A solid pitching staff will be led by Ed Figueroa, a 19-game winner, and by Sparky Lyle, the AL leader in saves with 23. The Yankees will win the AL crown in an exciting Championship Series but will be swept by Cincinnati in the World Series.

Mar 17— Commissioner Kuhn orders an end to the spring training lockout that began March 1. He believes progress is being made in contract negotiations between the players and owners over the new Basic Agreement.

— Billy Martin had little time to put his squad together. While the Yankees (10-7 in the exhibition season) responded to his style of aggressive, mistake-forcing baseball, they were picked by most experts to finish third, behind Boston and Baltimore.

Mar 24— Thurman Munson signs a new contract and becomes the sixth Yankee ever to make $100,000 in one season, joining Joe DiMaggio, Mickey Mantle, Bobby Murcer, Bobby Bonds and Catfish Hunter in that distinction. Thurman, who would have been a free agent following the 1976 season, signs a four-year pact calling for progressive salaries of $120,000, $155,000, $165,000 and $195,000.

Apr 10— In Milwaukee, the Yankees lead 9-6 in the bottom of the ninth when Sparky Lyle surrenders a grand slam homer to Don Money and the Brewers appear to have a 10-9 win. But first base umpire McKean says no; he had called time out just before the home run pitch. The Brewers lose both the obligatory argument and the game by a final score of 9-7.

Apr 15— In their first home opener against Minnesota, the Yanks treat 52,613 fans at renovated Yankee Stadium to an 11-4 win. Yankee starter Rudy May falls behind, 4-0, but the clawing Yanks battle back, scoring one run in the third, four in the fourth and six in the eighth. Mickey Rivers and Oscar Gamble each have three hits to lead the 14-hit attack. Dick Tidrow gains the win with a splendid relief effort.

— The crowd was just as pleased with the day's ceremonies and events in the "new" Stadium. James Farley, Toots Shor, Pete Sheehy and Mel Allen, all having long associations with the Yankees, were special guests, and Bob Shawkey, who pitched and won the 1923 opener, threw out the first ball. Bobby Richardson delivered the invocation and Robert Merrill sang the National Anthem. Joe DiMaggio, Mickey Mantle, Whitey Ford, Don Larsen, Mrs. Babe Ruth, Mrs. Lou Gehrig, Joe Louis, Frank Gifford, Johnny Lujack and Arnold Tucker were among those present. The "new" Stadium was beautiful. The only disappointments were the nonworking $3 million-plus scoreboard and the failure of the replicated Gothic facade to adequately replace the real, distinctive thing. The facade crowned the Stadium; the replication crowned the scoreboard. But the big thing was that fans no longer had to peer around support columns in the newly cantilevered Stadium.

Apr 17— Hours after being named the first Yankee captain since Lou Gehrig, Thurman

Munson, in a 10-0 win over Minnesota, becomes the first Yankee to hit a home run in the renovated Yankee Stadium.

Apr 21— Inside the Stadium's Memorial Park (located behind the left field wall), a new plaque is installed in honor of Joe McCarthy, "...one of baseball's most beloved and respected leaders..."

— Later in the summer, a similar plaque would be hung in tribute to Casey Stengel, a personality who "...brightened baseball for over 50 years with the spirit of eternal youth..."

May 4— In California, the Yankees win, 2-1, behind Dock Ellis and take first place in the AL East. New York will soon pull away from the pack and will take the division title in a runaway. Ellis will finish 17-8 and win Comeback Player of the Year honors (Lou Piniella was runner-up for the award).

May 20— A rumble marks the opener of a four-game series at Yankee Stadium with the Bosox. In the sixth inning, Lou Piniella becomes Dwight Evans' second victim at the plate. Sweet Lou is a dead duck and he does the only thing he can do, cleanly blasting into catcher Carlton Fisk. Piniella and Fisk come up fighting, as dugouts and bullpens empty. In the melee, Boston pitcher Bill Lee's eye is blackened and ligaments are torn in his pitching shoulder. When play resumes, the Red Sox overcome a 1-0 deficit and win, 8-2, with Carl Yastrzemski homering twice.

— Lee's injury disabled him for many weeks. Following a 17-9 record in 1975, the Spaceman would finish this year at 5-7. His loss was a severe blow to the Red Sox, and Lee was bitter over the incident. He would blame Nettles, Rivers and Martin and rap the Yankees whenever the mood struck him.

May 21— The Yankees beat Boston, 6-5, in 12 innings, after tying the score in the ninth on a pinch-hit double by Otto Velez and two fly balls. In the 12th, Denny Doyle commits a two-out error and Graig Nettles and Kerry Dineen follow with singles for the Yanks' victory.

— Last night's scuffle sidelined Piniella and Rivers, and Dineen, at Syracuse, received a 6 p.m. call to report to the Stadium. Traveling by airplane and George Steinbrenner's chauffeured limousine, Dineen made the scene by the fifth inning. His Yankee career was short but sweet: in a total of 11 games, Kerry hit .345 (10 for 29).

May 22— Catfish Hunter is marvelous, pitching 11 innings and allowing only three hits in beating Boston, 1-0. His own hitters make only five hits. Leading off the bottom of the 11th, Willie Randolph walks and is sacrificed to second by Roy White. Randolph scores the game's lone run on a single by Carlos May.

— This would be Hunter's last big-winning season. Even so, he would fall to 17-15 and for the first season since 1970 fail to win 20 games. But Catfish would pitch 299 innings and be the pitcher the Yanks counted on to win the big games.

May 23— Boston wins a see-saw battle, 7-6, and gains a split of the series witnessed by 167,267 fans. Nevertheless the Yankees have a record of 21-12 and retain a six-game lead over the Red Sox. Roy White's extra-base hit knocks in a run in the ninth but White is out trying for a triple and the rally fizzles.

Jun 15— In an attempt to strengthen their pitching for the expected rugged pennant stretch, the Yankees make two big deals. One, the purchase of pitcher Vida Blue from Oakland for $1.5 million, will be voided in three days by Commissioner Kuhn because of the large sum of money (and absence of other players) involved. From Baltimore, the Yankees accept Ken Holtzman (P), Doyle Alexander (P), Grant Jackson (P), Elrod Hendricks (C) and minor leaguer Jimmy Freeman in exchange for Rudy May (P), Tippy Martinez (P), Scott McGregor (P), Dave Pagan (P) and Rick Dempsey (C).

— This was a controversial trade, most observers feeling the Yankees were hoodwinked. In the short run the trade was good for New York. Concluding the season as Yankees, Alexander went 10-5, Holtzman 9-7 and Jackson 6-0. In the long run, the Orioles harvested the greater yield. May would have two big-win seasons in Baltimore, Martinez would be their ace left-handed reliever for many years, McGregor (the Yanks' top draft pick in 1972) would blossom into one of the league's premier southpaws and Dempsey would take his place among the game's top catchers. But back to the short run, the Yanks needed to make this deal to claim the 1976 AL pennant.

Jul 13— In Philadelphia, the NL wins the All-Star Game, 7-1. Hunter allows two runs in two innings, Munson goes zero for two at-bats, Rivers goes one for two and Chambliss is unsuccessful as a pinch-hitter. A fifth Yankee picked for the team, rookie Willie Randolph, has to be scratched because of an injury. Randolph will finish at .267, steal 37 bases and play second base like no other Yankee since Bobby Richardson. Randolph is the first AL rookie to have his name on the All-Star Game ballot.

Jul 16— In Texas, the Yankees win, 3-0, as Ken Holtzman hurls a two-hitter. Holtzman permits only a fourth-inning single by Jeff Burroughs and a seventh-inning single by Roy Howell.

Jul 25— The Yankees beat Baltimore, 6-5, at Yankee Stadium and complete a three-game sweep of their nearest rival. New York has opened up a 14½-game lead and the AL East title is all but sewn up. Ironically, the Orioles will win 13 of 18 games against the Yankees this season.

Aug 2— For the fourth time since joining the Yankees in mid-June, Doyle Alexander has a legitimate no-hit bid ruined. At the Stadium, he defeats Detroit, 1-0, on two hits. He keeps the Tigers hitless through six innings; Rusty Staub singles in the seventh.

Aug 7— In the bottom of the ninth, Chris Chambliss hits the first grand slam homer by a Yankee in more than two years, but it is not enough and Baltimore wins, 7-4, on Old Timers' Day. Chambliss will finish with 17 homers, 96 RBIs and a .293 average.

Aug 9— Yankee pitching coach Bob Lemon, who was 207-128 for the Indians from 1946-58, is inducted into the Baseball Hall of Fame. Lemon will have a successful season as a coach; his Yankee pitchers will lead the AL with a team ERA of 3.19.

Aug 25— The Yankees edge Minnesota, 5-4, in a 19-inning game at the Stadium that takes five hours and 36 minutes to complete. The Twins score all four of their runs in the second inning and are then held scoreless for 17 consecutive innings. Grant Jackson gets the win, when, in the bottom of the 19th, Gamble walks, takes second on Randolph's sacrifice and scores on Rivers' single. In the field, Randolph makes 13 assists and accepts 20 chances, both AL records for a second baseman in an extra-inning game.

— Rivers was a lead-off hitter who packed punch in the clutch. He drove in 67 runs, hit .312 and hit safely in 20 straight games at one point. He led Martin's Bronx Bandits with 43 stolen bases, the most by a Yankee since Snuffy Stirnweiss stole 55 in 1944.

Aug 27— In California, Yankee pitching is again first-rate, as the Yankees and Angels play a scoreless tie for 14 innings. In the 15th, New York scores five runs and Jackson finishes the whitewash, winning his second extra-inning game in three days.

Sep 11— The Yankees lead the AL East by 12½ games and Martin signs a new three-year contract, reportedly in the neighborhood of $300,000. But it is spiced with some provisions that will bother Billy in the future. For example, Martin is not allowed to criticize George Steinbrenner or the front office in matters of personnel, and Billy must meet with club officials upon their request. He can be fined or fired (without further pay) for the violation of any of the provisions.

Sep 12— A crowd of 52,707 journeys to Yankee Stadium to see the Yankees and Tigers split a doubleheader.

— The Yankees would draw 2,012,434 home fans this year, an increase of nearly three-quarters of a million over the 1975 season. They would top the two million mark for the first time since 1950.

Sep 25— The day after snapping a six-game losing streak, the Yankees win in Detroit, 10-6, and with Baltimore's loss, clinch the division championship. Doyle Alexander wins the clincher. But the real heroes are Billy Martin, who led his team to a remarkably peaceful and easy title, and George Steinbrenner, who in just his fourth season of ownership, put the club back at the top of the standings.

Sep 29— In Boston, Graig Nettles blasts a second-inning grand slam homer off Luis Tiant and the Yankees march to a 9-6 victory.

— After getting off to his customary slow start, Nettles peppered homers throughout the season's second half. He would win the AL home run crown with 32, five more than Baltimore's Reggie Jackson and Oakland's Sal Bando, becoming New York's first home run king since Roger Maris hit 61 homers in 1961.

Oct 9— The Championship Series between the Yankees and Royals opens in Kansas City and the Yankees win, 4-1, behind Catfish Hunter's five-hitter. The teams will split the first four games of the playoffs, trading wins back and forth.

Oct 14— Before a record-setting crowd of 56,821 at Yankee Stadium, the deciding game goes to the Yankees, 7-6, and New York wins its 30th AL pennant. Hitting stars of the game include Rivers, who has four hits and scores three runs; Munson, who has three hits and two RBIs; and Chambliss, who has three hits, three RBIs and scores two runs, and who led all batters in the playoffs with a .524 average. New York builds a 6-3 lead but in the eighth inning George Brett belts a three-run homer to tie. Leading off the ninth, Chambliss wallops Mark Littell's first pitch on a rainbow arc over the padded blue fence in right field for the pennant-winning round-tripper. Chris is mobbed by hundreds of fans as he attempts to circle the bases, touching off a wild celebration. New York City, the home of much mediocrity in professional sports teams in the 1970s and a city with severe financial problems, has a victory to shout about. "Thanks, Chris, we needed that," Mayor Beame tells Chambliss in the riotous clubhouse.

Oct 17— Cincinnati, already winner of Game 1 of the World Series, takes Game 2, 4-3, the closest game of the Series. It is the Yanks' first-ever attempt at night baseball in World Series competition and it is a freezing cold night in Cincinnati. Behind Catfish Hunter's last-stand pitching, the Yanks overcome a 3-0 deficit and tie the game. But with two out in the last of the ninth, Ken Griffey reaches second base on shortstop Fred Stanley's throwing error and is singled home by Tony Perez.

Oct 21— Behind Johnny Bench's pair of homers, the Reds win Game 4, 7-2, at Yankee Stadium and sweep the Series in four games. For the losers, Munson goes four for four and finishes the Series with six consecutive hits.

— Munson thus concluded a fantastic year that would gain him league MVP honors. He took his place among the majors' top hitters, hitting .302 in the regular season, .435 in the Championship Series and .529 in the World Series. During the regular season, Munson joined Lee May and Carl Yastrzemski as the AL's only 100-RBI men and he fell just four RBIs shy of May's league-leading 109. When Munson won the MVP, he would tell the press, "I'm proud that I won. I know it wasn't politics. I won this on my ability."

Nov 4— Baseball's first-ever free agent re-entry draft is held at the Plaza Hotel in New York City and the Montreal Expos make Reggie Jackson the first player selected. The Yankees are one of 13 clubs that obtain negotiating rights to Jackson.

Nov 18— The Yankees sign free agent pitcher Don Gullett to a reported six-year $2 million contract. Gullett is the first player to sign with the Yanks under the new rules. The injury-prone southpaw was 11-3 for Cincinnati in 1976.

— Gullett would have a fine season in 1977, going 14-4 despite more injuries. But Don would suffer a double tear in the rotator cuff of his pitching shoulder and on July 8, 1978, would pitch his last game. He would win 109 major league games and go 18-6 as a Yankee.

Nov 29— The announcement that Reggie Jackson has signed with the Yankees is made at the Americana Hotel in New York City. Reggie has agreed to a five-year pact for approximately $3 million, spurning offers of considerably more money because George Steinbrenner outhustled the competition, according to Jackson. Reggie is crowned a Yankee by Roy White, who places a Yankee cap on Reggie's head. Thurman Munson, who had advised Steinbrenner to sign the rightfielder, is also present. Reggie gives the quote-hungry press a good one right off the bat. "I didn't come to New York to become a star," says Reggie. "I brought my star with me."

— In five years with the Yankees, Jackson created excitement and contro-versy. He helped make the Yankees winners, hit 144 home runs and perhaps had a presence around town that no Yankee has had since Babe Ruth. But it was a double-edged sword; Reggie would have problems with some of his teammates, with Billy Martin, and, ultimately, with George Steinbrenner, his biggest supporter. Reggie would be an enigma in the Big Apple. He would be Number One, but he would pay a heavy price; he would be a Number One target for some as well as a Number One star for many.

George Steinbrenner, right, accepts the 1976 AL Championship Trophy for his team at the New York Baseball Writers' annual dinner. The Yankee owner is owed most of the credit for bringing the Yankees back to the upper ranks of baseball. Lee MacPhail, AL president and former Yankee executive, makes the presentation.

1977

The Yankees will finish first, 2½ games ahead of both Baltimore and Boston at 100-62. Graig Nettles (37 HRs, 107 RBIs) and Reggie Jackson (32 HRs, 110 RBIs) will lend power to an attack spearheaded by .326-hitting Mickey Rivers. Sixteen-game winners Ron Guidry and Ed Figueroa will lead a balanced mound staff, and Sparky Lyle will go 13-5 with 26 saves and win the Cy Young Award. The Yankees will defeat Kansas City and Los Angeles in the Championship Series and World Series to become World Champions for the first time in 15 years.

Jan 6— Thurman Munson signs a two-year extension to his contract, reportedly for $260,000 in 1980 and $275,000 in 1981. But almost immediately, Munson is upset; Reggie jackson is making more than he is.

— Munson's argument: When he signed his four-year deal last year George Steinbrunner assured him no other Yankee (save for Catfish Hunter) would draw a higher salary. Reggie's considerable deferred salaries had to be taken into consideration in fixing Munson's remuneration, the catcher argued. Differences and misunderstandings marked the Munson-Steinbrenner negotiations, but Munson finally got a new package, reportedly one that paid him $1.7 million over five years.

Jan 31— Joe Sewell is elected to the Baseball Hall of Fame by the Committee on Veterans. Sewell, who hit .312 lifetime playing for the Indians (1920-30) and Yankees (1931-33), was the hardest man in history to strike out. Sewell will be inducted into the Hall in Cooperstown, N.Y., on August 8.

Mar 1— Reggie Jackson arrives at spring training with a self-definition. "I think Reggie Jackson on your ball club is a part of a show of force. It's a show of power. I help to intimidate the opposition, just because I'm here." Jackson fails to endear himself with his new teammates who are understandably proud of last year's achievements—some wonder why they need Reggie in the first place. Backup catcher Fran Healy will be Reggie's only close friend on the club all year.

— The Yankees were into free agent baseball, not because they liked it, but because it was there. Baseball fans everywhere watched their every move, Yankee haters hoping for the worst. Mickey Rivers arrived in Ft. Lauderdale on this date upset about several front office requests. He wanted to be traded. Mickey Klutts, the heir-apparent at shortstop, would break a bone in his hand and lose his big chance. George Steinbrenner would explode at Billy Martin in the locker room after the Yankees lost to the Mets. Graig Nettles, one of several players unhappy with his contract, would jump the club, and Ron Blomberg would sustain yet another serious injury and end a Yankee career in which he hit .302 in 400 games. It would be a turbulent training camp.

Apr 5— New York acquires Bucky Dent (SS) from the White Sox for Oscar Gamble (OF), Dewey Hoyt (P), Bob Polinsky (P) and cash.

— With Klutts hurt, Dent was given the shortstop job over the popular and competent Chicken Stanley. Dent quickly won the respect of his teammates and the adulation of the fans. Although he would hit only .247 in 158 games, Bucky would give the Yankees the most consistent defensive play at shortstop since Tony Kubek's prime years.

Apr 7—   The season opens at the Stadium where 43,785 fans cheer a 3-0 win over Milwaukee and Reggie Jackson's impressive Yankee debut. Reggie gets two hits, runs the bases aggressively and sparkles in the field. Catfish Hunter pitches impressive three-hit ball for seven innings before being struck on the left instep by a line drive, the start of an injury-riddled year for the righthander who will finish 9-9. Sparky Lyle cleans up and collects a save.

Apr 21—   The Yankees beat Toronto,* 8-6, and for the second straight day Martin's pulled-from-a-hat line-up is successful. Jackson picks the names and the Yanks make 13 hits. Batting eighth, Chris Chambliss has a homer, two doubles and five RBIs. Now 4-8, the Yankees have climbed out of last place.

Apr 25—   Jackson returns to Baltimore where he played last year before becoming a free agent. He hits two doubles and a game-winning home run as the Yankees win their sixth straight, 9-6. An exciting baseball evening is marred by ugly and violent scenes in Memorial Stadium. The mood is mean. Reggie's every move is booed, he is hung in effigy and all night he has to dodge objects flung from the stands. Fights erupt everywhere and when the game ends, Nettles has to wrestle a fan and hold him for the police. The Yanks will take two out of three in "The Land of Pleasant Living."

Apr 29—   Since recently-obtained pitcher Mike Torrez has yet to show, Manager Martin gives Ron Guidry a starting assignment in Seattle. Ron, who has only one other major league start (in 1975), pitches into the ninth inning, and with relief help from Lyle, wins, 3-0.

May 5—   A candy bar, preliminarily named "Reggie, Reggie, Reggie," will indeed be named for Reggie Jackson. The idea was hatched several years ago when Reggie said that if he played in New York a candy bar would be named after him.

May 8—   The Yankees, now in first place, beat Oakland, 10-5, for their 14th win in 16 games. Munson has a home run, triple and two singles.

May 13—   Martin is fined $2,500 for comments he made about not having a third catcher and for his failure to meet with Gabe Paul on the matter. Ed Figueroa wins a three-hitter, 3-0, over California for his fourth consecutive complete-game win.

May 22—   The Yankees and Orioles complete a key five-game series with a double-header at the Stadium. Baltimore wins the opener for its third straight win. Guidry, in his third start, gains a nightcap victory, 8-2, and for the third time lasts until there is one out in the ninth.

May 23—   Boston wins, 4-3, at the Stadium, but the big story is just hitting the news stands; the latest issue of *Sport* magazine carries an article by Robert Ward quoting Jackson as saying "I'm the straw that stirs the drink. It all comes back to me. Maybe I should say me and Munson but really he doesn't enter into it...Munson thinks he can be the straw that stirs the drink but he can only stir it bad." Munson, the acknowledged leader of the Yankees, is furious, and so are many of his teammates. Back at the Stadium,

---

*The American League expanded this year to include Toronto and Seattle.

Reggie snubs his teammates after a homer by entering the dugout at the opposite end, not where they gathered to congratulate him. Then, in the eighth inning, Jackson overruns a single and allows the hitter to reach second, ultimately scoring Boston's winning run. Reggie compounds his problems.

May 29— Chris Chambliss hits a two-run homer and Jackson, who strikes out three times, has his handshake ignored by Munson who crosses the plate before Chambliss. The Yanks win behind Figueroa, 5-2, his seventh straight complete game.

May 30— Back-to-back homers by Nettles and Jackson help Torrez and the Yankees win in Boston, 5-4. Breaking the ice in their now chilly relationship, Munson shakes hands with Jackson after Reggie's homer. Rivers' throw to Munson in the ninth gets Butch Hobson and saves the game.

Jun 4— A second-inning rally, highlighted by two Jackson doubles, helps the Yankees to an 8-6 victory in Chicago where White Sox Manager Bob Lemon says, "I can't wait to get the papers every day and read what's going on with the Yankees. It's like *Mary Hartman, Mary Hartman*." But the Yankees are rolling and will be back in first place in four days.

Jun 17— The Yanks lose, 9-4, at Fenway Park. Boston's hitters belt six homers and Boston fans pelt Mickey Rivers in center field with various objects. The Red Sox leap over the Yankees into first place.

Jun 18— Before a national television audience, Billy Martin and Reggie Jackson nearly duke it out. Martin feels Jackson failed to hustle after Jim Rice's bloop hit which Rice runs into a double. Martin yanks Jackson, and when Reggie questions the move, Billy has to be restrained from taking on his rightfielder.

— The ugly scene was embarrassing in itself and disclosed still another rift— one between Martin, who never wanted Jackson in the first place, and Jackson, who believed Billy held him in low esteem as a ballplayer. It wasn't all Reggie's fault, of course, but in less than half a Yankee season he managed to alienate his manager, most of his teammates, Yankee fans and much of the press. Jackson was at a career lowpoint and he had only one ally who mattered, and he mattered the most—George Steinbrenner. Steinbrenner was extremely loyal to Jackon (an irony in that George would be accused, in a subsequent time, of dumping Reggie) in Reggie's darkest hour. As for Martin, he almost lost his job over the incident. Somehow— Steinbrenner and his diplomacy deserve the credit—the club survived a potentially explosive situation.

Jun 19— The Red Sox beat the Yankees, 11-1, completing a three-game sweep. Gabe Paul, Martin and Jackson, whose 14-game hitting streak ends today, have a meeting that goes badly, but tomorrow Fran Healy will help negotiate a truce.

Jun 24— The first-place Red Sox invade Yankee Stadium boasting a seven-game winning streak and a five-game lead over the Yankees. Most of the 54,940 spectators groan as the Bostons take a 5-3 lead. After the first two Yankees are retired in the bottom of the ninth, Willie Randolph laces a triple. Then comes the Yanks' single most important hit of the year: Roy White tags a two-run homer off Bill Campbell to send the game into extra innings.

Jackson's pinch-hit single in the 11th gives the Yankees a 6-5 win. New York will then sweep the series, which attracts 157,460 leather-lunged fans, 5-1 and 5-4.

Jun 30— In Toronto, the Yankees win, 11-5, and creep within a half game of first place as recently acquired Cliff "Heathcliff" Johnson hits two homers in one inning to tie a big league record, and three altogether in the game.

— In 56 Yankee games this season, Johnson would hit .296 with 31 RBIs. He would hit .381 against the Blue Jays and collect six of his 12 homers off them.

Jul 8— The Yankees win the first game of a four-game set in Baltimore, 7-5. Munson, batting .317, drives in four runs and Nettles knocks in the other three. The Birds will rebound to win the final three games and drop the Yankees to third place.

Jul 19— For the third time in history, the All-Star Game is played at Yankee Stadium and the NL wins, 7-5. Martin manages and plays five Yankees—Randolph, Jackson, Nettles, Munson and Lyle. Randolph sets an All-Star Game record for the most assists by a second baseman in a nine-inning game (6). In five at-bats, Willie has one hit and drives in a run. A crowd of 56,683 is on hand.

— That White should make the key hit was fitting in the eyes of many Yankee fans who considered the soft-spoken, sophisticated leftfielder the epitome of traditional Yankee class. He did his job, did it well and was lost in the neon lights of the Broadway stars who shared the same locker room. Roy was in his 13th Yankee season and made a lot of admirers overlook his weak arm, White's only flaw as a ballplayer. Batting second most of the time, Roy would display excellent bat control, hit 14 homers, steal 18 bases and score 72 runs.

Jul 24— The regular season resumes with New York three games behind first-place Baltimore and with rumors afloat that Martin will be fired. Gabe Paul assures Billy that he is still in charge. When Billy takes the line-up card out to home plate, a large Yankee Stadium crowd gives him one of several great ovations. Tomorrow Steinbrenner will reveal the Seven Commandments by which Martin will be judged.

Jul 26— The Yankees and Orioles open their final 1977 series. The Yanks trail, 4-2, when Cliff Johnson hits a pinch-hit two-run homer in the ninth inning. Jackson leads off the bottom of the 10th with a home run and the Yanks win, 5-4. The Birds will win tomorrow, 6-4, and the Yanks will take the finale, 14-2.

Aug 10— Opening a home stand, the Yankees beat Oakland, 6-3, behind Guidry's seven-hitter. From this date through the completion of the 1978 World Series, Guidry will go 37-4 in regular season and post-season play.

— The Yankees are starting some tremendous streaks of their own. After winning their final game on a West Coast trip, the Yanks returned home in third place, five games out of first (now occupied by Boston). Several changes are made. Jackson becomes the regular clean-up hitter (Steinbrenner wanted this and George would be proved correct); Piniella, who would hit .330 in 103 games this year, becomes an everyday player; and Torrez, who will go 14-12 for the Yanks, is put into a four-day rotation.

And the Yankees would win seven of the eight home games and 40 of 50 games down the stretch.

Aug 14— Emergency starter Dick Tidrow allows only two hits in six innings and the Yankees rout California, 15-3. Nettles hits a three-run homer and Rivers has a lead-off homer among his four hits.

— Because of injuries to several starting pitchers, Tidrow, a relief pitcher in recent years, was asked to make the first of seven starts. He would save the day by going 5-0 as a starter. Overall, Tidrow would finish 11-4 with a 3.16 ERA in 49 games.

Aug 23— In Chicago, the Yankees win, 8-3, and go into first place for the first time since July 9. Torrez wins his seventh straight complete game, Rivers goes five for five and Nettles hits his 30th homer to tie for the league lead.

Aug 28— Guidry on his 27th birthday allows only two hits as he faces just 28 batters, striking out eight, walking none and beating the visiting Rangers, 1-0. He will have another shutout in his next start, too, blanking the Twins.

Aug 30— Mickey Rivers, who hits at a .405 clip in August, leads off the bottom of the 11th inning with a home run and the Yankees beat Seattle, 6-5. It is Mickey's third hit of the game. For the second straight game, Lyle is the winner in relief, his 11th win.

Aug 31— In the bottom of the ninth, Graig Nettles wallops his second homer of the game and the Yankees beat Seattle, 5-4. Lyle wins in relief for the third consecutive game, an AL record.

Sep 10— Toronto bombs the Yanks, 19-3. It is the most runs scored against New York at the Stadium since a 19-1 Detroit win in 1925. Toronto's Roy Howell, who will finish with 44 RBIs in 103 games, knocks in nine runs.

Sep 13— Boston visits Yankee Stadium, trailing New York by 1½ games. Before more than 55,000 fans, Guidry strikes out the side on only 10 pitches in the first frame of the opener. The Red Sox take a 2-0 lead in the second inning, but the Yankees go on to win, 4-2. Guidry hurls a five-hitter and finishes strongly, fanning the final two Boston batters.

Sep 14— In perhaps the year's most tense game, Ed Figueroa and Reggie Cleveland pitch brilliantly, matching goose-egg for goose-egg through eight innings. Yankee outfielders sparkle, especially Jackson, who makes two spectacular catches. In the bottom of the ninth, Munson singles and Jackson steps in. On a full count, Reggie cracks a 430-foot homer into the right-center field bleachers for a 2-0 victory; Figueroa wins his 15th. The loss puts the Red Sox 3½ games back. Although they salvage the final game and will, within a week, win two games from the Yankees at Fenway, the Red Sox are dead.

— This was a great moment not only for Jackson but for Steinbrenner, the justification for signing Reggie now beyond any doubt. And Reggie had finally won over a good portion of the fans. He knocked in his 92nd and 93rd runs on his way to 110 RBIs, most by a Yankee since Mickey Mantle's 111 RBIs in 1964. His 39 doubles were the most on the club since Tommy Henrich's 42 in 1948. And he saved his best clutch hitting for the stretch run.

Sep 27— At Yankee Stadium, the Yankees pull out a 2-1 win over Cleveland. Tidrow pitches strongly into the eighth and Lyle gets the win. In the ninth, with the score, 1-1, Munson leads off with a single and moves to second on a wild pitch. Thurman takes third on a Piniella bunt and scores on another wild pitch.

— Munson finished fast to end up at .308 with 18 homers and 100 RBIs. It is the third straight season in which Munson hit .300 or better and knocked in 100 runs. For Munson, a catcher, to reach the twin .300/100 plateaus three seasons in a row was remarkable. The last American Leaguer to do it was Cleveland third baseman Al Rosen (1952-54).

Oct 1—   Baltimore beats Boston to eliminate the Red Sox from contention (the day after Boston had eliminated Baltimore) and the Yankees are division champs. The Yanks watch it all on TV as they sit through a rain delay of nearly three hours. The Yanks eventually lose, 10-7, to Detroit, but the loss is academic. The club celebrates with a champagne party and Billy Martin drinks with Gabe Paul and Reggie Jackson. The Yankees will win the meaningless finale the next day for their 100th win, most Yankee wins in 14 years.

Oct 6—   Having won yesterday's opener of the Championship Series, Kansas City runs into a Ron Guidry three-hitter and loses, 6-2, at the Stadium. The Yanks' Cliff Johnson ties the game, 1-1, with a fifth-inning homer and delivers a run-scoring double in a three-run sixth inning. A controversial play by Hal McRae in the top of the sixth arouses the Yankees and sets the tone for an intense, aggressive Series. McRae knifes through Willie Randolph on a brutal slide at second base while a tying run scores.

Oct 8—   Following a Royal win in Game 3, the Yankees rebound to win Game 4, 6-4, in Kansas City and force a deciding game. Nettles suffers from fuzzy vision after blasting Frank White in a takeout slide but remains in the game as New York takes a 4-0 lead in the early going. Kansas City cuts the lead to 5-4 in the fourth but Lyle puts out the fire and faces only 16 batters in getting the final 15 outs. The Yankees win, behind a 13-hit attack, four of the hits by Mickey Rivers.

Oct 9—   The Yankees win Game 5 in Kansas City, 5-3, and the pennant. Manager Martin benches Reggie Jackson, who is having a poor Series (he finishes at .125) and who has difficulty hitting southpaw Paul Splittorff. Paul Blair, the defensive genius, gets the nod in place of Jackson. The first inning is marked by a brawl at third base between Nettles and Brett, and going into the eighth inning the Royals lead, 3-1. Jackson delivers a pinch-hit run-scoring single. Kansas City, now trying to protect a one-run lead, opens the ninth with Dennis Leonard, author of a Game 3 four-hitter. Blair produces a lead-off single and Roy White walks. Larry Gura takes the mound and Rivers ties the game by singling home Blair. White goes to third. Mark Littell allows Randolph a game-winning sacrifice fly, and another run scores on a George Brett throwing error. Over the final 6⅔ innings, Torrez and Lyle blank Kansas City on only four hits, and Sparky is the winner for the second straight day. Johnson (.400) and Rivers (.391) are the Yanks' top hitters. In the victorious locker room, Martin pours champagne over George Steinbrenner and kids, "That's for trying to fire me." The owner roars in jest, "What do you mean, 'try'? If I want to, I'll fire you." Then they embrace. The Yankees are next treated to a wild welcome home by their fans at Newark airport.

Oct 11— The Yankees beat Los Angeles, 4-3, in 12 innings at the Stadium for their first win in World Series play since Game 6 of the 1964 Series. Lyle allows only one hit in the final 3⅔ innings to win his third consecutive post-season game. In the bottom of the 12th, Randolph, who homered earlier, leads off with a two-base hit. Munson is walked and Blair singles home the winning run. But the Dodgers will regroup to win Game 2.

Oct 14— The Series shifts to Los Angeles, and although another Reggie-Billy feud is threatening to upstage the Series, Mike Torrez gains the headlines with a fine seven-hitter. He outduels Tommy John and the Yankees win, 5-3. Torrez slips up only once, allowing a three-run homer to Dusty Baker to tie the game in the third. But Rivers, who has three hits, knocks in the winning run on a fourth-inning groundout. Torrez retires the final 11 Dodgers in order.

— Guidry would fire a four-hitter the next day, winning 4-2. Piniella would rob Ron Cey of a home run and Jackson would blast a homer. But then the Dodgers would pummel the Yankees, 10-4, cutting the Yanks' lead to three games to two.

Oct 18— Reggie Jackson belts three consecutive homers and thrills a crowd of 56,407 at Yankee Stadium as the Yankees win the Series in six games. Reggie goes three for three and walks, scores four runs (to tie a record) and knocks in five in the 8-4 New York triumph. In the second, Reggie walks and Chambliss belts a two-run homer to make the score, 2-2. In the fourth, Munson singles and Jackson lines a two-run homer. In the fifth, Jackson cracks another two-run homer and New York leads 7-3. Then in the eighth, Reggie—against a third pitcher and for the third straight time on the first pitch—wallops a tape-measure solo homer into the blackened bleachers. The Stadium rocks with chants of "Reggie, Reggie, Reggie." When Mike Torrez, who goes the distance for his second complete-game win of the Series, catches Lee Lacy's bunt pop-up for the game's final out, a wild celebration ensues.

— The locker room scene was wild and the focus was on Jackson who set a record with five homers in one World Series. Jackson also led all hitters in slugging (1.250), batting (.450), RBIs (8), runs (10) and hits (9). Reggie and Martin, who earlier in the day was assured that he was coming back in 1978 and was given a bonus, toasted each other. Martin was now a World Champion for the first time since he was a Yankee player in 1956. The Yankees would be given a tremendous ticker-tape parade through Manhattan as New Yorkers saluted their champion Yankees.

Nov 22— The Yankees sign relief pitcher Rich "Goose" Gossage, their No.1 pick in the recent free agent re-entry draft. The Gossage contract is said to be worth $2,750,000 over six years. Scout Birdie Tebbetts warns the Yankees against letting any American League contender get the Goose, who in 1977 saved 26 games and posted an ERA of 1.62 with Pittsburgh. Gossage is the most intimidating pitcher in the game.

— Ideally, the Yankees would have the perfect bullpen—righthanded Gossage, lefthanded Lyle and Rawly Eastwick (who would be signed in December) as the long reliever. But Lyle would become unhappy. He would regard the bullpen as overcrowded, keeping him from getting enough work in save situations. And one month after winning the Cy Young Award, Sparky would feel vastly underpaid.

The 1977 World Series belonged to Reginald Martinez Jackson. Especially his was Game 6, in which he hit three consecutive homers on three consecutive pitches. Top, Reggie acknowledges the cheers of the Yankee Stadium crowd after his return to right field following his second homer. Bottom, he admires the flight of his third homer off knuckleballer Charlie Hough. The ball goes into the black seats behind center field.

1978

The Yankees will finish at 99-63, in a first-place tie with Boston, whom they will beat in a single-game playoff. Ron Guidry goes 25-3 with a 1.74 ERA and has one of the most spectacular years in Yankee history. Ed Figueroa, at 20-9, is right behind Guidry and Goose Gossage leads the league with 27 saves. The power-hitting attack once again is led by Reggie Jackson (27 HRs, 97 RBIs) and Graig Nettles (27 HRs, 93 RBIs). In the post-season, the Yankees will down Kansas City and Los Angeles to win their second straight World Championship.

Jan 13— Joe McCarthy, Yankee manager from 1931 to 1946, dies at his farm outside Buffalo, N.Y. He was 90.

Feb 25— Spring training is four days old and Sparky Lyle arrives in Ft. Lauderdale where he is greeted by a high school band playing "Pomp and Circumstance," pompom girls, majorettes and a sign reading, "Welcome to Ft. Lauderdale, Sparky—Finally." It is George Steinbrenner's surprise party for Lyle, the ultimate practical joker. Lyle will go 9-3 with nine saves in 59 games this season.

Mar 16— Attempting a comeback after a 1977 arm injury, pitcher Andy Messersmith (who was 5-4 for Atlanta in 1977) is hurt again in an exhibition game. Cliff Johnson fields a grounder at first base but his toss to Messersmith, covering the bag, is behind the pitcher. Andy reaches back, falls and suffers a shoulder separation.

— Messersmith had been tremendous in camp and seemed a sure bet to make the starting rotation. He would pitch a few games this season (0-3) but his career is all but ended.

Mar 27— George Steinbrenner names Al Rosen Yankee president and says he will be less involved in club activities. Gabe Paul had resigned as president in December and returned to the Indians.

Apr 8— New York opens the regular season in Texas. The Yankees lose, 2-1, on Richie Zisk's ninth-inning homer off Goose Gossage. It is the first game with their new teams for both Zisk and Gossage, free agents after the 1977 season.

Apr 13— The Yankees beat Chicago, 4-2, behind Ron Guidry and before 44,567 fans at Yankee Stadium in the home opener. Roger Maris, in his first appearance at the Stadium in over 11 years, joins Mickey Mantle in raising the 1977 World Championship flag. The M&M flag raising was arranged by the resourceful producer of such dramas, George Steinbrenner. The crowd cheers, and cheers some more when Reggie Jackson hits a three-run homer off Wilbur Wood in the first inning. Reggie is showered with Reggie Bars—the candy named after him—which the fans are given.

Apr 14— The Yankees have an off day but are required to attend a charity luncheon. Sparky Lyle, Thurman Munson, Graig Nettles and Mickey Rivers are no-shows. Each is fined $500. "If this club wants somebody to play third base, they've got me. If they want somebody to go to luncheons, they should hire George Jessel," quips Nettles. Old-time comedian Jessel will send Nettles a telegram: "Thanks for getting my name in the paper."

Apr 17— Billy Martin and Earl Weaver nearly brawl during a 6-1 Baltimore win at the Stadium. After an Oriole batter is dusted, Weaver charges the field and threatens retaliation. Martin enters a swearing war with the enraged Weaver, who has to be restrained from attacking Billy—probably a stroke of luck for Weaver. The next day Jackson hits a ninth-inning homer off Tippy Martinez and the Yankees beat the Orioles, 4-3.

Apr 22— Roy White heroics. In the seventh inning he robs Milwaukee's Charlie Moore of a homer and in the 12th he knocks in the tally that produces a 4-3 Yankee win at Yankee Stadium. White will play in 103 games, his fewest as a Yankee since 1967 and will hit .269.

Apr 25— In Baltimore, Yankee righthander Jim Beattie, recently recalled from Tacoma, makes his major league debut against Jim Palmer, who is closing in on his 200th victory. Jim Spencer's 100th career homer helps New York win, 4-3, but there is a ninth-inning scare when Sparky Lyle allows two runs and has the tying run on third base and the winning run on first when he finally gets the third out.

May 7—   The Yankees beat Texas, 3-2, before some 50,000 fans in a 12-inning Helmet Day game at the Stadium. Chris Chambliss sends everyone home in the 12th with a fourbagger. The win goes to Goose Gossage, who pitches four hitless innings. After a shaky start, Gossage now has two wins and two saves in his last four games. New York's record is 15-10.

May 14— Two days after New York loses in Kansas City when outfielders Reggie Jackson and Paul Blair collide, allowing Amos Otis a gift inside-the-park homer, Kansas City again beats the Yanks, 10-9, when Mickey Rivers decides not to throw home as the winning run scores. On the plane, an upset Billy Martin yells at Lou Piniella (whose two-run double had tied the game) and has a loud and unfortunate argument with Thurman Munson whom he admired and loved like a son. Four days later, Rivers will replace an injured Roy White and escape from everyone's doghouse with a game-winning triple.

          — Rivers' inclinations to occasionally not be 100 percent in the game were more frequent this year, and there was no way to discipline him. Fines would only aggravate the problem. Rivers was upset over not being allowed to run at will; he would steal only 25 bases this year. He hit only .265. But when he turned it on, Mickey was a devastating offensive player.

May 26— Thanks to Jim Spencer's pinch-hit grand slam homer in the bottom of the seventh, the Yankees capture their fifth straight win by beating Toronto, 4-3, for reliever Sparky Lyle. Sadly, Catfish Hunter is forced to go on the disabled list and heads home to North Carolina, his great career in jeopardy. Hunter joins Don Gullett and Roy White on a growing disabled list.

May 29— New York wins in Cleveland, 2-0, as Andy Messersmith and Rawly Eastwick combine on a one-hitter. Jim Norris, a .283 hitter this year, singles in the first inning for the only Indian hit. Eastwick picks up one of his two Yankee wins when Graig Nettles belts a two-run seventh-inning homer. The Yankees will end the month three games behind first-place Boston, a club that goes 23-7 in May.

Jun 2—   Guidry wins his eighth consecutive victory in Oakland, 3-1. The Rajun Cajun strikes out 11. Gossage fans the final two A's, as two runners dance off the bases in the ninth.

Jun 7— Guidry extends his personal winning streak to nine games and ends a Yankee losing streak at four games by beating Seattle, 9-1. Ten Mariners go down on strikes. Reggie Jackson homers twice and Roy White and Bucky Dent also homer. But the Yanks have lost seven of their last nine games and reports that Billy Martin's managerial job is in jeopardy are rampant.

Jun 10— Besides absorbing a tough 4-3 loss in 12 innings to California, the Yankees lose Bucky Dent to a hamstring pull. Also this date, Yankee catcher Mike Heath earns the everlasting respect of Billy Martin. In the ninth inning, after Bobby Grich blasts into Heath (but is tagged out), the rookie catcher on the next play himself dishes out punishment to Carney Lansford steaming home, but Heath is ejected from the fray.

— Five games behind Boston, the Yankees traded Ken Holtzman (1-0) to the Cubs and received minor leaguer Ron Davis in what turned out to be a great deal for New York. Holtzman wasn't being pitched and Davis, who had been languishing as an inconsistent starter in the Cubs' system, would be successfully converted to a relief pitcher by the Yankees.

Jun 12— Guidry turns in another stopper performance in Oakland, winning 2-0 while fanning 11.

Jun 13— Roy White homers from both sides of the plate in the same game, as the Yankees defeat the A's, 5-3. But Willie Randolph hurts a knee and joins Dent on the disabled list. Making matters worse, Mickey Rivers also has knee problems.

— This was the fifth time White switch-hit homers, having done it in 1970, 1973, 1975 and 1977. He is second to Mickey Mantle in switch-hit homer games in the AL. Tom Tresh is the only other Yankee to do it up to this time.

Jun 14— New York edges Seattle, 10-9. Cliff Johnson's eighth-inning homer ties the game, and after the Mariners score twice in the top of the 10th, reserve outfielder Paul Blair hits a three-run, two-out homer.

— Also on this date, the Yankees acquired Jay Johnstone (OF) and Bobby Brown (OF) from the Phillies for Rawly Eastwick (P). The colorful Johnstone would deliver clutch hits for New York, and Brown would have a fine year in 1980. Eastwick never found his niche on the Yankees but through no fault of his own. He was to be one of the few new era free agents not to have great success with the Yankees. The next day the Yankees would make another key acquisition—outfielder Gary Thomasson, who would hit .276 (32 for 116).

Jun 17— Ron Guidry is remarkable, striking out 18 California Angels to set an AL record for lefthanders. A screaming, clapping throng at the Stadium sees the strikeout display fall just one short of the big league record of 19. (But Guidry breaks a 59-year-old Yankee club record held by Bob Shawkey.) New York wins, 4-0—Ron's 11th straight triumph.

— Guidry was on his way to 248 strikeouts, breaking Jack Chesbro's 1904 record of 239 strikeouts. Also on this date, Mickey Rivers went on the disabled list after being hit on the hand by a pitched ball, resulting in a hairline fracture. The Yankees had three middle fielders—Randolph, Dent and Rivers—disabled, while their fourth, catcher Thurman Munson, played in great pain. Boston, meanwhile, had a comfortable seven-game lead.

Jun 19— The injury-riddled Yankees go to Boston for three games. There the Red Sox, scoring six runs in the eighth inning of the opener, maul New York, 10-4. The Yankees are now eight games back and tied for third place.

Jun 20— The Yankees rebound by beating Boston, 10-4. The big hit—one of the most important of the season—is substitute infielder Fred Stanley's grand slam homer off losing pitcher and former Yankee teammate, Mike Torrez. Reggie adds a three-run homer.

Jun 21— Pitchers Jim Beattie and Catfish Hunter are roughed up by the Red Sox, 9-2. The first 1978 New York-Boston confrontation is thus a Red Sox victory.

— The Yanks left Beantown eight games down. In some circles, they were written off as contenders. Worse, Hunter was to be placed on the disabled list and the promising Beattie would be returned to Tacoma for seasoning. But Beattie would come back and would finish at 6-9 in 25 games.

Jun 26— Boston enters New York and extends its lead to 9½ games by winning the first of a two-game series behind Dennis Eckersley, 4-1, before about 50,000. Rumors say Billy Martin will be axed, but the Yanks say no. George Steinbrenner says the emphatic denial "should end the speculation that has been developing of late concerning Billy's job." Clyde King is added to the coaching staff and rightfielder Reggie Jackson becomes the designated hitter.

Jun 27— In a 14-inning, four-hour-plus marathon, the Yankees outlast Boston, 6-4, to split the series, Lyle winning in relief of Guidry. Graig Nettles, always reliable in the clutch, sends everyone home with a home run.

Jul 2— Guidry's record becomes 13-0, the best start in Yankee history, with a 3-2 win over Detroit in the first of two games at the Stadium. In the nightcap, Gary Thomasson's three-run homer with two out in the ninth inning helps beat the Tigers, 5-2. Gossage has a save and win on the day. Guidry in his next start will lose his first game as Milwaukee's Mike Caldwell (22-9) blanks New York, 6-0.

— It was solely Guidry's excellence that kept the Yankees within shouting distance of the Red Sox. In winning his first 13 decisions, Louisiana Lightning set a new Yankee record (breaking the record of the scout who signed him, Atley Donald). Guidry's 25-3 season record would compute to a winning percentage of .893, the highest in history for a 20-game winner. Ron's league-leading ERA of 1.74 would be the lowest in the AL since Luis Tiant's 1.60 in 1968. (But Tiant did not have to face designated hitters.) The league hit a feeble .191 against Guidry, who was also a stopper— 14 of his 25 wins came immediately after a New York defeat. And the Yankees would win 30 of the 35 games Ron started. Guidry would be only the second unanimous Cy Young Award winner. Ironically—and perhaps most amazing of all—on a club that the public perceived as made up totally of card-carrying millionaires, Guidry reportedly made all of $38,500 in 1978!

Jul 3— At Fenway Park, Dennis Eckersley personally defeats the Yanks for the third time in 12 days as the Red Sox win, 9-5. Injuries force Ed Figueroa (elbow) and Thurman Munson (knee) from the game. Tomorrow's game will be rained out and rescheduled for September.

Jul 9—   In Milwaukee, Don Gullett's arm is in pain as he pitches what turns out to be his last big league game. The Brewers beat New York for the third straight day (the Yankees will finish with an 0-7 record at County Stadium). The All-Star Break mercifully halts play, the Yankees 11½ games back of Boston, which has a phenomenal record of 57-26. Gullett is 4-2 in his last big league season.

Jul 13—   On the first day of the season's second half, George Steinbrenner and Billy Martin have a productive meeting, and some line-up changes are made. Steinbrenner meets with the team and vows that the pennant can still be won. "I'm not going to lie down and die like a dog, and neither are you," George tells the assembled Yankees in his first 1978 visit to the clubhouse.

Jul 14—   The Yankees defeat Chicago, 7-6, in an 11-inning game Goose Gossage wins in relief of Ron Guidry. Cliff Johnson's pinch-hit homer in the ninth ties the game and Graig Nettles' single wins it for the Yanks in the bottom of the 11th. Johnson will hit .184 this year.

Jul 16—   Kansas City prevails, 3-1, dropping the Yanks into fourth place, 13 games behind Boston. The Yankees have lost eight of their last 10 games. Thurman Munson's painful knees won't let him catch and a depressed Reggie Jackson is benched with lefthander Larry Gura on the mound.

Jul 17—   Jackson defies Billy Martin by bunting against orders and is suspended for five days. Failing one attempt to sacrifice in the bottom of the 10th, Jackson is signaled to hit away, but he continues bunting even after third base coach Dick Howser verbally tells him the sacrifice is off. Jackson strikes out on a foul bunt, the Yankees fail to score and Kansas City goes on to win, 9-7, in 11 innings. Billy Martin can barely control himself. The low point of the season is at hand. The next night Boston's lead would swell to 14 games. A Jackson-Martin blowup is inevitable.

              — Earlier in the day, Jackson told George Steinbrenner he was unhappy with being a part-time DH. After his suspension statement, Martin observed, "Nobody's bigger than this team. I sensed by Jackson's attitude when he came to the ballpark today that he was very upset about something. His attitude up until today has been tremendous. If he comes back, he does exactly what I say, period..." Jackson was feeling so low that when the team picture was taken earlier in the day, Reggie, usually camera-willing, bowed his head and stared at the ground.

Jul 19—   Today the Yankees begin a long climb. They remain in fourth place, 14 games behind Boston, but Ed Figueroa pitches a six-hitter and trims Minnesota, 2-0, in the first game of a key road trip. Tomorrow Guidry will win a four-hitter, 4-0. These two masterpieces give the Yankees a much-needed lift.

Jul 23—   In Chicago, the Yankees win, 3-1, behind Figueroa and Gossage for their fifth consecutive victory, cutting the slumping Bostonians' lead to 10 games. But Billy Martin, who was jovial in Reggie Jackson's absence, is upset over the returned Jackson's nonchalance. In a Chicago airport, Billy tells a couple of sportswriters that Jackson and George Steinbrenner "deserve each other." Adds Martin: "One's a born liar, the other's convicted."

Jul 24—   Billy Martin announces his resignation as Yankee manager in an emotional statement to the press and leaves Kansas City's Crown Center Hotel in tears. Al Rosen's old Cleveland teammate, Bob Lemon, becomes New York manager. With coach Dick Howser temporarily in charge, the Yanks' five-game winning streak is snapped by Kansas City, 5-2.

— Lemon realized all the implications, saying, "I know Billy was a favorite, and he's going to be a tough act to follow. He's been successful. He's always been my friend..." Lemon adds, "I don't think Boston has won it yet. It could be interesting."

Jul 25— In Bob Lemons's first game at the helm, the Yankees beat Kansas City, 4-0, as Ron Guidry hurls a six-hit shutout. Boston loses for the sixth time in seven games and New York is 9½ games out.

Jul 26— Cleveland leads, 1-0, at Yankee Stadium in the bottom of the ninth inning when Lou Piniella belts a three-run homer to win for the Yankees, 3-1. Sweet Lou will stroke a sweet .314 average in 130 games this year. Secretly, Martin and Steinbrenner meet to discuss Billy's future with the Yankees.

Reggie Jackson pops up a bunt in the 10th inning of the Yankees 9-7 loss to the Royals on July 17, 1978. Jackson ignored orders from Manager Billy Martin to hit away after his first bunt attempt failed to advance a runner. The Yankees suspended Reggie after the game.

Jul 29— The baseball world is stunned. As the Yankees celebrate their famous Old Timers' Day, Billy Martin is sequestered in a room at the Stadium while pre-game ceremonies unfold. The huge crowd is told that Lemon will manage the Yankees in 1979 and become general manager in 1980. Then Public Address Announcer Bob Sheppard says, "Managing the Yankees in the 1980 season and hopefully for many seasons after that, will be Number One, Billy Martin!" Billy runs onto the field, shocking all the pre-game participants, and receives a tremendous seven-minute ovation from the happy crowd. The ovation is believed to be even longer than ones afforded either Babe Ruth or Lou Gehrig. On the field, the Yankees beat the Twins, 7-3.

— To his credit, George Steinbrenner arranged the dramatic and historic baseball moment. He did not feel it right that Billy should be separated from the Yankees over a statement made in a moment of anger. "Somebody's got a touch of genius here," said Phil Rizzuto, and he was correct.

Jul 31— New York beats Texas, 6-1, and climbs within 7½ games of Boston, having picked up 6½ games in 11 playing dates. Bucky Dent is off the disabled list and the Yankees are playing their regulars for the first time since early June. The next day Catfish Hunter gives the team a big lift by beating Texas, 8-1.

Aug 2— Boston comes into Yankee Stadium as losers of 13 of their last 16 games and are seemingly ready for plucking. But before 52,701 fans, the Yankees blow an early 5-0 led and the 1 a.m. baseball curfew halts play with the score tied, 5-5.

Aug 3— Hopes that the Yankees are making a serious run at Boston are deflated. New York loses twice. Boston wins the previous night's suspended game, 7-5, then romps to a rain-shortened 8-1 victory in the scheduled game. The Red Sox leave a melancholy Bronx in the belief that the last New York challenge has been repelled. They lead by 8½.

Aug 4— Another low point. The ball club is in a hitting slump. Ron Guidry loses in a 2-1 heartbreaker to Baltimore. Doug DeCinces, one of the few players who hits Guidry well, blasts a homer into the Stadium's bullpen area. Yet Roy White's ninth-inning run-scoring single will beat the Orioles, 3-2, tomorrow and hope is rekindled.

Aug 6— Catfish Hunter pitches his first shutout in over a year, outdueling Baltimore's Jim Palmer. Catfish allows only five hits and raises Yankee expectations of him with a 3-0 win.

Aug 7— Larry MacPhail, the volatile but imaginative part-owner and president of the Yankees in 1945, 1946 and 1947, is inducted into the Baseball Hall of Fame. He had gained election in a vote of the Committee on Veterans this past January. Broadcasters Mel Allen and Red Barber, who once teamed in the Yankee booth, are awarded the Ford Frick Award and receive a special place in the Hall.

Aug 9— Entering the bottom of the ninth inning, the Yankees trail Milwaukee, 7-3. Dent singles, White flies out, Rivers homers (two runs), Randolph reaches on Robin Yount's error, Munson walks, Chambliss doubles (one run), Nettles is walked intentionally and the tying run scores when Jackson is beaned (but not hurt). Lou Piniella successfully lays down a suicide squeeze bunt and the Yankees have a stirring 8-7 triumph.

Aug 13— A controversial, rain-shortened Baltimore victory leaves a bad taste in the mouths of the Yankees and their fans. The Orioles' 3-0 lead is overcome in the top of the seventh when the Yankees rally for five runs. Then, as a rainstorm begins, Earl Weaver stalls until a field that was virtually unplayable at the game's start is covered. The Baltimore grounds crew dallies, skillfully enlarges outfield puddles—does what it can to get the game called. It *is* called, the score reverts to what it was after six complete innings, and the Orioles are the winners. New York drops nine games behind Boston.

Aug 27— At Yankee Stadium, Chris Chambliss and Graig Nettles hit two homers apiece and Catfish Hunter beats Oakland, 6-2. Boston also wins and the Yankees remain 7½ games back.

— Hunter thus completed a storybook comeback. In the month of August, Hunter went 6-0 with a 1.64 ERA. He would finish the year at 12-6, allowing only 98 hits in 118 innings.

Sep 3— New York bests Seattle, 4-3, and now trails Boston by only 5½ games. The Mariners threaten in the ninth, but Goose Gossage takes the mound, with runners on second and third, and strikes out the side on 11 pitches.

Sep 4— Ron Guidry wins No. 20, defeating Detroit, 9-1, in the first of a Labor Day doubleheader. A bases-loaded triple by Chris Chambliss, who is on his way to his third consecutive 90-RBI season, is New York's key hit in an eight-run seventh inning. The Tigers win the second game, but Boston also loses and the Red Sox lead is now five games. It will be a four-game lead after tomorrow's games.

Sep 7— The Yankees go to Boston for a four-game showdown with the uncertain Red Sox. The Yankees, spirited, confident and ready for a fight, smother Boston in the first game, 15-3. Willie Randolph leads the way with five RBIs. Catfish Hunter's pulled groin muscle forces him out of the game in the third inning, and Thurman Munson is beaned but shakes it off. Jackson leaves the hospital for the series.

— Randolph would soon fall to an injury that kept him sidelined through post-season play. But he played on his third pennant winner in three full seasons in the majors. Despite knee problems, Willie would play in 134 games, hit .279, score 87 runs, get 82 walks, steal 36 bases and team with Bucky Dent to give the Yankees the league's best double-play combination.

Sep 8— Led by home runs from Jackson and Piniella, the Yankees launch a 17-hit attack and overwhelm Boston, 13-2. Jim Beattie's would-be shutout is spoiled by two unearned runs in the ninth.

Sep 9— In possibly his greatest victory of a great season, Ron Guidry pitches a two-hitter at Fenway Park, the house of horrors for southpaws, and beats Boston, 7-0. The only hits Ron allows are by Jim Rice and Rick Burleson.

Sep 10— New York completes the Boston Massacre with a 7-4 win. The Yankees are now tied for first place. They make 67 hits and score 42 runs in the series sweep. It is the first time in 10 years that the Bosox are swept in a four-game series at Fenway. New York will go into undisputed possession of first place three days from today.

Sep 15— The Red Sox invade Yankee Stadium and get a case of deja vu as Ron

Guidry pitches his second straight two-hitter against them, winning 4-0. Fred Lynn and Rick Burleson make the only hits off Guidry. Nettles and Chambliss hit homers.

Sep 16— Thurman Munson's ninth-inning sacrifice fly scores Mickey Rivers to beat Boston before 55,091 fans at the Stadium. The Yanks open up a 3½-game lead.

— For the first time since 1974, Munson failed to drive in 100 runs or hit .300. Yet, despite playing with an assortment of painful injuries, Munson managed to get into 154 games and hit .297 with 183 hits. He was still the guts of this team.

Sep 17— Dennis Eckersley salvages some Boston pride on Sunday afternoon with a 7-3 win, a big win for the Red Sox as events would prove.

— By winning, Boston stayed in the race, only 2½ games back. The series attracted 165,080 fans to Yankee Stadium, the largest three-game total in the AL since 1950. The Yanks would lose four times in the next six games and Boston would claw to within one game of them.

Sep 24— At Cleveland, Ron Guidry pitches his third two-hitter in four starts and ties Babe Ruth's 1916 AL shutout record for southpaws at nine, as New York wins, 4-0. Both Indian hits are by Duane Kuiper. Ron raises his record to 23-3. The Yanks remain in first place by one game.

Sep 30— Ed Figueroa becomes the first native-born Puerto Rican to win 20 games in the big leagues and he does it in style, shutting out Cleveland, 7-0, and preserving the Yanks' one-game lead. Figgy wins his last eight decisions of the season.

Oct 1— On the final day of the regular season, Cleveland shocks the Yankees with a 9-2 win, while the Red Sox beat Toronto, 5-0, for their eighth consecutive win. Thus, the two AL East titans finish the season tied, necessitating a playoff. The Tribe's Rick Waits is just too tough, limiting the Yankees, who won 48 of their last 68 games, to five hits.

Oct 2— The second one-game playoff in AL history takes place in Fenway Park. It is one of the most memorable games ever played, and the Yanks are victorious, 5-4. The key hit is Bucky Dent's seventh-inning, three-run homer off Mike Torrez which puts New York ahead, 3-2. Thurman Munson would also knock in a run and Reggie Jackson belts a home run. Boston rallies for two runs in the eighth and in the ninth faces Goose Gossage, trailing, 5-4. With Rick Burleson on first and one out, Jerry Remy singles to right. Lou Piniella momentarily loses the ball in the blinding sun, pretends to have the play under control, and Burleson holds at second base. Gossage retires Jim Rice on a drive to right (Burleson going to third) and gets Carl Yastrzemski to pop up to Graig Nettles. The Yankees win the AL East in the most amazing comeback in baseball history! Guidry gets his league-leading 25th win and Gossage gets his league-leading 27th save. They are the difference between the two teams.

Oct 3— The Championship Series opens in Kansas City and the Yankees mop the floor with the unusually placid Royals, 7-1. Reggie Jackson paces the 16-hit attack with a three-run homer and safely reaches base five times. Jim Beattie and Ken Clay combine for an astonishing two-hitter. The Royals will win tomorrow, 10-4.

Oct 6—   Back in Yankee Stadium, the Yankees win exciting Game 3, thanks to a gritty
           Thurman Munson and in spite of George Brett's three homers. In the eighth
           inning, Munson blasts a 440-foot two-run homer to put the Yankees ahead
           for good. It is only the fourth homer hit into the bullpen area at the "new"
           Stadium.

Oct 7—   The Yankees beat the Royals, 2-1, capturing the series three games to one
           and winning their 32nd AL pennant. Graig Nettles and Roy White homer.
           Ron Guidry gives up a first-inning run, then puts the Royals on tough
           rations until the ninth when he allows a leadoff double. Goose Gossage
           enters and blows the Royals away for the final three outs. The Dodgers
           and the World Series lie ahead.

Oct 11—   The Dodgers, after winning Game 1 of the World Series in a rout at Dodger
           Stadium, win again, 4-3, in a game remembered for its high drama in the
           ninth. Reggie Jackson bats against rookie Bob Welch with two out and two
           runners on base and strikes out on a 3-2 pitch, ending the contest.

Oct 13—   The Series shifts to Yankee Stadium. Down two games to none, the Yankees
           hand the ball to Ron Guidry, who pitches a complete Game 3 to beat Los
           Angeles, 5-1. He is supported by a Roy White homer and by Graig
           Nettles' sensational fielding around third base. The Nettles' plays change
           the momentum of the Series. Not since Brooks Robinson's great 1970 World
           Series had a player's glovework been so instrumental in his team's victory.

Oct 14—   New York wins, 4-3, when Lou Piniella singles home the winning run in the
           10th inning. Los Angeles had jumped to a 3-0 lead but the Yanks score twice
           in the sixth, thanks largely to a controversial play concerning Reggie Jackson
           and Dodger shortstop Bill Russell. Attempting to complete a double play,
           Russell's throw hits Jackson's hip and a run scores while the ball bounds
           away—a run that counts despite the Dodgers' contention of interference.
           Thurman Munson's double scores the tying run in the eighth. Winner Goose
           Gossage is brilliant in relief.

Oct 15—   In a merciless rout, the Yankees send 18 hits all over Yankee Stadium in
           winning Game 5, 12-2. Impressive rookie Jim Beattie pitches a complete
           game and scatters nine hits. The Dodgers, now trailing three games to two,
           are reduced to making snide remarks about New York City and Yankee fans.

Oct 17—   Before a dazed Dodger Stadium crowd in Game 6, the Yankees breeze to a
           7-2 victory and capture the club's 22nd World Championship. Catfish Hunter,
           with relief help from Goose Gossage, is the winning pitcher with seven
           strong innings. Reggie Jackson delivers the coup de grace, a two-run homer
           off Bob Welch, his adversary in Game 2.

           — Bucky Dent hit .417 and won the Series' MVP Award, and rookie second
           baseman Brian Doyle, playing in the absence of injured Willie Randolph,
           batted .438 as the Series surprise. Dent and Doyle played excellent defense.
           Back in New York, the Yankees would be greeted with a ticker tape parade
           even more splendid than last year's.

Nov 10—   The Yankees obtain Dave Righetti (P), Mike Griffin (P), Paul Mirabella (P),
           Juan Beniquez (OF) and Greg Jemison (OF) from Texas in exchange for
           Sparky Lyle (P), Larry McCall (P), Dave Rajsich (P), Mike Heath (C) and
           Domingo Ramos (INF) and cash.

           —The Yanks stole some fine young arms in this deal, particularly Righetti,
           who is labeled "the next Ron Guidry." Lyle, who through the 1982 season

was still the Yanks' all-time leader in saves with 141, wanted to be traded. He would never again be the ace of a bullpen.

Nov 13— Free agent Luis Tiant is signed by the Yankees to a two-year contract with an option on a third year. Tiant joins New York after a 13-8 season at Boston. His career mark is 204-148.

Nov 22— Free agent Tommy John is signed to a five-year Yankee contract worth better than $1 million. John joins New York after a 17-10 season at Los Angeles. His career record is 171-133.

Nov 28— In Reno, Nev., Billy Martin has a fighting incident with a Reno reporter. All charges and suits are later settled out of court.

1979

The Yankees with a record of 89-71 will finish fourth, 13½ games behind first-place Baltimore. Reggie Jackson again will supply the bulk of the power with 29 homers and 89 RBIs; Graig Nettles will have 20 homers and 73 RBIs. Newcomer Tommy John will lead the pitching staff with a record of 21-9. This season will disappoint and, with the tragic death of Thurman Munson, sadden.

Apr 5— The Yankees lose their home opener to Milwaukee's Mike Caldwell who outduels Ron Guidry, 5-1, before 52,719.

— No one expected Guidry to repeat his sensational 1978 season. Nor did he; still, at 18-8, Ron had a fine year. And he might well have been a 20-game winner had he not volunteered for bullpen duty when Goose Gossage was injured. Ron had an 11-game winning streak on the season, had the league's best ERA at 2.78, and finished third in the Cy Young Award voting.

Apr 19— With the season only 12 games old, Goose Gossage and Cliff Johnson have a scrap that drastically alters Yankee prospects. Locker room joking (over Johnson's ability or inability to hit Gossage when the two were in the NL) leads to words and brief fisticuffs. Goose suffers a thumb injury.

— Goose would be on the disabled list from April 21 through July 9. By the time he returned, the Yankees were out of the race. Pitching sensationally after he returned, Gossage would finish with 18 saves and a 2.64 ERA. But in the meantime, the bullpen was a disaster: Sparky Lyle was gone; the usually reliable Dick Tidrow would have several bad outings and get traded; and Paul Mirabella would go winless in four decisions. Others would fail, too, but not Ron Davis, called from the minors in late May. His 14 relief wins (against 2 losses) would break the AL rookie record set by the Yanks' Wilcy Moore in 1927.

Apr 29— Two days after surrendering two pinch-hit homers in one game, the Yankee bullpen again fails when Tommy John pitches well for 7⅓ innings in Seattle and leaves leading, 5-3. The Mariners win, 6-5, with Mirabella, Davis and Tidrow unable to hold the lead.

— John would be the first-ever Pitcher of the Month for April. He finished the month with a 4-0 record and a 1.12 ERA. John would win his first nine decisions and extend a personal winning streak begun in 1978 to 10 games. He would become one of the few pitchers to win 20 games in both leagues.

May 2—   The Yankees complete a horrible West Coast swing in which they win only two of eight games, as Guidry loses, 1-0, to Nolan Ryan in Anaheim. Within a week Guidry will be working out of the bullpen, "if it will help the club," in his own unselfish words.

May 6—   At Yankee Stadium, Guidry relieves Catfish Hunter, pitches 3⅔ scoreless innings and gets the win when Jim Spencer delivers a run-scoring single in the 10th inning. The Yankees are back at .500.

May 20—   In Boston, Tommy John pitches a two-hitter and defeats the Red Sox, 2-0.

           — The Bosox would not be shut out again at home until the Yanks' Rudy May does the trick on July 2, 1980.

May 23—   New York trades pitcher Dick Tidrow to the Chicago Cubs for pitcher Ray Burris, who will go 1-3 with a 6.11 ERA in 15 relief games for the Yankees this year.

           — Tidrow's Yankee ERA was 7.83, and he had not replaced Gossage in any manner, shape or form. George Steinbrenner later admitted, however, that Tidrow's trade was a mistake. Tidrow was one of the most valuable swing pitchers in Yankee history—he could start, pitch long relief or short relief, and he was a team player. In six seasons with the Yanks, "Dirt," as his teammates referred to him with affection, was 41-33 with 23 saves. Of his 211 games, 59 were starts. Tidrow would continue to do fine work with the Cubs.

May 30—   In Milwaukee, Cliff Johnson crosses the plate with a Yankee run and slams into Umpire Lou DiMuro, who is sent sprawling. The massive Johnson, who comes in like a speeding freight train, never sees DiMuro until the collision.

           — DiMuro was carried off the field and hospitalized with a bruised spine. As a pedestrian, he would be killed in a traffic accident several years later. Johnson, having had the encounter that disabled Gossage, felt some responsibility for New York's slow start. He was played sparingly and would feel a sense of relief when traded to Cleveland for pitcher Don Hood on June 15.

Jun 2—   Jackson pulls a hamstring muscle and will go on the disabled list until June 27. Although Reggie will play in only 131 games, he will have one of his best years. His .297 average will establish a career high (to be broken next year). Reggie this year will also pass Yankee stars Yogi Berra, Johnny Mize and Joe DiMaggio on baseball's all-time home run list.

Jun 18—   The Yankees replace Manager Bob Lemon with Billy Martin. The club is in fourth place with a record of 34-31 and the next day Martin makes his season debut visible by coaching in the third base box. He receives a warm welcome from the Stadium faithful.

           — Lemon lost a son in an auto accident during the off-season and understandably lacked his old competitive fire. The club was loosely run and George Steinbrenner was distressed. Steinbrenner reportedly received a call from Reggie Jackson asking about the rumored switch to Martin, and was piqued at having a ballplayer inject himself in front office matters. Some cite this as the break in the special Steinbrenner-Jackson relationship. Ironically, Martin and Jackson got along well over the rest of the season. The Yankees' play would improve under Martin; they would be 55-40.

Jun 26—   Bobby Murcer comes home. The Yankees reacquire the outfielder from the

Chicago Cubs for pitcher Paul Semall and cash. Yankee fans show their appreciation by giving Murcer a tremendous ovation at the Stadium.

— Although Murcer was still a fine player, he had lost some of his luster. He had three good seasons after leaving New York but 1978 was something of an off-year. In 1979 he would hit .258 in 58 games for the Cubbies and .273 in 74 games for the Yanks. Bobby, now 33, could still deliver in the clutch as well as anyone in baseball.

Jul 2— A series between the Yankees and Red Sox sets a new four-day attendance record for Yankee Stadium of 206,016.

Jul 8— In Oakland, Luis Tiant pitches his finest game as a Yankee. He allows only one hit and makes only 84 pitches.

Jul 13— Nolan Ryan one-hits New York and becomes the third pitcher to hurl two one-hitters against the Yankees. A sell-out crowd of 41,805 and a national TV audience watch the Yanks nearly get no-hit for the first time in 21 years. Ryan is aided by the 5:15 p.m. start which makes his blazers harder to see, and by a controversial scoring decision. In the late innings, Jim Spencer's line drive to center field falls safely off the glove of Rick Miller, who nearly makes an incredible catch. It is obviously a clean hit but it is ruled an error. A tainted no-hitter would have gone in the record books had Reggie Jackson not singled cleanly in the ninth.

Jul 19— Al Rosen resigns as president of the Yankees and becomes an executive vice-president of Bally Manufacturing Corp. in Atlantic City, N.J. Rosen will return to baseball in October of 1980 as general manager-president of the Houston Astros.

Aug 1— With the Yankees in fourth place, 14 games out of first, Mickey Rivers, hitting .287 in 74 games and disabled most of July, is dealt to Texas. The original trade is vetoed by Commissioner Kuhn and the deal will not be completed until October. In the end, New York receives Oscar Gamble (OF), Amos Lewis (INF), Gene Nelson (P) and Ray Fontenot (P) in exchange for Rivers (OF), Bob Polinsky (P), Neal Mersch (P) and Mark Softy (P).

— Gamble came to the Yankees the next day and Yankee fans were glad to have this popular member of the 1976 team back. Gamble would hit .389 with 11 homers in 36 games for New York. Overall, the Big O hit .358, the highest average in the majors. But he lacked the needed number of at-bats (he had only 274) for the batting title. Rivers would finish the season hitting .300 for the Rangers.

Aug 2— Thurman Munson is killed in an airplane crash. While practicing takeoffs and landings as the pilot of his new twin-engine jet at the Akron-Canton, Ohio Airport on a Yankee off-day, Thurman's plane clips a tree and hits 1,000 feet short of the runway. It crashes and bursts into flames. Munson's two companions escape but Thurman is trapped inside and dies of asphyxiation. The shocked Yankees will go through the motions for the remainder of the season.

— The Yankees lost their leader of a decade and one of the greatest catchers in baseball history. Munson hit .292 over 11 seasons, .339 for three Championship Series and .373 for three World Series. He won three Gold Gloves and tied a Yankee seasonal record for fielding average at the catcher position. Simply put, Munson was among the handful of great all-time catchers and deserves to be given his place in the Baseball Hall of Fame.

Aug 3—   A crowd of 51,151 fans journeys to Yankee Stadium to pay tribute to Thurman Munson's memory. Banners are everywhere. Terence Cardinal Cooke eulogizes Munson as "a good family man." The pre-game message on the scoreboard reads, "Our captain and leader has not left us. Today, tomorrow, this year and next our endeavors will reflect our love and admiration for him." (These same words will be on a plaque dedicated to Munson next year at the Stadium.) The crowd stands and applauds for 10 minutes. The catcher's box remains empty as the Yankees take the field. Finally, Jerry Narron gets behind the plate and Baltimore wins, 1-0, in spite of a combined two-hitter by Tiant and Gossage.

Aug 6—   The entire Yankee team attends Thurman Munson's funeral in Ohio where eulogies are delivered by Lou Piniella and Bobby Murcer, two of Thurman's best friends. Piniella says, "We don't know why God took Thurman, but as long as we wear a Yankee uniform, Thurman won't be far from us..." Murcer ends his moving words with one last thought: "But in living, loving and legend, history will record Thurman as Number One." After the service, the Yankees fly back to New York in time to beat the Orioles, 5-4, in a stirring game. Without any sleep the night before, Murcer, with New York down, 4-0, in the seventh, hits a three-run homer. In the ninth, Bobby strokes a two-run single for the sudden victory. It is an incredible and very special tribute to Thurman Munson—or so it seems, at least.

Sep 16—   Catfish Hunter Day is held and Catfish tells the crowd: "Three people I wish were here today...Clyde Kluttz, the scout who signed me...My dad... and...Thurman Munson...Three guys (all deceased) who got me where I am today and I miss them." Making his major league debut, 20-year-old Dave Righetti pitches impressively against Detroit but has no decision. As one legend departs, a new phenom emerges to take his place; the baseball cycle is at work.

           — Hunter walked right out of baseball, having accomplished everything a pitcher could dream of achieving. His unhappy final season (2-9) record could never mar Catfish's great comeback in 1978 nor his career total of 224 victories, 63 for New York. Now the classy gentleman would return to country living in North Carolina.

Oct 10—   Billy Martin, his coaches, front office officials, scouts and George Steinbrenner meet to make rebuilding plans and to plan trades.

           — One Yankee standout, Roy White, who hit .215 in 1979, would not be back next season. He would enter the free agent re-entry draft, turn down several offers from big league clubs and elect to play in Japan where he would enjoy three fine seasons. White played 15 years with the Yankees. Only Mickey Mantle, Frank Crosetti, Bill Dickey, Lou Gehrig and Whitey Ford had longer Yankee-exclusive careers. Roy had good numbers, including a .271 lifetime average, 300 doubles, 51 triples and 160 homers.

Oct 23—   Billy Martin has an altercation with a marshmallow salesman in a hotel-bar in Bloomington, Minn. After a hunting trip with a friend, Billy is having a drink and becomes annoyed with one Joseph W. Cooper. Martin and Cooper step outside to settle matters and Cooper gets the worst of it.

Oct 28—   Martin is dismissed as Yankee manager and Dick Howser is named as his successor. George Steinbrenner says Billy's scrapes were not good for the Yankee organization.

— An obscure marshmallow salesman has altered Yankee history—and Oakland history, too. Martin will personally save the floundering A's franchise as the A's manager, 1980-82.

Nov 1— Dick Howser is presented at a press conference as Yankee manager and Gene Michael as the club's general manager. Both had served the Yankees since the 1960's (as players, coaches, etc.). Howser is leaving his one-year head coaching job at Florida State University to return to New York.

— While presenting Dick and Stick, the Yankees announced two blockbuster trades. They obtained Rick Cerone (C), Tom Underwood (P) and Ted Wilborn (OF) from Toronto for Chris Chambliss (1B), Damaso Garcia (2B) and Paul Mirabella (P). From Seattle, they wangle Ruppert Jones (OF) and Jim Lewis (P) for Juan Beniquez (OF), Jerry Narron (C), Jim Beattie (P) and Rick Anderson (P). The deals would glimmer in the 1980 season with Cerone, Underwood and Jones having fine years. The loss of Chambliss, who hit a combined .282 in New York (and it seemed all of his 954 hits came in the clutch), would sting.

Nov 8— New York signs free agents Rudy May (P) and Bob Watson (1B). They, too, will make outstanding contributions in 1980, May going 15-5 and Watson hitting .307. In the course of one week, George Steinbrenner has made the necessary changes to put the Yankees back on a championship course.

The Catfish waves to the crowd on September 16, 1979, Catfish Hunter Day at Yankee Stadium. It was a disappointing season for Hunter, shown with his family, but he left baseball with head held high.

THE 1980's
TRYING TO STAY ON TOP

1980

The Yankees at 103-59 will emerge on top after a tense pennant race with Baltimore, beating the stubborn Orioles by three games. Reggie Jackson will have his best Yankee season; his 41 homers will give him half ownership in the home run crown. Willie Randolph will hit .294 and lead the AL in walks with 119. Tommy John will lead the pitching staff with 22 wins and Goose Gossage will tie for the league lead with 33 saves. The Yankees, however, will finish the year with a bitter three-game defeat in the playoff at the hands of Kansas City.

May 14— At Yankee Stadium, Bucky Dent hits an inside-the-park homer, the Yankees beat Kansas City and they go into first place to stay on Manager Howser's 43rd birthday.

— After a mediocre (9-9) April, the Yankees had a splendid May (19-7) and June (19-9). New York would lengthen its lead to 9½ games over second-place Milwaukee by July 17. The Yankees would need a big cushion: Baltimore, which had a miserable spring, would have baseball's best post-June 15 record and would be breathing down the Yankees necks.

May 22— Yankee outfielder Joe Lefebvre homers in his first big league game (in Toronto), and righthander Mike Griffin gets his first win in the majors. Tomorrow, Lefebvre will strike a pinch-hit homer against the Blue Jays and become the first AL rookie to hit homers in each of his first two games.

— Lefebvre would hit eight homers in 150 at-bats and represent the remarkable depth of power hitters on this Yankee team. New York would belt 189 homers, most for the club since the 1962 Yankees hit 199 homers. No fewer than nine Yankees hit homers in double figures: Jackson (41), Nettles (16), Cerone (14), Brown (14), Gamble (14), Watson (13), Murcer (13), Spencer (13) and Soderholm (11).

May 26— Detroit Manager Sparky Anderson has his pitcher intentionally walk Graig Nettles three times to pitch to Rick Cerone, and the Yankee catcher three times foils the strategy. Cerone has six RBIs, four on a grand slam homer, and the Yankees have an easy victory. Cerone has the satisfaction of receiving a big hand from the "home" fans.

— Cerone, who grew up in the northern New Jersey portion of the Greater New York Metropolitan Area, had the pressure of replacing the great Thurman Munson. He would rise to the occasion, hitting .277 with 85 RBIs and performing marvelous all-round work behind the plate. But he was off to a slow start; this game seemed to turn things around for Rick.

May 31— Reggie Jackson, playing the best ball of his career at age 34, hits a game-winning homer against Toronto at the Stadium. On a 3-0 count, Jackson glances at the third base coach and then displays an angry look, first at the coach and then at Howser as though he had been given the "take" sign. Mock anger, as it turns out, because on the next pitch—grooved right down the middle—Jackson rips the fourbagger.

— Reggie was a happy ballplayer in 1980. He liked playing for Howser, adopted a positive leadership role and responded with his first-ever .300 season. Reggie's 111 RBIs were the most by a Yankee since Mickey Mantle's 111 in 1964. This year Jackson played like Mantle, hitting for power and average and hitting in the clutch.

Jun 6— Tommy John pitches a two-hitter in Seattle and wins his 200th game in the majors, 3-0.

    — John and Ron Guidry got off to terrific season starts. John, as of this date, was 7-0, and Guidry won his first six decisions. When they slowed down, Rudy May would pick up the slack and win the ERA title at 2.46. A fourth lefty, Tom Underwood, won 13 games.

Jun 13— The Yankees visit Oakland for the first time since Billy Martin took up the A's reins, and 47,768 are on hand for a twi-night doubleheader. The A's win the opener, 4-3, when former Yankee Mickey Klutts hits a ninth-inning homer off Guidry. But New York wins the nightcap, 6-4, as Jackson unloads his eighth career grand slam homer.

Jun 14— Oakland's Rick Langford (19-12) leads, 1-0, and is one out away from a gallant victory, when Bobby Murcer connects on a two-run, game-winning homer. Ed Figueroa, attempting a comeback after arm surgery the previous year, is the winner.

    — Figueroa had lost the old zip, and with a 3-3 record, would be dealt to Texas next month after 62 Yankee victories.

Jun 15— The Yankees win the finale in Oakland, 8-2. Jackson cracks his 14th and 15th homers of the campaign. Willie Randolph, hitting .318 with a league-leading .444 on-base percentage, is coming off a remarkable streak of getting on base 16 consecutive times on seven hits, six walks, one hit-by-pitch, one error and one fielder's choice.

Jun 30— In Boston, the Yankees win, 6-3, as Gossage records another save. In the ninth inning, with three Bostons on base, Goose fans Tony Perez on three pitches. Afterwards, Perez says Goose's third pitch—a hopping fastball on the outside corner—was the best pitch he'd ever seen in his long career.

    — Goose would have an awesome year. His 33 saves were the most in history by a Yankee righthander and tied Kansas City's Dan Quisenberry for the most in the majors. Goose would win six of eight decisions, have 103 strikeouts in 99 innings, pitch in 64 games and record an ERA of 2.27.

Jul 21— At Yankee Stadium, Graig Nettles blasts his 267th homer as a third baseman, breaking Brooks Robinson's AL record for the position. The Yankees beat Milwaukee, 3-0, Tommy John getting his sixth shutout.

    — The Yankees were about to receive the awful news of Nettles' hepatitis which would force him to miss 67 games. Nettles' absence—the absence of his run-producing bat and incomparable glove at third—would almost cost New York the division championship. Indeed, the Yanks would lose almost all of the 8½-game lead they had built up when Nettles' illness was discovered.

Jul 23— The Yankees entertain Milwaukee and win, 4-0; Guidry hurls his 19th shutout as a Yankee, tying Herb Pennock for 11th place on the club strikeout list in only Ron's fourth full season.

    — Guidry had been having trouble with his slider, and while the pitch eluded him, Ron had gone 5-6 with a 4.94 ERA in 11 starts—his first slump in the majors. Pitching Coach Stan Williams discovered a flaw in Gator's pitching delivery and the resultant adjustment paid dividends. Guidry would finish with a 17-10 record.

Jul 31— Jackson hits a key late-inning homer, something he does with amazing regularity this season. The Yankees are losing, 6-3, with two out in the ninth inning in Milwaukee, when Reggie wallops a three-run homer (his 10th in July). New York pulls it out in extra innings.

Aug 11— At Yankee Stadium, Jackson hits his 400th career homer. But Aurelio Rodriguez, obtained a week earlier to replace the ill Nettles at third base, is the hero of New York's 3-1 win over Chicago. Rodriguez hits a ninth-inning, two-run homer to make Rudy May, and his clutch four-hit pitching, victorious. Clutch because the Yanks are coming off three straight home losses to the fast-charging Orioles, who have suddenly thrust themselves into the division race.

Aug 14— In Baltimore, the Orioles, 3½ games behind the Yanks, get off to a quick start in a crucial five-game series with New York, Steve Stone (25-7) winning over Tom Underwood, 6-1. The Yanks' lone run comes on Jackson's 32nd homer. The Birds please a crowd of 49,952 with three homers, one off Underwood and two off Ron Davis.

Aug 15— Tommy John halts the Orioles' charge with a key 4-3 triumph. Gossage records the first of 17 saves he will tally in the stretch, striking out five of the final seven batters. Both Willie Randolph and Al Bumbry lead off with first-inning roundtrippers and Jackson adds a two-run clout.

Aug 16— Three days after joining the Yanks from Texas (for pitcher Ken Clay), Gaylord Perry wins the first, and most important, of his four Yankee victories. Perry goes seven strong innings before turning matters over to the Goose, and the Yankees beat the Orioles, 4-1. Highlights include a sensational catch by Ruppert Jones, who reaches over the seven-foot center field wall to rob Eddie Murray of a home run; home runs by Oscar Gamble and Eric Soderholm; and Earl Weaver's rendition of Saturday Night Fever—one of the most animated arguments with an umpire in history. Earl is ejected but the crowd loves it and Weaver has cleverly taken the pressure off his stumbling troops.

Aug 17— Scott McGregor (20-8) pitches an exquisite six-hitter, fans Jackson four times and beats Luis Tiant, 1-0. Jackson crashes into the right field wall making a spectacular catch and lies motionless while many in the Memorial Stadium crowd cheer. Reggie finally gets up and stays in the game, his only lingering injury a bruised forearm.

Aug 18— Baltimore wins the final game, remembered for the defensive heroics of Ruppert Jones, to take the series three games to two. Winners of six of eight August encounters with New York, the Orioles have reduced the Yankee lead to 2½ games. The series draws 253,636 to Memorial Stadium and is the best-attended five-day series in major league history.

Aug 22— The Yankee season is at its low point. The Yankees lose badly to the Angels and Baltimore climbs within a half game of the lead. Baseball is comparing the Yanks' fade with Boston's fold in 1978.

Aug 25— Ruppert Jones, in attempting a miraculous catch in Oakland, is hurt when he runs full speed into a padless outfield wall. The accident is similar to, but not as serious as, Earl Combs' 1934 collision with a wall. Still, Jones suffers a concussion and a serious shoulder injury.

— The accident had pronounced consequences. Jones was through for the year and Bobby Brown would play in center field, as he did once before (from May 27 to July 10) when the unlucky Jones, New York's RBI leader at the time, was sidelined after emergency surgery for an intestinal problem. Jones had played in his final regular season Yankee game. He would be lost through trading, having never had a full-season opportunity to demonstrate his wide-ranging baseball talents to Yankee fans.

Aug 28— The Yankees have lost 18 of their last 41 games but tonight launch a dramatic and successful stretch run. They begin a home stand with a late-inning win over Seattle on a Murcer home run, one of three hits for Bobby.

— For six days, Baltimore stayed within a half game of the Yankees. The Yankees, however, would capture 10 of 11 games on the home stand. A 23-4 spurt was more than enough to keep the Orioles at bay. This Yankee edition refused to fold. Especially courageous in the turnaround were Gossage, for his relief work, and Piniella and Murcer, for the their timely hitting.

Sep 6— The Yankees beat California, 5-4, as Gossage, with no outs and a runner on third in the eighth inning, strikes out Carney Lansford and retires Dan Ford and Jason Thompson on weak flies, then strikes out the side in the ninth.

— Over seven appearances from late August through early September, Gossage retired 28 consecutive hitters, one better than a perfect game. Over 18 appearances from early August through late September, he did not allow an earned run. He would awaken after pitching six times in eight games so tired that he could not raise his right arm. So Ron Davis, who would go 9-3 with a 2.95 ERA in 53 games, would take on even greater importance. Davis, too, was great down the stretch; he did not allow an earned run over his first 20⅔ innings in September. Gossage and Davis (seven saves) were the heart of a bullpen that set a club record with 50 saves.

Sep 21— Guidry pitches seven shutout innings and Gossage pitches two more as the Yankees down Boston, 3-0. Guidry, in command of his slider, strikes out nine batters in one of his best performances of the season.

Sep 23— New York scores a dramatic 5-4 comeback win against Cleveland. With two out in the bottom of the ninth, Eric Soderholm, who hit .287 in 95 games mostly as a DH, strokes a two-run single to win a game the Yankees need badly. Three days later in Detroit, Soderholm's grand slam homer will help the Yankees dominate, 7-5, in another much-needed win.

Oct 4— In the first game of a doubleheader at the Stadium, the Yankees clinch the division title with a 5-2 win over Detroit. Jackson unloads a three-run homer, his 41st (Milwaukee's Ben Oglivie will tie Reggie for league honors) and the third in as many games for Mr. October. Jackson will finish with a 13-game hitting streak.

Oct 5— On the season's final day, the Yankees defeat the Tigers, 2-1, for their 103rd win, most by a Yankee team since the 1963 club won 104. (The Yanks have won 100 or more games in 14 seasons.)

— The Yankees drew 2,627,417 fans in 1980 and broke the AL home attendance record set by Cleveland in 1948. (The Angels would break the Yanks' mark in 1982.) Under George Steinbrenner's winner-bent ownership, the Yanks' home attendance improved for the eighth consecutive season, beginning with Steinbrenner's first year with the Yankees in 1973.

THURMAN MUNSON
NEW YORK YANKEES
JUNE 7, 1947 - AUGUST 2, 1979
YANKEE CAPTAIN
"OUR CAPTAIN AND LEADER HAS NOT
LEFT US -
TODAY, TOMORROW, THIS YEAR, NEXT...
OUR ENDEAVORS WILL REFLECT OUR
LOVE AND ADMIRATION FOR HIM."

ERECTED BY
THE NEW YORK YANKEES
SEPTEMBER 20, 1980

On September 20, 1980, the Yankees added this plaque to the wall in Memorial Park beyond left field at Yankee Stadium. Thurman Munson's leadership has never been replaced.

New York in 1980 also became the first team in AL history to top five million in combined attendance, home and away.

Oct 8— After losing the first game of the Championship Series in Kansas City, the Yankees go down in gut-wrenching defeat in Game 2, a game that delivers what *Washington Post* sportwriter Thomas Boswell calls "one of baseball's most indelible plays." The Royals are protecting a one-run lead with two out in the eighth and Willie Randolph on first. Bob Watson, who will hit .500 in the Series, rips a double to left. The ball makes an agreeable return from the outfield wall for Willie Wilson, but Wilson's throw overshoots the cutoff man. Randolph is waved home by coach Mike Ferraro and the Yanks are victimized by a practiced play. Third baseman George Brett, positioned behind the cutoff man on line with the throw, receives the overthrow and fires to the plate to nail Willie. A would-be Yankee rally stalls in the ninth and the Randolph play proves the key to the game, which the Royals win, 3-2.

Oct 10— Kansas City's momentum cannot be halted at Yankee Stadium, and the Royals claim the AL pennant with a 4-2 win. The Yanks lead, 2-1, in the seventh when Willie Wilson bloops a two-out double. Gossage enters, and after U.L. Washington beats out a weak chopper, George Brett gets around on a fastball and stuns the crowd of 56,588 with an upper-deck three-run homer. The Yankees load the bases with none out in the eighth, but come away empty when Rick Cerone's wicked liner is speared by shortstop Washington, who doubles Reggie Jackson off second base.

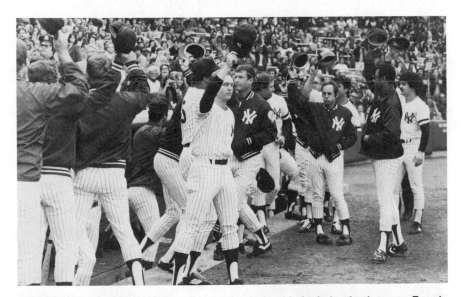

After clinching their division title October 4, 1980, with the help of a three-run Reggie Jackson homer, the Yankees showed their appreciation to the fans who cheered their victory. The more visible Yankees are Brian Doyle (looking at camera), Tommy John, Manager Dick Howser (cap held high), Bob Watson and Rick Cerone (far right).

— It was the greatest victory in Royal history. The law of averages caught up with the Yankees; they had beaten the Royals in 1976, 1977 and 1978. But the loss was still painful. While Yankee pitchers made mistakes, New York's biggest problem was an absence of clutch hitting; the Yanks scored only six runs on 26 hits. The team with baseball's best record would watch the World Series.

Nov 21— Yankee General Manager Gene Michael becomes the Yankees manager. He replaces Dick Howser who has been in a feud with George Steinbrenner. Howser, however, accepts a Yankee job as director of scouting in the Southeast. Front office executives Cedric Tallis and Bill Bergesch are assigned Michael's former duties.

— Somewhere along the way to a remarkably successful rookie season, Howser's relationship with Steinbrenner soured. The Yankee owner liked Mike Ferraro but not Ferraro's work as third base coach. Howser was firm on keeping Ferraro at third. The controversial decision to send Randolph home in the Championship Series was reinforcing to Steinbrenner. Later, when Steinbrenner announced that Don Zimmer (who got the managing job at Texas) could coach third base for the Yanks, Howser greased his own skid by publicly stating that his right to pick the coaching staff had been violated. Howser in 1981 would return to the majors as Kansas City's manager.

Dec 15— The Yankees sign free agent outfielder Dave Winfield to what is called the most lucrative contract in team sports history. The 10-year contract is said to be worth between $13-25 million, depending on whose figures are accepted and the consequences of certain stipulations.

— Winfield is a complete player blessed with great all-round skills. His finest season with San Diego was in 1979 when he hit .308, poled 34 homers and had a league-leading 118 RBIs. He has a great arm and fine speed and would switch from right field to left, the tougher of the flanking outfield positions at Yankee Stadium.

1981

A 50-day strike will split the 1981 season, giving birth to a "double season" format, the First Season made up of games before the strike and the Second of games after the strike. The winners of the two "seasons" would meet to decide the division title. The Yankees will be First Season winners by virtue of a 34-22 record and their two-game lead over second-place Baltimore. They will go 25-26 in what is for them a meaningless Second Season. They will win the AL East title by beating Second Season-winning Milwaukee, then overwhelm Oakland for the AL pennant. But they will fall to Los Angeles in the World Series. Jerry Mumphrey (.307), Dave Winfield (.294), Ron Guidry (11-5) and Rich Gossage (20 saves) are New York's top performers.

Jan 15— John Mize, a lifetime .312 power hitter, is elected to the Baseball Hall of Fame by the Committee on Veterans. Mize did most of his damage as a Cardinal and later a Giant but hit 44 of his 359 homers as a Yankee (1949-53). He will be inducted August 2.

Mar 1— Lou Saban is named president of the Yankees. Saban, a much-traveled football coach, had George Steinbrenner as an assistant coach at Northwestern University in 1954. Saban will return to college coaching in 1983.

Big Dave Winfield joined the Yankees in 1981 and gave the club its best strictly right-handed power since Joe DiMaggio. Winfield stands an impressive 6′6.

Mar 17— At spring training camp, Reggie Jackson explodes in anger and frustration at his inability to reach a contract settlement with George Steinbrenner. "I'm worn out," says Jackson. Preliminary talks with the Yankee owner about a new contract (Reggie's original five-year deal will run out after this season) had not only gone well but, according to Jackson's portrayal of them, were exploring exciting career opportunities for Reggie. Jackson reports to camp late and serious contract talks cease. Reggie's mood is affected by what he considers to be the cold shoulder from Steinbrenner.

— Jackson's 1981 play didn't recommend a big new contract. He hit a weak .237 and it took a great September to finish with decent strike-year numbers (15 HRs, 54 RBIs). It was embarrassing to watch Jackson, one of the game's consummate professionals, pass dispiritedly through almost an entire season. If George Steinbrenner's baseball braintrust was telling him Reggie was over the hill, Jackson did little on the field to argue with that appraisal. By late season, Jackson was planning his New York exit. He told an Oriole player that he wanted to play for the Angels.

Mar 31— New York trades Ruppert Jones (OF), Joe Lefebvre (OF), Chris Welsh (P) and Tim Lollar (P) to the San Diego Padres for Jerry Mumphrey (OF) and John Pacella (P).

— Mumphrey would play a decent center field for the Yankees in 1981, hit .307 in 80 games and have a 16-game hitting streak in May. But two years later, the Yankees would have to rue this trade, especially in light of Lollar's impressive development.

Apr 1— New York makes a splendid trade that Commissioner Kuhn will veto in two days. This April Fool's Day deal with Pittsburgh nets the Yankees a first baseman—slugger Jason Thompson for Jim Spencer and two other players and big money, reportedly $850,000. It is the large sum of money that bothers Kuhn and the Yanks lose out on Thompson, who, already regarded as a consistent slugger, will blossom into one of the game's dominant hitters.

Apr 9— A full house of 55,123 (new home opener record at the Stadium) enjoys a beautiful Opening Day at Yankee Stadium. Dave Winfield debuts as a Yankee with two singles, two walks and aggressive base running; Tommy John gets the win; and Bucky Dent hits a three-run homer. But it is Bobby Murcer who charms the crowd with a pinch-hit grand slam homer. The Yankees defeat Texas, 10-3.

Apr 28— Barry Foote, who as a Cub began the year taking an 0-for-22 collar, belts a home run in Detroit in his first at bat as a Yankee.

— Foote was obtained to help with behind-the-plate chores after Rick Cerone broke a thumb. Cerone would miss five weeks and 32 games before returning to action in late May. He would hit .244 in 71 games, Foote .208 in 40 games.

May 4— Twenty-year-old righthander Gene Nelson wins his major league debut, but Ron Davis grabs the headlines. The day after striking out the final five A's on only 20 pitches, Davis fans eight Angels in a row to end the game. This breaks Denny McLain's major league record of seven consecutive strikeouts as a reliever. In three perfect innings, Davis fans every batter he faces except the first, Don Baylor (who pops up), for 13 strikeouts in 14 hitters faced!

— Six days later in Seattle, in Davis' next outing, he would run his strikeout skein to 14 out of 15 over three games when he would fan the first opposing batter. In spite of his reliever's role, Davis by early June would lead the the league in strikeouts and would finish with 83 in 73 innings pitched. Usually pitching in long relief before handing leads over to Goose Gossage, Davis in 1981 became a star in his own right. The Yankee bullpen, which also featured Dave LaRoche, Doug Bird and later George Frazier, saved 21 games in the First Season. The Yankees brought a new dimension to the game—over the combined 1980-81 seasons, they went 130-5 when they took a lead into the seventh inning. Opponents desperately fought to keep from falling behind.

May 23— Dave Winfield, who hit his first Yankee homer April 29 in Detroit, has his first circuit clout at Yankee Stadium (off Cleveland's Rick Waits) and Dave Righetti has his first major league win.

— Winfield was a tremendous addition to New York. His first-year performance would include 13 homers, 68 RBIs in 105 games, nonstop fervent hustle and some of the greatest catches in Stadium history. One against Baltimore's Doug DeCinces, was unbelievably larcenous; big Dave literally picked a homer out of the left field stands. Another, against Oakland's Tony Armas in the playoffs, was nearly as beautiful. Winfield also played center field while Mumphrey was injured. And watching his long rapid strides turn a single into a double was worth the price of admission.

May 24— Before a near-capacity home crowd, the Yankees fall to Cleveland, 12-5. Their play is poor and Steinbrenner for the first time indicates he is not all that pleased with Manager Michael. Steinbrenner warns against further embarrassment as the club heads for Baltimore where the Orioles will sweep a three-game set.

Jun 2— Baltimore comes to Yankee Stadium for what the approaching players' strike will turn into the most important series of the year. Ron Guidry has a perfect game for six innings (but leaves in the seventh) and Winfield hits a towering 475-foot homer. With the score tied as the Yankees bat in the 11th inning, recently acquired Dave Revering hits a game-winning homer off Sammy Stewart and New York wins, 5-3. It is revenge for Revering. The righthanded Stewart began to pitch to him lefthanded in Baltimore recently, just to show him up.

Jun 3— The Yankees again beat the Orioles with an 11th-inning home run, this one a two-run shot by Graig Nettles to break a scoreless tie. With the homer, Nettles ties Roger Maris for sixth place on New York's all-time home run list, each with 203. Righetti keeps the Yankees in the game with eight shutout innings as the starter.

Jun 4— Gene Nelson allows Al Bumbry's lead-off hit, then refuses another Oriole hit until the ninth inning. By that time, Baltimore's three-run rally is immaterial; the Yankees romp, 12-3, to sweep the series. Mumphrey leads the attack with three doubles, each one in a different direction, and Murcer registers his 1,000th RBI in the majors with a single.

— From May 29 through June 9, New York won 11 of 12 games and this streak—the club's only impressive roll of the year—would be enough to carry the Yankees to their First Season crown. The fact that they were a combined 11-0 against Detroit and Kansas City didn't hurt, either.

Jun 12—   The major League Players Association goes on strike, with New York atop
           the AL East in spite of Reggie Jackson's current .199 batting average. On the
           strike's eve, the Yankees orchestrate a complicated deal in which they obtain
           veteran pitcher Rick Reuschel from the the Cubs. Among those given up
           is valuable swing pitcher Doug Bird.

           — Chicago had just beaten Bird to snap a professional baseball 18-game
           winning streak (including six wins at Columbus). Eight wins were for the
           Yankees over the 1980-81 seasons, after New York had resurrected Bird's
           career. Reuschel, who was 4-7 for the Cubs, would go 4-4 for the Yankees
           in the Second Season. A damaged pitching shoulder would sideline him
           for the entire 1982 season.

Aug 10—   The strike settled, the Second Season begins as did the First, with Tommy
           John facing Texas at the Stadium. And John again beats the Rangers in an
           opener, this time, 2-0. Graig Nettles and Oscar Gamble hit solo homers.

           — Having assured themselves, as First Season winners, of a berth in the AL
           East playoff series, the Yankees faced a Second Season that for them was
           the Season Without Incentive. Were they Second Season winners, the
           Yankees would still have to compete in a division playoff (with the best
           runner-up). Thus there was no pot of gold, nothing to attract extra effort.
           The Yankees would pass through the Second Season, 25-26, and that would be
           that. The situation could foster nothing but bad habits.

Aug 27—   Reggie Jackson undergoes a complete physical examination that is ordered
           by the Yankee front office. Reggie's slump is so pronounced that he has
           been pulled for a pinch-hitter, light-hitting Aurelio Rodriguez, no less. Taking
           the physical is humiliating to Jackson, but he submits to the examination
           and is found free of any physical problem. Jackson then goes on to play
           through the rest of the season like the competitive Reggie Jackson of old.

Aug 28—   Manager Gene Michael blasts George Steinbrenner. Michael tells the press
           that he has told the Yankee owner to "quit threatening me"—to fire him
           if that is his inclination. It is a declaration of independance that is bound
           to trigger a harsh response. Meanwhile, on the field in Chicago, Ron Guidry
           wins, 6-1. Guidry's 4-0 record for August will earn him league Pitcher of
           the Month honors.

Aug 29—   Jackson hits his first homer in 93 at-bats. He breaks a dry spell that began
           May 25 and is the longest of his career. Murcer hits a three-run pinch-hit
           homer and Winfield raps an inside-the-park homer, as the Yankees romp
           in Chicago.

Aug 30—   The bad news from Chicago is that Bucky Dent, upset over being hit by
           a pitched ball, tears hand ligaments in angrily sliding into second base
           and is lost for the year. The good news is Rudy May's five-hitter; it is
           the first route-going performance for New York in 49 games. And it snaps
           a personal losing streak for Rudy at seven games.

Sep 6—   Gene Michael is fired and Bob Lemon is named manager of the Yankees.
           George Steinbrenner waits for Gene to apologize for his late August
           outburst to the press, and when no apology is forthcoming, the Yankee
           owner says he is forced to let Michael go. Gene, who was personally close
           to his boss, had the team playing 14-12 ball in the Second Season, following
           a 34-22 division-winning First Season.

Sep 11— The Yankees and Red Sox finally meet for the first time in the 1981 campaign (thanks to a strike-contorted schedule). Righetti strikes out 11 Bosox and the Yankees win at the Stadium.

  — Righetti was 5-0 at Columbus before coming to New York where he would go 8-4. He would spin a 2.06 ERA, good enough for the ERA title except that he came up 1⅓ innings short of the necessary innings pitched needed to qualify for the championship. Dave would give up only one home run (to Milwaukee's Gorman Thomas) and would win AL Rookie of the year honors.

Sep 23— Recently subjected to several close pitches, Reggie Jackson has words with John Denny after the Cleveland pitcher knocks him down. Later Jackson connects for a mammoth homer, and, as he circles the bases, Denny tracks his progress in a challenging manner. Reggie no sooner touches the plate than he charges the mound and puts a headlock on Denny. Pried loose and bodily removed from the field by teammates, Reggie looks happier than he has all year.

Sep 26— With New York trailing Baltimore, 4-3, in the bottom of the ninth, pinch-hitter Bobby Murcer delivers a three-run, game-winning homer, his third pinch-hit homer of the year. Reggie Jackson has a long homer in this game and will hit another off Baltimore tomorrow, the ball traveling at least 450 feet and landing in the black bleachers in center field.

Oct 7— The best-of-five AL East playoff opens in Milwaukee and the Yankees win, 5-3. The combination of Guidry-Davis-Gossage holds the powerful Brewer bats, aided by a diving, rally-killing catch by Nettles. The key hits are Gamble's two-run homer and Cerone's two-run double. Tomorrow Righetti and Gossage will be the heroes of a 3-0 New York victory. Yankee pitching will record 26 strikeouts in the first two games.

Oct 11— The Brewers, by winning two games in a row, have made Game 5 necessary. Yankee nerves have been jangled by the Milwaukee comeback, but New York digs in at the Stadium and wins the clincher, 7-3. With the Yanks trailing, 2-0, in the fourth, Jackson, who gets three hits, wallops a two-run homer. Gamble follows with a homer and the Yanks are on their way. Cerone also homers and Righetti, pitching middle relief, gets his second win of the playoff series and Gossage his third save.

Oct 13— Billy Martin's Oakland A's come into Yankee Stadium to open a much-anticipated Championship Series. George Steinbrenner is among the many who are astounded at how far Martin has brought a team that, while having excellent starting pitching and a great outfield, has little else. The Yankees win Game 1, 3-1, on a three-run double by Nettles and the combined pitching of John-Davis-Gossage. Piniella and Nettles will each hit three-run homers tomorrow as the Yanks win in a 19-hit, 13-3 laugher.

Oct 15— The Yankees complete their three-game sweep in the Championship Series by winning in Oakland, 4-0, for their 33rd AL pennant. Righetti and Matt Keough exchange goose eggs until Willie Randolph's sixth-inning solo homer. Nettles' ninth-inning three-run double completes the scoring. It is the third three-run hit for Nettles, the Series' MVP, in as many games. Gossage, who was used sparingly in the Second Season, finishes the game. Goose has been on the mound for the Yanks' last five title-clinchers in post-season play (including three in 1978).

— As sweet as this victory was (and it was the first sweep by any Yankee team in the post-season since the 1950 World Series), it was to be slightly tainted when Nettles and Jackson got into a brief scuffle during a victory celebration. Nettles and Jackson had never been close, and neither had Nettles and Steinbrenner, but the Yankee owner made it clear he was upset with Jackson. Sportswriter Dick Young, who figured Reggie would re-sign with the Yankees, changed his mind after this incident.

Oct 20— The World Series opens at Yankee Stadium and Guidry beats Los Angeles, 5-3, with Gossage getting a save. The key hit is Bob Watson's three-run homer and the key play is Nettles' diving snare of a Steve Garvey drive to put down a Dodger uprising. Afterwards, Dodger Manager Tom LaSorda calls Nettles' play at third "so great that it makes me sick to my stomach to watch him." But Nettles will hurt his thumb attempting another great play in Game 2 and will miss three games on the West Coast. New York will win Game 2, 3-0, behind John and Gossage.

Oct 23— Today the Dodgers behind Fernando Valenzuela win, 5-4. The Dodger phenom delivers 145 pitches, allows nine hits and seven walks, and yet goes the distance. Down by one run in the eighth, the Yankees put runners on first and second. But third baseman Ron Cey turns a double play after making a beautiful catch of Bobby Murcer's pop foul bunt.

— New York would lose Game 4, 8-7, in a poor, loosely played game, then drop Game 5, 2-1, in a tight duel between Guidry and Jerry Reuss.

Oct 28— Back at Yankee Stadium, the Dodgers win their fourth straight game, 9-2, and the World Championship. The curtain is drawn on baseball's most rueful season. In the fourth inning of a 1-1 tie, Manager Lemon has Bobby Murcer pinch-hit for Tommy John (whose deep displeasure is caught on TV), with two on and two out. The strategy fails and so does a succession of relief pitchers. Poor George Frazier takes his third loss, while Dave Righetti, the winner of three playoff games, goes unused (Righetti pitched only two innings in the Series). Afterwards, Steinbrenner, who had a run-in with two New York haters following Game 5 in a Los Angeles hotel elevator, apologizes to Yankee fans for his club's performance, an apology that Jackson, for one, feels is unnecessary.

Nov 4— The Yankees obtain Ken Griffey (OF) from Cincinnati for Brian Ryder (P) and Freddie Toliver (P). Griffey has played out his option with the Reds and will be eligible for free agency, but the Yankees will be able to sign him before that happens.

— Griffey's acquisition virtually assured a Reggie Jackson exit. Griffey was, after all, a rightfielder, and Jackson had no desire to be a fulltime designated hitter. Indeed, Jackson would enter the free agent draft this month. This also marked the Yanks' search for a more balanced attack—more speed, less power. Several weeks later, speed-burning free agent Dave Collins would sign with New York.

1982

The Yankees at 79-83 will finish fifth in the AL East, only a game out of last place. The dismal season will not be without personal accomplishments. Dave Winfield will hit 37 homers and collect 106 RBIs, and 39-year-old Lou Piniella will post a .307 average.

Ron Guidry, at 14-8, and Rich Gossage, with 30 saves, will lead the starting corps and bullpen, respectively.

Jan 22— Reggie Jackson has shed his pinstripes. The charismatic Mr. October will ride with Gene Autry for four years at close to $1 million per year plus some of the Angels' gate. The signing is not unexpected. Reggie's desire to play for the Angels (and in California) has been known for some time. He will have a great 1982, belting 39 home runs.

— George Steinbrenner made no serious attempt to keep Jackson. His posture drew a negative response from many Yankee fans. Moreover, a number of baseball people questioned his judgment. All of this was ironic since Steinbrenner's bold signing of Reggie in 1976 sparked horrified reactions to Jackson's big-bucks contract. Also, Reggie appeared to be more popular with New York fans now that he was gone. Ater all, he never won over everybody and alienated many fans in his first two Yankee seasons. Now by some strange twist he seemed a hero.

Jan 29— Graig Nettles is named Yankee captain. He is only the sixth captain in club history. Nettles, who joined the Yankees in 1973 and is the senior player in point of continuous service, succeeds Thurman Munson.

Feb 9— New York's training camp opens about two weeks earlier than usual. The players are told that the early camp is voluntary, but they don't really believe that. And so attendance is good and morale predictably poor. Most players resent the early start with its emphasis on fundamentals, physical conditioning and speed. The idea for the early camp is a good one, but not a great one. Whatever virtue it may have will be difficult to assess since many of its participants would soon be on other clubs.

Apr 6— A rare April blizzard blankets New York City with a foot of snow, forcing postponement of the Opening Day game between the Yankees and Rangers at Yankee Stadium.

— It would take an incredible effort by the grounds crew to get the field playable for the rescheduled opener five days later (four games are post-poned). And on Easter Sunday, the Yankees would begin the season by dropping a doubleheader to Chicago.

Apr 10— The Yankees trade pitcher Ron Davis (along with two other players and cash) to Minnesota for shortstop Roy Smalley. This creates two Yankee problems. One, the bullpen is greatly weakened. Davis represents a distinct loss. After a poor start, and when he isn't feuding with Minnesota owner Calvin Griffith, Davis pitches with customary skill and saves 20 games for the Twins. Two, Smalley's insertion in the Yankee camp disturbs incumbent shortstop Bucky Dent, who has given the Yanks 5½ years of top-notch glovework. The unhappy Dent will play less and finally is traded (in August) to Texas for Lee Mazilli.

— Davis was the victim of unfortunate events. In the 1981 World Series, he allowed eight runs (six earned) in 2⅓ innings. Then he took the club to arbitration (the third to do it and the third to be traded). Finally, in late March, Davis surrendered a home run to the crosstown Mets in a one-run loss that infuriated George Steinbrenner. Besides Davis, New York between March 24 and April 23 traded away Bill Castro (P), Dennis Werth (C-1B-OF), Andy McGaffigan (P), Ted Wilborn (OF), Gene Nelson (P), Bill Caudill (P), Bobby Brown (OF), Brad Gulden (C) and Bob Watson (1B).

Apr 25—   The Yankees enter a Sunday afternoon home game against Detroit with
           a 5-8 record, including an 0-5 mark at the Stadium. The Yankees win, 3-1,
           but afterwards Bob Lemon is replaced as manager by Gene Michael. Lemon
           returns to scouting. Michael is taking over a club that is constantly changing
           personnel and is injury-afflicted.

           — Graig Nettles broke a thumb in this game and within a month Jerry
           Mumphrey and Rick Cerone also would suffer disabling thumb injuries
           and Doyle Alexander would break his right hand instead of the dugout wall.
           Dave Winfield, Ken Griffey and Rudy May would also suffer spring injuries,
           and those who were not hurt by early May would be "close to mutiny,"
           according to the New York Daily News.

Apr 27—   Reggie Jackson makes a triumphant return to the Stadium in an Angel
           uniform. Reggie hits a long homer, his first of the season, off Ron Guidry
           and many in the crowd of some 35,000 on this rainy night offer a chanted
           criticism of Steinbrenner.

           — The Yankees would be seen in many other teams' highlight films this
           year. Besides Jackson's big moment, there would be Seattle's Gaylord
           Perry's 300th win and Oakland's Billy Martin's 1,000th win as a big league
           manager, among others. And fine youngsters like Willie McGee, grown
           in the Yankee farm system, would be starring for other teams, in McGee's
           case the Cardinals. Yankee fans had their reasons for flinching.

Jun 13—   The Yankees lose in Baltimore and limp home after losing nine of 11 games.
           This saps the promise of a 17-10 May record and seems to render the
           Yanks unfit for any division race. New York will be 39-42 at the All-Star
           Break and out of contention.

Jun 26—   Dave Righetti, laboring with a record of 5-5, is sent down to the Yanks'
           Columbus farm club, but George Steinbrenner promises that Righetti will
           be back. In fact, Steinbrenner lets his talented southpaw down easily and
           even calls Dave's dad to explain the move.

           — Righetti would return to the Yankees and finish at 11-10 with a 3.79
           ERA. He never really mastered his control or knew whom to listen to for
           pitching advice. But in the view of at least some observers, he remained
           destined for greatness.

Jul 17—   At Yankee Stadium, Shane Rawley pitches his first complete game in the
.   majors and defeats Oakland, 4-1. This comes only 12 days after Rawley
           made his first start since 1979.

           — The Yankees obtained Rawley from Seattle 10 days before letting Ron
           Davis go—Rawley was slated to work in the bullpen and his presence made
           Davis expendable. He was less than effective in relief, but his season
           turned around once he began to start games. He was far more impressive
           than his 11-10 record indicates. He got to use his variety of pitches in
           a starting role and his class on the mound was showing. The Yankees,
           having shown good judgment in converting Ron Davis from starter to reliever,
           appeared equally wise in converting Rawley from reliever to starter.

Jul 31—   Tommy John and Bill Bergesch, a Yankee executive, have a club-
           house argument that nearly results in fisticuffs. John, unhappy about being
           relegated to the bullpen after a mediocre campaign, has been asking to be
           traded. Now, he threatens Bergesch over remarks the club official is said
           to have made to the press about John's sense of appreciation (for what

the club did for the Johns after their son, Travis, was seriously injured in a fall).

— John was no longer a golden boy in George Steinbrenner's eyes. There was a time when John frequently praised Steinbrenner, but he turned to making a public display of attacking the owner and demanding a trade to one of four AL clubs. He wanted out for Tommy John's sake and he would get his wish in one month when he and his 10-10 record were dealt to the Angels.

Aug 3—   The Yankees lose to Chicago twice, 1-0 and 14-2, and Stadium fans are offered a free ticket to another game, a compensatory gesture by an embarrassed ownership. Afterwards, Manager Gene Michael pays a price of his own; he loses his job.

— The firing of Michael was not precipitous. Steinbrenner had been considering the action for two weeks. With the club at 50-50, Clyde King took over for Michael, "reluctantly, but willingly," the Yankees announced. Michael need not have felt singled out. King was the season's third manager, to go along with the five pitching coaches the Yanks would have this year. The players would enjoy playing for King, a distinguished veteran of the baseball wars.

Aug 6—   The season is not without its lighter moments. Veteran Dave LaRoche, newly arrived from Columbus for the fourth time this year, excites a Yankee Stadium crowd with his version of the blooper pitch, the LaLob. He ends a Yankee 6-0 victory by striking out Texas' Lamar Johnson on a scintillating LaLob. Johnson swings in vain, screws himself into the ground and is counted out by the home plate umpire, as the house roars with delight.

Aug 7—   On the 36th annual Old Timers' Day at Yankee Stadium, honoring 80 years of Yankee history and 60 years of Yankee Stadium, a Yankee star of yesteryear—before there was a Yankee Stadium—is a special guest. He is Ray Fisher, now in his 95th year, who pitched for New York from 1910-17. Mr. Fisher receives an ovation in his first-ever visit to the Stadium. The Yankees celebrate with a 9-1 win over Texas.

Sep 4—   Sweet Lou Piniella goes four for four in Kansas City, running his streak to seven consecutive hits over two games. Piniella will hit .481 against the Royals this season.

Sep 5—   New York clobbers the Royals, 18-7, in a game that features a pair of three-run homers by Roy Smalley that are hit from different sides of the plate. Thus, Roy joins Mickey Mantle, Tom Tresh and Roy White as Yankees having the distinction of hitting righthanded and lefthanded homers in the same game.

— Smalley showed class in understanding reactions and emotions aroused in fans and teammmates when he was brought in to replace Bucky Dent. Smalley, who earlier in the season hit two grand slams, would finish with a flourish of homers. He would break Tony Lazzeri's official 1936 club record of 15 homers from the shortstop position, a record tied by Tresh in 1962. Roy finished with 20 homers (four of them hit as a third baseman).

Sep 8—   At Yankee Stadium, the Yankees snap Baltimore's 10-game winning streak, winning, 10-5, and Dave Winfield becomes only the fifth Yankee righthanded hitter to hit 30 homers, joining Joe DiMaggio, Joe Gordon, Bob Meusel and Bobby Bonds. Winfield is only the ninth player in history to hit 30 in both leagues.

— Winfield had a fabulous long-ball summer. His outstanding all-round skills were seen and appreciated over a full season in New York. Yankee fans were treated to seeing simply the best all-round player in the game. He would be the only Yankee to play in the All-Star Game, although a record 11 Yankees were on the ballot. Winfield would also be among those to have a conflict with George Steinbrenner.

Dec 1— The Yankees sign free agent Don Baylor, recently of the Angels, who had 24 homers and 93 RBIs in 1982. He is the take-charge hitter Steinbrenner wants in the middle of New York's line-up. The numbers bear out George's opinion. Through 1982, Baylor has 218 home runs and 820 RBIs.

Dec 9— The Yankees sign two more free agents, outfielder Steve Kemp and pitcher Bob Shirley and obtain pitcher Dale Murray from Toronto. In 1982, Kemp had 98 RBIs, Shirley was 8-13 and Murray 8-7. The Yankees are primed and ready for 1983. These announcements are made in Hawaii at the winter   meetings.

1983

Jan 11— What has been rumored ever since his dismissal from Oakland the previous October has come to pass. Billy Martin is returning as Yankee manager for the third time. The team promises to be successful and exciting with Martin back at the helm in 1983. And so, ladies and gentlemen, the more things change the more they remain the same.

Billy Martin, already so much a part of Yankee history, returned in 1983 for the third time, as skipper of the New York Yankees.